CO-ASZ-464

EDUCATIONAL DELIBERATIONS

Studies in Education Dedicated to
SHLOMO (SEYMOUR) FOX

EDUCATIONAL DELIBERATIONS

Studies in Education Dedicated to SHLOMO (SEYMOUR) FOX

Editors: Mordecai Nisan and Oded Schremer

Keter Publishing House

מכון מנדל למנהיגות
Mandel Leadership Institute

ISBN: 965-07-1391-3

Publishing Supervision: Asher Weill

Mandel Leadership Institute
P.O.B. 10613
Jerusalem 93553

Printed by Keterpress, Jerusalem, Israel 2005

Contents

A Biography of Seymour Fox   xi

Morton L. Mandel — Foreword   xvii

Mordecai Nisan and Oded Schremer — Introduction   xix

Acknowledgements   xxii

FROM CHICAGO TO JERUSALEM

Barry W. Holtz — Seymour Fox in America: Themes in a Career in Jewish Education   3

Chava Shane-Sagiv — Seymour Fox in Israel   16

David Finn — The Story of a Friendship   34

Daniel Marom — Theory in Practice   51

SOURCES

Moshe Greenberg — Reflections on the Story of the Garden of Eden: *Genesis* 2:4–3:24   71

David Weiss Halivni — *Sof hora'ah*: The End of Teaching; Teaching What?   76

Israel Scheffler — Five Dualities of Education　　　　　84

Jonathan Cohen — The Educational Significance of　　93
Modern Philosophical Midrash: Emmanuel Levinas —
"Temptation of Temptation"

Daniel Pekarsky — Dewey's Groundwork　　　　　119

PRACTICES

Barry W. Holtz — Teaching Torah as Truth:　　　　143
An Exploration of Pedagogic Goals

Robert Chazan and Benjamin M. Jacobs — Jewish History　157
from the Academy to the Schools: Bridging the Gap

Sam Wineburg and Pam Grossman — A Community of　181
Teacher-Readers

Philip Wexler — Chabad: Social Movement and　　196
Educational Practice

Jonathan D. Sarna — The Cyclical History of Adult Jewish　207
Learning in the United States: Peer's Law and its Implications

Burton I. Cohen — The Impact of Summer Camping Upon　223
the Major North American Jewish Religious Movements

Walter I. Ackerman ז"ל — Would You Want Your Child to be　247
a Hebrew Teacher?

CONSIDERATIONS

Michael Rosenak — Eldad and Medad: A Paradigm of Leadership　261

David K. Cohen — Professions of Human Improvement:　278
Predicaments of Teaching

Samuel C. Heilman — Ethnography and Biography:　295
The Stories People Tell of their Lives as Jews

Joseph S. Lukinsky — Mentors, Colleagues, and Disciples:　303
A Jewish Curricular Deliberation

Zvi Bekerman — Paradigmatic Change: Towards the Social and　324
the Cultural in Jewish Education

Daniel Gordis — "It is My Brothers I am Seeking":   343
Educational Responses to the Isolationist Trend
of Contemporary American Jewish Spirituality

Jennifer Glaser — Contemporary Sensibilities and their   373
Implications for Jewish Education

Eli Gottlieb — On the Corruption of Jewish Education by   404
Philosophy

Yehezkel Dror — A Jewish People Leadership Academy   430

Lee S. Shulman — Visions of Educational Leadership: 451
Sustaining the Legacy of Seymour Fox

Seymour Fox: List of Publications   473

Contributors   477

Contents of the Hebrew Volume

Together with the present English volume, a parallel volume in Hebrew has been published by the Bialik Institute and the Mandel Institute.

Mordecai Nisan and Oded Schremer: Introduction

Seymour Fox: From Chicago to Jerusalem

Barry W. Holtz: Seymour Fox in America: Themes in a Career in Jewish Education

Chava Shane-Sagiv: Seymour Fox in Israel

Daniel Marom: Theory in Practice

SOURCES

Moshe Greenberg: Reflections on the Story of the Garden of Eden

Marc Hirshman: Aleph- Bet, Oral Tradition and Education: An *Aggada* in Three Versions

Aviezer Ravitzky: Maimonides: Esotericism and Philosophical Education

Moshe Meir: The Story of the Wise Man and the Simpleton as a Critique of Reason

Shmuel Wygoda: "Remove the Vessels" on the Mutual Responsibility between Master and Disciple

PHILOSOPHY

Israel Scheffler: Five Dualities of Education

Yisrael Sorek: Philosophy as a Practical Science

Oded Schremer: Joseph J. Schwab - Knowledge and its Application

Marc Silverman: Janusz Korczak's Anti-Theoretical Educational Theory: First Reflections

POLICY

Rachel Elboim-Dror: Past Failures; Future Lessons

Zvi Lamm ז״ל: Educational Connotations of Leadership — Types and Levels

David Deri: On the Agenda and the Ability to Control

Varda Shiffer-Sebba: Is the Neo-Tocqueville Vision Realized in the Education Policy-making of Israel?

DELIBERATIONS

Freema Elbaz Luwisch: Teaching Story as Dialogue

Nehama Moshieff: Integrative Aspects of Schwab's Method for Curriculum Planning

Miriam Ben-Peretz: Deliberations in Teaching in the Affective Domain

Yoram Harpaz: Toward an Ontological Foundation of the Approaches to Teaching Thinking

Mordecai Nisan and **Yishai Shalif:** The Sense of Worthy as a Motivation for Studying: The Case of the Yeshiva

A Biography of Seymour Fox

Seymour Fox was born in Chicago on November 17, 1929, to parents who had emigrated from Poland. He grew up in Chicago, attended public school while also studying at an Orthodox yeshiva and being an active member of the Bnai Akiva youth movement. He entered college as a pre-med student and continued his Jewish education at the College of Jewish Studies in Chicago where he earned a Bachelor of Hebrew Literature degree and a Jewish Teacher's Certification. Among the distinguished scholars on the faculty, one who had a lasting and profound influence on Seymour, was the eminent Jewish philosopher, Simon Rawidowicz.

While pursuing pre-medical studies, Fox began his career in education as principal of a Jewish supplementary school in Chicago. In 1949, though accepted to medical school, Seymour Fox made the critical decision to leave medicine and devote his life to education. He began his doctoral studies in education at the University of Chicago (U of C) under the tutelage of the eminent Professor of Philosophy of Education, Joseph Schwab, who was to become the most important intellectual influence in his work. As his mentor, Schwab introduced Fox to many of the leading thinkers at the U of C with whom he subsequently studied; among them Ralph Tyler, in the fields of evaluation and curriculum, Bruno Bettleheim, psychoanalyst, Richard McKeon, philosopher, and Robert Maynard Hutchins, president of the University of Chicago. He wrote his Ph.D. thesis on the topic of "Freud and Education."

Louis Finkelstein, chancellor of the Jewish Theological Seminary of America (JTSA), asked his close friend, Robert Maynard Hutchins, to recommend a young scholar in the philosophy of education. Hutchins suggested Seymour Fox. At Finkelstein's invitation, Fox moved to New York and enrolled as a student at the Seminary.

At JTSA, Fox studied with many of the distinguished Jewish scholars of the day. Among those who were to guide him in his educational thinking and practice were Talmudic scholar, Saul Lieberman, and the philosophers Abraham Joshua Heschel and Mordechai Kaplan. He was ordained as a rabbi in 1956, and received a Master of Arts degree in Hebrew literature. Subsequently, he was appointed assistant professor of education at the Teacher's Institute (TI) and the Rabbinical School, and later was named dean of the Teacher's Institute.

As dean, Fox was guided in his educational innovations both by his professors at JTSA and those at the U of C. He worked with and introduced many of the latter to Jewish education. At JTSA, he worked closely with Wolfe Kelman, head of the Rabbinical Assembly of America (the organization of Conservative rabbis), and with Sylvia Ettenberg, dean of students of the TI. These working relationships developed into lasting friendships with both. It was also in these years that he began his enduring affiliations with outstanding community leaders, beginning with Samuel and Florence Melton of Columbus, Ohio, and later, after his move to Israel, with Jaime Constantiner of Mexico City.

The years at JTSA were fruitful and abundant in terms of a number of educational initiatives. In 1960, Fox established the first research center for Jewish education in the USA — the Melton Research Center for Jewish Education, with Louis Newman as its first director. The curricula for the teaching of Bible, developed at the Melton Center, were implemented in schools throughout North America. As director of Camp Ramah and later as dean of TI, of which Ramah was a division, Fox played a central role in developing and establishing the camp's educational ideals and practices. To this day, Ramah is considered one of the important Jewish educational institutions in North America.

In 1966, Fox accepted an invitation to be a visiting professor of education at the Hebrew University of Jerusalem (HU) from Nathan Rotenstreich, rector of the Hebrew University and Moshe Davis, head of its Institute for Contemporary Jewry. In the wake of the Six-Day War, he decided to remain in Israel permanently, and was appointed head of the University's School of Education, a position he held for 14 years.

As head of the School of Education, Fox was instrumental in establishing a close working relationship between the School and scholars in the natural sciences, the humanities, the social sciences, as well as with the Ministry of Education. Here, too, former U of C teachers as well as colleagues from other American universities were recruited to help guide and assist in his educational thinking and endeavors. Fox initiated new directions in research and innovative projects at the School. He established a unit to train specialists in curriculum development, and acted as advisor to a generation of doctoral students in the field of curriculum and philosophy of education. Among those whom he guided were Miriam Ben-Peretz, Michael Rosenak, Oded Schremer, Jonathan Cohen, and Nehama Moshieff, who helped Fox establish the early childhood education program at the School of Education, and with whom he continues to work on various projects.

It is through Fox's efforts and active encouragement that scholars and practitioners from the School of Education, as well as experts from abroad, were made available to Israel's Ministry of Education. He served as advisor to four ministers of education — Zalman Aranne, Yigal Alon, Aharon Yadlin and Zevulun Hammer — and helped shape policy in crucial areas of Israeli education as an active member of the Council for Higher Education and as chairman of the committee for the accreditation of the teacher-training colleges.

In 1968, together with Israel's Minister of Education, Zalman Aranne and the National Council of Jewish Women in the United States, Fox established the Research Institute for Innovation in Education at the School of Education, whose goal was to improve the educational achievement of disadvantaged students. Haim Adler was recruited to direct the Institute in 1970. Fox served as chairman of the Institute's board until 1981.

At the same time, Fox established the Melton Centre for Jewish Education in the Diaspora at the Hebrew University — the first program at HU in the field of Jewish education for the Diaspora. As head of its academic board, Fox worked with the directors, beginning with the first, Hanoch Rinot, then Michael Rosenak, Barry Chazan, Alan Hoffmann and Ze'ev Mankowitz.

In response to an initial request from Aryeh Dulzin, chairman of the Jewish Agency, Fox and Haim Zohar, then the general-secretary of the World Zionist Organization, proposed a program to train education leaders for Jewish communities in the Diaspora. The program, established in 1981, was the "Jerusalem Fellows." Fox served as its first director, recruiting an outstanding faculty that included Nathan Rotenstreich, Mordecai Nisan, Michael Rosenak, Walter Ackerman, Janet Aviad and Ze'ev Mankowitz.

The Jerusalem Fellows is based on an innovative concept of leadership education that emphasizes the centrality of vision and a sophisticated understanding of the relationship between theory and practice. Fellows receive a stipend for two years of study in Israel, with a commitment to return and enrich their home communities for a minimum of five years. Graduates of the program (known now as the Mandel Jerusalem Fellows) fill many of the leading positions in Jewish education throughout the world today.

At the Jewish Agency, Fox met one of the most prominent visionary leaders of the North American Jewish community — Morton L. Mandel, and developed a working relationship that has deepened into a lasting friendship. Their initial partnership was to guide a program established jointly by the Jewish Agency and the Ministry of Education to support innovative projects for Jewish education in the Diaspora.

When Mandel was invited to serve as chairman of the Jewish Agency's committee on education, he appointed Fox as his senior policy advisor, and with the years their collaborative work grew and intensified. In 1984, Annette Hochstein, director of Nativ Policy and Planning Consultants, joined the team. Four years later, Mandel established the Commission on Jewish Education in North America, and asked Fox and Hochstein to join with him and lead the staff work. The challenge was to set priorities and to recommend programs in Jewish education that could make a significant impact on the future of Jewish life in North America.

As chairman of the Commission, Mandel invited outstanding community leaders, scholars, rabbis and educators from the North American Jewish community to participate in its work. In 1990, the Commission published its report, *A Time to Act*, and created the Council for Initiatives in Jewish Education to carry out its recommendations. Alan Hoffmann, who was appointed director of the Council, began to implement the Commission's recommendations.

In 1990, Morton Mandel established the Mandel Institute in Jerusalem, with Fox appointed its president. An outstanding group of scholars, prominent thinkers, researchers and planners from the fields of education and Jewish studies were invited to advise and work with the Institute. Among them were David Cohen, James Coleman, Ernest Hilgard, Michael Inbar, Mordecai Nisan, Israel Scheffler, Lee Shulman, Marshall Smith, Yitzchak Twersky and Sam Wineburg. Two years later, the Mandel School for Educational Leadership (MSEL), was established by the Mandel Foundation, in partnership with Israel's Ministry of Education. Fox developed the program with Ami Bouganim, using the Mandel Jerusalem Fellows as a model. In 1993, Michael Gal was appointed director, and Mordecai Nisan director of the faculty, which included Joseph Bashi, Avi Ravitzky, David Dery and Chaim Adler, and from 1997–1999 Avital Darmon served as director.

Under Fox's leadership, all of the Mandel Foundation programs for the education of leaders were consolidated in 1998 to become the Mandel Leadership Institute (MLI). Directed by Annette Hochstein, and later by Varda Shiffer and then Daniel Gordis, MLI was encouraged to establish additional programs to enhance leadership potential. Programs for Israel's senior civil service were established, currently led by Neri Horowitz, offering training and enrichment to participants from the Ministries of Education, of Social Welfare and of Immigrant Absorption. In addition, a program was initiated for young educational leadership of the periphery. MLI graduates now serve with distinction in leadership positions throughout Israel and Jewish communities throughout the world.

In 2002, Fox was appointed Director of Program for the Mandel Foundation worldwide, and Annette Hochstein was appointed President of the Mandel Foundation — Israel. The Foundation turned to Fox to develop programs with notable institutions. At the Hebrew University of Jerusalem, an innovative program, "Scholion," directed by Israel Yuval, was established at the Mandel Institute of Jewish Studies. In North America, the first center for Jewish education at a general university, the Mandel Center for Studies in Jewish Education, was founded at Brandeis University in Waltham, Mass., under the direction of Sharon Feiman-Nemser.

Between 1992 and 2003, Fox initiated and headed a project for the Foundation — to develop visions of Jewish education for Israel and for Jewish communities throughout the world. He turned to his teacher and colleague of many years, Israel Scheffler, to be his partner in the project, and enlisted his student and colleague, Daniel Marom, to join them. Working with outstanding Jewish thinkers and educators, the results of the project were formulated in essays, and in 2003, Cambridge University Press published the volume, *Visions of Jewish Education*, edited by Seymour Fox, Israel Scheffler and Daniel Marom. The Hebrew version (*Medabrim Chazon*) will be published in 2005.

Throughout his entire career, concurrent with establishing groundbreaking institutions and programs, Fox has never stopped teaching and working with students, both in Israel at institutions such as the Hebrew University, and abroad at universities such as Harvard and the University of Chicago. His list of publications includes works on curriculum, philosophy of Jewish and general education and on the relationship between theory and practice for the field of education.

Seymour Fox is married to Sue Mogilner-Fox and lives in Jerusalem. He is the father of David, Eytan and Danny.

Foreword

Morton L. Mandel

For the last 25 years, I have worked with Professor Seymour Fox to explore, even dream, about "what could be" for the Jewish people. We have learned how to develop a vision, to constantly challenge that vision, and to be driven by it. Over these years, we have encountered much success, some failure, constant exhilaration, and great personal fulfillment. My association with Seymour and the exceptional team he has assembled, has been a joy.

Part of my pleasure comes from our joint participation in choosing Mandel Foundation people and projects. Through the years, Seymour and I have drawn on our combined experience in building for-profit and not-for-profit organizations, and we have been able to successfully lead the process of building the Mandel Foundation into a creative, vigorous, well-staffed, and highly principled institution.

It is indeed sufficient when an individual gives a grant to a charity. But there are very rich rewards in personal involvement – in personally helping to build a strong social institution. In our case, we have built an enterprise that has a clear mission, a deep, rich culture, is staffed with exceptional people, seeks constantly to raise an already high bar, has a clear and well-documented operating process, and is committed – in its own way – to changing the world.

More than anything else, the Mandel Foundation has become a platform on which rest multiple efforts aimed at increasing the effectiveness of nonprofit institutions, by strengthening their leadership. As we have become more sure of what we know and do well, and more aware of what we do not know, I have watched — sometimes in awe — as our team has created truly meaningful programs, with proven, measurable results.

In the end, the Mandel Foundation is all about "who." Who we are, how we define ourselves, the beacons we steer by, the personal example we set, the people we promote to high positions, how deep and extensive the knowledge we expect our leaders and faculty to possess, and how high and how often we raise the bar.

On a personal note, I am grateful to Seymour for the privilege and pleasure of working with him so closely over all these years. I have learned much from him. Without a doubt, this philanthropic experience has added considerable meaning to my life.

Morton L. Mandel
February, 2005

Introduction

MORDECAI NISAN AND ODED SCHREMER

In this book Prof. Seymour Fox's colleagues, friends and students got together to congratulate him on his 75th birthday with the gift of a collection of articles in Hebrew and English. Fox has worked in many areas of education, from teaching and mentoring students to leadership initiatives. Imbued with a love of Torah and of Torah scholars from the time he began working in education more than 50 years ago, his teaching has been defined by his commitment to his sources and his students. It is teaching that underlies all his activities in the educational arena: his writings on curriculum planning, on Jewish education, and on the development of a vision for education; his initiatives that came to life in the Ramah summer camps; his management of the Department of Education in the Rabbinical Seminary in New York; his revamping of the School of Education at the Hebrew University of Jerusalem; his establishment of the Jerusalem Fellows Program, the School for Educational Leadership, and the Mandel Leadership Institute; and his contributions as consultant and advisor to ministers of education, the Jewish Agency, the Jewish school system in the United States and other countries, and many educational institutions and personnel in Israel and abroad.

The focus of the book is the concept of mindful deliberation in education, in the sense of a dialectic examination of the issues under discussion in their real, complex, and dynamic contexts. It may be considered a process of deliberating on contemporary issues in the light of situational givens and their various possible interpretations. This concept is central to Fox's understanding of education; a view that is based on an awareness of the necessity of having a vision but refuses to be chained to particular ideals, principles or values. In essence, this implies that deliberations in education are concerned with concrete problems rather than abstract questions; they are committed to constructive intervention and not only the quest for knowledge and understanding. Fox has called on educationalists to consider the prospects of the application of educational decisions in the light of the diverse constraints that operate in the given reality: decisions in education must be based on anticipating the possible, and not simply on the basis of the desirable.

The educational deliberations that are discussed in the articles of this book are drawn from three interconnected sources that nourish one another. The first is Jewish and general philosophy, which constitutes the basis for fundamental concepts in education, such as its purposes, limitations and methods. This philosophy begins in the Holy Texts and continues to the present day in focused philosophical discussions. The second source of educational deliberations is experience in the range of areas connected with education, from teaching in schools to policy and administration. The third source is directed, methodical research on education in its psychological, social and organizational aspects.

* * *

The articles in this book are presented in two volumes, one of Hebrew articles and the other of articles in English. Each volume is divided into four parts. The first part of each volume is devoted to Fox's enterprise and educational method. The articles in the second part deal with sources of inspiration for education in Jewish culture — from the Bible, the Talmud and the Aggada to Maimonides and R. Nachman of Bratslav — and in general culture, in the theories of major 20th century figures in the philosophy of education, for example Dewey, Schwab, and Scheffler, who influenced Fox's thought deeply. The third part of the Hebrew volume includes articles on past and future educational policy. The corresponding part of the English volume discusses the development of various educational practices and examines their current application, with an emphasis on the Jewish reality in North America. The fourth part of both volumes presents examples of educational deliberations and analyses of educational practices. The wide variety of topics reflects the abundance of Fox's enterprise. What they all have in common is the attempt to create a general view of education that combines vision and practice, the desirable and the realistic, the universal and the particular.

Fox's work, which is always based on deep investigation of vision and practice in consultation with first-rate thinkers and researchers, gives expression to his admiration of, and even esteem for, the achievements of both theoreticians and researchers, along with his recognition of their limitations with respect to educational practice. In Fox's view, their work relies on a methodology which lacks sufficient sensitivity to the multi-faceted dynamics and contingencies of the life situations in which their subjects operate. The concept of deliberation and its inherent practical orientation shifts the center of gravity from theory and practice unto themselves, to the interface between the two. Fox discusses the problems that arise at this interface and calls for the examination and reformulation of problems from different perspectives. This poses unconventional demands on educationalists — not only teachers, but also researchers and thinkers; not only those in the field, but also educational officials and leadership.

These remarks also pertain to the group of articles that deal with Jewish education (primarily in the English volume). Jewish education in both Israel and the Diaspora is one of Fox's primary commitments, as expressed in his past and current activities. On this matter too he has clearly articulated his conviction that no discussion — including discussions of education — can afford to be detached from its specific social and cultural context and take place only on an abstract, general plane; and that such discussions must therefore involve a continual awareness of the situational reality.

The articles collected in these two volumes are presented to Prof. Seymour Fox with great respect, admiration, and deep gratitude.

Acknowledgments

The Editors

We would like to express our thanks to the following individuals whose contributions to the publication of this book were invaluable: Avi Katzman who edited the Hebrew volume, Vivienne Burstein who prepared the English volume for publication, Asher Weill who assumed responsibility for the publishing of the English volume; the various readers who offered critiques of the essays and helped to clarify and enrich them; the Mandel Leadership Institute and its director, Annette Hochstein, for encouraging and supporting publication of the book; and, last but by no means least, Haya Erez of the Mandel Leadership Institute who oversaw the work on the book from start to finish efficiently, meticulously and with sound judgment.

from
CHICAGO
to
JERUSALEM

Seymour Fox in America:
Themes in a Career in Jewish Education
BARRY W. HOLTZ

Not too long ago I had a conversation with a prominent American lay leader who had recently gotten to know Seymour Fox. I mentioned that I had had dinner in Fox's apartment in Jerusalem a few weeks prior. She turned to me with some surprise and said "does Seymour live in Jerusalem? I thought he lived in America."

Despite the fact that Seymour Fox made *aliyah* in the mid-1960s and has not lived in America for 35 years, in many ways he *does* live in America, at least symbolically — in the institutions that he created, in the ideas that he has promulgated, and through the individuals who were once his students. For those reasons words written by Joseph Lukinsky, the senior scholar in American Jewish education, are truly apt: "Fox's influence on Jewish education," Lukinsky wrote, "in this country and in the world is inestimable. . . . [H]e might validly be considered the most important figure in the field in this century." (Lukinsky, 1993, p. 629).

In the few pages that follow I will not attempt a full-scale biographical essay on Seymour Fox's life or even an intellectual biography tracing the roots and development of his thinking. I will not, in other words, give the detailed story of the many institutions that Fox created and influenced — Camp Ramah, the Melton Research Center, the Teachers Institute at JTS, the Commission on Jewish Education in North America, the Jerusalem Fellows, the Council for Initiatives in Jewish Education, the Mandel Foundation, etc. — nor will I enumerate the list of scholars and Jewish

3

educators that he trained and mentored. And this is not the place to explicate in detail the ideas that he developed in his work on Jewish education and general educational theory.[1] Rather I wish to outline some of the key *themes* in Fox's educational career, particularly as they have been expressed during the American phase of his activities. These themes have remained remarkably consistent over many years in his work in the field of Jewish education. And, I suspect, even in his work in general education — mostly realized in his life in Israel — the same themes, *mutatis mutandis*, also play an important role. I will, however, leave the Israeli part of career to someone with greater knowledge of his work in Israel and try to see how Fox has influenced American Jewish education.

* * * * * * * *

Biography, of course, does play a role here, and it is clear that Fox's upbringing in a traditional Jewish home that valued Jewish learning had a profound influence on his own thinking about the nature of Judaism and Jewish education. The family background set the scene for two elements that run as a kind of *leitmotif* throughout his academic career. One is a deep respect and admiration for scholars who exhibit great depths of Jewish knowledge. The second is an equally deep commitment to sharp intellectual inquiry and the value of asking penetrating questions.

Given Fox's upbringing it is no surprise that he was drawn to and worked with those individuals in the academic community who, along with their scholarly credentials, exhibited the kind of encyclopedic Jewish knowledge most valued in the traditional Jewish world. We see this consistently throughout his long career. Fox's relationships with scholars such as Saul Lieberman, Isadore Twersky and Moshe Greenberg are examples of this predilection. It is no accident, therefore, that during his years as a student and later a teacher and dean at the Jewish Theological Seminary, Fox developed close connections to both Louis Finkelstein and Abraham Joshua Heschel. This admiration for traditional Jewish learning is more than an interesting personal preference; as we shall see, it came to have a central influence on Fox's approach to his work in Jewish education.

---

1   Such as his explication and expansion of Schwab's educational approaches as found in Fox (1972) and Fox (1985). The recently published book *Visions of Jewish Education* by Fox, Scheffler, and Marom (2003) sums up a great deal of his work around the issue of goals and education.

A similar statement could be made about his commitment to intellectual inquiry. Although Fox himself claims to have learned this value from the traditional Jewish schools that he attended, it is hard to imagine that the kind of inquiry that characterizes his mind could ever have been fully realized within the constraints of old-fashioned Orthodoxy.

Traditional Jewish learning environments *do* encourage questioning, but the kinds of questions that Fox consistently asks go beyond the bounds of what is acceptable in the traditional world. As we read in one study of the Yeshiva world:

> A good question assures a student's reputation in the study hall much more than a decent answer. And yet there are questions that are not asked. On the one hand, the ultimate goal in the training of the Yeshiva student is to educate an inquisitive mind, on the other hand, however, there are questions that may not be voiced. Questions aimed at the meaning of the practice as a whole, inquires concerning theological and religious beliefs, historical contextualization and moral critique which might undermine claims for authority, are not part of the legitimate ongoing conversation. (Halbertal and Halbertal, 1998, p. 464).

Thus it is one thing to ask, as Fox is wont to do, "how do you know that?" It is another thing to ask questions at the meta-level — also typical of Fox's mind — like "why is this a good idea" or even "is this whole thing worth doing?"

For those kinds of questions the world of the Yeshiva is not the right place. Only in a university or place like JTS, which values university-like inquiry, can these questions be asked and discussed. It is surely significant that Fox did his doctorate at the University of Chicago during the time that the university was influenced by its visionary president Robert Maynard Hutchins. Fox clearly breathed the same air of open inquiry and "Great Books" that characterized the University of Chicago during those years. Like his connection to traditional Jewish learning, the orientation toward questioning and inquiry also came to have a profound influence on Fox's practical work in the field of Jewish education.

Jewish Scholars and Jewish Education

In the light of his own background, therefore, it is not surprising that one of Fox's most important influences on American Jewish education was a commitment to enlisting important Jewish scholars to the enterprise. Because of his own personal attachment to scholarship and individuals of great learning, Fox was, perhaps, the first person to recruit Judaica scholars — particularly from the academy — to do actual work in the field of Jewish education. It was rare indeed for major scholars to involve themselves in the work of Jewish education.[2] It is certainly true that prior to Fox significant work in American Jewish education was done by rabbis, but Fox felt that Jewish education required the insights of academics — individuals on the cutting edge of scholarship.

Fox had the opportunity to bring this about through his connection to two institutions working in the field. The first was Camp Ramah. Although Fox was not one of the original founders of Ramah, he early on came to have a key role in the Ramah camps, in essence becoming the chief educational theorist behind the camps' work in the 1950s and 60s.[3] Fox saw Ramah as an opportunity to realize a number of educational goals. One of these was developing the original idea of having a Jewish scholar, usually from JTS, in residence at each camp. The scholar's role was, as Fox put it, "to encourage intellectual ferment." (Fox, with Novak, 1997, p. 35). In addition, the scholar was simply to *be* there, as a role model for campers and staff of what a profoundly learned person looks like and does. Of course, scholars-in-residence did do other things — they taught the staff, they helped deal with questions of Jewish law and practice, they met with campers — but their main job was to be themselves.

Another Jewish institution closely associated with the Seminary allowed Fox a chance to involve scholars in Jewish education in an even more serious way. This was the Melton Research Center. The founding of the Melton Research Center is one of the great stories in American Jewish education and one that I will not recount in detail here. Suffice it to say that in 1959, Samuel M. Melton, a lay leader with a desire to change Jewish education (because of the unhappy experiences of his own children in supplementary school), met Seymour Fox, at that time a young administrator at JTS. Out of that encounter the Melton Research Center would come to be born. Later in this essay I will return to this story for a different reason, but here I will focus on the issue of Jewish scholars and Jewish education.

2   Perhaps the most significant exception to that rule was Rabbi Joseph B. Soloveitchik's close connection to the Maimonides Day School in Boston.

3   Ramah was an idea dreamed up by two JTS senior administrators, Moshe Davis and Sylvia Ettenberg. They, along with Rabbi Ralph Simon and lay leaders Maxwell Abbell and Joseph M. Levine, brought the first camps into existence. See Brown, 1999, p. 32.

As Fox began to work on the plan that Sam Melton eventually funded (what came to be the Melton Research Center), he built in a central role for Jewish scholars in the work of Jewish education. Following upon Joseph Schwab's work — Schwab was Fox's own teacher — he aimed to find a role for the subject matter specialist in the curriculum deliberation. This was first realized in the Melton Faculty Seminar at the JTS. The Seminar, led by Fox and Schwab, was a regular gathering of some of the brightest young stars on the Seminary faculty.[4] Fox saw this as an opportunity to expose these Judaica scholars to sophisticated thinking from the world of education. To that end he brought Schwab, Ralph Tyler and other major education scholars to meet with the JTS professors.

The first agenda on the docket was the educational and religious program at Ramah. As Walter Ackerman has pointed out, "the Seminar, under Fox's skillful guidance, provided a model of Deweyian deliberation, easily adaptable to the circumstance of camp; it also made clear that camping is worthy of serious intellectual inquiry." (Ackerman, 1999, p. 19).

The Melton Faculty Seminar set the stage for other significant involvement of JTS Judaica faculty in the work of Jewish education. Faculty members became resources for the Melton curriculum projects. Scholars were engaged to write books that interpreted contemporary scholarship so that teachers could construct lessons based on the latest thinking from the field. The first book of this sort was Nahum Sarna's *Understanding Genesis*, still in print 40 years after its publication. Some have suggested that the Melton Center's support for *Understanding Genesis* had another, quite unintended positive consequence. In writing a book for teachers, Sarna and the Melton team of advisers had created one of the first works to popularize Judaica scholarship for the general reader. It set the stage for a whole genre of works that were to follow.[5] Aside from these general background works for teachers, Judaica scholars came to have an important role reviewing Melton curriculum materials as they were being written.

4   For example, Gerson Cohen, later the Seminary's Chancellor, and Yochanan Muffs, an important Bible scholar, were both members of the Seminar.
5   Interestingly in this regard, in 1980 *The Jewish Almanac* edited by Richard Siegel and Carl Rheins, (New York: Bantam Books) chose *Understanding Genesis* as one of the 20 most important books since 1950.

General Education Scholars and Jewish Education

In all this work what Fox tried to accomplish was the actualization of Schwab's theory of curriculum deliberation in the domain of Jewish education. Implementing a major curriculum theory from general education in Jewish education was a large and original contribution to the field. In fact, the first appearance of the influential article by Schwab that later came to be known as "The Practical III" appeared in a volume edited by Fox for the Melton Research Center, *From the Scholar to the Classroom*. (1977).

Our discussion of the Melton Faculty Seminar leads us to another important element of Fox's contribution, the engagement of scholars from *general* education into the world of *Jewish* education. Although Schwab is the name most associated with Fox's work, we should remember that he was not the only academic from the world of education and psychology that Fox brought into the arena of Jewish education. In the years of the Melton Faculty Seminar, Bruno Bettleheim and Fritz Redl were involved. Later Lawrence Cremin and Israel Scheffler served as active members of the Melton advisory committee. Second only to Schwab was the consistent close involvement of the "father" of curriculum studies in America, Ralph Tyler.

The engagement of academics from general education in the work of Jewish education has remained a consistent theme in Fox's work. Even today in his role in the Mandel Foundation, Fox has enlisted general education scholars to advise the ongoing work. This group includes Israel Scheffler, David K. Cohen, Lee Shulman, Sharon Feiman-Nemser and Sam Wineburg. What Fox is seeking here is input from the wisdom of general education, a desire that Jewish education not be second-rate or behind the times.

But it should also be noted, that Fox has always been concerned about the dangers of importing theories from one domain (like psychology) into education and from general education into Jewish education. This is one of the themes of Fox's book *Freud and Education* (1975) and it explains why one of his oft-quoted articles is Schwab's "On the Corruption of Education by Psychology" (1978). The need to be careful about importing general education theories into Jewish education has been well articulated by one of Fox's best known former students, Michael Rosenak. Rosenak has described at length the complex ways that "translation" is necessary when one crosses these domains. (Rosenak, 1995).

Curriculum and the Ideals of Inquiry

Earlier I mentioned Fox's commitment to the idea of inquiry, a predisposition, I speculated, rooted in his early upbringing. The notion of inquiry appears in Fox's work in two different ways. First, it is essential to his understanding of the way that intellectual work actually happens *within* any given discipline. Here, once again, we see the influence of Schwab who wrote that "it is through the telling question that we know what data to seek and what experiments to perform to get those data. Once the data are in hand, the same conceptual structure tells us how to interpret them, what to make of them by way of knowledge." (Schwab, 1964, p. 12). In one sense we could argue that Fox extended Schwab's ideas about "enquiry" (in the quotation above Schwab is clearly speaking about science) into the subject matter of Jewish education. But Fox did not need Schwab to give him that idea. His own early Jewish training and his subsequent education at the Jewish Theological Seminary prepared him well to view inquiry as the heart of the nature of education in the disciplines and he saw inquiry as the key to creating the new Bible curriculum that the Melton Research Center began to develop in the early 1960s.

He had another agenda in mind as well. I once asked him why Melton decided to begin with Genesis rather than some other Jewish subject area or classical text. "So people would understand that the Bible wasn't junk," he tartly replied. As he explained, in the late 1950s and early 1960s, the so-called conflict between science and religion, (between the Bible and evolution, for example) came to be seen as a powerful attack on the Bible as a legitimate source of wisdom or area of study. In this conflict the Bible was losing — it was common to view the Bible as simply a primitive and outdated work. Educators did not have much of a response to this critique. What Melton tried to do in its curriculum work was to view the Bible simultaneously as a core text of values ("character education" was the phrase that Fox wanted to promulgate at the time) and as an interesting domain for academic, historical study. The Melton background works such as *Understanding Genesis* (1966) and teacher materials like Leonard Gardner's *Genesis: The Teacher's Guide* (1966) aimed at approaching both of those foci.[6]

The idea of inquiry had another dimension as well. Not only was it the

6   For more on this, see the discussion of the early years of the Melton Bible curriculum in Zielenziger, 1989.

value most emphasized *within* the academic disciplines that Melton was working on (and, it should be added, taught at Camp Ramah), inquiry defined the very approach to curriculum *development* that Fox introduced to Melton. This was, of course, Schwab's "curriculum deliberation," the ambitious attempt to engage the "four commonplaces" of any educational encounter in the process of creating curriculum: the teacher, the learner, the community and the subject matter were all essential partners in the preparing of the curriculum. Leading the process was the curriculum specialist, a role that Fox described in some detail in his *Practical Image of the Practical*. (Fox, 1972) The attempt to implement Schwab's demanding ideas in the real world of Jewish education was not without its difficulties. In the course of time Melton needed to adapt the process in the light of its own need to help provide service to the field, and some of its solutions to the difficulties of the "the practical" were inventive attempts to remain faithful to Schwab's ideas and yet accommodate the "practical" exigencies of time and the needs of the field.[7]

Another aspect of Fox's approach to curriculum development was his strong commitment to the need for teacher education. Fox learned an important lesson from the "New Math" and "New Science" curriculum projects that were being developed at around the same time as the early Melton curriculum: pedagogic materials without teacher education were likely to fail. Therefore, from virtually its earliest days, Melton invested both in intensive teacher training (often done at Camp Ramah in the summers) and in "field testing" of the new materials as they were being written.

But teachers who attended the Melton seminars and institutes did gain access to the new (often simply mimeographed in the days before photocopying) lesson plans. They tried them out at Camp Ramah under the watchful eye of Louis Newman, the first director of Melton, and reactions were discussed later by Newman, Fox, Sylvia Ettenberg and others in the JTS leadership group.[8] In fact, the testing of the materials was itself a form of teacher education. Later Melton curriculum writers came to see that the existence of Melton curriculum materials had a powerful impact on the novice teachers, even those with a minimal amount of training. In the early 1980s, while Fox was still involved as an adviser to Melton, Gail Dorph and Vicky Kelman began use Melton supplementary school materials with

7   I have discussed the way that Melton adapted Schwab's model to the realities of the field in Holtz, 1992.
8   See Zielenziger.

day school teachers and saw that the curriculum work could serve as the core of a very effective teacher education program. (Dorph, Kelman, and Holtz, 1983).

A Focus on People

The interweaving of teacher education with written materials for the classroom was always a hallmark of Fox's approach to curriculum development, as I have said above. But this is also indicative of another core element of Fox's educational thinking. He has always believed that the key to educational change was the importance of personnel. Ultimately, education depended on developing the people who could do the work. The Melton teacher seminars, therefore, were not only related to a desire to find ways to implement curriculum reform, but were themselves part of a larger strategy to improve the quality of educators in the field. As we survey his career this latter emphasis becomes particularly clear. It is easy, in fact, to see a direct line from the Melton work with teachers, through the establishment of the "Mador" — the staff training program — at Ramah, through the original Melton Fellows at JTS,[9] the establishment of a doctoral program in Jewish education at the Hebrew University and the creation of the Jerusalem Fellows.

The culmination of this focus can be seen in *A Time to Act* (1991), the document that was the final report of the Commission on Jewish Education in North America. Fox was the director of research and planning for the Commission and had a leading hand in the writing of the report. "Building the Profession of Jewish education" was the first recommendation of the report, and, it can be argued, that it was in this area that the Commission's influence has most clearly been felt in North American Jewish education — both in the work of the organization created by the Commission, the Council for Initiatives in Jewish Education (CIJE, later folded into the Mandel Foundation) and in the many programs educational personnel development initiatives that have been created throughout the continent in the years that followed.

I think it is appropriate to add another, less appreciated, aspect of this focus on people. Fox has always been a kind of talent scout for the field.

---

9   These were fellowships to allow talented individuals to do advanced work in Jewish education. The original group included Janet Aviad, Barry Chazan, Gail Dorph and Vicky Kelman, a pretty obvious success story by any standard!

Despite his work with establishment institutions, he has also had an eye toward bringing somewhat more unconventional types into the field. Of course, as I have mentioned above, this includes bringing professors of general education like Schwab and Scheffler into Jewish education, but it also includes recruiting a variety of poets, journalists, editors, dramatists and performers, musicians, film makers and others into Jewish education. Not all of these experiments have been successful, but in some cases they have been strikingly so. It is a surprising sidelight in Fox's career that is worth noting.[10]

A Focus on Vision

Since the publication of his article "Toward a General Theory of Jewish Education" in 1973, Fox has been associated — perhaps more than anything else — with the idea that the key missing component in Jewish education is careful attention to its goals and vision. Fox has argued that vision is not accomplished through shallow exercises in "visioning," a term he dislikes, but rather by rigorous, philosophical examination of the intellectual underpinnings of educational institutions and practices. It is only through this kind of careful endeavor, in Fox's view, that Jewish education can overcome its persistent blandness. The case for vision has been behind much of his work in recent years and is particularly expressed in the volume *Visions of Jewish Education* that he has recently completed with Israel Scheffler and Daniel Marom.[11]

Vision plays a roll in another aspect of Fox's work, the assertion of the need for new institutions. In his American career this was clear from the creation of the Melton Research Center, but later work in both Israel and

10 Now for a personal note: The present author came into Jewish education through a circuitous route that began with a PhD. in English and American literature. After teaching in a Jewish day high school for a few years, I found myself in Fox's office in Jerusalem close to 25 years ago armed only with three names who suggested that I see him: Joe Lukinsky, Sylvia Ettenberg and Mike Rosenak. In those days Fox was dean of the School of Education at the Hebrew University and sat in a corner office overlooking Jerusalem's Golden Dome from atop Mount Scopus. The view was intimidating in itself and I had been warned by many that Fox did not have a lot of patience for fools. Two friends, Mike Rosenak and Nessa Rapoport, had urged me to persevere in trying to meet him. That meeting in September, 1978, and Fox's openness and generosity essentially changed my life, so I am not a disinterested writer here. In retrospect, I see that I must have been one of the "unconventional types" that he has a soft spot for!
11 See Fox, 1973 and 1997a. Also relevant is Fox, with Novak, 1997. In addition, Pekarsky, 1997.

the United States confirm the same point of view. Whether it was the Jerusalem Fellows, the Melton Centre at the Hebrew University or, most dramatically, the Mandel Leadership Institute in Jerusalem, Fox has shown that there are times that the old institutions cannot do the job and new ones need to be created.

Partnerships with Community Leaders

A Time to Act argued that the two great enabling conditions for change in North American Jewish education were building the profession of Jewish education, as I mentioned above, and mobilizing community support for Jewish education. Creating new institutions needs the support of the Jewish community, particularly its lay leaders. Fox has shown such partnerships are possible and that the key to raising the funds to create new institutions and to support existing ones lies in inspiring communal leaders with great ideas and a sense of vision. As he himself put it, "if you treat potential donors as people who can join *with* you and help you in creating this new enterprise, you may get somewhere." (Fox, 1997, p. 37). Fox has understood that the key element in working with lay leaders was to see those very working relationships as itself part of education. The job is to educate the donor, not to sell him something. The story of Fox's original meeting with Sam Melton is the classic example. Melton had an idea to pay for placing a copy of the Ten Commandments in every Jewish classroom in America. Many would have denigrated this suggestion as unsophisticated or silly. What Fox did was to ask Sam Melton a series of very good questions about the project. "How would the children be able to understand the Ten Commandments?" "What would the teachers do?" "How would the parents react?" Fox took Sam Melton's simple idea and rather than reject it, he built on it and led Melton to an understanding of what the enterprise of education had to entail. It was out of this process that the first research center devoted to Jewish education was born. If Fox had not believed in that partnership and that mission of working educationally with the lay community, it never would have happened.

For Fox, of course, this work led to even larger engagements with Jewish educational issues both in Israel and on an international scale. During the past decade this work has been bound up with another remarkable lay leader, Mort Mandel and through Mandel the canvas has grown dramatically larger.

Fox committed himself to a career in Jewish education in North

America at a time when many of his contemporaries both at the Jewish Theological Seminary and at the University of Chicago saw the field as either a kind of backwater or completely nonexistent. Lay leaders who supported and cared about Jewish education were few and far between, as he himself has pointed out (Ibid, p. 36). He had the insight to understand that without a vibrant system of education and the people to work in that system, American Jewish life would face a crisis. Recognizing that need he abandoned thoughts about going into Jewish scholarship or the professorate in general education, as teachers at both JTS and Chicago had urged him. Instead he turned his energy to Jewish education and in doing so he built many of the institutions that needed to be created and inspired people with the ideas that could motivate change.

Fox's legacy in American Jewish education is, as I have tried to show, widespread and profound. His impact in Israel, emanating out of the Mandel Leadership Institute during the past six or seven years, is also deep. But that story calls for an essay of its own.

References

Ackerman, Walter. (1999). Becoming Ramah. In Sheldon A. Dorph (Ed.) *Ramah: Reflections at 50*. New York: National Ramah Commission.

Brown, Michael. (1999). Ramah in its first four decades. In Sheldon A. Dorph (Ed.) *Ramah: Reflections at 50*. New York: National Ramah Commission.

Dorph, Gail Zaiman, Kelman, Victoria Koltun, and Holtz, Barry W. (1983). The Melton curriculum in the Conservative day school. *The Melton Journal*. Spring.

Fox, Seymour, Scheffler, Israel, and Marom, Daniel. (2003). *Visions of Jewish education*. Cambridge: Cambridge University Press.

Fox, Seymour, with Novak, William (1997). *Vision at the heart*. Jerusalem: Mandel Institute.

Fox, Seymour. (1997a). From theory to practice in Jewish education. Paper delivered at the World Congress of Jewish Studies, Jerusalem, Israel, July.

Fox, Seymour. (1985). The vitality of theory in Schwab's conception of the practical. *Curriculum inquiry 15 (1)*.

Fox, Seymour. (1973). Toward a general theory of Jewish education. In David Sidorsky. (Ed.). *The future of the American Jewish community*. New York: Basic Books.

Fox, Seymour. (1972). Practical image of 'The Practical.' *Curriculum theory network 10*.

Halbertal, Moshe and Halbertal,Tova. (1998). The Yeshiva. In Amelie Oksenberg Rorty. (Ed.). *Philosophers on education*. London: Routledge.0

Holtz, Barry W. (1992). Making 'The Practical' real: The Experience of the Melton Research Center in curriculum design. (Hebrew). *Studies in Jewish education 6.*

Lukinsky, Joseph. (1993). Forum: Response to Brian Tippen. *Religious education 88 (4).* (Fall).

Pekarsky, Daniel. (1997). The place of vision in Jewish educational reform. *Journal of Jewish Education, 63 (1&2).* (Winter/Spring).

Rosenak, Michael. (1995). *Roads to the palace: Jewish texts and teaching.* Providence: RI: Berghahn Books.

Schwab, Joseph J. (1964). Structure of the disciplines: Meanings and significances. In G. W. Ford and Lawrence Pugno. (Eds.). *The structure of knowledge and the curriculum.* Chicago: Rand McNally & Co.

Schwab, Joseph. J. (1978). *Science, curriculum, and liberal education,* In Ian Westbury and Neil J. Wilkof. (Ed.). Chicago: The University of Chicago Press.

Siegel, Richard & Rheins, Carl. (Eds.). (1980) *The Jewish almanac.* New York: Bantam Books.

Zielenziger, Ruth. (1989). A history of the Bible Program of the Melton Research Center with special reference to the curricular principles on which it is based. Unpublished PhD dissertation, The Jewish Theological Seminary of America.

Seymour Fox in Israel

Chava Shane-Sagiv

Seymour Fox has been dedicated to promoting education in Israel and the Diaspora since his arrival in Israel in the mid-1960s. He has invested vigorous effort in developing educational leadership, creating partnerships with communities and promoting ideas to generate change in the nature of education and the functioning of society. It is still too early to assess the full extent of his contribution in these areas, but even a cursory glance at the list of institutions and initiatives he has created demonstrates his role in shaping education in Israel and Jewish education in the Diaspora.

This article is an initial attempt to describe Fox's extensive achievements in Israel to date. It is not my intention to mention all of the educational activities in which he has been involved, but rather to outline his contribution in general and in chronological terms and to suggest a basis for further in-depth study of his philosophy and life's work.[1]

1   I would like to thank the many people whom I interviewed for this paper; responsibility for any errors is of course my own: Shlomit Aviad, Professor Haim Adler, Minister Zevulun Orlev, Dr. Michael Gillis, Hannah Gafni, Annette Hochstein, Susan Hochstein, Haim Zohar, Dr. Uri Haklai, Dr. Jonathan Cohen, Rabbi Dr. Daniel Tropper, Professor Zvi Lamm, Dr. Nehama Moshieff, Dr. Daniel Marom, Professor Mordecai Nisan, Professor Michael Rosenak, Eliezer Shmueli, and Professor Oded Schremer. Special thanks are reserved for the staff of the Mandel Foundation in Jerusalem, especially Haya Erez, Akiva Maybruch and Rachela Levanon.

Fox and the Hebrew University (1967–1981)

"Good men who are good philosophers and who are willing to run the extraordinary occupational hazards, moral and mental, of university administration, are a race which appears to be extinct." (Robert M. Hutchins)[2]

Fox arrived at the Hebrew University of Jerusalem in 1966 as a visiting professor at the School of Education, in response to an invitation by the rector of the university, Nathan Rotenstreich. At that time, Fox was already a well-known and esteemed figure in the world of general and Jewish education in the United States, where he lived and worked. He was dean of the Teachers Institute of the Jewish Theological Seminary (JTS) and a key figure at Camp Ramah. His commitment to bold, creative initiatives for developing Jewish education in those years was manifested in his establishment of the first research center for Jewish education at the Jewish Theological Seminary with the support of the American Jewish philanthropist, Samuel Melton.[3]

The School of Education of the Hebrew University was located in 1966 in the Levy Building on the Givat Ram campus. Ernest A. Simon and Karl Frankenstein, two recipients of the Israel Prize, were dominant figures in the School. The faculty at that time included scholars who laid the foundations of research in education in Israel, such as Zvi Adar, Avraham Minkovitz and Aharon Kleinberger and younger research fellows such as Haim Adler, Rachel Elboim-Dror, Moshe Caspi, Zvi Lamm, and Mordecai Nisan.

Fox joined the faculty as an expert in curriculum planning, a speciality he had developed through his academic study in the United States. Fox was raised in an Orthodox Jewish home in Chicago, Illinois. He later chose to pursue rabbinical studies and Jewish thought alongside general studies. His years as a doctoral student in education were spent at the University of Chicago in the early 1950s, at a time when the influence of the university's past president, Robert Hutchins, was enormous and scholars such as Joseph Schwab and Bruno Bettelheim were part of the faculty.[4]

---

2   Hutchins (1947, 1966 edition), pp. 148–149. For a comprehensive, in-depth and critical study of Hutchins and his philosophy, see Dzuback (1991).
3   Concerning Fox's years in the United States, see the article by Barry Holtz in this volume. Concerning Fox's contribution to Ramah, see Aviad (1988). For Fox's views on Ramah, see Fox with Novak (2000).
4   For a summary discussion of the intellectual character and heritage of Robert Hutchins and Joseph Schwab, see Shils (1991), pp. 185–196, 452–468. On Hutchins' path as an educator (together with Adler), see McElroy (2002), pp. 18–21.

In the two courses Fox taught in 1966, "Developments in the Philosophy of Curriculum Planning" and "Theories of Personality and Their Effect on Educational Processes," he presented students with up-to-date research in the field of curriculum planning as well as with an analysis of Freudian theory in an educational context. Aside from textual analysis, based on the evaluation of the logical reasonability of arguments, Fox endeavored to foster in his students "rhetorical analysis" in the spirit of Schwab's ideas. He stressed that the value of a theory is dependent on its actual contribution to a useful act.

In 1967, during the Six-Day War, Fox accepted an invitation to direct the School of Education and decided to live in Jerusalem. These were exciting days for the Hebrew University and the State of Israel. The swift victory in war and its ramifications for the young state also swept the university into a period of prosperity. When restoration and expansion work began on the Mount Scopus campus, Fox was integral in the creation of a building for the School of Education. A metaphor for the 14 years Fox served as dean of the School of Education at the Hebrew University is that during his tenure, the School grew from one floor on the Givat Ram campus to an entire building on Mount Scopus.

Fox was, at one and the same time, dean, teacher and educator, involved in the educational issues that occupied Israeli society and its political leadership. His attitude to his role as head of the School of Education differed from that of his predecessors as well as from those who followed: in contrast to scholars who viewed administrative roles in the university as a burden that distanced them from research, Fox accepted his administrative function as a privilege and an obligation because he saw this position, as did Hutchins, as one that could bring about change.

The administrative staff with whom Fox worked describes an energetic and devoted dean who invested many hours in planning new initiatives. He did not flinch from complex undertakings which required extensive financing, as long as he was convinced of their justification and that all aspects of their execution had been thoroughly considered, including the comments of critics. He urged those around him to consider not only the immediate consequences of projects under normal conditions, but also further ramifications that might ensue from unexpected circumstances and their long-term effects.

We may learn of Fox's days as dean of the School of Education from his enthusiastic support of Zvi Lamm's initiative to fundamentally change the approach to training high school teachers. Lamm, who headed the department for teacher training in 1970, suggested a new position for high school teachers who, as part time lecturers in the university, would organize a program of tutoring. He asked Fox for 20 part-time positions for teachers who had a talent for connecting educational theories and practice. The tutors were to work with the students to synthesize the theoretical knowledge learned in their university courses with the practical knowledge of teaching a specific subject in high school.

This requirement contained within it a revolution in the understanding of teacher training in Israel. Previously, student teachers had studied theory at the university and then spent a brief period as student teachers in schools. As a result of severing theory from practice many teachers duplicated their mentors' work methods without any reference to their university studies in education. The vision was that tutors should bridge academia and practical pedagogy in schools, by virtue of their commitment to both. Lamm instructed the tutors in their work and Fox, who saw to it that the required resources for the project were available, provided guidance.

The changes in the department of teacher training were only one aspect of a larger process of professionalizing the school. This reform process included dividing the school into disciplinary units, such as the philosophy of education, psychology of education, and so on. He also established a department for early childhood education. While undergraduate students were required to choose courses from among these units without specialization, the advanced degree students were for the first time selecting a particular unit in which to focus their studies. Fox taught in the department of philosophy of education and led the department of curriculum development.

The course with which Fox is most identified in the School of Education is a workshop for building curriculum that he taught for more than 20 years. Participants in this workshop, which combined theory and practice, were themselves writing curricula in their fields while in the workshop. Pioneering research that examined curriculum in the light of theory was published by Fox and Leah Adar on the history curriculum. (Adar and Fox, 1978).

As a teacher, Fox mentored a generation of researchers in school curricula. This cadre eventually took up positions in universities and teacher colleges throughout the country and at the Ministry of Education.

While encouraging new endeavors in the School of Education, Fox worked hard to improve its status within the Hebrew University and in international research in education. He strove to increase the interaction between university scholars and the School of Education. For example, when a topic in the psychology of education was discussed, he asked that members of the Department of Psychology be consulted. Moreover, he encouraged staff members of the School of Education to strengthen relations with the international community in their fields of research and he succeeded in his endeavors.

In order to strengthen the potential contribution of international research in education to Israel, Fox invited the best contemporary scholars to visit the School of Education and to advise him. Among the luminaries Fox hosted at the university in the 1970s were Bruno Bettelheim, Ernest Hilgard, Ralph Tyler, James Coleman and Joseph Schwab. Visits by world-renowned scholars to Jerusalem demonstrated the standard of excellence that Fox sought to encourage in the field of education in Israel.

From the beginning Fox saw the School of Education as more than an institution for the production of academic-theoretical knowledge. He strove to increase the influence of academic research in education beyond the walls of the university. To this end, with the support of the president of the university, Avraham Harman, and the assistance of donors, he established two academic and pragmatic institutions in the School of Education that operate to this day and serve Israeli society as well as Diaspora Jewry: The Melton Center for Jewish Education in the Diaspora and the Research Institute for Innovation in Education.

The Melton Center for Jewish Education in the Diaspora[5]

The establishment of an academic institute to research and develop programs in Jewish education in the Diaspora was a joint initiative of Fox, as dean of the School of Education, the heads of the university and the faculty of the Institute for Contemporary Judaism. The Center was created during the period of celebration following the Six-Day War, at which time relations between Israel and Diaspora Jewry were greatly reinforced. The Center was established in the School of Education and Sam Melton, with whom Fox had engaged in joint projects in the past, granted the Center a perpetual endowment fund in 1976.

Studies began in the Center in 1968, with Chanoch Rinott as director.

5   During the years that Fox was active in the Center, it was called "The Melton Center for Jewish Education in the Diaspora." In the late 1990s, the name was changed to "The Melton Center for Jewish Education." The recent name change is an external sign of the Center's growing involvement in education in Israel.

The Center's mandate was four-fold: to be a focus for academic scholarship on Jewish education, research that would be not only theoretical but would also develop educational programs for the Diaspora; to train teachers from the Diaspora in Jewish education, both in their countries of origin and in the Center in Jerusalem; to establish a generation of scholars who would specialize in the field of Jewish education; and to provide professionals in the field of Jewish education with advice, assistance and a pedagogic library.[6] The Center continues work in these areas, as well as taking on new directions.

In the first days of the Center some scholars in the university voiced discomfort concerning the idea of developing Jewish education, which was perceived as having an ideological strain inappropriate to an academic institution. Critics claimed that Jewish education is not a field of academic study since there was little scientific research in this area. There was also apprehension that ultimately the Center would duplicate the work of the Jewish Agency.

For Fox, the development of an academic infrastructure for Jewish education at the highest level was essential and he resolved to address these challenges. Fox believed that in order to advance the practice of Jewish education, academic theory was necessary. He saw the Center for Jewish Education in the Diaspora as a way to attract scholars from the fields of Jewish studies and education and to create a new field of Jewish education.

His contribution to the Center was in securing support for its establishment and operation and in introducing his doctrine of the translation of Jewish and educational philosophy into the curricula. He nourished a conviction among the Center's staff that is remembered to this day: "Nobody likes to be second best." That is to say, the staff at the Center should not communicate to Diaspora educators that their proposals are better than what has already been accomplished in Jewish education in the Diaspora. One must approach working with Diaspora Jewry in a spirit of partnership rather than of superiority.

The establishment of the Center for Jewish Education in the Diaspora at the Hebrew University, as the continuation of his work in setting up the first Melton Research Center for Jewish Education at JTS, was one of the salient points of Fox's endeavors in Israel. His aliyah to Israel did not sever

---

6 The four aspects are depicted in an article by Professor Michael Rosenak on the Melton Center. See Rosenak (1980). See also the document produced by the Center in 1976, "A Proposal to Establish the Samuel Mendel Melton Center for Jewish Education in the Diaspora".

his connection to developments in Jewish education in the United States. On the contrary, his aliyah became a motivating force for commitment to these developments and to Israel's contribution to them.

The Research Institute for Innovation in Education

In the 1960s, the education system in Israel, headed by Minister of Education Zalman Aranne, faced public criticism concerning the standard of pupils' achievements and the lack of progress in the social integration of the masses of immigrants who had arrived in the 1950s (Sheinin, 1996, p. 230). As dean of the School of Education, Fox assisted Aranne in contending with these challenges. The two convinced the National Council of Jewish Women (NCJW), which had donated funds to the School of Education, to establish an institute at the University that would conduct research and operate experimental educational programs for the advancement of the at-risk segments of the Israeli population.

In 1968, the Research Institute for Innovation in Education was established at the Hebrew University. Haim Adler accepted Fox's invitation to direct the Institute, and served in this capacity for over 20 years.[7] As articulated in its Newsletter, the Institute "aims to address the special educational problems and needs of children and youth, and thereby to promote their educational and social advancement... The accumulated knowledge and expertise attained through these activities also lead to the Institute's professional contribution to deliberations associated with public educational policy."[8]

In the years in which Fox directed the School of Education, he gave researchers in the Institute the freedom and support to direct their studies, which resulted in the development of a number of programs. An example of these programs is *Ha'etgar* ("Hippy") a home instruction program for parents and their children aimed at improving the development of children whose parents have little formal schooling.

This program, developed by Avima Lombard, started out as an experiment in the years 1969–1973 with 100 families from the Tel Aviv area. By 1985, more than 50,000 families across Israel had taken part in the program. Since the 1980s, the program has been offered for implementation abroad and operates in various countries, such as Australia, the USA,

---

7   Immediately upon the establishment of the Institute, the acting director was Professor Avraham Minkovitz.

8   Newsletter of the Research Institute for Innovation in Education 23 (2002).

Germany, and South Africa, under the guidance of local coordinators, with local funding.

As dean of the School of Education, Fox also served as advisor to ministers of education on issues pertinent to Israeli society. From the beginning of his tenure as director of the School of Education, Fox worked closely with Minister of Education Aranne (Aranne, 1971, pp. 15–20). With his knowledge and academic and personal connections in Israel and abroad, Fox assisted Aranne with the educational challenges of the day, including improving the scholastic achievement and integration of new immigrants.

In 1968, the reform in school organizational structure was authorized and middle schools were gradually established, something for which Aranne had consistently and vigorously striven. The reform demanded a change in teacher training; Fox supported Aranne on this issue and was appointed chairman of the Central Committee for Teacher Training and Professional Enhancement. While the changes in teacher training as a result of the Committee's activities were limited, its principal contribution was to place the academization of teacher training on the public agenda and to involve the universities in this cause.[9]

Following Aranne's retirement, Yigal Alon was appointed minister of education, followed by Aharon Yadlin. Fox served as academic advisor to each throughout their terms of office. In the course of the 1970s, Fox continued to engage in the academization of teacher training as chairman of the National Academic Council sub-committee of the Council for Higher Education, and as a member of other committees. These committees and the reports he participated in writing during these years ultimately led to the granting of academic standing to the David Yellin College and subsequently to other teachers colleges (Sheinin, 1996, pp. 243–259).

In 1977, Zevulun Hammer was appointed minister of education, and he and Fox became especially close. Hammer appreciated Fox as both a friend and as a professional. He established the Committee for Planning and Budgeting, of which Fox was chairman. In Hammer's view, Fox was gifted with a strategic vision of the education system, lacking narrow interests and excelling in profound understanding; he therefore tended to adopt Fox's ideas. During this period, Fox accepted the position of

9   For Fox's part in the academization of teacher training in Israel, see Dror (1992), pp. 24–25, and Sheinin (1996), pp. 210–213.

Director of the Department of planning and Budgeting at the Ministry. Their relationship took on a more prominent role in Fox's activities in the 1990s, when Hammer was reappointed minister of education.

Fox, the Jerusalem Fellows and the Mandel Institute (1982–1990)
From Zion will go forth the Law (Isaiah 2:3)

In the summer of 1981, Fox took a sabbatical from the Hebrew University and completed his work as dean of the School of Education. In subsequent years, Fox continued to teach curriculum planning at the School of Education and remained involved in the activities of the Melton Center.

Upon completing his term as dean of the School of Education, Fox become the director of a new program for training educational leaders in the Diaspora: The Jerusalem Fellows, a long-term program in Israel for educators from the Diaspora that he established with Haim Zohar, Director of the World Zionist Organization and who directed the Pincus Fund for Jewish Education in the Diaspora under the auspices of the Jewish Agency. Aryeh Dulzin, who headed the World Zionist Organization, supported the institution, as did the chairman of Bank Leumi L'Israel.

In the late 1970s, Minister of Education Zevulun Hammer and Prime Minister Menachem Begin arrived at a joint decision that, in light of data on Jewish assimilation in the Diaspora, Jewish education should be placed on the public agenda in Israel. It was decided that the government of Israel and the Jewish Agency would create a world council on Jewish education in the Diaspora. The government and the Jewish Agency allocated five million dollars to the Pincus Fund, which worked to strengthen Jewish education in the Diaspora, and a new council called the Joint Program for Jewish Education in the Diaspora was set up in 1989.

Daniel Tropper headed the Joint Program, and Haim Zohar served as co-director of the program. Fox was an active participant in the committee for the program which, as opposed to the Pincus Fund, did not invest resources in the Diaspora but rather encouraged and funded programs in Israel that would serve the Diaspora. The Fund fostered training programs for teachers from the Diaspora at a variety of universities in Israel and the creation of new curricula, and encouraged students from abroad to study in Israel.

This spirited activity in Israel for Diaspora Jewry was the background against which, at the beginning of the 1980s, the Jerusalem Fellows program grew. The objective of the Jerusalem Fellows was, in Zohar's words, "to find inspiring people, with intellectual and emotional power, and to train them so that they would be able, by virtue of the strength of their personalities and talents, to create around them dynamic centers for Jewish education, whose influence would affect many others."[10] From the very beginning, the founders anticipated that the program would develop leaders' personalities, and they would contribute to changing Jewish communities throughout the world, both as individuals and as a group.

In 1982, Fox and Susan Hochstein, administrative director of the program, constructed the program and screened candidates for admission. They consulted with academic experts while keeping representatives of the Bank Leumi L'Israel involved. The target audience for the program was talented educators or those from other fields who sought to influence education. The duration of the program was determined to be three years for each cohort, with full scholarships available for participants.

Fox's aim was for the program to provide a significant and pleasurable experience for participants, an aim that became a guiding principle for the selection of staff and facilities. It was decided that the program would be run in Hebrew, a decision that took into account the fact that while this might prevent some candidates from participating in the program, it expressed a commitment to Hebrew as the lingua franca in Jewish education.

The Jerusalem Fellows program was intended to train senior personnel for Jewish education throughout the world. Fox defined this objective as "the creation of a common language" among all those involved in Jewish education. The assumption was that the Fellows' time together in Israel, their independent study, and the group curriculum would together produce a professional field of Jewish education in the Diaspora, with its own language. So as to create this field, Fox believed there was a need to develop an academic discussion of the issues that arise in the field and to harness the best minds from both inside and outside of the academic world.

Ten candidates from the United States, Britain, France and Argentina were selected as the first group of Jerusalem Fellows. They studied Jewish philosophy, education and Jewish education, and contemporary Judaism in a group for one and a half days a week, taught by the program's academic staff, which included Fox, Rotenstreich (chairman of the academic committee), Janet Aviad, Walter Ackerman, Mordecai Nisan and Michael Rosenak. During the remaining days of the week, the Fellows participated

---

10 From the address of Haim Zohar at the Jerusalem Fellows inauguration ceremony, July 13, 1981.

in university courses and studied with tutors. The choice of course contents
and teachers reflected Fox's perception of the philosophical basis essential
for considering educational issues.

The program's attitude was that the Fellows are the elite amongst Jewish
educators in the Diaspora and, accordingly, maximum resources must be
invested in them. Fox believed that the Fellows should meet with the
leading thinkers in the fields of the education and Jewish education, in
order to learn from their characters and thinking. Therefore, the Fellows in
the early groups met with Nehama Leibowitz and others. The event which
perhaps best reflects Fox's vision concerning the Jerusalem Fellows was
the first colloquium held in Jerusalem in the summer of 1984 upon the
completion of the first year of studies.

The colloquium opened in the Jewish Agency building with greetings
that were followed by a festive dinner and lecture by Rotenstreich on "The
Face of our Generation and Jewish Education" at the Van Leer Institute.
During the following four days, the program hosted lectures and seminars
in which the Fellows and the outstanding international education scholars
participated. Among the guests who had come from the United States to
attend the colloquium were Ralph Tyler, already a legend in the field of
curriculum development, Israel Scheffler, Lee Shulman, and Sam
Scheffler. All the lectures had simultaneous translation into Hebrew and
English. The scholars did not present papers prepared in advance but rather
responded to the presentations of the Fellows in the program. It was a very
exciting conference for the Fellows and expressed the essence of Fox's
outlook that the Fellows are part of the discourse of the leading specialists
of the time in education and Jewish education.

In retrospect, it is clear that the Jerusalem Fellows program
distinguished itself as the first long-term program in Israel that aimed to
promote Jewish education in the Diaspora on its own terms, rather than as
a platform for promoting aliyah. The program was built upon the genuine
belief in cooperation between Israel and the Diaspora on the basis of
equality, and expressed a policy different to that of the *shaliah*, (emissary),
which had been customary up until that time and even today in the Israel-
Diaspora relationship. Rather than sending Israelis to the Diaspora for a
limited period of time to work in Jewish education, Israel's best intellectual
and other resources were invested in Diaspora Jews, in people who would
return to their communities and continue to exert their influence
throughout their lifetimes.

During the same years that the Jerusalem Fellows program was getting
underway, Fox was an advisor for Morton L. Mandel from Cleveland,

Ohio, chair of the steering committee of the Joint Program for Jewish Education. Mandel discussed with Fox and his other advisors how to reach the leadership of Jewish communities in the Diaspora and to urge them to deepen their involvement in education. Leaders of Jewish communities were already committed to founding and supporting Jewish schools and they were now asked to contribute also to shaping their content and goals. Fox argued for an in-depth discussion on a sufficiently high level on Jewish education had not yet taken place. He claimed that borrowing knowledge from general education is not enough, and he strove to have Jewish education recognized as a unique field of interest and research. For this purpose, a committee was established to convene an international conference on the subject of Jewish education. Fox made the arrangements for the conference together with Haim Zohar, Herb Millman, Carmi Schwartz, Avraham Infeld and others. The World Leadership Conference for Jewish Education, the first conference for Jewish community leaders from around the world, opened in Jerusalem in June 1984. The conference was held in the presence of Chaim Herzog, President of the State of Israel, Prime Minister Yitzhak Shamir and Education Minister Hammer, and was attended by 250 Jewish community leaders belonging to the various streams of Judaism, from 27 countries.

In the words of conference chairman, Morton Mandel, the objective of the 72 intensive hours of the conference – which was comprised of discussions and workshops on Jewish education in an age of assimilation and distancing from tradition – was "to encourage the top echelon of world Jewry to pick up the torch of Jewish education" (Mandel, 1984).

The decision to address the community leadership and not just the professional educators, was a change of direction. The conference was a public expression of the State of Israel's intent to actively support Jewish education in the Diaspora. In his speech to the conference, Fox articulated his vision for the partnership between Israel and Diaspora Jewry in Jewish education: "In the field of education, we have the opportunity to develop a deep, creative and meaningful partnership between Diaspora Jewry and Israelis. A partnership that means working, thinking and creating together: the meeting of the academic from the Diaspora with the Israeli scholar, the artist from the Diaspora with the artist from Israel, where by way of joint efforts they search for new forms and expressions for Jewish education. This kind of partnership may change the status of Jewish education among communities throughout the world, and lift the morale of the Jewish educator, two salient points that are so significant to the success of education" (Fox, 1984, p. 6).

Following this international conference on Jewish education, Fox continued in his role as advisor to Mandel to promote the work of the Jewish Education Committee. One of the Committee's undertakings following the conference was to conduct a comprehensive study of the Jewish Agency's existing educational programs in Israel on behalf of Diaspora Jewry. To carry out the study, in the summer of 1984 Mandel and Fox recruited Annette Hochstein, who at the time was the head of the Nativ Consultants for Policy and Planning firm and conducted studies on public policy. The study was conducted over a period of one and a half years, during which time a great deal of material was collected, creating, for the first time, an extensive factual database on Diaspora youth visits to Israel. In 1986, a detailed report on "Israel Experience" programs was submitted to the Jewish Agency. The report opened up the opportunity for discussion of their strengths and weaknesses and made recommendations for action. (Hochstein, 1986).

In the late 1980s, Mandel decided to withdraw, together with Fox and Hochstein, from Jewish Agency activities and to work independently on behalf of Jewish education, with the assistance of his family foundation, the associated Mandel Foundation. The data that began to be formulated at that time concerning the growing number of Jews in North America who were losing their connection to the Jewish heritage and even assimilating completely greatly disturbed Mandel and he decided to take action. Upon consulting with Fox, Mandel established a commission with the participation of the top echelon of Jewish leadership in the United States and Canada that would assemble to discuss the situation of Jewish education in North America.

The Commission on Jewish Education in North America, headed by Mandel and led by Henry Zucker, was active between 1988 and 1990. Fox and Hochstein, among the Commission's senior advisors, were responsible for planning and setting up the research that formed the basis of its meetings. The Commission was comprised of 44 key figures from North American Jewish communities. During the meetings, proposals were made for the improvement of educational systems and their ties with the communities. At the end, the Commission formulated a document that presented the data and proposals, and called for action.[11]

At the same time, in 1989, Mandel and Fox began discussing the establishment of an independent institute that would serve as a central address for issues in Jewish education. The idea was to set up a professional

11 *A Time to Act* (1990).

headquarters for pooling wisdom on Diaspora Jewish education, and which could advise the various organizations involved in the field.

The Mandel Institute was founded in Jerusalem in 1990. At its head stood Fox as president and Hochstein as director. From the start, the Institute received requests to promote Israeli education along with Jewish education in the Diaspora. With Mandel's leadership, Fox began to work ardently with the Institute's staff on ideas for the professional development of education in Israel. One of the central ideas that was repeatedly raised was to train senior personnel for the field.

Fox, the School for Educational Leadership and the Mandel Foundation (1981 to the present)

"If you have toiled and found — believe" (Megillah 6b)

In the early 1990s, Fox met with the minister of education and culture, Zevulun Hammer, and familiarized him with the work of the Mandel Institute. The two old acquaintances discussed the establishment of an institute similar to The Jerusalem Fellows that would train a cadre of senior educators for the Israeli education system. Hammer expressed his enthusiasm and a meeting between Hammer and Mandel, chairman of the Mandel Institute's board, followed. This meeting resulted in the decision to establish the School for Educational Leadership, with the support of the Ministry of Education and Culture.

Fox and Hochstein spent 1990–1991 working with Mandel Institute staff member Ami Bouganim on the establishment of the School for Educational Leadership. The three consulted with experts in Israel and abroad on the importance of the idea and methods of implementation. They also visited world-renowned institutions specializing in the training of senior personnel and examined several models of leadership training (Ettinger, 1997).

The School for Educational Leadership accepted its first cohort of Fellows in October 1992.[12] This was made possible by the support of the Mandel Foundation, additional Diaspora-based foundations, Felix Posen and the Israeli Ministry of Education and Culture. Michael Gal was appointed as the School's first director.

The framework of studies at the School for Educational Leadership, modeled on The Jerusalem Fellows, was a two-year program for mid-

---

12 On the opening of the School, see Efrati (1992).

career Israeli educational personnel and those from other fields of expertise who wished to become involved in education. During two years, Fellows received a stipend for living expenses to allow them to devote themselves full time to the program. The theoretical group studies took place two days a week and encompassed three principal fields of study: Education, led by Joseph Bashi; Humanities and Jewish Studies, led by Aviezer Ravitzky; and Policy, Planning and Social Studies, led by Hochstein. The remaining days of the week were devoted to individual studies with tutors, and to the development of individual projects. This model, though it has changed, continues to be the basis for studies today.

The School for Educational Leadership appeals to experienced mid-career educators who have a vision for the advancement of Israeli society. From its inception, the School's uniqueness was in the positioning of the Fellows' individual visions at the forefront and providing them with the tools to realize these visions. For Fox, "the two most important characteristics of a candidate to the School for Educational Leadership, in addition to having vision and commitment, are self-motivation and stamina in the face of failure; for it is not sufficient to choose people with excellent skills, inspiration and commitment — we must ensure their success on the rocky path of translation from vision to practice."[13]

The School for Educational Leadership strives to offer its Fellows tools to assist them in bringing about positive change in Israeli education and society. The School introduces the Fellows to top researchers, thinkers, and resources in order to promote their personal development and the development of their vision. The learning experience is structured around meetings with leading experts on social and educational issues, and on meetings among the Fellows. The diversity of the group is also a source of learning and of the Fellows' personal development. As one Fellow stated, "the group's pluralistic nature, be it in their fields of interest and expertise or the various agendas, forces me to listen and ask myself if I have understood the other. If I have not, I must ask why this is the case. Studies in the framework of a top quality, albeit diverse, group often require of the individual a certain amount of discipline."[14]

In the course of their studies, Fellows are required to participate in a group exercise and also to create their own individual project. The project is expected to be a focus in which the various study units come together, a process overseen by a tutor. Several graduates of the School have chosen

---

13 *Beit ha-Sefer le-Manhigut Hinukhit*, p. 8.
14 Ibid., p. 22.

to implement their projects immediately upon graduation or at later stages of their careers. Other graduates have assumed senior positions in the educational and social infrastructure.

The School for Educational Leadership, the first of its kind in Israel and worldwide, was designed along the lines of Fox's vision as an institute of high academic standing for training educational personnel that requires of its graduates more than academic output. Unlike a university, which does not hold itself responsible for the actions of its graduates, this institute is judged by its graduates' contribution to society. In many cases, the School's graduates maintain ties amongst themselves with their return to work and have created networks along educational-professional lines for improving social-educational realities.

In the mid-1990s, the Mandel Institute adopted the Jerusalem Fellows program and it ceased to operate under the auspices of the Jewish Agency. Today The Mandel Jerusalem Fellows and the Mandel School for Educational Leadership operate side by side and thus programs for the training of senior personnel for Jewish education in the Diaspora and for education in Israel are housed in the same location. In the past years, the Institute has also begun to offer additional programs, such as in-service programs for training senior staff for the civil service.

These programs merged under one roof in the late 1990s and now reside together in the Mandel Leadership Institute located on Hebron Road in Jerusalem. Fox, in his former role as president of the Mandel Foundation Israel and his current position as Director of Programs of the Mandel Foundation, continues to play a leading role with the Institute, where every year additional programs are instituted, new people attend, and objectives are reviewed.

During the 1990s, Fox led a project within the Mandel Institute that engaged in the philosophical formulation of alternatives for Jewish education. This project dealt with the ways in which Jewish education in various contexts can embody and maintain systematic vision. A vision in education, according to Fox, is not merely a vague idea about general direction or a concept of desirable outcomes. It is, instead, an approach to education that relies on fundamental assumptions about education in general, and Jewish education in particular.

For ten years, within the context of the project, Fox and his colleague Daniel Marom led a colloquium of six prominent philosophers of Jewish life and education: Menachem Brinker, Moshe Greenberg, Michael Meyer, Michael Rosenak, Israel Scheffler and Isadore Twersky. Each scholar wrote a conception, or vision, of Jewish education. The scholars then read and responded to one other's ideas. They also attended seminars with teachers and educators who were engaged in translating vision into reality in the realm of education.

The project began as a spirited and dynamic educational voyage, with no limits on its output, and eventually resulted in the publication of *Visions of Jewish Education* (Fox, Scheffler and Marom, 2003). This volume will also be published in Hebrew under the title *Medabrim Hazon*. The book reflects the unique experiment in which a variety of philosophic perceptions grapple with the objectives of Jewish education today.

* * *

At this time, Fox and his colleagues are working on new avenues of activity, combining the resources and goals of the Mandel Foundation and other institutions. The connections between the Mandel Foundation and universities, government agencies and non-profit organizations produce cooperative initiatives, all acting with the goal of improving education in Israeli society and Jewish education in the Diaspora.[15] The initiatives, alongside the institutions he has founded, are an expression of Fox's determination and his belief that with the combined effort of people, ideas and community support, it is possible to succeed and to improve the quality of life. Clearly these successes are the result of Fox's own careful, detailed adaptation of ideas to practice and the understanding that mistakes are an inevitable part of the process. In Fox's words:

"To make words on a page come alive in a community means to experiment, to learn from mistakes, to try a new approach, sometimes to fail, and inevitably to reformulate the initial idea in light of experience. No-one can write a step-by-step manual for success. Rather, success is the consequence of the ability both to justify an idea and demonstrate its implementations." (2003, p. 256).

References

A Time to Act: The Report of the Commission on Jewish Education in North America. (1990). University Press of America: Lanham-New York-London.

15 One example of this collaboration is the creation of "Scholion" – an interdisciplinary center in Jewish Studies at the Hebrew University, Jerusalem and the establishment of the Mandel Center for Studies in Jewish Education at Brandeis University.

Adar, Leah and Fox, Seymour. (1978). *Nituah Tokhnit Limmudim be-Historiah u-Vitzuah be-Batei Sefer* (Analysis of a history curriculum and its implementation in schools), Jerusalem: The Hebrew University.

Aranne, Zalman. (1971). *Hevlei Hinukh*. (The pangs of education). Jerusalem: Ministry of Education and Culture.

Aviad, Janet. (1988). Subculture or counterculture: Camp Ramah. *Studies in Jewish Education 3*.

Dror, Yuval. (1992). *Bein 'Akademizatziah' le-'Huminizatziah' be-Hakhsharat ha-Morim be-Yisrael me-Reishit ha-Meah ad Sof Shnot ha-80*. (Between academization and humanization in teacher training in Israel from the beginning of the century until the end of the 1980s).

Derakhim le-Hora'ah. (Ways to teach). Jerusalem

Dzuback, Mary Ann. (1991). *Robert M. Hutchins: Portrait of an educator*. Chicago: University of Chicago Press.

Efrati, Yael. (1992). *Mehanekh me-Zan Hadash Tzomeah be-Moshavah ha-Germanit*. (A new kind of educator is being raised in the German Colony). In *Ha'aretz* (10 November).

Ettinger, Leah. (1997). *Beit ha-Sefer le-Manhigut Hinukhit, Ekronot, Derakhim ve-Tokhniyot: Reishit ha-Derekh*. (The School for Educational leadership: principles and programs: The beginning). Jerusalem: School for Educational Leadership.

Fox, Seymour. (1984). *Yisrael ve-haHinukh Hayehudi baTefutzot*. (Israel and Jewish Education in the Diaspora). *World Leadership Conference for Jewish Education*, 18–20 June.

Fox, Seymour with Novak, William. (2000). *Vision at the heart: Lessons from Camp Ramah on the power of ideas in shaping educational institutions*. Monographs from the Mandel Foundation: Jerusalem.

Fox, Seymour, Scheffler, Israel and Marom, Daniel. (2003). *Visions of Jewish education*. Cambridge: Cambridge University Press.

Fox, Seymour. (2003). "The art of translation." In Fox, Scheffler and Marom, *Visions of Jewish Education*.

Hochstein, Annette. (1986). "The Israel Experience educational programs in Israel" *Summary report submitted to the Jewish Agency's Committee for Jewish Education*.

Hutchins, Robert M. (1947). "The administrator." In Robert B. Heywood. (Ed.) *The works of the mind*. Chicago: University of Chicago Press. (1966 edition).

Mandel, Morton L. (1984). A summary report of the Conference. *World Leadership Conference for Jewish Education, June 18–20*.

McElroy, G. C. (2002). Great Men of the Great Books. *University of Chicago Magazine 94:9* (August), pp. 18–21.

Rosenak, Michael. (1980). The Melton Center for Jewish Education in the Diaspora. *Scopus* 32, (Autumn), pp. 18–19.

Sheinin, Nissan. (1996). *HaTahalikh ha-Akedemi shel Hakhsharat ha-Morim be-Yisrael* (The academic process of teacher training in Israel). Jerusalem: The Magnes Press.

Shils, Edward. (Ed.). (1991). *Remembering the University of Chicago: Teachers, scientists and scholars*. Chicago: The University of Chicago Press.

The Story of a Friendship

DAVID FINN

It is said that a sign of true friendship is when people feel close to each other even when they don't see each other for long periods of time. That wise observation was called to my attention by Seymour Fox because it explained so clearly the relationship we have had for over 40 years. True friends have a sense that they are always on each other's minds whether they see each other often or not. There is continuity to their friendship that is never broken by distance or time. That is why our friendship has grown ever stronger as the years have gone by even though we have only seen each other intermittently.

This brief essay will not be about Seymour's accomplishments as a thinker and educator, but rather a personal story about his influence on my life and the lives of my family. In that sense it is more a description of his character than of his work.

We first met in the 1960s after Seymour graduated from the Jewish Theological Seminary and he became the head of the Teacher's Institute and Camp Ramah. I knew that my uncle, Louis Finkelstein, the Chancellor of the Seminary, considered Seymour a brilliant young man with an extraordinary future ahead of him. Although Seymour was a few years younger than I was and Louis a good deal older, I felt there was a magical quality about my friendship with both of them. I thought that they each had a quality of greatness about them.

Seymour had a special relationship with Professor Saul Lieberman as well as with Louis Finkelstein, and we used to talk about both of them in those early years. There is a curious story about their friendship that indirectly reveals something about Seymour's character. I had long admired the portraits in the Seminary of Professors Ginsberg and Marx, two giants of an earlier generation whom I had known when I was a boy, and I suggested to Louis that the time had come for a portrait of him to hang on the walls along with the others. I had asked Louis' close friend, the art-historian Meyer Shapiro, if he could recommend a painter for the project, and he suggested Wolf Kahn, a young artist who had done mostly landscapes in the past, but whom Meyer thought was well suited to capture Louis' personality. But Louis, who tended to be quite self-effacing despite his charismatic leadership, felt it was inappropriate to have an image made of him to hang on the walls of the Seminary. He proposed that Wolf paint a portrait of Professor Lieberman instead. Professor Lieberman then came up with the idea of a double portrait — of Louis and him together. It would be a portrait of a friendship rather than of an individual. Louis agreed that this would be appropriate, and not long afterwards a sensitive painting of the two of them together joined those of professors Ginsberg and Marx. In a way the portrait was a tribute to their humility as well as their friendship, and I believe that Seymour has some of the same characteristics. One almost never sees a picture of Seymour in connection with his various activities, and he tends to take a back seat when a spotlight is thrown on the accomplishments of the organization he heads. Somewhere Sigmund Freud had written that mature persons seek credit for their work rather than for themselves, and there couldn't be a more striking example of that wise observation than the personality of Seymour Fox. Everybody around him knows that he is responsible for enormous achievements, and that in his personal relationships he has had a profound effect on many individual lives. Yet he is literally the last person who would make such a claim for himself.

When I write about Seymour I think of my life as a Jew, which is unusual for me. I have written elsewhere about my life as a businessman, as a public relations practitioner, as a photographer and a painter, but I have written practically nothing about my life as a Jew. The one special opportunity I had to do so was when I was invited to write one of *The New York Times* op-ed advertisements for the American Jewish Committee on the theme "What Being Jewish Means to Me." There I recounted my embarrassment when as a child, my father who was a writer, adopted the pen name of Jonathan Finn and my name was changed officially from

Finkelstein to Finn. I worried that people would think I was trying to hide my Jewishness when in fact I was very proud of my Jewish heritage. I wrote that in my family, being Jewish meant devotion to study and commitment to ethical behavior. Seymour was, to me, the personification of those values, and knowing him over so many years has enhanced and deepened that sense of pride.

Seymour's first major involvement in the lives of our family came about in the early 1960s, when my oldest daughter, Kathy, who was about 12 years old at the time, announced to my wife, Laura, and me that she had decided to become a Catholic. The reason was that some of her friends at public school who were Catholics had invited her to go to church on Sundays, and she had been profoundly moved by the deep spirituality of their prayers. It was very different, she said, from the atmosphere she had experienced in our local synagogue on high holidays, when she thought people seemed to be more interested in gossiping with each other than in paying attention to the service. We were, of course, dumbfounded, but we suggested that before she took any drastic action she should write Uncle Louis about her feelings.

She did write a very thoughtful letter, and to my delight Louis wrote a most impressive reply, in which he not only responded to her points but invited her to have lunch with him at the Seminary. (Years later I asked Louis if I could publish that exchange of letters, but he refused. He said that it was a private correspondence between him and his grand-niece and was not written for public distribution.) Kathy was a little uneasy about the meeting, but I assured her that I would accompany her. So she accepted his invitation and shortly afterwards we were having lunch together in Louis' office at the Seminary.

The discussion that took place was between Louis and Kathy — I had promised myself that I would listen but not participate. It soon became clear that Kathy had done her homework and studied both the Hebrew Bible and the New Testament and was prepared to make a convincing case for her new beliefs. Louis was impressed, and as they talked he readily agreed that Jesus was a great teacher. That wasn't enough for Kathy because the New Testament described him as the Son of God. Louis talked about our many ancestors who had been killed in his name over the centuries and our responsibility to remember their sacrifice. Back and forth they went until Kathy found herself unable to continue and grew silent. She was overwhelmed by what Louis had to say and didn't know how to reply. Her head was bowed and tears started rolling down her cheeks. There was a long moment of silence, and then Louis said in the most gentle way that he didn't want to make Kathy feel bad, nor did he want to take away any of the beautiful thoughts she had about Jesus. But he wanted to make a proposition to her. He said that Camp Ramah was established to give young people a positive and joyous sense of what it meant to be Jewish, and he would like her to spend the coming summer at one of the camps to learn what is beautiful about her own religion. Afterwards, he said, it would be all right with him if she made up her mind as to what she wanted to do. Would she agree to that? he asked. She nodded her head. She thought it was a fair proposal and agreed to do as Louis requested. Louis explained that Camp Ramah was a Hebrew-speaking camp, which he knew would be a problem for Kathy, but he was sure that the problem could be solved. He would ask Seymour Fox, who was in charge of Camp Ramah, to arrange for a special teacher.

When Kathy came home she announced that she and her three siblings would all go to Camp Ramah that coming summer "to give Judaism its last chance," as she put it. We all met with Seymour and he assured us that he would arrange everything. He found an excellent teacher, Gail Dorph, who came to our home several times a week and gave our children Hebrew lessons. Although they would obviously have a more limited background than other children at the camp, Seymour was sure they would be able to manage. He decided that they should go to the Wisconsin Camp Ramah with which he had a special relationship, and when the time came they all went off together — with determination but very little enthusiasm.

This was the first contact my wife, Laura, and I had with Seymour, and we were enormously impressed with his sensitivity and understanding. He was interested to know about my involvement in the arts (I was chairman of the board of the Jewish Museum at the time), as well as my business involvement as co-founder of a growing public relations firm, Ruder Finn. He also developed a warm relationship with Laura who had a keen sense of her Jewish roots, although neither of us was religiously observant in our daily lives. We both recognized that Seymour had an extraordinary mind, and that he was a most unusual listener as well as teacher. When we talked about religion or philosophy or family issues, we knew that he respected our feelings and at the same time we were grateful for the new insights we gained from him about matters that were important to us. We very quickly became the closest of friends.

What we didn't know at the time was that Kathy had persuaded her younger sister, Dena, to become a Catholic as well! They had even taken an oath not to be swayed by the Camp Ramah experience in any way and to stick to their commitment to change their religion regardless of what they might experience at Camp Ramah. Presumably they thought the other two siblings were too young to be involved in such a plot. But Kathy turned out to be more flexible than Dena, and as soon as she made friends and began to enjoy herself, she forgot all about their promise to each other. When Dena realized that Kathy was having a good time, she felt deserted. Her counselor, who happened to be Seymour's sister and a sensitive psychologist, noticed that Dena was being very quiet and withdrawn. When she asked what the problem was, Dena was at first non-committal, but eventually she burst into a flood of tears and explained that Kathy had forgotten all about their oath, while she, Dena, was trying to stick to their commitment and not be taken in by their experiences at Camp Ramah. Seymour's sister persuaded her that she, too, could be free to change her mind and enjoy her camp experiences, and Dena ended up having a good time as well. When they returned from camp, the idea of becoming a Catholic had long been forgotten.

We had a chance to spend more time with Seymour when he came to New Rochelle, where we lived, as an alternate rabbi at Temple Beth El on High Holidays. We once even organized a series of evening get-togethers with neighbors who weren't sure how they felt about Judaism, in which Seymour led a thoughtful conversation about human values. In the time the two of us spent together, Seymour and I talked about our varied interests and activities — about my life in public relations and the different books I was working on as a photographer and writer on art, and about his life at the Seminary as a teacher, and organizer of new programs for Jewish education.

In one of our many conversations, I told Seymour that I had a strong sense of identity with my Jewish heritage, but I was not what might be called a practicing Jew. I didn't keep kosher, didn't put on tefillin, didn't go to shul on Shabbat — although my family had been observant on all counts when I was a child. I even said that as an adult I sometimes had negative feelings about the practices of Judaism. It seemed to me that my religion was telling me what was wrong to do, what sins should not be committed, what punishment to expect for wrongdoing, but not what joys or exaltations could be achieved through spiritual experiences. I once told Louis Finkelstein that I remembered being in his apartment as a child, playing on a Saturday afternoon with his daughter Hadassah, with whom I was quite close, when somehow my hand passed close to a light switch. He became very tense, and warned me to be very careful not to turn on the light by mistake. That was what Judaism meant to me — beware of breaking even the smallest law of observance, rather than be inspired on a day of holiness. Louis understood why such childhood experiences could create negative feelings, and Seymour did as well.

Some family tragedies in my early life had led my mother, who had been devoutly orthodox as a young woman, to completely change her point of view and virtually abandon religion as an element in her life. My father was not as negative as she was. He had great respect for his father and his brother who were distinguished rabbis, and he used to say that not being observant did not mean we were not religious. I used to enjoy going with him to the Seminary on High Holidays mostly because it was a time to be together, and also because I found the scholarly air in the services and prayers especially moving. In later years, Laura and I always appreciated the holidays as a time to bring our family together and attend services at our local temple in New Rochelle, NY, but those experiences rarely gave us a profound feeling about Judaism as an important part of our lives.

All of that seemed to us to be a limited and even superficial relationship with Judaism, which I often discussed with Seymour. He was not at all surprised or critical of us when we told him how we felt. I knew that he was much beloved by the congregation in New Rochelle, but I also knew that he completely understood and respected our feelings. Judaism, he said, was meant to be a positive element in our lives, and he encouraged us to find our own way to identify with the values that meant the most to us. He convinced me that the many positive experiences I was having in my involvement in Jewish affairs, in my friendship with Jewish leaders and intellectuals, in my reading of books on Jewish life, represented a deep bond with Judaism, which I should continue to strengthen.

My friend Alfred Kazin, with whom I published a book called *Our New York* (his text and my photographs), once noted that Sholom Aleichem wrote about "Jewishness" as if it were a gift, a marvel, an unending theme of wonder and delight. I could identify with this even though what he described was not part of my way of life. At the same time, there were moments when I have been deeply moved by prayer. This has been particularly true when in later years I have said *Kaddish* for my loved ones — my father, my mother, my sister, my brother, my father-in-law, my mother-in-law, and my wife's grandmother — all of whom were very close to me. In those prayers, I have always felt an uncanny closeness to them, believing to the depths of my being that I am as much in their presence while I am praying as I was when they were here. It has been a healing and uplifting experience, and it remains as intense today as it ever was, even though decades have passed since many of them died. It is not the meaning of the words I recite that touches me so deeply, it is the sense that my ancestors for hundreds of years have uttered the same words for the same reason over and over again. The words are to me like "old stones that cannot be deciphered" to use a phrase from T.S. Eliot's "Four Quartets." Seymour understood how I felt about all this, and he helped me realize that these experiences were as strong a foundation for my sense of Jewish identity as anything else I might do.

But there was much more in our relationship than an understanding of Jewish identity. In my mind, Seymour's greatness, and I don't use that word lightly, lies in his ability to help others realize their potential for expanding their horizons in whatever field they might be working. It is hard to describe what there is in his nature that enables him to achieve this, and I worry that he will be embarrassed when he reads what I have written. I don't think he realizes that he has that charismatic effect on people, and would rather just think of himself as a good friend to those who are close to him and a good teacher to his students. Others know that he is much more than that. If the course of his life had been different and he had chosen to be more active in public life, I'm sure that he would have become one of the most distinguished intellectual and spiritual leaders of our time. Indeed, I was so certain of his capacity to become such a leader that, along with other good friends, I tried my best to encourage him to move in that direction. But that's not where his heart was. As far as he was concerned, if he could help develop leadership abilities in others — even a few hundred gifted individuals, he would feel his life's mission would be accomplished. His gift to the world would not be recognized in personal fame or glory, but in the achievement of others who would themselves become inspired teachers through his efforts.

When Seymour moved to Israel and became a member of the faculty of Hebrew University, we continued to see each other regularly. And when we had another crisis in our family, it was Seymour whom I turned to for guidance.

At the time, my son, Peter, was a student at Brown University, and he had fallen in love with a fellow student, a fine young woman named Sarah Duncan. One day Peter announced that he and Sarah had decided to get married. We loved Sarah but unfortunately she was not Jewish. Her parents were Protestants and had been married by Algernon Black, the head of the Ethical Culture movement. I knew Algernon Black and admired him, but a possible intermarriage in our family was a serious problem for us, and I didn't know how to cope with it. When we spoke to Peter, Laura found it difficult to be restrained. As far as she was concerned they just couldn't get married unless Sarah became Jewish. Peter said that he and Sarah wanted to spend the rest of their lives together, and he could no more ask Sarah to convert to Judaism than she could ask him to convert to Christianity. If we didn't want them to get married, they would simply live together as an unmarried couple. Laura said she couldn't deal with it, and that it was up to me to find a solution.

I decided to call Seymour who was in Israel at the time to ask his advice. Seymour was very wise, as usual, and he urged us to calm down. He was going to be teaching in Harvard that summer and he would arrange to spend time with Peter and Sarah to talk about their future. He had confidence that everything would work out. When I told Peter about my conversation, he was extremely skeptical. He said that if Seymour could solve the problem, he would be a genius. But he had great respect and affection for Seymour and was sure that Sarah would feel the same way. They would have no reservations about spending time with him.

And so a series of conversations between the three of them began. Once a week Peter and Sarah went to Boston and had dinner with Seymour. They were all obviously enjoying getting to know each other. Peter said that he and Sarah found their discussions very stimulating, and Seymour said that things were progressing well. I asked Seymour what they talked about in their weekly sessions, but he wouldn't tell me. I wondered if he was giving them some background about Judaism. Seymour told me once again to relax. They were discussing all sorts of things — life, philosophy, love, etc. He found both Peter and Sarah to be wonderful young people, and he had confidence that their conversations would bear fruit.

By the end of the summer, we were thrilled to learn that Sarah was inclined to convert to Judaism. Then Peter told me one evening that every time Sarah went home from school, she became uncertain again. Her parents told her it would be all right with them if she decided to convert if it was what she wanted to do and not because of pressure from Peter's parents. Peter said that she felt we *were* pressuring her, and that made it difficult for her to decide. I was surprised, because neither Laura nor I had talked to Sarah about it. But according to Peter, Sarah knew how concerned we were, and that was a problem. I told Peter that I wished I could tell Sarah how I really felt, that it was not because I thought being Jewish was better than being Christian. It was something else that I wished I knew how to express. Peter thought it would be a good idea for me to try to explain my point of view. So that night I stayed up late writing a long letter to Seymour telling him what I thought I would like to say not only to Sarah but to Peter as well. I wanted to show the letter to Seymour before writing to them because I had such a high respect for his remarkable sensitivity to the whole issue, and because of his confidence that their talks had been fruitful. I still didn't know what they talked about in their many conversations, but I wanted to be sure that what I wrote did not in any way run counter to what he had said. Seymour telephoned me as soon as he received my letter and assured me that it would be OK to write the same letter to them. His warm encouragement gave me the feeling that he understood my perspective completely – or to put it another way, I came to think that through my friendship with Seymour I had been able to clarify in my own mind how I felt about Jewish continuity.

So with his encouragement I re-addressed the letter, and sent it off to Peter and Sarah. Laura and I were tremendously relieved when shortly afterwards Peter told us that Sarah had decided to convert to Judaism.

That was 26 years ago, and they have been happily married ever since. They have two brilliant children, Noah and Emily.

There is a sequel to that story. Over the years, many friends of mine have confided in me about children of theirs who had fallen in love with someone who wasn't Jewish, and when I told them the story of Peter and Sarah, they asked for copies of my letter to give to their children. I don't know how many copies I have given to friends over the years. I even gave one to my friend, Ed Klein, the editor of *The New York Times* magazine section, who had married a Japanese woman and was bringing up his children as Jews, and he wanted to publish my letter as an article. However he said he would have to mention all our names, and we felt it would that would be inappropriate since it was a private matter for our family. Now, because of our affection for Seymour and the influence he has had on our lives, Peter and Sarah have given me permission to publish the letter here for the first time.

October 2, 1975

Dear Sarah and Peter,

There's a line of Robert Frost's which I always loved but which I am not sure I remember accurately…it goes something like "We dance round in a ring and suppose/But the Secret sits in the middle and knows." I feel a little like that about this letter. Whether it says what I wanted to say I couldn't quite make up my mind; whether I should have written it in the first place I couldn't decide. Perhaps I'm being oversensitive about it. Perhaps it honestly says how I feel and it is foolish of me to hesitate.

It is hard to write to the two of you without referring to one or another in the third person (as if I were writing to someone else about you), but I'll do my best.

The immediate provocation of the letter is a talk Peter and I had late into the night (or morning, to be more precise) about Judaism and Christianity. As we talked, I think we both felt that we were pretty much on the same wavelength about almost everything — including a sensitive understanding of exactly how Sarah, who was brought up as a Christian, must feel about the whole thing. Peter explained that one of the major problems that the two of you have had to cope with is the sense of pressure from us — Peter's parents — and if this pressure had not existed it might have been much easier for you to work things out in your own minds. I found myself speculating about the nature of that pressure — and then suddenly realized that we had never talked to Sarah about it… and the "pressure" (and here I purposely put quotes around the word) could only be something one sensed in the air, or as interpreted through Peter rather than something actually exerted in a direct relationship.

As I thought about this, and talked to Peter, it occurred to me that "pressure" was not at all descriptive of the kinds of feelings I have on the subject, and that I really wished I could tell Sarah what my thoughts actually were. As a sort of experiment, I then told Peter what I would say to Sarah if she were here — and when I was through, Peter sighed (I thought) half in relief and half in frustration. He said it might indeed be very good if I did say all that to Sarah, but that undoubtedly such a conversation — even at best — would be a difficult one, that Sarah might find herself agreeing with my point of view as we talked — that it might even help clear the air — but Peter was worried that when Sarah was by herself again, and thought some more about it, she would feel just as upset and uncertain about the whole thing as she was before. That was when I decided on the unusual idea of writing you both a letter to tell you how I feel.

To begin with, I should explain that Peter brought back with him from his visit to Louisville (Sarah's parents) a copy of Sarah's paper on the Meaning of Judaism (I forget the exact title) — a paper she wrote for a course on Judaism that she took at Brown University, I think a couple of years ago (in any case before she met Peter). Both Laura and I read the paper and were amazed; it was as fine an explanation of what Judaism is all about and why Jews feel the need to perpetuate their

44   The Story of a Friendship

heritage as we had ever read. Laura and I said jokingly that if Sarah
would read this paper she would understand exactly how any sensitive
Jew feels about the past and future... and Peter hastened to say that
Sarah was afraid that this was exactly what we would think.

However as Peter and I talked about it, I couldn't help observing how
curious it was that all of us are pretty good about appreciating or being
responsive to religious (or anti-religious) ideas that are different from
our own. After all, I had worked on my book on Donatello for ten years
(as a photographer), and Donatello was one of the most devout Christian
artists of the 15th century (unlike many others of the time, he was very
deeply involved in the religious content of his work), and Fred Hartt
(who wrote the text for the book), was especially sensitive to the
religious elements of the various works. Moreover, I have just finished
my book on the three Pietas of Michelangelo, which in a sense is even
more religious (and might even be used by the Catholic Church as part
of its education program). As if that weren't enough, I have
concentrated for the past few years on a series of paintings on T.S.
Eliot's "Four Quartets" which is one of the most deeply religious
(Christian largely, but with traces of Buddhism and Hinduism) poems in
the English language. Although I have read a fair amount of Jewish
literature, history and philosophy, and been very moved by it — and
have also been involved with the Jewish Museum for many years —
obviously I have been most profoundly affected — in a personal sense —
with the works that have been the basis for my photographs and
paintings for these past many years. In that sense, my own experience is
very much like Sarah's in writing her paper about Judaism. Nobody
would have any difficulty believing that I understand — and am
responsive to — the basic concepts of Christianity, any more than one
could have any difficulty believing that Sarah understands the basic
concepts of Judaism.

If one wanted to extend this, one only has to think of Louis
Finkelstein's relationship to Bertrand Russell, and their great mutual
admiration, even though Russell was an avowed atheist and Louis one
of the great religious thinkers of our time. As a matter of fact, the
Institute of Religious and Social Sciences, the only school in the world
where priests and rabbis and ministers study together, is a school
developed by Louis Finkelstein because of his lifelong desire to share
the wisdom of all faiths.

So where does our problem come from? If I had not been born a Jew
and had been born in another religion that had no hang-ups about the

past and the future, I'm sure I would have felt free and flexible about the family's attitude towards — or against — religion. (I hasten to add that I am proud of being a Jew for reasons that don't need to be spelled out... it is just that if I had not been, my attitude towards religion might have been more in keeping with people like Bertrand Russell — and with P.B. Shelly (I have just finished reading a brilliant biography of him written by a young Englishman) who was a passionate atheist because he didn't like — or couldn't stand — the tyranny of an all-knowing all-powerful god.) In that sense I admire Sarah's parents who have brought up their children, I gather, with a complete sense of freedom to choose their own way of life. I think this is most sensible, most rational, most logical — and everything in me says I agree with it.

However, I was born a Jew, and the whole shape of my life has been affected accordingly. By the shape of my life, I mean that I feel that I cannot abide the thought of violating the responsibility, which has been placed on me by centuries of suffering, centuries of struggling for survival, centuries of striving to find a just life in the midst of some of the greatest trials ever borne by any segment of humanity. This is an obligation of history that is not necessarily tied to my ideas of spirituality, or universal truths, or beliefs in ultimate reality, etc. About those matters I feel completely free to follow my own, independent thinking. But about being a Jew, about accepting without reservation my identification with all those who have been part of the past and will hopefully be part of the future, I have no doubt. This somehow is a must for me, and imperative in the true Kantian sense.

Now, of course, this is not an imperative which anyone else need pay any attention to. It is certainly not one that anyone not born a Jew need feel in the slightest way concerned about. There is no particular logic or rationale about it. It certainly says nothing about the relationship between Judaism and Christianity or any other religion — the virtues of one over the other, the exclusive truths in one and absent in others, or any other such matters. No such considerations have any reality in my mind. And I am very puzzled about the thought of how one who is not born a Jew should ever bother to consider such an obligation for himself or herself. If one felt as I do, I could see no earthly reason to "convert" to Judaism to try to kindle in my own soul that sense of obligation (which could seem more like a burden — a cross to bear, to use an inappropriate metaphor — than a blessing) which only someone born a Jew need to suffer with.

This is how I feel, putting myself in Sarah's shoes. Brought up to be free, believing completely in the logic of this freedom, why accept a bond or link or chain that seems to go against everything I believe in?

The only reason I feel someone like Sarah can possibly think about this is that if one should happen to be in love with a Jew — a Jew who feels this innermost sense of responsibility in some fashion (hard to verbalize, hard to identify, hard even to understand — and something, I believe that grows deeper and more penetrating as one grows older), and one thinks of spending one's life with such a person. Perhaps the only way this can be done in a sense of total union is if the person not born a Jew decides to share the commitment which the one who was born a Jew cannot escape. This is an odd kind of action to take — for if the definition of what I am referring to is rooted in the fact of being born a Jew, how does one who was not born a Jew accept such a definition for oneself? The only way I can answer this in my own mind is an act only explainable through the union of two souls — "a further union and a deeper communion" in Eliot's phrase — in which two people become a unity, and the two can accept what was a before a fact only in the life of one.

The use of the word "convert" bothers me in thinking about this whole subject. It implies — or in fact states by definition — that a person is changing one's belief to a new belief which one considers better. (Webster defines *convert*: to bring over or persuade...to a particular belief, view, course, party of principle often from a previously held position....."). In this sense why on earth should one "convert" from Christianity to Judaism, or from rationalism to Christianity — unless one is profoundly affected by the religion one is adopting in the way that Eliot was affected by Christianity. (Stephen Spender, in his recent biography of Eliot writes about Eliot's "conversion to Christianity" even though he was born a Unitarian, because what he embraced was in effect a new religion for him, and it changed his whole way of life, indeed his whole attitude towards man and the universe... or more accurately, the conversion was a function of the change which had taken place within him). I know that Sarah has no such experiences, and I certainly don't, so I could never convert to Judaism in this sense. (I once talked to Laura about converting to Quakerism because of its profound beliefs in peace... that was before I knew Nixon was a Quaker!) If I were Sarah, and I thought Peter's parents wanted me to convert to Judaism for this reason or in this way, I know my back would be up, and I would resent that. It would be just as logical for Peter to convert to Christianity — that is, if there were any logic at all to the idea that husband and wife had to have the same religion. And I'll bet that's exactly how Sarah feels.

The trouble is that I don't know the right word to describe what I have in mind. Rather than converting, it has something to do with sharing, sharing the obligation to a trickle of humanity through the long stretches of history — and that's about it. As far as beliefs and way of life — I see nothing but complete freedom, just as I feel — with books on the *Pieta*, *Four Quartets*, atheism — or if one should ever get interested, the Jewish concept of justice…it doesn't matter. This is not a question of imposition or belief, or even going through the motions to make it appear that one has been "persuaded." Such an idea would revolt me. I am talking about the reality I feel — and which I am sure Peter feels in some way, too, and which I am sure Sarah completely understands — not some sham for appearance sake.

I have a feeling that if Sarah knew how I feel, that instead of the "pressure" which seems to have been in the air, that it is this curious strain (or stain) in our souls as Jews that we are struggling with, she might be very much relieved. At least I hope that is the way she would feel. The trouble is that it is so hard to talk about this. My guess is that the two of you must have talked about some aspect of this — at least that is my impression from what Peter told me. But he also said that Sarah was still troubled by a great deal of uncertainty and unhappiness about the whole subject…and I'm sure the whole thing hangs like a cloud over their heads. The only reason I decided to write this was because of Peter's comments about the negative effects of the "pressure" which Sarah has felt from us, and my sudden realization (helped by reading Sarah's paper and reflections on my own books and paintings) that our feelings might appear to be something drastically different from what they really are. And if Peter felt the removal of this (I think illusory) pressure would help, I at least wanted to go to as many pains as possible to explain exactly how I — (and I am sure Laura agrees with me) feel about the subject. I don't know if it will help, but at least it's the truth as I see it. If it does help to clear the air, I will be enormously happy, because I think Sarah is a wonderful person and it is a joy to see Sarah and Peter together, and it would be marvelous if the problem which has plagued the two of you could be resolved and free you to concentrate your energies on all the other important things which two people have to deal with in building your lives for the future.

Perhaps a final word — and that about Sarah's parents whom I haven't met, but have heard a lot about, and admire a great deal. I'm sure they wonder, too, about this whole business of "conversion" and the unfortunate, parochial view of some Jews who think theirs is the "true" religion. I would love to tell them how I feel also, and I somehow have a feeling they would respect what I would say. I recently learned that Algernon Black married them, which says something about their own broad views about religion. I have known Algernon Black over the years (I once debated with him about ethics and business at Barnard), and certainly respect his views about ethics and religion. I hope some day that my feeling about all this will be expressed to Sarah's parents — I'd like to tell them myself, or perhaps this letter says it, because I know that someone like Sarah must have a deep respect for her parents' feelings. I cannot imagine that Sarah would be comfortable about any step she would take unless she felt that her parents thought it made sense.

And the last thing I would want Sarah's parents to feel would be that Sarah was "knuckling under" the pressure from Peter's parents.

That's pretty much what I wanted to write. A much longer letter than I originally intended — but there it is, for what it is worth.

All the best,

P.S. Peter also reminded me of two other points I made during our late night discussion. The first was that I really felt terrible for Sarah about this whole business. I could sense how difficult all this was for her — and I also realized that she had done nothing to deserve this trouble. If only she had fallen in love with someone else, or if we were not a family that felt as we do, she would have none of these problems, and it was a great pity that she should have to go through all this just because we — and Peter — were who we were. I also made the point that being in love, contemplating the prospect of marriage at some future time, should be a joyful — certainly a positive experience. It should not be something which is dominated by the idea of making some kind of sacrifice about one's own origins and beliefs. I have a realistic view of what it means for two people to adjust their lives to each other — I'm not talking about that truism. I am talking about the special difficulty in this case which makes the contemplation of a union something of an enormous problem to be solved rather than the beginning of a common destiny. I hope some of the points I have made in this letter help to relieve the tensions for both of you.

* * * *

There were many other times when my friendship with Seymour had a great influence on my life, but the most intense professional work we did together had to do with the conferences organized by Mort Mandel that took place between 1988–1990 in which Jewish leaders attempted to assess the state of Jewish education in the world today. Mort's goal was to develop a long range, comprehensive plan to improve what threatened to be a disastrous state of affairs. These conferences held under the auspices of The Commission on Jewish Education in North America, proved to be the first time that the heads of the Reform, Conservative, Orthodox and Reconstructionist movements in the U.S. met together with some of the top education scholars in America and the leaders of major Jewish organizations and foundations to discuss this most compelling issue. I was amazed at the number of outstanding scholars and religious leaders as well as lay leaders that had been assembled for these conferences. It was a wonderful example of how effective the joint efforts of Mort and Seymour could be. Between the two of them, they were able to persuade these distinguished individuals to devote a substantial amount of time and effort to reach a consensus on a whole series of critical issues in Jewish education. Seymour and his colleagues had commissioned a number of excellent research papers to be prepared for the conferences in order to make sure that the discussions would be serious and well-informed, and Mort was a master at organizing and leading the conferences themselves. This was quite a revelation to me, for I had known Mort in his business role almost as long as I had known Seymour, and it was amazing to see the fruits of his organizing ability combined with Seymour's intellectual and leadership skills working so well on such a significant undertaking.

In the course of preparing for the conferences, Seymour told me of his many discussions with Lawrence Cremin of Teachers College of Columbia University, Israel Scheffler and Isador Twersky of Harvard University, Theodore Sizer of Brown University, and many other leading educators. It was clearly Seymour's vision to combine the best thinking in the field of general education with insights into the current state of Jewish education. This was not to be a superficial overview, but rather a profound, in-depth analysis of how and why Jewish education had failed and how it could be transformed into a far more serious and well thought-out function in the years ahead. Seymour was not interested in simply organizing a series of conversations, but in calling upon the best minds of our time to provide a solid foundation for a new era in Jewish education in America. So carefully was this thought out, that those in attendance felt that the future of educational activities in Orthodox, Conservative, Reform and Reconstruction Movements depended on how thoroughly and creatively they addressed the issue together.

At Mort's and Seymour's request, I attended the conferences as an observer, and when they were over, I met with Mort, Seymour and Annette Hochstein, who was the other key person in the Mandel Foundation involved in its education programs, to see what we could do with the mountain of paper that had been accumulated. The decision was made that Seymour, Annette, and I would take on the task of putting it all together into a single publication.

Writing what we called *A Time to Act* proved to be a monumental undertaking. The three of us sat in my office for days and eventually weeks framing the report. We each took turns at the computer writing drafts of the text as we exchanged thoughts. When we finished the first draft we had no idea whether Mort and those who had participated in the conferences would feel we had done justice to the discussions that had taken place, but to our delight all those involved felt that we had managed to pull it all together. Subsequently we had several telephone conferences with the different parties to make a few modifications, but finally the text was completed, approved and published. The response to that publication from the entire Jewish community has been a source of great satisfaction to all concerned.

Since then, Seymour and his wife, Sue, and Laura and I have continued our close friendship, talking frequently on the telephone and seeing each other as often as we can. Seymour never fails to tell me proudly of the accomplishments of his three sons as well as Sue's five children, and he shares our pride in the achievements of our four children and ten grandchildren. He is still the first one any of us would turn to when seeking sound judgment and wisdom on any major issue we face, and we know that his understanding and guidance would be of the highest order.

This is at best a partial description of what Seymour's friendship has meant to my family and me. Usually one does not have an opportunity to write about such friendships — one just takes them for granted. They are an integral part of our lives. But I welcome the opportunity to tell this brief story as a contribution to a collection of essays about Seymour's work. He is one of those rare individuals whose influence on our time is likely to be far more significant than is generally recognized, and I congratulate those of his colleagues who took the initiative of producing this record of his accomplishments.

Theory in Practice*

Daniel Marom

Introduction

In a class on governance at the Mandel Leadership Institute, a student once interrupted Seymour Fox's lecture and challenged him to analyze a failed exchange she had experienced in a hurried meeting with a director-general of the Israeli Ministry of Education. By her own admission, this was a missed opportunity that she had regretted for years. She wanted to understand where she had gone wrong and what she could have done that might have succeeded. On the spot, Fox asked her to simulate the exchange and then spent 30 minutes studying it with the group. The theoretical principles he had expounded in his lecture were now applied to this case. As the corrective to the failure became glaringly evident, it was difficult not to be mystified by Fox's capacity for extemporaneous response. How could he have produced such a profound and practical solution so readily?

Working as Fox's assistant at the time, I realized that such applications are the essence of his everyday work life. Yet, characteristic as this vigorous movement between the domains of theory and practice may be of Fox as educator, it is easy to underestimate just how fundamental it is in

* I would like to thank Annette Hochstein, Mordechai Nisan and Israel Scheffler for their critical suggestions after having reviewed earlier drafts of this paper. I would also like to thank Erin Henriksen and Avi Katzman for their patient and meticulous editorial assistance.

his larger approach to education. Only by focusing on the rigorous interplay between theory and practice in Fox's educational theory and practice can one grasp what is most profound in his approach to education.

How can such a focus be possible if it is not fully evident to those who limit themselves exclusively to reading Fox's theoretical writings or to getting an account of his practical achievements? In confronting this challenge, I am helped by one of Fox's own essays in which a unique form of description of theory-practice interplay appears. In "A Practical Image of the Practical," Fox provides us with an "annotated protocol" of the deliberations of a team of experts he led in the development of a curriculum in botany. (Fox, 1972). In the protocol, the reader is given an illustration of Fox's practice as the leader of the deliberations in the form of a line-by-line record of the curricular team's discourse. Alongside the protocol, Fox discloses the theoretical principles that guided him in his choice of directives and interventions in the deliberation. Reading the protocols in light of these interpretive comments thereby enables one to arrive at a clearer understanding of the theory and practice of managing a curriculum design process.

Using this methodology as my guide, I have chosen to present Fox's work in education through a series of interpreted vignettes.[1] The vignettes derive from my direct encounters with Fox, both as a student in his courses in curriculum development and as his associate at the Mandel Foundation and the Mandel Leadership Institute. The interpretations explicate Fox's educational practice in terms of its guiding theoretical assumptions as I learned them from his oral presentations and his writings. What follows is one interpreted vignette relating to Fox's conception of the role of theory in educational practice.

* * *

"Decisions of Principle": The Example of Driving

It was my privilege to assist Fox as he presented his conception of training for educational leadership to staff members in the programs that he founded for the development of senior personnel in Jewish and Israeli education. My role included researching the field of administrator training

---

1   This essay is an abridgement of a larger work I have written on "The Rigorous Interplay of Theory and Practice in Seymour Fox's Educational Theory and Practice" to be published by the Mandel Foundation.

in education, preparing the members of the staff group for each session, and summarizing the ensuing deliberations around Fox's conception.

In his presentation, Fox referred to a paper by the philosopher of ethics, R. M. Hare, entitled "Decisions of Principle" (1959). Fox clarified why he drew on a reference from the field of ethical philosophy in order to articulate his ideas on the training of educational leaders: educational leadership and ethics both focus on guiding practical behavior with theoretical principles.

According to Hare, a person cannot be trained to be ethical merely by being taught ethical behavior. Since every ethical act involves applying a moral principle to specific circumstances, the focus of ethical training would rather have to be on enhancing a person's capacity to make decisions about his or her behavior in light of moral principles. In order to illustrate his point, Hare refers to learning how to drive a car — a task that he sees as similar to ethical training:

"I am told, for instance, always to draw into the side of the road when I stop the car; but later I am told that this does not apply when I stop before turning into a side-road to the off-side — for then I must stop near the middle of the road until it is possible for me to turn. Still later I learn that in this manoeuvre it is not necessary to stop at all if it is an uncontrolled junction and I can see that there is no traffic which I should obstruct by turning. When I have picked up all these modifications to the rule, and the similar modifications to all the other rules, and practice them habitually as so modified, then I am said to be a good driver, because my car is always in the right place in the road, traveling at the right speed, and so on. The good driver is, among other things, one whose actions are so exactly governed by principles which have become a habit with him, that he normally does not have to think just what to do. But road conditions are exceedingly various, and therefore it is unwise to let all one's driving become a matter of habit. One can never be certain that one's principles of driving are perfect — indeed one can be very sure that they are not; and therefore the good driver not only drives well from habit, but constantly attends to his driving habits, to see whether they might not be improved; he never stops learning." (Ibid., pp. 76–77).

Fox refers to Hare's line of thinking in order to argue against the sort of leadership training that limits itself to tooling educators with management techniques. That would be as limiting as teaching a person to be moral, or even to drive, with a manual. Instead, Fox seeks to equip the educational leader with a strong command of the principles of education and to enhance his or her capacity to work with these principles in making everyday professional decisions.

Being privy to the process which led Fox to Hare in the first place, I could appreciate how committed he was to the principle of making "decisions of principle" in his own educational leadership. Hare's article was pointed out to him at one of his regular meetings with his cherished consultant, Professor Israel Scheffler. This may come as no surprise to those familiar with Scheffler's career as a philosopher of education. At Harvard University's Graduate School of Education and its Philosophy of Education Research Center, which he co-founded, Scheffler has explored the deeper implications of central ideas in education such as the conditions of knowledge, human potential, and the educated person.

Scheffler's mention of Hare's article was only incidental to the purpose of this meeting. Fox was consulting with Scheffler as a kind of "intellectual braintrust" regarding the theoretical soundness of one of his recent initiatives. It was a mode of working he carried out with his mentor and life-long teacher, the philosopher of education Joseph Schwab until his death. Much later, during the years I worked with Fox, I noted that he rarely takes a step forward in implementing any of his plans — the establishing of a new institution, the convening of a commission of community leaders, or designing curriculum — without first checking its conceptual infrastructure with Scheffler.

They often spend hours examining the theoretical principles that led Fox to the initiative under discussion. Fox wants to learn more from Scheffler as to where he is relatively strong or weak in his guiding assumptions, what alternatives he is ruling out in his applications, what arguments might be made against his moving forward, and so on. These insights influence Fox's thinking, sometimes even change it. Whether or not he agrees with Scheffler, he always takes his comments and criticisms very seriously.

Inevitably, as with the Hare article, tidbits from Scheffler's comments also creep into Fox's work with others, at board and staff meetings, in his exchanges with community leaders and professional associates in deliberations on his next initiatives, in his teaching. In this manner, Scheffler helps Fox to base the decision-making process at the Mandel Foundation and the curriculum and pedagogy at the Mandel Leadership Institute on sound ideas.

Equally demonstrative of Fox's commitment to "decisions of principle" is his own everyday practice. Though any random topic in Fox's work life might illustrate this point, allow me to remain with Hare's motif of automobile transportation. My point is choosing such a mundane topic is not to trivialize the role of theory in Fox's educational practice, but rather to show just how far it stretches.

Early in my association with Fox, I was given the assignment of ordering a taxi for a distinguished guest. Twenty minutes before the end of our appointment, Fox asked me if I had already ordered the cab. When I responded negatively, he took me aside to give me a two minute lesson on the principles for ordering cabs in Israel. That the cab had to arrive early was taken for granted, as an expression of the seriousness of the Jewish educational undertaking. The question here was how to order a cab in Israel so that it would come on time.

According to Fox, the consumer culture in Israel was not based on the principle "the client is the boss." Rather, clients are often treated preferentially on the basis of the volume of their business and the urgency of their commissions. This is a roving principle, so that at any given time, the preference for one client over another may change. It is not uncommon in Israel for a cab driver to ask the person who hailed the cab where he or she is going, and then, on the basis of the response, to decide whether or not to be for hire.

Consequently, Fox explained, one has to order a cab far in advance of the time it is needed, with the explanation that it is for an important meeting and a request that the cab wait for the client even if she/he does not exit the building at the said time. "Tell them that while waiting, the driver should turn the meter on," he added, "but also that he should not honk the horn, because the meeting inside should not be disrupted. Then, a second call has to be made an hour before the pickup time in order to double check that the order has indeed been registered and accurately so."

Before I could express my bewilderment regarding this approach, Fox continued by arguing for the necessity of a third call, ten minutes before the appointed time. This one was to be made in order to check whether the cab was on its way, and if so, how far was it from our offices. "If there is any hesitation in the dispatcher's answer," Fox added, "a threat should be made as to the prospect of our continued business with that company."

Overwhelmed by the amount of effort Fox was demanding for this simple task, I did not take in too much more of Fox's instructions about the fourth and fifth calls. Reasoned as Fox's arguments were, I found them to be counterintuitive. Still, as soon as he finished, I rushed to order the cab. Then, as was the case in so many of Fox's seemingly excessive calculations, his practical wisdom was borne out by ensuing events. By the third time I saw our guest check his watch, waiting impatiently for the cab to arrive, I had learned my lesson. From then on I began to notice cabs waiting silently for Fox in front of our Foundation offices. I soon learned that the administrative support staff at the Mandel Foundation had been trained to work with the same principles as I had regarding ordering cabs.

The second car-related incident took place a few years later. By then, I had become accustomed to Fox's standards of practice, especially with distinguished guests, and I could now give lectures as to his guiding principles regarding their treatment. I do not say this facetiously. Students and associates marvel at Fox's ability to collaborate with outstanding community leaders and scholars in joint educational endeavors. Many even testify to their sense that this accomplishment had an ennobling effect on their otherwise undervalued profession.

As it turns out, I found it necessary to share some of what I had learned from him on this topic with an angry dinner-date companion! I had explained that I would have to change the time of our engagement to comply with Fox's request that I accompany a community leader from the airport. Though there was no problem changing the time, my companion felt that Fox's request was in principle outrageous. She knew that this community leader visited Israel many times a year. To accompany him from the airport would be insulting, she argued. It would insinuate that he was incapable of making it to the hotel on his own. "This sycophantic catering is not only humiliating," she posited, "but it also arouses suspicions of manipulation for the purposes of fundraising."

Goaded by a sense that the only way I could be respectful of my date was to convince her to the contrary, I summarized some of the principles behind his request. First, I explained, Fox's unequalled success as a fundraiser for Jewish education had to reflect a trusting rather than manipulative relationship with community leaders. Indeed, much of his work was guided by the assumption that the success of Jewish education was contingent on genuine partnership between professionals and community leaders.

Fox's method of pursuing this genuine partnership, I continued, went beyond the meeting table. Of course, the crux of that relationship did hinge on honest businesslike discourse about Jewish education. Still, the authenticity of the partnership needed to find consistent expression in other areas as well. If the professionals were really relating to the community leaders not merely as instruments for the advancement of their own plans, but rather as representatives of the community, they had to be treated as such. It was important to invest conscious effort in order to demonstrate that the partnership went above and beyond the immediate agenda.

That did not mean one had to cross the boundaries of a working relationship between educators and community leaders and seek out personal intimacy. That would be manipulative. Nor did it mean self-denial or forfeiting one's own dignity. The point is to honor the educator-community leader relationship by giving it a proper pedestal.

In this case, the application of Fox's principle was clear. The community leader flew over to Israel to discuss collaboration on the development of Jewish education in his own community. Whether or not we found a way to work together, this leader and his community should be treated with reverence and collegiality. Accompanying him from the airport to the hotel, using that time to answer preliminary questions about our institutions, our meetings, participants around the table, what's going on in Jerusalem or in Israel, making sure he was comfortably settled in at his hotel, personally delivering a schedule, agenda and extra background materials, could all contribute to establishing a true sense of partnership around the meeting table.

Apparently, the thing I left out of this analysis was the methodological question: What is the guiding principle for how to appropriately convey to one's date one's regret at having changed dinner plans because of an urgent matter at work? My date might have been convinced by my arguments, but somehow, she was not amused.

Some consolation was given me by what followed. At the meeting the next day, the community leader publicly announced his appreciation at having been accompanied to the hotel from the airport, claimed that he had not too often been treated so well in the world of Jewish education, and saw this as a hopeful sign for the quality and content of the coming discussions. As it turned out, we did strike up a fruitful collaboration.

The last example is for me the most powerful of the three. It took place at the outset of my years of collaboration with Fox and Scheffler on a project dedicated to the development of alternative conceptions of Jewish education. Much of this project involved close work with some of the leading Jewish studies scholars in the world.

Among these was Professor Isadore Twersky, of blessed memory. A scholar of medieval Jewish philosophy, Twersky served as the dean of Judaic studies at Harvard University and rabbi of the Talner Beit Midrash in Brookline, Massachusetts. Though I had never met Twersky, his reputation as a leading academic and as a compelling spiritual figure preceded him. When Fox asked me to bring him to our first meeting, I was more than happy to comply. The same principles that applied to community leaders applied to Twersky.

As it happened, however, one of my associates at the Mandel

Foundation overheard Fox's request and pleaded with me to allow him to replace me in picking up Twersky. This associate was a former student of Twersky and had remained his adoring and faithful disciple. As Twersky would benefit from the same kind of treatment from this person as he would from me, I forfeited.

When the two of them entered the room for the meeting, Fox noticed that my associate had picked him up instead of me. He was furious with this exchange. Asked for my justification, I invoked Fox's own principles concerning the treatment of scholars. His shaking head and rolling eyes signaled to me that there was obviously another principle at work here.

Circumstances did not allow Fox to explain what it was to me right at that time, but when I mentioned this story to another associate, he explained it. Since he, like Fox, had grown up in the world of Orthodoxy, the guiding principle was clear to him. Smiling at Fox's insight, he explained that the job of driving a distinguished rabbi around is a privileged one in Orthodox circles, not only because of the honor of serving a great man, nor solely because of the precious time this role offers for dialogue with him, but also because of the opportunity to learn about moral and religious life by watching a model of it up close. This was a form of apprenticeship, he explained, one that is traditionally referred to as *shimush talmidei chachamim* (literally, tending to Torah scholars).

I made sure to take Twersky back from our meeting to his hotel. In fact, from then until he died a few years later, I never once relinquished the opportunity to drive Twersky back and forth from our meetings every time he came to Jerusalem. Twersky and I developed a deep professional and personal relationship on the basis of our discussions in my car.

At first, this relationship developed because Twersky would use our time in the car to "unpack" what had transpired at our work meetings. His schedule was extremely busy and this was one of the times he had available to think over what was going on. In these discussions, he came to trust my insights and I used the opportunity to take in as much as I could from his scholarly wisdom, his religious fervor, and his personal example. As the years went by, our discussions in the car grew deeper. Twersky took a great interest in my professional and personal life and I encouraged him enthusiastically about the prospects of his continued engagement with issues of Jewish education and persisted in my efforts to make his visits to Israel and work with our Foundation as comfortable as possible. We stretched the drives to include a regular trip to the Western Wall and to the homes of Twersky's relatives. Following traditional custom, Twersky and I agreed that I had a *chazakah*, an established right, to accompany him to the *kotel*.

About three years after we first met, my car was stolen. It was just when I was supposed to pick Twersky up and take him somewhere. His response was to ask me how much time the insurance company allotted to the police to find the stolen car before enabling me to buy a replacement. After hearing that it was 45 days, he took it upon himself to send me hand-written letters from Boston every few days to ask if the car had been found. As Twersky himself confirmed long after, this was a compelling expression of his effort to live by (rather than simply pronounce) the biblical principle of *ve'ahavta le're-echa kamocha* ("Love thy neighbor as thyself.") Twersky knew that when he returned to Boston, the discomfort of not having a car would be mine alone, so he took it upon himself to share the discomfort with me by inquiring about the stolen car every few days...

When Twersky passed away, I wrote Fox a letter, thanking him for his initial insistence on my driving Twerksy in my car.

* * *

A tight fusion between theoretical principles and practical decisions lies at the heart of Fox's approach to education. This fusion derives from what might be the cornerstone of this approach: a profound faith in the practical significance of educational theory.

Fox's case for the expediency of educational theory flows from his definition of education as a practical field and his belief that one of the central characteristics of educational practice is accountability. Fox's propensity to challenge any and every educational practice with the question "Why is this a good idea?" is well known. Far from being facetious, the aim of this question is to invite the educator who designs a particular practice to justify it being adopted in terms that go beyond first-hand impressions.

All educational practice involves intervention, Fox explains, and as such it lays claim to advancing the well-being of the learner in some way. Given that this is not always the case, that the intervention might move the learner backwards or even cause damage to his or her growth, the need to justify that claim is built into the practice of education. Neither educators, nor the policymakers in education who grant them the right to intervene in the lives of learners, can afford to avoid the demand for accountability. They must be able to expose the outcomes that the intervention seeks to attain and to defend the choice of these aims over others. Furthermore, they must be able to demonstrate how the practice is designed to obtain those objectives, and to defend the selection of that practice over alternatives.

Finally, they must also be able to identify the indicators by which they will evaluate the results of practice — were the outcomes it sought to attain indeed achieved, were they worthy outcomes, were the means chosen to pursue those outcomes appropriate?

Compelling as the argument for this kind of accountability in education might be, such justifications are not pervasive in contemporary educational practice. It is the rarer case when the guiding assumptions of educational practices are put on the table for systematic evaluation. Old ideas are often accepted as givens, on the basis of habit or inertia. Good intentions frequently provide a sufficient basis for practice without theoretical justification. New ideas, on the other hand, take hold without advance consideration of their possible negative impact. Conflicting approaches run side by side, as if the contradiction between them was irrelevant.[2]

Fox advocates a commitment to professional accountability in education on a number of levels. First, he seeks reform through the development of educational leadership. If current practice is to be improved, it must happen at the highest levels. Fox's ideal educational leader values theory and uses it in order to make responsible decisions and devise effective programs, and revisits it in light of experience. He or she will always engage with the tension between the daily practice of education and the larger picture of what it is all about. Where this method becomes the standard for educational leadership, Fox believes, room will be made for theory to play a central role in practice. Policymakers and practitioners will pay others and/or will get paid to inquire, to deliberate, to evaluate, to experiment — not only to do.[3]

Conventional approaches to administrator training seek primarily to equip educational leaders with management skills. Fox has designed a curriculum and pedagogy to enable them to be guided by theoretical ideas in the design, implementation and evaluation of their professional practice. This approach emphasizes the study of fundamental theoretical concepts and categories in philosophy and the philosophy of education. In addition to freeing trainees from slogans and bandwagons that capture professional attention from time to time in education, such study is designed to deepen and broaden educational leaders' theoretical perspective on their practice.

2   On this point, Fox points to a claim made by the policy analyst, David K. Cohen, regarding the "intellectual bankruptcy" of American secondary school education in light of teachers' incapacity to rule out certain goals for their educational practice. See Cohen, Farrar, and Powell, 1985, pp. 305–308. See also, Graham, 1984, pp. 29–57.

3   Fox often refers to Robert M. Hutchins' conception of administration as a source of inspiration for his own ideas on that topic.

Through this study, they should be able to envision and articulate the larger educational aims of their institutions and programs, to choose among various means for their attainment, to oversee the effective implementation of these means, and to evaluate the results constructively.

Fox devotes substantial amounts of time in such training programs for analysis of Israel Scheffler's works on the philosophy of education.[4] His aim here is to teach educational leaders to discern fundamental principles in education, to better distinguish between schooling, teaching and education, between various kinds of educational relevance, between computer hard disks and learner's brains, between a definition of cognition as inclusive of emotion versus one that is not, and among different ways of reconstructing traditional culture so that it deals with challenges of modernity... The use of such material in administrator training is rare.[5]

Fox further pursues the development of accountability in education through the area of historical research. Fox views the history of education as contributing studies of past educational theory and practice to the design and implementation of educational theory and practice in the present. With a critical mass of such research in place, educators would have available to them a literature through which they could be inducted into the profession and to which they could contribute studies of their own. This approach departs significantly from what is often called "history of education," which is really a sub-division of research in social history that tries to understand societies by looking at them through the prism of their educational institutions. In a sense, Fox's conception extends his repeated call for the study of failures in education (including his own[6]).

Fox's approach might, for example, ask the researcher studying the career of a great educator, to focus on that educator's theoretical view of education (implicit or explicit). Then, the researcher must describe the educator's professional career in terms of its translation of that theory into practice. Such a description could enable educators today who are committed to the same theory to re-evaluate it in light of the historical figure's practice. Alternatively, they may invent new ways of translating the same theory into practice, taking into account contemporary circum-

4 See for example, Scheffler, 1960; 1965; 1973; 1985; 1991; and 1995.
5 In his discussion of his teacher, Joseph Schwab, Fox suggests that an important topic for research is the didactic theory that is to be developed out of Schwab's writings. See Fox, 1985, pp. 83–85). A similar case could be made regarding the pedagogical theory that is implicit in Fox's theory and practice of training educational leadership. I include here not only Fox's teaching in groups, but his mode of tutoring educational leaders as well.
6 See for example, Fox's comments on "Where Ramah Failed" in Fox, with Novak, 2000, pp. 51–55.

stances. The same method could apply to the study of educational institutions, theories, pedagogies, curricular processes, and so on.[7]

Fox's view of the relationship between theory and practice in education has sometimes been misunderstood. A good example is the belief that his approach to education is rigidly rationalistic, that it is ruthlessly, even obsessively, in search of a perfect correspondence between ideas and practice that simply does not and cannot exist in the real world. As I see it, Fox's emphasis on decisions of principle is not driven by a desire to arrive at a totally harmonious relationship between reason and reality. If anything, it is based on an assumption that education is an open system that will always be too complex for someone to grasp or control. Indeed, that is one of the bases upon which Fox rejects the search for a single comprehensive theory of education from the outset.[8]

Fox's assumption is that, at best, theoretical principles can provide mental handles and levers within the infinity that defines educational reality. They can facilitate attempts to make one's way through it by suggesting or ruling out a particular route. Without theoretical principles, one is left to the whims of intuition and the limitations of narrow visibility. With them, however, one might be able to navigate in a particular direction, without the final destination being fully in sight. If one can employ theoretical principles in order to account for educational practices without treating them as total validations, if one can hold theoretical commitments with a measure of tentativeness, if one can relinquish the search for guaranteed proof in theory and use it instead as a means of maximizing one's clarity of vision in a messy situation, then will the full practical value of educational theory be realized.[9]

For Fox, the reification of theoretical principles is a cardinal sin, the punishment for which must necessarily be bamboozlement in the realm of practice. Fox is never surprised by failure. One of his driving assumptions is that the things that can go wrong in the design and implementation of

7   This was a framework that defined my doctoral research on the Zionist educator, Ben Zion Dinur. See Marom, 2000, especially pp. 28–30. (The reference applies to the extended version of this research.)

8   I have expanded on this point considerably in the larger work mentioned in note 1 above.

9   Fox rejects the idea that educational decisions can be based on intuition alone, arguing that he knows of no theoretical justification for such an approach. In my opinion, there is a need for further clarification on this point, since Fox's argument (and his practice) does not rule out altogether the appeal to intuition, nor is it easy to account for Fox's own successes in practice without appealing to his extraordinary intuitive powers. I would argue that Fox's approach necessitates an "education of the intuitions" rather than their total rejection. On the role of intuitions in medical practice, see Gawande, 2002, pp. 228–252, 263–264.

any plan of action are boundless. There is never any waste when educators prepare for as many aspects or scenarios of failure as are imaginable. Expedient practitioners may get impatient with such an approach, but Fox sees it as being much more respectful of the practical world than one that solely emphasizes doing. When, having covered oneself in advance for many of the negative potentialities, things run simply and smoothly, or when an idea that initially seemed to be good is thoughtfully rejected, even at the last minute, Fox sees this as an expression of cognitive wit more than of technical administrative skill.

Fox's emphasis on theory should not be construed as being so pragmatic, however, that it blocks the educator from thinking creatively. For Fox, it is the kind of decision-making that does not take theory into account that risks being locked into existing realities. Fox warns about the dangers that accrue when "what works" becomes the standard of educational thinking. While the occupation with "what works" bestows a sense of relevance on the educator, a sense of gaining more control over familiar realities, Fox sees this approach as paradoxically eternalizing the very reality that often needs to be changed.

A crude analogy can be made to medicine, which often concentrates solely on providing responses to illness and disease once it sets in. While this may produce an impressive array of medical strategies and solutions, it may ignore the benefits of focusing on prevention. Mastery over hundreds of cases of disease treatment will not change this orientation for the training medical practitioner, particularly when it provides effective tools for treating disease.

Principled distinctions such as that between the disease treatment and disease prevention facilitate the kind of unconventional thinking that might liberate one from fixed notions of practice in any profession. Fox sees such distinctions as being an important source of ingenuity and innovation in education. Clearly, such distinctions lie at the heart of Fox's initiatives. A well-known example is his appeal to the distinction between "necessary" versus "sufficient" conditions as the basis for educational reform. This distinction lies behind his choice to focus on the development of infrastructural elements in education (e.g. building the profession, mobilizing community support) over and above initiatives in domains with programmatic agendas (e.g. developing programs on the teaching of the Holocaust or undertaking research in family education).[10]

---

10 See Commission on Jewish Education in North America, 1990, pp. 47–50.

In his teaching, Fox often uses the distinction his teacher Joseph Schwab makes between "objectives" and "problems" in the development of curriculum. Conventional wisdom posits "objectives" as the departure point of planning a curriculum, with "problems" being dealt with subsequently. Schwab's approach, as Fox explains and expands upon it, works in the opposite direction, first investing much energy in identifying the "problem" and then setting "objectives" accordingly:

> "In contrast to an approach to curriculum development that begins with the search for objectives, Schwab's deliberation begins with the search for "the problem"…[O]ne characteristic of the practical is that the problem is not a given but must be located and/or discovered. This has led us in our work in curriculum development, to make a distinction between what may *appear* to be the problem, namely symptoms, and what the curriculum group, through deliberations, ultimately agrees is the "problem" that the curriculum will have to respond to.
>
> Failure on achievement tests, student boredom, teacher unrest, criticism by parents or academics for example, may all be symptoms that can instigate the call for curriculum revision. Any one of them can lead us to the formulation of a problem other than how to revise or develop a new curriculum. After a careful deliberation, we may decide that our problem is how to improve instruction or motivate teachers to utilize the existing curriculum more effectively. Therefore our solution might be teacher re-education and not a new curriculum project. We may even decide tentatively that our problem is the curriculum, but we may not know how to improve the existing one; or the improvement may involve the investment of time and money that is not available; or the project for curriculum improvement may be feasible for experimental classes, but not for large numbers of teachers and students." (Fox, 1985, pp. 81–82).

Another distortion of Fox's approach to theory-practice interplay in education would be to see it as moving unidirectionally from theory to practice. This view would see Fox's probing questions and tireless positing of alternatives for consideration as "show-stoppers" designed to halt people in their tracks, to get them to freeze their activities and enter into a "theory zone" in a never-ending search for infallible logic before actually deciding to do something.

Such a distortion would be more understandable had Fox's success in the world of practice been less impressive, had he not succeeded in implementing his own approach to education in such areas as institution building, training and fundraising, or had he not been asked repeatedly to play the role of advisor to ministers of education in Israel and to various philanthropic foundations on topics such as budgeting and planning, curriculum and teacher education.

One could argue, perhaps, that his constant appeal to rationality and his repeated use of traditional philosophic terminology in the discussion of education — for example, "categories," "assumptions," "hypothesis," "justification," "validity" — lend themselves to the association of his approach with a linearity that always precedes theory to practice. This mistaken association might also be motivated by Fox's insistence on allowing theoretical and practical inputs to educational planning to be initially considered exclusive of each other, prior to being brought into dialogue. Fox does indeed allot time and space for separate treatment of theory and practice. He does so, however, to ensure the richness of each input into the ensuing dialogue, to keep the dialogue between theory and practice from being reduced to a monologue right from the start.

The dialectical relationship between theory and practice is axiomatic in Fox's approach to education. As Fox's approach factors practical concerns into the theoretical design of education from the outset, it is hard to see how it could be construed as moving only from theory to practice. Fox sees practice as theoretically instructive, and as such, its inclusion in the design of educational theory is an ongoing necessity. The capacity of practical concerns and outcomes to alter theoretical assumptions is not reduced at any time. Given this assumption, the question of where to begin is moot. One might equally begin with the implementation and evaluation of a given practice of education as with the invention of a new theory of education and its implied methods.[11]

---

11 Within this dialectical relationship between theory and practice, the movement from practice to theory finds expression in Fox's work on many levels. In one of his articles on curriculum planning, for example, he makes suggestions about how school principals can be brought into the deliberation group from the very outset of the planning process, so as to help the group anticipate and confront issues that could emerge from the world of practice. See Fox, 1983. Similarly, in his teaching and in the development of a curriculum in Bible at the Melton Center for Research on Jewish Education at the Jewish Theological Seminary, Fox emphasizes making room for experimental implementations of a curriculum so that teachers can bring their experience with it in the classroom to inform its final articulation. See Fox, 1977. One of the outcomes of this approach is the development of extensive teacher's guides alongside published curriculum, sometimes two or three times as long as the curriculum itself. See, for example, Gardner and Newman, 1966, especially the "Foreword" by

Conclusion

Many Jewish and Israeli educators owe our own training and professional careers to Fox having committed himself to working with Mort Mandel and other community leaders in building the profession of education. Those of us who have had the great fortune of studying and working with Fox up close up know that this achievement represents but one application of his larger approach to education — one he chose to emphasize because of his analysis of the urgencies of Jewish and Israeli education today.

This awareness requires those who have benefited from Fox's efforts to continue being in dialogue with his teachings about education as we fill the institutions he has founded and the fields to which he has so profoundly contributed with our own ideas and practices. It is not out of literal adherence to his approach to education that I make this claim. Rather, the standards by which Fox's ideas and practices have been developed should apply equally to those of us who have benefited from them. We cannot enjoy the fruits of his labor without assuming at the same time that we ourselves must be judged by the very same standards that enabled Fox to further our professional field of activity. Undoubtedly, one way of accomplishing this is by continuing to grapple with Fox's approach to education as we devise our own.[12]

References

Ben Peretz, Miriam. (1977). *Analysis and comparison of some high school biology curricula in Israel; Theoretical and practical considerations in the process of curriculum development*. PhD dissertation, the Hebrew University of Jerusalem.

Cohen, David K., Farrar, Eleanor, and Powell, Arthur G. (1985). *The shopping mall high school: Winners and losers in the educational marketplace*. Boston, Houghton Mifflin.

Newman on pages i-xi. On another level, together with Leah Adar, Fox made a valuable contribution to Israeli education by undertaking a systematic "content analysis" of a curriculum that was used for this history teaching in the public schools for many years. (Fox and Adar, 1978.) In her doctoral research, with Fox as her advisor, Miriam Ben Peretz undertook a similar study in the area of Israeli biology curricula. See Ben Peretz, 1977.

12 That Fox's contributions to Jewish education are of historical proportions has already been asserted by Lloyd Gartner. See Gartner, 1983, p. 392. At the time of Gartner's assertions, Fox had only built his first set of programs and institutions. Now that he has also established a second and third set in Israel, there is a need for research on Fox's role in the history of Jewish education worldwide.

Commission on Jewish Education in North America. (1990). *A time to act: The report of the Commission on Jewish Education in North America*. Lanham, University Press of America.

Fox, Seymour. (1972). A Practical Image of the Practical. *Curriculum Theory Network*. (Fall) pp. 44–55.

Fox, Seymour. (1977). The scholar, the educator and the curriculum of the Jewish school. In Seymour Fox and Geraldine Rosenfield. (Eds.) *From the scholar to the classroom: Translating Jewish tradition into curriculum*. New York, Melton Research Center for Jewish Education of the Jewish Theological Seminary of America, pp. 104–112.

Fox, Seymour and Adar, Leah. (1978). *An analysis of the content and use of a history curriculum*. (Hebrew) Jerusalem, The Hebrew University School of Education.

Fox, Seymour. (1983) The role of the principal in curriculum development. (Hebrew) In M. Nisan and U. Last. (Eds.). *Between Education and Psychology: Essays dedicated to the memory of Professor Avraham Minkowitz*. (Hebrew) Jerusalem, Magnes Press.

Fox, Seymour. (1985). The Vitality of Theory in Schwab's Conception of the Practical. *Curriculum Inquiry (15) 1*.

Fox, Seymour. (2000). Where Ramah failed. In Seymour Fox, with William Novak. (Ed. Nessa Rapoport). *Vision at the heart: Lessons from Camp Ramah on the power of ideas in shaping educational institutions*. Jerusalem, Mandel Foundation, (2nd edition), pp. 51–55.

Gardner, Leonard and Newman, Louis. (Eds.). (1966). *Genesis: The teacher's guide, experimental edition (Companion volume to Understanding Genesis)*. New York, The Melton Research Center of The Jewish Theological Seminary of America.

Gartner, Lloyd. (1983). Jewish education in the United States. In M. Sklare. (Ed.). *American Jews: A reader*. New York, Behrman House.

Gawande, Atul. (2002). *Complications: A surgeon's notes on an imperfect science*. New York, Metropolitan Books.

Graham, Patricia Albjerg. (1984). Schools: Cacophony about practice, silence about purpose. *Daedalus 113 (4)*, pp. 29–57.

Hare, R. M. (1959). Decisions of principle. In Israel Scheffler. (Ed.) *Philosophy and education*. Boston, Allyn and Bacon. pp. 72–86.

Marom, Daniel. (2000). *The educational thought and practice of Ben-Zion Dinur*. PhD dissertation. The Hebrew University of Jerusalem. (Advisor: Z. Lamm). An extended version of this research, which includes an analysis of Dinur's develop-ment as an educational leader, can be found at the Dinur Center at the Hebrew University.

Scheffler, Israel. (1960). *The language of education*. Springfield, Charles C. Thomas.

Scheffler, Israel. (1965). *Conditions of knowledge: An introduction to epistemology and education*. Chicago, Scott, Foresman and Company.

Scheffler, Israel. (1973). *Reason and teaching*. London, Routledge and Kegan Paul.

Scheffler, Israel. (1985). *Of human potential*. London, Routledge and Kegan Paul.

Scheffler, Israel. (1991). *In praise of the cognitive emotions*. New York, Routledge and Kegan Paul.

Scheffler, Israel. (1995). *Teachers of my youth: An American Jewish experience*. Dordrecht, Kluwer Academic Publishers.

SOURCES

Reflections on the Story of the Garden of Eden: *Genesis 2:4–3:24*[1]

MOSHE GREENBERG

The major challenge to understanding the stories of Genesis lies in overcoming the narrative gaps, be they gaps in the plot's continuity, or the omission of motives behind the characters' actions, which the reader is required to supplement. For example: Would the first humans have remained immortal had they not sinned? Who planted the serpent in the garden? It appears that the narrator had no use for embroidery of narrative details. He was interested in reworking the stylized materials at his disposal into a clear and consistent plot line, while at the same time remaining loyal to the language of his original sources. The result — our scriptural narrative — reveals ellipses that were effected in order to focus the mind of the reader on what the narrator deemed most important. An example of such an ellipse is the case of the Tree of Life. It is likely that the Tree of Life played a larger role in earlier versions, not limited solely to its role as the reason for the banishment of the man and woman from the Garden (3: 22–24).

Observe the economy of the narrator's art. He does not waste a word to explain how the serpent and the woman were informed of the prohibition against eating from the Tree of Knowledge (the prohibition was

---

1   I am grateful for this opportunity to express my gratitude to Seymour Fox for all the kindness bestowed on myself and my family, by dedicating this essay on education to him.

communicated explicitly only to Adam). Nor does the narrator relate how Adam responded to the woman's suggestion that he violate the prohibition. The reader, therefore, is obliged to pay close attention to the scriptures, until he may, with all due humility, surmise if and how each gap should be filled. The goal of study is to develop a comprehensive view of the narrative episode, a view which will enable the reader to distinguish the central plot line from ancillary issues which merely stir up controversy. In the following paragraphs I attempt to present a comprehensive view of the story, without entering into debate with other interpreters (indebted as I am to all from whom I have learned), and without documenting or referring to narrative parallels in the Hebrew Bible or in other ancient literature.

After the couple had sinned by eating of the Tree of Knowledge, God declared: "Now that the man has become like one of us knowing good and bad…" It becomes clear that the serpent was not misleading Eve when he said to her: "but God knows that as soon as you eat of it your eyes will be opened and you will be like divine beings who know good and bad." On the contrary, God reproduces the serpent's words almost exactly; the outcome of the sin was just as the serpent had predicted; the sinners did not die, but gained knowledge which likened them to God.[2]

This narrative aims to answer the question: How did the world (that is, human society) devolve from its primal, ideal form to its current corrupt state? According to the story, man's unique moral consciousness "to know good and bad" is a feature of corruption. The first man was created perfect,

2   "Elohim" here refers to all superhuman entities such as angels ("we shall surely die, for we have seen a divine being" Judges 13:22, from verse 9 onwards the same entity is called "an angel of the Lord"); spirits of the dead ("I see a divine being coming up from the earth," 1 Samuel 28:13). The same superhuman entities are called "sons of God" in Job 1:6, 2:1 and "heavenly entourage" in rabbinic Hebrew. The locution "know good and bad" has several meanings, in this context "to distinguish between good and bad" (1 Kings 3:9) makes the most sense, as the following examples demonstrate: 1. Deuteronomy 1:39, "your children who do not yet know good from bad"; 2. 2 Samuel 14:17 "like an angel of the Lord, understanding everything, good and bad"; 3. 2 Samuel 19:36: "I am now eighty years old. Can I tell the difference between good and bad?"; 4. Isaiah 7:15: "By the time he learns to reject the bad and choose the good." In all these instances the locution signifies the ability to distinguish good from bad. In examples 1 and 4, the lack of ability to distinguish good from bad is characteristic of infancy and childhood; in example 3 this ability is taken from the very elderly who experience a "second childhood": their senses dim, their interest in the world diminishes; they are not capable of following a complicated issue. Such a shell of a human being, Barzilai says, is not suited for such an intense lifestyle. In example 2, "to hear (*shama'*) = to understand (cf. Genesis 11:7; Deuteronomy 28:49, etc.) See 1 Kings 3:9 "Grant then, Your servant an understanding mind to judge your people, to distinguish good and bad…"

innocent and devoid of fleshly desire. This accords with the story that Adam did not sense loneliness until God made him aware of it. Only when God created animals and presented them to Adam for naming did the first man realize his difference: he had no partner.[3]

From the moment that he was created, Adam had the technical skill to tend God's garden, to classify and to distinguish between male and female. What he was not imprinted with initially, the normal "knowledge of good and bad" i.e. the moral dimension, had been, until Adam's transgression, the unique province of God, which set him apart from all creatures. Prior to this stage, Adam was like an infant in his innocence: "the two of them were naked, yet they felt no shame." (Genesis 2:25).

The next stage was recognition of the moral dimension: there is good and bad in his world — and only in his world. This recognition becomes actualized when Adam encounters an authorized, legitimate power, which demands that he obey commands that limit his actions.

Two wills collide here: the will of one who wishes to realize his independence by executing his own desires opposing the will of the authority that deserves obedience. Submission to that authority is perceived as good, rebelling against it is perceived as bad. Moral consciousness, and the concomitant experience of free choice, is realized, according to the Hebrew Bible, under the following conditions:

   a. The individual confronts an authority that prevents him from carrying out his own will.

   b. The individual is free to choose between obedience and rebellion.

Just as Adam becomes aware of his uniqueness through an external factor, so he becomes conscious of the moral dimension as the result of external agents, namely:

   1. God who forbids eating the fruit of the Tree of Knowledge. Owing to Adam's innocence, the announcement of the prohibition produces no reaction.

   2. An inciter, represented as external to man — a perverse and unruly creature who urges man to rebel against authority, by interpreting the prohibition as a means to preserve the singularity of the commanding

---

3   However the narrator does not explicitly recount how Adam discovered his difference from the other creatures. This accords with what was said above — the biblical narratives ignore elements of the story which might distract the reader from the plot-line. An additional example may be found in the story of the binding of Isaac, which conceals from the reader how and when God revealed the place of the sacrifice to Abraham (Genesis 22: 4–5).

authority — a singularity, whose essence, according to the serpent, is possession of knowledge of good and bad. (He lied, since immortality is his other unique feature).

Adam is enthralled by the serpent's promise that violation of the prohibition will make him like God, a knower of good and bad. The difference between him and God lies in the fact that only God knows good and bad; Adam's dependence on this divine monopoly becomes intolerable to him as a result of the serpent's incitement. The couple captivated by the serpent's temptation, violate the prohibition, and immediately lose their childlike innocence. They sense their nakedness.

This odd fact (for what connection is there between the sense of nakedness and the "knowledge of good and bad"?) points to another parallel between the Eden story and the course of human development. Distinguishing good from bad (the moral sense) is particularly powerful in the realm of sexuality — a realm hedged by many guilt-inducing prohibitions. The age when awareness of nakedness develops coincides with the age when moral concepts develop (i.e. the process of socialization).

As claimed above, the story's purpose is to explain humankind's current state as a fall from a primeval state of innocence and bliss. Knowledge of good and bad is a characteristic of man's fallen state. It is the loss of an early childlike innocence, a state achieved through sin, but once achieved, permanent. Ever since, this awareness is implanted within the heart of every human as a unique sense — the conscience, which enables him to make moral evaluations.

Man's knowledge of good and bad is not dependent upon divine revelation. Since the case of Cain, humans have been judged for their evildoing, despite the fact that they did not receive the Torah or any other divine instruction. The same applies to Lemech and Amalek. On the other hand, a gentile who has not received the Torah can exhibit moral behavior (such as the sailors in the book of Jonah) and a sense of justice ("the fear of God") which enables him to admire the sublime qualities of Israel's Torah (Deuteronomy 4:6: "Surely that great nation is a wise and discerning people").

Those who lived by the Torah of Israel would not have been surprised by the lofty morals reflected in the Mesopotamian laws or in Egyptian wisdom literature. For God had already declared in respect to the progenitor of all humankind: "Now that the man has become like one of us, knowing good and bad..." Adam broke the divine monopoly over this realm and became independent of God. This was the realization of his maturity, his moral maturation. But the price of this freedom is high: humans are liable at any moment to be confounded in their judgment by the incitement of passion. But the movement is irreversible: the prophetic images of the end of days speak of restoring peace and unity among humans and between humans and beasts; they do not speak however of a return to nudity or of the loss of moral judgment (cf. Isaiah 11:1–9)

The passage from infancy and childhood is irreversible, and the story of the Garden of Eden reflects its ambivalence. Man's original primeval state is described as an idyllic innocence, a perfect correspondence between man and his creator — a passivity whose reward is bliss. Loss of this innocence is inevitable; one might even say that the creator laid the groundwork for it when he planted the serpent in the Garden. The loss of innocence implies a confrontation between human will and divine will, and a simultaneous arousal of moral consciousness and a sense of guilt and shame. The parallel between the phases of development of the first human and of human maturation in general is apparent, and points to an almost tragic world view: maturity necessarily entails a loss of original innocence. Maturity is the offspring of sin, which procured for humans a singular quality. This quality will continue to exist in humans even in the future — when the world will be renewed.

"*Sof hora'ah*"
The End of Teaching; Teaching What?

David Weiss Halivni

A single statement in tractate Bava Metsia 86a has had a determining effect upon the study of the Babylonian Talmud's redaction, from the earliest commentaries until the most recent scholarship:

Rabbi and R. Natan [are] the end of mishnah (*sof mishnah*); Ravina and R. Ashi the end of instruction (*sof hora'ah*).

Almost all commentators on the Talmud understand *sof hora'ah*, — the "end of instruction" — to denote the close of the Gemara itself. That is to say, when Amoraic teaching, or *hora'ah*, ceased, according to this view, the finished text of the Babylonian Talmud was left as the precipitate of that activity, almost exactly as we find it now, with the acknowledged exception of occasional brief accretions added by early inheritors of the text for the sake of elucidation. The most traditional view, based upon the above statement from Bava Metsia 86a, holds that just as R. Yehuda ha-Nasi was both the final Tana and the codifier who shaped the Mishnah into its present formulation, Rav Ashi and Ravina both completed and compiled the Gemara. Even in those academic circles most emancipated from the constraints of religious commentary, the prevalent view has seen the Amoraic age as the essential generative period of the Talmud, not only of its attributed legal positions, but also of its interstitial discursive fabric, its overall textual structure and character.

In the view which the following discussion will introduce and defend, *sof hora'ah* does indeed denote the end of Amoraic teaching; but rather than marking the point at which the Talmudic edifice reached its final form, *sof hora'ah*, in the sense we believe is intended in Bava Metsia 86a, means the time at which the primary building blocks of that edifice — the concise, Amoraic legal dicta, called *memrot* or *okimtot* – ceased to be produced as such. (Inasmuch as these rulings are the *result* of disputation, but are presented in terse, official, and finalized formulation, we shall refer to them as *apodictic* statements.) Following *sof hora'ah* – understood as the end of apodictic, Amoraic rulings — until the actual close of the essential Talmudic corpus, there intervened, as we shall demonstrate, a formative period. During that time, the officially codified material of the Amoraim, as well as the less formal legacy of the Amoraic epoch, was studied, queried, developed and interconnected, and was then finally crafted into the finished, stylized pericopae of Talmudic exposition and disputation — the familiar *sugyot* — which comprise our Gemara. These sugyot, after this formative redaction, differed substantively from those that we find today in the form of certain self-contained supplementary additions, which are not essential to the main-lines of their reasoning.

Additionally, we shall see that whereas, by way of adulation, the author of the statement concerning *sof hora'ah* in Bava Metsia 86a designated Ravina the First and his counterpart Rav Ashi as personifying the end of Amoraic productivity, the Talmud clearly recognizes several subsequent generations of Amoraim. Thus, the Talmud's actual redaction, occupying a significant period following the very last Amoraim, must be dated much later than the time suggested by R. Sherira Gaon's influential epistle.

Once we have established that the intended sense of *sof hora'ah* in Bava Metsia 86a is the end of Amoraic, apodictic rulings, we must then account for the discursive matrix in which these dicta are embedded in our Talmud — the largely unattributed *shakla vetarya* (dialogical give-and-take) which characterize the Gemara. We shall conclude that the Babylonian Talmud as we know it is a post-Amoraic oeuvre. To be sure, the primary endeavor of its redactors was to preserve earlier material; yet the distinctive textual character, and much of the substance of the Gemara, is the work of these redactors themselves. Although their focus on the discursive in the formation of their opus was an innovation, we have argued elsewhere that the redactors' dialogical style of compilation and composition was rooted in, and modeled upon, the less formally preserved traditions and modalities of earlier rabbinic periods. ("Midrash, Mishnah and Gemara," Harvard University Press, Cambridge, Mass. and London, 1986) Here we are concerned with determining the original sense of *sof hora'ah*.

The Meaning of *Hora'ah*

As stated, almost all of the Rishonim regard *hora'ah* in Bava Metsia 86a as synonymous with gemara, thus implying that R. Ashi and Ravina who are acclaimed in Bava Metsia 86a — whose precise identities we shall discuss below — concluded the composition of the Babylonian Talmud, just as R. Yehudah ha-Nasi had concluded and finally edited the Mishnah. Just as the material of the Mishnah is thought to have been virtually complete by the time of Rabbi, so too the prevailing school of thought in Talmudic study sees the Gemara as we know it taking shape gradually throughout the Amoraic age so that the final Amoraim — like the Mishnah's final Tana, Rabbi–might be regarded as the final editors of the corpus. In the traditional perspective, no essential, substantive development of the Gemara as a whole took place after the ostensibly final Amoraim named in Bava Metsia 86a. Accordingly, classical commentators, among them Rashi, assume the anonymous interstitial voice of the Talmud to be that of R. Ashi, just as the Mishnah's unattributed statements represent the prevailing Tanaitic opinions based on the teachings of Rabbi Meir. In order to evaluate this traditional position with regard to the Talmud, we must ask, first of all, whether *gemara* or *talmud* — denoting either a complete corpus or a distinctive modality — are accustomed meanings of *hora'ah*, or likely meanings in Bava Metsia 86a.

The answer is, emphatically, no. From the Mishnah through both Talmudim, overwhelmingly, *hora'ah* does not suggest lengthy exposition or disputation, or a corpus composed of such *shakla vetarya*, but rather denotes the pronouncing of concise, halakic rulings. "*Talmud*," by contrast, from the period of the Tanaim onwards, is the word used by the rabbis to indicate the discursive argumentation which becomes the Gemara's distinguishing characteristic. (See Rashi in Sukkah 28a, "Talmud").

In order to uphold his position that the Ravina and Rav Ashi of Bava Metsia 86a represent the close of the Gemara as a work containing not only terse legal rulings, but also discursive material, R. Sherira Gaon was obliged to understand *hora'ah* in an unaccustomed way, as the totality of the Babylonian Talmud, including also the discursive. This reading runs against hundreds of places in the Gemara itself in which *hora'ah* clearly means apodictic, legal ruling. Indeed there is the whole tractate of Horayot in which the term *hora'ah* consistently indicates final, legal instruction.

Late defenders of R. Sherira Gaon, notably Isaac Halevi, can point to only one passage in the Babylonian Talmud itself that supports his unusual usage of *hora'ah*. This is the exegesis in Berakhot 5a, "'To instruct them' —

this refers to *talmud' (lehorotam — ze talmud*)," which appears in the course of a word-by-word midrashic exposition of Exodus. 24:12., It must, first of all, be noted that this exegesis appears in a creative, aggadic reading of a verse, in which accustomed definitions are likely to be less rigidly preserved. The exegesis in Berakhot 5a almost certainly does not assign the scriptural word "*lehorotam*" to *talmud* because it deems *hora'ah* to be the best term for discursive learning, but rather because, having already assigned the word "*vehamitzva*" (and the commandment) to the Mishnah, which epitomizes the genre of terse, legal prescription, "*lehorotam*" is the single word left in the biblical verse which can be made to fit *talmud* as a modality or genre.

Moreover, we should note that this exegesis of Exodus 24:12 is reported in the name of a Palestinian sage, R. Shimon Ben Lakish, and there is a related idea, preserved in two loci in the Palestinian Talmud, in the name of Shemuel, which may account for the association of "instruction" with *talmud* among Palestinian Amoraim. This is the statement in Y. Peah 2:4(17a) and its parallel in Y. Hagigah 1:8(76d):

"One may not learn [law] (*ein lemedin*) from the *halakhot*, and not from the *aggadot* and not from the *tosafot* (that is, from *baraitot*), but only from *talmud*."

This passage does indicate "*Talmud*" as the *means* to authoritative rulings. Yet rather than strengthen R. Sherira Gaon's interpretation of *hora'ah* as *talmud*, this passage from the Palestinian tradition in fact more strongly distinguishes between terse, apodictic, legal statements and the modality of discursive learning, or *talmud*. One does not arrive at practical law merely by quoting codified legal positions, "*halakhot*," according to Shemuel; rather one learns the law through the examination and discussion of such statements, that is, through *talmud*, as *distinct* from *halakha* or *hora'ah*. This principle is made explicit several lines later in Y. Peah, with the statement of R. Hananiah in the name of Shemuel, "One does not learn law from *hora'ah* (*ein lemedin min hahorayah*)." Rather, as Shemuel opines, one derives law through *talmud*.

Similar to the position of Shemuel is the Tannaitic tradition — and its Tanaitic, Amoraic (and anonymously edited) explanations — found in Sotah 22a:

"It is taught: The *tanaim* destroy the world.
They 'destroy the world?' Can one think this?
Said Ravina, [It means] that they teach law on the basis of their *mishnah* (*shemorim halakha mitoch mishnatan*).

A teaching affirms this: Said R. Yehoshua, Do they truly destroy the world? Are they not the sustainers of the world (*meyashvei olam*) as it is written, 'His ways are eternal (*halichot olam lo*)?'[1] Only that they teach law on the basis of their *mishnah*."

Here, the *tanaim* – meaning not the Tanaitic rabbis, but the specialists in memorization whose job it was to preserve and recite the rulings of the sages — are accused of destroying the world, since they presume to rule on matters of law on the sole basis of the official traditions that they hold memorized (*morin halakha mitoch mishnatan*). In this discussion, received rulings are not sufficient for arriving at new decisions. *Hora'ah* alone is incomplete, and without circumspection it can easily be misapplied with perilous consequences. Transmitted traditions must be examined and studied in the mode of *talmud* as a means to new pronouncements.

Rashi (Berachot 5a) links this tradition of "*tanaim mevalei olam*" to the exegesis "*lehorotam — ze talmud*," saying that the word "*Talmud*" indicates "the understandings of the meanings of the mishnayot, out of which proceeds instruction (*hora'ah*)," and adding, "But those who rule halakha [directly] from the Mishnah are called destroyers of the world in tractate Sotah [22a]." Thus, the source in Berakhot 5a which substantiates R. Sherira Gaon's reading of *hora'ah* as meaning the entire Gemara, including the discursive mode, in fact implies only that discussion (*talmud*) is a necessary means to instruction (*hora'ah*). Talmud is an essential activity to those who would give rulings (*lehorortam*), but this is a far cry from calling the Babylonian Talmud, in its entirety, *hora'ah*, as though this were its essential nature.

One must contrast this opinion of Shemuel, and of the tradition in Sotah 22a, with a contradictory baraita recorded in the Babylonian Talmud's Bava Batra 130b:

"One does not learn law (*ein lemedin halakha*) from *talmud*, nor from anecdote (*ma'aseh*) unless [the Sages] say [that it is] practical law (*halakha lema'aseh*)."

At first glance, this source seems to conflict with those that we have seen so far; but, in fact, it is in accord with them, for it intends to indicate that discursive argumentation, *talmud*, should not be mistaken for definitive, legal instruction (*hora'ah*). Understood thus, this Tanaitic

---

1   This verse is the subject of a famous exegesis in the name of Tana debey Eliahu, praising the daily recitation of laws, that plays upon the similar words "*halikhot*" (ways) and "*halakhot*" (laws) and upon the meanings of "*olam*" as "eternal" and as "world."

tradition in Bava Batra 130b does not undermine what we have already said. This baraita does not deny that *talmud*, as a modality, is essential in reaching legal decisions. Rather, the authorship of this baraita seems intent upon ensuring that statements made, and examples cited, in the course of discursive argumentation, not be taken for final, halakhic rulings unless they have been officially ratified and formulated. Thus this baraita too makes a clear distinction between *talmud* and *hora'ah*, and it proves the additional point that both modalities were current in the Tannaitic period.

Clearly, the highly unusual association of *hora'ah* and *talmud* in the one midrashic instance of Berakhot 5a — so out of keeping with the usual usage of the terms — cannot support the view that *sof hora'ah* in Bava Metsia 86a means the end of the Gemara's discursive, investigative modality. *Hora'ah*, generally, means final, apodictic instruction, and the end of such official instruction by the Amoraim is what is meant by *sof hora'ah* in Bava Metsia 86a.

We must also consider a less often quoted source, from the Babylonian Talmud's tractate *Keritot*, which might be raised in defense of R. Sherira Gaon's equation of *hora'ah* and *talmud*. The source may be less often cited in support of the traditional view because, whereas the *tana kama* (the first, anonymous, authorial voice) of the baraita cited here might associate *talmud* with *hora'ah*; as we shall see, R. Yose b.R. Yehuda, on the other hand, dissents, and Rav, who was the principal legal decisor of Babylonia, says that the law in this case follows R. Yose b.R. Yehuda. The source in question, an exegesis of Lev. 10:10–11, enumerating the kinds of discourse which are forbidden to an inebriated person, reads as follows:

> "'And that you may differentiate between the holy and the unholy' — this refers to values and valuations, tithes and donations;
> 'and between the clean and the unclean' — this refers to [the laws of] purity and impurity;
> 'and that you may teach (*ulehorot*)' — that is *hora'ah*;
> 'all the laws' — this refers to exegeses (*midrashot*);
> 'which God has spoken' — this refers to *halakha* [that is, tradition attributed to Sinaitic revelation][2]
> 'by the hand of Moses' — this refers to *talmud*.
> Might *mishnah* also [be forbidden to an inebriated person]?
> We learn otherwise from the scripture, 'and that you may teach (*lehorot*)'".

R. Yose son of R. Yehuda says, Might *talmud* [be forbidden to an

2   See the second chapter of Weiss Halivni (1997).

inebriated person]? We learn otherwise from the scripture, 'and that you may teach (*lehorot*).'

First we must note that this source, another word-by-word exegesis, constrained by the diction of the verse it exposits, can hardly be conclusive with regard to definitions or regular usages. Shortly we shall also see that the variants of this text, found in other sources, render it even more questionable as a support for an equation of *hora'ah* and *talmud*.

Dealing first of all with the text we have before us in our printed Gemara, we must note that the *tana kama* of the baraita does seem to elevate *talmud* to the same status as *hora'ah* with respect to it being forbidden for an inebriated person. By the same token, the *tana kama* of this version of the baraita dissociates *mishnah* from *hora'ah*. When the anonymous voice of the baraita asks whether *mishnah* might also be forbidden, it responds, "We learn otherwise from the word '*lehorot*'." Only discourses to which the term *hora'ah* may be applied are forbidden to a drunkard. *Mishnah* here is excluded from the category of *hora'ah*, whilst *talmud* seems to be included by the *tana kama* in the realm of *hora'ah*. Even this turn of argument, however, falls far short of equating *hora'ah* and *talmud* in a terminological sense. In this connection we must recall what we have learned from the baraita in Sotah 22a and the statement, "the *tanaim* destroy the world." We may conclude that an intoxicated person is permitted to recite *mishnayot* because such recitation will not be taken as definitive instruction. As Rashi points out once more in his comment upon this source, "one does not teach law [directly] from the *Mishnah*." A drunkard may recite *mishnah* by rote, just as any other person, according to the *tana kama*, since there is no danger of his thereby innovating a mistaken point of law. Even if he misquoted his *mishnah*, the ensuing sober *talmud* required for new decisions would presumably correct the error. *Talmud*, on the other hand — as the rigorous, probing discourse that leads to new *hora'ah* – is forbidden to an inebriated person. Again, we must differentiate here between *hora'ah* as the term for a body of material, of which the *Mishnah* is an example, and *hora'ah* as an activity, which cannot arise from *mishnah* alone but must ensue from the discursive modality of *talmud*, for which a drunkard is unsuited.

As quoted, R. Yose b.R. Yehuda disagrees with the foregoing view. When he asks rhetorically, "Is it possible that *talmud* [also is forbidden to a drunkard]?" and answers, "We learn otherwise from the word "*lehorot*," R. Yose b.R. Yehuda implies that *talmud* and *hora'ah* are not equivalent. We have noted that this is the opinion accepted by Rav, the leading Amora of Babylonia, which may account for the infrequency of this source's being cited in defense of R. Sherira Gaon — the refutation is so readily at hand.

We should also note that only the version of this baraita found in the Babylonian Talmud includes the midrash, "'By the hand of Moses' — this refers to *talmud*," which is in any case a somewhat improbable exegesis. Much more expected is the version of this text in the Sifra (Shemini, Chapter 3, 1:9), "'By the hand of Moses' — this refers to scripture." It is not unthinkable that the version of the baraita found in the Babylonian Talmud, which raises *talmud* into a category with *hora'ah*, arose and became current because of the esteem in which the modality of *talmud* was held among the Babylonian Amoraim. Here we may note again that it is Shemuel, a Babylonian sage, who is cited in the Palestinian Talmud (Y. Peah 2:4[17a] and Y. Hagigah 1:8[76d]), saying that one learns law only by means of *talmud*.

We must also note that only the *Romi* manuscript of the Sifra includes the *tana kama's* question and response, "Is it possible that *mishnah* also [is forbidden]? We learn otherwise from the scripture, 'that you may teach (*lehorot*)'". The other witnesses of the Sifra do not dissociate *mishnah* and *hora'ah* as does our Gemara. On the other hand, while R. Yose b.R. Yehuda's question and response do not appear at all in the standard edition of the Sifra, in the *Romi* manuscript, he is quoted as saying, "Is it possible that translation (*targum*) also is forbidden? We learn otherwise from the scripture, 'that you may teach (*lehorot*)'". Thus, that version of the Sifra does not dissociate *talmud* from *hora'ah* in the name of R. Yose b.R. Yehuda as does our Gemara. We must therefore admit the possibility that it was the version found in the *Romi* manuscript to which Rav referred when he said that the law followed R. Yose b.R. Yehuda. Rav's view might then be in keeping with the tendency of the Babylonian Amoraim, which we have just suggested, to elevate the status of *talmud* as does the *tana kama* in the Babylonian version of the baraita. Still this would not amount to the kind of terminological equation of *talmud* with *hora'ah* which would be necessary to support R. Sherira Gaon's view that *sof hora'ah* means the end of the Gemara, including its discursive, interstitial fabric.

We therefore conclude that *sof hora'ah*, in Bava Metsia 86a, was originally intended to mean the end of Amoraic, apodictic rulings.

References

Weiss Halivni, David. (forthcoming). *The Torah reclaimed*
Weiss Halivni, David. (1997). *Revelation restored: Divine writ and critical responses*, Westview: Boulder, Colorado.

Five Dualities of Education

ISRAEL SCHEFFLER

Introduction

In significant respects, cognition, learning, and teaching are dual. I believe this fact has important bearings on the theory and practice of education. Only recently have I begun to realize how often I have illustrated such duality in various of my writings on education, without stating it explicitly. In what follows, I shall explain what I mean by "duality" and I shall elaborate five such dualities together with their educational consequences.

1. Cognitive Duality

The task of cognition is typically construed as uniformly positive. It is to construct broader and broader theories that continue to explain the growing body of observational information in increasing approximation to the truth. This simple and appealing uni-directional picture masks two facts. First, it underplays the point that cognitive advances occur not alone when a theory is constructed but also when it is demolished. If it is a cognitive virtue to propose a theory that explains the data, it is no less a virtue to search out its flaws and to relinquish it when it turns defective. Secondly, cognition is in any case not a matter of progressing smoothly from one satisfying theory to another, the whole series converging on an ideal limit. In sum, the

84

typical picture ignores the cognitive importance both of falsification and of theoretical divergence.

To take the first point first, "cognition is…two-sided and has its own rhythm. It stabilizes and coordinates; it also unsettles and divides. It is responsible for shaping our patterned orientations to the future, but it must also be responsive to the insistent need to learn from the future. Establishing habits, it must stand ready to break them. Unlearning old ways of thought it must also power the quest for new, and greater expectations." (Scheffler, 1991, p. 15).

Regarding the second point, that of a presumed convergence of successive theories, science does not in general proceed in a fixed theoretical direction, its results converging on a limit which it ever more closely approximates. "The theoretical agreements of one period are often uprooted and superseded by conflicting agreements at a later time." (Scheffler, 1999, p. 428). The net result of both points is that cognitive advances may be marked not only when accepted theories are rejected but, furthermore, when their implicit theoretical directions are abandoned.

A realistic education should prepare our children for such dualities of cognition, for disconfirmations as well as confirmations, for divergences from, as well as concordances with familiar theoretical habits, for unlearnings as well as learnings, for the loss of cherished beliefs as well as their acquisition. Education should also instill in our students the courage deliberately to court the risk of such loss by pressing accepted beliefs into ever new situations in which they may be tested. The dualities here noted do not imply separations or rifts. They are reversals of cognitive direction, each reversal motivated by what went before. The losses in question result from applying the very gains previously accrued, and they in turn energize the quest for further, and more adequate gains. This interlocked bi-directional pattern needs to be acquired if our students are to avoid the fantasy of uniform steady advance.

2. Decisional Duality

Decisions shape the future, but the future test of a decision must refer to the past. For such a test lies in the decision's consequences: Have such consequences turned out as expected at the time of decision? Did they occur as predicted, and did they exhibit the values hoped for? To answer these questions, the consequences of a given decision must be checked as they occur, against the past judgments of fact and of value that went into its formation. An accurate memory of such past judgments is essential to proper assessment, in turn required for critical review of the action or policy initiated by the decision.

Such critical review is the very opposite of blind adherence to a line of action initiated by a decision — endorsing its future embodiment in similar decisions and forgetful of the circumstances of its birth. The popularity of the idea of commitment underplays the equal importance of criticism. "The role of the policy-maker, construed critically, involves not simply the making of decisions for the future but also the checking of past decisions by monitoring their presently discernible outcomes. He thus not only shapes policy but may also contribute to its improvement." (Scheffler, 1985, p. 114)

Such a critical role toward one's ongoing policies is difficult to realize. "It requires a double consciousness demanding energetic fulfillment of commitments already undertaken while at the same time demanding a skeptical reserve vis-à-vis assumptions underlying these very commitments.... Not only is the mere 'doubling' of consciousness a hardship; the two attitudes seem to be in conflict." (Ibid.) Once a policy is undertaken, the inertia it generates defends it against revision, while the critical attitude toward its continuing flow of consequences threatens just such revision. This apparent conflict poses what seems an impossible choice: either resolutely defend policies already in force or put such policies on indefinite hold while scrutinizing the unending flow of consequences.

The apparent conflict between resolute but uncritical action and critical but passive intelligence is, however, spurious. No law, either in logic or in nature, forbids all but dogmatists to act and all but passive persons to reason. What is needed is practical ingenuity in relating decision and criticism in the realm of policy. The critical professional appears a model of what is required and what has already been achieved in certain domains. "What the wise physician does in providing definitive therapy and in critically revising such provision in light of new evidence is what the policy maker needs to do. He should feel obliged to offer, at each juncture, the guidance best warranted by contemporaneous evidence. In striving to do so, he may take pride both in his active practice and in his welcoming changes in such practice indicated by the evidence. Criticism of his past practice is no longer necessarily a threat, nor does it in any way suggest that practice is to be shunned in the future." (Ibid, p. 115).

What holds for the policy maker in political, social and educational realms indeed holds for each of us insofar as we all continually make decisions and formulate consecutive lines of action affecting our lives. We need, therefore, throughout education to cultivate the doubleness of consciousness required for action that is not only resolute but critical, firm while open to revision based on experience. This duality is not fatal. It is overcome by treating policies bi-focally, that is, taking them as present guides that are also answerable to the future.

3. Duality in Teaching

The teacher strives to represent and to advance specialized forms of thought by handing them on to the novice. This process occurs largely through explanation and interpretation. It requires the teacher to occupy two different intellectual worlds, that of the specialist and that of the novice. Moreover, the teacher needs to engage in a two-way translation project, one requiring the interpretation of specialized concepts in terms accessible to the novice, the other translating the understandings of the novice into the language of the specialist. In this translational or explanatory role, "he functions willy-nilly as a philosopher." (Scheffler, 1973, p. 36). For, by contrast to the specialist, whose domain he is charged to represent to the novice, the teacher cannot isolate himself within the protective walls of some specialty. He "requires something more — the ability to step out of the inner circle of specialists and to make their jargon intelligible to novices aspiring to sophistication." (Ibid.) Further, he needs to show how the concepts of the specialist gain traction in the novice's world by reformulating the novice's queries in terms treatable by the specialty.

This intellectual bilingualism is a primary qualification for excellence in teaching, the task of which is not simply to confront the student with the specialty as a given to be taken on trust, but rather to motivate such specialty by providing its rationale in terms already available to him. Nor ought the teacher to conceive the student's world as a fixed domain preventing its inhabitants from growth through contact with worlds beyond their own.

Respect for the world of the novice is essential in communicating with him. It is, moreover, indispensable if the specialist's achievements are to find ultimate application in that world. The case of the professional strikingly illustrates this point. Hoping to apply his special training to the alleviation of human problems, the professional needs to understand such problems as originally expressed. "The patient feels pain or cannot walk;

the bridge sways or is too narrow to accommodate rush-hour traffic; the child is having difficulty reading. Each of these descriptions is couched, not in the specialized language of a discipline, but in the idiom of everyday life. Each expresses…the character of a situation affecting human beings who are disposed to notice and respond to it in one way or another… Such expressions, in whatever language is natural to the persons in question, are essential to identifying the problems which professions must treat." (Scheffler, 1985, pp. 5–6)

The teacher, concerned to transmit the content of disciplines, is also bound to transmit a sense of their scope and application. Thus, the teacher is required not only to occupy two worlds himself, but also to convey a sense of the two worlds apparent in applying the disciplines to ordinary experience.

4. Duality of potential

Educators and parents focus on the enhancement of their children's potentials and this focus scants the fact that some potentials are desirable, others not. The popular slogan "Be all that you can be" fosters the myth of uniformly valuable potentials, overlooking the fact that value judgments are required to separate the potential for kindness, for example, from the potential for cruelty (see Scheffler, 1985, pp. 15–16), the former to be fostered, the latter destroyed.

But the natural shrinkage of desirable potentials must also be acknowledged. "Certain educational moments must be caught or they are gone forever…. The capacity to learn is not an unlimited resource which can be lightly squandered. The child's curiosity, sufficiently blocked, may be dulled beyond awakening. The impulse to question, thwarted repeatedly, may eventually die." Moreover, the existence of certain critical intervals for learning is a fact to be reckoned with in various areas of development. Chess, the violin and ballet need to be learned early in life; certain aspects of the visual system and of language acquisition mature, in favorable cases, within relevant periods. "Potentials here today may, in short, be gone tomorrow." (Ibid., pp. 12–13).

The parent and educator need to promote the development and realization of desirable potentials not yet manifest, while capitalizing on those now in place but shortly to wane or disappear without nurture. The future, in short, should not be the sole focus of parent or educator. A hopeful imagination of the student's future desirable potentials must be combined with a realistic appreciation of those now present and, perhaps, only temporarily possessed. "Striving to overcome present lacks through future possibilities, the educator is also constantly haunted by the specter of past opportunity wasted. The pressure of educational time forces him to look in both directions at once." (Ibid.)

The idea of education as preparation, increasingly fostered by our more and more competitive society, skews the vision of parent and educator alike. As Dewey and other progressive theorists have repeatedly stressed, education must concern itself with the present quality of the child's life and not solely with that life as a stage en route to the future. Attending to the child's desirable present potentials is as crucial as planting the seeds of those to emerge only later.

5. The duality of creativity

Creativity is innovation, but innovation is never *ex nihilo*. It employs available means and springs from themes and issues inherited from the past. "Originality in science presupposes immersion into the methods, conceptions, lore, and practices of prevalent science, without which even the most radical scientific innovations could not be formulated. Originality in literature implies a mastery of the available language, without which new literary content could not be articulated. Einstein could not have produced his theory of relativity without a grounding in Newtonian conceptions; James Joyce could not have written *Ulysses* without a mastery of ordinary English; Picasso could not have revolutionized the traditions of artistic representation without a prior mastery of those very traditions. It would, in sum, be ridiculous to counsel a student aspiring to originality in any field to avoid initiation into the fundamental traditions of the field in question." (Scheffler, 1995/1996, p. 91). The heritage of the past is indeed the ground of the new, but it by no means determines its character. Our students will need to "reshape the very heritage of knowledge we now teach them" in ways we cannot foresee (Scheffler 1991, p. 129). We need to avoid giving them "the idea that our heritage is a seamless web of settled facts... The plain fact is that [it] has gaps and fissures, jagged edges and incomplete contours...contradictions and enigmas...deep difficulties and disagreements." (Ibid.) Acquisition of a heritage is, as Michael Oakeshott has described it, "initiation into an inheritance in which we have a life interest, and the exploration of its intimations." (Ibid., p. 130). The ignorance of the future which borders the heritage we bequeath is thus "not a mere void, but an infinite space rich with educational possibilities to beckon the active young mind. Far from being an embarrassment, ignorance should be given a proud and central place in our curricula." (Ibid.)

The duality we confront here is faithfully to represent the accumulated materials of our heritage and concurrently to instill the courage in our students to reach beyond it. Respect for the past and the willingness to edit, supplement or abrogate it: are these not flatly contradictory? Yet both are necessary. Respect for the past is indeed largely respect for our forebears' accumulated innovations, all of which have built upon or departed from still earlier stores of achievement. No matter how seemingly conflicting as ideals, erudition and experimentation are both essential to hold in view, for our children as well as ourselves.

The settled heritage is indeed a source of security to one who has acquired it. But it is precisely such security that enables one to risk departing from it. The situation commonly associated with adolescents, whose development vacillates as they negotiate the boundary between the security of childhood and the risks of adulthood — taking two steps forward and one step back — is pervasive in all efforts to appropriate a heritage with its dual demands. The very security it affords is prerequisite to the risk-taking required if it is to survive.

Each element of our heritage thus demands a dual response, as a unique object of understanding and appreciation, and as an incarnation of creative process. "To view past works — whether of art, or science, or architecture, or music, or literature, or mathematics, or history, or religion, or philosophy — as given and unique objects rather than as incarnations of process is to close off the traditions of effort from which they emerged. It is to bring these traditions to a full stop. Viewing such works as embodiments of purpose, style, and form revivifies and extends the force of these traditions in the present, giving hope to creative impulses active now and in the future... Appreciating the underlying process does not, by any means, exhaust the possibilities of understanding. But the understanding it does provide is a ground of further creativity in thought and action." (Scheffler, 1991, p. 41).

Conclusion

The five species of duality I have discussed highlight the often unacknowledged complexity of the educational process:

Cognitive duality denies the typical conception of learning as a uniform progressive advance of knowledge. It expresses the *bi-directional* rhythm of inquiry: on the one hand, consolidating the patterns of the known and, on the other, dismantling such patterns when they fail.

Decisional duality contradicts the idea that decisions move us forward into the future, thus enabling us to "put the past behind us," as the saying goes. But decision making as critical process is *bifocal*; it requires us to look backward as well as forward, to see how well the initial assumptions of our decisions have been borne out. Resoluteness in execution as well as critical assessment in process — both place demands on the agent, who needs to cultivate a double consciousness to do them justice.

Duality in teaching contravenes the still prevalent notion that teaching is a matter of mastering some special domain and then presenting it to the student. This duality requires *bilingualism* of the teacher, consequent upon his double occupancy — of the world of the specialist and the world of the novice. His task is largely translational, not merely to present his subject but to communicate it, to couch it in terms accessible in the novice's world, and to reformulate the novice's statements in terms that resonate for the specialist.

The duality of potential opposes the popular idea that the educator must simply determine or enhance the child's potentials and then attempt to actualize them, the underlying myth being that they are all desirable, all consistent, and all invariable. This duality, requiring acknowledgment of the value differences among potentials as well as their temporal variability, expresses the educator's *bifocal* concern both with selecting a consistent set of future desirable potentials, and with nurturing present desirable ones, especially those whose days may be numbered.

The duality of creativity counters the prevalent view that creativity springs anew out of spontaneous inspiration, producing works to be appreciated as givens, in and for themselves. Such duality recognizes that creative responses presuppose the heritage of the past while going beyond to edit, refine or otherwise alter it for cause. Creative works are thus *bi-valued*; they are to be prized for what they represent in themselves, but also appreciated as embodiments of style and form inherited from those who came before and bequeathed, under intelligent transformation, to those who come after.

References

Scheffler, Israel. (1999). A plea for pluralism. *Transactions of the Charles E. Peirce Society, 35 (3)*. Summer.
Scheffler, Israel. (1995/1996). The concept of the educated person. In V. A. Howard and I. Scheffler. *Work, education and leadership*. New York: Peter Lang.
Scheffler, Israel. (1991). *In praise of cognitive emotions*. New York: Routledge.
Scheffler, Israel. (1985). *Of human potential*. Boston: Routledge and Kegan Paul.
Scheffler, Israel. (1973) *Reason and teaching*. Indianapolis: Hackett.

The Educational Significance of Modern Philosophical Midrash: Emmanuel Levinas – "Temptation of Temptation"

JONATHAN COHEN

I could not begin this essay without first acknowledging its origin in insights gained through study with Prof. Seymour Fox. In the early 1970s, as a young student completing a teacher's certificate at the Hebrew University, I had the privilege of participating (together with Michael Rosenak, Nechama Moussaeff, Oded Schremer and others) in a course taught by Prof. Fox called "Recent Developments in Curriculum Theory." Among the readings he assigned for the course was an article by Joseph Schwab called "Enquiry and the Reading Process." (1978) At the time, I found the text extremely difficult. I was determined to penetrate it, however, and I remember re-reading it many times. Although the article was written from within the Deweyan pragmatic tradition, I felt nonetheless that it was describing and implementing the kind of close reading that I had internalized unreflectively in the course of my traditional Jewish education. In articulating the didactic practice entailed by what he termed "rhetorical analysis," Schwab urged teachers not to ask students "what does the text say?" (a question that can invite only paraphrases), but to insist that they address the question "what is the text *doing*?" (a question that turns students' attention to strategies of composition), (Ibid., pp. 158–160). This maxim served as my guide when I began teaching Jewish thought and philosophy at the Hebrew University High School shortly thereafter, and has oriented my teaching and research at the Hebrew

93

University ever since. It is in the spirit of the kind of close reading that gives due attention to the choices made by an author with regard to words, themes and compositional structure that this study of the educational strategy underlying one of Levinas' best-known Talmudic lectures is respectfully contributed to this festschrift.

As regards the application of close reading to Jewish philosophical texts, I must also acknowledge my indebtedness to Prof. Eliezer Schweid. It is he who directed my attention, both in his lectures and in his published writings, to the organic interconnection between literary form and philosophical content in classic Jewish texts. One has only to consult his brilliant analysis of the art of dialogue in the Kuzari, published over 30 years ago, for evidence of this motif in his research (Schweid, 1970). In this connection, mention should also be made of Leo Strauss' still remarkable essay: "The Law of Reason in the Kuzari" wherein startling conclusions are drawn from a rigorous literary analysis of the placement and deployment of the various arguments brought forth by the Jewish sage in defense of the "despised faith." (Strauss, 1952). More recently, Prof. Schweid has published two analyses of individual texts, one on Maimonides' introduction to *Perek Helek* (1998), and one on Gordon's *Le'Berur Ra'ayonenu Meyesodo*, in which attention to composition is again in the forefront (Schweid, 1997). In these works, more explicit reference is made to the manner in which the text is structured and textured such that the reader is led through an educational process of philosophical maturation. In the following analysis of Levinas' "Temptation of Temptation," as well as the brief contrast I wish to draw between this much-appreciated lecture and another well-known exemplar of modern philosophical midrash, Soloveitchik's "Lonely Man of Faith" (Solo-veitchik, 1965), I will follow Schweid's example in focusing on the connection between literary composition and educational strategy aimed at philosophical reorientation.

In the last two decades, Levinas scholarship has proliferated far beyond the radius of French and French-Jewish culture. Three recent studies focus intensively on the very essay we have chosen for compositional and educational analysis: Levinas' suggestive Talmudic reading entitled "Temptation of Temptation." Prof. Zev Harvey seeks to clarify Levinas' understanding of "integrity" and "naiveté" by comparing insights gleaned from "Temptation of Temptation" with key passages from his philosophical essay "Substitution." (Harvey, 1993). Prof. Lawrence Kaplan places Levinas' interpretation of BT Shabbat 88 in the the context of medieval and modern commentaries on the same Talmudic passage (Kaplan, 1998).

Shaul Wachstock, in a recent master's thesis, devotes two chapters to "Temptation of Temptation," and takes issue with Kaplan's characterization of the difference between the Maharal's and Levinas' interpretations of the *sugya* (Wachstock, 1999).

I am particularly indebted to two colleagues for their recent work on the connections between form, content and educational strategy in the Talmudic readings of Emmanuel Levinas. Annette Aronowicz points to Levinas' use of the humor born of discrepancy and incongruity (Aronowicz, 1990, pp. xv–xvi). By humorously highlighting the blatant anachronism involved in the midrashic conflation of traditional story-elements with contemporary events and figures, Levinas demonstrates his own "distanciation" from the texts he is interpreting. This move creates safe space for his critical listeners or readers to "appropriate" those same texts through the mediation of a critically aware teacher.[1] Michael Gillis, as well as Aronowicz, refers to Levinas' analysis of the minutest details of midrashic narrative as the literary performance of a philosophical-educational ideal, namely that to be an educated Jew does not mean to dissipate particularity into universality. (Gillis, 1998, Chap. 3, especially pp. 142–143).[2]

I believe that our appreciation of the interconnections between forms of discourse and their philosophical-educational purport can be further enhanced by additional studies based on the analysis of selected individual texts chosen from the corpus of contemporary Jewish thought. It is through such treatment that we can view a thinker's typical "moves" against the background of the plan of a whole discourse, and thereby observe a text in the process of teaching itself. We propose, then, to examine the overall structure, as well as some typical modes of expression, that can be observed in Levinas' philosophical midrash "Temptation of Temptation." The bulk of our comments will be devoted to an analysis of this by now

1   For the terms "distanciation" and "appropriation" see Ricoeur, 1982, pp. 131–144.
2   In the context of this festschrift, featuring research by past and present fellows and faculty of the Mandel School, I gratefully acknowledge what I have learned from other studies of Levinas written by former Jerusalem Fellows. In addition to the studies by Annette Aronowicz, Michael Gillis and Shaul Wachstock, mention should be made of the penetrating and original doctoral thesis written by Ami Bouganim entitled "L'Autre dans la Pensee d'Emmanuel Levinas" (1990). Among many other insights, Bouganim claims to have disclosed a religious, quasi-gnostic motivation underlying Levinas' non-theological "epiphany" of the Other. Further mention should be made of Shmuel Vigoda's master's thesis at the Hebrew University much of which is devoted to uncovering an explicit and implicit critique of Heidegger in Levinas' Talmudic writings. His forthcoming doctoral thesis contains many interesting comparisons between Maimonidean and Levinasian ethics.

well-known Talmudic reading. We hope to show that the structure of this discourse, as well as some of its chosen forms of articulation, reflect a coherent educational strategy. In the course of our presentation, we will distinguish between what has been called a "dialogical" hermeneutic, and the mode of interpretation we have chosen to call "philosophical midrash," as one key to appreciating the educational thrust of this composition.[3] At the end of our presentation, we will make some brief remarks comparing the philosophical-educational plan of "Temptation of Temptation" with the strategy underlying another well-known essay that originated in a spoken address, also composed in the mid-sixties, namely Rabbi Joseph Soloveitchik's "Lonely Man of Faith."

The Talmudic reading known as "The Temptation of Temptation" was given at a colloquium of French intellectuals held in December, 1964. The circumstances surrounding these colloquia have been dealt with extensively by Aronowicz (1990, pp. xxxii–xxxiii, and *passim*) and others. The first part of this discourse might be titled "opening remarks, disclaimers and rules of the game." (Ibid, pp. 31–32).[4] It is here that Levinas justifies his presentation in the light of remarks made earlier in the colloquium, apologizes for confining himself to Aggadic material, ironically attributing this move to his supposed intellectual inadequacy, and disavows any access to a mystical numerology that might "decode" the Talmudic text. He advises his hearers that he will proceed on the assumption that seemingly disconnected fragments of Talmudic discourse can be shown to reflect "unity and progression of thought." Most importantly, however, Levinas lays out the philosophical "ground rules" that will constrain him in his discourse. Although the discourse will consist of a commentary on a traditional Talmudic text, the interpretation will be undertaken within the horizon of humanly accessible experience. No revelatory knowledge of the attributes or "psychology" of God will intrude upon the discussion. There will be no theological or theosophical assumptions about God's will, his cosmic purpose or historical plan. Should a transcendent dimension become visible in the discussion, it will be by way of human ethical experience, necessitating no claim to discrete theological knowledge.

3   I deal more extensively with the distinction between the "hermeneutics of dialogue" and the hermeneutic mode I call "philosophical midrash" in Cohen, forthcoming, "Carrying the Past into the Future: Texts and Teaching in Contemporary Jewish Education."

4   It is recommended that the reader follow the passages referred to in the discussion. All references will be to Aronowicz's excellent English translation. Those who wish to consult the original French are referred to Levinas' *Quatre Lectures Talmudiques* (Paris, Editions de Minuit, 1968), pp. 67–109. Quotes can be located within the textual units indicated in the notes following.

The next section of "Temptation of Temptation" represents an articulation of what Levinas considers to be the structure of experience underlying both the Western tradition and the contemporary European sensibility.[5] It should be noted that Levinas makes a point of diagnosing the European condition in this rather long section with virtually no reference to Jewish sources. This passage, which precedes his active commentary on BT Shabbat 88a–b, can be further divided into four subsections, separated by clear literary markers. The first, rather short, subsection speaks of the contemporary Westerner's hunger for rich and manifold experience in non-philosophical language, in the rhetoric of feeling and desire, although he calls this posture Western man's "moral attitude." Western man, says Levinas, is "for an open life, eager to try everything, to experience everything, 'in a hurry to live, impatient to feel....we cannot close ourselves off to any possibility. We cannot let life pass us by!" This hankering for experiential intensity is then contrasted with innocence and naiveté, regarded as childish and, at best, "provisional." The section is then marked off by a remark as to the possibility of an alternative to this orientation (termed for the first time "the temptation of temptation," without an explanation) an alternative Levinas hopes to extrapolate from his forthcoming commentary.

In the next subsection, Levinas probes deeper into the European sensibility, locating its roots in the Western philosophical tradition (the "reasonable City" of Plato that "must have everything") and the Christian tradition (the dramatic life of the saints who live in constant temptation).[6] More essentially, however, he draws connections between the moral posture implied in being "tempted by temptation" and the epistemological deployment of the knower and the known. The Westerner wishes to traverse as much of experience as possible, yet experience harbors both good and evil. The Westerner, however, contrives to place himself, by his own lights, "beyond good and evil" by withholding himself from commitment and full engagement with what he is experiencing. He builds a subject-object structure, wherein he can *know* the object of his experience, perhaps even sympathetically and deeply, yet always retreat to the safe haven of subjectivity. The knowing subject never really leaves the self-subsistence of his status as knower, always maintaining a safe distance from the known. He is constantly tempted by the temptation of giving himself over to that which he experiences, whether good or evil, but

5   ibid., pp. 32–33: "The temptation of temptation.......in that direction."
6   Ibid., pp. 33–34: "In the *Republic* ..... shows us the way?"

keeps from being tainted by evil or entering into a pact with the good, by a judicious withdrawal, whereby the experienced "other" becomes integrated into his fund of knowledge without commanding his commitment. A connection is made, then, between a moral posture of studied neutrality vis-à-vis good and evil, and the Western epistemological structure of subject and object. From the language of feeling and desire, we have moved to the language of ethics and the threshold of epistemology. This section is also marked off by a remark that the forthcoming Talmud commentary will explore an alternative to this orientation.

The third subsection of this first, non-commentative section of Levinas' presentation moves further into the realm of philosophical discourse.[7] At this juncture, Levinas offers a penetrating phenomenological analysis of the experience of "experiencing without experiencing," or knowledge. On the one hand, we want all experience to pass through our own selves, and we do not want to limit the scope of our experience. On the other hand, we do not want to act or commit before having "gone and seen for ourselves," before investigating and gathering direct evidence. As Strauss has so wisely put it, the philosopher is an "investigator." (Strauss, 1952, p. 17). On the one hand, there is the courage to search out everything. On the other hand, the philosopher wishes to be "secure in truth." Secure in his subjectivity, without having risked himself, he beholds the truth-system within which he has integrated all the objects of his experience. Unfortunately, this kind of irresponsible curiosity also penetrates the world of what Plato called societal "opinion," promoting a climate of "immodesty," "abdication of responsibility" and moral "incapacity." It should be noted that, as Levinas articulates his account of the European sensibility-become-philosophy, he makes sure to include himself as heir to and participant in the Western tradition: "...courage within security, the basis of *our* old Europe." The author presents himself as a fellow inhabitant of the same epistemological universe that the reader has come to recognize as his own. Yet, this orientation is revealed as vulnerable to a radical ethical critique.

In the fourth and final subsection of this pre-commentative excursus, Levinas offers an actual formal *definition* of philosophy as "the subordination of any act to the knowledge one may have of that act."[8] (In so doing, he is subtly foreshadowing the issue of the proper order

---

7   Ibid., pp. 34–35: "One can perceive.....guides this commentary."
8   Ibid., pp. 35–36: "Philosophy, in any case.......even conditions, these notions."

between "knowing" and "doing" that will occupy him in the Talmud's response to the Biblical "We will do and we will hear.") All action will be preceded either by the calculations of practical reason or the subsumptions of theoretical reason (i.e. the placing of the "other" in either a cosmic or historical "perspective.") In a manner uncannily reminiscent of Strauss, the attitude opposite to that of philosophy is cast as naiveté or innocence, seen as the indispensable condition of spontaneous, generous action.[9] Before beginning his commentary, Levinas intimates the possibility of a primordial experience, preceding cognition, which is yet not childlike innocence and naiveté. Naturally, the reader becomes curious as to what this non-naive pre-reflection could possibly consist of. Apart from a small number of oblique hints and only one direct, and unessential midrashic reference, Levinas has unfolded this diagnosis of the European condition from within the horizon of human experience, without recourse to insights derived from canonical texts.

As a transition from section one to section two of his discourse, from independent phenomenology to commentary, Levinas interpolates a brief reflection on reason and revelation.[10] For the addressees of Levinas' discourse, the transition from the phenomenological to the commentative mode is by no means self-understood. It must be justified in terms of humanly accessible experience. The move to what have been considered to be texts that partake of Revelation must be justified within the domain of philosophy. But does not this very move dissipate the uniqueness of the category of Revelation, a form of knowledge held to be of a different order than that of Reason? Anticipating these reactions in his listeners, Levinas makes some explicit remarks on his understanding of Revelation, its relation to Reason, and the status of the canonical text he has chosen to interpret. In so doing, he plays with different meanings of the word "revelation" at different points in his transitional interpolation. At first, he says that there is a certain "Revelation at stake" in the text to be interpreted, and that this "revelatory" text will disclose an order of experience wherein there is something prior to subject-object cognition that is neither innocence nor naiveté. "Revelation" in this sense means something that "recommends itself" to one's "discernment" (sagesse), something that "comes to mind"

---

9   See Strauss, 1983, pp. 160–161. See also Strauss, 1979, pp. 111–113.
10 Aronowicz, 1990, p. 36: "The Revelation.....has acquired for us." The play on the word "revelation" is as plain in the original French as it is in Aronowicz's English translation. See *Quatres Lectures Talmudiques*, p. 79–80.

without being located beyond consciousness.[11] Such an understanding of Revelation makes the traditional Western dichotomy between Reason (the human horizon) and Revelation (in the sense of extra-rational knowledge) irrelevant. In the traditional understanding, adherence to revelatory knowledge must involve either "fideism" or "blind faith" in the transmitters of the alleged revelation. Levinas proposes to reinterpret the category of Revelation such that it can function within the human horizon. "Revelation," becomes, then, for Levinas, "elements that are accepted because they already recommend themselves to the discernment of the one who accepts them." It is this kind of "revelation" that Levinas wishes to extrapolate from the ostensibly "revelatory" texts that he will comment on forthwith. In a final play, Levinas remarks that the text chosen for commentary occupies itself precisely with the question of the manner of acceptance of a revelatory message by its addressees (whether freely or by coercion, and if by coercion, by what kind of coercion?) It would seem that before Levinas can get down to the business of commenting on a text both *of* and *on* Revelation, he must both thematize and reinterpret the category of Revelation for his addressees for whom the traditional category of Revelation has little normative significance.

At this point, Levinas moves into the core of his discourse, the analysis of a passage in Shabbat 88a–b, which is likewise divided into four parts, this time according to what Levinas perceives to be links in the chain of Talmudic discussion. There is much richness in Levinas' analysis, and we will take note only of certain features that have a bearing on his educational plan. Levinas is intent on demonstrating that the seemingly dissociated elements of the Talmudic discussion reflect a coherent sequence. This, to enhance his hearer's respect for a text they might have thought to be the product of a primitive, non-systematic intelligence. He is also intent on translating the pictorial images and narrative elements appearing in the Talmudic texts into concepts or experiential structures that are recognizable to his listeners, yet carry them beyond what they have already encountered to a consciousness of commitment they might only have intimated. It is likewise of great importance to Levinas that the spiritual option he presents to his listeners, that of a response to a call for commitment made before the weighing of evidence, be looked up to as an ideal of maturity, rather than looked down on as a reflection of childish innocence and rashness.

---

11 The words "comes to mind" are taken from the title of Levinas' book *De Dieu qui vient à l'idée* (1982).

In the first literary sub-unit interpreted by Levinas, Mount Sinai is described as being held over the people of Israel "as a tub."[12] This is followed by the objection that such coercion could be seen as duress, liberating the Jewish people from their obligation to obey the commandments of the Torah. The sub-unit is concluded with the reassurance that what was forcibly imposed in the days of Moses was freely appropriated in the days of Mordechai and Esther. The image of the mountain held over the Israelites is translated by Levinas into a challenge posed to his listeners: "Is one already responsible before one chooses responsibility?" On the one hand, he assumes that such a formulation will not suggest itself to his hearers without reservation. On the other hand, he seems confident that such a situation will not be perceived as entirely out of the range of their experience. We have all been thrust into situations whereby a certain course of action seemed "imposed by the logic of things," leaving no real freedom of choice in the matter. Sometimes we feel compelled to consent to certain courses of action before "inspection" of "evidence." The image of the suspended tub, then, becomes an emblem of inescapable responsibility, of the urgency of action before inspection. At this stage, Levinas purposely refrains from "fleshing out" the concrete circumstances of such an experience. Initially, he is most concerned to establish, in the consciousness of his hearers, the *formal* possibility of an orientation-toward-action that is not dependent on the total freedom of the ego.

In commenting on this first subsection of the *sugya*, Levinas articulates his insights in two forms we feel are consistent with the overall educational thrust of his discourse. As we have seen, the direction of Levinas' presentation could be called, after Peter Berger, "inductive" rather than "deductive." (Berger, 1979, pp. 56–60). He is not interested in what Fackenheim has called "top-down" theology, whereby implications for the human condition are drawn from a conception of God, Creation, Providence, Prophecy, Revelation, etc. (Fackenheim, 1968, p.101). His is most definitely a "bottom-up" approach to transcendence, beginning with a phenomenology of human experience. In keeping with this orientation, he makes two moves in his interpretation of this subsection. First, he engages in what might be called a particularly modern form of "negative theology." Rather than speaking of God by way of negative attributes, as Maimonides and others did in the Middle Ages, Levinas points to the transcendent by heightening the experience of human

12 Aronowicz, 1990, pp. 37–40: "And they stopped at the foot of the mountain......is a beyond-freedom."

limitation. In a telling passage, speaking of the ethical compulsion symbolized by the overturned mountain, Levinas says: "the truth (the primordial awakening to responsibility) or death (only through such responsibility is life justified) would not be a dilemma that man gives himself." When we experience the imperative of responsibility, we find ourselves in a situation of which we are not the authors. Who, then, is the author? Of this Levinas does not speak in a discourse which has promised to remain within the horizon of human experience. The transcendent as the Other par excellence "Who situates us" ethically[13] is only hinted at, and not thematized or articulated. If there is to be any positive approach to a transcendent sovereign, it will only "come to mind"[14] by way of our own sense of the limitations of human sovereignty as mediated by the ethical realm.

As a further instanciation of Levinas' "inductive" orientation, we can observe him portraying archetypal situations that could be said, again in Berger's terms, to be "signals of transcendence." (See Berger, 1969, pp. 52–75). One of these is the educational experience itself. In his words: "Would the choice between truth and death be a reference to education, the process by which the mind receives training under the master's rod in order to rise toward comprehension? That the mind needs training suggests the very mystery of violence's anteriority to freedom, suggests the possibility of an adherence prior to free examination and prior to temptation." Then again, further on: "Freedom begins in what has all the appearance of a constraint due to threat. The text might be teaching us this pedagogy of liberation. But is it a pedagogy? Is it a method for children?"

It should be clear that the above is not a policy statement about the efficacy of corporal punishment. "Violence," in this context, means "adherence" not given to choice, or "constraint." Later on in his discourse, Levinas is at pains to cast the experience of primordial, non-assumed, responsibility in terms that would do away with the liberty-violence dichotomy altogether. In Berger's terms, Levinas is pointing to a "signal of transcendence;" a recognizable experience that points beyond itself to something essential about the human condition, both with regard to cognition and ethics. If we were to turn to educational thinkers, such as Dewey or Shulman, we might say that Levinas is "psychologizing" or teaching by analogy.[15] He is searching for a situation within the

---

13   This is a play on Fackenheim's expression "the Other who situates us humanly" used at the end of his *Metaphysics and Historicity* (1961), pp. 89–90.

14   See note 11.

15   See Dewey, 1956, pp. 22–31, and Shulman, 1986, pp. 4–14, esp. pp. 9–10.

experiential horizon of his listeners that could be seen to reflect human situatedness in general. Ironically playing on the phrase "pedagogy of liberation," Levinas implies that education for liberation cannot concern itself only with emancipation and empowerment. True liberation can be gained only by way of a prior, indissoluble bond. Unlike R.S. Peters, Levinas does not see non-freedom as a mere propadeutic to a freely assumed morality (See Peters, 1966). What children must go through is paradigmatic for what we must all face again and again, namely constraint calling for response, rather than free choice autonomously assumed. Such a posture represents, for Levinas, an ideal of maturity, rather than a concession to immaturity.

In moving to his interpretation of the second literary unit composing the Talmudic *sugya*, Levinas articulates what he considers to be a conscious insight embedded in the very transition between the two sections.[16] This serves to reinforce his explicit assumption that analysis into parts will yield coherence, and that the subsections of the Talmudic text can be seen to present and then augment an overarching vision. In his words: "this anteriority of acceptance in relation to freedom does not merely express a human possibility but ... the essence of the Real depends on it. In this anteriority lies hidden the ultimate meaning of Creation." The text, then, "extends the meaning of the situation we have examined above to the entirety of Being." At this point Levinas proceeds to interpret that part of the Talmudic text that asks why and how the earth both trembled with fear and was calmed at the time that God "uttered His judgment." Why did the earth tremble, then? God had told it that if the people of Israel do not accept the Torah, He would return it to a state of chaos. The completion of Creation on the sixth day was made dependent on Israel's acceptance of the Torah on the sixth day of Sivan. Annette Aronowicz and Michael Gillis have already written eloquently on Levinas' tendency to universalize without sacrificing particularity.[17] His interpretation of this passage is a most illustrative case in point. On the one hand, Levinas universalizes: Israel and the Torah become mankind and ethics: "Being has a meaning. The meaning of being, the meaning of creation, is to realize the Torah. The world is here so that the ethical order has the possibility of being fulfilled." On the other hand, demythologization does not dissipate particularity, for the insight that Being rests on ethics, and not vice versa, is considered to be the basis of Israel's special witness.

16 Aronowicz, 1990, pp. 40–41: "This introduces.....the temptation of temptation."
17 Aronowicz, 1990, Tran. Intro. to Levinas, pp. XXIX–XXXI. Gillis, Michael, see note 2.

Let us return for a moment to Levinas' tendency to see quotidian experience as the locus for transcendental insight, and to his predilection for "psychologizing" and "analogizing." This second literary unit of the Talmudic text is presented in something like the classic *petichta* form.[18] There is a passage from the Writings, in this case from Psalms, which is assumed to correspond to a passage from the Pentateuch. In our case, the Talmud assumes that the passage from Psalms: "From the heavens Thou didst utter judgement: the earth feared and stood still" refers to the giving of the Torah at Sinai. Levinas knows that his audience is "suspicious" of the midrashic tendency to connect disparate passages, and so he purposely problematizes the assumption that "Psalm 76 has to do with the giving of the Torah." He temporarily shares his audience's "hermeneutic of suspicion" in order to lead them on to a "hermeneutic of trust."[19] He tries to elicit greater trust by claiming that the psalmist is merely doing something that we all do, namely ascribing meaning to classical texts on the basis of our own experiences. Levinas asks: "Don't we moderns say: Here are the circumstances that finally made me understand such and such a saying in Pascal or Montaigne? Aren't the great texts great because of their capacity to interact with the events and experiences that shed light on them and which they guide?" In the end, says Levinas, the psalmist, who has a sense of the fragility of Being in the presence of Judgment, interprets the event of the giving of the Torah as the paradigmatic event wherein the world trembled at a normative message. So, says Levinas implicitly, what I am doing — finding the transcendental implications of recognizable experiences and uncovering the experiential base of received tradition ("psychologizing") — is something we all do, and something that the texts themselves do among themselves. Levinas' educational assumption here would seem to be the following: Observed continuity between the interpretive experience of my listeners and the interpretive activity of classical Jewish texts will enhance trust in those texts and counteract suspicion.

In his analysis of the third subsection of the *sugya*, Levinas continues to point to "signals of transcendence" within human experience, to translate images and figures from the Midrash into concepts, and to characterize the

---

18 See note 16. On the *petichta* form, see Heinemann, 1970, pp. 12–17.

19 For the concept "hermeneutics of suspicion," see Ricoeur, 1970, p. 34. I have coined the term "hermeneutics of trust" by way of contradistinction to the "hermeneutics of suspicion." Ricoeur's preferred terms for this "trustful" orientation are the hermeneutics of "recollection of meaning" or "recovery of meaning."

human ideal held up by the Talmud as a paradigm of maturity.[20] This part
of the *sugya* speaks of the crowning of the Israelites by the angels as a
result of their having chosen to do before they hear. Firstly, as before,
Levinas expresses solidarity with the difficulty his Western, critical
audience must have in relating sympathetically to an ideal that places
acceptance before knowledge. Says Levinas: "This shocks logic and can
pass for blind faith or the naiveté of childish trust..." As a philosopher-
educator, it is important for Levinas that his hearers know that he has
experienced the same recoil at this notion that they have. To gain their
trust, he must appear as heir to the same rational-critical tradition. In the
educational context within which he is operating, it will not do for him to
claim dogmatic "extraterritoriality" for the text he is interpreting.

Immediately afterwards, however, Levinas recounts a human experience
he hopes will provide a bridge between the ideal purveyed by the text and
the human possibilities available to his listeners: "....yet it is what
underlies any inspired act, even artistic, for the act only brings out the form
in which it only now recognizes its model, never glimpsed before."
Inspired action is cast here as a "signal of transcendence," as a form of
committed involvement that points beyond itself. Inspiration, whether in
ethics or the aesthetic realm, begins with activity or creation. It is not
preceded by a "conception" which is only later "applied." Rather its
conception becomes intelligible only in the course of the activity itself.
Levinas hopes that his audience has experienced such moments of
inspiration, whether directly or vicariously, and that this "signal of
transcendence" will contribute to the legitimation of the overall existential
orientation spoken of by the Talmud.

Throughout this subsection, the image of angels recurs. It is they who
crown the Israelites when they commit before investigating, it is they who
remove their crowns when they immediately sin, and the act of
engagement before inspection is spoken of as the angels' "secret" and
"mystery." For Levinas, the angels represent the highest possibility of
spiritual maturity, as opposed to the lowest, that of childhood. Throughout
his discourse, and particularly in this section, Levinas is intent upon
reorienting his audience's notions of maturity and immaturity.[21] This issue
is of paramount educational significance, for it concerns itself with the

---

20 Aronowicz, 1990, pp. 41–46: "We are coming.......secret of subjectivity."
21 Elsewhere, I have discussed Levinas' understanding of religious maturity. See Cohen,
   2002.

human ideal to be held up as the end product of the educational process, as well as with stages that must be reached or overcome on the way.

Levinas is wary, as we have seen, lest his audience identify the attitude of "doing before hearing" with childish naivete. Such naivete, however, for Levinas means "an unawareness of reason in a world dominated by reason." First of all, the commitment spoken of by the Talmud is actually more rational than the posture of autonomous choice by an ego, because it is phenomenologically more radical and primary. The awareness of responsibility to the other is more primordial even than the subject-object distinction.[22] In fact, as Levinas never tires of saying, selfhood itself is constituted by acts of responsibility. Secondly, as Levinas emphasizes in the last section of his discourse, the posture of unconditional responsibility has need of reason to aid it in the prioritization of obligations to various "others."[23] Both practical reason and theoretical investigation into the conditions of human existence are essential for the realization of the ideal of commitment. The Talmud, then, does not praise unconditional responsibility out of an ignorance of, or an abdication of reason. Secondly, childhood is not to be idealized, as it often is in the cherubic images of the Christian tradition, for childhood stands unfortified against temptation. The human being must be advised, by reason, of the various temptations that surround him.

If unconditional commitment is the most mature ideal, and childhood is not to be idealized, what of the sophistication so often associated with adulthood? In this third section of his Talmudic discourse, Levinas takes on what often passes for sophistication in Western culture. In so doing, he deliberately articulates what he means by the difference between "temptation" and the "temptation of temptation." According to the Talmudic midrash, the crowning of Israel by the angels (when the Israelites said "we will do and we will hear") and their de-crowning by a double contingent of angels when they immediately sinned, both took place at Mount Horeb. It would seem that the response of unconditional commitment and the falling into temptation happen almost simultaneously in time and space. The Torah also mentions that, as a sign of their shame, the Israelites surrendered their "adornments" after their sin. Levinas

---

22 For a discussion of the origin and meaning of the phrase "ethics as first philosophy," see Adriaan T. Peperzak's introduction to the collection by that name: *Ethics As First Philosophy: The Significance of Emmanuel Levinas for Philosophy, Literature and Religion* (1995), pp. IX–XIII.

23 See the end of "Temptation of Temptation" in Aronowicz, 1990, p. 50. For Levinas' conception of the "third party," see also Levinas, 1989, pp. 25–40.

interprets this sequence to mean that the posture of absolute commitment does not automatically make one into a saint. Temptation lies in wait, and can succeed. Yet the person oriented toward a primordial pact with the good will never "adorn" his sin by calling it "experience," or by placing himself "beyond good and evil." Should he sin, he will understand his act as "unadorned sin;" he will surrender all adornment, and this will leave the path of repentance open to him.[24] The person "tempted by temptation," however, insists on the fullness of experience without commitment — he wishes to exist in a condition of abiding temptation and stimulation. The "sophisticated" person will have knowledge of a great many things, but he will have withheld himself from commitment to any one of them. His brushes with evil in his hankering for experience will never elicit guilt, only the satisfaction that comes with rich and intense living. I would suggest, in light of passages from Levinas' other writings, that this posture be characterized as his understanding of "adolescence."[25] Here, as elsewhere, Levinas offers educators a compelling image of the mature person, contrasted with both childishness and the false maturity of adolescence.

It is worth dwelling briefly on another Talmudic image translated by Levinas in this section, for this is the image that helps to characterize this whole discourse, as well as his other interpretations of Talmudic texts, as "philosophical midrash." This is the image comparing Israel to a tree that bears fruit before it sprouts leaves. Levinas' reaction to this image is enthusiastic: "Marvel of marvels: A history whose conclusion precedes its development. All is there from the beginning…The fruit is there from all eternity. History does not grow but extends." This, and other passages in Levinas, bear a remarkable resemblance to the manner in which Gershom Scholem has characterized rabbinic midrash. Note the following passage from Scholem: "The meaning of revelation unfolds in the course of historical time — but only because everything that can come to be known has already been deposited in a timeless substratum.…..Truth must be laid bare in a text in which it already pre-exists." (Scholem, 1970, pp. 289–290).

We believe that Levinas, in leading his readers from a "hermeneutics of suspicion" to a "hermeneutics of trust," is not embodying or espousing a "dialogical" hermeneutic, and in this matter I would like to take issue with

---

24 In the French, the "unadornedness" of sin is rendered "il reste peche triste sans couronnes."

25 See again Cohen, 2002, for a discussion of what could be construed as a Levinasian understanding of "adolescence."

Michael Gillis.[26] In philosophical midrash, there is no reciprocity or parity between the reader and the text, just as no such parity obtains between the bearer of responsibility and the "other" in Levinas' ethics. It is the text that is regarded as the inexhaustible source of wisdom and guidance, and the reader as the one summoned to devote himself to it such that it might disclose its meaning for his time and place. The relation between the interpreter and the text is dialectical and paradoxical, but not dialogical. The eternal fruitfulness of the text is the fountainhead for the seeming originality of the interpreter. Levinas' educational task is indeed very great. He must lead his listeners from suspicion, and a false sense of superiority — not only to respect for the text as partner, but to devotion to the text as an inexhaustible wellspring of wisdom.

The hermeneutic service performed by the reader, in order that the text disclose its import for his time and place, is taken up thematically at the beginning of Levinas' commentary on the fourth and final subsection of the Talmudic *sugya*.[27] In so doing, he weaves the images and motifs that have occupied him until now: fruit and leaves, history, childhood and hermeneutics, into one meaningful strand, in true homiletic fashion. The Torah, the repository and emblem of the epistemological primacy of ethics, is given as a ripe fruit, as a fully self-evident truth, and does not grow as the result of the explorations of the maturing child. History does not consist in an evolution of meaning from the "lower" to the "higher." It is rather, in a felicitous phrase I first heard from Prof. Michael Rosenak, an "unfolding agent;"[28] it "lays open" the pre-contained, what has "already been thought." Against this background, the arresting image that opens the fourth subsection of the *sugya* takes on meaning. The text's deepest insight, its lifeblood, courses in its veins, below the layers of its surface. The image of Raba rubbing the skin of his foot so hard that blood flows out becomes symbolic of the service performed by the interpreter for the text. The encrustations that have accumulated on the text's surface by centuries of dogmatic interpretation and philological presumption must be scraped away. The lifeblood of the text has been there all the time. It is not generated, even partially, by the interpreter. Although the interpreter is vigorously active, his activity only serves to release a pre-existing

---

26 See Gillis, "1998, p. 140. There he characterizes Levinas' orientation to the Talmudic text as taking its model from the Talmud's own approach to the Bible, an approach he terms a "dialogic process."

27 Aronowicz, 1990, pp. 46–48: "But here is the final section........crafty and industrious."

28   In conversation with the writer.

meaning. In dialogical interpretation, generation and appropriation of meaning are divided as equally as possible between text and interpreter. In philosophic midrash, on the other hand, the text is the sole repository of meaning, while the interpreter, though intensely active, is ultimately an enabler and not an originator. We cannot be sure if the structure of Levinas' discourse, and the forms of articulation he employed, did indeed lead his readers from suspicion to service. He seems, however, to have left little room for doubt that this is the hermeneutic reorientation he wished to bring about.

In concluding the commentative centerpiece of his discourse, Levinas remarks on the substance of the exchange between the Sadducee and Raba, who was "rubbing his foot until it spurt blood." The Sadducee accuses the Jewish people of being rash in consenting to obey a Law they had not yet scrutinized and understood. Raba counters by holding up the image of the Tamim, the upright person who allies himself with the good without calculation, as the human ideal. Prof. Harvey could be right in interpreting "Temimut" as "substitution" in light of parallels with Levinas' famous essay by that name. (See Levinas, 1989a). In the context of the structure of this particular discourse, however, Levinas would appear to be doing two things in concluding his Talmudic reading. Until now, Levinas seemed to be intent on legitimizing the possibility of a commitment that precedes and conditions free choice, yet is not childish naiveté. While intimating that such a possibility was to be found within the realm of the ethical relation, it remained largely a *formal* possibility. The primordiality of freedom is no longer to be regarded as self-understood. Now, finally, Levinas speaks *materially* of the structure of ethical experience, using terms that can be found throughout his philosophical works intermingled with terms drawn from the Jewish tradition: " ...the reception of Revelation — can only be the relation with a person, with another. The Torah is given in the Light of a face. The epiphany of the other person is *ipso facto* my responsibility toward him: seeing the other is already an obligation toward him. A direct optics — without the mediation of any idea — can be accomplished only as ethics. Integral knowledge or Revelation (the receiving of the Torah) is ethical behavior." The question gathering force in the listener — "How do we sense this compulsion-before-freedom you have spoken of?" — has finally been given satisfaction.

It is important for Levinas, however, that the human ideal of the Tamim, the upright person, should not be cast as an alternative to philosophical integrity. Levinas wishes to leave his hearers and readers with the claim that moral integrity is also logically and rationally superior to the subject-object perception. Exorcision of the primordial consciousness of the obligation to the other is tantamount to an epistemological lobotomy. "Excluding adherence" is arbitrary and therefore "*logically* tortuous." By the criterion of phenomenological primacy alone, the ethics of the Torah is a corrective to Western philosophy. Levinas leaves the commentative mode with an implicit, but immediately recognizable polemic against Descartes' *cogito*. Descartes saw the subject's perception of its own thinking as the "direct optics" forming the bedrock of philosophical certainty. Levinas, on the other hand, regards ethical perception as even more foundational and axiomatic for thinking conducted within the human horizon alone.

Just as Levinas began his Talmudic reading with a diagnosis of the European condition with virtually no reference to canonical texts, so he ends his address with "philosophical considerations" unattached to the Talmud or the Bible.[29] True, he does not determine whether these considerations have generated his interpretation, or whether they have *grown out* of his interpretation. In terms of literary form, however, Levinas leaves commentary behind and once again resorts to the kind of phenomenological discourse that characterizes so many of his other, non-commentative writings. This concluding section forms the mirror image of the opening section that preceded that commentary itself. While the opening section presented a phenomenology of neutral stimulation of the kind exhibited by the European sensibility, this concluding section consists in a digested phenomenological articulation of the consciousness that looks out upon the world through ethical lenses. It is here that we hear echoes of the images and metaphors that Levinas has deployed throughout his oeuvre in order to conjure up the lack of security and repose characteristic of primordial ethical experience: "substitution," "hostage," "uncondition,"" undone,"" lack of leisure," etc.[30]

In this rich final section, Levinas makes a multiplicity of moves within a very limited space, and we do not have the room to follow all his allusions here. I wish to call attention once more, however, to an additional instance of Levinas' particular, modern brand of "negative theology," indicative as it is of his overall inductive orientation. At one point, Levinas characterizes responsibility as a kind of acupressure on the self-subsistence of Being applied by individuals at discrete places and times. He then continues; "This weight is called responsibility. Responsibility for the creature — a

---

29 Aronowicz, 1990, pp. 48–50: "Allow me to add.......knowing how to sacrifice oneself."
30 For reference to such terms as "substitution," "hostage," "unconditon," "undone," "lack of leisure," see, for example, Levinas, 1989.

being of which the ego was not the author — which establishes the ego."
Again: who is the "author" of this being? Levinas does not speak
positively of God's thoughts or activity in this discourse. Once again, the
possibility of transcendence is intimated by moments in which human
sovereignty is perceived by all to be limited. Earlier, Levinas said that the
existential choice: to justify being by ethics or witness the undoing of the
world, is not one of our own making. Here, the fact that we are confronted
with the needs of vulnerable, dependent "creatures" is also imposed on us,
without our having exercised freedom in the matter.

In summarizing the integral connection between the philosophical-
educational structure of Levinas' discourse and some of the typical moves
he makes within it, we could say that he wishes to expose his hearers to the
imposed by way of a non-imposed medium. What Prof. Michael Rosenak
has called the "explicit" dimension of religious experience (Levinas would
not approve of the phrase "religious experience"), the dimension of the
imposed and received, is to "come to mind" by way of an "implicit," or
humanly generated milieu — phenomenological reflection (See Rosenak,
1987, Chap. 6). The "explicit" dimension will not be treated explicitly.
Even the so-called "explicitly" normative texts of the tradition, such as the
Talmud, will be read only within the horizon of "implicit," humanly
generated and accessible experience. This philosophical-educational
strategy is undertaken on the basis of the diagnosis that the audience to
be addressed, as well as the teacher himself, will accept nothing as given in
advance, unless the "givenness" of the given can be made manifest by way
of an independent discourse accessible to all.

This explains the basic tripartite structure of "Temptation of
Temptation." After his introductory remarks (what we called disclaimers
and rules of the game), Levinas begins the formal body of his discourse
with an independent phenomenological articulation of the condition of
Western consciousness, proceeding from more everyday usage to
formulations more typical of formal philosophy (performing what he calls
"the life of Western man becoming philosophy.") After a transitional
reflection on the possibility of understanding "revelation" as the discernment of the force or logic of things within a human horizon, he proceeds to
derive the possibility of a commitment that precedes choice from the close
reading of a canonical text. Levinas, then, first meets his audience in an
independent, human realm, devoid of imposed texts. He then leads them
on an excursion into the world of these texts, but only insofar as their
intimations of the imposed can be disclosed by way of a non-imposed
medium: universal human experience. At the end of his discourse, Levinas

leaves his audience where he found them — with an independent, humanly accessible, phenomenological analysis of the ethical bond, again without a running commentary, although isolated Hebrew "memories" from the excursion persist even at this stage ('*Temimut*," "*Bogdim*," "*Yesharim*," etc.).

The educational message underlying the literary structure of the discourse would seem, then, to be the following: Although speaker and audience meet on the common ground of the European sensibility-become-philosophy, this common ground can be problematized without being delegitimized. The ethical problematic inherent in the subject-object orientation propels both speaker and hearers to search for an alternative sensibility within the milieu of philosophically interpreted Jewish texts. The alternative sensibility mined out of the traditional texts, however, does not effect a transfiguration or conversion. The hearers are left on the same ground on which the engagement began. The same human perspective is taken and the same philosophical language is spoken. Yet, the excursion into the substance of the Jewish tradition has reconstituted the Western world of Reason and Justice on a new basis and illustrated the possibility of a reorientation of philosophical consciousness that does not, for that, cease to be philosophy. On the contrary, philosophy is deepened according to the very criteria of philosophy: lucidity and radicality. The insight gleaned from the Talmud has established philosophy, qua philosophy, on even firmer ground than before.

The audience, then, has been led through a process of re-orientation within philosophical parameters. Having been engaged within the human horizon of philosophy, the audience then receives an epistemological infusion from the Hebrew tradition by way of philosophic-midrashic commentary. This infusion is meant to change their philosophical perspective, but not to induct them into a new order of extra-philosophical knowledge.

Specific educational "moves" made by Levinas in the course of his presentation corroborate the educational project of reorientation within the human horizon reflected in the tripartite structure we have just analyzed. Levinas' particular brand of "negative theology," pointing as it does to the possibility of a sovereignty other than the human from within the human experience of limitation and situation, is one of the means he uses to make the experience of subordination to an Absolute vivid. His recourse to "signals of transcendence" from within everyday human experience — education, inspired action — also help his listeners to visualize situations of compulsion conditioning reason and freedom without invoking some extra-experiential authority. In leading his listeners from their (and his own) inherited hermeneutic of suspicion to a hermeneutic of trust and service, Levinas points to a continuity of experience between the way moderns and traditional texts make meaning. Finally, Levinas insists that he is not advocating a retreat to a childlike faith. Uprightness, Temimut is a mature ideal. The "angels' secret" of succor before calculation and perspective is neither cherubic nor ethereally inaccessible. It is an ideal accessible to fully developed human beings who do not abdicate reason.

In order to further emphasize the uniqueness of Levinas' philosophical-educational strategy, we feel it might be useful to compare the structure and typical forms of articulation in his Temptation lecture with certain aspects of the structure and some of the characteristic "moves" of another master of philosophical midrash, Rabbi Joseph B. Soloveitchik. The framework of this essay does not permit us to report the results of a close reading of "The Lonely Man of Faith" at length. Nonetheless, a few brief remarks will serve to highlight some significant differences between the educational approach of the two thinkers. First of all, it is important to note that Soloveitchik spoke, and then wrote, to a very different kind of addressee. Rather than confronting a colloquium of Europeanized French intellectuals, he tells us in his opening footnote that "the basic ideas of this paper were formulated in my lectures to the students of the program 'Marriage and Family — National Institute of Mental Health Project — Yeshiva University, New York.'" (Soloveitchik, 1965, p. 5). Though Soloveitchik makes ample reference to general disciplines, particularly philosophy and psychology (as befits a program directed to students with a more-than-adequate secular education, and in keeping with his own predilections), the lectures in question took place within a confessional institution, identified with so-called "modern orthodoxy," and were first published in the organ of that movement — *Tradition*. These socio-educational circumstances, as well as Soloveitchik's standing as a rabbinical authority, have much to do with the composition and tone of the essay.

Soloveitchik also opens on a personal note with a section which could be similarly titled "opening remarks, disclaimers and rules of the game." (pp. 5–10). His point of departure is a confession of personal loneliness (immediately engaging the reader, who wonders why such a personage should experience such an oppressive feeling), and an attempt to place this loneliness in a larger perspective (the paradigmatic and perennial loneliness of the man of faith in the face of the secular-minded majority, and the unique loneliness of the contemporary man of faith in the light of modern secularity). He disclaims any presumption to a new theoretical account of the human condition, or to an authoritative philosophy of Halahah. Most interestingly, however, for a comparison with Levinas, are those lines in which he lays out what, for him, will be the constraining framework of his discourse: "Before beginning the analysis, we must determine within which frame of reference, psychologico-empirical or theologico-Biblical, should our dilemma be described. I believe you will agree with me that we do not have much choice in the matter; for, to the man of faith self-knowledge has one connotation only — to understand one's place and role within the scheme of events and things willed and approved by God, when He ordered finitude to emerge out of infinity and the Universe, including man, to unfold itself." (p. 9). As distinguished from Levinas, who wishes to avoid God-talk and theology, and confine his discourse to the philosophical realm that does not presume an a priori faith commitment, Soloveitchik presents himself immediately as a "man of faith," who, as such, must have recourse to discrete theological insight derived from the sacred text of the Bible. True, Soloveitchik also gives an account of such categories as Creation, Revelation and Redemption in terms of a phenomenology of religious experience as perceived by human beings. Yet, he has no qualms, as does Levinas, about attributing will and action to God throughout the essay. Such talk would most certainly have the effect of alienating Levinas' Europeanized audience, including Levinas himself, who was wary of discourse on "religious experience" as such.[31] For Soloveitchik's modern orthodox audience, on the other hand, such rhetoric might actually have a galvanizing effect. Solovetchik is not intensely hortatory or sanctimonious in this text, yet he is heard to be speaking in a recognizable religious "home-language."

Another telling point of comparison has to do with the "envelope" that encases the structure of the two discourses. As will be remembered, Levinas begins the formal part of his talk with an independent phenomenological analysis of the condition of contemporary Western consciousness. Only afterwards he begins his commentary on the Talmud, a commentary that is devoted to mining an alternative mode of consciousness out of the text. Finally, he returns to independent philosophical discourse, giving material substance to the largely formal possibility he has derived from the Talmudic *sugya*. Soloveitchik, while

---

31 For Levinas' wariness of talk of the "sacred," see his essays "The Diary of Leon Brunschwig" and "Place and Utopia." Both appear in his collection *Difficult Freedom* (1990), pp. 43–45, 102.

briefly inveighing against the utilitarian character of contemporary Western society in his opening, personal remarks, nonetheless immediately begins the formal part of his essay with his famous analysis of the contradictions that can be found in the early chapters of Genesis. (pp. 10–11) He opens with a close reading of those chapters, and expands on themes he derives from Biblical plot-elements and metaphors throughout the essay. As the essay proceeds, there is much phenomenological "space" between direct references to Biblical phrases, like "the image of God," "dust of the earth" "breath" "deep sleep," etc. However, the net of the text is spread over the whole essay. His major analysis of the aesthetic-utilitarian character of Western civilization and culture is not presented as an independent phenomenological insight, but emerges out of his interpretation of the Bible. The Bible actually approves and sanctions the utilitarianism and aestheticism of "Adam the First," as long as they do not get out of hand. (pp. 11–16). In true midrashic form, Solovetchik displays *all* phenomena through the lenses of the canonical text, and the essay is never really cut loose from its Biblical moorings.[32]

In the closing section of his long essay, Soloveitchik once again undertakes a close interpretation of a Biblical text quoted in full, the story of the transformation of Elisha from successful farmer to a "lonely man of faith." (pp. 65–67) While Levinas has met his audience as a philosopher who has entered the commentative world of the Hebraic tradition and thereby enhanced philosophy, Soloveitchik meets his audience as a man of commentary who has accessed philosophy for a deeper understanding of the Biblical charge, never really departing from what Levinas called the "square letters," and always returning to them. While Levinas remains within what Rosenak has called the "implicit" dimension, allowing his hearers a glimpse of the "explicit" dimension only from within its parameters, Soloveitchik's excursion into implicit religious consciousness is undertaken altogether within the framework of the constraints of an explicitly binding text. His modern orthodox hearers can rest assured that although they have been led deep into the forest of phenomenology, as well as other Western philosophical modes of discourse, their path has been consistently marked by Biblical signposts erected in advance by their guide. While the reorientation hopefully undergone by Levinas' listeners involves a deepening of philosophy through access to insight derived from Hebrew sources, the reorientation Soloveitchik hopes will affect his

---

32 For an understanding of the way the rabbinic consciousness views the world through Biblical "lenses," see Fraenkel, 1971, pp. 80–99

audience consists in the illumination that insights derived from the philosophical tradition can deepen their understanding of the canonical texts; texts that carry a charge they have already accepted, though they may chafe under its yoke.

Once again, space does not permit a more elaborate analysis of other elements in Soloveitchik's presentation. Neither do we make the claim that the way Levinas and Soloveitchik transmit their insights in these particular essays exhausts their ultimate philosophic positions. Still, we believe, and hope to have shown, that the structural-literary analysis of discursive texts can shed much light on the philosophical-educational strategy of their writers.

References

Aronowicz, Annette. (1990). Trans. with Introduction. Emmanuel Levinas. *Nine Talmudic Readings*. Bloomington and Indianapolis: Indiana University Press.

Berger, Peter. (1979). *The heretical imperative*. Garden City, NJ: Anchor Press.

Berger, Peter. (1969). *A rumor of angels*. Garden City, NJ: Doubleday.

Bouganim, Ami. (1990). L'autre dans la pensée d'Emmanuel Levinas. [The Other in the thought of Emmanuel Levinas]. Unpublished PhD thesis. The Hebrew University, Jerusalem.

Cohen, Jonathan. (forthcoming). Carrying the Past into the Future: Texts and Teaching in Contemporary Jewish Education. New York: Memorial Foundation for Jewish Culture.

Cohen, Jonathan. (2002). Postponing spiritual gratification: Levinas' conception of religious maturity as an orienting notion for Jewish education. In B. Cohen and A. Ofek. (Eds.) *Essays in education and Judaism in honor of Joseph S. Lukinsky*. New York: Jewish Theological Seminary Press, pp. 345–365.

Dewey, John. (1956). *The child and the curriculum*. Chicago and London: The University of Chicago Press.

Fackenheim, Emil. (1968). An outline of a modern Jewish theology. In Emil Fackenheim. *Quest for past and future*. Blomington and London: Indiana University Press.

Fackenheim, Emil. (1961). *Metaphysics and historicity*. Milwaukee: Marquette University Press.

Fraenkel, Jonah. (1971). Bible verses quoted in the tales of the Sages. In Joseph Heinemann and Dov Noy. (Eds.). *Studies in Aggadah and folk-literature* (*Scripta Hierosolymitana, XXII*, Jerusalem: Magnes Press.

Gillis, Michael. (1998). Hermeneutics and Jewish Education: The Case of Rabbinic Literature. Unpublished PhD dissertation, Melbourne, Australia, Monash University.

Harvey, Zev. (1993). Levinas al temimut, naiviyut ve'AmAratzut. [Levinas on innocence, naiveté and ignorance]. *Da'at 30.* (Winter), pp. 13–20.

Heinemann, Joseph. (1970) *D'rashot Be'Tzibbur Be'Tekufat Ha'Talmud* [Public Sermons in the Talmudic Period]. Jerusalem: Mossad Bialik.

Kaplan, Lawrence. (1998). Israel under the mountain; Emmanuel Levinas on freedom and constraint in the Revelation of the Torah. *Modern Judaism 18 (1)*, pp. 35–46.

Levinas, Emmanuel. (1990). *Difficult freedom.* London: Althone Press.

Levinas, Emmanuel. (1989). The ego and the totality. In Emmanuel Levinas. *Collected philosophical papers.* Dordrecht: Martinus Nijhoff, pp. 25–40.

Levinas, Emmanuel. (1989a). Substitution. In S. Hand. (Ed.). *The Levinas Reader.* Oxford: Blackwell Publishers, pp. 88–125.

Levinas, Emmanuel. (1982). *De Dieu qui vient a l'idee.* Paris: Vrin.

Levinas, Emmanuel. (1968). *Quatre Lectures Talmudiques* [Four Talmudic Readings]. Paris, Editions de Minuit.

Peperzak, Adriaan. (1995). *Ethics as first philosophy: The significance of Emmanuel Levinas for Philosophy, Literature and Religion.* New York and London: Routledge.

Peters, R. S. (1966). Reason and habit: The paradox of moral education. In Israel Scheffler. (Ed.). *Philosophy and education.* Boston: Allyn and Bacon, pp. 245–262.

Ricoeur, Paul. (1982). *Hermeneutics and the Human Sciences.* Cambridge, Cambridge University Press.

Ricoeur, Paul. (1970). *Freud and Philosophy.* New Haven and London: Yale University Press.

Rosenak, Michael. (1987). *Commandments and concerns.* Philadelphia: Jewish Publication Society.

Scholem, Gershom. (1970). Revelation and tradition as religious categories in Judaism. In Gershom Scholem. *The messianic idea in Judaism.* New York, Schocken Press, pp. 289–290.

Schwab, Joseph. (1978). Enquiry and the Reading Process. In Joseph Schwab. *Science, curriculum and liberal education.* Chicago and London, Chicago University Press, pp. 149–183.

Schweid, Eliezer, (1998). *Mi'Talmid Le'Rav: Darko HaChinuchit Shel HaRambam Be'Shlav Ha'K'dam-Philosophi — Nituach Mashma'ut HaMivneh HaSifruti Shel Hakdamat Perek 'Chelek,'* [From student to master: Maimonides' educational approach to the pre-philosophical stage — An analysis of the literary structure of the Introduction to 'Perek Chelek']. In Aviezer Ravitsky. (Ed.). *Me'Romi Le'Yerush-alayim: Sefer Zikaron LeYosef-Baruch Sermonetta.* [From Rome to Jerusalem: Anthology in memory of Joseph Baruch Sermonetta]. Jerusalem, The Hebrew University.

Schweid, Eliezer. (1997). *Ha'Mivneh Ha'Philosophi-Chinuchi Shel Machshevet A. D. Gordon.* [The philosophical-educational structure of the thought of A. D. Gordon]. *Iyyun 46.* (October), pp. 293–414.

Schweid, Eliezer. (1970). *Omanut ha'dialog be'Sefer 'ha'Kuzari u'Mashmautah ha'Iyyunit* [The art of dialogue in the Kuzari: Philosophical implications]. In Eliezer Schweid. *Ta'am Ve'Hakashah* [Feeling and speculation]. Ramat Gan, Massada Press.

Shulman, Lee. (1986). Those who understand: Knowledge growth in teaching. *Educational Researcher 15 (1)* (Jan.).

Soloveitchik, Joseph. (1965). Lonely Man of Faith. *Tradition 7 (2)*. (Summer), pp. 5–67.

Strauss, Leo. (1983). Jerusalem and Athens: Some preliminary reflections. In Leo Strauss. *Studies in Platonic Political Philosophy*. Chicago and London, The University of Chicago Press.

Strauss, Leo. (1979). The mutual influence of Theology and Philosophy. *The Independent Journal of Philosophy 3*.

Strauss, Leo. (1952). The Law of Reason in the Kuzari. In Leo Strauss. *Persecution and the Art of Writing*. Glencoe, Il., The Free Press, pp. 95–141.

Wachstock, Shaul. (1999). *Na'aseh Ve'Nishmah — Iyyun BeShiur Talmudi Shel Emmanuel Levinas* [We shall do and we shall hear — A study in a Talmudic reading by Emmanuel Levinas]. Unpublished Master's thesis, Jerusalem, The Hebrew University.

Dewey's Groundwork*

Daniel Pekarsky

Imagine that an educator (or anyone with an interest in deliberating more thoughtfully about education) asks you to recommend a single chapter of a single book that will offer the guidance needed to think intelligently about educational practices and proposals. What would you do? If you were of the School of Shammai, you might very well send this person away with a whack from your walking stick and a comment about the frivolity of the request. But, if you were of the School of Hillel, you might place in his or her hands a copy of "Criteria of Experience," the third chapter of John Dewey's *Experience and Education*, (1963, pp. 33–50) with the instruction to examine it patiently and in depth.[1] True, there is much educational wisdom that is not embodied in this chapter, and it would therefore be a misleading exaggeration to add, as Hillel does in response to the heathen, that all the rest is just commentary. But it is certainly true that some of the best writing on education since Dewey's day is actually implicit in, or a

* I wish to express my thanks to my colleague Professor Herbert Kliebard for his helpful comments on an earlier draft of this paper, as well as to Lisa Gann-Perkal for her editorial suggestions.
1 The reference here is to a famous episode in ancient times. When a heathen approaches the forbidding Rabbi Shammai with the request that he explain to him the whole of the Torah while he, the heathen, is standing on one foot, Rabbi Shammai unceremoniously shoos him away. But when the heathen approaches Rabbi Hillel with the same request, Hillel responds: "What is hateful to you, do not do to your neighbor. That is the entire Torah. The rest is commentary. Go and learn it."

corollary of, Dewey's discussion in chapter 3 of that book, even if some of those whose work falls into this category are unaware of this connection to his ideas. Put differently, the perspectives, distinctions and guiding principles embodied in chapter three of *Experience and Education* represent many of the basics that a thoughtful person requires to analyze educational practices, transactions and proposals fruitfully.

Over and above its power as a tool in educational deliberation, I would like to draw attention to the analytic framework suggested in "Criteria of Experience" for three reasons. First, some of its core ideas are frequently misunderstood not just by students and lay people but also by notable educational theorists.[2] Second, Dewey in effect camouflages this framework by intertwining its core-ideas with other ideas, without explaining that these other ideas arise *within* the framework rather than being part of it. It may therefore be useful to throw this framework into high relief by separating its core elements from the ideas Dewey presents alongside them.

My third reason for undertaking an examination of this Deweyan framework of analysis is intimately connected with the fact that this paper has been developed and offered in honor of Professor Seymour Fox. My explanation of this point begins with a portrait of Seymour Fox as teacher.

Seymour Fox at Work: What's Going on Here?

In the powerful mental image I have of Seymour Fox as a teacher, he is not standing at a podium, but sitting around a table with a group of from three to 20 people. One member of the group has put forward an idea — perhaps a thesis concerning an educational issue, or a curricular or policy proposal. As the idea is presented, Seymour listens quietly, periodically writing down a note or two, now and then looking up toward the speaker. When the presentation is concluded, he continues to sit quietly as a number of people offer their reactions. Finally, Seymour enters the discussion, and everyone present immediately senses that the conversation has moved to a new, more serious stage. A dialogue follows — a dialogue very much in the Socratic sense — between Seymour and this individual, with Seymour playing the role of questioner.

In these dialogues, Seymour's questions are not all of a kind; nor do they

---

2   For example, both E. Callan and R. F. Dearden have misconstrued key elements in Dewey's guiding framework in at least one of their respective writings. For specifics, see Pekarsky, 1990, pp. 283–294.

succeed each other in any obviously predictable order. While some questions appear to be designed simply to clarify his conversation-partner's position or proposal so that the discussion can proceed intelligently, others seem designed to elicit the thinking behind, or the evidence for, what has been asserted or proposed. While some questions draw attention to the unarticulated or unexamined assumptions about human nature that are implicit in a practical proposal, others invite reflection on the conception of success that it embodies — what it is, whether and why it is worthy, whether it is achievable via the proposed practice, how we would judge whether it has been achieved, and so forth. Some questions take the form of extremely simple probes, for example, "Why do you think this?" or "How is this idea consistent with that one?" Others help Seymour's interlocutor realize that his/her remarks could be interpreted in three different ways, each with radically different implications, and invite this person to explain which of these interpretations he/she has in mind. These questions may also introduce powerful counter-arguments to the idea that has been advanced and invite an effort to salvage it in the face of these challenges. And while some questions focus on the internal logic of the presenter's position, other questions draw attention to important considerations that have not yet been taken into account.

As these transactions move along, one has the sense that Seymour, like a great chess player, is a few steps ahead of the conversation — that when he asks a question, he has already anticipated three possible responses, for each of which he has prepared an additional question of his own. One also senses that Seymour's questions vary not just in their intellectual direction, but also in their motivation. While, for example, some seem designed to help him and/or his conversation-partner better understand the latter's ideas, others seem designed to highlight problems with these ideas or holes in this person's thinking, with an eye toward guiding the person into new inquiries and/or deflating pretensions to adequate knowledge.

For the person being questioned by Seymour, the experience can prove an uncommonly challenging intellectual adventure. Not infrequently, Seymour's interlocutor discovers along the way that his/her beliefs are not as well developed or grounded as he/she may have believed. One is reminded of Meno's comment describing the result of his conversation with Socrates on the subject of virtue, about which Meno had previously thought himself very knowledgeable:

"Socrates, even before I met you they told me that…you reduce others to perplexity. At this moment I feel that you are exercising magic and witchcraft upon me and positively laying me under your spell until I am just a mass of helplessness…[You] are exactly like the sting-ray that one meets in the sea. Whenever anyone comes into contact with it, it numbs him, and that is the sort of thing that you seem to be doing to me now. My mind and my lips are literally numb, and I have nothing to reply to you. Yet I have spoken about virtue hundreds of times, held forth often on the subject in front of large audiences, and very well too, or so I thought. Now I can't even say what it is." (Plato, 1956, pp. 127–28).

Meno's comments would undoubtedly be echoed by many who have undergone questioning by Seymour Fox. But many of them would also agree that the experience proved extraordinarily illuminating for themselves, as well as for everyone present. For as it unfolded, deeply held assumptions, insights that are intriguing but perhaps not yet articulated, careless steps, and missing links were brought to the surface; critical questions were raised; and new inquiries and possibilities emerged.

An additional feature of the kinds of dialogue just described is, for our purposes, especially worthy of notice. The room in which they transpire is typically pervaded by a sense of awe at Seymour Fox's capacity to grasp so quickly the intellectual infrastructure of a text or a presentation and to guide its creator to a clearer recognition of its implications, strengths and limitations. And when the dialogue is over, those who have witnessed it find themselves nodding in disbelief and asking one another, "How does he do it?"

Responses are likely to include references to Seymour's extraordinary mind, to his intuition and to his capacity to size up people and situations; and such explanations are surely an important part of the story. But there is also something else at work in these educational transactions. Seymour brings to them an array of highly illuminating mental maps. By a 'mental map' I am referring to a web of integrated concepts, principles and theories that give structure and meaning to the field to which they are applied. Just as a landscape artist, a botanist, an ecologist and an evolutionary biologist bring different mental maps to bear on my garden — each capturing a different dimension of this sliver of reality — so, too, in the intellectual realm, the maps we bring with us structure what we see, suggesting meanings, connections and questions that would otherwise remain beyond our purview.

This idea of a mental map is at work in Dewey's *The Child and the Curriculum*. Here he suggests that a large part of the educator's wisdom consists of the capacity to apply such maps — each representing a mature but different perspective on the world — to the understandings, impulses and activities of the child. Writes Dewey:

> "What we need is something that will enable us to interpret and to appraise the elements of the child's present puttings forth and fallings away, his exhibitions of power and weakness in the light of some larger growth-process in which they have their place… [The] subject-matter of science and history and art serves to reveal the real child to us. We do not know the meaning either of his tendencies or of his performances excepting as we take them as germinating seed, or opening bud, of some fruit to be borne. The whole world of visual nature is all too small an answer to the problem of the meaning of the child's instinct for light and form. The entire science of physics is none too much to interpret adequately to us what is involved in some simple demand of the child for explanation of some casual change that has attracted his attention…So much for the use of the subject matter in interpretation." (Dewey, 1902, pp. 14–16).

No one who has watched Seymour Fox in action would suggest that his brilliance in the kinds of conversations I have described can be reduced to the mental maps that inform what he sees and hears. Yet the fact that he possesses them must be recognized in an attempt to explain his extraordinary ability to interpret and question the ideas and arguments of those with whom he enters into dialogue.

And this brings me to my last reason for undertaking an examination of chapter three of *Experience and Education* on this occasion. For this chapter embodies one of the mental maps that Seymour Fox brings to his analyses of educational transactions. Indeed, Seymour Fox at work in dialogue beautifully exemplifies the power of the infrastructure of ideas contained in this chapter to illuminate the actual and proposed work of educators. Given that there are also, as suggested earlier, other important reasons for revisiting the ideas Dewey develops in this chapter, the fact that they figure significantly in Seymour Fox's thinking makes such a discussion especially appropriate for a volume in his honor.

Two Levels of Discourse in Dewey's Writings

It will be useful to begin by elaborating on my earlier suggestion that in Dewey's writings — including chapter three of *Experience and Education* —

ideas at basic and less basic levels are typically presented as an undifferentiated whole. To draw the distinction crudely, Dewey's "basic ideas" (what I am calling Level 1 ideas) define the guiding framework within which Level 2 ideas — specific theories, hypotheses and insights — arise and are tested. I would characterize these theories, hypotheses and insights, both empirical and moral, as 'less basic' relative to the first cluster of ideas.[3]

Let me illustrate this point by examining a passage from Dewey's *Democracy and Education* that exhibits the two levels of inquiry and the way in which they are unselfconsciously intertwined in Dewey's writing. The passage is drawn from the chapter entitled "Vocational Aspects of Education," which is informed by Dewey's critical perspective on the U.S. workplace. According to Dewey, work should be an arena in which human beings are challenged to grow and to become aware of themselves and others as making meaningful contributions to the well-being of one another and to the community at large. In actual fact, however, work is pure drudgery for most people, wounding rather than nourishing the human spirit. As Studs Turkel expresses this point in the opening lines of the introduction to his book *Working*:

> "This book, being about work, is, by its very nature, about violence — to the spirit as well as to the body. It is about ulcers as well as accidents, about shouting matches as well as fistfights, about nervous breakdowns as well as kicking the dog around. It is, above all (or beneath all), about daily humiliations. To survive the day is triumph enough for the walking wounded among the great many of us." (Turkel, 1974, p. xiii).

But whereas this passage seems to imply that it is in the very nature of work to do violence to those who carry it out, Dewey, as noted above, believes that work has the potential to become an intrinsically rewarding activity that is a source of growth and a contribution to humankind. The key to achieving this potential is education! The view as a whole is expressed in the following passage, which begins with Dewey's sketch of an as yet unachieved community in which work is more meaningful than it now is:

---

3   It is, however, worth noting that there is nothing inherently more basic about one of these sets of ideas relative to the other. It is entirely conceivable that, in the context of a different discussion, beliefs which appear "less basic" in the present discussion would prove "more basic," or that none would stand out as more basic than others.

"The desired transformation is not difficult to define in a formal way. It signifies a society in which every person shall be occupied in something which makes the lives of others better worth living, and which accordingly makes the ties which bind persons together more perceptible — which breaks down the barriers of distance between them. It denotes a state of affairs in which the interest of each in his work is uncoerced and intelligent: based upon its congeniality to his own aptitudes. It goes without saying that we are far from such a social state... But...there are more ample resources for its achievement now than ever there have been before. No insuperable obstacles, given the intelligent will for its realization, stand in the way.

Success or failure in its realization depends more upon the adoption of educational methods calculated to effect the change than upon anything else...[We] may produce in schools a projection in type of the society we should like to realize, and by forming minds in accord with it gradually modify the larger and more recalcitrant features of adult society." (Dewey, 1916, pp. 369–370).

It is not my purpose to evaluate Dewey's proposed vision of a better society. What I do want to highlight is that this vision is not sharply distinguished in this passage from a different, and more basic, idea that is expressed alongside it. The idea is this: instead of continuing to fashion our schools in the image of the society that in fact exists, it is possible to build schools in the image of the society we would like to exist, and in so doing advance toward this kind of society. Put differently, this passage contains what I am calling a very basic idea (that schools can and should be organized around our vision of a better society), and a less basic idea (namely, Dewey's particular vision of what this better society will look like). The very basic idea does not entail the less basic idea, and it is entirely possible to accept Dewey's understanding of the role that schools can play in society without accepting his particular idea of what a better society would look like.[4]

Dewey's educational writings thus operate on two distinct levels: Level 1 offers a framework for capturing and highlighting significant dimensions of an educational theory (in this case, a conception of the role of education in society); Level 2 advances specific empirical and moral claims that, in

4   Though not immediately relevant to our discussion, it is also noteworthy that Dewey's vision of a better society can be accepted without endorsing his conception of the role of education in society.

conjunction with this framework, give the educational process concrete content and direction. As I have already suggested, both levels of discourse are at work in chapter three of *Experience and Education,* and therefore my effort to identify the Level 1 ideas that make up the guiding framework will require separating these ideas from the accompanying Level 2 ideas. My guiding assumption in undertaking this effort is that whether or not one accepts the Level 2 empirical hypotheses and moral convictions represented by a quintessential liberal like Dewey — and there are certainly students of education (including many educational and social conservatives) who will *not* accept them — this framework will serve educators of many ideological stripes very well in their efforts to analyze educational ideas, practices and policies.

Core Elements of Dewey's Guiding Framework

My attempt to clarify and distinguish between the key elements in this guiding framework will be organized around the following themes: principles of experience, educative and miseducative experiences and, finally, corollaries of the foregoing ideas.

Principles of experience. At the heart of *Experience and Education* is Dewey's suggestion that educational theories and inquiries often go awry because they are grounded in inadequate understandings of experience. Careful reflection on the nature of experience (the kind of reflection which most people ordinarily regard as irrelevant philosophical reveries) will, Dewey believes, yield extraordinarily useful practical results, laying the foundation on which any adequate educational theory must be built.

Dewey's own account of experience is organized around two core ideas that he regards as universal principles of experience: interaction and continuity. Let us begin with interaction. The principle of interaction advances the proposition that experience — any and every experience — is an interaction between the individual and that individual's environment, an interaction whose character depends on both parties to the transaction.

Three points may help clarify the nature of this principle. First, the principle of interaction is not an evaluative claim. As far as Dewey is concerned, good and bad, desirable and undesirable experiences are all interactions. That is, the principle applies to all experiences. Second, the principle of interaction is not an empirical generalization, based on scrutinizing numerous instances of experience. Rather, experience as an interaction is to be understood as a guiding principle, the justification of which is pragmatic. "By their fruits ye shall know them" is, according to Dewey's teacher C.S. Peirce, the key pragmatic idea. The justification for interpreting a concept this way rather than that is that — ultimately, overall and in the long run — this interpretation will yield better results. Understanding experience as an interaction, rather than as something that goes on in an individual, is ultimately justified on the grounds that this way of thinking about experience will illuminate enormously our understanding of encountered situations and will enhance our capacity to influence their unfolding and resolution. In this sense, understanding experience in this way will yield more satisfactory results.[5]

Third, if one is to understand Dewey's principle of interaction, one must guard against interpreting it in the narrow sense in which it is already embraced by many educators who view themselves as facilitating an interaction between the minds of their students and the subject-matter. Dewey would have no reason to deny that such interactions regularly take place or that they are important. But he insists that the interaction identified by the principle of interaction is much broader and more complex, encompassing a transaction between a total self and a total environment. In the situation just described, the mind may very well be interacting with a body of ideas as proposed by the educator, but the interaction is, inevitably, much richer than this suggests. Because we are incapable of leaving everything but our minds out of the classroom, the self that participates in the experience is necessarily more than just a mind. It is a being with a history of experiences, with feelings, beliefs, attitudes, an attention span of a certain kind and so forth. Similarly, while the environment with which this self comes into contact will include the body of ideas presented, it will also incorporate many other features. It will be cold or warm, both physically and interpersonally; it will be defined by norms of a certain kind; it will be fast-paced or slow; cooperative or competitive; inviting and friendly or threatening; tightly or loosely organized and so forth. Though the educator may have a special interest in a particular facet of this interaction (say, that between subject-matter and mind), it is a serious, sometimes educationally fatal, mistake to believe that this is the sum total of the interaction. On the contrary, the complex, multidimensional

---

5 For a very illuminating discussion of controversies surrounding the concept of "satisfactory results" in relation to pragmatism, see Scheffler, 1974, pp. 100–116.

interaction between the learner's attitudes, tastes and sensibilities, on the one hand, and the social environment of the classroom, on the other, often proves to be — as we will soon see more concretely — at least as important as the more narrow spectrum of the interaction on which a teacher may be focusing.

The nature of the principle of interaction can be further clarified by identifying two very different understandings of experience that Dewey rejects when he asserts experience to be interactive. One of them, which is very close to what some have described as the environmentalist hypothesis, resembles Locke's idea of the individual as a *tabula rasa* on which the environment inscribes itself. This approach views the self as relatively passive in the determination of its experience. The objective conditions surrounding the self are decisive: what we see, hear, smell, feel and believe — and, more generally, who and what we become — is, as it were, thrust on us by these objective conditions.

Dewey believes this understanding of experience to be misguided. In his view, even in what seem to be paradigm cases supporting the environ-mentalist hypothesis, the experience is in fact an interaction to which the self makes an essential contribution. Consider, for example, the experience of an ill-clad person standing outdoors in minus 30 degree weather. On the surface, the experience of feeling cold would seem to be thrust on us by the environment. But when we think about the ways in which hypnosis might relieve the person of the experience of coldness, we quickly realize that the experience of coldness depends as much on the self as it does on the environment. To take another example, although most of us would likely feel sheer terror were a lion to pounce into our living room one quiet evening, the belief that our terror is a natural response thrust on us by the environment is quickly dispelled when we consider that people who, by virtue of their cultural assumptions, regard the appearance of the lion as a sign from heaven, or an incarnation of an ancestor, or an opportunity to exhibit their courage, are likely to respond very differently. In sum, on inspection it becomes clear that experiences seemingly thrust upon us by circumstances are what they are not just because of these circumstances, but also because of the self's active contributions.

Analogous considerations apply to the polar opposite view, which Dewey also rejects. This view suggests that the character of our experience is principally a function of the self, depending little on environmental circumstances. One can distinguish at least two variants of this view. One of them — what might be described as the 'rugged individualist' variant — is discernible in the judgments of the person who, having triumphed over adverse circumstances, points disapprovingly at others for allegedly failing to take similar control of their destiny. "I am the author of, and am responsible for the character of my experience" are the watchwords of this perspective. The other variant of this view ascribes a certain biological nature to individuals, a nature so powerful that it dictates the course of their experience. Although these variants differ sharply in their understanding of why we must principally look to the individual to understand his or her experience, they are, as noted above, alike in viewing the power of the environment as relatively negligible by comparison.

There may be cases that lend a measure of credibility to one or both variants of this general view yet Dewey believes that closer inspection of instances allegedly supporting this general outlook will actually support an interactionist perspective. Consider, for example, the kinds of character-istics we often take to be attached to selves and to view as environment-independent — characteristics like shyness, hyperactivity or even capacity to learn. If we look carefully, Dewey believes, we discover that such characteristics are not tied to selves in any hard and fast way but are properties of the interaction between the self and its environment. Thus, the person who seems 'to own' the attribute of shyness (as though it were a possession carried into one and all situations) turns out to be warm, outgoing and perhaps even boisterous under certain social conditions, and the person who appears incapable of learning is found to be exceptionally quick when placed in certain unfamiliar conditions. In other words, characteristics that we take to be properties of the self, and sufficient to explain its experience and performance, are revealed actually to be properties of the relationship between the self and its environment.

Paralleling Dewey's conviction that we will deepen our understanding of experience by rejecting the either/or perspectives that dominate everyday thinking and adopting an interactionist outlook is his belief that our capacity to understand — and influence — the course of experience will be enhanced if we take his second principle, that of continuity, into account. This principle asserts that every experience — every individual/ environment interaction — affects the course of future experience by transforming the self that enters into future experiences, as well as the environment. Like Dewey's principle of interaction, his principle of continuity is not an evaluative principle. It does not, as some people believe, assert that experiences *ought* to be continuous. Rather, it asserts that — for better and/or for worse — experiences are inevitably and universally continuous with one another, in the sense that each experience affects the future course of experience.[6] In addition, just like Dewey's principle of interaction, his principle of continuity should be understood as a pragmatically justified guiding idea, and not as an empirical generalization based on observation. Though we might well be able to come up with what seem like strong counter-examples, Dewey suggests that our inquiries and our practice will be stronger overall if we accept the principle of continuity as a guiding assumption.

The principle of continuity represents a challenge to those who believe that the meaning or significance of an experience is discernible at the moment of its occurrence. Says Dewey: since every experience affects the course of future experience, the meaning of the present experience must, at least in part, be identified with its future consequences. Therefore, it does not make sense to assess the value of an experience only by observing it unfold in the present. An experience that seems very positive at the moment of its occurrence may be evaluated very differently once we understand how it shapes the future outlook or dispositions of the person who undergoes it. Dewey exemplifies this point with the case of the spoiled child:

> "The effect of over-indulging a child is a continuing one. It sets up an attitude which operates as an automatic demand that persons and objects cater to his desires and caprices in the future. It makes him seek the kind of situation that will enable him to do what he feels like doing at the time. It renders him averse to and comparatively incompetent in situations which require effort and perseverance in overcoming obstacles." (Dewey, 1963, p. 37).

Though each instance of getting what he/she wants may leave the child feeling very satisfied, if we examine the impact of such experiences on the way the child approaches future experiences, Dewey believes that we will discover that such experiences are actually destructive. And, once we become aware of the destructive future impact of such experiences, this awareness enters into our characterization of them at the time they occur. Thus, the over-indulgent parent is not just "catering to the child's desires" but is "nurturing dispositions that will prove injurious to the child."

---

6   This is not to deny that, in daily conversation, we often use the term 'continuous' in an evaluative sense to describe experiences that build on one another in a desirable way. Dewey himself encourages educators to foster these kinds of experiences for the learner. But continuity in this narrower and evaluative sense is to be distinguished from the kind of continuity that is identified by the principle of continuity.

The case of the spoiled child thus effectively exemplifies Dewey's point that an assessment of the meaning or value of an experience must take its future consequences into account. It also illustrates Dewey's tendency to shuttle back and forth between what I have called Level 1 and Level 2 ideas without even hinting that these ideas have a very different standing in his overall system of thought. The principle of continuity lies at the very foundation of Dewey's intellectual universe. It is a presupposition not just of his understanding of education, but also of his understanding of science, since the idea of predicting — and based on this controlling — the course of events depends on the operation of the principle of continuity. But, though he does not say so, Dewey's view about the effects of what he characterizes as over-indulging a child is no more than an ordinary, fallible empirical hypothesis. It is an open question whether this hypothesis will survive the test of critical examination. What is clear, however, is that this critical examination requires the principle of continuity as its presupposition.[7]

Educative and miseducative experiences. Although, as I will suggest below, the principles of interaction and continuity offer powerful lenses for examining educational ideas and practices, the analytic framework embedded in chapter three of *Experience and Education* also points us toward another essential dimension of educational analysis. This dimension concerns the basis for discriminating between desirable and undesirable educational outcomes. The need for this dimension becomes obvious when we perform the following simple thought-experiment. Suppose that, using the principles of interaction and continuity as well as our empirical knowledge, we succeed in exhaustively and accurately identifying the immediate quality and the many consequences of a particular educational transaction for a particular individual. Would we then be in a position to judge whether, educationally speaking, something good has happened? The reader who carefully performs this experiment is likely to arrive at Dewey's insight that we are in no position to judge this in the absence of a criterion or set of criteria that enables us to identify desirable educational outcomes. The framework of analysis Dewey develops in chapter three guides the reader to think about this important matter.

In the relevant sections of this discussion, Dewey weaves a conceptual web with three central points. First, he labels those experiences that

---

7   Some students of child development will likely disagree with Dewey both about what counts as over-indulging a child and about the effects of the kinds of behavior he identifies with over-indulgence.

culminate in desirable educational outcomes "educative." Second, he proposes "growth" as the basis for identifying educative experiences. Third, he defends growth as a criterion by asserting that there is an intimate and indissoluble connection between the ideal of growth and democratic social arrangements, such that the full flowering of each requires and supports the flowering of the other.

What Dewey exactly means by growth and whether it offers a defensible basis for judging whether an experience is educative are beyond the purview of this paper.[8] For our purposes, the critical point is that Dewey's invocation of growth represents a possible (but by no means necessary) answer to the question: "How do we decide whether an experience is educative?" Put differently, Dewey's invocation of growth represents a Level 2 answer to a Level 1 problem. At Level 1, Dewey correctly reminds us that any full-fledged educational theory must provide a basis for judging whether an experience is educative. At Level 2, Dewey offers us his own particular answer to this question, which happens to be growth. The fact that this answer may not prove clear or compelling to everyone should not distract Dewey's critics or supporters from heeding his suggestion that any credible theory purporting to guide the educational process must offer and defend *some* conception of educational value that can serve as a basis for identifying educative experiences. Certainly, an examination of this guiding conception must be central to any serious, comprehensive assessment of an educational proposal or practice.

Since our purpose in elucidating Dewey's ideas about educative experiences is to further build a Deweyan framework that will facilitate educational analysis, our discussion of this topic would be incomplete were we not to highlight the important observations concerning *miseducative* experiences that accompany Dewey's discussion of educative experiences. Dewey insists that educative experiences (those that promote our educational purposes) must be distinguished not just from non-educative experiences (those that are educationally neutral), but also from what he calls miseducative experiences (those that adversely affect our educational progress, as judged by the same criterion we use to identify educative experiences). Dewey's reference to miseducative experiences is a reminder that although, as the principle of continuity states, all experiences change us, not all experiences change us for the better! Some change us for the worse. Kafka once quipped: "A man was astonished at how easily he went the eternal way; he happened to be rushing backwards

---

8   For further discussion of this matter, see Pekarsky, 1990, and Pekarsky, 1991, pp. 61–74.

along it."(Kafka, 1948, p. 286) So, too, there are times in education when, unbeknownst to us, we may be going backwards rather than forward.[9] Put differently, granted that educators are typically motivated by good intentions, sometimes those intentions are misguided, so that achieving them undermines the learner's development. And, even when the intentions are worthy, things sometimes go awry with negative results. Or else, as sometimes happens, the educator's worthy intentions are achieved, but at the price of negative by-products that outweigh them (see the discussion of *collateral learning* below). For these reasons, it is as important for educational analysts to be on the lookout for a practice's potential to prove miseducative as it is to consider its potential to be educative. Certainly, they should not assume that a practice is likely to be educative rather than miseducative just because it is called "an educational practice" or because it takes place in "an educational institution."

Corollaries of the foregoing ideas. The principles of interaction and continuity suggest a kind of two-dimensional grid on which educational transactions can be mapped. The distinction between educative and miseducative experiences gives this grid an all-important third dimension. Taken together, the two principles and the educative/miseducative distinction point to a number of key questions that should be asked of educational proposals, institutions and practices. Dewey himself suggests some of them in the chapter of *Experience and Education* that we are considering; others are readily derivable from his discussion. Identification of these questions will also serve to summarize the different strands of the preceding discussion, strands that jointly define the powerful analytic framework offered in that chapter.

1. The basis for distinguishing educative from noneducative and miseducative experiences: As we have discussed earlier, a minimally adequate framework for examining proposed and actual educational practices and institutions must guide its users to examine the values that they explicitly or implicitly espouse. Hence, the need to ask questions such as: Does the educational proposal, practice or institution under consideration explicitly or implicitly embody a conception of success that can

---

9   This represents a rejection of the comforting idea that all of our experiences educate us. All of our experiences *change* us, says Dewey, but it does not follow that they *educate* us, i.e. change us for the better. Dewey's writings suggest that while any experience is potentially educative, i.e. capable of changing us for the better, in actual fact many experiences prove miseducative, that is, change us for the worse.

meaningfully discriminate between educative and miseducative experiences? Is this conception articulated, adequately defended and defensible? And are the proposed or actual criteria for evaluating the effectiveness of an educational practice, as judged by changes in the learner, coherent with this conception of success?

2. *Two dimensions of evaluation:* The principles of interaction and continuity indicate two dimensions of any experience. The interaction between the individual and the environment has an immediate quality, as well as consequences for the course of future experience. In assessing whether an educational experience is worthwhile, it is therefore insufficient to determine whether it has a positive immediate quality. It is also essential to consider whether it has a desirable impact on the future course of the individual's experience, as judged (in the spirit of *corollary number 1* above) by a defensible conception of success. To describe an experience as educative is to predict that it will contribute positively to the future course of the learner's experience. And because, human nature being what it is, such predictions are all-too-frequently influenced by our hopes, it is not only fair but also important to ask the forecasters to offer convincing reasons to think their predictions reasonable. Thus our second critical question: Is there good reason to believe that the educational intervention in question will prove both meaningful in the present *and* conducive to the long-term growth of the learner (as judged by our criterion for distinguishing educative from miseducative experiences)?

3. *No inherently educative environment:* As the principle of interaction emphasizes, every experience is defined by the interplay between an individual and his/her environment. And, because every individual differs from every other individual, there is no reason to assume that any particular set of objective conditions is inherently educative. The same conditions that may be immediately rewarding and conducive to development in one individual or sub-group may interact negatively with the attitudes, skills and dispositions of other individuals and sub-groups. If the set of objective conditions that seems to work with some groups is not efficacious with others, the inference to be drawn is not that these latter groups are deficient, but rather that the particular set of conditions is not tailored to their cognitive, attitudinal or physical equipment. The educational challenge, therefore, is not to separate the able from the unable. Rather, the challenge is to identify what it is about a particular educational environment that impedes the progress of certain individuals or populations, and to search for conditions that will bring out the best in them. Hence the importance of the third question that grows out of Dewey's discussion: Is the educational environment tailored to the needs, capacities and circumstances of the learners? Is the 'fit' between the environment and the learners appropriate — and if it isn't, how can this fit be rendered more adequate?

4. Transfer: The principle of continuity asserts that every experience affects the future course of experience. In fact, education is typically predicated on a particular corollary of this assumption — namely, that what is learned in the educational setting will be available to the learner under actual life conditions. This is the assumption of transfer. But since, as Dewey emphasizes, the effect of an experience is not immediately evident, one cannot reasonably assume that the learner will be capable of meaningfully employing what is learned under real life conditions, just because it *can* be demonstrated in the school setting at the moment it is acquired. Since learning often does not transfer, it is important to consider carefully whether the learning context has been organized in order to maximize the likelihood that what is being taught will be remembered *and* appropriately used under real life conditions. Thus, question 4: Are the educational practices under consideration justified on the grounds that what is to be learned will be used meaningfully in other settings — for example, 'in the real world'?[10] If so, has the learning environment been organized to make this a likely outcome?

Before moving on to the fifth question, we may note in passing that Dewey's discussion of transfer offers another excellent example of his tendency to interweave what I have described as more basic, or Level 1 ideas with less basic, Level 2 ideas. The ideas concerning transfer in the preceding paragraph are what I have characterized as Level 1 ideas, i.e. ideas about education that can meaningfully inform our inquiries across a variety of ideological divides and that are compatible with a host of competing empirical beliefs about the conditions of transfer. But, once again, these Level 1 views are presented alongside some particular ideas

---

10 As indicated in the main body of the text, Dewey's discussion of transfer in "Experience and Education" puts a powerful question in the hands of the educator: Is what is learned, learned in such a way that it will carry meaningfully into the learner's other transactions with life? At the same time, this formulation may seem unduly instrumental to those who think about learning as *Limud Torah LiShma* ("studying Torah for its own sake.") Whether this tension is more apparent than real deserves discussion, but is beyond the scope of this paper.

concerning when and why transfer is unlikely to take place. Thus, in explaining why school learnings often do not transfer to our transactions with the outside world, Dewey writes:

"Almost everyone has had occasion to look back upon his school days and wonder what has become of the knowledge he was supposed to have amassed during his years of schooling, and why it is that the technical skills he acquired have to be learned over again in changed form in order to stand him in good stead...One trouble is that the subject-matter was learned in isolation; it was put, as it were, in a water-tight compartment. When the question is asked, then, what has become of it, where has it gone to, the right answer is that it is still there in the special compartment in which it was originally stowed away... But it was segregated when it was acquired and hence is so disconnected from the rest of experience that it is not available under the actual conditions of life. It is contrary to the laws of experience that learning of this kind, no matter how thoroughly engrained at the time, should give genuine preparation." (Dewey, 1963, pp. 47–48).

These speculations concerning the conditions of transfer are very interesting. But — and this is an essential point for our purposes — these are Level 2 ideas: they represent particular, fallible and empirically testable responses to more basic Level 1 concerns and questions concerning transfer.[11]

5. Collateral learning: As discussed earlier, the principle of interaction holds that the transaction between the individual and the educational environment is an interplay between the totality of the individual (including his/her beliefs, attitudes, dispositions, inclinations, skills, needs,

11 In fact, Dewey's beliefs concerning the conditions of transfer (beliefs for which he offers no empirical evidence) are, as generalizations, questionable. Although they may well hold up as explanations for the failure of transfer for certain sub-groups in the population, there is no *a priori* reason to believe (and there is probably good reason to doubt) that they will hold up for all groups. Dewey's own principle of interaction, which warns us against assuming that there is an inherently educative environment, would also caution us against believing that any particular set of educational arrangements is inherently miseducative. Taken seriously, this principle would lead us to approach Dewey's hypotheses concerning the conditions of transfer with a measure of skepticism. This skepticism will only be strengthened by an examination of recent work concerning the kinds of educational environments that appear to be conducive to learning for economically disadvantaged African-American children in the United States. See in this connection Delpit, 1995, pp. 11–20.

both psychological and physiological, etc.) and the totality of his/her environment. This means that the interaction between mind and subject matter envisioned by many curriculum developers is, at best, only one dimension of a highly complex transaction. The teacher may be interested in this particular dimension of the transaction. But, like it or not, and whether the teacher is aware of it or not, the interaction is proceeding along many other dimensions as well. Among other things, attitudes toward self and other, toward learning and toward the subject matter are all being acquired. In short, much more is being learned in typical classroom settings than teachers think they are teaching. And, not infrequently, some of these other learnings have a more profound impact on the learner's development than the intended influence. As Dewey writes:

"What avail is it to win prescribed amounts of information about geography and history, to win ability to read and write, if in the process the individual loses his own soul: loses his appreciation of things worth while, of the values to which these things are relative; if he loses the desire to apply what he has learned and, above all, loses the ability to extract meaning from his experiences as they occur?" (Dewey, 1963, p. 49).

In other words, educators must ask themselves and seriously investigate the following questions: In what unintended ways do the environment in which learning proceeds, the pedagogy being employed and the content of instruction affect the learner's beliefs, attitudes, values and dispositions?[12] And are these learnings consistent with our (i.e., the educators') deepest educational aspirations?[13]

---

12 I am indebted to the students in Hasha'ar (a New York-based program of Jewish studies and professional development for future day school educators) for helping me realize that, along with educational environment and pedagogy, instructional content can also give rise to collateral learnings.
13 Dewey's discussion of collateral learning offers another, but more ambiguous, example of his tendency to mix Level 1 and Level 2 ideas. Along with his general Level 1 point that collateral learning is ongoing, Dewey intimates some Level 2 beliefs concerning the effects of the traditional educational arrangements described in chapter three. He suggests (without actually asserting) that these educational arrangements operate to undermine the desire to continue learning, common sense, and other conditions of a thriving life. See Dewey, 1963, pp. 48–49. Such ideas are clearly fallible, Level 2 hypotheses. They should not be taken as elements of the guiding framework of analysis that Dewey offers educators in this chapter.

Conclusion

As suggested above, the analytic framework composed by these five inter-
related themes focuses one's attention on critical dimensions of educational transactions, on the very things that thoughtful persons need to
consider when seeking insight concerning educational phenomena and
ideas. A mental map of this kind is thus an invaluable tool. But, as
suggested earlier, we would be unwise to assume that such a tool is
sufficient to enable an educator to guide others into productive reflection
concerning their educational beliefs and commitments. Even a very
powerful mental map of the pertinent terrain is no substitute for good
educational instincts, for what William James, seeking to dispel the illusion
that knowing psychology would transform people into good teachers,
felicitously called that "happy tact and ingenuity…that are the alpha and
omega of the teacher's art…" (James, 1958, p. 24).

No doubt Seymour Fox possesses, and in his teaching effectively
employs, the mental map I have tried to describe, as well as many others.
But he also possesses — and this is critical to note if we are to understand
his effectiveness — the "happy tact and ingenuity" that allows him to ask
the right question at the right time in the right way. A mental map that
articulates the pattern of *his* intellectual moves is not likely to be drawn
soon — unless we can persuade the map-makers at Hogwarts to get busy
with what would prove to be, even for them, a formidable challenge.[14]

References

Delpit, Lisa. (1995). Skills and other dilemmas of a progressive black educator. In Lisa
    Delpit. *Other people's children.* New York: New Press, pp. 11–20.
Dewey, John. (1902). *The child and the curriculum.* Chicago: The University of
    Chicago Press.
Dewey, John. (1916). *Democracy and education.* New York: Macmillan Company.
Dewey, John. (1963). *Experience and education.* New York: Collier Books.
James, William. (1958). *Talks to teachers.* New York: The Norton Library.
Kafka, Franz. (1948). *The great wall of China.* New York: Schocken Books.

14 For those muggles who have not yet had the opportunity to encounter them, the allusion
    here is to J. K. Rowling's series of books dealing with the adventures of Harry Potter
    and other members of the wizard community.

Pekarsky, Daniel. (1990). Dewey's Conception of Growth Reconsidered. *Educational Theory, 40 (3)*. (Summer) pp. 283–294.

Pekarsky, Daniel. (1991). Burglars, Robber-Barons and the Good Life. *Educational Theory, 4 (1)*. (Winter).

Plato. *Protagoras and Meno*. W. K. C. Guthrie. (Trans.) Baltimore: Penguin Books, 1956.

Scheffler, Israel. (1974). *Four pragmatists*. New York: Humanities Press.

Turkel, Studs. (1974). *Working*. New York: Avon Books.

PRACTICES

Teaching Torah as Truth:
An Exploration of Pedagogic Goals
BARRY W. HOLTZ

More than any other individual, Seymour Fox has placed the issue of goals on the agenda of Jewish education. Over the course of many years, as both scholar and teacher, Fox has argued that discourse about the goals of education, rather than a mere frill or philosophical tangent, lies at the heart of good educational practice. In the spirit of Kurt Lewin's famous adage, "there is nothing so practical as a good theory" Fox has asserted that all practice is rooted in theory and all theory is tested in practice. Ultimately, the process is interactive.

In his influential article, "Toward a General Theory of Jewish Education" Fox posited that "the most urgent problem facing Jewish education today is its lack of purpose and, consequently, its blandness."(1973, p. 261).[1] In his view, only a serious philosophical deliberation about the goals of education can address this crisis. In that spirit, this article will explore the purposes of teaching the Bible, investigating both ways to approach the issue of goals for Bible teaching and some of the difficulties that teachers might encounter in implementing their goals.

We like to say that studying the Bible, like other great academic pursuits, can potentially transform a student's life. This suggests that the Bible inhabits a particular and very special universe, a place where the primary concern is nothing less than the pursuit of truth. As R. S. Peters puts it:

1   Also see Fox, 1997, and Pekarsky, 1997.

"Being concerned about truth has another type of worth. It can be regarded as having a worth which is independent of its benefit. Indeed, the state of mind of one who is determined to find out what is true ... can be regarded as an ultimate value which provides one of the criteria of benefit. ... Someone who values truth in this way may find the constant effort to free his mind from prejudice and error painful; he may sometimes find it wearisome and boring; but it matters to him supremely, even if he falls short of the ideal which he accepts." (Peters, 1966, p. 100).

What does it mean to be concerned with "truth?" What does it mean to teach Torah as a repository of truth? How can such a view influence goals for teaching the Bible? In this paper I will try to suggest various approaches to these knotty issues, hoping to reflect some of the ideals impressed by Seymour Fox upon his colleagues and students during his remarkable career.

We will begin with the thinking of the contemporary philosopher Hans-Georg Gadamer.[2] Gadamer is particularly relevant because for him the essential goal in confronting a text[3] from the past is to experience its *truth*. In this regard, Gadamer pushes us to listen carefully, respectfully, to works of the past and to take those texts seriously, without rushing to judgment. As one scholar has claimed, for Gadamer:

"... the first principle of a hermeneutical interpretation of a text is to come to an agreement about the truth of the subject matter in question. But to come to an agreement or understanding, one has to recognize the integrity and independence of the viewpoint of the other." (Zuckert, 1996, p. 90).

That is, we need to take the text's claims of truth very seriously indeed.[4]

2   The relevance of Gadamer for religious education has been explored by a number of writers in recent years, in particular Hass, 1993; Cutter, 1993; Kerdemon, 1998; and Levisohn, 2001.
3   It should be noted that Gadamer also includes works of art in general, along with texts in this category.
4   An interesting, but very different, approach to the question of "truth" in teaching has been raised by the literary scholar Robert Scholes in his book *The Rise and Fall of English* (1998). Scholes is not so much concerned with the truth of texts in the lives of individuals but rather with the problem of teachers in making truth claims in an academic world of relativism. One of the reasons that professors in the humanities "feel bad" he says, "is that we have become reluctant to make claims of truth about the matters we teach. Powerful voices in our field have taught us to be embarrassed by the word *truth*, and thus either to avoid it or condemn it." (p. 39.)

Gadamer views much of modern hermeneutics as an attempt to run away from the question of textual truth and replace it with attention to the historical or personal circumstances under which the text was composed. Gadamer attributes this move to the German philosopher Friedrich Schleiermacher (1768–1834) and his attempt to do what Gadamer views essentially as an impossible task: To "reveal the true meaning of a work of art and guard against misunderstanding and anachronistic interpretation" by reproducing "the writer's original process of production" and the historical context in which he or she lived. (Gadamer, 1999, p. 166) Instead of truth, the interpreter in the Schleiermacher mode strives to "reconstruct the original intentions of writers … and the circumstances of their lives…" (Warnke, 1978, p. 14). Especially in a world holding claims of truth suspect to begin with, the "romantic" hermeneutics of Schleiermacher, Wilhelm Dilthey (1833–1911) and others — with their focus on the historical, contextual dimension of interpretation — came to play an increasingly significant role in intellectual life. Still, Gadamer believes that resorting to historical context and writers' motivations is an inadequate response to texts of the past:

"Hermeneutic work is based on a polarity of familiarity and strangeness; but this polarity is not to be regarded psychologically, with Schleiermacher, as the range that covers the mystery of individuality, but truly hermeneutically — i.e. in regard to what has been said: the language in which the text addresses us, the story that it tells us. Here too there is a tension. It is in the play between the traditional text's strangeness and familiarity to us, between being a historically intended, distanciated object and belonging to a tradition. The true locus of hermeneutics is this in-between." (Gadamer, p. 295).

The tension between the familiar and the strange abides at the heart of Gadamer's interpretive view. In essence, the Schleiermacher approach collapses the familiar-strange polarity into a merely psychological focus (specifically on the artist) or a contextual focus (on the world in which the text has been created). And, according to Gadamer, this destroys the crucial tension involved in taking any traditional text seriously. The problem Gadamer describes here parallels quite closely the approach of biblical studies, at least in the world of the university, during the past century. Gadamer would, I believe, criticize biblical studies in which scholars tried to "explain" the Bible by putting their energies into describing the historical, linguistic and cultural context in which the Bible was produced. These scholars, Gadamer might charge, mistakenly believe that they should read the Bible in the hermeneutical manner of Schleiermacher.

By not seriously confronting the potential truth of the text, Gadamer believes we have abandoned the most important dimension of interpretive work, which is "to understand the content of what is said, and only secondarily to isolate and understand another's meaning as such." (Gadamer, p. 294).

In what way can a text like the Bible teach truth? A number of contemporary writers have grappled with this question regarding the study of literature, and how it may have an impact on students' lives. Their views have important implications for the study of Bible. Though, as I will try to show below, there are also significant differences for the particularities of biblical study.

The philosopher of education, Harvey Siegel, has articulated one approach to the questions, "How can fiction teach? What are the pedagogical possibilities of fiction? What sorts of lessons can be taught?" (Siegel, 1989, p. 116). He argues that novels:

"... can add to our understanding of philosophical issues by making clear to us the motivations and felt reasons undergirding alternative views. A very fine novelist can make such reasons come alive and drive home sorts of reasons not open to more conventional modes of teaching." (Ibid, p. 131).

In *The Brothers Karamazov*, for example, Dostoyevsky deals with a number of powerful philosophical issues, including the problem of evil, the meaning of suffering and the conflict of belief and unbelief. "Felt reasons" a phrase Siegel uses as a kind of technical term, have a "visceral quality" that allow us to "feel the force of reasons... in entirely different ways than we feel the force of the ... same reasons in other circumstances." (Ibid. p. 125) It is *not* that Dostoyevsky offers philosophical ideas that are "particularly original or forceful, if taken out the context of the novel." (Ibid.) Rather, the context of the fiction changes our experience of the reasons offered. The living, breathing characters of a novel, enmeshed in circumstances that are, if not familiar, extremely *real* to us, make reading a novel by Dostoyevsky about the nature of evil palpably different from reading a work like Hume's *Dialogues Concerning Natural Religion,* even though both may deal with some of the same issues. The felt reasons presented in fiction do not differ "from ordinary propositional reasons.

[They are] ordinary reasons whose power to move people is made obvious or manifest by the way in which those reasons... are portrayed. Felt reasons are not a different kind of reason; they are rather a particular *kind* of *presentation* of reasons." (Ibid., p. 129).

Reading literary works of this sort is crucial to the practice of (and here Siegel uses Scheffler's term) "the rationality theory of teaching, which places the offering and exchange of reasons at the center of teaching activities." (Ibid, p. 123). Fictional examples represent points of view in intense and living ways, bringing them to life for the reader or learner.

The embodiment of philosophical disputation in fiction allows us to view reading and teaching literature as a kind of moral enterprise — it is meant to have an effect on the reader that is not "merely" aesthetic. The reading and teaching of great literary works can, in the view of some, actually make us better, more ethical human beings.

We can follow this line of argument into other realms as well. Richard Rorty, for example, argues that certain books can "help us become less cruel." (1989, p. 141). He divides these books into two types: books like *Uncle Tom's Cabin* that "help us see how social practices which we have taken for granted have made us cruel" and books "about the ways in which particular types of people are cruel to other particular sorts of people." (Ibid.) These latter books might include George Eliot's *Middlemarch* or Dickens's *Bleak House*. When we read these books, we begin to realize the ways that "our private obsessions with the achievement of a certain sort of perfection may make us oblivious to the pain and humiliation we are causing" (Ibid.) Rorty's definition of the power of books to affect the way we think about others and the way we could avoid causing cruelty, might influence a pedagogic stance toward the teaching of a biblical text like the story of Jacob and Esau. When Esau realizes that Jacob has tricked him out of Isaac's blessing, we read one of the most poignant scenes in the entire Bible. "'Have you but one blessing, Father? Bless me too, Father!' And Esau wept aloud" (*Genesis 27:38*). Teaching such a text, Rorty would surely argue, has the potential to distance the student from cruelty.

Siegel and Rorty consider literature a tool in the reader's ethical development. This position has been most powerfully articulated in the work of two other thinkers, Martha Nussbaum and Wayne C. Booth. We shall first look at Nussbaum's work and then turn to Booth's contribution.

In Nussbaum's collection of essays, *Love's Knowledge*, (1990), the author states her desire to look at works of literature as "indispensable to a philosophical inquiry in the ethical sphere: not by any means sufficient, but sources of insight without which inquiry cannot be complete." (pp. 23–24).

Such a view, according to Nussbaum, swims against the tide of most literary criticism of a variety of stripes. As she says, writing that assumes

"… that any work that attempts to ask of a literary text questions about how we might live, treating the work as addressed to the reader's practical interests and needs, and as being in some sense about our lives, must be hopelessly naïve, reactionary and insensitive to the complexities of literary form and intertextual referentiality."

Such "ethical criticism" need not lead to overly simplistic, moralistic tracts, Nussbaum argues. Rather, "far from insisting that all literature must play some single, simple role in human life, the best ethical criticism, ancient and modern, has insisted on the complexity and variety revealed to us in literature, appealing to that complexity to cast doubt on reductive theories." (Ibid, p. 22).

Love's Knowledge tries to demonstrate such an approach with essays on a variety of literary works, including novels by Henry James and Dickens. This is a rich and complex work, impossible to summarize in a few pages. The main point of relevance to us is Nussbaum's belief that we can find in fiction ways of thinking about the fundamental question "how should one live?" Fiction does this in a number of different ways, but one of the most salient is that it shows us "the ethical crudeness of moralities based exclusively on general rules, and [demands] for ethics a much finer responsiveness to the concrete…" (Ibid. p. 37). In another book, *Poetic Justice*, Nussbaum seeks to enumerate how literature "has the potential to make a distinctive contribution to our public life." (1995, p. 2). How? By giving us the ability "to imagine what it is like to live the life of another person who might, given changes in circumstance, be oneself or one of one's loved ones." (Ibid. p. 5).

Nussbaum clearly leans toward fiction of a particular sort. The "realist" novels of Dickens, George Eliot and James well represent her interest in the "concrete" and the "ordinary." (Ibid., pp. 7, 9, and *passim*) Her writing shows far less interest in Joyce, for example. But if we use Nussbaum as a lens to look at the goals of teaching the Bible, the perspective she offers is particularly attractive. Of course this is not because the Bible resembles a 19th century realist novel. One major difference is that the Bible consists of many genres, not just the realist narrative. Alongside familiar narratives we find law, prophesy, "wisdom literature" (e.g. *Proverbs*) and poetry. But for educators the *narrative* portions of the Bible are those most often taught and here the power of "ethical criticism" is relevant indeed.

The gap between the Bible and modern fiction entails much more than genre. There are vast differences between, say, the Joseph story and

James's *Princess Casamassima*. The fine details of place and nuanced readings of internal states that one finds in Henry James are not present in the Bible. Nor will we find in the Bible the careful descriptions of a character's appearance or the assured voice of an omniscient narrator such as we might encounter in a novel by Jane Austen or George Eliot. The *way* the Bible tells its stories is markedly different from the way that later fiction, like the novel, tells its stories.[5]

But despite these discrepancies between the novel and the Bible, congruities of great significance make comparisons between these two literatures very instructive for our pedagogical project. Biblical person-alities struggle with questions of right and wrong, death and life, good and evil, all in muted tones of gray, similar to the complexities of presentation found in the fiction admired by Booth and Nussbaum. In what way was Joseph to blame for the troubles he encountered with his brothers? How was his father Jacob culpable as well? What did it mean to be the favored son? How was the multi-colored coat both a symbol and a burden? Looking at Edward Greenstein's article *An Equivocal Reading of the Sale of Joseph* (1982), for example, we see what Nussbaum calls "the worth and richness of plural qualitative thinking." (Nussbaum, 1990, p. 36). In the David and Batsheva story (particularly as read by Meir Sternberg (1984), we see exemplification of Nussbaum's comment that the "choice between two qualitatively different actions or commitments, when on account of circumstances one cannot pursue both, is or can be tragic." (Nussbaum, 1990, p. 37).

We dwell on narrative not only because some of the most enduring and memorable elements of the Bible are its narratives, but also because narrative itself has such a deep hold on the human species. We *live* through narratives; they define us as individuals and as parts of a larger society. Thus reading and teaching biblical narratives help us and our students make sense of their lives as human beings, as part of a culture. Asks Mark Johnson:

"Why is it that we turn to literary texts for our moral education? Why do we learn more from narratives than from academic moral philosophy about what it is to be human, about the contingencies of life, about the kinds of lives we most want to lead and about what is involved in trying

---

5   The Bible differs from other ancient texts as well — see Erich Auerbach's classic "Odysseus' Scar" in his *Mimesis* (1971): pp. 3–24. On how the Bible tells its stories see, among many other possible sources, Sternberg, (1985), Joel Rosenberg, (1984), Edward L. Greenstein and Robert Alter, (1981).

to lead such lives? ...The key to the answer is that *our lives ultimately have a narrative structure* [emphasis added]. It is in sustained narrative, therefore, that we come closest to observing and participating in the reality of life as it is actually experienced and lived." (Johnson, 1993, p. 196).

Placing narrative at the heart of the curriculum of biblical studies, then, is no whim and no attempt to dodge the difficulties of other biblical genre. It might in fact be our first obligation to those we teach, of any age. As Alasdair MacIntyre memorably put it:

"...man is in his actions and practice, as well as in his fictions, essentially a story-telling animal. He is not essentially, but becomes through his history, a teller of stories that aspire to truth. But the key question for men is not about their own authorship; I can only answer the question 'What am I to do?' if I can answer the prior question 'Of what story or stories do I find myself a part?' We enter human society, that is, with one or more imputed characteristics... and we have to learn what they are in order to be able to understand how others respond to us and how our responses to them are apt to be construed. It is through hearing stories about wicked stepmothers, lost children, good but misguided kinds, wolves that suckled twin boys... that children learn or mislearn both what a child and what a parent is, what the cast of characters may be in the drama into which they have been born and what the ways of the world are. Deprive children of stories and you leave them unscripted, anxious stutterers in their actions as in their words. Hence there is no way to give us an understanding of any society, including our own, except through the stock of stories which constitute its initial dramatic resources." (MacIntyre, 1984, p. 216).[6]

Of all the writers exploring "ethical criticism" there is arguably none as influential as the literary critic Wayne C. Booth. Particularly in his profound and monumental volume *The Company We Keep: An Ethics of Fiction* (1988), Booth has explored the complex ways in which books can affect the reader's life.[7] This lengthy and far-ranging work is impossible to

6   The literature on "narrative" is immense — in literary criticism, anthropology, psychology and education, among other disciplines. In education one may look at Jerome Bruner's classic 1986 essay; and at McEwan and Egan, 1995.

7   Booth has been an important influence of Martha Nussbaum. See her important review "Reading for Life" in Nussbaum, 1990, pp. 230–244.

summarize here. But I will focus on one aspect of Booth's thinking, namely, the *way* that learning has an impact on one's ethical sensibility. Or, as Nussbaum puts it, "what becomes of readers *as* they read?" (1990, p. 233).

Booth invents the term "coduction" to refer to the kinds of conversations that we need to have in order to "arrive at our sense of value in narrative." (Booth, p. 70). Whenever I read a text, I am constantly viewing it against the "backdrop of my long personal history of untraceably complex experiences of other stories and persons." (Ibid. p. 71). Moreover, I am engaged in a *community* of like-minded readers, who are also trying to unravel the moral implications of what I have read. The work is then "transformed by us as we hold our conversations about it." (Ibid. p. 74) With his strong emphasis on the power of conversation, Booth is referring to a model of teaching. There are no clear answers to the questions of "truth" here, no moral prescriptions. Instead there is a generating of moral vision and self-reflection within the classroom discourse. Booth's analysis of hermeneutical principles is, it turns out, an argument for a kind of pedagogy.

I have spoken here about the "Bible as truth" in terms of the text's ethical power, and as adumbrated by Nussbaum and Booth. But it is appropriate to add another dimension of truth. The Bible may speak to the student in ways that are personally revelatory, psychologically meaningful or spiritually profound. This goes beyond the ethical (if one can say such a thing) into other kinds of truth. Consider, for example, Buber's comments about what "the man of today" must do in reading the Bible:

> "He must face the Book with a new attitude, as something new. He must yield to it, withhold nothing of his being, and let whatever will occur between himself and it. He does not know which of its sayings and images will overwhelm him and mold him, from where the spirit will ferment and enter into him, to incorporate itself anew in his body. But he holds himself open." (Buber, 1968, p. 5).

What does Buber have in mind? It is clear that some models of interpretation find ways of drawing biblical texts into the realm of personal or psychological meaning. One classic example is the way in which early Hasidism reinterpreted biblical texts in deeply personal ways. Gershom Scholem described this as the "process of spiritualization which biblical or rabbinic terms and concepts have undergone in Hasidic exegesis." (Scholem, 1971, p. 200). Scholem goes on to say that, although this was not a novel idea in Hasidism, its "radical application, the hypertrophic use of this device" was remarkable. Classic concepts like Egypt, *galut* (exile) and *ge'ulah* (redemption) were turned into allegorical catchwords no longer denoting only their definition, but standing for a personal state of mind, for an amoral condition or, as we would say in contemporary jargon, for existential situations of man. Notions like these have lost their concrete historical or geographical meaning; they no longer have to do with the fate and future of the nation, but with the individual's struggle for his own salvation. (Ibid.)

In this mode of interpretation, the Exodus from Egypt becomes metaphorized into an expression of a person's personal redemption from spiritual lethargy or sin. Even such a prosaic biblical passage as "the servants of Isaac, digging in the valley, found a well of living waters" (*Genesis* 26:19) becomes an opportunity in early Hasidism for a personalized spiritual message:

> "The patriarchs opened up the channels of mind in the world teaching all who were to come into the world how to dig within themselves a spring of living waters, to cleave to their fount, the root of their lives." (Nahum, 1982, p. 189).[8]

Hasidism expresses itself in the language and modalities of an intact religious culture. But even in a more secular era, such impulses can be perceived. Michael Fishbane, a scholar of the Bible and its exegesis, has tried to articulate what it might mean today for "an individual [to read] texts in a wholly personal manner." (Fishbane, 1989, p. 132)[9] seeking to make sense of a text deemed "sacred" in a more secular age:

> "Here, we may say, modern readers prowl around texts like wolves around Sinai — to paraphrase Kafka's well-known parable. Indeed we prowl around many texts, the Bible included, and wrest from these encounters fragments of various sorts. So viewed, we are, in part, a living texture of ideas derived from our reading. ... Accordingly, the Bible may become sacred to us insofar as its images and language shape our discourse, stimulate our moral and spiritual growth, and simply bind us to past generations which also took this text seriously. Indeed, the

---

8   See Green's introduction to this volume, particularly pp. 9-16, for more on the "personalizing" tendency in Hasidic thought.

9   Later in this article, the author deals with the "communal" dimension of reading texts.

Bible may become sacred in this way because — together with other texts — it helps establish our personhood and outline our possibilities; and because it may provide the words and values through which we may cross over from the private to the interhuman realm. No denial of death is this. It is rather a transcending of selfhood and its limitations through concourse with other texts and other selves." (Ibid.)

Thus, in Fishbane's view, the Bible becomes sacred in a number of different ways, even in a secular age. It provides a set of images and words by which our own language and metaphoric substructures are shaped. We lose our own Gardens of Eden; we wander years in our wildernesses; we cast our bread upon the waters and hear the still, small voice. It pushes us, in the manner of Nussbaum and Booth, toward moral development. It helps elicit our own spiritual growth. And it links us back across the generations to all those people who have lived and died for this enduring text.

What does it mean to say that studying the Bible helps "establish our personhood and outline our possibilities"? In the Bible we learn new things, to be sure, but perhaps more importantly we learn both to see familiar things in a new way and to rediscover truths that we had known before and forgotten. Gadamer points out, in the words of Georgia Warnke:

"... [in] so far as works of art are mimetic, they are therefore not only representational but pedagogical. In picking out certain features of their objects they teach their views or readers more of their objects than that audience previously understood... On the one hand, we learn from a work of art... On the other, we recognize this new way as something familiar, as something we knew or should have known." (Warnke, 1987, p. 59).

* * * *

Where, one might well ask, does the exploration I have undertaken here leave the Jewish teacher in facing his or her students? I have tried to argue that teachers of the Bible should place the question of truth on their educational agendas, but in ways that differ from conventional Jewish education. On the one hand, it seems to me that Gadamer has helped us see that "truth" and "the historical context of the Bible" are not coterminous. Teaching the Bible as an interesting text reflective of the ancient world in which it was born may work in the academy — in scholarship or even in the university classroom. But it will be inadequate for other educational contexts, whether schools for children or adult education programs.

On the other hand, teaching the Bible as a fundamentalist repository of plain "truths" will not work either. The preparation of sophisticated students — students who will view the Bible as a powerful source of personal identity — will not be aided by advocating the Bible as a sourcebook of simplistic "values" or by focusing on the historicity of the biblical narrative.

Instead, I have argued for teaching the ethical dimension of the Bible in ways articulated by thinkers like Siegel, Nussbaum and Booth. Their approach views the Bible as a complex and challenging ethical work, a work whose very pedagogy entails the potential for ethical engagement and development.

Moreover, the Bible leads students toward other kinds of growth. As suggested in distinct ways by Buber, Scholem and Fishbane, the Bible can — through the careful planning of good teachers — become a locus for personal identification and psychological insight. Proust articulates this for the act of reading, in comments that hold equally true for the experience of teaching and learning:

"In reality, every reader is, while he is reading, the reader of his own self. The writer's work is merely a kind of optical instrument which he offers to the reader to enable him to discern what, without this book, he would perhaps never have experienced in himself. And the recognition by the reader in his own self of what the books says is the proof of its veracity." (Quoted in de Botton, 1997, pp. 24–25).

The Bible offers teachers these potential rewards, the opportunity to find truth through an exploration of the biblical text. But the enumeration of potential pedagogical goals, such as those I have attempted to raise in this paper, does not bring the teacher's story to a close. Indeed, perhaps most of the great challenges have just begun.

References

Auerbach, Erich. (1971). Odysseus' scar. In Erich Auerbach. *Mimesis*. Princeton, NJ: Princeton University Press.
Booth, Wayne C. (1988). *The company we keep: An ethics of fiction*. Berkeley, CA: The University of California Press.

de Botton, Alain. (1997). *How Proust can change your life*. New York: Pantheon Books.

Bruner, Jerome. (1986). Two modes of thought. In Jerome Bruner. *Actual minds, possible worlds*. Cambridge: Harvard University Press, pp. 11–43.

Buber, Martin. (1968). The man of today and the Jewish Bible. In Nahum N. Glatzer. (Ed.). *On the Bible*. New York: Schocken Books.

Cutter, William. (1993). Reading for ethics — Renouncing simplicity. *Religious Education 88:2*. (Spring), pp. 212–225.

Fishbane, Michael. (1989). *The garments of Torah*. Bloomington: Indiana University Press.

Fox, Seymour. (1997). From theory to practice in Jewish education. Paper delivered at the World Congress of Jewish Studies, Jerusalem, Israel, July.

Fox, Seymour. (1973). Toward a general theory of Jewish education. In David Sidorsky. (Ed.). *The future of the American Jewish community*. New York: Basic Books.

Gadamer, Hans-Georg. (1999). *Truth and method*, In Joel Weinsheimer and Donald G. Marshall. (Trans.) Second revised edition. New York: Continuum.

Greenstein, Edward L. (1982). An equivocal reading of the sale of Joseph. In Kenneth, R. R. Gross, Louis and Ackerman, James S. (Eds.). *Literary interpretations of biblical narratives*, Vol. II, Nashville, TN: Abingdon Press, pp. 114–125.

Greenstein, Edward L. and Alter, Robert. (1981). *The art of biblical narrative*. New York: Basic Books.

Hass, Ernest. (1993). Practical biblical interpretation. *Religious education 88 (2)*. (Spring), pp. 190–211.

Johnson, Mark. (1993) *Moral imagination*. Chicago: The University of Chicago Press.

Kerdemon, Deborah. (1998). Some thoughts about hermeneutics and Jewish religious education. *Religious education 93 (1)*. (Winter), pp. 29–43.

Levisohn, Jon. (2001). Openness and Commitment: Hans-Georg Gadamer and the Teaching of Jewish Texts. *Journal of Jewish education 67 (1–2)*. (Spring/Summer), pp. 20–35.

MacIntyre, Alasdair. (1984). *After virtue*. Second ed. Notre Dame, IN: University of Notre Dame Press.

McEwan, Hunter and Egan, Kieran. (Eds.). (1995). *Narrative in teaching, learning, and research*. New York: Teachers College Press.

Nahum, Menahem. (1982) *Meor eynaim* ["The light of the eyes"]. In Arthur Green. (Ed. and trans.). *Upright practices; The light of the eyes*. New York: Paulist Press.

Nussbaum, Martha. (1990). *Love's knowledge: Essays on philosophy and literature*. Oxford: Oxford University Press.

Nussbaum, Martha. (1995). *Poetic justice*. Boston: Beacon Press.

Pekarsky, Daniel. (1997). The place of vision in Jewish educational reform. *Journal of Jewish education, 63 (1&2)*. (Winter/Spring).

Peters, R. S. (1966). *Ethics and education*. New York: Scott, Foresman and Company.

Rorty, Richard. (1989). *Contingency, irony, and solidarity*. Cambridge: Cambridge University Press.

Rosenberg, Joel. (1984). Biblical narrative. In Barry W. Holtz. (Ed.). *Back to the sources*. New York: Simon and Schuster/Summit Books, pp. 31–82.

Scholem, Gershom. (1971). The neutralization of Messianism in early Hasidism. In Gershom Scholem. *On the Messianic idea in Judaism and other essays on Jewish Spirituality.* New York: Schocken Books.

Scholes, Robert. (1998). *The rise and fall of English.* New Haven, CT: Yale University Press.

Siegel, Harvey. (1989). Teaching, reasoning, and Dostoyevsky's The Brothers Karamazov. In Philip W. Jackson and Sophie Haroutunian-Gordon (Eds.) *From Socrates to software: The teachers as text and the text as teacher.* NSSE Yearbook, Part I. Chicago: National Society for the Study of Education.

Sternberg, Meir. (1985). *The poetics of biblical narrative.* Bloomington: Indiana University Press.

Warnke, Georgina (1987). *Gadamer: Hermeneutics, Tradition and Reason.* Stanford: Stanford University Press.

Zuckert, Catherine H. (1996). *Postmodern Platos.* Chicago: The University of Chicago Press.

Jewish History from the Academy to the Schools: Bridging the Gap

ROBERT CHAZAN AND BENJAMIN M. JACOBS

The Hebrew Bible — the foundational text of Judaism — projects history as the plane within which the divine-human relationship is realized. History is thus central to religious vision and religious life. It is hardly accidental that so much of the Hebrew Bible comprises historical narrative. The first five books of the Hebrew Bible — the Torah — constitute the most religiously meaningful element in the entire corpus; they comprise a running narrative of events from creation through the death of Moses. The subsequent six books advance the story from the demise of Moses through conquest of the Holy Land and until the destruction of Jerusalem and the First Temple. A number of subsequent biblical books — Ezra, Nehemiah, and Chronicles — are likewise entirely historical in format. Even the utterances of the prophets, which abandon the narrative format, focus on the meaning of historical events — the appearance of Assyria; the destruction of the northern kingdom; the ascendance of Babylonia; the destruction of the southern kingdom, its capital Jerusalem, and its sanctuary. History lies at the very heart of Israelite consciousness; it is the plane upon which the covenant between God and his people is realized.

As conceived by the biblical authors, history is directly controlled by God. God set history in motion through creation of the world, and God manipulates the workings of history in order to fulfil his covenant with the Israelite people. As powerful as the empires of the Assyrians and Babylonians might have appeared, they were in fact merely pawns in the

157

real dynamic of history, which encompasses the Israelites and their fulfillment or rejection of the covenant between themselves and God. Rejection of the covenant and its demands entails divine punishment; fulfillment of the covenant brings divine blessing.

Given the centrality of history in the biblical vision, the Israelite past obviously had to be pondered regularly and taught incessantly. The Bible is replete with injunctions to the people of Israel to remember — to remember God's role in creation, to remember what God has done for his people throughout history, to remember the demands and workings of the covenant. The commandment to remember is both a religious obligation and an educational imperative. The rabbis obliged Jews to recall constantly their past and to teach their children the Torah, as it presents key aspects of Israelite — and indeed all — history.

It has often been suggested that post-biblical Judaism has lost its sense of history. Post-biblical Jews wrote relatively little history, and what history they did write was often lost to Jews and preserved by others (for example, the books of the Maccabees and Josephus). In the most penetrating study of this issue to date, Yosef Hayim Yerushalmi (1982) claims that Jews never lost their sense of history. Rather, argues Yerushalmi cogently, post-biblical Jews concluded that they knew what they had to know of history — its essential mechanisms — from the biblical corpus.[1] From the Bible, they learned what history was all about: namely the punishments that befell errant Israelites and Jews and the rewards bestowed upon those loyal to the covenant. Little purpose would be served by heaping example upon example of human failure and divine punishment.

In the Yerushalmi view, Jews were constantly involved in the study of history through their regular immersion in the Hebrew Bible. The annual cycle of Bible reading in synagogues around the world constituted ongoing and intense historical study; endless rumination on the Bible in the most diverse modes of exegesis possible constituted the Jewish version of historical study. Instruction in Jewish history for both young and old was carried on through the annual cycle of Torah reading, through homiletic interpretation of the Torah text for the Jewish masses, through other synagogue liturgy, and through the key rituals of the Jewish year, with their focused attention on the past. (Ibid.)[2] To be sure, according to Yerushalmi,

---

1   The first chapter of this important study focuses on the biblical and rabbinic periods.
2   The second chapter focuses on the Middle Ages and the traditional ways in which the scheme of Jewish (and in fact all) history operates.

Jews were rarely exposed to much beyond the core historical paradigm adumbrated in the Bible, but that was because what came later seemingly had little of value to impart.

In the world of antiquity, there was another major paradigm of historical writing and teaching. The Greeks viewed history as the theater of human action, both dignified and debased. While rooted in a sense of relationship with divine forces, the Greeks wrote histories that diverged markedly from those of the Israelites. Their histories focused on human beings and involved a patriotic sense of human heroism or shortcoming in service of community or an anthropological sense of curiosity at the varieties of human thought and behavior.[3] These interests stimulated ongoing writing of histories. Because the range of human activity was so diverse and was free of constriction by an overarching paradigm, the writing of histories was genuinely valued and encouraged. One could never know what new story might hold the promise of a valuable illumination of the complex human scene.

We know now that the rigid distinction between the world of Israel and that of the Greeks is untenable. Judea of the Second Commonwealth period was part of the Hellenistic world of late antiquity, and the Jews were deeply affected by Greco-Roman modes of business, government, and thought. Josephus was surely a member in very good standing of the Jewish upper class in first-century Palestine, and his writing evidences the impact of Greek historical thinking. Nonetheless, Greek modes of thought did not affect profoundly the Jewish focus on the Israelite paradigm of history as controlled by God in the name of the covenant. The sibling religion — Christianity — was ultimately far more affected by Greco-Roman attitudes toward history, largely as a result of its fuller expansion throughout the Mediterranean basin. Even Christianity, however, did not stray in principle from the notion of divine control of history in the name of the covenant, which Christians of course saw in different terms than Jews.

During the Middle Ages, Jews wrote very little history, but continued to immerse themselves in their legacy of historical thinking. Alternative views surfaced occasionally and briefly as a result of new influences or new challenges. Two examples are useful. The first involves the heroic view of history that emerged briefly in the vigorous and creative Jewish community of Spain under Muslim rule. There, Samuel ibn Nagrela, Jewish vizier of the kingdom of Granada, wrote an epic poem detailing his

---

3   Thucydides emphasized the patriotic; Herodotus the anthropological.

military exploits, out of his sense that the God of Israel stood by to assist him at every step. (Schirman, 1954–56, I, pp. 85–92). A slightly milder version of this same heroic sense is found in the closing chapter of Abraham ibn Daud's *Sefer ha-Kabbalah* in which the author extols the achievements of the courtly circles of Iberian-Jewish culture of the tenth and eleventh centuries.

In northern Europe, the younger but equally vigorous and creative Jewish communities of Ashkenaz adumbrated their own unusual view of history — again distinguished by an emphasis on human heroism. In this case, the stimulus came from the outside, specifically the sporadic but devastating Crusader assaults during the spring of 1096. Fired by a zeal as intense as that of the Crusaders, the besieged Jews saw themselves and were seen by those who chronicled their actions as heroic warriors engaged in a battle of religious faith. Indeed, these Jewish chroniclers saw their embattled brethren as the genuine giants of the First Crusade, whose heroic commitment far exceeded that of the Christian warriors who successfully conquered Jerusalem. While God remained the ultimate controller of history, the Jews of 1096 were projected into an unusually grand role in the cosmic scheme.[4] Like that of Ibn Nagrela and Ibn Daud, this view was anomalous for medieval Jewry, which largely continued to see history in terms derived directly from the biblical legacy.

A new style of historical consciousness emerged during the 18th and 19th centuries, largely in Western Europe. The emergence of this new style reflected larger changes taking place in Western society. As the scientific revolution displaced God from his central position in the cosmos, the physical and then the biological world were increasingly seen as a setting within which natural forces interacted, without divine interference. As part of this evolving mentality, notions of history inevitably changed as well. To place this within the framework of our earlier observations, it was inevitable that the Judeo-Christian sense of history as divinely manipulated on behalf of a covenant would increasingly yield to a more Greek notion of history as the stage on which intersecting forces — physical, biological, and human — would play themselves out.

Several major, inter-related implications of this changing view of history should be noted. First, God receded from his influential role on the world scene, and with him the role of his chosen peoples. History could no longer be seen in terms of the fate of Israelites, Jews, Christians or Muslims. Secondly, the clerical leadership, which exercised disproportionate power

4   For an analysis of this history writing, see Chazan, 2000.

in medieval societies, was quickly challenged and, in many instances, displaced. This shift in leadership had important implications for educational systems, which had long been the province of clerical authority in Jewish, Christian, and Muslim societies. Finally, more democratic notions of governance and power emerged. If government was to be a natural system of power distribution intended ultimately to serve the interests of human society as a whole, then human society deserved better representation in the exercise of governmental power. These changes coalesced into a thorough rethinking of old pillars of thought and practical programs for total societal reorganization.

Jewish reactions to and absorption of the new societal ideals, including the new conceptions of history, were complex but overwhelmingly positive. These new views — with their displacement of God and his chosen peoples — offered dazzling new opportunities for the Jews of Europe. The displacement of chosen peoples in concert with the notion of government on behalf of the governed combined to offer Jews a position of legal and social equality, something rigorously denied them in pre-modern Christian societies. To be sure, in order to prove themselves worthy of a place in the new order, Jews had to participate fully in the new societies and to share their innovative assumptions. While this raised some difficulties for Jewish thought, and while some Jews were inclined to reject the demands and the gift of emancipation, the Jews of Europe and the New World largely accepted both. These Jews well understood that acceptance of the benefits and demands of emancipation would have an impact on every aspect of Jewish religious thinking and life; they embraced emancipation nonetheless.

The majority society's demand for Jewish acceptance of the new patterns of thinking should not be over-emphasized. Beyond feeling pressured to acculturate into a rapidly modernizing social setting as a way of gaining emancipatory rights, Jews felt a genuine and powerful desire to do so. They perceived the liberating force of the new science and its corollaries. At some level, Jews certainly understood that changes that had evolved among their Christian neighbors over centuries had to be introduced into Jewish life much more quickly, within decades. Jewish life in 19th century Europe thus exploded in many innovative and creative directions.

One of the most obvious elements of change involved displacement of the old internal Jewish leadership. Jewish communities throughout Western Europe wrestled with their own versions of entrenched clerical and aristocratic leadership. The rabbinic hierarchy and with it rabbinic constructions of the Jewish past had to be dismantled, and were. In the same way, the increasingly democratic tendencies of the majority made themselves felt among the Jewish minority. A wider circle of Jews demanded inclusion of their own perspectives on the past within the Jewish sense of history. A new and more diversified set of guardians of the Jewish past was created, with a new set of ideas about what Jewish history was all about.

As early as 1819, a group of young Jewish intellectuals articulated an ambitious program for reconfiguring the story of the Jewish past. These visionary Jewish intellectuals projected a three-pronged enterprise. The first element in their undertaking would involve amassing a large, diverse, and uncensored body of data. No longer would the clerical leadership of the Jewish world control the flow of information. Libraries would be combed and archives would be ransacked in search of new and untapped evidence on the Jewish past. Stage two of the program would be to write a series of histories of major Jewish communities. Recognizing correctly that the Jewish past was hardly linear and that different Jewries had evolved in diverse directions, the new Jewish historians set out to trace the divergent lines of Jewish historical development. This set of fully elaborated histories would pave the way, it was believed, for stage three: an overall appreciation of the essence of Jewishness and Judaism. New and richer data would lead to more accurate histories, which would in turn permit a full and fair statement of the essence of Jewish experience and Judaism.

This ambitious program engendered an exciting effort to rewrite the history of the Jewish people and reconceptualize Judaism. Success varied. The first stage, involving data gathering, was gloriously successful. Copious new sources were uncovered; long obscured Jewish communities resurfaced; long neglected aspects of Jewish life re-emerged. The history-writing stage was highly successful as well, although quickly fraught with unanticipated problems, to which we shall shortly turn. However, the hope that better histories of the Jews might lead to a clear and unambiguous statement of the nature of Judaism and Jewishness was utterly frustrated. In a real sense, the diversity of Jewish life uncovered during the data-gathering phase of the new enterprise made it impossible to distill any pithy statement about the nature of Judaism.

Not surprisingly, the dismantling of prior Jewish views was somewhat easier to achieve than the adumbration of a comprehensive and satisfying restatement of the Jewish past. It was not terribly difficult to dismantle constricting rabbinic constructions of the Jewish past. The uncovering of new materials — long suppressed by Jewish clerical leadership — itself altered perceptions of the Jewish past. Thus, for example, the newly discovered corpus of medieval philosophical treatises and Hebrew poetry dispelled the rabbinically inspired sense of Jewish intellectual life constrained exclusively within the four ells of the Law. Jewish intellectual life was revealed as rich and multi-faceted.

At the same time, the democratization of Jewish life made it nearly impossible to attain a comprehensive and widely accepted view of Jewish history. Competing views of the Jewish past would henceforth be the norm. These would result, in part, from the alternative interests of the historian/observers of that past and, in part, from the pressures of current events and contemporary issues, which inevitably affected the reconstructions of the past offered by historians of the Jews to their non-Jewish and Jewish readers. A number of troubling yet stimulating questions surfaced during this period. We shall deal with only two. The first involved the foci of interest of the historian/ observer; the second and more important concerned the narrative framework encompassing the evidence of the Jewish past.

Let us first examine foci of interest. What should attract the historian's eye in the plethora of new materials unearthed from libraries and archives? In former times, the answer would have been fairly simple. For the pre-modern Jewish observer, the information of utmost interest would have involved the great rabbis and rabbinic thinkers — their lives, their books, their thoughts. Again, the new and more democratic inclinations broadened the range of interest. Jewish business, Jewish community organization, Jewish political thinking, Jewish negotiations with the non-Jewish world — all these issues and more captured the imagination of the new Jewish historians.

The first of two striking examples of new foci of interest involves the quotidian aspects of past Jewish life — the realities of daily Jewish existence. One of the masterpieces of recent historical research into the Jewish past is Shlomo Dov Goitein's five-volume *A Mediterranean Society* (1967–1993). Grounded in Goitein's meticulous analysis of thousands of mundane documents from the Cairo Genizah, this monumental study follows everyday realities of medieval Jewish self-governance, economic activity, family structures, housing, food and clothing — all topics hardly conceivable in earlier phases of Jewish history writing. A second new topic emerged from the feminist revolution of the past few decades. The history of Jewish women has now emerged as an exciting new area of historical research. Their story is being reconstructed and is shedding valuable light on many further aspects of Jewish existence.

Now to our second, more important, and more problematic, issue. Again, the simple and compelling narrative framework provided by the Hebrew Bible was, for many Jews, no longer tenable. It was replaced by a sequence of difficult questions. What exactly should be the narrative framework within which the rich new data are to be embedded? Should it be a narrative of leadership, of community, of sets of communities, of religious literature and beliefs, of folkways and customs, of the life of reason, of mystical yearning, or of national aspiration? Should it focus exclusively on the Jews, or should it highlight Jewish interaction with the outside world? Does some kind of evolution form the core of the historic Jewish experience, some kind of teleological movement toward full realization of the Jewish potential or the Jewish mission?

Reconstruction of the Jewish past was in fact quickly and inevitably linked to the realities of the 19th and 20th century Jewish scene. As new Jewish inclinations and movements emerged, they generated innovative Jewish narratives. Two tendencies are evident among the earliest generations of new-style Jewish historians. The first involves politics and was occasioned by the unprecedented opportunities offered and pressures imposed by the emancipation of European Jewry. This window of opportunity, already noted in passing, resulted in a new and exciting narrative framework for telling the tale of the Jewish past. Firstly, this framework highlighted the limitations and persecution endured by earlier generations of Jews, a tale of suffering intended to suggest that the majority societies owed a profound debt to 19th century Jewry. Concurrently, telling the tale in this way echoed a note of appreciation for the changes seemingly underway.

Limitation and suffering were only half the story — the half imposed from the outside. For 19th century Jewish historians, pre-eminently Heinrich Graetz, the glory of pre-modern Jewry was its capacity not only to endure the suffering inflicted by the outside world, but also to rise above it. The most striking manifestation of this capacity for overcoming limitation and pain lay in the ceaseless Jewish commitment to learning — learning distinguished by its purported rationality. While this view is rooted in medieval Jewish polemical literature, with its complementary claims of Jewish rationality and Christian irrationality, the new historical narrative brought this message home in an especially emphatic and effective way.

The second tendency in the new style of 19th century Jewish history writing involved religion and the need for religious flexibility and change. 19th century Jews were doubly influenced in this direction. On the one hand, they shared the general discomfort with traditional religious behaviors and thinking that was endemic to the period. At the same time, as they were emerging from a long period of distancing from majority society and under pressure to accommodate as quickly as possible, Jews felt a particular urgency to alter the forms of their religious life. To an extent, such alteration could be rationalized in terms of sheer need, especially the need to maintain Jewish commitment among an increasingly disaffected younger generation. At the same time, deeper minds were unwilling to remain satisfied with the appeal to dire necessity; they were attracted to examining the record of the Jewish past. It is no accident that many of the most important 19th century Jewish researchers participated in the movements that wrestled with religious change in one way or another. Convinced that the Jewish past, including its religious ideals and practices, was hardly monolithic, these researchers focused much of their attention on the divergences and changes in Jewish religious practice and thinking over the ages. The result was a set of narratives that highlighted prior Jewish religious adaptability and responsiveness to changing circum-stances.[5]

With the emergence of Jewish nationalism toward the end of the 19th century, an entirely new set of interests emerged. Again unwilling simply to argue contemporary necessity, the Jewish nationalists, like their earlier assimilationist confrères, began intensive investigation of the past in order to discern the roots of their yearnings and to legitimize these longings. Studies of Jewish migration to the Holy Land abounded, as did analyses of the place of Zion in earlier Jewish thinking. The so-called Jerusalem School of Jewish History emerged in the 20th century as one of the most powerful voices on the Jewish intellectual scene. These researchers — giants such as Dinur, Baer, Ben-Sasson, and Ettinger — by no means abandoned the commitment ot unearthing new sources. At the same time, they embedded their findings in a historical narrative that was both informative and compelling (Myers, 1995). Not accidentally, many of them were deeply involved in the budding educational enterprise of the Jewish *Yishuv* in what was then British-controlled Palestine.

By the end of the 20th century, Western historians had largely abandoned the search for an objective and monolithic history. This has by no means entailed the dismissal of data or the acceptance of shoddy and tendentious historical reconstruction. What it has meant, rather, is growing acknowledgement that an exhaustive and definitive perspective on the past

5   For a number of valuable essays on this history writing, see Schorsch, 1994.

is not possible. Despite constant expansion of data, historians will always encounter developments for which evidence is sparse. Sometimes these developments are of great significance, for example the early history of the Israelites, of rabbinic Judaism, and of Christianity. For such developments, the alternatives are abandonment of the effort to write history (not feasible in most cases) or imaginative reconstruction. Even — or perhaps especially — where data are copious, it is increasingly acknowledged that history is written by an engaged observer. The very first step in writing history — the selection of focus — can hardly be construed as an objective move. In the process of selecting focus (and methodology as well), certain patterns immediately become possible, and others are dismissed. Likewise the choice of narrative framework provides and precludes possibilities. History writing has come to be recognized as part science and part art, with perhaps even a nod in the direction of art. History writing is seen as disciplined creativity, the product of both empirical data and personal imagination. While rigor has not been abandoned, there is a growing consensus as to the limits of rigor and objectivity in the historiographic enterprise.

* * * *

The remainder of this essay will examine the educational implications of the loss of the old historical framework and its replacement by fuller and less constricted data, the new focus on a wider range of human experience, and the search for a new narrative framework or frameworks for telling the tale of the Jewish past. How do these developments impinge on the educational endeavor? Do they enhance or impede it? While the ramifications of this new history writing are far from clear, it is fair to assume that the striking changes in the reconstruction of the Jewish past should have a significant impact on the teaching of that past. The new histories being written must make some impression — in structured or unstructured ways — in the classroom. What follows is an effort to grapple with the new Jewish history writing and its meaning for contemporary Jewish education.

A caveat: our analysis will be limited in several crucial ways. First, we will only assess these changes in one sector of the Jewish world, namely the Diaspora community of North America. Nevertheless, we will be grappling with some of the same issues as our Israeli colleagues, who have been engaged in a fascinating and highly charged debate over the rewriting of Israeli history textbooks. Second, we will not attempt to deal with every element in the diverse educational network in North America. This network includes denominational and community schools, supplementary and day schools, and primary and secondary schools. Most notably, the highly traditional religious school system — largely resistant to the developments of modernity — lies beyond our purview. What we hope to outline is a general view of Jewish history education that would probably be most appropriate for liberal and community day high schools in North America, one of the most rapidly developing sectors of Jewish schooling today. We believe that this view could be adapted to multiple settings as well. Finally, we acknowledge that statements regarding the current state of Jewish history education are largely anecdotal or impressionistic, because research on the subject is perilously scarce.[6] At the heart of this study lies the conviction that the time has come for major work to be undertaken in the field of Jewish history education.

* * * *

Jewish history education is as ancient as Jewish history itself. We have already described the essential correlation of the Bible, history and education in the pre-modern Jewish world. To study the Bible meant to glean from a historical text important religious, moral, and life lessons that could be applied in any time and place. Accordingly, until the early part of the 20th century, the teaching of Jewish history in the schools primarily entailed children memorizing and reciting Bible stories. Emphasis was placed on heroes, miraculous events, wars and conquests, or tragic situations (e.g. destruction of the Temples), as well as God's role in shepherding his chosen people through history.

It stands to reason that the developments in modern Jewish historiography described in the previous section — namely, the establishment of Jewish history as a discipline; the secularization of Jewish studies; the expansion of scholarship to include political, economic, social, as well as intellectual Jewish historical circumstances; and the development of alternative Jewish historical narratives — would necessitate a significant reconfiguration of the way Jewish history would be taught in Jewish schools. No longer could Jewish history education rely solely on the Bible as its primary textbook or on a providential view of historical development. Rather, Jewish history courses would need to teach the emergent and

---

6   The only recent major study of the field is Goldflam, 1989. For a useful literature review, see Gereboff, 1997.

expanding corpus of critical Jewish historical scholarship, adapted for pedagogical purposes. Put another way, Jewish history — now a separate and distinct component of academic Judaic studies — would need to be a separate, distinct, and altered component of the Jewish school curriculum.

However, the transition from the academy to the schools has not been an easy one. We will elaborate three significant constraints on curriculum reform in Jewish history education. First, continuity and articulation is lacking between university-based and school-based Jewish learning in America. Second, the research arm of the field of Jewish education is underdeveloped. Third, the liberal, democratic, pluralistic ethos that underlies American general education has yet to encroach fully on Jewish parochial schooling.[7]

The first limitation can best be understood in light of the historical development of American history instruction in the public schools. In the mid-19th century, as history was emerging as a scientific discipline, American historians made a concerted effort to establish a place of prominence for themselves within the modern university. Recognizing early on that the expanding public high school system would serve as both a training ground for future American citizens and a feeder for university history seminars, American historians distinguished themselves by becoming major actors in the development of curricula, methods of instruction, and standards of assessment for school history and civics courses. Their activities in the schools would be advantageous for two reasons. First, by introducing young students to some of the most current scholarship and methods being advanced in the universities, they would potentially create a cadre of disciples ready for the next level of research. Second, and more important, by directly involving themselves in public education — and citizenship education in particular — they would gain a highly visible and influential public face for themselves and their trade. (Whitman Hertzberg, 1988).

While American historians have long been among the chief advocates for history education in the public schools, Jewish historians have been conspicuously absent from direct involvement in Jewish schools. Unlike their counterparts, Jewish historians in America did not secure a place of integration, prominence, or even comfort in the universities until the mid to late 20th century. (See Ritterband and Wechsler, 1994). In the early part of

---

7   Whether or not American public education is in fact liberal, democratic and pluralistic has been the subject of much debate, but is beyond our current focus. The point remains that public education is generally more liberal, democratic, and pluralistic in principle than Jewish education.

the century, academic Judaic studies were largely confined to rabbinic seminaries and colleges of Jewish studies. Only a handful of Jewish historians held academic chairs in major research universities. Moreover, a significant number of colleges and universities had Jewish admission quotas in place. Slowly, as universities began to open up to academic Judaic studies and to Jewish students, Jewish historians concentrated on normalizing Jewish studies, as well as bolstering their own reputations in the universalistic and humanistic world of the academy. For many of these academics, this meant highlighting scholarly rigor, professionalism and dispassion, rather than serving as public advocates for models of Jewish education. In other words, it meant shying away from involvement in Jewish communal causes such as the Jewish education enterprise.

To date, few professional Jewish historians have paid much attention to the ways in which their discipline is presented and studied in Jewish schools. Few scholars have chosen to dedicate their knowledge and talent to the educational enterprise — few articles have been written on the subject, few curricula have been designed or implemented, and few sourcebooks have been produced. There are some notable exceptions. First, Judaic studies scholars have collaborated with educators at seminaries, colleges of Jewish studies, movement-based education offices, and national and local curriculum agencies to develop outlines and source materials for Jewish history courses. The work of the Melton Research Center for Jewish Education stands out in this regard. Second, popular histories written or shaped by academic historians — such as the *Heritage: Civilization and the Jews* books and videos — are valued classroom materials. But the fact remains that most school administrators and teachers are developing Jewish history/curricula in isolation from the academy. Moreover, although there are certainly some knowledgeable and talented instructors out there, most teachers of Jewish history are hardly trained as Jewish historians.[8] Hence, it is unlikely that the most current thinking in the field is being presented (even the Melton materials and *Heritage* series are decades old). Rather, in many schools, Jewish history subject matter lags as much as a generation behind Jewish history scholarship.

The second major problem with curricular reform in Jewish history

---

8   The issue of how Jewish history teachers should be trained is worthy of further explication, but beyond our current scope. Issues that need to be addressed include: how much content (Jewish history) knowledge and how much craft (education) knowledge must good teachers have, what are the best ways of conveying this knowledge to teachers, how do we certify these competencies in teachers, and how do teachers maintain and/or expand their knowledge base while in the field?

education is the lack of curriculum research being conducted in the field of Jewish education. The expansion and flourishing of academic Jewish studies did not have its counterpart in the development of academic Jewish education. In fact, until very recently, Jewish education was almost entirely beyond the scope of major research universities and schools of education in North America. Consequently, the infrastructure for academic research in Jewish education lags at least a generation behind other education disciplines.

Again, seminaries and colleges of Jewish studies, as well as denominational education offices and bureaus of Jewish education deserve much of the credit for the research that has been done to date. The massive *Bibliography of Jewish Education in the United States* (Drachler, 1996) is a testament to this work.[9] More recently, national Jewish education agencies, such as the Jewish Education Service of North America and the Coalition for the Advancement of Jewish Education, as well as private foundations such as Mandel and Avi Chai, have made significant contributions to the knowledge base. Each of these organizations has published major lengthy studies within the past few years.

Nonetheless, research in Jewish education remains limited. In part, this is because the central research paradigm is more quantitative than qualitative. The national organizations, community leaders, funders, boards of directors, and administrators who are conducting most of the major studies are generally concerned with financial and enrollment figures or with data on parents, students, and teachers' backgrounds and religious commitments. In the absence of the humanistic educational research frameworks found in universities — such as philosophy of education, history of education, and subject-specific curriculum studies — we are left with very little evidence about what has gone on, what is actually going on, and what should go on in Jewish schools today. Major philosophical and pedagogical questions regarding the Jewish education enterprise have yet to be addressed adequately: What is Jewish pedagogy? What should be the aims and outcomes of Jewish education, and why? What curricula have succeeded and failed in the past, and what can we learn from these experiences? How do intended Judaic studies curricula become operational, and how are they received? In sum, who is teaching what, why, how, and to

9   At nearly 700 pages, Drachler's bibliography is the most comprehensive in the field. For the present discussion, it is interesting to note that only about ten pages are dedicated to the place of Jewish history in the curriculum (although there are large sections specifically on Holocaust and Israel education, which include some pieces on history instruction).

what effect? Certainly, major curriculum reform in Jewish education cannot be achieved if these issues remain unexamined.

The final major constraint on curricular reform is that the liberal, democratic, pluralistic ethos underlying American public education has yet to encroach fully on Jewish schooling. Historically, Jewish education in America has attempted to balance membership in two cultures — one religious and corporate, the other secular and liberal. Negotiating this landscape meant seeking the best of both the American and Jewish educational worlds — either through supplementary religious schools, which allow children to receive a part-time Jewish education while reaping the benefits of full-time public schooling, or through day schools, which provide a dual Judaic studies and general studies curriculum. It also meant endeavoring to make the Jewish school system perfectly compatible with the public school system, not only in terms of administration, methods of instruction and the like, but also in terms of outlook and mission. Mordecai Kaplan and Samson Benderly, the founding fathers of American Jewish education, were both committed to the growth and development of a normalized Jewish life in harmony with American civilization. Jews should not separate themselves from American life, they argued. Rather, all educational efforts should be directed toward the students' self-fulfillment both as Americans and as Jews. To this end, Kaplan and Benderly advocated progressivist forms of Jewish education that would ostensibly demonstrate continuities between Jewish and American ideals.

Much of this overt commitment to acculturation was supplanted, however, in the latter decades of the 20th century. On the one hand, Jewish schooling did become entrenched in the American educational scene, as excellent day schools developed general studies curricula and college preparatory programs on a par with those in first-rate private and public schools. On the other hand, the Holocaust, the establishment of the State of Israel, the self-actualization of third generation American Jewry, the growth of movement-based American Judaism, the Six-Day War and the Arab-Israeli conflict, the 1990 National Jewish Population Study and a host of other factors, all contributed to a degree of parochial retrenchment in Jewish schools. We do not necessarily mean that schools have become increasingly theocentric. The parochialism we are describing is more cultural and ethnic in nature, stemming from what have been the mantras of American Jewish communal life for years now — identity and continuity. These issues have impinged on Jewish education in subtle and not so subtle ways. It suffices to note here that the emphasis on positive identification and social conservatism in Jewish schooling is at odds with the emphasis on pluralism and liberalism in American schooling. Consequently, Jewish schools often send mixed messages. In US history courses, American pioneers are criticized for the injustices of Manifest Destiny, while in Jewish history courses, Zionist pioneers are valorized for the workings of *Shivat Zion*. The field of Jewish education has yet to fully reconcile the particularistic nature of Jewish education with the universalistic nature of American education.

What might be done to narrow the gap? If, for example, tendentious "Jewish history" gave way to a more critical, universalistic, humanistic "history of Jews," might parochial "Jewish history education" eventually yield to a more rational, liberal, democratic "history education of Jews?" This is certainly the model we find in university-based Judaic studies programs. Of course, the comparison is limited, because the mandate of Jewish schools is broader than merely replicating the ideal of pure academic study found in universities. Jewish schools are expected to engage students in identification and effective response, not only in the dispassionate analysis favored by most academics.[10] Nevertheless, we are convinced that building bridges between the enterprises is both feasible and desirable.

To this end, in the last section of this essay, we will suggest some prospects for the teaching of Jewish history in the schools that are compatible with the contemporary study of Jewish history in academia. We will begin with an overview of the aims of Jewish history education. Next we examine what ways, for what purpose, and to what effect, can modern Jewish historiography be translated into the Jewish history curriculum. Finally, we will ask, how might Jewish history education help transform the field of Jewish education as a whole?

*   *   *   *

Traditionally, the aims of Jewish history instruction have been (1) to develop within students an emotional appreciation of Jewish values, ideals, hopes, and struggles through history, (2) to inspire students to identify with Judaism and with the Jewish people, and (3) to give students the ability to interpret contemporary Jewish life in light of Jewish history. Above all, the rationale for Jewish history education stems from the community's desire to develop in its children a full appreciation of Jewish life, so that the

---

10 For an interesting discussion of these issues, see Levstik and Barton, 2000.

children will trust the cultural environment, be loyal to it and become active participants in it.

On the surface, it might seem natural for Jewish history and Jewish education to be intimately linked, as both are concerned with the transmission and perpetuation of cultural identity. History serves to record and preserve cultural inheritances that are deemed of most worth to the present generation, while education serves to transmit and sustain cultural elements of enduring value from one generation to the next. Jewish history seems to teach that, despite periods of adaptation and adjustment in response to internal and external catalysts, Jews have consistently chosen to preserve their distinct way of life based on their commitment to a normative tradition. In other words, there seems to be an historical essence embedded in Jewish tradition that makes it continuous and enduring. In this view, Jewish education should be normative, emphasizing the transmission of the "traditions of our fathers" in order to continue the historical perpetuation of a standard Jewish culture.

The normative education paradigm has long been regnant in most Jewish education venues. Thus, it should not be surprising that most Jewish history courses have made little provision for presenting the dispassionate, critical versions of Jewish history found in academia. Instead, it has been observed that Jewish history education seldom extends beyond a rather rudimentary coverage of major trends, heroes and landmark events, with a concentration on chronological sequencing, facts and dates. Subject matter is generally presented through didactic instructional methods, especially relying on lectures and textbooks. Moreover, and perhaps most importantly, teachers tend to emphasize triumphalist, mythical, or polemical Jewish historical constructs, based on the assumption that celebratory narratives have the power to instill pride in Jewish students.[11]

To cite but one example, in many schools, the Jewish history course ends with the establishment of the State of Israel. Subsequent historical developments spanning 50 years are essentially treated as Jewish current events. Why end with the State of Israel? We can surmise three possible rationales. The first is theocentric — if Jewish history begins with the covenantal promise of Eretz Yisrael to Abraham (the "first Jew"), then it seems reasonable to end the course of Jewish history with the promise fulfilled. The second is teleological — if the destruction of European Jewry

---

11 A number of schools are committed to more secular, dispassionate, and critical approaches to Jewish history instruction. See Goldflam, 1989, pp. 33–34.

during the Holocaust is catastrophic and disheartening, then the establishment of Israel provides some sort of providential denouement. The third is nationalistic — if most schools hope to inculcate a love of Israel in their students, then presenting Israel as the antidote to the Holocaust lends credence to the Zionist idea that Israel is at the apex of Jewish civilization.

If, as we have suggested, theocentric, teleological and nationalistic versions of Jewish history are increasingly being transcended in academia, then it seems problematic that these versions continue to hold sway in the schools. Pedagogically, it is also problematic that teachers consciously or unconsciously end up imposing belief in providence, the superiority of one or another religious view, or the legitimacy of Zionism on their students by almost exclusively perpetuating these versions of Jewish history. The didactic approach can prevent students from developing their own insights regarding the subject matter. Students digest ideas emanating from teachers and textbooks, and classrooms can even become hostile environments for students who find certain beliefs or interpretations to be unacceptable or inapplicable to their own lives. Student autonomy and initiative are quashed. Learning becomes a tedious exercise of memorizing and retaining facts, rather than a stimulating process of understanding and internalizing ideas. As a result, students lose interest and motivation in the study of Jewish history. Thus, the didactic approach to Jewish history education may actually be self-defeating, because many students come to view Jewish history as boring and irrelevant. They come to consider Jewish tradition as dead and static, or even a source of resentment.

A potential solution to this problem lies in the deliberative education model. Deliberative education rejects the transmission model and aims instead to empower students to grapple with the problems that have arisen in past Jewish life and to project potential solutions that might bear implications for their own times and lives.[12] Deliberative educators argue that learners should develop skills to make reasoned and principled decisions as to how knowledge affects their own motives for action, their own commitment and their own communal involvement. From the deliberative educator's perspective, Jewish tradition will hold no meaning for students unless they are allowed to confront, question, analyze, interpret, and understand issues of Jewish history for themselves, on their own terms. If students construct their own understanding of Jewish

---

12 For a full consideration of normative versus deliberative models of Jewish education, see Rosenak, 1995.

tradition, they will assume ownership of their own Jewish values, ideas and identities.

While the deliberative approach seems appealing, it is not without its drawbacks. A more deliberative version of Jewish history instruction would place limits on the sense of shared community that schools might be hoping to foster. It would also entail challenging traditional reconstructions of the Jewish past. Thus, if the aim of Jewish education is to inspire positive Jewish identity and continuity, a problems-based approach to instruction might be considered counter-productive to the Jewish education enterprise.

Yet, the alternative — to continue to inculcate in students a normative, heavily ideological version of Jewish history — is also untenable. Modern Jewish historiography and the modern Jewish experience have repeatedly demonstrated that neither Jewish history nor Jewish education is monolithic. To reiterate an earlier point, the democratization of Jewish life in the modern world has made a comprehensive and widely accepted view of Jewish history unattainable. Competing views of the Jewish past have become the norm. To claim that Jewish history follows one simple pattern from ancient to contemporary times is therefore irresponsible, doctrinaire and neglects the spirit and standards of modern historical inquiry. To assume that Jewish education exists to inculcate a monolithic approach to tradition is likewise irresponsible, for it is indoctrinating and neglects the spirit and standards of modern liberal education.

This latter point is especially crucial for Jewish education in North America. American Jewish education serves a dual purpose — to inspire students' commitment to Judaism and to train students to be intelligent citizens of the American Jewish community. Effective participation in both Jewish and American communal life requires that children learn the ideals, habits and attitudes of American Jewry. Certainly, standards and norms have been defined in multiple ways within the community, leading to significant tension between its segments. Nonetheless, if there is a single value that all American Jews have historically embraced, it is democracy. In fact, the community has distinguished itself as one of the staunchest defenders of democratic rights and freedoms. Jewish school curricula, accordingly, have long been replete with lessons about civil liberties, separation of church and state, social justice and the like. Parents and teachers hope that American Jewish children will perpetuate the community's commitment to democratic values in the future.

However, the point has been made cogently in American education circles that democratic education is a process, not a product. In other words, democratic education requires more than education about democracy — it requires a liberal, humanistic, democratic form of education. Indeed, *what* students learn is a function of *how* they learn. Democratic values such as freedom, equality and opportunity might be perceived as personally stifling when taught through didactic methods such as lecture and recitation. If we want students to learn the workings of democracy and the value of democracy, they need to experience democracy in the classroom. As one thoughtful observer put it: "If we took freedom seriously, we would encourage each student to develop his or her own perspective on the nation — its past, present, and future. And if we took democracy seriously, we would require these students to argue and deliberate with one another about the leading public issues of their day." (Zimmerman, 2001, p. 56). Given that American Jewish children will eventually determine the fate of American Jewish society, our schools must give Jewish children the skills to make choices wisely.

What does all this mean for the Jewish education enterprise? If we take the mandate for democratic education seriously, the aim of Jewish education should not be to force children to learn a traditional canon for its own sake, because students may come to view Jewish tradition as a dead letter or even a source of resentment. Rather, Jewish education should be about the search for *meaning*. It should arouse in children the desire and capacity to *choose* Jewish history and tradition as an inspiration for personal and communal conduct. In short, Jewish education should be an exercise in open-ended inquiry. In such a scheme, modern Jewish historiography — with its inherent commitment to open-ended inquiry — would finally gain a vital link to the school curriculum. Jewish history courses in the schools, as in the academy, can be forums for discussion, debate, intellectual rigor, and the pursuit of meaning in Jewish history.

The first step in achieving this paradigm shift is for teachers to become role models of intellectual honesty and curiosity. Teachers' behavior needs to reflect a respect for reason and openness to alternative points of view. Teachers must also acknowledge why they select particular content and what lessons they hope students will learn from it. In this way, students will be introduced to critical questions regarding Jewish history education, such as: What Jewish historical knowledge is of most worth? Are certain historical events more significant and enduring, and are certain historical interpretations more illuminating than others? What personalities, events, and facts are Jewish children supposed to know and be able to retrieve as signposts of their identification with Jews and Judaism?

Regarding methods of instruction, teachers should use a variety of pedagogical techniques, from activity-based projects to lectures, based on whichever methods most effectively direct the subject matter to the desired results of the lesson (lectures can be useful for covering a large amount of background material efficiently, but should not be the only instructional procedure used in an inquiry-based classroom).[13] Overall, teachers should see their roles as co-learners and facilitators who share knowledge rather than as experts and overlords who impart it.

Second, students need to be able to judge the credibility of various claims to historical truth emanating from primary sources, secondary sources (i.e. historians), teachers, each other, and themselves. Jewish history is laden with values and commitments; learning and making history entails value judgments. Decision-making skills in history include identifying and defining problems, devising critical questions, evaluating evidence, judging biases, searching for concepts and patterns, understanding cause and effect, identifying alternatives, validating statements with specific references to evidence, predicting consequences, drawing conclusions, and justifying decisions. Indeed, these are many of the same activities in which professional Jewish historians are engaged. This is not to say that young students will be able to achieve the same sophistication as historians or students in academia. However, by working as "student Jewish historians" they should be able to construct their own independent and thoughtful judgments.[14] This entails engaging primary and secondary sources at their level of meaning, and asking questions such as: What does the author intend to convey in this source? What narrative structure is in use in this source, and for what purposes? In what ways does this source impinge on my (the student's) understanding of Jewish history? What sorts of commitments does this source inspire?

Third, students should be exposed to the warts of Jewish history as well as the wonders. This means entering areas that may previously have been closed to discussion or debate.[15] Complex and controversial issues such as the documentary hypothesis, the Christian schism, the Talmud's views on women, the Zionist settlement of Palestine, and Jonathan Pollard, should all be open to rational dialogue and be accorded balanced treatment. Not only would this offer students a more complete picture of issues and problems in Jewish history, it would show them the shortcomings of the past and present, so as to imbue them with a passion for changing the

13 For an extensive discussion of methods of history instruction, see Thornton, 2001.
14 Exemplary models of history instruction using primary sources can be found in Holt, 1990, and Kobrin, 1996.
15 The idea of opening "closed areas" is explored in Hunt and Metcalf, 1968.

future. Debate and dialogue would allow students to encounter and address controversial issues in a safe space, among trusted peers and mentors. This collaboration would result in the creation of a pluralistic group, whose members will presumably continue to value, respect, and be loyal to one another when they become citizens of the adult Jewish community.

Fourth, a wide range of Jewish historical experience should be open to investigation. Selecting subject matter and devising a scope and sequence to study three thousand years of history is certainly not an easy task. Perhaps this is why most Jewish history courses have focused on major ideas, trends, heroes and landmark events. But we are in a period today of remarkable Jewish historiographic creativity. New research and new histories abound for every period of the Jewish past. Entirely new themes have emerged, alongside old and established interests. And more sectors of the Jewish community have become the subject of intensified research: Jewish women, Sephardic Jewry, Russian Jewry, small town/rural European and American Jewry. All these sectors deserve to be studied as well, not necessarily at the expense of the "greats," but alongside them. Primary historical sources such as letters, diaries and journals of common folk can be especially meaningful and useful when used in conjunction with the traditional historical narratives about landmark people and events.

Last, students should be encouraged to develop the art of historical writing. The process of marshalling, arranging, analyzing, and presenting evidence entails both technical accuracy and creative finesse, so that a responsible, convincing, and engaging argument can be made. History writing is also the combined byproduct of empirical research and personal reflection. Thus, in the process of constructing their own histories, students may come to feel intellectually and emotionally linked with their heritage, and intellectually and emotionally self-aware, for it reminds them that Jewish history and memory are fundamentally about *them*, about how they identify themselves as Jews.

In sum, we envision a Jewish history classroom in which teachers will encourage openness and use a variety of pedagogical techniques; students will be trained in the skills of inquiry and decision-making; Jewish history will be taught warts and all and include a variety of sectors of the Jewish community; and, students will be encouraged to express their own perspectives on the subject matter by practicing the art of historical writing.

What we are proposing is a middle ground between normative and deliberative education. An emphasis on issues and problems, criticism, multiple perspectives, and choice need not come at the expense of conveying content lessons or inculcating allegiances and values. Indeed, the content and texts to be studied will have to be carefully selected and should be representative of the major strains of Jewish culture and thought. Furthermore, at its core, the discussion is rooted in Jewish history, which tells us the many ways in which Jews have adapted to changing environments and circumstances while preserving that which they consider essential to their cultural identity.

Neither side of this equation — creativity or continuity — should be disregarded in Jewish education. The key is ensuring the proper balance between the normative and the deliberative, which we might call "healthy skepticism." If students become critical thinkers about Jewish history, they can devise creative solutions to the challenges of continuity that Jews have faced in any given time and place, including our world today.

Thus conceived, Jewish history education has the potential to serve at the vanguard of Jewish education. Ultimately, if students are able to learn, think, and care about Jews and Judaism in their own terms, they will be able to understand their own Jewish values and grow into thoughtful, responsible members of the Jewish community. If they are trained with the proper tools for inquiry, they may someday be able to create their own forms of Jewish history, culture, literature and thought.

References

Chazan, Robert. (2000). *God, humanity, and history: The Hebrew first crusade narratives*. Berkeley: The University of California Press.

Drachler, Norman. (1996). *A bibliography of Jewish education in the United States*. Indiana: Wayne State University Press.

Gereboff, Joel. (1997). Can the teaching of Jewish history be anything but the teaching of myth? In S. Daniel Breslauer. (Ed.). *The seductiveness of Jewish myth: Challenge or response?* Albany, NY: SUNY Press, pp. 43–69.

Goitein, S. D. (1967–93). *A Mediterranean society: The Jewish communities of the Arab world as portrayed in the documents of the Cairo genizah*. 6 vols. Berkeley: The University of California Press.

Goldflam, Dov. (1989). Survey of current practices and attitudes of Jewish History teachers in the high Jewish day schools in the United States. Unpublished Ph.D. dissertation, University of Miami.

Holt, Tom. (1990). *Thinking historically: Narrative, imagination and understanding*. New York: College Entrance Examination Board.

Hunt, Maurice P. and Metcalf, Lawrence E. (1955/1968). *Teaching high school social studies*. 2nd ed. New York: Harper and Brothers.

ibn Daud, Abraham. (1967). *Sefer ha-Qabbalah*. [The book of tradition]. Gerson D. Cohen. (Ed. and trans.) Philadelphia: Jewish Publication Society.

Kobrin, David. (1996). *Beyond the textbook: Teaching history using documents and primary sources*. Portsmouth, NH: Heinemann.

Levstik, Linda S. and Barton, Keith C. (2000). Committing acts of history: Mediated action, humanistic education, and participatory democracy. Paper presented at the Annual Meeting of the American Educational Research Association, New Orleans, April.

Myers, David. (1995). *Reinventing the Jewish past: European Jewish intellectuals and the Zionist return to history*. New York: Oxford University Press.

Ritterband, Paul and Wechsler, Harold S. (1994). *Jewish learning in American universities: The first century*. Bloomington, IN: Indiana University Press.

Rosenak, Michael. (1995). *Roads to the palace: Jewish texts and teaching*. Providence, RI: Berghahn Books.

Schirman, Haim. (1954–56). *Ha-shirah ha-'Ivrit be-Sefard uve-Provens*. [Hebrew poetry in Spain and Provence]. 2 vols. Jerusalem: Bialik Institute.

Schorsch, Ismar. (1994). *From text to context: The turn to history in modern Judaism*. Hanover, NH: Brandeis University Press.

Thornton, Stephen J. (2001). Subject specific teaching methods: History. In Jere Brophy. (Ed.). *Advances in research on teaching, Vol. 8: Subject specific teaching methods*. Greenwich, CT: JAI Press.

Whitman Hertzberg, Hazel. (1988). Are method and content enemies?. In Bernard Gifford. (Ed.). *History in the schools: What shall we teach?* New York: Macmillan Publishing Company.

Yerushalmi, Yosef Hayim. (1982). *Zakhor: Jewish history and Jewish memory*. Seattle: University of Washington Press.

Zimmerman, Jonathan. (2001). Talking about terrorism. *Education Week*. 10th March.

A Community of Teacher-Readers

Sam Wineburg and Pam Grossman

In the West, literacy has traditionally been the province of the cleric, and the monastery in which he dwelt was our first library. In the monastery of late antiquity, the religious scholar withdrew from the hustle-bustle of urban life seeking tranquility and serenity, often in desolate outreaches of civilization. The monk engaged in silent contemplation and prayer in the solitude of his cell, seeking to experience his God directly, without intermediary. Silence filled the air and voices, when audible, were hushed to allow the Divine response to be heard.

The monastery is important because it bequeathed to us the modern institution of the library which, despite its secularity, bears a striking resemblance to its religious predecessor. The defining feature of the library is its solitude, a quiet oasis where one can plumb one's interests protected from the din of the outside world. Signs like "Quiet Please" underscore the conventions parodied in cartoon strips and children's stories. Even the library's physical structure reinforces features of solitude. The individual study carrels, reminiscent of the monk's cell, communicate beliefs about how we think we learn: by ourselves, set apart from others, in well-lit, enclosed capsules. The message is clear: We should not talk to others but to our books.

Compare the library to the *Beit Midrash*, or study hall of the traditional yeshivah. In it there are no study carrels. Indeed the very idea of the carrel is foreign. So is silence. The *Beit Midrash* hums with overlapping voices in spirited debate. The outsider is struck by the seeming disorder of it all:

students do not sit quietly in rows of neatly arranged desks but bob up and down in their seats, thumbs pointed upward cutting the air for emphasis. Students do no learn individually but in *hevruta*, pairs, and the text before them is not read but probed. Indeed, Hebrew usage reflects this distinction: one do not 'read' Torah, but 'studies' it.

Until recently, the conduct of Western schooling and the enterprise of educational research that accompanied it could claim lineage back to the tradition of the monastery, but not to the Beit Midrash. In our professional journals and research projects, reading is understood to be a solitary act, individually assessed and measured, and best done in quiet moments immortalized by an acronym known to every American school child: SSR or, Sustained *Silent* Reading. While educational researchers have experimented with various forms of group or cooperative learning, in most cases these interventions did little to alter the fundamental status of reading as an individual act, conducted in silence.

One of the few venues in the secular world in which people learn to "read in public" is the literature classroom, where groups of students, guided by a single teacher, consider a common text and explore its meaning in discussion. But these discussions are marked by a fundamental inequality. For the teacher, the text is not read so much as remembered, drawing on the teacher's previous encounters with it in university or previous years of teaching. For students, the experience with *Hamlet*, *Heart of Darkness*, or *Huckleberry Finn* is a virgin encounter, often resulting in confusion or, worse, boredom. The ensuing discussion typically bears little resemblance to the give and take between equals but instead has been characterized as a "gentle inquisition" (cf. Eeds and Wells, 1989), in which teachers ferret out in discussion predetermined answers to predetermined questions.

Where, then, are teachers of the textual disciplines, literature and history, to find renewal as readers if most of their time is spent delivering shopworn answers to remembered texts rather than formulating new questions to fresh texts? It is this question — the lack of professional development opportunities for teachers in the humanities — that led us to experiment with an idea at once radical and simple: the creation of a reading group for teachers in the walls of their own school.

Background

In 1995, with a grant from the James S. McDonnell Foundation Program "Cognitive Studies in Educational Practice," we located ourselves in the midst of an urban high school. Our long-term goal (and the reason the project attracted the school's attention) was to bring teachers together from two different departments to create an interdisciplinary curriculum exploring the disciplinary principles of history and literature. But before we engaged in curriculum writing, we needed to lay the intellectual groundwork for communal understanding.

To do this, we sought to build a teacher community around the reading of texts, seeking to import the social form of the book club (or, in Europe, the "café klatch") from the comfort of the middle class living room to the confines of the dilapidated urban high school. Grant monies, along with enthusiastic support from the local school district, allowed us to do what few projects have done: we were able to buy teachers' time on a bi-weekly basis, permitting them to leave the classroom for an entire day (while the grant provided substitute teachers) to come together to read full-length pieces of history and fiction, to discuss disciplinary principles, and to deliberate over curriculum design (see Grossman, Wineburg and Woolworth, 2001; Thomas, Wineburg, Grossman, Myhre and Woolworth, 1998; Wineburg and Grossman, 1998; 2000).

Our plans were grand. We planned to compare our own readings of texts to the responses of high school students to the same texts; we would free up teachers to observe in each other's classrooms, where they would engage students in clinical interviews about disciplinary knowledge; we would videotape teachers as they tried out new forms of classroom discussion and then show the tapes during our group meetings where, as a community, we could engage in the process of the design, revision, and reformulation of instruction. Informed by the writings of Ann Brown (1992), Allan Collins (1992), Barbara Rogoff (1994); Rogoff, Baker-Sennett, Lacasa, Goldsmith (1995) and others, we argued that rather than locating our work on a bucolic college campus (typically the site of professional development in the humanities in North America) we should create a reading community amidst the meandering hallways, aluminum sided trailers, and classrooms-without-telephones of the high school. In short, we had time, we had resources, we support from the local district as well as the particular school, and we had willing teachers who saw the project as a gift from heaven. We were ready to hit the ground running.

After one of our first all-day meetings, Dave, an experienced literature teacher, called to tell us that he was leaving the project. He had spent the morning reading texts in a small-group activity with some of his younger colleagues and complained that he didn't "have the stomach" to read with colleagues who did not share his deep knowledge of literature or his commitment to intellectual inquiry.

By the fifth group meeting, we began to notice that Heather, an articulate literature teacher relatively new to teaching, had grown quiet. In contrast to our early meetings in which Heather had been a lively contributor, she now said little. In an interview at the end of the first year, Heather explained that she had become aware of the costs of talking about books and "making mistakes" in front of her department chair, the person who would seal her fate by assigning her to teach freshmen or seniors, regular or honors students. Heather's contributions to discussions now passed through a filter in which she weighed risks and benefits in a complex personal and vocational calculus.

By the end of the first year, Lee, a history teacher, and Barb, a literature teacher, had settled into a predictable routine of head-to-head disputes (cf. Hamel, 2001; Wineburg and Grossman, 2001). At issue were questions at the intersection of history and fiction: What is the role of the reader vis-à-vis the text? How stable is the text and what is the "truth" of an interpretation? How do we judge competing interpretations and arrive at criteria for assaying intellectual claims? In these discussions we heard echoes of the heady epistemological issues that have injected fresh life into discussions in the humanities since the linguistic turn, (cf. Wineburg, 2001). Yet the teachers in our project heard something different. To them, these exchanges were emblematic of personality conflicts played out in public view. For many, airy questions of epistemology were eclipsed by issues of gender, identity, and forms of power exacted through discourse.

Among our 22 participants, Grace immediately stood out. Unlike her liberal colleagues, who espoused progressive educational and social ideals, Grace was conservative in her beliefs and, at least in the early phase of the project, willing to share them. But as the project matured, Grace began to sense a hostile atmosphere when she expressed ideas that ran afoul of the prevailing current. All diversity is tolerated in this group, she once remarked, on the condition that it is the "right diversity." The books we read and the issues we broached — from the topic of gang rape in Nathan McCall's (1994) *Makes Me Wanna Holler* to notions of Eleanor Roosevelt's alleged homosexuality in Doris Kearns Goodwin's (1994) *No Ordinary Time*; to issues of silencing the other in Stephan Ambrose's (1996) *Undaunted Courage* and the moral dilemma of "justified" murder in Bharati Mukherjee's (1989) *Jasmine* – touched on questions at the heart of the humanities: what does it mean to be human, in its darkest or most sublime dimensions? On more than one occasion, when Grace spoke her truth, eyes rolled and muttering under the breath began. Over time our group meetings became a place for Grace to mask her real self — not reveal it.

Were we guilty of choosing the wrong school for our project? Were the teachers we recruited small minded and petty? Were they less generous and more callous than the rest of us, unrepresentative of other adults who might gather at other schools? We believe, in fact, that the opposite is true. If other projects do not experience similar obstacles on the way to creating community, we bet that they either began with self-selected volunteers or met for only a limited time.

Indeed, many teacher development projects are configured to prevent issues of self and professional identity from entering into the workplace and thus end up tinkering at the margins of teacher change (cf. Miller and Lord, 1993). Ironically, the typical profile of the teacher who seeks professional development in the humanities is the person who needs it least, a self-starter already motivated to learn, to read, and to stretch beyond his or her present understanding. But what about teachers who would never choose to travel to a university campus in the summer to attend a professional development institute? Because our project offered compensation for participation, and because of the convenience of locating ourselves in their workplace, we attracted teachers who would not have otherwise participated. Furthermore, because we intervened at the departmental rather than at the individual level, our allies were the two department chairs, strategic lynchpins typically overlooked in discussions of high school reform (Grossman, 1996). In several instances, department chairs "strongly recommended" that individual members participate in this project, creating a subgroup we refer to as *impressed volunteers* (Grossman, Wineburg and Woolworth, 2001); teachers who technically volunteered but only because their department chairs strongly pressed them to do so. Our final group of 22 teachers, drawn from English and history, with representatives from English as a Second Language and special education, was a mix of eager and reluctant learners, fence sitters and those who came under gentle duress. In this sense, our group better reflected the overall make-up of teachers in the school than would participants at a special summer program or brief workshop.

Our work of reading together was transacted on a public stage, and our community members were "worse than perfect strangers." Strangers may not have a strong basis on which to build community, but they are at least not burdened by history. In some cases, teachers in our project had been working side-by-side for decades, but had never before seen each other teach. Instead, they brought to the table years of hearsay from legions of 14 and 15-year-old informants. These impressions created a charged atmosphere that highlighted the disjuncture between participants' *performed identities* and their *perceived identities* by the group (cf. Goffman, 1959). The social framework that our 22 participants enacted as they and we came together constrained and enabled, setting our parameters and changing them as we went along. Collectively, we resembled the proverbial Geertzian spider caught in webs of interaction that we ourselves had woven and from which we would have to extricate ourselves in order to create community.

Affect was the common thread in issues that marked our project in its first year: feelings of tension, anger, fear, exposure, denial, face-saving, positioning, ego-protecting, and embarrassment. Although we hoped to create a "Cognitively-Based Model for Teaching," we quickly realized that we were in a mine field: the psychological research tools we knew best, think-alouds, clinical interviews, and task analyses, would have to wait. Our most pressing concerns as project facilitators, researchers, and members of the group had most to do with creating and sustaining a safe place for adult learning in the day-to-day grind of the urban school. The challenges of creating such a space constituted a daunting and draining intellectual task. We put down our educational research books and turned to other literatures not because our familiar sources were wrong, but because they were mute about the practical problems of school change that confronted us at every turn (cf. Fox, 1985).

Pseudocommunity

In our naïveté, we thought that by offering teachers time and resources we were offering succor to weary travelers. But as change agents we failed to understand the weight of tradition. There is simply no history in American city high schools of teachers spending chunks of time together reading and arguing about texts. When teachers do meet, the focus is on administrative tasks — new initiatives for scheduling, new testing programs for students, or new forms of school governance. Unlike the people with whom we form voluntary associations — in our synagogues, social clubs and neighbor-hoods — our workplace colleagues are often people with whom we would not, had we our druthers, choose to associate. This is particularly true in the American public school, in which choices about hiring are made by a centralized district office and not the teachers working in a given school.

Schools that are characterized by a congenial working climate deal with the diversity of teachers and the different views they hold by establishing (mostly tactic) forms of interaction that allow people to get along in a friendly manner, never treading on each other's toes or invading another's personal space. But we should not mistake such surface friendliness as "teacher community." Typically, in large schools, it represents something that we refer to as *pseudocommunity*.

As social groups start to form, individuals have a natural tendency to *play community*, to act as if they are already a community that shares values and common beliefs. Playing community, or pseudocommunity, draws on cultural notions of interaction often found in middle-class, well-educated settings. The imperative of pseudocommunity is to "behave *as if* we all we agree." An interactional congeniality is maintained by a veneer of friendliness, hyper-vigilant to prohibit any trespass of personal space.

The maintenance of pseudocommunity pivots on the suppression of conflict. Groups regulate face-to-face interactions with the tacit under-standing that it is against the rules to challenge others or press too hard for clarification. This arrangement paves the way for the *illusion of consensus*. Because there is no genuine follow-up, conversation partners are able to speak at soaring levels of generality that allow each to impute his or her own meanings to the groups' abstractions. For example, if notions of "critical thinking" or "interdisciplinary curriculum" are never defined, every participant can agree to the common cause without giving it so much as a second thought.

Pseudocommunities regulate speech by appointing a facilitator to control discussion or by allowing a group member — often the most voluble or pushy–to seize the conversational reins. These mouthpieces emerge not because they express the collective will of the group (a will that remains ill-defined, in any event) but because they are verbally agile or because no one else is willing to challenge their dominance. The implicit rules of pseudocommunity dictate that discussion leaders make no attempt to elicit the thoughts of the whole group in order to bring to the surface underlying tensions or disagreements. Silence goes unquestioned because the rules of interaction prevent direct interrogation or unexpected exchanges, such as publicly turning to the person next to you and asking, "What is *your* position on that last point?"

At the heart of pseudocommunity is the distinction between hidden and revealed or, to use the dramatalurgical language of Erving Goffman (1959), the distinction between back stage and front stage. The key to maintaining a surface ésprit de corps is the curtain separating front from back stage, and the fact that only some group members are allowed behind it. So, while nonverbal behavior may be noticed and registered by the group, it becomes the topic of back stage rather than front stage discussion. "Did you see Ed roll his eyes when Ann started speaking" is whispered furtively near the coffee dispenser but never brought before the whole group for public inspection. Even if the whole group hears a hurtful remark, such as a barb that masquerades as an innocent joke, the victim's wound is dressed off-stage (in the restroom, in the parking lot after the meeting, on the phone that evening). If some type of redress is demanded of the offending party, it is an issue between individuals rather than a topic for the entire group. This fact reveals the lie at the heart of pseudocommunity: *there is no authentic sense of shared communal space but only individuals interacting with other individuals.*

The predominant mode of interaction in pseudocommunity is what Goffman calls "impression management," where individuals "perform" identities that typically (but not always) reflect positively on them. We say 'not always' because some social roles are performed not because they flatter the performer but because they achieve other desired ends. Individuals may don the mask of victim who, through expressions of incompetence, hurt, or low self-esteem, seeks the group's sympathy. The execution of roles in pseudocommunity goes smoothly as long as everyone gets to play the role he or she wants without being challenged. But a threat to pseudocommunity — one which looms larger as brief, infrequent meetings turn into longer, more frequent ones — is the question of authenticity: Is a given player "authorized" to give a particular perform-ance? In teaching, where social norms prescribe the role of the competent, committed educator, the question before the group is the fit between an individual's publicly performed identity and the "book" on the performer in the region hidden from view. This hidden region is, of course, the classroom — seen daily by scores of students but largely veiled from the eyes of co-workers. Because information from this region can disrupt one's performed identity, it is viewed as dangerous territory, access to which is guarded, and information from which is tightly controlled.

Beyond Pseudocommunity

By creating a book-club in the workplace and by providing teachers with more time for professional development than they ever imagined, it became harder and harder to pretend that there was general agreement on the central issues of teaching the humanities. After six months together it because impossible to ignore the cracks in pseudocommunity. Incidents of eye rolling, ridicule, and muttering under the breath continued to occur. Often this behavior came clothed in a jocularity that provoked laughter but left a sting in its wake. When Frank, a history teacher and coach of one of the sports teams, suggested a book for our upcoming summer institute he was cut off with the comment, "We're *not* going to all read the sports page!" Chuckles echoed, but the intent of putting Frank in his place was unmistakable.

Four months after we launched our project, our group of 22 teachers had divided into multiple factions and alliances. Pre-existing workplace conflicts, normally held in check by the limited contact during the school day, were given new life by our lengthy meetings. As project leaders we knew we needed to do something to hold the group together. In our darkest moments we feared that our three-year project would finish two and a half years ahead of schedule. As we saw it, the most pressing need was to formulate some ground rules for civil discussion, some way to restore a safe space for all participants.

We sensed from the outset that the social issues of adults coming together to read texts in the workplace might present new challenges. But in our theoretical models as well as in the primary literatures in which we located our work, these issues occupied the shadowy margins. Indeed, in the context in which we competed for grant monies, it is unlikely that we would have received funding had we showcased the social aspects of our work and downplayed the cognitive ones. To be sure, there was a recognition that teachers had to be motivated to do this work, and had to find a way to work together, but these issues were often viewed as items to be checked off before the real work could proceed.

Emotions in our project spanned the range from despair to elation. Positive affect, in fact, was the glue that ultimately held the project together, that made the struggle worthwhile. The joy of learning in a group, the élan that develops among people who work hard together, is also a missing element from the literature on cognitive change. Even the now-fashionable formulations of "distributed cognition" ignore issues of desire, fondness, affection, and respect — feelings that ultimately determine our willingness to learn from and with others (cf. Schwab, 1978). The emotional context underlying social forms of learning must be addressed as we move from highly individualistic models of cognition to models of cognition as a social enterprise. Groups can possess tremendous social and intellectual capital, but if the individuals in them are not ready to relinquish prior grudges and start over, the rich cognitive resources of the group will go untapped.

Even though we have provided here various examples of charged and tense manifestations of affect, our project could not have progressed had we not also experienced moments of goodwill and ésprit de corps. And so, Dave, who left the project in its early months, returned out of respect for a colleague's report that good things were in the making. With his deep background in literature, Dave had little to learn about subject matter. But the group offered Dave a chance to craft a professional identity that took seriously his own responsibility for the learning of new department members. Grace also left the project for a while. She, too, rejoined at her colleagues' urging, ultimately forging close relationships with people whose political views she strongly opposed. With time Heather got over her reluctance to speak and after three years of the project emerged as one of its leaders, responsible for extending the book club model from two departments to the entire school.

Obstacles to Community

Our experience vividly demonstrates that time and resources are necessary but insufficient ingredients for building community. In planning this project, we thought we had addressed the primary desiderata that had foiled previous efforts at creating learning environments. We located our work in the midst of the teachers' workplace, believing that a group that took root in its everyday context had a much greater chance of survival than one imported from a more distant locale. We tried to steer a middle course between individual and whole-school change by focusing on the department. We had buy-in across multiple levels of the system — from the district, principal, department chairs, and teachers themselves. And we had the luxury of day-long meetings once a month, in addition to the more rushed, and typical, after-school meetings.

In providing time to reflect and read together, we thought we were responding to teachers' stated needs. What we didn't fully understand is that in offering resources of time and space, we unwittingly created an unfamiliar social forum that demanded new forms of social and intellectual participation (cf. Rogoff, 1994; Rogoff et al., 1995). Our first lesson as change agents/researchers was that structural arrangements alone cannot teach people how to interact differently. By providing an extended forum for teachers to meet and engage in discussion about provocative texts, we inadvertently created a public stage on which co-workers could enact longstanding conflicts and question each other's credibility.

In retrospect, we should have known how difficult it would be to change the familiar folkways of schooling. Privacy persists in the urban high school for good reasons, shielding both outstanding and weaker teachers from the public gaze (cf. Little, 1990). Few teachers entered the profession to work with other adults. When pressures develop from working with other adults in crowded and often financially-strapped settings, retreating to the classroom provides a convenient escape. In a setting in which teachers do not necessarily share common visions and pedagogical philosophies, it is far easier to mark papers alone than to work through conflicts with other adults who do not share your beliefs.

In contrast to the idealistic visions sketched in the advocacy literature on teacher community, bringing teachers together can hurt as well as help. Reducing isolation can unleash workplace feuds that were, ironically, kept in check by the very isolation in which teachers work. To assume that just because teachers have experience in creating environments for children, they can spontaneously organize themselves into congenial social units reflects a romanticism that misrepresents the realities of group dynamics (cf. Hargraves, 1996). Teacher community works most smoothly when teachers self-select into groups of like-minded colleagues. Longstanding teacher collectives, such as the Brookline Consortium in Massachusetts or the San Francisco Bay Area Writing Project, most often consist of such self-selected volunteers. Similarly, discussions of school community often focus on sites such as New York City's Central Park East where teachers are chosen because of their adherence to the school's clearly articulated mission and philosophy. Such schools may represent an ideal, but they are far from representative of the typical urban comprehensive school, which draws together teachers with a dizzying mix of philosophies, educational backgrounds, subject matter commitments, political and religious beliefs, and beliefs about students and learning.

Community and Diversity

A primary goal of a community of learners in a pluralistic society is to learn to see difference as a resource rather than a liability. We experienced momentary recognition of this possibility, even as we struggled to hold on to it. We have consciously refrained from claiming that we "attained community," in part because we believe that community is always in flux, always an attempt by imperfect human beings to move closer to a utopian goal. Despite our ability to traverse a good stretch of the territory between a group of teachers and a community of teacher-learners, we remain painfully aware of the fragility of the group that came together. For us, community is a journey rather than a destination, a verb rather than a noun.

Grant monies and incentives allowed us to put together a diverse group of teachers who, left to their own devices, would not have chosen to spend time together. The group mirrored various fault lines, from ethnic, racial, political and religious differences to differences that matter in the context of school: differences in educational philosophy, subject matter perspectives, pedagogy, and beliefs about students. As the group began to coalesce, individuals who saw themselves and were seen by the group as deviating from the mainstream were pushed to the margins. This process of defining both a center and a periphery is a natural process in any collective dedicated to maintaining a diverse membership. But our experience refutes idealistic notions of the community's desire for diversity. *Community and diversity are in constant tension.* As individuals forge a common vision, the centripetal forces of community pose a constant threat to the centrifugal force of diversity. By its very nature, community presses for consensus and suppresses dissent. Without constant vigilance, diversities of many kinds may not survive the community's formation. Left on their own, large groups retreat from the public space and begin to disperse into smaller units based on perceived or actual similarity. Given this constant threat to diversity, much care has to be given to fostering experiences that bring — and keep — a group together.

Common experiences provide a foundation on which to build community — hence the team-building exercises that have become so popular in the corporate as well as the educational world. We too realized the importance of common experience as a counterbalance to the centrifugal forces of diversity. But instead of trekking through the woods or scaling a mountain, we located the common experiences for our project in something much closer to the spirit of schooling and the humanities: We shared common texts.

In the beginning, these texts only highlighted our differences, but this was a crucial step that pushed us beyond the limitations of pseudocommunity. Our collective growth came not because we lost the distinctiveness of the different readings we brought to *Good Scent from a Strange Mountain* and *No Ordinary Time, Makes Me Wanna Holler,* and *The Organic Machine,* but because we came to understand these differences more fully.

In the humanities, which seek to expand and enrich understanding of the human condition in all its multiplicity, a good text is one that can be pushed, pulled, and stretched to cover this vast terrain. As our list of common texts grew, we also began to understand how individuals responded to certain types of texts or to particular themes. People came to know each other in new ways as a result of our joint readings. We came to realize that our collective readings were far richer than the reading of any one member, and the process of reading together changed the reading we did alone. As in a successful book club, seminar, or Beit Midrash, we began, in a Bakhtinian spirit, to hear the "voices" of group members as we read alone. Our way of reading came to be shaped by our anticipated responses to predicted readings of other group members. To be sure, our readings continued to reflect the predispositions, predilections, and tastes that each individual brought to the group. But at the same time, the communal space of listening, learning, and arguing over books stretched us in ways that no one could have anticipated (Grossman et al., 2001).

Conclusion

If the last five years of field research have taught us anything, it is that we cannot treat issues of social context, workplace and vocational norms, interpersonal histories and issues of identity as someone else's theoretical problem. These issues are not prerequisites before we turn to the "real" work of school change. If we want to create a form of education research that has relevance outside of the controlled setting of the laboratory we must, in a Lewinian spirit, make the social world our laboratory. In schools, universities, hospitals, prisons, accounting firms, or anywhere where people work together on a daily basis, individuals bring to the table histories of beliefs, grudges, fears, insecurities, and needs for approval. Working through these issues — indeed, creating the structures for group cognition that deal with these issues systematically — must be at the forefront of our collective research agenda. Otherwise, we will continue to experience success in changing isolated parts of the school day — tinkering with one section of the science, reading, or math curriculum — but we will not, in any fundamental way, alter the cognitive, social, or moral landscape of the workplace.

References

Ambrose, S. E. (1996). *Undaunted courage: Meriwether Lewis, Thomas Jefferson, and the opening of the American West.* New York: Simon and Schuster.

Brown, A. L (1992). Design experiments: Theoretical and methodological challenges in creating complex interventions in classroom settings. *Journal of the Learning Sciences, 2,* pp. 141–178.

Collins, A. (1992). Toward a design science of education. In E. Scanlon and T. O'Shea (Eds.). *New directions in educational technology.* New York: Springer-Verlag, pp. 15–22.

Eeds, M., and Wells, D. (1989). Grand conversations: An exploration of meaning construction in literature study groups. *Research in the Teaching of English, 23,* pp. 4–29.

Fish, S. (1980). *Is there a text in this class?* Cambridge, MA: Harvard.

Fox, S. (1985). The vitality of theory in Schwab's conception of the practical. *Curriculum Inquiry, 15, pp. 63–88.*

Goffman, E. (1959). *The presentation of self in everyday life.* New York: Anchor.

Goodwin, D. K. (1994). *No ordinary time.* New York: Touchstone.

Grossman, P. L. (1996). Of regularities and reform: Navigating the subject-specific territory of high schools. In M. W. McLaughlin and I. Oberman. (Eds.). *Teacher learning: New policies, new practices.* New York: Teachers College Press, pp. 39–47.

Grossman, P., Wineburg, S., and Woolworth, S. (2001). Toward a theory of teacher community. *Teachers College Record, 103,* pp. 942–1010.

Hamel, F. (2000). Disciplinary landscapes, interdisciplinary collaboration. In S. Wineburg and P. Grossman (Eds.). *Interdisciplinary curriculum: Challenges to implementation.* New York: Teachers College Press.

Little, J. W. (1990). The persistence of privacy: Autonomy and initiative in teacher professional relations. *Teachers College Record, 91,* pp. 509–536.

McCall, N. (1994). *Makes me wanna holler: A young black man in America.* New York: Random House.

Miller, B., and Lord, B. (1993). *Staff development in four districts.* Newton, MA: Educational Development Center.

Mukherjee, B. (1989). *Jasmine.* New York: Fawcett Crest

Rogoff, B. (1994). Developing understanding of the idea of communities. *Mind, Culture and Society, 1,* pp. 209–229.

Rogoff, B., Baker-Sennett, J., Lacasa, P., and Goldsmith, D. (1995). Development through participation in sociocultural activity. In J. Goodnow, P. Miller, and F. Kessel (Eds.), *Cultural practices as contexts for development.* San Francisco: Jossey-Bass.

Schwab, J. (1978). Eros and education. In I. Westbury and N. J. Wiklkof (Eds.). *Science, curriculum, and liberal education.* Chicago: University of Chicago Press.

Schwab, J. J. (1978). Education and the structure of the disciplines. In I. Westbury and N. J. Wiklkof (Eds.). *Science, curriculum, and liberal education.* Chicago: The University of Chicago Press.

Thomas, G., Wineburg, S., Grossman, P., Myhre, O., Woolworth, S. (1998). In the company of teachers: An interim report on the development of a community of teacher learners. *Teaching and Teacher Education, 14*, pp. 180–195.

Westheimer, J. (1998). *Among school teachers: Community, autonomy, and ideology in teachers' work.* New York: Teachers College.

Wineburg, S, and Grossman, P. (2000). Scenes from a marriage: Some implications of interdisciplinary humanities curricula in the comprehensive high school. In S. Wineburg and P. Grossman (Eds.). *Interdisciplinary curriculum: Challenges to implementation.* New York: Teachers College Press, pp. 57–73.

Wineburg, S. (2001). *Historical Thinking and Other Unnatural Acts: Charting the Future of Teaching the Past.* Philadelphia, PA: Temple University Press.

Wineburg, S., and Grossman, P. (1998). Creating a community of learners among high school teachers. *Phi Delta Kappa, 79.*

Wineburg, S., and Grossman, P. (Eds.). (2000). *Interdisciplinary Curriculum: Challenges to Implementation.* New York: Teachers College Press.

Chabad: Social Movement and Educational Practice

PHILIP WEXLER

Preface

I have been a sometime student of "Tanya," the Lubavitch Hasidic textual guide for the "intermediate person;" a beginning reader of the late Rebbe's "Sichos" in Yiddish; and, perhaps more professionally appropriately, an interpreter of the Hasidic concept of *dvekut* in relation to Max Weber's sociology of religion. (Wexler, 2002).

Here, I want to offer some comments on social theory, social change and education — in the hope that they might somehow stimulate the work of primary scholars of Chabad in particular, and Hasidism more generally; some of whose front ranks were represented in a recent conference focused on scholarly analyses of Chabad that was organized by Yitchak Kraus (2001) and held at Bar Ilan University, in Ramat Gan. In what follows, I elaborate the comments I made at that conference which, on the whole, took a surprisingly critical political/religious stance toward the Chabad movement. My "positive" view was hardly representative of the collective mood of the conference. In addition, I also want to encourage rethinking of the connection between social movements and education.

While the work of a number of the academic researchers of Chabad Hasidism centers on its internal, religious, ideational history — an interest recently advocated and comprehensively displayed by Kraus (2001) in his dissertation — their work goes beyond Chabad, Hasidic, and even Jewish,

196

history, to draw upon more general sociological analyses of religion, which leads them to interpret the ideas and practices of the Lubavitcher Hasidic movement in relation to wider social contexts. Perhaps it is this interdisciplinary willingness of Jewish studies scholars to venture forth into social science, and into sociology in particular, that emboldens me to offer some preliminary sociological approaches to the study of Chabad.

Elior (1998), for example, uses the cognitive dissonance model of failed prophecy, and Ravitzky (1994) suggests that Chabad concepts atypical to Jewish history do, however, show similarity to contemporary sociocultural trends in America. And, while the *theoretical and practical expressions* of Chabad, notably its messianism, are explained in terms of Jewish history, especially as response to the Holocaust, but also in relation to the Litvak yeshiva movement (Friedman, 1994), or as an "alternative model" to Zionism (Ravitzky, 1994), Chabad's *origins and expansion* are explained simultaneously as a protective response against the secularizing European enlightenment of modernity, and as a result of the benefits of modern technology and affluence in modern American society.

It also makes good sociological sense to assimilate, as scholars of Chabad often do, social explanations of the religious movement to more general analyses of religious fundamentalism and apocalypticism, which rely so strongly on an understanding of these movements as defensive reactions to modernity. Both the specific work on Chabad, and the contemporary social analysis of religious movements more generally, focus on the context of modernity; both as a social context and as a theoretical framework.

I want to take a more speculative and less popular view that starts with the assumption that the social, contextual and theoretical frameworks for understanding Chabad may more fruitfully be initiated from perspectives arising from post-modern social conditions and from post-modern social theorizing. Beyond that, even if I can show how to work from a so-called "post-modern" vantage point, there too, for example, in the landmark work of Castells (1997), religious social movements are explained as "defensive reactions." Instead, I emphasize how such a movement may not only be a reaction against modernity, or against post-modernity seen as a social transformation, one that Castells and many others encapsulate as the "information age." I want to emphasize instead Castells' "projective" possibility for social movements, and to suggest that we can see such movements, perhaps with Chabad as an example, as anticipations, rather than simply as reactions; to understand them as prophetic movements, though their prophecy may be found less in their messianic and apocalyptic ideas, and more in the form of their embodied social, educative practices.

I specify how these practices represent the collective social psychological work of reconstituting the meaning of the sacred within postmodern social conditions. By actively and practically redefining sacredness, they also work not only to solve individual problems and dilemmas, but also shared, social ones. By so doing, a refigured sacredness contributes to the revitalization of society in general. In this sense, I am simply following the arch-modern sociologist, Durkheim (1995), in seeing the practices of the sacred as the source of societal energy. But, I want to think about these sacred social dynamics, these "mystical mechanics" — as Durkheim (1995) called the social process of regular religious revitalization — less in his terms of a unified process of aggregation and centralization ("assembly" or "congregation"), and more in terms of a post-modern sense of a multi-dimensional, even multi-planal, field of sometimes contradictory, disparate, yet interrelated processes. An apparently "unholy alliance" of social psychological, formative or educative (the German word "*bildung*" seems most precise) practices — notably, re-personalization and re-narrativization or re-cosmicization — can be taken together as examples of how sacredness and society are being reconstructed in postmodern conditions. From this vantage-point, Chabad provides an empirical case not only of a fundamentalist cult reaction against modernization or even, post-modernization. Rather, it exemplifies new modes of constituting the domain of the sacred in society that are adopted by prophetic, messianic social movements. Chabad can thus be taken as an ideal type case, not of the sort of defensive identity reaction of the social movements which Castells (1996) emphasized, but of an anticipatory, "projective" harbinger of a more de-centered reconstitution of sacredness by different means under significantly altered social conditions.

In this practical, social, formative ("bildung") work of reconstituting individual, self-identity and collective, cultural meaning, Chabad is an exemplary form of educational practice. Weber (1946, p. 426), in his all too brief, and too rarely discussed "comments" on a "sociological theory of pedagogical ends and means," prefigures — by reflection on the pre-modern — our late postmodern interest in a prophetic, revitalizing education (Wexler, 2000).

Not surprisingly for students of Weber's general sociology, this pre-modern, "ancient" education is the charismatic "polar opposite" of "rational" "bureaucratic (modern)" social organization and education. It serves not as a secularized instrument of rational domination, but as an education that "awakens" a "new soul" to "be reborn" (Weber, 1946, p. 426). Here, we begin to see how the interest in religious social movements can be related to education. A description of how contemporary social movements that reconstitute sacredness can be an example both of the specific ways in which prophetic movements are educative, and, more generally, of ways to reconceptualize educational practice itself as integral to social movement.

Post-modern Social Theory: Short Course

Sociology was late to jump on the post-modern bandwagon. But jump it, it did, and the most recent Handbook of Social Theory (Ritzer and Smart, 2001) is replete with post-modern perspectives. There is no simple way of summarizing all this work, which, in proper post-modern fashion, crosses and erases boundaries between sociology, literature, philosophy, and the post-modern hybrid, cultural studies. In "Mystical Society" (Wexler, 2000), I emphasized the social structural version of post-modern theorizing, that was a reaction to the privileging of textual and cultural aspects of change against the economic and organizational dimensions. Here too, while there is a sense of a less clearly bounded, more dispersed culture, and a de-centered, culturally 'saturated self' (Gergen, 1991), the emphasis for both Harvey (1989) and for Castells (1996/7) is on the economic transformation in production that includes not only new technologies, but also the overall social organization of production. A new society is being created, where fundamental assumptions about time and space are altered, where the intensity and internalization of change are unprecedented, and where there is an empirically demonstrable social basis to Foucault's (1988) portrait of an historic, unique combination of processes that combine individualization and totalization, in which our very understandings of what is 'social' and 'cultural' are altered.

There are now, I think, post-modern revisions of the aporias of the "classical," modern (Lemert, 1995) social theories of Marx, Weber and Durkheim. Marx's emphasis on the material world where social relations shape the refashioning of the natural, object world is 'post-modernized' by Knorr-Cetina (2001), who now writes of a "post-social" society, in which the human solidarity, and its pathologies that modern sociology chronicled, is replaced by "object-centered environments." The Marxist contradiction between economic productivity and human alienation is resolved by a post-social form of post-modernity, in which a world of the ever-expanding production of "unfolding objects" is itself the means for overcoming the alienation of human social relations.

Similarly with Weber's (1965) deep and abiding contradiction between rationalization and routinization on the one side and charisma and ecstasy on the other. The cultural basis of modernity now appears, in the postmodern world, according to Ritzer (2001), as a pervasive mass consumption unforeseen by Weber. "Contemporary sites of consumption," 'consuming palaces' are at once rationalized, but also re-enchanted, spectacular mega-shopping malls, Las Vegas casinos and Disney-worlds.

Along with the reconfiguration of production and consumption, Durkheim's (1995) dynamic in which the sacred/profane dichotomy powers and defines the meaning of the social, now has also to be historically reconsidered. Society is divided into two realms, two worlds, two orders of being, in which the mundane, economic and more "dispersed" profane is almost mystically energized by the "assembled" and "concentrated" more intense world of collective communion which defines the sacred activity of society. Society creates force and power for itself by worshipping the totemic gods that incarnate energy. "God and society are one and the same," for the vital source is the "collective effervescence" stimulated by the very act of social congregation. And, it is the type of oscillating, wave-like movement that alternates the centripetal and the centrifugal, where the core of the social is the sacred and where the sacred is always kindled at the aggregated hearth of processes of collective, de-differentiating communion emblematized by the ecstatic frenzy of the aboriginals' ceremonial "corroboree."

Vitalization of social structure by social aggregation, despite its apparently endless potential in secularized versions, becomes, I think, less viable under broad-scale social conditions of dispersion, decentralization, and dissolution of the recognizable social-cultural domain. Simultaneous individualization and totalization, self and cosmos, identity and meaning, set a new and different stage for the vitalizing power of the sacred, in the context of post-modern social movements, such as Chabad.

Social Movements

With the rise of sociological post-modernism, there is a renewed interest in social movements, and in the relation between social movements and religion, even to the extent that Beckford (2001) sees religion as once again important on the agenda of mainstream social science. Religion is being "used" in social movements, as a "cultural resource," and the post-modern emphasis on individual "identity formation, social inclusion and boundary maintenance" makes the sacred more salient for collective action.

The way that this occurs, in Castells' (1997) comprehensive account of contemporary social change, is that identities are being reconstructed in defensive communal reaction against the effects of globalizing informationalism. "Defensive identity" is "an identity of retrenchment of the known against the unpredictability of the unknown and uncontrollable." Social movements may be communal collective action, but they are focused on a "hyper-individualism" of identities which represents "defensive reactions against the global disorder and uncontrollable, fast-paced change." They are a "refuge" against a "hostile world," where the need for a meaning that has been imploded and destroyed by the timeless time and de-located space of network technology information flows is met by "reverse information flow." As Castells puts it: "God, nation, family and community will provide unbreakable, eternal codes, around which a counter-offensive will be mounted against the culture of real virtuality." (Castells, 1997, p. 66).

Social movements of defensive identity "use" religion as a stronger coding to effect meaningful integration. The collective memory of religious meaning, in its eternity, is more powerful than space and time, delimited ethnicity, or even nationality, as a social basis for identity. Rappaport's (1999) 'sacred postulates' of unquestionable meaning are a 'cultural resource' for an anti-globalizing process of protective individualization.

Sacralized social movements go beyond defensive strategies. Social movements, while taking place on the grounds of historical social conditions, are not simply defensive reversals of those conditions. As Wallace (1966) and, later, Fernandez (1986) showed, social movements also represent processes for the re-vitalization of collective as well as individual life, and religion is a common medium for the shared social labor of re-vitalization.

Sacred, Post-modern Durkheim — and Chabad

Instead of a reverse flow, mirror-imaging a centralized globalization processes that de-centers time, space, meaning and identity, imagine that societal change sets new arenas of collective problem-solving. On the one hand, from modern alienation through post-modern self-saturation, the problem of self-diminution and desiccation is intensified as individualization proceeds to displace collective sociality. At the same time, boundary-smashing of all but the most protectively-coded meanings implies that culture needs to become increasingly cosmic to achieve meaningful coherence.

Re-vitalization, under these conditions, is not about the communion of ecstatic collective aggregation as periodic revivals, in the face of dispersed, low-intensity profane economic activity — Durkheim's description of the sacred. It is not simply part of an oscillating wave driven by, in Durkheim's (1995) account, the "electricity" of the power of the social — at its moment of disintegration. Rather, it is a multi-dimensional process, not a duality, and one where the sacred is constituted in the interplay of those dimensions.

The desiccation of the self, and the global, emptying, flattening digitalization of meaning, are the new sites of the sacred. The sacred is no longer the unified tribe's collective representation. Instead, I am suggesting that it is composed of the combined, and sometimes conflicting, processes of re-personalization and re-narrativization.

Re-personalization returns needed vitality to the hyper-individualized self by re-'auratizating' that which the "mechanical reproduction" of the commodity destroyed (Benjamin, 1985). Re-narrativization needs to go beyond the empirical social story to effect an integration of meaning by countering chaos with a new totalization, a re-cosmicized narrative. Following Rappaport's (1999) informational approach to the "discursive" (sacred) and "numinous" (experiential) constitution of "the holy," religious un-verifiability is reinforced by informational minimalism, as a perverse method for creating meaningful order.

Acquisition of personal aura is obtained by the production of exemplary individual auras which can be identified with, from whom auratic power can be transferred, to work at the level of the self. Religious re-auratization, as a method of mass re-personalization means that stars, gurus and rebbes are not as "Critical Theory" (Horkheimer and Adorno, 1972, pp. 120–168) taught, mere iconic forms of self-alienation. On the contrary, by investing the super-person with more vital personal power, there is more, as Idel (1995) described the shamanic aspects of Hasidic *shefa* (energic abundance), to be distributed. This re-investment of selfhood by identification and transfer (*dvekut* or attachment/identification) from "rebbe" to vital self, threatens — as *Mitnagdim*, or historical opponents to Hasidism, understood — the integrative power of discursive meaning, in Torah and text. There may be conflicts between personal (experiential) and narrative (discursive) foci. They may alternate temporally, or divide spatially. Or, they may integrate, constituting a "holy" (Rappaport, 1999) alliance of the sacred and the numinous.

Messianism emphasizes, even over-codes and reinforces, these social psychological processes. The auratic power of a de-temporalized guru or rebbe is multiplied by making him the dramatic repository of a transferable selfhood that is securely anchored in the end of time. The ego-ideal of the guru which replenishes the globally-assaulted boundary and energy of the individuated self becomes even more idealized with a messianic mantle. The narrative resource for an ordering re-integration of meaning, that replaces the story of an empirical, historical society with one of a transcendental cosmos, is expanded and strengthened by the dramatic emphasis on imminent redemption.

If the post-modern sacred is multi-dimensional, if it is a shifting alliance of processes of re-personalization through re-auratization (or re-enchantment) and transfer on the one hand, and on the other, of a re-narrativization by re-cosmicizing (see Toulmin, 1985) meaning, then messianism can strengthen both constituent processes by making them even more transcendental, expansive and invulnerable. Prophecy never really fails. It can always be revised and reinvented. Chabad is a social prophecy, not simply in its ideas, but in its social psychological practices. It exemplifies in its everyday practices both of these dimensions of the post-modern sacred (Kraus, 2001; Werczberger, 2003).

As Kraus (2001) interprets the writings of the seventh Lubavitcher Rebbe, the "Ramam," re-personalization is made explicit. Not only is salvation individualized — "*geula pratit*" (personal, private redemption) — but even more directly, guru-energy, reinforced by messianic boundlessness, is expressly mass-distributed for collective purposes of re-vitalized selfhood: "*She bechol yehudi yeshno nitzutz shel meshiach* (In every Jew there is a spark of the messiah)." Indeed, there is now a revelation of a "*nitzutz hameshichi haprati*, (personalized messianic spark)." In other words, personalized revitalization through messianism. An efficient re-cosmic integration and restoration of meaning is accomplished by what Kraus describes as Chabad's "acosmicism." "*Ein od milvado* (There is nothing outside of him)." The process of providing orienting, integrative meaning where the social narrative is digitally dissolved, is best accomplished with the least information — an acosmic, cosmic narrative.

Chabad offers an example of an embodied social prophecy, of an actualized instance of strongly coded post-modern sacredness. Perhaps more than a defensive reaction against globalization, Chabad is prospective rather than simply reactive, in its practical demonstration of how central post-modern aporias are actively resolved by sacralized social movement. As an ideal type, Chabad enacts its own belief in practical embodiment and inner-worldly mysticism. Perhaps Chabad represents less of a reaction and more of an anticipation, an educational hint of a general model of sacred social action in the new world (Wexler, 2000).

Indeed, Werczberger's (2003) recent empirical case study of a Chabad women's group aims to describe how participation in Chabad activities by newly-religious women serves educative, self-transformative purposes. The feminist irony of its patriarchal, guru-centered ideology is revealed in the character of social practices. Even more specifically than self-revitalization or the reintegration of meaning, Werczberger shows how these women's Chabad activities enhance their sense of self power or "agency" and furthers their sense of meaningful social connectedness or "relationality." These particular observed effects undermine traditional, liberal feminist ideas about the effects of religious social movements on women's autonomy and relationality, as strategies of identity and meaning. In addition to placing in question the stereotypical view of the effects of social movements on identity and meaning, it specifically indicates how contemporary forms of alienation are countered by social practices that are self and socially formative rather than disintegrative, which is to say, "educationally developmental (bildung)."

Speculation about Chabad as a post-modern movement and a preliminary empirical study of its educative effects from a critical, feminist vantage-point ought to encourage more thought and research about how social movements work educationally. Beyond that, a social movement focus on the analysis of social life generally (Melucci, 1996), induces further reflection on how earlier paradigms of education as a socializing, functionalist process or a class, cultural reproductive one, may be fruitfully replaced by rethinking the elements of institutional and informal education (Beckerman et al., in press) as one of multi-dimensional, historical, collective action.

Weber's early, fragmentary observations on a "typology" of "pedagogy" provides some hints toward analyzing our own present. Rather than the "critical" opposition to the rationalized, specialist education of modernity that we have seen in contemporary social, educational thought (Wexler, 1987), his analysis suggests a rethinking of what "cultivated" and "charismatic" types of social action mean — educationally — in our current situation.

This "positive" alternative to the educational present may look to social movements as historical examples, and to educational thought for analytical models. "Visions" of education that place practice in historical cultural movements are also part of this rethinking of the relation between social movement, social change and education (Fox, Scheffler and Marom, 2003). Fox's "The Art of Translation" (Fox, 2003) and Merom's "Before the Gates of the School" (Marom, 2003) show how practice, implementation, and the "everyday world" of education provide a testing not only for the feasibility of the translation of theory into practice, but also of the articulation of theory and vision from embodied educational practice. Chabad is indisputably a contemporary mass educational practice. What theoretical, visionary and practical implications we wish to draw from its this-worldly successes as a social and educational movement, are still less evident, and appropriately ambiguous for a postmodern social context.

References

Beckford, James. (2001). Social movements as free-floating religious phenomena. In Richard Fenn. (Ed.). *The Blackwell Companion to Sociology of Religion.* Oxford: Blackwell Publishers.

Bekerman, Zvi, Burbules, Nicholas C. and Silberman Keller, Diana. (Eds.). (In press) *Learning in places: The Informal Education reader.* New York: Peter Lang.

Benjamin, Walter. (1985). Art in the age of mechanical reproduction. In Walter Benjamin. *Illuminations.* New York: Schocken Books, pp. 217 -253.

Castells, Manuel. (1996). *The rise of network society.* Cambridge, Mass: Blackwell.

Castells, Manuel. (1997). *The power of identity.* Cambridge, Mass: Blackwell.

Durkheim, Emile. (1995). *The elementary forms of religious life.* Karen E. Fields. (Trans.) New York: Free Press.

Elior, Rachel. (1998). The Lubavitch messianic resurgence: The historical and mystical background, 1939–1996. In Peter Sachfer and Mark R. Cohen. (Eds.). *Towards the millennium: Messianic expectations from the Bible to Waco.* Leiden and Boston: Brill Academic Publishers.

Fernandez, James W. (1986). The argument of images and the experience of returning to the whole. In Victor W. Turner and Edward M. Bruner. (Eds.). *The Anthropology of Experience*, Urbana: University of Illinois Press, pp. 159–187.

Foucault, Michel. (1988). Technologies of the self. In Luther H. Martin, Huck Gutman and Patrick H. Hutton, (Eds.). *Technologies of the self: A seminar with Michel Foucault.* Amherst: University of Massachusetts Press, pp. 16–49.

Fox, Seymour, (2003). The art of translation. In Seymour Fox, Israel Scheffler and Daniel Marom. *Visions of Jewish Education.* Cambridge UK: Cambridge University Press, pp. 253 -295.

Fox, Seymour, Scheffler, Israel and Marom Daniel. (2003). *Visions of Jewish Education.* Cambridge, UK: Cambridge University Press.

Friedman, Menachem. (1994). Habad as messianic fundamentalism: From local particularism to universal mission. In M. E. Marty and R. S. Appleby. (Eds.). *Accounting for Fundamentalism.* Chicago: The University of Chicago Press.

Gergen, Kenneth J. (1991). *The saturated self: Dilemmas of identity in contemporary life.* New York: Basic Books.

Harvey, David. (1989). *The conditions of Post-Modernity.* Cambridge, Mass: Blackwell.

Horkheimer, Max and Adorno, Theodor W. (1972). The culture industry: Enlightenment as mass deception. In idem. *Dialectic of enlightenment.* New York: Herder and Herder, pp. 120– 168.

Idel, Moshe. (1995). *Hasidism: between ecstasy and magic.* Albany: State University of New York Press.

Knorr-Cetina, Karin. (2001). Postsocial relations: Theorizing sociality in postsocial environments. In Goerge Ritzer and Barry Smart. (Eds.). *Handbook of Social Theory.* London: Sage Publications Ltd.

Kraus, Yitzhak. (2001). Living with the times: Reflection and leadership, theory and practice in the world of the Rebbe of Lubavitch, Rabbi Menachem Mendel Schneerson. Unpublished Ph.D. thesis. Bar Ilan University.

Lemert, Charles. (1995). *Sociology after the crisis.* Boulder, Co.: Westview Press.

Marom, Daniel, (2003). Before the gates of the school: An experiment in developing educational vision from practice. In Seymour Fox, Israel Scheffler and Daniel Marom. *Visions of Jewish Education.* Cambridge, UK: Cambridge University Press, pp. 296–331.

Melucci, Alberto. (1996). *Challenging codes: Collective action in the information age.* Cambridge University: Cambridge.

Rappaport, Roy A. (1999). *Ritual and religion in the making of humanity.* Cambridge, UK: Cambridge University Press.

Ravitzky, Aviezer. (1994). The contemporary Lubavitch Hasidic movement: Between conservatism and messianism. In M. E. Marty and R. S Appleby. (Eds.). *Accounting for fundamentalism.* Chicago: The University of Chicago Press.

Ritzer, G., Goodman, D. and Wiedenhoft, W. (2001). Theories of consumption. In George Ritzer and Barry Smart. (Eds.). *Handbook of social theory.* London: Sage Publications.

Ritzer, George and Smart, Barry. (2001). *Handbook of Social Theory.* London: Sage Publications.

Toulmin, Stephen E. (1985). *The return to cosmology: Postmodern science and the theology of nature.* Berkeley, CA: The University of California Press.

Wallace, Anthony. F. C. (1966). *Religion: An Anthropological View.* New York: Random House.

Weber, Max. (1963). *The Sociology of Religion.* Boston, MA.: Beacon Press.

Werczberger, Rachel. (2003). Feminized messianism and messianic feminism: An ethnography of a women's class at the Triangular Thread Club. Unpublished MA thesis, School of Education, The Hebrew University, Jerusalem.

Wexler, Philip. (2000). *The mystical society.* Boulder, Co.: Westview Press

Wexler, Philip. (2002). Social Psychology, the Hasidic ethos and the spirit of the New Age. *Kabbalah: Journal for the Study of Jewish Mystical Texts, 7,* pp. 11–36.

Wexler, Philip. (1987). *Social analysis of education.* London and New York: Routledge.

The Cyclical History of Adult Jewish Learning in the United States: Peer's Law and its Implications*

JONATHAN D. SARNA

No one has championed the importance of "vision" in Jewish education more strongly than Seymour Fox; and no vision has been more central to Jewish education than that of lifelong learning (Fox, with Novak, 1997). Yet, as in so many other areas of Jewish education, we have only a hazy idea of what lifelong Jewish learning has meant historically, much less how it has been achieved. This problem is especially acute in the United States where, as I have argued elsewhere, the history of Jewish education has been far-too-little studied and all-too-inadequately analyzed. (Sarna, 1998).

Here I focus on adult Jewish learning, which has undergone a dramatic revitalization over the past decade, spurred by programs like Wexner Heritage, Me'ah, and the Melton Mini-Schools. Throughout the United States in recent years, the quality of adult Jewish education programs has markedly improved and the number of those participating in such programs has multiplied. We know almost nothing, however, about how to contextualize these developments historically. What, for example, did adult Jewish learning mean to earlier generations of American Jews? How and why have programs of adult Jewish learning changed over time? Most

* An earlier version of this paper was delivered at the Brandeis University conference on Adult Jewish Learning, cosponsored by the Hadassah International Research Institute on Jewish Women.

importantly, what can we learn from history about the conditions under which programs of adult Jewish learning have succeeded or failed?

None of these questions can be answered in any definitive way given the current state of our knowledge. The standard histories of American Jewish education ignore adult Jewish learning. And the best one-volume study that we do have — Israel Goldman's *Lifelong Learning Among Jews* (1975) — devotes only about 5 percent of its pages to the United States. Most of these deal with the period commencing in the late 1930s.[1]

Rather than be comprehensive, this discussion will therefore be selective and suggestive. Starting from a law articulated by Robert Peers concerning the relationship between interest in adult education and eras of rapid change, this examination aims to shed light on a few significant moments in the history of adult Jewish learning in the United States, in hopes of gleaning insights that may prove relevant to contemporary developments in the field as well.

* * *

Adult Jewish learning in the United States builds on a tradition dating all the way back to Moses in the wilderness. The well-known biblical commandment (Deut. 31:9–12) declared that the Torah was to be read aloud "in the presence of all Israel," including "men, women, children and the strangers in your communities." All were required to gather, so that they might "learn to revere the Lord your God and to observe faithfully every word of this Torah." Without exaggerating the impact of this biblical commandment on modern Jews who scarcely know of its existence, one can nevertheless discern some important values from the text that may have helped to shape programs of adult Jewish learning, even unconsciously.

Thus, for example, the text makes clear that *Torah* (in this case Deuteronomy, but by extension all Jewish learning) is not the private preserve of priests, elders or teachers, but must instead be shared with everyone. This democratization of learning — the idea that Jewish learning belongs to the Jewish people as a whole, not just to the elite — has underlaid Jewish attitudes toward learning throughout the centuries. It helps to explain both widespread Jewish literacy and the idea that Jewish learning should continue throughout life.

---

1   More historical details may be found in Elkin, 1955. For additional sources, see Drachler, 1996, pp. 390–397, 647–648.

Interestingly, the biblical text placed adults *before* children in the performance of this commandment: old and young alike were required to hear and to learn. Louis Ginzberg believed that this reflected the priorities of antiquity. "In the olden time," he wrote, "the opinion prevailed that the fathers were to be educated first and then the children, not in the reverse order." (Ginzberg, 1928/1958, p. 87). According to this view, adult Jewish learning was once even more important than the education of children. While rarely the case in the United States, or for that matter in any other modern Diaspora Jewish community, the antiquity of this idea may nevertheless have contributed some added measure of legitimacy to adult Jewish learning. Even if, over time, adult Jewish learning became a stepchild in the field of Jewish education, practitioners could recall that it had once been the favorite child.

Finally, it should not escape our attention that the biblical text specifically mentioned women in the list of those told to gather to "hear and...learn" Torah. While the Talmudic rabbis, perhaps influenced by Hellenistic views, debated the issue of women's learning, the Deuteronomist was quite clear that the commandment of gathering to hear the Torah read aloud applied to women no less than to men.

For our purposes, the importance of this biblical text lies in the scriptural basis it provided, and the values it may have imparted, to those engaged in adult Jewish learning. Details of how the field developed between the biblical period and the present may be found in Israel Goldman's *Lifelong Learning Among Jews.* We will focus here on what happened when the tradition of adult Jewish learning crossed the Atlantic and came to the New World.

Before turning to this question, however, a critical point of terminology must be clarified.[2] Contemporary educators prefer the term "adult Jewish learning" to "adult Jewish education." This is no accident. By current definition, "adult Jewish education" refers only to what takes place in formal "instructional settings" where the teacher defines the process and the student is relatively passive (as in a university classroom). Adult Jewish learning, by contrast, "often occurs outside of such settings and is more determined by the individual's own purposes." It includes informal learning — what adults learn from family and friends, from lectures and libraries, from television and travel. The distinction, to be sure, is not always clear-cut. But the conceptual point is very important. *Adult Jewish*

---

2   On this point, Peterson and Associates, 1980, pp. 7–8, 16–17.

learning is not and was not confined to the classroom. In many places where we find no record of formal adult Jewish education — no classes, no Talmud study, not even a regular discussion of *parashat hashavua* (the weekly Torah portion) — a great deal of Jewish learning may nevertheless have taken place.

So it was, I think, in early America. Until the time of the American Revolution no more than a few thousand Jews lived in all of the colonies put together, and only five communities boasted synagogues that assumed responsibility for providing the essential features of Jewish life. None of these synagogues, so far as we know, offered any formal program of adult Jewish education. Nevertheless, a considerable degree of adult Jewish learning took place informally, in at least three different ways. First, adults learned from one another through regular conversations in the course of which they shared accumulated wisdom. A more learned Jew like Joseph Carpeles or Hayman Levy would impart information to those who were less learned, and the information would then be passed on. Second, adults gained information by reading books, which could be imported freely, and in some cases were even printed in America. The works of Josephus, for example, were printed in America as early as 1719. Abigail Franks' letters are filled with references to books that she read, many of them sent to her from England by her son, Naftali. By the early 19th century, New England religious historian Hannah Adams, a proponent of evangelization, wrote extensively about Jews and Judaism simply on the basis of books available to her in Boston and her correspondence with Jewish informants. Jews learned about their faith in similar ways. Finally, synagogue sermons served as vehicles for transmitting Jewish learning. Sermons were only delivered infrequently in the colonial synagogues, but they inevitably contained textual and spiritual messages designed to educate as well as to edify. Haham Isaac Carigal delivered a particularly famous sermon entitled "The Salvation of Israel" in Newport on Shavuot 1773. It is hard to know whether those in attendance listened to the sermon, delivered in Spanish, or simply marveled at the exotic speaker adorned in a "fur cap, scarlet robe, green silk damask vest, and a chintz undervest — girt with a sash or Turkish girdle," as well as dangling *tzitzit*. (Chyet, 1966, p. iii). But the sermon was subsequently published in English and contained many learned references. The point is that periodic opportunities for enhancing an adult Jew's learning existed even in the far off wilderness that was early America. Those early American Jews who thirsted for Jewish knowledge had some wells from which to draw, even in the absence of formal classes and study groups.

New Immigrants and New Technologies

More comprehensive programs of adult Jewish learning appeared in America in the 1840s. The obvious question is why? The answer brings us to an extraordinarily important finding articulated first, to my knowledge, by Robert Peers in his *Adult Education: A Comparative Study*, published in 1958. "The most active periods in the history of adult education," Peers declared, "have always been those in which there has been the greatest rapidity of change." (p. 3). The history of adult learning, according to this discovery — Peers' Law — is neither static nor linear; it is cyclical and responds directly to the pace of change. Among Jews, as among non-Jews, there have been periods of greater and lesser interest in adult learning. Eras of heightened social, cultural and technological change stimulate interest in adult education; eras of stagnation stifle it.

The 1840s offer a case in point. During this decade of change, Jewish immigration to the United States mushroomed. An estimated 6,000 Jews were in the country in 1830, 15,000 in 1840 and 50,000 in 1850. This enormous population growth, principally from Central Europe, transformed American Jewish life. It was then, for example, that the first ordained rabbis came to the United States, beginning with Rabbi Abraham Rice, who arrived from Bavaria in 1840 and settled in Baltimore. The changes wrought by immigration — upon new Jewish immigrants and long-time residents alike — stimulated Jewish learning at every level. In addition, this era witnessed a great democratization of print culture. Printing technology improved, the price of printing and paper fell, and so there was a tremendous growth of religious journalism, and of books, tracts and publications of all kinds (the mass-market newspaper, the so-called penny press, also dates to this era.)[3]

For Jews, this "media explosion" — the sudden availability of books, newspapers, magazines and so forth, many of them explicitly evangelical — represented both a challenge and an opportunity. The challenge came from their need to defend themselves not just from hired missionaries, but more seriously from their religiously awakened neighbors, who asked difficult questions of them (or, even worse, of their children). The opportunity, of course, was to use this stimulus — plus the same printing technology employed by their Christian neighbors — to strengthen American Judaism through enhanced Jewish learning.

The two foremost American Jewish religious leaders of the 19th

---

3   My thinking on these matters has been influenced by Hatch, 1983.

century, Isaac Leeser (1806–1868) of Philadelphia, and Isaac Mayer Wise of Cincinnati (1819–1900), understood the challenge and the opportunity. Concerned about the lack of quality Jewish education and eager to strengthen Jewish religious life — one as a proponent of Americanized Orthodoxy and the other of Americanized Reform — both men mounted vigorous programs to upgrade Jewish learning, largely through print media such as books, pamphlets, and newspapers. Between them, they produced almost 150 different works, and edited three of the community's foremost periodicals: Leeser's *The Occident and American Jewish Advocate* (1843–1869), and Wise's *Israelite (*founded in 1854 and renamed the *American Israelite* in 1874) as well as *Die Deborah* (1855–1902), a German newspaper aimed especially at women (Sarna, 1995; Goren, 1987; Singerman, 1984).

Both men looked to the printed word to promote Jewish learning. Their objectives, as Leeser explained in 1845 when he founded America's first, rather short-lived Jewish Publication Society, were twofold. First, to provide American Jews with "a knowledge of their faith" and second, to arm them with the "proper weapons to defend…against the assaults of proselyte-makers on the one side and of infidels on the other."(Mendes-Flohr and Reinharz, pp. 461–63).[4] These same two objectives — Jewish education and communal defense — would remain central themes of programs aimed at strengthening American Jewish learning forever after.

Jewish newspapers and books were the primary vehicles for disseminating Jewish learning in the 1840s, and for at least a generation thereafter. They reached into hundreds of communities, some of them places where only a single Jew resided (Glanz, 1972/73; Glanz, 1974). They transmitted a broad range of news and learning — everything from serious scholarship to popular fiction and helpful advice. They aimed to educate men and women alike. And they promoted among their far-flung readers a sense of community and group identity — feelings of fellowship, mutuality and interdependence.

While all of this was accomplished without any formal classes, adult Jewish education was not totally solitary. In fact, there are references to formal classes and lectures beginning in the 1840s in big cities like New York and Philadelphia.[5] We also know from Jewish newspapers that

---

4   Isaac Leeser, "Address of the Jewish Publication Committee to the Israelites of America," preface to *Caleb Asher*, no. 1 of the series *The Jewish Miscellany*; (Philadelphia: Jewish Publication Society of America, 5605 [1845]): pp. 1–4, reprinted in part in Mendes-Flohr and Reinharz, 1995.
5   Goldman, 1975, p. 282 provides a few examples.

Jewish men and women, usually separately, organized literary discussion groups. Most importantly, the Jewish Sunday School movement, pioneered by Rebecca Gratz in Philadelphia in 1838, also spurred adult Jewish learning, especially as the movement spread in the 1840s and 1850s. Gratz had specified that Sunday School teachers were to be "young ladies." As a result, the Jewish Sunday School movement, like its Protestant counterpart, was a women's movement. Women founded the schools, directed them, taught in them and insisted that their daughters be free to attend them on a par with boys. What is important for our purposes is that these "young ladies" (some of whom were only young in spirit: Rebecca Gratz was 57 at the time and continued to be active in the movement until she was a "young lady" of 84) needed to be adequately educated in order to teach. Indeed, women spurred adult Jewish learning, formal and informal, in this period. They wanted to learn in order provide their children with proper religious nurturing which, in America, was part of the women's domain. In some cases, they also wanted to learn in order to teach in the Jewish Sunday School system (Ashton, 1997).

This first spurt in adult Jewish learning in the United States thus took place amid an era of enormous social and economic change. Taking full advantage of new technologies and new media, America's first Jewish educational activists introduced the Jewish newspaper and the cheaply produced book or tract as vehicles for promoting adult Jewish learning. They also devoted significant efforts to the education of Jewish women. Just as the Peers' Law predicted, an era of rapid change correlated directly with a boon in adult learning.

The Great Awakening

The second period of heightened activity in adult Jewish learning took place in the late 19th and early 20th centuries. This era witnessed a great awakening of young native-born American Jews, and many remarkable strides in organized adult Jewish educational activities for American-born and East European immigrant Jews alike.

Not surprisingly, given Peers' Law, this was also a period of massive social and economic transformation. More than two million Jews, mainly from Eastern Europe, migrated to America's shores along with about 20 million non-Jewish immigrants. Electricity came into widespread use during this era. The railroad and the steamship tied distant regions together, and urban transportation systems like the subway and the trolley-car bound the big cities. The telegraph and the telephone revolutionized business and personal communications during these years. This is the period, in short, when America experienced what historians call "the second industrial revolution." (Chandler, 1977 and 1991).

This is also the period when forward-looking American Jews, especially young people, became deeply worried about Judaism's future prospects. Beginning in the late 1870s, young Jews lost confidence in the liberal assumptions of their day — the hope for a "new era" of universal brotherhood — and concluded that Judaism and Jewish education needed to be revitalized in order for the community to be saved. This was based on their concerns about assimilation, intermarriage, the growth of Ethical Culture (the liberal non-Jewish religious movement founded by Felix Adler, son of a prominent Reform rabbi), and a sharp rise in anti-Semitism. The subsequent onrush of East European Jewish immigrants only heightened American Jewry's sense of crisis and foreboding.

I have described the resulting "great awakening" in American Jewish life at length elsewhere.[6] What is important here is the fact that this revitalization movement resulted in the strengthening of Jewish education, particularly among young adults (in their late teens and twenties) and older adults. Raising the level of adult Jewish knowledge became a prime objective of those who concerned themselves with the era's crisis of continuity. Their response was to create an unprecedented array of new and carefully targeted educational undertakings. These included the establishment of:

- educational programs for Jewish singles at the Young Men's and Young Women's Hebrew Associations;
- institutions such as the Jewish Theological Seminary (1886), the Jewish Publication Society (1888), Henrietta Szold's Baltimore Night School for Russian immigrants (1889), the American Jewish Historical Society (1892), the Jewish Chautauqua Society (1893), the National Council of Jewish Women (1893) and Gratz College (1893);
- publications such as the *Jewish Encyclopedia* (1901–6);
- organizations such as Hadassah (1912);
- Jewish library collections across the United States for native Jews and immigrants alike.

All of these developments — and this list is by no means complete — reflect

6   For what follows, see Sarna, 1995a.

an extraordinary moment, perhaps unmatched until the present, when adult Jewish education stood near the top of American Jewry's communal agenda and was considered vital to its future.

Some general observations about this exciting and formative era in adult Jewish education may be in order:

First, to a considerable extent, it was institutionally driven. The Jewish community had become larger and much better organized in a country that itself had become an organizational society. In addition, modern communications and transportation systems enabled national institutions to function much more easily and efficiently than before. As a result, unlike the 1840s, new developments in adult Jewish learning took place primarily at the institutional level. In many cases, developments were centrally directed, distributed by leaders at a central office to affiliates nationwide. Such was the case, for example, with the Hebrew Sunday School Union, the National Council of Jewish Women and later Hadassah.

Second, adult Jewish learning during this period again involved women as well as men. Although we have no precise figures, women probably played a more active educational role than did men. This is not surprising. Late 19th century Jews looked to women as the "saviors of Jewish life," and believed that women were more innately religious and spiritual than men (who, in any case, were supposedly working too hard to take time off to study). In its early years, the National Council of Jewish Women maintained a vigorous Jewish education program. In the 20th century, Hadassah became the Jewish women's organization most committed to adult Jewish learning, as the Council moved onto immigrant work. It is also important to recall that the new teachers' colleges — Gratz, the Teacher's Institute of the Jewish Theological Seminary, Hebrew Teachers College in Boston and the like — were all open to, and often dominated by, women. In these institutions, women achieved, for the first time, access to *advanced* Jewish learning. It was through these colleges that women gained the knowledge and skills that would, in time, enable them to claim an equal place in Jewish life. More than is generally recognized, these teachers colleges were the crucible of the Jewish feminist movement.

Third, adult Jewish learning during this period was divided institutionally and educationally into various levels, from rarefied scholarly learning to the education of beginners. In the earlier era, adult Jewish learning was more individualized. Now, clear demarcations developed among both men and women between those who knew more and those who knew less, and especially between those who knew Hebrew and those who did not. American Jewish life as a whole became much more socially and culturally stratified during these years, and Jewish education followed suit.

Finally, adult Jewish learning existed largely outside the world of the synagogue. Synagogues, especially those following East European traditions in the larger East Coast cities, continued to house traditional *hevrot* (associations) that met for the purpose of studying Talmud, Mishna or *Ein Yaakov*. Most of these associations were exclusively male preserves; only a few admitted women, and even fewer consisted only of women.

The revolution in adult Jewish learning that we are discussing took place in national or communal institutions that explicitly were *not* synagogue centered. Partly this is because the idea of the institutional synagogue, the synagogue-center committed to a range of educational and social functions beyond prayer, was still in its infancy (see Kaufman, 1999). But it is also important to realize that, at this time, Jews viewed education as a *communal* responsibility. Thus Talmud Torah schools and, later, bureaus of Jewish education were communal rather than congregational. Moreover, Jews traditionally believed that Jewish learning was a unifying factor in Jewish life, the heritage of all Jews. While synagogues divided Jews from one another and fostered communal fragmentation, Jewish learning, it was hoped, could unite Jews and show them what they all held in common.

One of the organizations that developed during this period deserves special notice because its mission, in terms of advancing adult Jewish learning, was particularly ambitious and innovative. This was the Jewish Chautauqua Society, founded in 1893 by Rabbi Henry Berkowitz of Philadelphia, and now largely forgotten (today it is part of the Reform movement's National Federation of Temple Brotherhoods and does somewhat different work). Both its objectives and its failure are illuminating.[7]

As its name implies, the Jewish Chautauqua Society was modeled on the Protestant Chautauqua movement, founded by the Methodist Episcopal Bishop John H. Vincent in 1874. Originally, the aim of Chautauqua was to bring together and educate Sunday school teachers, but it soon broadened

---

7   For what follows, I have drawn upon Henry Berkowitz's history of the Jewish Chautauqua Society in Berkowitz, 1932, pp. 123–196; Berrol, 1986, pp. 206–212; and Pearlstein, 1993.

into a much wider and more popular agency for the diffusion of knowledge, especially through summer assemblies on Lake Chautauqua that combined learning and upscale entertainment. The idea was "to make of study a pleasant pastime, and of pleasure a wise pursuit." In addition, Chautauqua created home study groups, which it supplied with educational texts, and sent lecturers on a circuit to isolated communities.[8]

Jewish Chautauqua emulated all three prongs of this great adult education program: (1) It created curricula for "reading circles" which it operated in conjunction with the National Council of Jewish Women and B'nai B'rith, and later expanded into correspondence courses. (2) It provided lecturers who traveled to far-flung communities in an effort to bring Jewish education to all corners of the country. (3) It ran summer assemblies in Atlantic City and elsewhere, bringing together the leading minds of the American Jewish community as well as liberal non-Jews. Even Theodore Roosevelt once addressed the Jewish Chautauqua Society Assembly. Indeed, the Jewish Chautauqua programs read like a forerunner to the modern-day programs of CAJE in that they combined Jewish learning at various levels with displays of new pedagogic material and impressive cultural activities. Throughout its history, the rhetoric of Jewish Chautauqua was rousingly democratic and pluralistic. It spoke of the "Democratic idea in Jewish education," described itself as "an educational agency of, for and by the people," and boasted of how it welcomed to its platform "laymen and rabbis, women and men, Gentiles as well as Jews… It has believed in and acted upon the dictum '*Kol Yisroel Achim,*' All Israelites are brethren." (Berkowitz, 1932, pp.189–191).

Yet, notwithstanding this lofty rhetoric, and notwithstanding Jewish Chautauqua's far-reaching contributions, by the 1920s it had largely abandoned the field of adult Jewish learning. Instead, it became an organization devoted to sending Jewish lecturers to speak about Judaism to non-Jews, particularly on college campuses where Jewish teachers, at that time, were scarce. Its bold and far-reaching program for promoting Jewish learning among Jewish adults was quietly forgotten — so much so that Israel Goldman, in his aforementioned history of *Lifelong Learning Among Jews*, makes no mention of this organization at all.

Yet, its efforts richly deserve to be recalled for a least two reasons. First, the history of the Jewish Chautauqua Society underscores the cyclical

8   Chautauqua still exists today in upstate New York, and for all of its White Anglo-Saxon Protestant character, it continues to attract a surprisingly large and impressive Jewish attendance.

nature of adult Jewish learning. Success (as Seymour Fox knows from experience) should never lull Jewish educators into complacency. The record of the past is strewn with programs, like Jewish Chautauqua's, that succeeded for a while and then disappeared when popular interest waned. Second, the collapse of the Jewish Chautauqua Society seems to have been brought about primarily by lack of funds. As the priorities of the Jewish community changed, and fighting antisemitism became the community's number one priority, adult Jewish learning returned to the status of community stepchild. The Jewish Chautauqua Society could only stay alive by abandoning its mission to educate Jews in favor of educating non-Jews, an enterprise that was connected with the battle against anti-Semitism and could therefore win funding. Had the Jewish Chautauqua Society built up a strong endowment, perhaps things would have been different. Whatever the case, the society's failure serves as a sober reminder that adult Jewish learning can only succeed when it has community backing and proper funding. Otherwise even the most exciting programs inevitably collapse.

Revival of Jewish Learning

Adult Jewish education began to crest for the third time in American Jewish history beginning in the late 1930s. In response to Nazism, domestic anti-Semitism and the waning of the Great Depression, interest in Jewish learning revived among American Jews. This grew partly as a form of spiritual resistance against the forces of anti-Jewish hatred, and partly (and increasingly, after the Shoah) in recognition of American Jewry's new responsibility for preserving and promoting Jewish culture in the face of the destruction of the European centers of Jewish learning. The Conservative movement's National Academy for Adult Jewish Studies was founded in 1940; Shlomo Bardin's Brandeis Camp Institute for college-aged young adults was established in 1941; and the Department of Continuing Education of the Union of American Hebrew Congregations came into being in 1948, the same year that B'nai B'rith began its Adult Institutes of Judaism (Goldman, 1975, p. 308; Dash Moore, 1981, pp. 230–233).[9] The Jewish Publication Society, which promoted Jewish education and culture through books rather than formal instruction, also roared back to life with the waning of the Depression. Its total income increased five-

9   B'nai Brith's Committee on Adult Jewish Education was founded in 1950.

fold between 1935 and 1945, and the number of books it distributed tripled (Sarna, 1989, pp. 183–184). Other publishers of Judaica, including university presses, experienced similar increases in Jewish book sales (Madison, 1967–68; Zipin, 1984–85). Finally, Jewish organizational life as a whole surged during this period. In 1945, the *American Jewish Year Book* reported that "a larger number of new organizations... formed during the past five years than in any previous five-year period, forty seven new organizations having been established since 1940." (*American Jewish Year Book, 47.* 1945–46, p. 559)

Adult Jewish education promised to prepare the community for the new responsibilities that it faced in the wake of the European Jewish catastrophe. "American Jews," the *American Jewish Year Book* reported as early as 1941, "are realizing that they have been spared for a sacred task — to preserve Judaism and its cultural, social and moral values." That same year, Hebrew Union College historian Jacob Rader Marcus, who would himself soon shift the central focus of his scholarship from Europe to America, also pointed to the American Jewish community's new historic role. "The burden is solely ours to carry," he declared: "Jewish culture and civilization and leadership are shifting rapidly to these shores." (*American Jewish Year Book, 43.* 1941–42, pp. 28, 780, 789).

The establishment of the State of Israel and the postwar move to the suburbs furthered the new interest in Jewish learning, particularly on the part of synagogues, which in this period were deeply involved in fostering adult Jewish learning activities as part of their mission. Major Jewish organizations like Hadassah and B'nai B'rith also showed new interest in adult Jewish learning, and made strong commitments to their promotion.

Of course, the postwar era also witnessed a great deal of interest in adult education among Americans generally. It was estimated in the 1940s that some 60 million American men and women were enrolled in one or another study program for adults. As before, the larger culture's support for adult learning was closely related to developments inside the Jewish community (Goldman, 1975. See also Cohen, 1965).

By the 1960s, the third era in adult Jewish learning in America had run its course. A study published in the *American Jewish Year Book* served, unconsciously, as the obituary for innovations introduced 25 years earlier. While the study confirmed that adult Jewish education had "grown into an effort of major proportions and national impact," it noted that new methodologies developed in the general field of adult Jewish learning had not been employed by Jewish educators "to any great extent." The five most frequent activities that synagogues and organizations did employ —

"the lecture, formal class, study group, discussion group and forum" — were "not truly efficacious." (Cohen, 1965, pp. 287–90). The great social and cultural changes of the 1930s and 1940s stagnated in the 1950s and, just as Peers' Law predicted, adult Jewish education stagnated as well.

* * *

The American Jewish community today stands in the midst of its fourth great era of adult Jewish learning.[10] Seymour Fox and his disciples have helped make this era happen, and have contributed to the excitement that surrounds adult Jewish study programs in many communities, including where I live in Boston. How long this will last and what its final legacy will be cannot yet be predicted. What is clear is that this new era of adult Jewish learning, however much it is about "getting adults, from recent college graduates to retirees, to recognize the gaps in their Jewish learning and get excited about filling them in," (Tye, 2001, p. 129) is also much more than that. It is, in addition, closely tied to the pace of social, cultural and technological change in recent decades, and represents another confirmation of Peers' Law: "The most active periods in the history of adult education, have always been those in which there has been the greatest rapidity of change."

Looking back at the whole history of adult Jewish learning in America, we might describe it as a very moving and inspiring saga. Adapting conclusions drawn from the general history of adult learning, we could even characterize our story in heroic terms as:

> "... the epic struggle of ordinary Jews to catch up with the knowledge necessary to enable them to live useful Jewish lives, to understand the Jewish world about them, to appreciate the Jewish ideas which are significant to the situations in which they find themselves, and above all to break through the barriers which previously cut them off from their fellow Jews and walled them about with spiritual loneliness."[11]

But a closer look suggests that this history is better described in cyclical terms: as the periodic recognition on the part of American Jews that they need to deepen their Jewish knowledge in order to face the looming challenges posed by contemporary Jewish life. The most successful

10 On the recent proliferation of adult Jewish learning, see Wertheimer, 1999.
11 Adapted from Peers, 1958, p. 335.

programs, through the years, have taken cognizance of these challenges. To meet them, they have taken advantage of new conditions, new media, and new technologies. They have shamelessly borrowed successful ideas from other faiths and from the general field of adult learning. And they have employed diverse and eclectic means of achieving their aims, not a one-size-fits-all approach.

Yet, as Peers' Law reminds us, the long-term success of these programs is by no means guaranteed. Indeed, even as Jewish educators work to sustain the many exciting programs that have been developed in recent years, it behooves them to look back and learn from previous eras in adult Jewish learning. Both past successes and past failures suggest lessons for the future.

References

American Jewish Year Book, 43. (1941–42).

American Jewish Year Book, 47. (1945–46).

Ashton, Dianne. (1997). *Unsubdued spirits: Rebecca Gratz and women's Judaism in America.* Detroit: Wayne State University Press.

Berkowitz, Max E. (1932). *The beloved Rabbi.* New York: Macmillan

Berrol, Selma. (1986). Jewish Chautauqua Society. In Michael Dobkowski (Ed.). *Jewish American voluntary organizations.* New York: Greenwood, pp. 206–212.

Chandler, Alfred D. (1977). *The visible hand: The management revolution in American business.* Cambridge: Harvard University Press.

Chandler, Alfred D. (1991). Industrial revolution. In Eric Foner and John A. Garraty. (Eds.). *The reader's companion to American history.* New York: Houghton Mifflin, pp. 559–563.

Chyet, Stanley F. (Ed.). (1966). *Rabbi Carigal preaches in Newport.* Cincinnati: American Jewish Archives.

Cohen, Samuel I. (1965). Adult Jewish education. *American Jewish Year Book, 66,* pp. 279–290.

Dash Moore, Deborah. (1981) *B'nai B'rith and the challenge of ethnic leadership.* Albany: SUNY.

Drachler, Norman. (1996). *A bibliography of Jewish education in the United States.* Detroit: Wayne State University Press.

Elkin, Harry. (1955). Adult Jewish education developments in the United States during the 19th and 20th centuries. *Jewish Education 26* (Summer). pp. 40–54.

Ginzberg, Louis. (1928/1958). *Students, scholars and saints.* Philadelphia: Jewish Publication Society.

Glanz, Rudolf. (1974). The spread of Jewish communities through America before the Civil War. *Yivo annual of Jewish Social Science, 15,* pp. 7–45.

Glanz, Rudolf. (1972/73). Where the Jewish press was distributed in pre-Civil War America. *Western States Jewish Historical Quarterly, 5*, pp. 1–14.

Goldman, Israel. (1975). *Lifelong learning among Jews*. New York: Ktav.

Goren, Arthur A. (1987). The Jewish press. In Sally M. Miller. (Ed.). *The ethnic press in the United States*. New York: Greenwood Press, pp. 203–228.

Hatch, Nathan. (1983). Elias Smith and the rise of religious journalism in the early Republic. In William L. Joyce, et al., (Eds.) *Printing and society in early America*. Worcester: American Antiquarian Society, pp. 250–277.

Kaufman, David. (1999). *Shul with a pool: The "Synagogue-center" in American Jewish history.* Hanover, NH: Brandeis University Press/University Press of New England.

Pearlstein, Peggy Kronsberg. (1993). Understanding through education: One hundred years of the Jewish Chautauqua Society, 1893–1993. Unpublished Ph.D. dissertation, George Washington University.

Madison, Charles A. (1967–68). The rise of the Jewish book in American publishing. *Jewish Book Annual, 25*, pp. 81–86.

Mendes-Flohr, Paul and Reinharz, Jehuda. (1995). *The Jew in the modern world: A documentary history*. Second edition. New York: Oxford University Press.

Peers, Robert. (1958) *Adult education: A comparative study*. London & New York: Routledge and Kegan Paul/Humanities Press.

Peterson, Richard E. and Associates. (1980). *Lifelong learning in America*. San Francisco: Jossey-Bass Publishers.

Sarna, Jonathan D. (1998). American Jewish Education in historical perspective. *Journal of Jewish Education 64*. (Winter/Spring) pp. 8–21.

Sarna, Jonathan D. (1989). *JPS: The Americanization of Jewish culture*. Philadelphia: Jewish Publication Society.

Sarna, Jonathan D. (1995). The history of the Jewish press in North America. *The North American Jewish press: The 1994 Alexander Brin Forum*. Waltham, MA: Cohen Center for Modern Jewish Studies of Brandeis University.

Sarna, Jonathan D. (1995). *A great awakening: The transformation that shaped Twentieth Century American Judaism and its implications for today*. New York: CIJE.

Singerman, Robert. (1984). The American Jewish press, 1823–1983: A bibliographic survey of research and studies. *American Jewish History, 73* (June). pp. 422–444.

Tye, Larry. (2001). *Home lands: Portraits of the new Jewish Diaspora*. New York: Henry Holt.

Wertheimer, Jack. (1999). Jewish education in the United States: Recent trends and issues. *American Jewish Year Book, 99*, pp. 82–84.

Zipin, Amnon. (1984–85). Judaica from American University Presses. *Jewish Book Annual. 42*, pp. 172–182.

The Impact of Summer Camping Upon the Major North American Jewish Religious Movements
BURTON I. COHEN

Over the past half-century there has been an increasing recognition within the North American Jewish community of the significant ongoing contribution that was being made by the summer camps of the Conservative and Reform Movements, and other camps under Jewish institutional sponsorship, towards the development and strengthening of these movements and the Jewish community in general. A recent statement in a widely read American Jewish publication is characteristic of how the impact of these camps is viewed.

> "Community-based studies across the United States consistently show that Jewish campers consistently marry Jews more often and belong to *shuls* in greater numbers than non-campers. Most Jewish professionals, whether at the pulpit, in the classroom, in the community at large — say they discovered or consolidated their Jewish identity in summer camp." (Zelon, 2000, p. 82).

We will chiefly deal with the impact of camping upon the Conservative and Reform movements. Unfortunately, the diffuse organizational character of American Orthodoxy (and also the lack of the types of data about Orthodoxy about which we shall report in the other movements) makes it difficult to authoritatively cite the impact of residential camping upon that trend in American Judaism. However, there seems to be little

223

question that many Orthodox educators have been well aware of and supportive of the role that camping might play in strengthening the Jewish backgrounds and identity of the youth affiliated with the various expressions of Orthodoxy. In an article which appeared in 1978, marking the fifteenth anniversary of the founding of Camp Morasha, the premier educational camping expression of Modern Orthodoxy, Zvi Reich, the founding director states:

> "After intensive and lengthy deliberation [the members of the Metropolitan Commission on Torah Education] decided to establish an informal educational institution with the goal of transmitting the values of Judaism in a Jewish-Zionist ambience which was filled with "love of Israel," respect for Torah, and observance of the mitzvoth." (Reich, 1978, p. 329).

The esteem with which the ultra-Orthodox movements view the educational potential of camping is expressed in a publication of the educational department of the Lubavitch movement. "The camps of Chabad-Lubavitch are based upon the insight that camp is a unique institution that provides an especially effective environment for imbuing children with the Jewish lifestyle, in a milieu where they are totally insulated from corrosive influences." (Rivkin, 1982, p. 189).

By and large, the recognition given to the achievements of the camps has been limited to their profound educational, or identity-building, impact upon the individual children and youth who have participated in the camp programs. Relatively little attention has been paid to the impact that the camps may have had upon the central institutions of the movements themselves.[1]

This paper will endeavor to demonstrate that the Ramah (Conservative) camping movement and the UAHC (Reform) camping movements have been a major influence upon their movements far beyond their impact upon the camper/students. I hope to demonstrate that insufficient attention has

1   The Reform Movement and the Conservative Movement each have an academic "fountainhead," an organization of affiliated synagogues and a federation of affiliated rabbis as their major institutions. For the Reform Movement these are the Hebrew Union College — Jewish Institute of Religion, Union of American Hebrew Congregations and the Central Conference of American Rabbis; for the Conservative Movement they are the Jewish Theological Seminary, United Synagogue for Conservative Judaism and the Rabbinical Assembly. Both movements are headquartered in New York City, but also are represented by academic institutions in Los Angeles. The Reform Movement maintains its original academic institution in Cincinnati as well.

been given to the impact of the camping programs upon developments within the central institutions of the movements themselves. It will be suggested that certain characteristics of these camping programs facilitated this institutional impact.

While the examples I have drawn upon to illustrate the impact these camps have had on the development of the movements come from different periods in the short history of the camping movements (each about 50 years), I would assert that the relative stability of the camping programs over time, enables us to speak of these developments collectively. What I say is primarily based on the Conservative experience, to which I have had extended personal exposure, and which has been extensively documented.[2] Michael Brown has documented the problems which Ramah at times presented to the central Conservative institutions, especially in the arena of finances. I would hope to demonstrate, however, that despite these problems, on the whole, the impact of camping has been to strengthen the role of those institutions. I have been impressed, by what appear to me to be significant similarities between the Reform and the Conservative experiences, and hope that I have not erred in drawing inferences in this regard.[3]

The Development of Jewish Movement Camping

It was in the aftermath of World War II and the Holocaust that Conservative and Reform Jews embarked upon the creation of networks of summer camps. Shuly Schwartz in her history of the early years of

---

2   Several books and dissertations, and many articles have analyzed and summarized the development of the Ramah camping movement. Among them are the following, which all include additional bibliography: Ettenberg and Rosenfield, 1989; Dorph, 1999;

3   There are far fewer scholarly publications on the history of Reform camping as compared to Conservative (Ramah) camping. A significant volume is currently being prepared on the history of the Olin-Sang-Ruby Institute, the first of the Reform camps, and Reform camping in general. One aspect of this book will be to document the impact of Reform upon the North American Reform Movement. A recent personal communication from Gary Zola, the editor of this volume, describing the chapters of this book, asserts as much:

"Rabbi Hillel Gamoran contributed a fine essay on the history of OSRUI's significant (though little known) Hebrew speaking unit for high schoolers: Chalutzim. This unit has played a pivotal role in nurturing future leaders of the Reform movement and it was shaped and founded and shaped by Reform rabbis who, in their youths, were influenced by Hebrew speaking camps such as Achvah and Massad." (Personal e-mail from Gary Zola to the writer, August 6, 2001.)

Ramah Camping gives a fairly clear explanation of the process by which the Ramah camping network was created (Schwartz, 1987). Based on her examination of the sources relating to the founding of the first Ramah camp in 1947, and a series of interviews which she conducted, she demonstrates that it was the goal of the camp founders to deepen and broaden the nature of the Jewish educational programs offered to the children and youth of these movements so as to increase their Jewish knowledge and Jewish observance, and strengthen their Jewish identity (however that may have been defined). To those involved, at that critical juncture in Jewish history, this seemed to be an urgent and even holy task.

Today, we might tend to regard with skepticism, a suggestion that serious problems of Jewish life, such as the dilute quality of the education provided by synagogue religious schools, might be solved through the development of a network of summer camps based on the North American recreational camping model.[4] Yet, we need to recall that this was yet at a time when the Sunday School was the major agency of elementary Jewish education for the North American Jewish child, when non-Orthodox day schools were virtually non-existent, and even the Orthodox day school movement had barely gained a toehold. To a group of venturesome educators, utilizing the summer months to bolster synagogue religious education seemed to be a very sound idea,[5] an idea which had long been promoted by Benderly, the pioneering creator of the central institutions of Jewish Education in North America (Winter, 1966, pp. 31–43).

While requiring a significant investment of always scarce economic and human resources, as will be demonstrated, the decision to embark upon the camping initiative was to prove a sound investment for the national religious agencies beyond the extent to which it enriched the quality of the Jewish education received by the children and youth affiliated with the movement. For one thing, it appears that the founding of the camping movements may well have been the catalyst in stimulating a group of movement-wide initiatives which would foster the now routinely accepted rich panoply of Jewish educational programs in which the children and teenagers of synagogue-affiliated families participate in addition to the synagogue religious school or day school (e.g. youth activities and Israel programs). Later, this paper will describe how United Synagogue Youth (USY), the mass youth organization of the Conservative Movement was born out of the 1947 experience of Ramah staff members. The Ramah

---

4   For a history of recreational camping, see Eels, 1986.
5   See section titled "Summer Camps" in Davis, 1958.

Israel Seminar, the first organized Israel experience for Conservative youth, first engaged the participation of Ramah campers and staff in the summer of 1962.

While in many ways the camping programs developed in the Conservative and Reform movements were quite similar (notably with the exception of the commitment of the Ramah founders to conducting their camp totally in the Hebrew language), their origins were quite different. For the Conservative camp founders, notably Sylvia Ettenberg and Moshe Davis, it was their exhilarating experiences in the Cejwin and Massad camps (Schwartz, 1987, pp. 17ff.), which inspired their interest in Jewish educational camping. Cejwin, with its stress on Jewish communal living, was established in 1919 by the Central Jewish Institute, a Manhattan Talmud Torah, and was the first Jewish camp in North America established by an individual institution. Ettenberg spent a number of years in Cejwin, working closely with Abraham Schoolman, the founding Cejwin director (ibid.). As a result of their working together in the *Hanoar Haivri* [Hebrew Youth] Organization, Ettenberg and Davis were close collaborators of Shlomo Shulsinger who established Massad, a Hebrew-speaking camp which aimed to realize the goals of the organization in a camp setting. Its first summer as an overnight camp on its own site was 1941 (Ibid., pp. 18–19).

According to a published account, the founders of the first Reform camps were mainly German-born rabbis who had come to study at Hebrew Union College in Cincinnati before the outbreak of World War II. It was their familiarity with the successful European Jewish youth movements and camps and their observation of Christian youth camping in North America that convinced them of the potential significant role for camping in Reform Jewish education (Goldberg, 1989). In both cases, the founders of the religious camping movements were convinced that the summer camp offered a very sound solution to the problems of a skimpy religious school education and of the lack of potential indigenous candidates to prepare for professional leadership roles in the movements.

The founders of the movement camps were also well aware that recreational summer camping had long been accepted by American Jewish families as a desirable and appropriate summer pastime for their children.

"The "lure of camp" spread quickly within the American Jewish community, cutting across internal distinctions of class, religious affiliation, politics and culture. Initially circumscribed, limited to the children of the very rich or very poor, camping became "universal" by the 1930s, a mass phenomenon whose appeal engaged the collective imagination of the left and the right, the working class and the newly affluent..." (Joselit, 1993, p. 15).

In his recently published study of Yeshiva University students in the student body of the Jewish Theological Seminary, Gurock points to an additional motivation for the founding of a Conservative camping movement. He suggests that there is evidence that the founding of Ramah, and its coordinate elite youth organization LTF, was part of a calculated program by the Seminary leadership to replace the defecting Yeshiva College graduates students who regularly enrolled in the Seminary Rabbinical School with indigenous young Conservative Jews (Gurock, 1997, pp. 498, 500). Combining Gurock's and Schwartz's conclusions, we can surmise that the readiness of the Seminary to found and support Ramah camping may not simply have been a way to strengthen elementary Jewish education and to seek a means of replacing the European sources of Jewish religious leadership lost in the Holocaust (though surely it was), but also a way to diminish these Orthodox inroads.

Significantly, in the fall of 1952, five years after the first Ramah season, three of the 1947 campers, then high school students from families affiliated with Conservative synagogues — in Chicago, in Des Moines and in New York City — all began their rabbinical studies at the Seminary. Their numbers were to increase significantly in the years to follow (Davidson and Wertheimer, 1987). A similar impact within the Reform Movement is cited by Lawrence Hoffman.

"Over the last few decades Reform Jews have discovered the tremendous impact of summer camps on teenagers. . . . A simple glance at the list of applicants for the rabbinate, the cantorate, and other professions relating to the Jewish community reveals a highly disproportionate number who have elected these callings because of their positive experience as teenagers in a summer camp." (Hoffman, 1988, p. 75).

As was mentioned earlier, at the time these camping movements were established, in the decade following the end of World War II, other significant Jewish educational camps, among them, Cejwin, Massad, Yavneh, and Modin were operating with great success (Symposium on Jewish Camps, 1946, pp. 6–44). Building on the models presented by those Jewish camps, and the widespread model of the American recreational camp, the Ramah Camps of the Conservative Movement and the UAHC/NFTY Camps of the Reform Movement, grew into formidable educational camping empires which were to exercise a unique and far-reaching influence within these movements.[6]

It should be noted that following the typical pattern of American residential recreational camping, the Jewish educational camps developed a program of activities mainly focused around land and water sports and the arts (music, drama, arts and crafts and Israeli dance). Nature and camping activities, always central to the programs of American recreational summer camps, were offered sparingly in the early years, but as ecological concerns came to the fore in American society, beginning in the 1960s, the camps invested more heavily in staff, equipment and programming in these areas. To these typical American camp activities, the founders added an intensive regimen of Judaic and Hebraic classes, daily prayer, and the observance of Shabbat and other Jewish rituals, especially those connected with days like Tisha B'Av which appear on the summer Jewish calendar, and all types of informal learning activities which took Jewish life and Jewish tradition as their themes.

The Camps as Official Arms of the Synagogue Movements

Established in conjunction with the national institutions of the Conservative and Reform Movements, these camps had the advantage of being connected horizontally to the headquarters of the movements and vertically to the hundreds of synagogues dispersed across the continent which made up the organized local membership units of the movements.[7] The horizontal connection gave the camps the supervisory support and at times financial support of the parent agency. Conversely, the parent agency could rely on the camps for assistance in the achievement of its goals, e.g.

---

6   For up-to-date descriptions of these two camping networks, see these two websites: for the Reform camps, *http://www.uahccamps.org/* and for the Conservative camps, *http://www.campramah.org/*

7   Significantly, Camps Cejwin and Massad, despite their distinguished educational pedigrees and the impressive scope of their operations, were compelled to close, toward the end of the century, while the movement camps prospered. It appears that lacking the kind of institutional support which the religious movements provided to their camping networks, they could not long survive the combined pressures of recruiting campers in the face of changes in the complexion of the Jewish community, budgetary shortfalls, and failure to replace the vigorous leadership of the founders who had retired from active leadership.

as a site for testing curricular materials or a location at which to strengthen the Jewish backgrounds of potential students.[8]

The horizontal connection meant that in their recruitment efforts, the camps, had easy access to the children of member families in the affiliated synagogues (Cohen, 1987). This was a critical factor in the success of the camps because it was recognized from the very start that such a camp, in order to recruit an adequate enrollment, would need to draw campers from many synagogues in many communities.[9] The recruitment task of the camp directors was inestimably lightened by their having relatively free access to the memberships of the synagogues. It was not only for the sake of movement loyalty that the synagogues were inclined to give the camp directors such access; clearly, they perceived their own educational programs would be strengthened by the impact of the camps upon their students.[10]

Opening Camps Results in a Reshaping of the Seminary's Role of Leadership in the Conservative Movement

As indicated, it was The Jewish Theological Seminary, the rabbinical and teacher training institution of the Conservative Movement, which took the

8   In this regard one could cite the use of the classes in the Ramah Camps as locations for testing out the Bible curricula developed by the Seminary's Melton Research Center as described in Zielenziger, 1989. Also, potential Seminary Rabbinical School students were at times sent to a Ramah Camp to strengthen their Hebrew backgrounds and to expose them, perhaps for the first time, to a pattern of intensive Jewish ritual observance.

9   The 90 campers recruited for the summer of 1947, the first Ramah season, in Wisconsin, were drawn from an area spanning the eastern half of the United States. Some of the camps founded subsequently were able to draw their camper populations from narrower geographic areas: Ramah Poconos — Metropolitan Philadelphia; Ramah Berkshires — Metropolitan New York City.

10 The relationship between the camps and the local synagogues was not without tension, especially as regards religious policy. See interviews with Moshe Davis in *The Melton Journal,* 17 and in Shulsinger, 1989. While the camps had significant impact upon the synagogues through the strengthened Judaic backgrounds of returning campers, the reverse phenomena also took place. Davis describes the sensitivity of the Seminary administration to the religious policies of the rabbis and synagogues in the areas sending campers to each camp. In later years, when the Seminary gave latitude to the Ramah camps to provide greater opportunity for the participation of women in ritual, certain rabbis from the right wing of the Conservative Movement took steps to withhold their students. This, as well as a desire to have the camps reflect the pluralism of the Seminary and of the movement in general resulted in the Seminary requiring each camp to offer dual prayer minyanim: *im* (with aliyot for women) and *b'li* (without aliyot for women). This was fully implemented in the Berkshires Ramah camp and to a lesser extent in the other Ramah camps.

initiative to found the first Ramah Camp, Camp Ramah in Wisconsin in the summer of 1947. That the Seminary should take steps to sponsor a summer camp was unique in at least two ways. First, the Seminary had never before established a branch or outpost institution outside its own walls. Second, one would have thought that were the Conservative Movement to establish a camp for children and youth that it would be established by the United Synagogue of America, the synagogue arm of the Conservative Movement. The chief emphasis of the Seminary's program had always been upon fostering scholarship, publishing academic books and training rabbis (Wertheimer, 1997); while the United Synagogue, in its program of service to the affiliated congregations sponsored a youth organization for post high school youth (Young Peoples League) as well as an active Department of Education, which offered educational services to the affiliated congregations.

In her study of the early years of Ramah cited above (Schwartz, 1987), Schwartz has pointed to the convergence of two factors which brought about this unlikely Seminary initiative. One was the presence in key positions in the Seminary administration of Moshe Davis and Sylvia Ettenberg, individuals highly skilled and experienced in Jewish educational camping, who were aching to establish such camps under Conservative auspices. The other was the initiative of Rabbi Ralph Simon of Chicago, a Seminary alumnus, who approached the Seminary asking for assistance and support in establishing such a camp for the Conservative youth of Chicago. It was this convergence of willing minds in New York and willing hands in Chicago that resulted in the founding of the first Ramah Camp and eventuated in the establishment of the network of Ramah summer camps, day camps and Israel programs, all under the aegis of the Seminary. Even granting the accuracy of Gurock's suggestion of underlying *realpolitik* (see above), without these two favorable factors, there surely would have been no camp.

And so the Seminary agreed to extend itself beyond its normal regimen of scholarly and academic activities to sponsor and supervise a children's camp.[11] It committed itself to providing staff and program for this camp.

---

11 It should be noted that under the leadership of Ettenberg and Davis, during the previous two years the Seminary had already deviated from its academic emphasis when it had inaugurated a training program for teachers in Jewish nursery schools ("Atid") and an elite youth group (LTF). Concerned with the budgetary drain of sponsoring these two programs, Davis was made to choose by President Finkelstein between Atid and Ramah. He chose Ramah. As for the LTF program, for the next three decades, it served as the winter continuation of Ramah for high school age students. See Brown, 1999,p. 34.

More distinctive yet was the authority it established for itself to set the religious policies that would govern camp life. (See Gottfried, 1993, pp. 8–9) It was one thing for the Seminary administration to govern religious life on its own premises, but quite another to govern religious life on a property a thousand miles away for children from families affiliated with Conservative synagogues. In the Conservative movement, determination of religious policy (halacha) beyond the halls of the Seminary (i.e. in the affiliated congregations) had traditionally been in the hands of a subcommittee of the Rabbinical Assembly, the organization of Conservative rabbis. Now the Seminary undertook to set policies for the distant camp setting, to some extent infringing on the rabbis' prerogatives.

Some took it as a radical break with the established practice when major halachic changes regarding religious matters (such as the ordination of women, establishing an egalitarian minyan on its premises, etc.) were enacted by the Seminary in the 1980s. Actually, in retrospect, it was not so radical a step, because (aside from establishing the religious policies followed on the Seminary premises) the Seminary had been long performing this role for the Ramah Camps (Rabinowitz, 1986).[12]

It has already been noted that in the case of the Seminary, key Seminary administrative figures like Moshe Davis and Sylvia Ettenberg were founders of the Ramah camping movement. Seymour Fox was another key Seminary administrator who also played a major role in the early years of the Ramah movement. He entered the Rabbinical School of the Seminary in the fall of 1952. Fox served at the Wisconsin Ramah camp as Director of the Junior Counselor Training Program in the summers of 1952 and 1953, and as Camp Director in the summers of 1954 and 1955. He completed his rabbinical studies at the Seminary in the fall of 1955, at which time he assumed a post as assistant to then Chancellor Louis Finkelstein. Subsequently he became acting dean of the Seminary's Teachers Institute. During the entire time that he served as a Seminary administrator (approximately a decade), he maintained his intense interest and involvement in the Ramah camping movement. Many of the significant changes and innovations in Ramah which took place during that period can be traced to his initiatives. The presence in key Seminary administrative posts of such an individual, possessing first-hand knowledge and deep

---

12 In this article, Rabinowitz cites Ramah along with the Rabbinical Assembly as one of the official sources for halachic practice in the Conservative Movement. See pages 16, 18, 25, 28, and 31.

commitment to the Ramah camping model served to further cement the relationship between the Seminary and the camps.

The founding of the first Ramah Camp was to lead to the establishment of a Ramah Camping Movement (Brown, 1997). The first summer, despite serious problems relating to the facilities and commissary, was deemed successful (Brown, 1999, p. 37ff.) and led to the leasing of facilities for a second Ramah Camp in Maine the following summer. Though the camp in Maine was deemed unsuccessful and abandoned after two seasons, the continued success of the Wisconsin camp led to the purchase of Camp Ramah in the Poconos in summer of 1950 and the acquisition or development of the rest of the camps in following summers. In the Conservative Movement as well as in the Reform Movement, there was enthusiastic response to the camping initiatives. As new camps were opened and often oversubscribed, it led, with the support of local laypeople, to the opening of more new camps, to provide additional camper spaces. As new camps were opened they extended the leadership role of the central institutions to areas of the country where they were less well known, and/or in ways that they had previously not extended their authority.

Working Through the Local Synagogues Gives Access to Committed Lay Leadership

Because the initiative for founding the camps came from or with the support of the central organizations or their regional arms, the bulk of their camper recruitment was done within the affiliated synagogues. As a result, the fledgling camps were able to elicit the participation of laypeople already dedicated to and actively involved in the movement to serve as leaders on the camp committees.[13]

If Ramah served the Seminary as a builder of *chutzpah* (audacity/ courage) to establish itself afield institutionally (see below), it also served as a means of cementing for the Seminary the loyalty of lay leaders and contributors around North America, whose previous chief relationship to the Seminary came in the course of writing a check at an annual Seminary

---

13 Some of the most significant figures among these camp lay committees were *not* parents of campers but simply committed mature synagogue lay leaders with a strong commitment to the synagogue movement and an appreciation of the potential educational achievements of the camps. See for example, Winer, 1993. Winer was a long time leader and financial supporter of Camp Ramah in Wisconsin and the National Ramah Commission. At the time he began his involvement in Ramah, he was active in synagogue life, but had no children who were campers at the camp.

function. It is always difficult for Jewish institutions located in one city (e.g. in New York, in Cincinnati, or in Israel) to activate local lay people on behalf of the institution, when activity must be limited to occasional visits to the site of the institution, but mainly to participating in fundraising activity. Several of the camps proved to be unusually attractive projects to the leadership of the local Seminary campaigns.

One thinks of Camp Ramah in Wisconsin where men such as Louis Winer, Joseph Levine and Bert Weinstein were leaders of the camp board but also served as stalwarts of the Seminary campaign. The same is true of Philadelphia where Abe Birenbaum, a leader of the Seminary campaign literally went out and bought a site for the camp (Schwartz, 1987, p. 31). Here we have a consequence, not foreseen by the Ramah founders at the Seminary, but perspicaciously perceived by the Seminary's fundraising field representatives.[14] They saw that the time which they spent working with and supporting the work of the Ramah committee members on behalf of the camp would ultimately redound to the success of their Seminary campaigns. So we see, that as the camping movement spread to new locations, so the direct influence of the Seminary on the local communities was strengthened.

The same held true in the Reform movement as is attested to in a recent alumni bulletin column written by the then current chair of Olin-Sang-Ruby Institute, the first of the UAHC camps.

"... we must remember that lay leadership also played a significant role in the creation of the first Union Institute...it is good to recall names such as J. S. Ackerman who served as the first chair of the camp board . . . and Dr. S. S. Hollander and Sidney I. Cole ... both of whom served as national presidents of UAHC ... Our Camp and your synagogue thrive on lay leadership and dedication. As Maurice N. Eisendrath, former President of the National UAHC, wrote on February 29, 1952 [prior to the first season] to J. S. Ackerman: "I cannot tell you what a tremendous thrill I received when I read your letter and when I held in my hand the actual certificate of ownership in the first, 'Union Institute of The UAHC' ..." (Kol Noar, 2000)

---

14 During the 1960s and 1970s, when the writer served as director of Camp Ramah in Wisconsin, headquartered in Chicago, he had numerous informal conversations with Jack Goltzman, the Seminary's field representative in Chicago, aimed at fostering synergy between the work of the camp committee and the Seminary's annual campaign.

The Camps as Forerunners of Movement Expansion

In the Conservative Movement, the success of the Ramah Camps was followed by institutional expansion in other areas. In short order, while continuing its sponsorship of the growing Ramah movement, the Seminary was to embark on expansion to the West Coast with the opening in Los Angeles of the University of Judaism and to Israel with the opening of its American Student Center (Wertheimer, 1997, I, pp. 793ff, II, pp. 212ff). One can surmise, that given the relative caution with which Seminary President Louis Finkelstein approached the notion of sponsoring a camping movement (Brown, 1997, p. 829), and his reluctance to devote funds to activities not academic in nature, that had Ramah failed, these latter steps, and those that followed them might not have been taken.

It does not seem to have initially struck the Ramah founders, and certainly not Finkelstein, that these children's summer camps could ultimately provide important support for the academic and scholarly programs of the Seminary. However, when a world wide map was produced in the 1960s showing the "campuses" of the Seminary, the six Ramah camps were pinpointed along with the Seminary in New York, the University of Judaism in California, the American Student Center in Jerusalem, and the Jewish Museum in New York (Cardin and Silverman, 1987, p. 204). Ramah was no longer under the supervision of the Seminary; it was a *part* of the Seminary.

In a similar vein, Rabbi Marshall Meyer the dynamic apostle who brought Conservative Judaism to South America, having spent a summer in Ramah while yet a Seminary student, embraced the Ramah concept as a key part of the movement and institutions that he established in Argentina. Campamento Ramah and the Seminario Rabbinico Latin-americano were established simultaneously. Graduates of the Seminario, as they went to serve in other countries, followed his example and established their own camps. Levi Soshuk, one of the early Ramah camp directors was sent by the Seminary to assist Meyer in the founding of the Argentinean camp.

In a certain sense then, for the Conservative Movement, the camps became the regional extensions of the Seminary throughout North America as well as abroad. In Canada where the official legal name of the camp's governing body was the Jewish Theological Society of Canada, the existence of the camp provided a legal foundation for the Seminary's fundraising activity.

Establishing Low Cost Beachheads for the Parent Institutions

The camps had the capability to spread the image and the philosophy of the parent institution to distant locations at low cost. For families affiliated with the synagogues, but unfamiliar with the parent organizations or institutions, attendance at the camps could provide a pathway to guide campers and their parents toward knowledge of and involvement in the parent institutions (Cohen, 1987). Also, the camps provided the parent institutions with locations, often quite distant from the parent institution, through which its message could be disseminated to the members of synagogues in the distant region sending campers to the camp. This public relations work was done directly through the instrumentality of the camp director, Seminary students who filled staff roles and, in Ramah, through the professor-in-residence (a member of the Jewish Theological Seminary faculty who spent the summer in a Ramah camp). It was done indirectly, and in very powerful fashion through the medium of the camp program which was structured so as to reflect the values of the parent institution.

When a camp was established to serve a geographical region of the movement, it created a parcel of real estate in that region owned by the national organization (see description above of the president of UAHC receiving the deed to the first Reform camp) or by the Conservative or Reform religious community in that area. Brown describes some of the tugs-of-war in the Conservative movement between the lay boards governing the local camps and the national institution over control of these properties and the income derived from them in the form of tuitions. Because the Seminary itself made loans to the camps, or because it guaranteed substantial bank loans by the camps, at times, when the camps could not make timely payments, there were sharp disputes between the local camps and the parent institution (Brown, 1999). So for all its educational achievement, not infrequently, the camps were a "bone stuck in the throat" of the Seminary.

Though probably not established with that in mind, building or buying a camp in a rural area was a relatively cheap way of bringing the presence of the parent institution to an area. The Museum of the Southern Jewish Experience, constructed on the grounds of UAHC Henry S. Jacobs Camp for Living Judaism in Utica, Mississippi in 1989, is a telling example of how the establishment of a camp, a thousand miles away from the parent institution provided the opportunity for an activity under the aegis of the parent institution that would likely not have occurred and certainly not been connected to the parent organization, were it not for the presence of the summer camp in that location. It was done through the mediation of Rabbi Alexander Schindler, UAHC president, who introduced the camp director to the Southern foundation which made the gift which made construction of the Museum possible (Footlick, 1987, p. 10; Blackman, 1990, p. 16).

As camps became firmly established, the camp grounds became the locations of retreats, family education programs and other types of activities in furtherance of the goals of the parent organization. Camp Ramah in California was, early on, viewed as a part of the campus of the University of Judaism (some 70 miles away). Staff quarters at this camp were built attractively and comfortably so that they could house the summer staff and also serve as an attractive retreat center for the Conservative Movement in the West and Southwest during the rest of the year. The camp owned an attractive set of motel-style furniture, kept in storage during the summer months, and installed in those staff quarters once the damage-prone campers and camp staff had departed at the conclusion of the summer season.

Educational Significance of Remote Camp Locations and Seasonal Operation

A number of factors might be suggested which encouraged the innovative modes of education characteristic of the camps. As a result of these factors, educational programs in the camps often differed in significant aspects from the curricula of the synagogue schools which the campers attended during the winter months.

Among the factors were these: a) Camps tend to be located at a distance from the metropolitan areas from which campers originated or in which movement headquarters were located. These remote locations tended to foster a "disconnect" between the camp administration and local bureaus of Jewish education or movement headquarters thereby giving the camp staff a more or less free hand to be innovative as they designed and implemented the camp curriculum. b) To expect an educational staff to follow a curriculum or adhere to educational guidelines requires a degree of professional training and experience. Over 99 percent of the camp staffs were summer employees (many for only one season) so very likely they were receiving their training as counselors, as educators and as proponents of the ideology of the movement over the course of the summer while they were working with the children and youth. These employees may have excelled in Jewish loyalty and convictions, but often lacked any deep knowledge of the parent institution and its expectations. Further, as non-professionals, they did not feel constrained to offer the types of educational activities that characterized the standard practice of teachers in Jewish schools. To some extent, this might explain the ease with which a "reformer" like Newman could establish a new type of educational program in the Wisconsin Ramah camp which significantly made changes and additions to the model devised by Ramah's founders (Schwartz, 1984, pp. 7–22). While school faculties usually are bound by a fairly stable curriculum given to them by the school principal, in camp the staff often felt compelled to create, "on the spot," educational programs responsive to the needs of the campers and to events taking place in the world outside the camp which they deemed to be of particular relevance to the Jewish community.

These factors, among others, may help explain the comments of observers of Reform camping regarding the strong impact of the camp experience upon certain areas of movement ideology and activity. In the eyes of these camping historians, the experience of Reform youth in the movement's camps could be identified as responsible for the shift from cognitive to experiential (i.e. informal) learning activities in the Reform religious school; the spread of camp-type music throughout the synagogues of the Reform Movement; and even for a radical change in the theology of Reform Jews (Salkin, 1989, pp. 17–25). What was achieved in the Reform camps, and specifically, what took place in the Reform camps as regards developing a new style of communal prayer and liturgical music is well documented as a result of the discord which it created throughout the movement.

"Over the last few decades, Reform Jews have discovered the tremendous impact of summer camps on teenagers. It is generally assumed, and quite rightly so, that nothing rivals the camp in its ability to educate children in religious values and to socialize them in a religious way of life...

Part of the [camp] experience is prayer conducted in such a way as to reflect the worshipping group. The music has a soft, folk-rock character; songs led by a guitarist are sung in unison. Creative prayers are composed and read by group members, who emphasize in what they write the underlying concerns of the teenagers present... Camp graduates return home imbued with the desire to continue their experience in their local synagogues.

Unfortunately, that does not usually happen. One of the reasons worship works at camp is that all the other camp systems reinforce the worship system there. At home an entirely different network of systems must be confronted." (Hoffman, 1988, p. 75).

So significant was the conflict generated by the type of liturgical music developed in the camps, that the Reform cantorate dedicated a conference to discussing this topic:

"A controversy over what is proper synagogue music . . . became the central theme of the mid-winter conference of the [Reform] American Conference of Cantors ... the "new trend" is largely a product of the UAHC camps and the youth groups of the North American Federation of Temple Youth (NAFTY). The new songs show the influence of American rock and folk songs and popular Israeli melodies. Accompanied by guitar, they lend themselves to group participation... many cantors are concerned that the new songs do not maintain high enough standards and should not be used in the synagogue." (Galed, 1981, p.1).

There may be good reason to conjecture why such substantive impact was more likely to occur in the Reform Movement than in the Conservative Movement. In the Reform Movement, the camping and youth movements were integrated in one UAHC department so that youngsters and staff summering in the camps might have relatively easily maintained the attitudes developed in camp upon returning home. In the Conservative Movement, Ramah was under the Seminary while USY, its mass based youth movement was a department of the United Synagogue, so that Ramah influences were likely to have had a more limited influence upon the movement.

Though always working within the parameters set by the parent organizations, early on, camp staffs found that they had relative freedom to create the educational programs of the camps. Over time it gave them the opportunity to add to the traditional subject matter of Jewish schools (Hebrew language, Siddur, customs and ceremonies, and Torah) such contemporary subjects as the Holocaust and the persecution of Soviet Jewry. The Holocaust was regularly added to the content of the Tisha B'Av observances in camp—it seemed to fit very well into the main theme of the day, a recitation of the national disasters of the Jewish people going back to the destruction of the First Temple at the hands of the Babylonians, and continuing with the destruction wreaked upon European Jewry by the Crusades, and the exile of the Jewish community from the Iberian Peninsula.

Staffs took advantage of the opportunity which camp provided to offer far-ranging activities, such as programming social action projects which involved taking the campers beyond the camp setting. These new study topics and types of experiential learning were offered in the camps long before they were taught or introduced into the synagogue schools. Because of the examples seen in the camp programs, these educational innovations were brought back to the synagogues by staff members or simply by "word of mouth" and were adopted in the schools (Ackerman, 1993, pp. 125–26).

The Camps Strengthen Jewish Education in the Movements

One of the failures of Jewish education in the liberal movements has always been their frequent inability to provide the students with teachers who were models of Jewish living and Jewish commitment for the students to emulate. The teachers in synagogue religious schools were often not the type of individual who could strike a spark with their students. Though aware of the fact that they may have been non-religious or too religious (i.e. Orthodox), they were hired by the synagogue educational directors because they possessed the necessary knowledge base to teach the year-long curriculum. In the camps, this was not the case. The camp director could more easily hire charismatic college and graduate students possessing a basic knowledge of Judaism and the Hebrew language, attuned to the ideology of the movement, who were ready and able to adapt to the demands of the summer camp commitment.

Here we see another outcome of the camping programs, beyond their benefit for the campers, and redounding to the benefit of the religious movements and the broader Jewish community. The camps provided a structure for involving university-age members of the movement in intensive educational activity which could deepen and solidify their commitment to Conservative/Reform Judaism. The idealism of the young campers and especially teenagers was often ignited under the influence of these attractive young role models who fired up their enthusiasm for Jewish observance, further and more intensive Jewish study, visiting or studying in Israel and preparation for professional roles in Jewish life.

In each region where camps were founded they provided children and youth with centers for intensive Jewish study, far beyond what any one synagogue, or city or region could offer (with the exception of the day schools, in certain localities, once these were founded). Because they operated during the summer, when students were out of school, in a certain sense the camps were like two-month boarding schools catering to the Jewish education needs of the youth from Conservative and Reform synagogues in a certain geographic area. During a two year period (February-May, 1974 and 1975), the Reform Movement carried the concept of utilizing camp as school to its fullest implication and during these years operated a one semester study program for high school seniors at the UAHC Institute in Oconomowoc, Wisconsin. In addition to providing an intensive Judaic study program, students devoted their weekends to serving on the faculties of Reform religious schools in communities surrounding Oconomowoc which is located in the exurban area between Chicago and Milwaukee (Full-Time Education Program Initiated in Chicago, 1973; Ma'ayan Experience Inspires Commitment to Jewish Living, 1975).

In the Conservative Movement which established a smaller number of camps (though with larger camp populations) than the Reform Movement, campers often had to travel great distances to reach camps. Ramah campers in Florida and throughout the South, for example, were assigned to the camp in New England. (This was the case until the summer of 1997 when Ramah Darom in Clayton, Georgia opened.) What on the face of it might appear to be a disadvantage turned out to be an advantage in that it fostered long-lasting relationships between far-flung groups of campers, all under the aegis of the camp. Each camp constituency comprised a vital youth community for its campers that continued throughout the winter months. Long before the easy communication of the e-mail era, these young people remained in regular contact through the media of telephones and the mail and yearly mid-winter *kallot*.

The atmosphere of the camp settings was such that campers and staff would often carry away with them a lasting commitment to what was learned in the camps and feel a strong desire to apply it or follow through on it in their own personal and institutional settings, once they returned home. Campers absorbed from the camp setting Jewish rituals which were not included in the religious school curriculum. Many learned *Birkat Hamazon* (Grace After Meals) or *Havdalah* (the Sabbath concluding ritual), and participated in daily prayer or a *Tisha B'Av* service for the first time in their lives. The camps, to some extent because of the extended time they offered for study, augmented the curriculum of the synagogue religious school with areas of Jewish study or ritual skills previously deemed unattainable in a non-Orthodox setting. By encouraging campers to attend camp, synagogue religious school directors and rabbis were augmenting the outcomes of their schools and youth programs without changing the local educational program.

Extending the Educational Reach of the Parent Institution

While the camps, were established to be agencies of education for children and high school youth, much less note has been taken of the extent to which they served as significant agencies of Jewish education for staff who were college-age and graduate students. In both the Conservative and Reform movement camps high level teachers of Judaica were brought into the camps to serve as teachers for staff. One of the great strengths of the Reform camps has always been the extent to which rabbis serving in congregations from throughout the region served by a camp came up for periods of two or three weeks to serve on staff; also HUC-JIR professors also came up to the camps. In the Ramah movement, from the start, it was institutional policy to station a JTS faculty member as professor-in-residence at the camp. Only at a later period did Ramah encourage congregational rabbis to spend time at the camp. The Ramah professor-in-residence served as teacher to staff, consultant to the camp director, and to all a walking encyclopedia of Judaica and a model of a learning Jew.

While initially it was intended that these rabbis and scholars should benefit the camps by providing a living and breathing fount of Jewish learning within the camp; from another point of view, it made it possible for each movement to spread and exhibit its scholarly resources more widely. It made it possible to serve and influence a much broader population than were these rabbis and teachers who were limited to serving in a local pulpit or in the central rabbinical training institution. Conversely, the camp experience enriched the rabbis and scholars by exposing them to the realities of Jewish life on the frontiers of their movements and to the challenge of creating anew, each summer, educational programs responsive to the needs of the campers and qualifications of the staff.

The Seminary's Ramah Camp Inspires Creation of the United Synagogue's Youth Movement

Finally, the manner in which the first Ramah camp influenced the creation of USY, United Synagogue Youth, the mass youth organization of the

Conservative Movement, provides an interesting example of the potential for camps to have a far reaching impact within the parent movement. Appropriately, USY is an arm of the United Synagogue for Conservative Judaism but, surprisingly, the impetus to found such an organization for the youth in Conservative synagogues came from Ramah (an arm of the Seminary), through the persons of Ramah staffers Rabbi Kassel Abelson and his wife Shirley.

Newly ordained at the Jewish Theological Seminary, Abelson came to his first rabbinic position as assistant to Rabbi David Aronson at Beth El Synagogue in Minneapolis, in the fall of 1948, after having served, with his wife Shirley, as bunk counselors at Camp Ramah in Wisconsin in the summer of 1947, its first season. The Abelsons were inspired by the Ramah experience which had demonstrated to them the potential of informal Jewish educational programs, like Ramah, for strengthening the Jewish education received by the children and youth of the movement. Within a few months of their arrival in Minneapolis, they concluded that there was both need and room for a youth organization that would serve all of the synagogue-affiliated Conservative youth in the Twin Cities of Minneapolis and St. Paul. The organization, United Synagogue Youth as they named it, was established with the cooperation of the three local Conservative rabbis and their synagogues, and soon after was organized throughout the Midwest Region of the United Synagogue. The Midwest initiative caught the imagination of the United Synagogue leadership in New York, and in a short time a national organization was created. In summary, the Camp Ramah initiative under Seminary auspices, with the Abelsons serving as intermediaries, gave birth to the United Synagogue's youth organization. While they were not directly involved in the creation of national USY, the presence of the Abelsons at Ramah and then in the Twin Cities facilitated establishing a nexus between an activity of the Seminary and an activity of the Conservative Movement's synagogue organization (something not frequently seen over the next half century). (Abelson, 2000).

The important point to note here is the manner in which individuals as a result of their private experiences in the camp setting can have an impact upon the settings to which they return from camp. The Abelsons drew their own conclusions regarding the value of the type of informal Jewish education experiences that they had seen in the camp and as a result took steps to create a new kind of youth organization.

Conclusion

In this paper, we have tried to describe in broad outline the impact of the summer camps upon the religious movements. We are convinced that there is much more that will be revealed about this topic as more of the history of American Jewish camping is brought to light.

* * *

This paper is written in tribute to Professor Seymour Fox, an esteemed teacher and dear friend. It is written in recognition of his major contribution to Jewish camping and American Jewish education through his work at the Jewish Theological Seminary. It is also written in recognition of his teaching and personal encouragement for which I am deeply grateful.

References

Abelson, Kassel. USY Memories. (2000). Personal e-mail. Posted 17 October.

Ackerman, Walter. (1993). A world apart: Hebrew Teachers Colleges and Hebrew-speaking camps. In Alan Mintz. (Ed.). *Hebrew in America: Perspectives and prospects*. Detroit: Wayne State University Press.

Blackman, Michael. (1990). Rescue and Rededication: Museum of the Southern Jewish Experience. *Reform Judaism, 16.* Summer.

Brown, Michael. (1997). It's off to camp we go: Ramah, LTF, and the Seminary in the Finkelstein Era. In Jack Wertheimer. (Ed.) *Tradition renewed: A history of the Jewish Theological Seminary of America*. New York: JTSA.

Brown, Michael. (1999). The most important venture ever undertaken by the Seminary: Ramah in its first four decades. In Sheldon Dorph. (Ed.). *Ramah reflections at 50: Visions for a new century*. New York: National Ramah Commission.

Cardin, Nina and Silverman, David. (Eds.). (1987). *The Seminary at 100: Reflections on the Jewish Theological Seminary and the Conservative Movement*. New York: Jewish Theological Seminary and Rabbinical Assembly. Jewish Theological Seminary and Rabbinical Assembly: New York City.

Cohen, Burton. (1987). From camper to National Director: A personal view of the Seminary and Ramah. In Nina Beth Cardin and David Silverman. (Eds.). *The Seminary at 100: Reflections on the Jewish Theological Seminary and the Conservative Movement*. New York: Jewish Theological Seminary and Rabbinical Assembly.

Davidson, Aryeh and Wertheimer, Jack. (1987). The next generation of Conservative rabbis: An empirical study of today's rabbinical students. In Nina Beth Cardin and David Silverman. (Eds.). *The Seminary at 100: Reflections on the Jewish Theological*

Seminary and the Conservative Movement. New York: Jewish Theological Seminary and Rabbinical Assembly.

Davis, Moshe. (1958). The ladder of Jewish education. In Mordecai Waxman. (Ed.). *Tradition and change: The development of Conservative Judaism.* New York: The Burning Bush Press.

Dorph, Sheldon A. (Ed.). (1999). *Ramah reflections at 50: Visions for a New Century.* National Ramah Commission: New York City.

Eels, Eleanor. (1986). *Eleanor Eels' history of organized camping.* Martinsville: American Camping Association.

Ettenberg, Sylvia C. and Rosenfield, Geraldine. (Eds.). (1989). *The Ramah experience: community and commitment.* New York: Jewish Theological Seminary and National Ramah Commission.

Footlick, Robbyn. (1987). Camp Jacobs: Portal to Southern Jewry. *Reform Judaism: 10* Summer.

Fox, Seymour, with Novak, William. (2000). *Vision at the heart: Lessons from Camp Ramah on the power of ideas in shaping educational institutions.* Jerusalem: The Mandel Foundation.

Full-time education program initiated in Chicago. (1973). *Reform Judaism.* April.

Galed, Elli C. (1981). Synagogue music controversy. *Reform Judaism.* June.

Goldberg, Edward Cole. (1989). The beginnings of educational camping in the Reform Movement. *Journal of Reform Judaism, 36 (4).* Fall.

Gottfried, Pamela Jay. (1993). Camp Ramah: Origins, Problems and Partial Solutions: An Interview with Moshe Davis. *The Melton Journal 27.* Autumn.

Gurock, Jeffrey S. (1997). Yeshiva students at the Jewish Theological Seminary. In Jack Wertheimer (Ed.), *Tradition renewed: A history of the Jewish Theological Seminary.* New York: Jewish Theological Seminary. Vol. I.

Hoffman, Lawrence A. (1988). *The art of public prayer: Not for clergy only.* Washington D.C.: The Pastoral Press.

Joselit, Jenna Weissman. (1993). The Jewish way of play. In Jenna Weissman Joselit with Karen S. Mittelman (Eds.) *A worthy use of the summer: Jewish summer camping in America.* Philadelphia: National Museum of American Jewish History.

Kol Noar: News from Olin-Sang-Ruby Union Institute and The Youth Department, Great Lakes Region, UAHC. Fall 2000.

'Ma'ayan' experience inspires commitment to Jewish living. (1975). *Reform Judaism.* May.

Rabinowitz, Mayer. (1986). Towards a Halachic guide for the Conservative Jew. *Conservative Judaism, 39 (1).* Fall.

Reich, Zvi. (1978). Camp Morasha (Hebrew). In Meir Havatzelet. (Ed.) *Kovetz Massad: Essays in Hebrew literature and thought by friends of Massad Camps.* New York: Massad Camps.

Rivkin, Mayer S. (Ed.). (1982). *The Rebbe: Changing the tide of education.* Brooklyn: Lubavitch Youth Organization.

Salkin, Jeffrey K. (1989). NFTY at Fifty: An Assessment. *Journal of Reform Judaism.* Fall.

Schwartz, Shuly Rubin. (1984). Ramah philosophy and the Newman revolution. In

Alexander M. Shapiro and Burton I. Cohen. (Eds.). *Lilmod U'Lelamed: Studies in Jewish Education and Judaica in honor of Louis Newman*. New York: Ktav Publishing House.

Schwartz, Shuly Rubin. (1987). Camp Ramah: The early years: 1947–1952. *Conservative Judaism, 40 (1)*. Fall.

Shapiro, Alexander M. and Cohen, Burton I. (Eds.) (1984). *Lilmod u-Lelamed: Studies in Jewish Education and Judaica in Honor of Louis Newman*. New York: KTAV Publishing House.

Shulsinger, Shlomo. (Ed.). (1989). *Kovetz Massad II*. Jerusalem: Massad Organization.

Wertheimer, Jack. (Ed.). (1997). *Tradition renewed: A history of the Jewish Theological Seminary of America*. (2 Vols.) New York: JTSA.

Winer, Louis. (1993). *My first 89 years*. (no publisher).

Winter, Nathan. (1966). *Jewish education in a pluralist society: Samson Benderly and Jewish education in the United States*. New York: New York University Press.

Zelon, Helen. (February 2000). Camp Comeback. *Moment Magazine*.

Zielenziger, Ruth. (1989). A history of the Bible Program of the Melton Research Center. D.H.L Dissertation, Jewish Theological Seminary of America.

Would You Want Your Child to be a Hebrew Teacher?

WALTER I. ACKERMAN

I

The proper functioning of a community or any other human organization depends in large measure on the skill and competence of its leaders, professional or voluntary. Many societies, ancient and modern alike, have developed sophisticated forms of recruitment and training for those who intend to devote themselves to the service of the common good. The examination system which spawned the Chinese literati in ancient and pre-modern times and the highly selective *ecoles superieures*, whose graduates are the backbone of the French civil service are but two examples. A medieval document (Kanarfogel, 1992) of unknown provenance, *Sefer Hukai Torah*, pushes the idea of an elite of service to an ultimate. The model of the biblical Levites who were enjoined to separate themselves from their families in order to "... teach your norms to Jacob [and] your instruction to Israel" (Deut. 33: 9–10) leads the author to call upon Jewish families of Kanarfogel's time to dedicate one son to the study of Torah. The youngster elected to the task joins other *P'rushim* who were separated from home and family for seven years to devote themselves exclusively to the study of Torah. The American Jewish community is no exception to the universal need for professionals whose background and training equip them to deal with the manifold issues which are the hallmarks of post modern times.

247

Recent years have witnessed a welcome proliferation of programs and allocation of resources designed to attract and retain young people of ability, intelligence and motivation to the various branches of Jewish communal service. Despite the many efforts — some of which date back to the turn of the 20th century — there is still a shortage of manpower in many communities; people with only the most minimal of qualifications, and sometimes even without that, function in positions in schools, social service agencies, volunteer agencies, and the other settings which constitute a well organized community.

The rich experience of the various training programs available in the United States notwithstanding, we do not have as much information as we would like regarding the factors which influence young people in their choice of a career in Jewish education or some other area of communal service. The lack of data complicates the task of planning for recruiting, training and retaining of personnel.

The idea of career choices is, of course, a function of an open society. Young people are free, theoretically at least, to choose what kind of work they want to do. Talented youngsters of secure economic background can look to a wide array of possibilities as they contemplate what they "want to be." The theory of career choice teaches that the choice of an occupation is an expression of personality, itself in part a product of an individual's early environment, and not a random event, even though chance sometimes can play a role. Moreover people look for work settings which let them exercise their skills and abilities, express their attitudes and values and take on agreeable problems and roles (Brown and Brooks, 1990). This paper examines the explanations of their choice of Jewish education as a profession given by a group of young American Jewish educators. The material is drawn from the autobiographical essay which is required of applicants for acceptance by the Jerusalem Fellows program.

The Jerusalem Fellows program was established in 1982 for the express purpose of training educational leadership for the Jewish people in the Diaspora. Participants in the program, from Jewish communities around the world but predominantly American, spend one or two and sometimes even three years in residence in Jerusalem. More than 90 graduates of the program today hold senior positions in Jewish education in their communities of origin.[1] Applicants for admission to the program must

---

1   A condition of acceptance to the program is a commitment to serve in the Diaspora for a period of three to five years, depending on the time spent in Jerusalem. A number of former Fellows have settled in Israel following the fulfillment of their obligations.

be under 40 years of age, hold a master's degree in education, Jewish studies or some relevant discipline, and have at least three years of experience in Jewish education or a related field. The latter condition together with the time spent in Jerusalem and the assumption of the obligation to continue service in Jewish education upon completion of the program is surely adequate evidence of long term commitment to Jewish education as a profession.

The admissions procedure to the Jerusalem Fellows requires, among other things, an autobiographical essay which includes reference to the candidate's understanding of the factors which led to a choice of a career in Jewish education. As already indicated, this paper is based on an examination of these essays. Our sample consists of American applicants only because of their predominance among applicants. It did not appear that admission to the program was a relevant variable for our purpose. Altogether, 56 essays were analyzed — 43 and 13 written by men and women respectively.

The distribution between sexes does not reflect the increasingly significant role that women have come to play in American Jewish education. One possible explanation of the imbalance is that male spouses are unable to leave their work in order to accompany their wives for the extended period of time which participation in the program requires.

Despite the problems inherent in self-composed life histories as accurate and objective accounts of the writer's past, we believe that the material before us is essentially reliable. In addition to the narrative, candidates are required to impart vital statistics-places of schooling, extra-curricular activities and other particulars permit a kind of external validation. In addition to submitting written material, candidates are interviewed by members of the faculty of the program; on occasion, graduates or other persons familiar with the Jerusalem Fellows and its purpose serve as interviewers. The interview provides an opportunity to explore seeming discrepancies or incongruities in the written narrative. Experience has taught that candidates from all over the world are aware of these procedures. The circumstances of composition are also important: application for acceptance to the Jerusalem Fellows signifies a readiness for change both in place of residence, even if only temporary, and very often also of job after completion of the program. Despite the possibility that a candidate's essay is guided by a notion of what he/she thinks the program is looking for, it is reasonable to assume that the request for an autobiography leads candidates to reflect and report as faithfully as possible on how they understand their having become what they are.

II

A group profile of the Fellows drawn from application forms and the responses to a questionnaire distributed in 1992 — the tenth anniversary of the program and the occasion of an overall review — provides a helpful framework for a more detailed analysis.

By and large, the educational background and work history of the Fellows meet the minimum requirements of eligibility — a master's degree and at least three years of experience in some sort of educational setting.[2] The overwhelming majority of those who had participated in the program in the first decade of the operation describe themselves as belonging to middle class families, even though slightly less than a quarter of their parents are college graduates. As a group the Fellows are decidedly "mainstream" — the schools they went to and the places in which they worked prior to arriving in Jerusalem are "centrist," whether Conservative, Orthodox or Reform. The few secularists who have participated in the program are far from any radicalism, either of the left or the right. All this reflects the coloration of organized Jewish education all over the world. It is also possible that the characteristics of the program and the composition of the faculty-academicians are fairly well known in mainline Jewish education — as developed over the years and described by participants — discourage consideration by educators and others who think themselves outside the "in-house" norms of the Jerusalem Fellows. The coloration of the group may also be conditioned by the unfortunate fact that the Jerusalem Fellows is one of only a few settings in contemporary Jewish life which bring together people of varied religious identification and allegiance for an extended period of time. While participation does not necessarily imply an acknowledgment of the worth of each of the different understandings of Judaism represented in the group, it does indicate a willingness to accommodate to the demands of a pluralistic setting.

Most of the Fellows attended public colleges and universities on both undergraduate and graduate levels. Among those who indicate that they are Orthodox, Yeshiva University is the most favored institution. As might be expected, most of them majored in the humanities and only one or two, surprisingly, in the arts. The Jewish educational background of the group ranges over the possibilities available in organized Jewish communities.

---

2   The latitude explicit in the formulation is intentional; its aim is to encourage applications from people whose experience has been outside the regular framework of Jewish education, formal or informal.

Applicants to the program are largely in their thirties or late twenties.[3] A goodly number reported that they had reached a point in their professional lives at which they welcomed the opportunity to recharge batteries and even consider a change in jobs. The collective employment history of the Fellows is a map of the job structure of Jewish education in the United States and elsewhere — teacher, principal, youth group leader, director of education in a summer camp, Shaliach,[4] subject coordinator in a day school, curriculum writer, professor in a Jewish studies program, Hillel rabbi, program director in one of the educational departments of the WZO; and somewhat off the beaten track — editor of a children's magazine, film producer, computer specialist, family educator.

The experience of most of the Fellows has been on the level of direct service, immediate contact with learners in a variety of settings. The rules of the game of Jewish education probably account for this skew; access to executive positions in settings distanced from hands on work generally requires a period of experience which places the practitioner beyond the age eligibility of the program. It is also possible that educators who have reached a certain level of position do not consider the program altogether suited to their needs.

Exceptions to the level of job described here are most frequent among Israelis. Both the life history and work experience of the Israelis are considerably more varied than those of the Americans who constitute the majority and set the tone. The decision to permit Israelis to apply to the program, adopted during the first year of operations and after considerable debate, led to a significant change in its ambiance.

When we move from the wide frame of the group portrait to a reading of the autobiographical essays, we find a convincing similarity of pattern in the stories the Fellows tell about themselves. Very few of the accounts — their number is insignificant in the language of statistics — report a critical moment, a chance event, or an accidental contact with a charismatic personality which became a turning point in the individual's sense of Jewishness. On the contrary, the overwhelming majority of the accounts describe an incremental progression consisting of well-defined and easily recognizable elements.

The influence of the family is central to all but a few of the accounts.

---

3   Forty is the ceiling of eligibility.
4   Educators living in Israel whose work in Jewish education in the Diaspora makes them eligible to apply to the program.

Indeed, the appreciation of the role of family is so pervasive as to leave little doubt regarding its critical role:

> "…My earliest influence was my grandfather who sought and saw God all the time…"
> "I grew up in a family that breathed social service in general and Jewish education in particular."
> "My father started me on my path by imbuing in me a love of Jewish and American values."
> "The highlight of my Jewish childhood experience was attending *Shul* with my dear grandfather. We walked two miles each way to attend the closest Young Isroel shul. I enjoyed the warmth and intensity of that special relationship and the love of Yiddushkeit which emerged from it."
> "I learned commitment to Jewish life and the Jewish community through my parents."

In many instances the recollections of family life are accompanied by a sense of having belonged to a community:

> "As a young man I was exposed to a complex of neighborhood, schools, synagogues and youth movements."
> "My childhood world was a very Jewish one. I grew up in a committed Conservative home, in the totality of the Jewish community."
> "…a home where Jewish observance, education and involvement in the community were important."

The kind of family described here designs, almost inexorably and totally in keeping with its commitments, a particular pattern of educational experience for its children — day schools, summer camps and time in Israel. At the time that the members of the sample were of elementary school age, the idea of the day school had not yet gained the kind of public support among American Jews it enjoys today; it was then completely identified with Orthodoxy. The choice of such a school at that time was a socially significant statement.

Even though the reports of schools attended sometimes refer to the influence of teachers — "My earliest Jewish perspective was shaped by two of my teachers" — there is almost no reference to the process of schooling itself. With the exception of one writer who notes that the move from a Yeshiva high school to the more "open" climate of a university was "exhilarating" and even "overwhelming," our material provides no sense of what such schools were like. The uninitiated reader would find it difficult, if not impossible, to learn anything about what distinguishes such a school from others, how tensions between general and Jewish religious studies are resolved and other matters including the way in which it shapes sensibilities.

The camp experience, mainly among non-Orthodox writers and almost completely absent from other accounts, suffers from no such lack of attention:

> "I lived for my summers at Ramah."
>
> "...The experience of Ramah set in motion a lifetime of conversations and relationships with persons for whom the issue of Jewish living and moral responsibilities were serious domains for serious thinking."
>
> "The Union Institute summer camp had a powerful effect on me. The intensity of the Jewish experiences at camp filled a personal need for me...and created one, the need for the continuation of the same experience."
>
> "Ramah was a moment of self-discovery. Some time during that summer I woke up and realized that I was a Jew."
>
> "The experience that had the greatest impact on my life was Camp Massad. There I blossomed, there I flourished."

This is not the place for an analysis of the elements of the camp experience which elicit such responses. Considering, however, the possibility that all kinds of camps, including commercial ones, have a similar influence, it is worth noting, even on pain of repetition, that enrollment at Ramah or a camp of the Reform movement is not a matter of accident. Like attending day school, it flows from a commitment to a certain way of living.

Even though the essays contain fairly frequent mention of membership in youth groups — Bnei Akiva, USY, NFTY — there is next to no description of what went on in those settings. Unlike many retrospective accounts of the transformational effect of participation in a classical youth group, no one here recalls a counselor who served as a model of focus and identification. The following statement stands out for its singularity:

> "I became involved in Hashomer Hatza'ir by chance... Much of my Jewish world view was influenced by the movement's scathing critique of religion and the American Jewish community in favor of an alternative Israeli community based on secular Judaism... My identity is

inextricably intertwined with Israeli culture and the values of the kibbutz."

The lack of detail regarding youth groups may perhaps be accounted for by the fact that there was not really so much about them that was different — they were simply a seamless extension of a world already familiar to the youngster.

Slightly more than a third of the essays note time spent in Israel. The settings vary from Yeshivat Aish HaTorah through organized summer programs for tenth graders to two and a half years in the "Gush."

For many people from whom our material is drawn, a period of time in Israel during a school career or immediately afterward is considered a must. Here, too, it is difficult to discern exactly what it is about Israel that heightens identification and quickens resolve to work for the good of the Jewish people. Descriptions of the Israeli experience range from

"...The two years I spent in the Gush were beyond question the most spiritually and intellectually enriching years of my life..."

to mere mention of the fact that the writer had spent some time there.

Our reading of the essays leads to a picture composed of a number of elements worth noting:

1) Almost without exception, the writers depict families for whom Jewishness — no matter how defined — is central to their lives. The fact of Jewishness is often embedded in a communal framework.
2) A day school education figures prominently, particularly among those who identify themselves as Orthodox. There is no one in the group who did not attend a Jewish school of some sort. We do not, however, find any information regarding the nature of the school experiences. Aside from teachers recalled with great appreciation, there is little to learn here about the way in which attendance at a Jewish school shaped attitudes or behavior.
3) The configuration of educational experiences includes youth groups, summer camps, and visits to Israel — sometimes one of these and sometimes all of them. The memory of each of these settings and its meaning is too personal to point to any generalization about its relative significance. It does seem safe to say that all of them are related one to another — once you are in school, for instance, a summer camp and a trip to Israel seem more probable.

4) As already noted, only a small minority of the writers reports a transformational experience which brought about a major change in lifestyle and career plans.

5) There is almost no mention in the essays of the intellectual — books, ideas and other encounters of the mind — which shaped perceptions and molded commitments. Fairness requires us to note that this omission is possibly a function of the circumstances of composition.

All the foregoing describes a common ground which nurtured the resolve to pursue a career in Jewish education. The testimony of the essays is evidence that the decision was a matter of choice, attractive opportunities in other fields notwithstanding. This is in welcome contrast to the traditional image of the hapless *melamed* whose presence in the classroom is dictated by the fact that he is unsuited for any other employment.

"The Jewish people had no need for another computer programmer but could seriously use an educator who could relate to teenagers."

"A process evolved in which as I grew more confidant in my abilities, the idea of foregoing the American dream (i.e., becoming a lawyer) in order to pursue what I really loved grew more realistic..."

For some, a successful teaching experience or summer in camp as a counselor set the stage for a professional career. All of the essays stress the commitment to the survival of the Jewish people as an important variable in the decision. Some of the writers are children of survivors of the Holocaust; more than one of these thinks that engagement in Jewish education is payment of an obligation to perpetuate the beliefs and traditions for which their parents suffered. Perhaps more typical, however, are the following observations:

"I experienced first hand the power of a good education and I felt that I had the capacity and therefore the responsibility to educate others as well."

"Even at an early age I knew that my life would be dedicated to our nation and Jewish education."

"By my senior year I found that I was drawn to work with people and to accomplish something more meaningful. After some soul searching, I decided to enter Jewish education."

"The essence of my major life choice was wound up in my Jewish identity and in the pleasure and significance I derived from educating others."

Common to all the essays is a commitment to the future of the Jewish people:

"I desperately did then and still do now [want] to help ensure the survival of the Jewish people."

III

We can compare what has been brought out here with findings from two other studies. Teachers in Jewish schools of all kinds in Boston and Providence reported that the most important persons, events and experiences which influenced their choice of profession were, in descending order, "the general nature of their home life, the influence from a Jewish professional, Jewish teacher, and parents." (Frank, Margolis and Weisner, 1992, p. 13). Senior educators,[5] organized into focus groups in several American cities revealed that they had "...reached their positions 'by accident' rather than through a long period of training and advancement; ...that most started in the field as part-time supplementary school teachers or youth workers; ...had strong Jewish upbringings ... punctuated by an intensive experience of one sort or another, particularly youth groups, Jewish educational camps, or a trip to Israel..."; and the influence of mentors who "...inspired them to deepen their Jewish commitment, work as educators [or] enter the field of Jewish education." (Cohen and Wall, 1987, p. 36) The material presented here, together with the findings of the studies cited, is clear about one thing at least: very few people are likely to "walk off the street" into Jewish education. While entry is sometimes accidental, even then it is against a background of long term formal or informal educational experiences. Whatever the valence of any particular element of the configuration, the family and the life it leads is crucial.

---

5   Senior educators were defined as principals, consultants and directors of bureaus of Jewish education, camp directors, regional and national youth directors and other related positions.

The implications of our findings seem quite obvious:

1) The idea of Jewish education must be broadened to include educational opportunities outside of school, particularly during adolescence and college years.
2) Young people should be provided with opportunities and encouraged to act as "educators" — camp counselors, teachers' aids, youth leaders — during adolescence.
3) Families already "in the fold" rather than those "out there" deserve pride of place in the allocation of communal resources.

References

Brown, Duane, Brooks, Linda, and Associates. (1990). *Career choice and development; Applying contemporary theories to practice.* (2nd ed.) San Francisco: Jossey-Bass Publishers.

Cohen, Steven, and Wall, Susan. (1987). *Recruiting and retaining senior personnel in Jewish education: A focus group study in North America.* Jerusalem: Jewish Education Committee of the Jewish Agency.

Frank, Naava, Margolis, Daniel, and Weisner, Alan. (1992). *The Jewish school teacher: Preliminary report of a study.* Boston: Bureau of Jewish Education.

Kanarfogel, Ephraim. (1992). *Jewish education and society in the High Middle Ages.* Detroit: Wayne State University Press.

CONSIDERATIONS

Eldad and Medad: A Paradigm of Leadership

MICHAEL ROSENAK

For many years, Seymour Fox has taught — and put into practice — his conviction that the future of Jewish life depends largely on the discovery and advancement of leaders who can ultimately position themselves effectively within appropriate educational frameworks. What characterizes leaders? Are they born or bred? Are such people simply to be discovered and then cultivated by study and apprenticeship, or targeted and systematically trained? Are there rules and guidelines that apply equally to all leaders, or are leaders each so unique that they require distinct regimens of education and different measurements of success? The following exploration will address these issues and also briefly examine a Midrashic source that may be a useful resource in Jewish discussions of educational leadership.

The Yeshiva and the University of Chicago

How is such a discussion conducted? What are its rules and its aims?

Let us begin with Fox himself, and examine where biblical narrative, midrashic commentaries and talmudic teaching should, in his view, inform educational inquiry and deliberation.

In thinking about leadership — for example, in planning and creating the monumental project of the Mandel School for Educational Leadership, where he has been both philosopher and practitioner — Fox has held several principles firmly in mind. He has insisted that good educational practice must be informed by theory, and that theories are never neutral. Hence, he has maintained, all Jewish educational *philosophies* set limits for what constitute legitimate educational *theories*, that is, for determining which theories may be judged acceptable and useful for Jewish educational *practice* (Fox with Novak, 2000, p. 37).[1] In short, Jewish education, like all educational enterprises, requires a body of congenial theory that will formulate and illuminate guidelines for concrete educational activity. And it is philosophy that is to determine which theories are acceptable.

Educational philosophy, then, may be defined as giving systematic and principled direction to bodies of congenial theory. But Fox has further insisted that the various philosophies (of Judaism) are presaged in classic Jewish ideals, and that norms are built around them. These ideals and norms await the disciplined efforts of the Jewish educational thinker to locate them in varied philosophies of Judaism and then, though the prism of these philosophies, to "translate" their "value concepts"[2] into educational thought and practice. Thus, for example, Fox has enlisted talmudic principles — such as *shimush hakhamim*, or putting oneself at the service of the wise (*Avot 6:6*) — to clarify worthy relationships between teachers and pupils. He has also urged his students to unearth and "translate" such cultural and religious principles into operative ideals, in order to bridge the gap between the scholar and the classroom.

Not surprisingly then, Fox consistently wrote, taught, encouraged and supervised exploration of Jewish thought *for* Jewish education. This area of study ("Jewish thought for Jewish education") systematically articulated and contextualized what talmudic discussion, exegesis and Midrashic narrative had established as the valuative language of Jewish life. Hence, the philosophy of Jewish education that Fox proposed to Jewish educational leaders was formed in the crucible of talmudic and biblical teachings, and refined by philosophical reflection upon them.

Given Fox's insistence on both text and philosophical discourse upon it, it is not surprising to find among his terms of reference for leadership in education both "the Yeshiva" and "the University of Chicago" as two

1   For an earlier exposition, see Fox, 1968. The "congeniality" of theory, in Fox's view, is required not only on philosophical or Jewish grounds, but extends to a consideration of what is appropriate in practice for each of the four "commonplaces" (learner, teacher, subject matter and environment) of education and how diverse theories affect the interaction of the commonplaces. See Fox, 1983.
2   For the idea of "value concepts," see Kadushin, 1972, Chapter Two.

dimensions of the educational ambience. The University of Chicago, like the Yeshiva, represents a significant feature of Fox's own education and maturation as a philosopher and educator. It also represents an ideal and aspiration, namely that the resources of Jewish tradition be passed through the prism of modern, albeit classically hued, sensibility. The Yeshiva approach brought Jewish texts to the fore. The University of Chicago perspective presented Fox with opportunities to "translate" philosophies, and even educational theories, from within the entire Western tradition for potentially fruitful use, *if they were found to be congenial to Judaism and Jewish education.* Hence, Fox has insisted on careful study of Plato and Dewey, as well as Hutchins and Schwab. He has found thinkers who linked philosophy to the practice of leadership particularly congenial. To Fox, these thinkers embodied the talmudic value that "the study of Torah is secondary to its practice"(*Avot 1:10*), that study should spark the practical endeavor that talmudic sages and their interpreters considered to be the end goal of all "theoretical" study.[3] It is not accidental that Fox has always aligned himself with philosophers who were also practitioners, and with men of action who engage in life-long learning of guiding ideas and fructifying theories.

What is Leadership?

The question of what constitutes leadership and its constituent elements has long engaged Fox and other educational thinkers. Moreover, Fox has been a pioneer in locating and honing particularly Jewish perspectives on leadership throughout two decades of planning, ongoing evaluation and innovation at The Jerusalem Fellows program and the Mandel School for Educational Leadership.

"Leadership" is indeed a controversial and complex issue. It involves creative and critical faculties that sometimes distance the leader from his or her society. It requires an innovative perspective. It usually involves some measure of authority. All of these features of leadership bear internal complexities and even paradoxes, and call for precise definitions and also qualifications. For example, creativity may be wise or foolish. The Talmud puts this dilemma succinctly in saying, "When the young [i.e., the inexperienced or foolish] construct, consider it destruction and when the

---

3   Note the unequivocal statement of Maimonides: "Since the Torah is truth, the purpose of knowing it is to do it."" Introduction to *Perek 'Helek'* in Twersky, 1972, p. 405.

old [i.e., the wise] destroy, consider it construction" (*Megillah 31*). Not everyone can be relied upon to know what to preserve and what to discard. Thus, who is to be trusted with leadership's creativity? Similarly, criticism — an important feature of leadership — may be courageous or simply an outburst of incomprehension, perhaps even alienation. The teacher of leaders will thus wish to know: *How much* criticism is required for *which* leadership role?

As for authority, some leaders seem to have little or no authority, yet flourish that way. Others, in different contexts, clearly require authority and must learn when to express it in explicit, and when in implicit, ways. So, we may ask: On which bases must authority exist and alongside what else? In terms of Weber's well-known categories, (Weber, 1948, p. 78) we raise the question: Is educational authority mainly rational-legal, deriving from a role filled competently within a social structure? Is it charismatic, reflecting the unique ability of a vision-driven leader to inspire others? Or is it perhaps traditional, deriving from a tradition of reverence for certain time-hallowed models of leadership, say that of the *talmid hakham*? How does each version of authority function in the realm of education? And in each case, what are its limits?

We expect leaders to possess distinct abilities and virtues, but here too there are different views, contexts and nuances. On the basis of Aristotelian categories and concepts, we may ask: Should the educational leader be one who possesses virtues that endow him or her with the character to allow just or moral or wise actions to flow "naturally" from his or her "perfections"? In other words, should this person do just or moral or wise acts because she is just, moral or wise, and thus "performs these acts in the way that just and self-controlled men do?"[4] If so, must we conclude (as Aristotle) that one who takes fine actions but lacks the qualities of soul that "dictate" such actions, might at best be a competent "master of an art" and professional instructor, but is (to be) precluded from educational leadership? Or, to move to the conceptual framework suggested by Rabbi J. B. Soloveitchik in his classic essay "The Lonely Man of Faith" (1965): Is the leader she who inspires and commands others and thus gains "majesty" in the functional world of "Adam the first," where the ethos is achievement-oriented and the leader-doer is "impressively" in control of matters?

Yet Rabbi Soloveitchik presents us with a different yet complementary model, the covenantal world of "Adam the second." In this second world, human beings seek redemption rather than "worldly success." This leads to

---

4   Aristotle, 1979, pp. 38–39.

a very different kind of leader: lonely individuals, seeking to walk in the footsteps of Moses, Judaism's great covenantal leader. Scripture describes this leader as singularly unimpressive: he stutters, is 80 years old at the start of his ministry, easily shaken in his conviction that he has the capacity for leadership, and "more modest than any man on the face of the earth." Yet this leadership is described as having the power and the audacity to bring the Torah down from Heaven, against the will of the ministering angels (*Shabbat 88b*).

As noted, we shall examine some of these questions and the ideals that consequently suggest themselves through a brief exploration into a biblical narrative and related talmudic and midrashic exegesis on this narrative. The relevance of the subject of our study, Eldad and Medad as leaders, will not emerge ready-made from this discussion. However, our deliberation on leadership and leadership education may be enriched by incorporating this readily accessible source into the sum of materials that guide us in our educational conversations.

Eldad and Medad: Prophesying Within the Camp

The Torah presents us with various personality and leadership types. There is Rebecca, somewhat deviously guiding the destiny of her son, Jacob — i.e., Israel — from behind the scenes; Joseph, the confident and cunning politician who senses that God, while silent, is watching. There is Aaron, the man of reconciliation who at least once, when he built the golden calf, learned that the leader's capacity for rapprochement and "peace" can easily and instantly slip into appeasement and surrender of authority. And there is Moses, the prophet-king, who most comprehensively is called upon to represent the leadership of God Himself.

The Torah also tells us about two young men,[5] Eldad and Medad, who stand "within the camp" and yet apart from it. The leadership of these two comes to fruition through the distance they somehow place between themselves and all others, including Moses. They lack social authority and seem too young to be trusted with their immature perspectives. Yet they are clearly charismatic, for the spirit of God rests upon them.

---

5   That they are young may be deduced from the midrashic tradition that they assumed the leadership of the people after the death of Joshua (see below) and that they were not among those destined to die in the desert. They must, therefore, have been under the age of 20.

Who are these people? As the Torah describes it, they appear at a time of crisis in leadership, when its authoritative and compassionate aspects seem disjointed. The People of Israel have been encamped at Sinai for almost one year. They have received the Torah. They have constructed a tabernacle which, Moses taught them, assures that God will dwell among them even as they march forward and distance themselves from the place of revelation. This divine presence is graphically clear to them, for God — like a provident parent — is sending them manna for their daily sustenance.

The first anniversary of the Passover has come and gone, duly celebrated as a memorial of past salvation and a promise of total redemption. Those who were ritually impure on that day have been given a chance to celebrate the festival one month later. By His legislation of *Pesach Sheni*, God has shown that even His seemingly most arbitrary and restrictive laws reflect His care for all. The camp has been organized for the march to the Land of Israel, each tribe in its place, each with its distinctive banner, with the Ark of Covenant present in their midst. Trumpets have been fashioned for celebration and calls to assembly. God Himself will lead the people, with a pillar of cloud by day and of fire by night. He will guide their march, but also provide for rest. The divine leader and His lieutenant are in charge; the redemptive future seems assured. The leader(s) clearly know what they are doing.

A Dream Unraveled

The Exodus, then, is over; the conquest of the Land is about to begin. Moses can be exuberant as he tells his father-in-law Hovav-Jethro that "we are setting out for the place of which the Lord has said, 'I will give it to you.'" He invites the Midianite to join Israel and share in the largess of God's providence. Rashi, following the Midrashic *Sifre* on this verse, has Moses saying to Hovav, "Immediately, within three days, we shall enter the Land" (on *Bamidbar 10–29*). It seems a moment of happy fulfillment.

So the march toward the land of promise begins, and continues for three days until things begin to go wrong. The procession begun so festively and joyously slows and, with its own deathly dynamic, culminates in the episode of the twelve spies who report that the people living in the Land are too powerful to be defeated. The march grinds to a halt. Whispers, cravings, fear and panic are everywhere.

The dream begins to unravel when the people start to complain bitterly. The complainers are the *erev rav*, the "mixed multitude" that left Egypt together with the Israelites, when the punishing fire sent by the Lord breaks out at "the outskirts of the camp." Then the *assafsuf*, the riffraff, declare their craving for meat, an obsession with which they infect the People of Israel, who take to "weeping." Suddenly everyone remembers how good it was in Egypt where one ate meat, or at least fish, together with juicy appetizers and vegetables. The sense is that "the camp" is moving in the wrong direction. Absurdity dominates consciousness. How else to explain that the Israelites look back on their abject slavery in Egypt as a blessed time, of eating "free of charge"?

Moses, the leader, appears at a loss. His mood changes radically, in line with the mood of his people. He complains to God of the burden of leadership. He cannot do it alone, he says. God has dealt ill with him. If things go on this way he prefers to die and thus be taken out of his wretchedness. How can he supply meat to a whole people who are no longer content with manna?

There had also been problems on the journey from Egypt to Sinai. But then God was patient and understanding. He provided manna, and also quail. He showed Moses how to sweeten bitter waters. It was easy to be a leader then. Now the atmosphere is different, charged. God feels, as it were, that Israel has rejected Him, that they do not want to enter the Land He is giving them. Now their dissatisfaction is rebellious.

God's response to the rebellion is harsh toward the people, and ambiguous and distant toward Moses, who has lost control or, at least, self-control. Therefore, says the Lord, Moses must take 70 elders to the Tent-Tabernacle and God will draw from the spirit given to Moses, transferring it to these elders. As if to say, 'if you do not wish to be leader or even to live, perhaps I should begin distributing your authority and power to others.' As for the people, they are promised quail to eat, but this time the intimation is sinister. May they choke on it! Moses has no cause to doubt that God can provide miraculous food. But miracles are not always providential; they may be a punishment!

In the wake of these developments, Moses must address the people. Does he tell them that the quail will not come from heaven, as did the manna, but from beyond the camp, from 'the other side', like the *assafsuf*? Does he report that it is ominous and menacing? That like the slavery which now seems so attractive and delicious, it draws them to death? That all will become nauseated by the quail after 30 consecutive days of eating it, and that some will choke in their gluttony? That these days could have been devoted to the conquest of the Land? Did Moses tell them that he was happy to be sharing leadership with 70 elders, or that he considered this "favor" a rebuke? Did he tell them to beware of undeserved "miracles"? Apparently not.

The enthusiasm and fervor of the departure for *Eretz Yisrael* has quickly become a distant memory. Initial doubts about victorious entry into the Land will soon become grim certainties of defeat; the spies are about to tell them that the entire venture of conquest is "impossible." Moreover, through despair and disobedience, death has entered the picture. (Shortly it will be decreed for the entire generation of the wilderness.) And we can imagine that Moses himself is no longer certain that he, who led the Exodus and took the people to Mount Sinai, will lead them into the Land.

After the fanfare and the anticipated three-day journey to the Land of Israel, the People of Israel is lost. The clear goal and the straight line to redemption have been blurred. Something has gone wrong. God is still in their midst, but the grace has gone out of His presence. He is sitting, so it seems, on the seat of *din*, of harsh judgment, rather than on His seat of *rahamim*, or mercy.

Modest — Or Arrogant?

Eldad and Medad are on the list of the 70 elders who were to "solve" Moses' problem by sharing his leadership. But they are not part of that scene. They do not show up at the Tent of Meeting. Or perhaps they are not really invited. Here is the Torah's description of what happened:

> "Moses went out and reported the words of the Lord to the people. He gathered seventy of the people's elders and stationed them around the Tent. Then the Lord came down in a cloud and spoke to him. God drew upon the spirit that was on him [Moses] and put it upon the seventy elders. And when the spirit rested upon them, they spoke in ecstasy, but did not continue [thereafter to do so]. Two men, one named Eldad and the other Medad, had remained in camp; yet the spirit rested upon them. They were among those recorded, but they had not gone out to the tent — and they spoke in ecstasy in the camp. A youth ran out and told Moses, saying, 'Eldad and Medad are acting the prophet in the camp'! And Joshua, son of Nun, Moses' attendant from youth, spoke up and said, 'My lord, Moses, restrain them' But Moses said to him, 'Are you wrought up on my account?' Would that all the Lord's people were prophets, that the Lord put His spirit upon them." (*Numbers 11:24–29*).

Eldad and Medad are strange characters. They arouse the wrath of Joshua, yet win Moses' approval. Why weren't they at the Tent with the others who were "stationed" there? Where did they get "the spirit"? Why, instead of sitting with Moses in council, do they end up prophesying or speaking "in ecstasy" in the camp? What did they say? How were these matters connected, if at all, to the "words of the Lord that Moses reported to the people" about the 70 elders, or the quail?

Joshua, faithful to his teacher Moses, demands that the leader's authority be used and seen. He urges that these men be restrained or locked up. They are not playing by the rules. Young men who were chosen to be mere members of an advisory board, they snub their noses and do their own thing. They make speeches. Perhaps they are planning to usurp Moses' prophetic role and status. But Moses will not abide Joshua's suggestion. "Would that all the people of God were prophets," he says. Can he mean this seriously? Or is it the statement of a fatigued leader ready to be released, in any way that suggests itself, from the burdens of authority? Or is he saying that one who is only a prophet, however impressive, lacks power and constitutes no threat to the "authorities"?

As for the young men, what is their story? The Talmud records a controversy about this:

> "Our rabbis taught: 'And two men remained in the camp.' Some say that they [i.e., their names] stayed in the urn. [And the background to this urn:] when the Holy One, blessed be He, said to Moses, 'Gather Me seventy men of the elders of Israel' Moses said [to himself]: How shall I do this? If I select five from each tribe, there will be ten too few; if six from one [tribe] and five from another, I will create jealousy among the tribes. So what did he do? He selected six [from each tribe] and brought seventy-two [lottery] slips; on seventy he wrote 'elder' and two he left blank. He shuffled them and put them in an urn. He said to [those 'recorded']: 'Come and draw your slips. To those who drew slips bearing the word 'elder' he said, 'Heaven has already consecrated you.' To those who drew a blank slip he said, 'The Omnipresent has rejected you, what can I do?' (Sanhedrin 17a).

Here Eldad and Medad seem to be the two rejected ones. They were "recorded" (among the 72 candidates). But, having been rejected, they "stayed in the camp" while the 70 new "leaders" were consulting with Moses, even temporarily "prophesying." But Rabbi Shimon understands their remaining in the camp differently:

"When the Holy One, blessed be He, said to Moses, 'Gather Me seventy men,' Eldad and Medad said, 'We are not worthy of that dignity.' The Holy One said, 'Since you have humbled yourselves, I shall add yet more greatness to your greatness.'

According to Rabbi Shimon, God allowed Eldad and Medad to prophesy continually whereas the others, who were chosen by Moses, "spoke in ecstasy" only once. Moreover, unlike the 70 elders who received "the spirit" from Moses, God Himself endowed Eldad and Medad.

What did these two men prophesy about after receiving the divine spirit? The Talmud cites three opinions. According to Rabbi Shimon, they prophesied: "Moses will die and Joshua will bring Israel into the Land." Abba Hanan said in the name of Rabbi Eliezer: "They prophesied concerning the quail." Whereas Rav Nahman said: "They prophesied about Gog and Magog."

Within the context of these prophecies, the Talmud also discusses Joshua urging his master, "My lord, Moses, restrain them." If Eldad and Medad prophesied about the death of Moses, Joshua's outburst is understandable, says the Talmud; one can see why there might be an element of rebellion in this prophecy, spoken publicly at this politically unstable moment. But why should they be locked up for prophesying about the quail or even about the future, yet remote, war of Gog and Magog? The answer given: It is impudent for "disciples to teach without the approval of their master (Moses)." The Talmud concludes that what Joshua might have meant by "restrain them or lock them up" was, "Impose civic duties upon them and they will stop (prophesying) by themselves." However, the *Sifre* cited by Rashi on *Numbers 11:28* opines that Joshua's suggestion was harsher still: those who proclaim evil tidings should be locked out of the world (i.e. put to death).

The elders, as we have seen, were meant to help Moses, perhaps to get things back to normal so that the historical events could proceed as intended. The elders speak and act with his spirit; they are temporary *mitnavim*, in a state of ecstasy, perhaps intoxicated with the promise of power, however slight, that makes them part of the spiritual establishment. Eldad and Medad, on the other hand, receive God's spirit directly. They too begin in ecstasy, but Moses perceives them as having moved beyond that, from the state of *mitnavim*, ecstatics, to genuine prophets, *neviim*.

Yet the talmudic controversy about how Eldad and Medad received the spirit betrays ambivalence about such people. Perhaps they didn't really deserve to be among the elders; perhaps God rejected them as leaders.

Perhaps their prophesying was no more than a youthful ego trip, a destructive venture of building. On the other hand, perhaps they were *too good* for the establishment? In this case, their humility may have appeared self-serving and, paradoxically, arrogant.

Joshua, with a disciple's zeal, but perhaps also a practiced eye for evaluating leadership candidates, wishes to shut them up. The Talmud expresses his contempt pithily: They should be put to work, given civic positions. We can almost hear Joshua saying: Troublemakers! No wonder they allow themselves such prophecies. They are detached, irresponsible. They have too much time on their hands. Let them dirty their hands in the nitty-gritty of community service instead! Joshua might have added today: They have too many fellowships. Theorists! Intellectuals!

Good News and Bad News

The three prophecies ascribed to Eldad and Medad suggest that they think it their task to "tell it like it is". They see themselves as realists, perhaps as critics of the establishment that made promises, raised hopes, and caused the pain of disillusionment. They seem to assume that the people have the "right to know", although this too causes pain. Whether that makes them leaders or a problematic presence, even Moses and Joshua disagree. If they are indeed prophets, what can be said against them (Moses' point of view)? And, if they are not, how can their demoralizing influence be countered (Joshua's dilemma)? In any case, on that day of crisis, when the elders were probably deliberating about how to calm and reassure the people, the tidings of Eldad and Medad were sad, touched with irony, perhaps bitter. Though all their prophecies consisted of good and bad news, the bad news — as is usually the case with "good news and bad news" scripts — is the real message. Eldad and Medad pierce the illusion that the causes of recent murmurings would pass. There is tribulation ahead. It must be faced.

Perhaps their prophecies attribute the gloom of that hour to the people's rebellion, to fear, to an indisposition to conquer the Land. But matters will certainly not proceed according to plan or promise. You thought that Moses would bring us into the land, perhaps within days? No, he will die; the conquest is to be delayed for a generation. You await the miracle of ample meat? So it will be, and it will bring calamity. You imagine redemption as the immediate, self-understood and painless outcome of the Exodus? It will take place only at the end of days, after the apocalyptic war of "Gog and Magog" against the messiah on the hills of Israel (*Ezekiel 38–39*), and long after we are all dead.

How should one relate to such people? What shall parents and teachers do with such disturbing Eldads and Medads now sitting before them as children at the table, in the classroom? Certainly these children are convinced that they will not grow up to become the helpers or supporters of the regime. Perhaps they envision leadership roles for themselves by virtue of their clear-sightedness — and criticism of society. In the modern parallel, we may consider them the intellectuals of the next generation. In their "prophesying within the camp" and their apparent indifference to the spiritual establishment of elders, they remind us of newspaper columnists whose verdict on events is eagerly awaited, yet also feared. They are like the best playwrights and novelists, those who seem, at least to solid citizens, to be in permanent ecstasy — that is, mad. We know that these children are even now getting ready to claim their critique as the truth without which society is doomed. Rather annoyingly, they are already insinuating that they possess the spirit of God, or whatever spirit they believe to guide them. In fact, many of them will be bribed by promises of socially regulated spirit. Some will refuse to conform. Some will be admired for their individualism. And some will be locked up.

Our relationship to these potential leaders is complicated. We are happy to have them, for we believe that education for leadership, among other things, cultivates critical thinking and the ability to criticize society. And these young people appear to have attained this on their own. But we are unsure. We don't know whether we want to teach critical thinking, or even whether it can be taught. To what extent should we try to teach it and to whom? Should intellectuals "carry their share of the load" to cure budding leaders of their presumptions or should they be protected, even pampered, because they represent a type of leadership without which society will grow even more obtuse? And yet, how do we know that the future leadership they represent is not destructive? Is this good-news-and-bad-news sarcasm useful? Disillusioning? Perhaps it is manipulative? When should these people be restrained? How do we know whether they really have "the spirit of God" in them, whether they deserve our attention? Maybe it is a ruse!

Like the Talmud, we are ambivalent. Are these now and future critics unworthy or endowed with spiritual power? Is what they (will) do really leadership, or irresponsible "ecstasy"? For example, we know things never work out exactly as planned, but is the dissemination of that somber reality helpful or demoralizing? Will it make our children and pupils cynical and apathetic if we actually *teach* them to be critical?

John Passmore, in an important essay entitled 'On Teaching to be Critical' (1967), helps us resolve the first dilemma. He notes that while we can impart critical skills and habits, these cannot alone create a genuinely critical mind. Nothing is easier than teaching a person to say, "I question that" about everything. But getting children to understand when and how criticism is appropriate is another matter. Being a true critic, Passmore suggests, testifies less to skill and more to character. It is a character trait, a gift. To move closer to the biblical view, one is endowed with a critical nature. Wise teachers — like Moses himself — can encourage it, but it comes from God.

Secondly, is critical nature a good thing? Should it be encouraged? Who really is imbued with the spirit of God and who should be restrained? The rabbinic supplement to the story and talmudic discussion of Eldad and Medad suggests an answer. A Midrash (*Numbers Rabbah III:7*) tells us that Eldad and Medad, still young men just after the Exodus, became the leaders of Israel after Joshua's death. They outlived the leader who questioned their right to live, who once opined that they undermined leadership and society. They "dirtied their hands" in communal leadership. They were not simply knee-jerk critics. They had not developed the habit of always saying, "I question that"; they were not detached intellectuals.

Why did they deserve to lead? Even when Eldad and Medad bring bad news, they also offer good news, or good advice. True, when the quail comes it will be destructive, yet knowing this might help us realize the self-control needed to save lives. True, the redemption will not play itself out "in three days," but ultimately Israel shall be redeemed. Gog and Magog will be defeated. *Eretz Yisrael* will be conquered; the Exodus was not in vain. Bearing these ambiguous good tidings, Eldad and Medad indeed "prophesy within the camp"; they belong to it and care about it. They do not compromise their honesty for their commitment. And, if we pick up on Rabbi Shimon, there is nothing arrogant about them. Although speaking the truth, they are yet concerned that they may be unworthy. Such critics, messengers of God, are the boon of their societies. They are impassioned yet loyal, truthful yet loving.

Teachers are aware of the danger posed to every society by false prophets, men and women of false ecstasy, whose profession it is to defame or flatter, but always without love. Yet no true teacher will belittle pupils who look to become true disciples of Eldad and Medad. Their ecstasy may at times seem a bit crazed, certainly to such policy-conscious people as Joshua. They are irritating; they get on one's nerves. Yet teachers, observing them in the midst of the camp, will recall the prayer and blessing of Moses: "Would that all the people of the Lord were prophets!" In instructing Joshua, Moses may have overstated his point, but that should not keep us from understanding and appreciating his meaning.

The Educator Reflects

Let us now, very briefly, initiate the educational conversation that began in "the Yeshiva" and was mobilized by the sensibilities of "the University of Chicago." What philosophical and theoretical questions may arise in the study of our *sugyah*, or subject?

1. Eldad and Medad are prophetic types. Like true leaders in the covenantal mold, they are modest and, indeed, seem to have no authority. Yet their powers of perception and insight make them potentially dangerous critics. Prophets are never *parve*. Is there anything that education can do to mitigate the dangers of prophetic fervor, or is this a case where the rule, "do not touch my anointed ones" must prevail? (*I Chronicles 16:22*)[6]

2. Do Eldad and Medad represent one of several types of leadership? If so, do we require different theories of education for different types of leaders? Or are Eldad and Medad instances of another conception, namely that leadership is a quality allowing for more than one type of application? After all, the "intellectuals" who annoyed Joshua did become political leaders. The Torah was "passed on to them" as elders, *together with the reins of government.*[7] May we then learn from them not to compartmentalize leadership teaching and leadership roles; that there are stores of general talent, pertaining to all leaders, to be fostered in all leadership education?

3. The elected elders received their leadership roles from Moses. In Weberian terms, we would say they "merely" fulfilled a role for their

6 On this verse, the talmudic sages comment, "These are the pupils sitting before their teachers" (*Shabbat 119b*).
7 The Midrash, in identifying the elders who outlived Joshua as Eldad and Medad (*Joshua 24:31*), seems to assume that they were leaders, since this verse views the elders as leaders. Note that this verse states that as long as these elders lived, the people remained faithful to God. Note also that, in the opening Mishna of *Pirkai Avot [Ethics of the Fathers]*, we are told that "Moses passed the Torah on to Joshua, and Joshua passed it on to the elders".

charismatic teacher. Eldad and Medad received their leadership directly from God, but we note that they were outsiders. They were either rejected as members of the socio-political scheme of things, or they decided it was "not for them, they were not worthy." Are they politely saying that authority issued from an urn is beneath them? Or that official leadership requires social graces and political acumen that they do not possess?

4. Leaders often appear to be outsiders. Yet they must also be caring and involved individuals who understand social and political situations, who are not easily offended by reality or disillusioned, misanthropic. If this is teachable, what modes and models can help potential leaders learn to negotiate the delicate balance between intellectual remoteness, genuine caring and participation?

5. Is the Eldad-Medad model sufficient? It seems pristinely biblical, underlying the concept of the "judge," the surrogate of God and, of course, the prophet. In the Bible, the charismatic dimension of "the spirit of God" also factors into political leadership. Recall the first formal agreement between Joshua upon assuming leadership, and the people: They say to Joshua that "All that you have commanded us we will do, and we shall go wherever you send us. As we obeyed Moses in all matters, so will we obey you." But then they utter what sounds like an innocent blessing, but is certainly a veiled threat as well: "Only be it so that the Lord your God be with you as He was with Moses...(*Joshua 1: 16–17*). We shall follow you, the people seem to be saying, as long as God is with you, and not for a moment longer. Disciples of the University of Chicago approach, and of the Yeshiva orientation as well, may find this model instructive, but would not consider it comprehensive. Leadership, they would maintain, cannot be confined to what Gershom Scholem (1973) called the *hasid*, the man of single-minded zeal or "prophetic" extremism. Jewish leadership, states Scholem, places the *talmid hakham* at the top of its hierarchy. This is the "man of Halacha," the student and scholar who also leads the community, establishing its norms and teaching its ways.

6. But the Midrash cited above asks us to reconsider. After all, Eldad and Medad may themselves be envisioned as assuming this Halachic role when they become elders. Yet the teacher of potential leaders in contemporary society may well ask: Is Halachic discipline, careful scholarship and intellectual restraint only the end product of a life of leadership? Or, in an age rife with idolatry that speaks in the name of

God, should practice and thoughtful reflection upon it not have pride of place, even in the early stages of life and leadership? Should we not always keep in mind that, without the spirit of God, Halacha and rational scholarship can both lead to pettiness, irrelevancy and arrogance? The spirit of God, in the sense that we require it of leaders, probably cannot be taught. For those who don't have it, the nearest thing is to "appoint them to spiritual grandeur" so that they will momentarily "speak in ecstasy" and then stop.

Our midrashic exploration indicates the complexity of leadership as a social and educational ideal. It also illustrates the significance of Fox's insistence that the rabbinic tradition has a vital role to play in Jewish educational deliberation; that we may discover models and methods for education from Torah study seen through the prism of educational philosophy and theory. For example, as a result of the type of learning session we have conducted here, we may decide again to wonder whether the Mandel School should be structured more for *cultivation* of leaders than for their *training*. We may find ourselves asking once again: how do we best *locate* leaders in order to provide them with space for study, reflection and community-building. We may also be encouraged by studies such as this to consider that potential leaders, despite their different inclinations and talents, should, perhaps possess stores of general wisdom and competence. Then they may well take on different responsibilities, having been moved to assume them by a strange blending of modesty and the spirit of God.

References

Aristotle. (1979). *Nicomachean ethics*. 18th printing. Martin Ostwald. (Trans.) Indianapolis: The Liberal Arts Press, Inc.

Fox, Seymour, with Novak, William. (2000). *Vision at the heart: Lessons from Camp Ramah on the power of ideas in shaping educational institutions*. Jerusalem: The Mandel Foundation.

Fox, Seymour. (1983). Theory into practice (in Education). In Seymour Fox. (Ed.). *Philosophy and education*. Jerusalem: The Van Leer Jerusalem Foundation.

Fox, Seymour. (1968/5729). Prolegomenon to a Philosophy of Jewish Education. (Hebrew). In *Kivunnim Rabim, Kavannah Ahat* [Essays in Education: Theory and Research]. Jerusalem: Hebrew University, School of Education, and the Ministry of Education and Culture, pp. 145–154.

Kadushin, Max. (1972). *The Rabbinic mind*. New York: The Jewish Theological Seminary of America.

Passmore, John. (1967). On teaching to be critical. In R. S. Peters. (Ed.). *The concept of education*. London: Routledge and Kegan Paul, pp. 192–204.

Scholem, Gershom. (1973). Three types of Jewish piety. *Ariel Quarterly Review 32*, pp. 76–93.

Soloveichik, Joseph B. (1965). The lonely man of faith. *Tradition 6 (2)*. New York, Doubleday.

Twersky, Isidore. (Ed.). (1972). *A Maimonides reader*. New York: Berman House.

Weber, Max. (1948). Politics as a vocation. In H. Gerth and C. Wright Mills. *From Max Weber*. London: Routledge.

Professions of Human Improvement: Predicaments of Teaching*

DAVID K. COHEN

The developed world has seen a remarkable change in ambitions for schools. Policymakers and some educators in the 1980s began to say that schools must offer intellectually challenging instruction that is deeply rooted in the academic disciplines. Under Margaret Thatcher and John Major, British schooling was re-vamped to exert much greater pressure for academic work. Reformers and policymakers in the U.S. also urged more thoughtful and intellectually ambitious instruction, arguing that students must become independent thinkers and enterprising problem solvers. Meanwhile, reformers and some policymakers in Singapore and Japan, whose academically excellent schools were the envy of many American commentators, began trying to push instruction toward more flexibility and creativity.

Far-reaching changes in politics and policy were proposed to achieve these goals. The British government centralized considerable influence over state-maintained schools, and placed much more stress on examinations and common curricula. Many states in the U.S. instituted

* This is a revised version of one chapter in a larger, unpublished volume, *Teaching: Practice and its predicaments*. Thanks to Charles E. Lindblom and Janet A. Weiss for discussions that led to this work, and to Mary Magdalene Lampert, Deborah Loewenburg Ball, and Suzanne Wilson, for helpful comments on several earlier versions.

aggressive systems of assessment and accountability, arguing that states tests would push instruction toward greater heights. Prominent politicians, businessmen and analysts argued that schools should be judged by their results in student performance, not the adequacy of the resources allocated to them.

These ideas seem hopeful to some and unwise to others, but whatever one's view, they mark serious change. Resource allocation had been the chief method of judging schools' adequacy, and professionals had considerable leeway. One difficulty for the reforms, common across many different systems, has been political. Power and authority have been dispersed, either by the growth of powerful interest groups — like teachers' unions in Britain, Israel, and Japan — or by federalism in the US, or some combination of the two. Could state or national agencies actually mobilize the influence required to steer teaching and learning in thousands of classrooms, when central influence was so dispersed?

A second difficulty is educational, and arises from the idea that teaching and learning should be much more thoughtful and demanding. Teachers are urged to help students to understand mathematical concepts, to interpret serious literature, to write creatively about their own ideas and experiences, and to converse thoughtfully about history and social science. Whatever we think of these ambitions in principle, they are unfamiliar in practice in many schools in many nations. Most classroom work is frontal, instruction centers on teachers, and, aside from some academically crack classes, intellectual demands are modest. In several nations, few teachers have deep knowledge of any academic subject, especially in elementary schools, and the instruction that reformers propose has mostly been confined to protected enclaves in a few public and private secondary schools. Hence the second difficulty is whether anyone can steer teaching and learning away from established practice.

If intellectual excitement is to be the meat and potatoes of teaching, much would have to change. What would it take to make the changes? What might be required to transform teaching from a largely routine and unimaginative practice into an intellectually ambitious and adventurous enterprise, and why has such a transformation been so difficult in the past?

Many researchers have investigated teaching. By World War II it was already America's most investigated profession, the object of many studies, much disappointment, and proposals for reform. The post-war explosion of higher education, the consequent growth of the social sciences, and increasing efforts at school reform fueled a huge growth in research on education. Investigators scrutinized teachers' education and politics, the conditions of their work, the unions they join, the salaries they earn, how and why they make decisions, and many related subjects. But even in this accelerating blizzard of studies, there has been little about teaching, conventionally so-called. Researchers have probed this profession from dozens of angles and produced boxcar loads of studies, but only a few have asked what sort of a practice teaching is, and what kinds of problems must teachers solve.

Practices of Human Improvement

Teaching seems plain enough: An older or more educated person holds forth for those younger or less knowledgeable. Children sit at small desks, adolescents slouch in lecture halls, and grown-ups gather in half-circles. Someone older or more learned almost always stands in front, almost always talking. So when we ask "What sort of a practice is teaching?" the answer seems simple: One in which knowledge and skills are transmitted.

All true, but not all that is true. One might also say that teachers try to improve their students' minds, souls, and habits. There are of course many important differences among such improvers. Some teach in kindergarten while others do so in graduate school. Some teach sub-atomic physics, others inculcate religious belief, and in religious schools, teachers often do both. If the range of teachers' aims is vast, so are the situations in which they labor. Some work in one-room schools while others instruct in universities that enroll forty thousand. Some tutor a single student while others face four thousand. But through all these differences, teachers work at the profession of human improvement. Like psychotherapists, social workers, pastors and organization developers, they work directly on other humans in efforts to better their lives, work, and organizations.

Professions of human improvement share extraordinary ambitions. Practitioners seek to improve skills, deepen insights, broaden understanding, cope with feelings, take another's point of view, and increase honesty. These are occupations in which practitioners seek to transform minds, enrich human capacities, and change behavior. Learning is central to all of them, and in all it is seen as the key to betterment. Practitioners regularly remind us that their work is crucial to modern life. Teachers cultivate practical intelligence, theoretical reason, and the capacity to solve problems, without which many believe a modern economy would falter or collapse. Organizational consultants improve effectiveness, productivity, and even honesty in organizations. Some of these professions, like psychotherapy and organization development, are quite new, the progeny of the idea of progress that has distinguished Western civilization since the Enlightenment. Others, like teaching and pastoral work, are ancient, but have been reconceived in light of modern ambitions.

Practitioners in all of these unusual trades face several common predicaments. One is that while special expertise is these practitioners' chief qualification to work with clients, it is insufficient. For no matter how well educated and professionally informed they may be, practitioners have no conclusive expert solutions, even to many rudimentary issues of practice. Schoolteachers and academic experts regularly disagree about the purposes of practice. Many argue that teachers should instill obedience and respect for authority in students while others insist they should cultivate critical intelligence and the disposition to question authority. Some contend that students should learn the basics while others argue for much more intellectually elevated work. There is no scientifically conclusive way to decide such disputes — indeed, the disputes thrive as much in social science as in popular discourse. Americans also dispute the best ways to reach academic goals. Some fans of basic education argue that 'hands-on' experience and practical work are the best way to teach reading or arithmetic, while others urge rigorous academic study. Observers and evaluators also disagree about how to judge success. In teaching reading or arithmetic, as in any profession of human improvement, what seems to be the same improvement can be defined in different ways, each plausible from some perspective but all different. Different means to achieve any improvement can be identified, each plausible and many backed by some evidence of success. Professional knowledge and social science inform these views, but conclusive evidence is rare.[1] Practitioners in every human improvement profession struggle with similar problems, as do commentators on these professions. Expertise is essential to practice, but also is essentially inadequate.

---

1   There are several sources for these ideas about uncertainty. One is the historical literature on the rise of education and other social services, which traces expanding aspirations and arguments (see Perkinson, 1995; Cremin, 1980). Another is philosophical discourse about epistemology, especially in the philosophy of science (see Toulmin, 1972; Kuhn, 1962). Still another is argument about the nature of social science knowledge (see Lindblom, 1965; Lindblom and Braybroke, 1963; Lindblom and Cohen, 1979).

Predicaments of Human Improvement

Some readers will demur, saying that the progress of science or professional education will solve these problems. Prediction about matters of this sort is impossible, and the historical record is not encouraging. Uncertainty and dispute about human improvement have not diminished in the century just past, during which the entire enterprise expanded enormously, professional education in human improvement professions grew into a vast undertaking, and social research was applied on an increasing scale. Contrary to the hopes of many advocates for the saving power of science, these developments were accompanied by increasing dispute and uncertainty. As each profession prospered, so did rival schools of thought and practice within it. Jung and Freud founded the first great systems of psychoanalysis, and disagreements multiplied thereafter. Psychotherapy grew greatly, but much of the expansion was in contending treatments, and much of the professional literature has been consumed with disputes about them. Thus, as early skepticism about the efficacy of psychic therapy declined, it was replaced by a blizzard of critiques of particular treatments and some bitter attacks on the entire therapeutic enterprise. One particularly striking example is the view that madness is essentially rational and that psychotherapy is the cause of human misery rather than its cure — ideas advanced by leading psychiatrists. (See Szasz, 1978; Laing, 1960).

A similar story can be told about teaching. Disputes about the best ways to instruct are as old as public education. In the U.S., some people in the early 1800s saw instruction as a fierce struggle with depravity while others saw it as a gentle cultivation of humanity's goodness. While that old division is still with us, a myriad of other theories and practices sprang up in the intervening decades, including, among others, Montessori education, Anarchist schools, Progressivism, Behavior Modification, Open Education, Free Schools, and Christian Fundamentalist schools. Levels of education, literacy, and humanity in instruction have grown greatly since Horace Mann campaigned for public schools in the 1840s and 1850s, but so too have competing ideas about instruction and attacks on teaching as a cause of oppression and ignorance. The progress of education has been accompanied by increasingly bitter critiques and multiplying disputes about whether there has been educational progress at all. Some commentators now portray schooling as a vicious attack on innocent children, or a calculated means of holding entire populations in intellectual and political bondage, ideas that were almost entirely absent from early debates about education. (See, for instance, Goodman, 1964; Friedenberg, 1965; Bowles and Gintis, 1976). The growth of formal education evidences both an expanding faith in the possibilities for human improvement and increasing doubts about teachers' capacity to deliver the goods.

The limits on special expertise are also evident in the proliferation of self-help improvement schemes. Books, magazines, tapes and video recordings promise emotional peace without therapists: we need only perform therapy upon ourselves. Various experts propose education without teachers: we need only read manuals, or use computers. Managers are urged to improve organization in five minutes by reading a book or listening to a tape. These schemes testify both to an irrepressible faith in human improvement and to deep doubts about practitioners' expertise. If we can find peace without therapists, education without teachers, and decent organizations without consultants, how important are practitioners, and how weighty their expertise?

To date, the progress of human improvement and knowledge about it seems to have increased uncertainty rather than diminishing it, and complicated practitioners' work rather than simplifying it. Practitioners must solve more problems, learn more, and work more skillfully, yet doubts about their expertise multiply along with these demands. As efforts to improve humanity have grown, so have our ambitions, our sophistication and our critical capacities. There is no doubt that better scientific and professional knowledge could help, by informing practitioners' understanding and their work, but there is also good reason to doubt that such knowledge would end dispute or uncertainty. The more these professions prosper, the better we can see what has been done, how much remains undone, and what might have been done better. Such insight seems to be part of progress in human improvement.

I mention only a few bits of evidence among many that might be marshaled on these points, but the bits are basic, touching on the ends and means of improvement. Practitioners and commentators argue about whether such uncertainties and disputes are but a temporary problem that will be eliminated with the progress of social science and professional knowledge, or a permanent feature of such work. They debate whether these professions are sciences, practical arts, or social engineering. Unlike carpentry or plumbing, the very nature of these professions, and of their practitioners' knowledge and skill, are matters of continuing uncertainty and often ferocious dispute.

Practitioners' efforts to manage the limits on their expertise is complicated by a second predicament, arising from their dependence on clients. A carpenter can produce results if he has the skills and knowledge of the trade, the will to work, and passable materials, but all of a teacher's pedagogical art and craft will be useless unless students embrace the purposes of instruction as their own and seek them with their own art and craft.[2] This is no theoretical matter, for human improvers and their clients often differ about the aims of their work. Teachers who are eager for Shakespeare or medieval history regularly encounter students who want accounting or auto mechanics. In such cases the purposes of practice must be negotiated and renegotiated within practice, for clients' commitment is essential. Improvement cannot go forward without willing participants, yet clients regularly fear improvement, or doubt its possibility, or are indifferent, or prefer something other than what practitioners offer.[3]

Practitioners' dependence ramifies everywhere in their work. It can affect the politics of practice, for mobilizing and sustaining clients' commitment is a key task: practitioners cannot succeed without clients who work with them toward that success. But the social organization of practice is a potent influence on the mobilization of commitment. American and Israeli teachers persistently try to find ways to "motivate" their students, for they work in unselective institutions to which all students are admitted. In contrast, most psychiatrists, psychoanalysts, and other therapists in private practice typically select clients, treat patients' payment for service as a motivating force, and use it as such. Mobilizing commitment is managed differently in various sectors of each profession. Private practitioners who select clients that seek assistance and pay for it have a less acute problem of client motivation than do their colleagues who work in public facilities that accept all comers, for the social arrangements of practice manage the mobilization of commitment for the private practitioners, while their publicly practicing colleagues are effectively delegated the task of mobilizing their clients' commitment. One way that professionals in all sectors cope is to delegate large responsibilities to clients. Therapists often assign patients a key role in deciding what problems should be solved and when they have been solved. Organization consultants regularly invite clients to decide on the goals they will seek and when they have been achieved. Teachers often try to anticipate what particular students will find appealing, and make suitable assignments.

2   Psychiatrists and teachers of course also require ideas and inanimate materials, but these are ancillary to their work on people.
3   Commentators on teaching have long noticed the importance of resistance to teaching. (See, for example, Eggleston, 1957; and Waller, 1965.)

Practitioners' dependence on clients imposes limits on skill and knowledge that go beyond those arising from uncertainty. If a neurotic patient refuses to discuss his problems the therapist's special expertise is of little avail. If anything helps, it may be the little-skilled suggestion that therapy cannot proceed unless the patient cooperates, and the long silence that often follows. If eight year-olds reject their teacher's plan for a French lesson, no amount of instructional knowledge of French is likely to help. Often unspecialized coaxing by the teacher, or a stern admonition from a parent, or a trip to the principal is what does the trick. In such cases and many others, practitioners' expertise is insufficient to produce results, or even get started, for no improvement can occur until clients agree to a course of action and set to work on it.

Practitioners must supplement their own expertise with clients' consent, and the knowledge and skills they subsequently may be able to bring to bear. Clients' commitment is an essential companion to practitioners' expertise, and often nearly a complete substitute for it. That would be true even if all practitioners were exquisitely skillful, for teachers, psycho-therapists and organization developers work on other human beings whose commitment to improvement is essential to the mere opportunity to practice, let alone to success. No amount of improvement in professionals' knowledge and skill could supplant clients' commitment and the many essential but little-skilled things that many practitioners must do to mobilize and sustain it.[4] But here again, the problem is managed differently with varied social arrangements of practice. Practitioners in private practice, or in very selective public settings, can count on selectivity to comb out those clients whose will to improve needed mobilization, while their equally skillful colleagues in unselective settings must labor to mobilize that will.

Practitioners are pulled in contrary directions as they try to manage their dependence. Since professional success depends on clients' improvement, there are powerful incentives to press for dramatic change, since the greater the client's accomplishment the greater the practitioner's success. But human improvement can be both risky and difficult, for more ambitious improvements are more difficult to achieve, and pose greater risks of

---

4   This account is only the beginning, for apart from disagreement over the ends and means of practice, no practitioner can anticipate how clients will respond in classes, therapy sessions, and other settings. Teachers are regularly surprised by students' interpretation of a story or their solution to a math problem, and they are often compelled to revise their own approach in consequence. Practitioners of human improvement cannot work without their clients, but interaction opens up uncertainty.

failure. Old ideas or habits must be revised or abandoned if clients are to change, whether in learning physics, improving emotional health, or increasing organizational effectiveness. Yet the old ideas and habits did work, however roughly, and casting them aside is rarely easy. Clients must also acquire new skills, habits, understanding, or states of organization, which is often difficult and risky, for if clients cannot change as much as they had hoped, perhaps they cannot become the people they wished to be, or were told they should become. In a world that sets human improvement as one of its highest ambitions, such failures count.[5]

The more that practitioners seek ambitious successes for their clients, the greater the likelihood that they will provoke resistance, precipitate failures, or both. Since things that are risky and difficult for clients threaten practitioners' prospects of success, practitioners have incentives to define improvements that clients will not resist or can easily accomplish, for modest or even trivial improvements may be better than none at all. Teachers, therapists, and colleagues in sister practices regularly worry about whether they should aim high in order to gain great improvement in their clients and equally impressive accomplishments for themselves, or aim low in order to avoid the risk of total failure for clients and achieve at least some success for themselves. The problem yields to no lasting or generally satisfactory solution, but it must be managed somehow if work is to continue. (Berlak and Berlak, 1981; Lampert, 2001).

These predicaments are unique to professions of human improvement. Teachers and organization consultants need the will to work in addition to their specialized knowledge and skill, and in this respect they are just like carpenters and architects. But carpenters and architects do not require the will — the consent and commitment — of their wood or ideas. Only teachers and colleagues in related practices require clients who bend their own wills to the work, along with practitioners. Workers in these professions thus face a unique predicament. They have special status, social position, authority, and influence, while their clients are defined as unskilled, or deficient, or problem-ridden, or even pathological. Yet professionals are useless without their clients, and often are powerless with them. Patients who doze on the couch and students who read comic books impede not only their own improvement but also practitioners' progress

---

5   There is occasional recognition of difficulty and risk in educational commentary, but it has not been seen as a central problem. In contrast, difficulty and risk have been viewed as central in psychotherapy. Such differences in theories about practice can be very influential in setting expectations for what practitioners can accomplish.

as professionals. Practitioners can work only if their clients will work with them. They can succeed only if their clients strive for and achieve success. If students, patients, and members of organizations do not become practitioners of their own improvement, professionals cannot succeed. Clients' will and capabilities are no less important than those of practitioners — indeed, professionals' work in these trades is aimed centrally at cultivating their clients' will to better themselves, and relies heavily on their skill at such work. Whatever their own attainments and position, practitioners depend on their less skilled, less mature, or less healthy clients for their own success and satisfaction.[6]

The two predicaments that I have been discussing operate jointly, for practitioners are regularly caught between their claims to special knowledge and their dependence on clients. Their expertise is essential for access to clients, for their clients' trust, for fees or salaries, for social position, and for results. But practitioners' expertise is always far from sufficient, and they must rely on other resources or arrangements, supplementary to their specialized knowledge and skill, to sustain their work. Some of these supplements belong to clients — their will to work and their knowledge and skill. Others belong to practitioners and include everything from the courage to face uncertainty to the generosity of spirit that enables one person to devote himself to help others. Improved knowledge and skill are sorely needed in teaching and its sister practices, but no matter how well-educated and experienced they may be, practitioners need much more than specialized knowledge and skill to do good work.

It therefore seems fair to say that professions of human improvement are impossible.[7] I do not mean that teachers, therapists, and organizational consultants constantly tear their hair: they do go to work every day like anyone else, and struggle with boredom as well as other common problems. Yet these professions require the management of deep difficulties that have no entirely satisfactory or lasting solutions, and the solutions that practitioners patch together regularly come unglued.[8] To say, however, that these predicaments must be managed is not to say that practitioners must manage them constantly or attentively. Practitioners and clients can mutually regulate how much they need attend to the problems discussed here. If psychotherapists and patients use behavior therapy and simple reinforcements to induce weight loss or to end smoking, they need not

---

6   Willard Waller recognized this point in Waller, 1965; as did Bidwell, 1965.
7   I take the term from Malcom, 1981.
8   On teachers' management of dilemmas, see Lampert, 2001, and Berlak and Berlak, 1981.

struggle with great uncertainty about the ends and means of improvement. In contrast, uncertainty and doubt increase if practitioners use traditional "insight" therapies to help patients understand why they overeat or smoke, to decide whether they can do something about it, and then try to do it, for doubt and uncertainty are essential elements in such therapies.

Practitioners and clients can thus increase the risk and difficulty of their work by embracing relatively complex and ambiguous purposes and methods, or they can ease matters by adopting clear and simple objectives and methods. They are not absolutely free agents, but they can regulate work together from the inside, by varying the ends they seek and the means they use. Such regulation is a central element in human improvement professions, for it allows practitioners and clients to shape how large the predicaments of human improvement will loom, and to shape the skills, knowledge, and other personal resources they must deploy.

Yet practitioners and clients are not Robinson Crusoe and Friday, parked on islands all their own. Their work is also regulated by society, economy, and culture. Some teachers work in institutions that admit only talented and committed students and dismiss them if their performance is poor; the chances are slim that these teachers will struggle much with dependence on students. Yet many equally committed and skilled teachers work in slum schools or community colleges that accept all applicants and cannot dismiss any without extraordinary effort; they are more likely to struggle with dependence. Some teachers and students work in schools or societies that have strong consensus about educational results, and are unlikely to be plagued by uncertainty about the ends and means of schooling. Yet equally able colleagues work in schools or societies that persistently dispute those matters, and that improves the chances that they will struggle with uncertainty. Social arrangements in these professions increase the likelihood that the predicaments of improvement will be called painfully to mind in some cases while reducing their visibility in others. These arrangements also increase the probability that extraordinary expertise will be required to get barely decent results in some situations, while making it possible to get fine results with only modest expertise in others.

To attend to the predicaments of human improvement thus is not to claim that all practitioners constantly worry about them, for attentive coping is not the only way that these problems are managed. Professionals and clients can diminish or increase the attention they give to these predicaments by internal regulation of their practice, and professions or societies can do so by the ways in which they configure the social arrangements of practice. Much can be learned by figuring out why some practitioners and clients are little troubled by the predicaments sketched here, while others are plagued by them. The predicaments are distinctive to these professions, but they are not always at the top of practitioners' minds. I propose them as a useful way to interpret these professions, whatever practitioners may be worried about.

I should also note that my claim that these occupations are distinctive is not a claim that they are utterly unique, for the work of human improvement bears remarkable similarities to other work. In the last years of the 20th century all occupations could make some claim to human betterment, and most do. Social progress is an increasingly fundamental value everywhere, and more and more occupations and enterprises explain and justify themselves with reference to human improvement. Advertisers assert that they are improving our capacity to satisfy emotional needs. Managers claim that they are improving our capacity to be productive, or to enjoy work. Soap manufacturers even announce that their products are "caring" for our children. Whatever one thinks of these claims, only teachers, psychotherapists, and their colleagues work directly on other humans with the primary aim of improving their minds, skills, souls, and organizations.

But someone will ask: What about many other occupations, ignored thus far, in which practitioners work directly on others? Cosmetic sales clerks work on their customers, surgeons work on their patients, "human resource" managers in large corporations work on their employees, and prison guards work on prisoners. Great promises for human improvement are regularly made for facial cosmetics, management, and involuntary detention. Can one deny that these practitioners also produce human improvement?

Consider the improvements and the means by which they are cultivated. Surgeons do not try to make their patients into apprentices,[9] nor do salesmen try to improve their clients' capacity to sell vacuum cleaners or encyclopedias. Most managers avoid trying to help subordinates become managers, let alone better managers. In occupations like sales, physical medicine and many branches of management, practitioners typically strive for a distinctive sort of result: Items sold or manufactured, profits earned, bones and organs repaired, and the like. Improving clients' minds, souls, knowledge and skills are subsidiary at best, and typically either irrelevant

9   Changes in medical practice and the reduction of many common diseases in advanced industrial societies have greatly changed medical practice, so that many doctors now also deal with a broad range of social and psychiatric problems.

or merely decorative. In guarding prisons or other police work, practitioners typically are more custodians than meliorators; their assignment is to keep people away from trouble, not to improve their capabilities. (See Muir, 1978).

In contrast, teachers succeed only by helping students to acquire some elements of their own specialized expertise: knowledge of a subject, skill in communicating about it, a repertoire of strategies for solving problems, and the like. When psychotherapists succeed it is typically by helping their patients to acquire elements of their own distinctive therapeutic expertise: insight into emotional problems, understanding their sources, skill in noticing symptoms, and a grasp of the barriers to improvement. Only teachers and practitioners in sister trades must cultivate their clients' capabilities to become adept practitioners of their own improvement, for only in these professions must clients become such practitioners in order for professionals to succeed.

Though there are elements of human improvement in many modern occupations, there are also important differences between human improvement professions and other occupations in which people are processed. But it would be unwise to draw hard and fast lines between these types of work, for the distinctions are plastic and contested. Some human resource managers in firms define their goal as profits made or units produced, but others define them as understanding achieved, knowledge acquired, and capacities improved. Some prison managers define their results in custodial terms but others energetically seek rehabilitation. Some prison guards act as though they were teachers while others are brutal or indifferent. And if some teachers act like prison guards, others seek social and intellectual liberation for their charges.[10] The shape that these professions take in any given case depends on organizational differences and professional preferences, among other things.

Another reason to eschew rigid distinctions is that all occupations exist in time, and are subject to change. Just five or six centuries ago, what little school teaching there was dealt either with simple skills useful to commerce and administration or with otherworldly salvation. The problems of human improvement were not on anyone's plate because secular betterment was not an explicit enterprise. Professions of human improvement are an invention of the last several centuries, progeny of the

10 More and more commentators maintain that teachers really are a species of thought police, helping to keep us all in an invisible intellectual or political prison, but others see teachers as a liberal and liberating force. (Bowles and Gintis, 1976; Lindblom, 1990).

idea of progress. One result of the invention was the transformation of several ancient professions. Pastoral work, which was focused on otherworldly salvation for centuries, has gradually been oriented to human improvement. Pastors still offer guidance on mysteries beyond experience, but even to do that they borrow from social work, psychotherapy, and education, so that even such otherworldly work now includes elements of secular human improvement.

The boundaries of human improvement professions also blur because these trades are not similarly constituted in all societies, and are often contested within them. The speed of modernization varies among nations, as does enthusiasm for various doctrines of progress. Psychotherapy has been much more popular in America, with its established Protestant passion for self-improvement, than in more traditional and Catholic European countries where it grew up. Teaching addresses a more limited range of purposes in Asian societies than in the US, but even Americans disagree deeply about the extent to which it should attend to human improvement. Religious fundamentalists of all sorts regard teaching in quite traditional terms, arguing that it should orient students to salvation. Some secular educational reformers and practitioners think that teaching ought to be restricted to traditional academic matters, eschewing broader improvement. But the ubiquity of human improvement is evident here as well. Fundamentalists explain their view of school as an alternative to secular eschatologies, and conservatives argue against the same broad secular values — economic progress, political justice, and social peace — that most human improvers pursue.

These arguments will persist, waxing and waning with circumstances, but they all are variations on an essential modern theme: humanity's capacity to better self and society, to repair mind, soul, and organization, with specialized knowledge and skill. It is unprofitable to define these professions tightly because history and social variation overgrow any such tidy borders. We can see that some professions of human improvement (teaching, psychotherapy, and organization development), are further down the modern road than others, at least in the U.S., and more clearly exhibit the distinctive puzzles of this most modern work. We also see that the same practices seem to be moving in a similar direction in less modern societies, and can imagine that the movement may become more pronounced or widespread in the future.

It would in fact be surprising if the momentum of human improvement did not increase, pulling more occupations and enterprises into channels that others have already taken. In a few decades many sales clerks may become practitioners of consumer therapy, using goods, services, and clinical insight in this cause. There is already plenty of evidence that consumers search for emotional improvement in the goods and services they purchase, and that many salespeople skillfully assist them in this quest.[11] Though I can delineate the leading features of professions like teaching and psychotherapy today, it seems reasonable to expect that ambitions for human improvement will continue to grow tomorrow, assuming no convulsive rejection of modern civilization, or collapse. Such expansion would be difficult to avoid in a civilization that identifies progress so closely with increased technical mastery, personal comfort, and satisfaction of individual wants.[12] The boundaries of this new family of practices thus will probably remain indistinct, weakly defined, partly because they lie along an uneven and shifting frontier.

* * *

This account throws a little additional light on my claim that human improvement professions are impossible. Since they make the great modern promises for secular betterment, they open up many of the great modern puzzles. Of course, each profession organizes these matters differently, for each employs a distinctive approach to setting and solving the problems. Psychotherapy is mostly centered around the discourses of emotional renewal and self-discovery; practitioners and clients focus on defining and solving problems by probing personal history, or practicing new habits, or both. In contrast, teachers set and solve human improvement problems in the discourses associated with various academic subjects, or theories of learning and schooling, or some combination of the two. But if the specific terms of reference vary from one human improvement profession to another, they still have much in common. Professionals all try to better the human condition in some specific aspects by increasing their clients' capacity to think, to feel, or to act. As a result, practitioners and clients are regularly confronted with certain common problems. How will we define human improvement in this case: what can this person become? How best to achieve that progress: what methods of human betterment are most appropriate? And how will we know if we have done well, or well enough, or whether we have done anything constructive at

---

11 Today, for instance, "color therapists" advise clients on what hues are most likely to improve their dispositions, and prescribe clothes and housing accordingly.

12 Oswald Spengler argued that this imperial spirit of progress was essential to modern Western (he wrote "Faustian") civilization (Spengler, 1991).

all? Ought practitioners urge their clients to great things, taking an expansive view of human possibility and pressing for great improvement? Or should they restrict their dependence by setting simpler and easier goals?

Workers in these unusual trades thus face versions of the problems of producing and assessing human progress that all modern societies confront in national social policy. To undertake a profession of human improvement is to do the most essentially modern work. Because teachers, therapists, and organizational consultants try to deliver on these most distinctive promises of modern civilization, they also wrestle with the problems of defining and justifying human improvement with which entire societies have struggled through the modern centuries. But they confront these problems at the level of particular individual efforts to improve other human beings, rather than engaging them on the grand scale of social policy. Academic analysts can make hay from the predicaments of human improvement, but practitioners must somehow find ways to manage them that are good enough to warrant continued work with the person in the next seat, the next hour, or the next consultation.

References

Berlak, Ann and Berlak, Harold. (1981). *Dilemmas of schooling: Teaching and social change*. London: Methuen.

Bidwell, Charles. (1965). The school as a formal organization. In J. G. March (Ed.), *Handbook of organizations*. Chicago: Rand McNally, pp. 973–1023.

Bowles, Samuel and Gintis, Herbert. (1976). *Schooling in capitalist America*. New York: Basic Books.

Cohen, David K. (n.p.). *Teaching: Practice and its predicaments*.

Cremin, Lawrence. (1980). *American education, The national experience, 1783–1876*. New York: Harper and Row.

Eggleston, Edward. (1957). *The Hoosier schoolmaster*. New York: Sagamore Press.

Friedenberg, Edgar. (1965). *Coming of age in America*. New York: Random House.

Goodman, Paul. (1964). *Compulsory mideducation and the community of scholars*. New York: Vintage.

Kuhn, Thomas. (1962). *The structure of scientific revolutions*. Chicago: University of Chicago Press.

Laing, R.D. (1960). *The divided self: A study of sanity and madness*. Chicago: Quadrangle Books.

Lampert, Magdalene. (2001). *Teaching problems and the problems of teaching*. New Haven: Yale University Press.

Lindblom, Charles E. (1990). *Inquiry and change*. New Haven: Yale University Press.

Lindblom, Charles E. and Cohen, David K. (1979). *Usable knowledge*. New Haven: Yale University Press.

Lindblom, Charles E. (1965). *The intelligence of democracy*. New York: The Free Press.

Braybroke, David, and Lindblom, Charles E. (1963). *A strategy of decision*. New York: The Free Press.

Malcom, Janet. (1981). *Psychoanalysis: The impossible profession*. New York: Vintage.

Muir. (1978). *Police: Streetcorner politicians*, Berkeley: The University of California Press.

Perkinson, Henry. (1995). *The imperfect panacea: American faith in education*. Boston: McGraw-Hill.

Spengler, Oswald. (1991). *The decline of the West*. New York: Oxford University Press.

Szasz, Thomas. (1978). *The myth of Psychotherapy: Mental healing as religion. rhetoric, and repression*, Garden City, N.Y., Anchor-Doubleday.

Toulmin, Stephen. (1972). *Human understanding*. Princeton: Princeton University Press.

Waller, Willard. (1965). *The sociology of teaching*. New York: J. Wiley.

Ethnography and Biography: The Stories People Tell of their Lives as Jews

SAMUEL C. HEILMAN

The Connection between Ethnography and Biography

In his classic exposition of the "several ways in which the organized life of man can be viewed and understood," anthropologist Robert Redfield has suggested that one useful approach involves the examination of a "typical biography."(Redfield, 1956, pp. 11, 1). This approach recognizes that while "particular men and women come and go, and make life's passage in varying ways," nevertheless, "in any stable community there is a characteristic passage." (p. 52). Accordingly, the ethnographer's role is often, therefore, to try, by means of looking at particular individuals' passages, to discover what is general and characteristic about these life experiences. In doing this, ethnography goes beyond telling those particular stories but actually uses such individual narratives to discover that general character of the community and in turn make it visible and comprehensible, even as the emphasis may appear to be on specific people's lives (p. 52). Put simply, the character and even the personality of a community, something very difficult to articulate, emerges in the lives of those people who call it home.

Faced with the sometimes overwhelming task of trying to discover and articulate the character of contemporary American Conservative Judaism and in particular its synagogue life, I used this ethno-biographical strategy among others. Underlying this research decision was the realization that the synagogues I observed were not simply places of worship but were — at least for most of their core membership (those who participate in its activities on some sort of regular basis) as well as for a good many in the periphery (those who come relatively less often but still feel a sense of sufficient affiliation to pay their dues) — enduring little communities. As such, the Redfield conception of examining 'typical biographies' seemed a particularly fruitful research strategy. I set out therefore to gather biographical sketches of synagogue members and construct out of them a series of typical biographies that could in turn help me uncover the features of the general Conservative Jewish face.

Part of the research task was of course to decide whom to interview and subsequently to select among and edit the many personal narratives collected. In general, a familiarity with the basic nature of contemporary American synagogue life — what in social anthropology is called 'cultural competence' — made it possible for me to discern the basic synagogue member types I was seeking. These included finding those who were actively involved (core) members and those who were passive (peripheral) members. It also included exploring the backgrounds of some of the young and especially of those who were just beginning new families as well as of those in their middle age who were into the most intense years of raising children and creating a home. I also looked for the so-called 'empty-nesters,' people who, having completed those years, were now reassessing what their ties to the synagogue and Jewish life should be. I talked to people who related to the synagogue and their Judaism in a variety of ways — from those who saw it as a spiritual experience to those who saw it as a social one, from those who focused on the school to those who went only to a house of worship.

I was of course limited by a number of factors. I could only talk to those who were willing to talk to me and who responded positively to my request that they share the story of their Jewish lives. At times I could get people to participate in one-on-one interviews, while on other occasions they agreed to be part of a focus group of several who serially shared their life stories. The variations in the results that these different situations fostered, I shall speak about presently. For now, I would simply note that in both situations, getting those to whom I talked to put the facts into some sort of coherent narrative was also a challenge. People are not always articulate or able to summon the facts of their lives in an order that weaves their experiences and outlooks into an autobiography. In some cases, for them to do so required just a few simple questions from me which served as a trigger to a barrage of recollections. In other cases, responses were brief, thin descriptions that needed to be thickened by responses to a whole series of concrete queries. In some cases, respondents lingered over or explored the points raised by some of these questions in far greater depth than they would have had they been asked only to tell a kind of stripped-down story of their lives.

Exploring these various biographies, therefore, I concerned myself always not only with individual stories, but I looked for themes and patterns which enabled me to fit the details I learned into the mosaic of the particular synagogue's life. This gathering of personal stories also offered a way of discovering and demonstrating how over the course of a lifetime, people could change their relationships to the synagogue and Judaism, how they might move from one to another synagogue category and how that movement could be bi-directional.

Sitting down with these people I began by simply asking them to tell me how their personal Jewish history had brought them to become members of their particular synagogue and lead the kind of Jewish lives they now led. For those who were stymied by this open question, I would add questions about their Jewish education, relations with the Judaism of their parents, the nature of and frequency of their trips to the synagogue at various stages of their lives, the trajectory of their religious life and particularly their college experiences, relationship to Israel, the Jewish consequences of their marriage and parenthood, and of course at the end of this once again why they had selected to lead the kind of Jewish life they now led. I would also occasionally simply ask people to expand, if their answers seemed too abbreviated. Moreover, when the narratives were carried on in groups, people in the group occasionally asked one another questions; and of course the way one person told his or her story often set the tone or served as a model for the other narratives, either for comparison or contrast. As Redfield has reminded us, "if the native is induced to sit and reflect, if he finds it interesting to arrange his thoughts so as to communicate them to someone, perhaps an ethnologist, the structure of the world view grows and develops." (p. 91). As James Clifford explains, the ethnographic process of gathering narrative accounts can lead to "the construction [or maybe a kind of re-construction] of self."(Clifford, 1986, p. 23). This is evidence that, as anthropologist Renato Rosaldo has correctly observed, "stories often shape, rather than simply reflect, human conduct."(Rosaldo, 1986, p. 129).

People I interviewed reflected on their current level of synagogue and Jewish involvement and why and how that involvement could be articulated in their Conservative Judaism, a denomination that each one of them agreed was for them a matter of choice rather than default. They talked about the current nature of their Jewish lives and how it compared to what they once were when they were younger and where they thought they might be in the future. In this they also tried to articulate their reasons for having become the kind of members they were as well as accounting for their current level of involvement.

Moreover, in their narratives those I spoke with also constructed (some tacitly and some explicitly) basic definitions of the nature of Conservative Judaism and Judaism in general and what each demanded of those who identified as such. Often they admitted that their definitions were not necessarily authoritative, yet at the same time they declared them to be sufficient because — as one woman put it — "it is just my experience." In other words, they often conflated their own stories with what we might call the story of American Conservative Judaism. To this quite a few would add something to the effect that they did not need an institutional or authoritative endorsement to their interpretations of Judaism and Conservative Judaism. In the words of one, "we feel comfortable in our Jewishness, and I don't feel I need to answer anybody about it." In other words, quite a few seemed genuinely to see this as a chance to reflect seriously about their Jewish commitments and concerns in ways they had not done in a long time — if ever.

Finally, when I had recorded and collected these narratives, I inserted them or parts of them into my manuscript and then sent my written work to those whose stories I used for their response and reaction, explaining my willingness to correct any errors or misperceptions. For all my efforts at using biography as a tool in ethnography, there were some unintended consequences that I had not bargained for.

Unintended Consequences

The first of these was the extent to which the very act of looking at and telling the story of one's life could transform the people I was talking to (and by extension the Jewish setting in which they found themselves). Many had never thought about a life trajectory having a synagogue as one of its endpoints. To frame the narrative with the synagogue as its destination made them see some of their life choices in a far more Jewish and communal light than they would otherwise have done. This happened because for some I interviewed, this look at themselves as Jews and synagogue members was a wholly new experience, as if they were forced to listen to their narrative in a key that they usually did not use to understand the meaning of what they had done. In fact, the very asking of the question stimulated in them a kind of reflection and self-examination that became for some a religious experience in itself. One group was so moved by the process, so engaged by their own and others' accounts, that they quickly embraced one member's suggestion that such gatherings for Jewish autobiography become an organized synagogue activity.

This transformed ethnography into Jewish self-scrutiny and therapy. I found people turning my sessions with them into an opportunity to confess their own religious shortcomings — after one interview one man actually followed me out to my car and held onto me in the darkness while he movingly explained how our interview made him meditate upon his Jewish life and recognize perhaps for the first time about where he had made wrong choices which he now believed had perhaps led to his son marrying a non-Jew, and who, like his son, was not particularly interested in Jewish life or concerned about its continuity. In response to my questions, one couple seemed to notice that while they had tried to escape what they perceived as their parents' forced imposition of religious values upon them, they had in fact begun imposing their religious world-view on their children in no less absolute a manner. As she repeated the Jewish choices of her own life, yet another woman seemed suddenly to realize that even as years before she had resented her Reform Jewish parents' "flat-out" refusal to her request join a Conservative Jewish youth movement because they had a different idea about the sort of Judaism they wanted for her, she had now responded with a similar "flat-out" refusal to her own children's recent request to go to a Schechter day school rather than the afternoon Hebrew school she had in mind for them. One women who had been a convert to Judaism from Catholicism found herself telling me how she now recognized that in her decision to make her kitchen kosher, she had endorsed standards of Jewish conduct that put her at a distance from her friends who did not do the same and who now thought of her as Orthodox, which she hastened to add she was not. Another woman found herself admitting that while she went to the synagogue regularly, "I don't believe there's a God. I go to synagogue because it's uplifting. I like the people; I like the music; I like the rabbi," and although she enjoyed joining in prayer, "I don't believe anyone's listening; it's comforting but I don't think anyone's answering me." These and other reflections like them were braided into the biographies people helped me construct but also had the quality of perhaps leaving some of those with whom I spoke Jewishly changed, a consequence that as an ethnographer I find troubling (though as a committed Jew, I might find reassuring).

A second unintended consequence of the ethno-biographical approach occurred when people, at a later point in time, reviewed their words as written on a page and woven into unified narrative. In line with my agreement with the synagogues studied, I sent them drafts of my account. The realization that, even though they would not be identified, they would find their lives "immortalized" in a published text served to make people sometimes reconsider and seek to recast their biography. Many now chose to remodel what they had said — some going so far as wanting to rewrite not only what they had said but also my own interpretations of the cultural and religious implications of those words.

Sometimes it was not simply their biographies they sought to recast. Sometimes they engaged in a contest to define Judaism, not simply as they did for themselves, but in objective terms. In other words, they wanted the final text of the manuscript not simply to tell their lives and versions of Conservative Judaism but to present theirs as *the* only true version of Conservative Judaism or Judaism in general. They sought validation for their Jewish biography in the ethnography.

In some cases, those interviewed sought to reconstruct the images of their Jewish life that came from their original accounts because they did not fit into their desired or idealized self image. This is a kind of analogue to the client who wants a commissioned portrait to show only what the client considers to be the most flattering features. Two examples: So disturbed did one woman become with one of her candid declarations of a fact in her life, as I reiterated it in the manuscript — her explanation that she would not have considered conversion to Judaism "if it weren't for her husband," — that she demanded that I delete that comment, even though my purpose in using this statement was to demonstrate that this women who now lived a committed and active Jewish life had not come to Judaism out of a personal religious awakening or dissatisfaction with her religion of birth but, by her own admission, out of the fact that her husband was a Jew and had wanted to have a Jewish family.

Yet another man wanted me to change his original statement, "I went to Hebrew school too long," so that it would appear less ambiguous when its ambiguity was, it seemed to me, most revealing and emblematic of his ambivalence about much of his early attitude toward Judaism. As a respected leader of the congregation, and a supporter of its Hebrew school to which he had sent all his children, he did not want this sentiment of his to be public. But of course an ethnography is not such a commissioned self-portrait; it is closer to a mug-shot.

The third unintended consequence of my research strategy was the discovery of how the very act of gathering life narratives could turn into a contest between the interviewer and the interviewee over the definition of what Judaism requires of its adherents. Part of this no doubt occurred because of my own public position as an occasional columnist whose opinions about Jewish life are widely known — or at least were by a number of those interviewed. Moreover because a number of those I talked to knew that my own personal Jewish commitments were not identical with Conservative Judaism, (and those who did not know, asked), they turned some of their life narrative into a kind of cultural challenge. For one man, the issue was egalitarianism and the role of women in Judaism which he believed needed bolstering in Conservative Judaism, a position he wanted me to somehow endorse, both as a sociologist and Jew. Another person explained how what had attracted him to Conservative Judaism was its endorsement of the principle that Jews could "pick and choose" those aspects of Jewish life and ritual with which they were most "comfortable." When I noted that the movement had certain *halachic* demands to which it remained committed and wondered how he related to these in his life, this question launched him into a debate about what is properly Conservative Judaism. When such questions came up in focus groups, moreover, the debates about the nature of Conservative Judaism grew even more animated. Indeed, the interview and its responses created opportunities for "cultural performances," situations in which people discovered who and what they were part of and dramatically projected that discovery onto a canvas for all to see.

The aim in the bio-sketches that make up a large part of my Conservative synagogue ethnography is to provide for an opportunity to understand the character of community. Yet in their execution they became Judaism and Conservative Judaism, "as felt," experienced, "good or bad, desirable or not to be desired" by the people of the congregations studied (Redfield, 85).

Conclusions

To be sure, when I was in the midst of carrying on the field work and collecting these personal accounts, I did not always see these consequences coming. Narrative analysis, the capacity to build some sort of analytic framework out of a set of stories, as Rosaldo reminds us, "makes sense only after the fact."(Rosaldo, 132). Hence the patterns and themes that emerge from all these biographies and associated outlooks on Conservative Jewish life only became discernible for me in the course of the actual writing of my ethnography. Of course, some will argue that this simply points out my own failings as an ethnographer. Perhaps so. Maybe this is just another cautionary methodology tale, reminding those who collect narratives how much the process of such collection can make an impact on the stories being collected, particularly where the focus of them is biographical and religious. Some might also see in my experience the risks one encounters when the people whose lives one documents come from a sufficiently close cultural milieu and share enough with the ethnographer so as to challenge not only his facts but his capacity to interpret them — Margaret Mead never had this problem with the Samoans whose lives she documented, nor Malinowski with his Trobriand Islanders.

Yet I believe this example also serves as an important lesson for Jews who seek to document the religious lives of other Jews and who seek to do so in the pluralistic context of American life. The challenges and contests over particular constructions of Judaism and Conservative Judaism demonstrate that the effort to interpretively comprehend — *verstehen* as Max Weber called it — the religious life of one Jew by another is not a simple ethnographic investigation, no matter how disciplined the researcher tries to be. Rather it may become — sometimes implicitly but at other times quite explicitly — a dispute in the ongoing battle to define the meaning and identity of Judaism in a society where a variety of such definitions and identities are contending with one another for legitimacy and authority. The Jewish ethnography of Jewish life would best be forewarned.

References

Clifford, James. (1986). *Writing culture: The poetics and politics of ethnography.* Berkeley: The University of California Press.

Redfield, Robert. (1956). *The little community.* Chicago: The University of Chicago Press.

Rosaldo, Renato. (1989). *Culture and truth: The remaking of social analysis.* Boston: Beacon Press.

Mentors, Colleagues, and Disciples:
A Jewish Curricular Deliberation
JOSEPH S. LUKINSKY

Introduction

This essay explores facets of mentorship and colleagueship pertinent to the consciousness and development of Jewish educators. It also proposes some pedagogies for encountering these modalities in an educators' workshop.

En route to creating or enhancing noteworthy general and Jewish educational institutions, Seymour Fox has been a colleague and mentor to many; I am honored to be among them. Fox has an uncanny knack for communicating even to those marginally involved in one of his projects, that they share in *devarim ha'omdim berumo shel olam!* Sustained by sound Jewish values, he doesn't get mired in what he has already accomplished and perseveres in generating new ideas, always moving forward in accord with the best thinking he can find.[1]

---

1   Seymour Fox is also a remarkable *disciple*. I recall, (mostly limited to the non-Israeli context, from the time I first met him in Chicago in 1949) his collaborations with great mentor-colleagues such as Shimon Rawidowicz, Louis Finkelstein, Saul Lieberman, Shraga Abramson, Abraham Joshua Heschel, and Natan Rotenstreich, among others. In addition, education greats Joseph Schwab, Ralph Tyler, Lawrence Cremin, and Israel Scheffler, were attracted to Jewish education projects by Fox. We were privileged to share their impact *with*, as well as *through*, him. Seymour Fox practices the values of *Shimush talmidei hakhamim* and *kavod hamoreh*, not only in his mentors' presence, but also in the way that he honors their thought and work in his own.

A few years ago I was invited to teach at a seminar-conference for day-school principals. The principals had been working for two years in a grant-supported project, sharing their experiences and their accumulating wisdom. Each principal consulted with an experienced mentor-principal.

I will describe how I created a curricular activity for this seminar, stressing mentor-student and colleague-colleague relationships. I did not record the sessions that I led; nor did I do a systematic analysis or follow-up of the results. I have, however, always held that even one lesson plan is a *curricular* activity and that there is value in reconstructing and sharing the process of creating it.[2]

A first assay took place in my graduate class in curriculum, "From Scholarship to Curriculum," at the Jewish Theological Seminary of America where, as a curricular exercise, we worked through early draft-versions of the activity that I was planning for the Principals' Conference. The trial took two or three sessions and led to refinements in the final plan.

A year after the seminar-conference, I worked on the same Jewish text studied there with my class in "Experiential Techniques in Jewish Education" at the Hebrew University's John Dewey School of Education. Here the focus was on the pedagogy of group inquiry. Some of the lessons of these experiences have been drawn upon here, but sorting out the threads of the two resources is beyond the scope of this paper. I am grateful to both groups for helping move many ideas from theory to practice.

After introductory reflections on the roles of mentors and colleagues, I will follow a description of the Day-School Principals' Program with my deliberations about how to conceptualize and use a classic Jewish text as a resource, and close with a depiction of the activity that emerged.

Mentors and Colleagues[3]

"...a mentor not only has a love of learning, but above all a love of students. A mentor directs rather than dictates, and offers guidance that inspires rather than smothers. A mentor respects students' urges to broaden their own vision of who they are and what they might become, and a mentor lives a life that embodies the beliefs that he or she

2 While my description of this experience does not meet some of the criteria of a "case" as delineated by Lee Shulman (Shulman, 1992), it does partake of what he calls "the relatively new genre of research in which the author is systematically studying his or her own practice in a disciplined manner..." (p.29).

3 See Palmer, 1998, esp. pp. 21–25. See also Kridel, et al. 1996.

espouses. And when we think of a teacher as mentor, most often we remember a person whose technical skills were matched by the qualities we associate with a good and trusted friend." (Boyer, 1996, p. xii).

It is mentors and colleagues who create and define a profession. True, a profession is advanced by research and writing, but, as actors with a script or musicians with a score, mentors and colleagues embody and enact a tradition. They become what Abraham Joshua Heschel called "textpeople," (Heschel, 1966, p. 237) and transmit tradition expansively, beyond any text, to the next generation. This normative *"Torah she-b'al peh"* process can be negative; it can diminish as well as distort. But at best, the horizontal and vertical interactions between mentors, students, and colleagues amplify tradition so that it grows in complexity, flexibility and sophistication. Only part of this can be recorded. Through the resourcefulness of mentors and colleagues responding to challenges great and small, the ongoing narrative of a tradition erupts through the boundaries and bondage of the past. It is not photocopied, as it were, from generation to generation. Something spontaneous happens, an interaction between the processes of receiving, transmitting and transforming. Each receiver, ostensibly receiving the same tradition along with others, may, in fact, do something different with it. In reader-response literary theory, each reader is viewed as reading a different book; some would go so far as to avow that a reader is a "co-author"![4] While this may be an exaggeration, each receiver of tradition is, for good or ill, more than a conduit of literal transmission. The pertinent considerations are: How do teachers, *as mentors*, communicate this unwritten content to students who bring different resources to the same encounter? Transmission often takes place in groups. How does group process affect the interchange? The tapping of mentors' and colleagues' knowledge may or may not produce new insight. What then accounts for that rare transformation into something new in which the old retains some force and valence?

I am interested in the parameters of discipleship and mentorship.[5] How

---

4   See the work of critics like Stanley Fish, for example, in Fish, 1980.
5   See Schwab, 1978. Schwab suggests that the "eros" for the mentor, when teaching succeeds, is transformed into a love for what the mentor loves, imitation leading to creativity. Going beyond the question of what makes a great mentor, Parker Palmer asks a "question that opens the deeper purpose..: What is it about *you* that allowed great mentoring to happen?" For Palmer, "Mentoring is a mutuality...not only are the qualities of the mentor revealed, but the qualities of the student are drawn out in a way that is equally revealing." (Palmer, 1998, p. 21). Palmer's whole section on heart and the one on mentors are moving and relevant.

far may a student diverge from a teacher and still be a "disciple" or even be considered *that* teacher's student? If several students all hear the same message, how is it possible to distinguish the traces of that message as reflected in their individual renditions of it? How does a mentor know if the message is getting across at all, in spirit if not in letter? In short, continuity of a tradition is problematic. What is to be continued? Why should it be continued at all? How is continuity maintained, and where does it come from if students change what they have been taught? How do we evaluate students' versions of their teachers' teachings? How do teachers and students negotiate the line between spontaneity and the simple restatement of what has been said before?

These questions were a central worry of J. L. Moreno, the creator of Psychodrama.[6] tradition, or what he calls "cultural conserve," is, at most, a takeoff point — a setting for spontaneity and creativity. People need to break out of their conserve, not to be bound to following scripts, re-playing old tapes, or being "exegetical"; rather, they must respond from the depths of their personal resources. What is creative in one instant of time becomes at another, "tradition," with a propensity for becoming mechanical, stultifying, doing and thinking what has been done and thought before. We ought not be "hung up" on our cultural conserve. The transfer of tradition from mentor to student is fragile, and preserving the spark of spontaneity is both difficult and crucial. For Moreno, tradition, by its very nature, may stifle, even as it may spur creativity. But tradition needs to exist, as it were, to have something to push *against*, or off *from*, a wall to break through.

At another point on the continuum, Max Kadushin,[7] in his studies of rabbinic thought, shows a different way of looking at continuity, in which the core is preserved even as the new is created.

In his generative research on rabbinic literature, Kadushin suggests tools that may help us view connections among mentors, students, and colleagues. These tools are embedded in the transmission of basic "value concepts." The *terms* that identify value concepts may not be used *as such* in the multi-dimensional rabbinic texts, but they reside beneath the surface, springing to life as texts encounter one another, different nuances emerging in the different configurations. How readers identify these terms is influenced by what they bring to each unique setting. Yes, they are

6   See Moreno, 1987, pp. 39–59, *passim*. I use Moreno here to create a continuum. Others could have been chosen, but the whole issue is Moreno's emblem.
7   See Max Kadushin, especially Kadushin, 1938 Also see the many essays in Peter Ochs, 1990 and Joseph Lukinsky, 2002.

subjective constructions in part, but the meaning of the terms is affected by real circumstances that awaken the latent value concepts to life.

In the texts that I will consider here, and in the workshops in which I taught them, it was the responses of those who joined me in study that established the meaning for themselves and for me, for *that* time and *that* place. Scholarship was a "control," but there was room for creativity too, *makom l'hit-gader bo*. It does not mean that these interpretations were the only ones possible, or that they were artificially read *in* to the text. They were valid constructions among others, in this case generated by our focus on colleagueship and mentorship.

The Principals' Program

Here I will describe the Day-School Principals' Seminar program, tell about what I was asked to do, and how I prepared for it.

Though I knew most of the participants (many had been my students), I had not yet worked with this project group which would shortly come to a close. I was given some background by the coordinator of the program who had invited me. The long-term goals of the program were associated with conveying the wisdom and skill of the experienced principal-mentors to the new and inexperienced principals, to create a sense of colleagueship amongst the latter, as well as a shared sense of purpose and a conviction of the significance of their educational efforts. They were also to gain from opportunities to collaborate, from joint problem solving, from sharing techniques, and responding to one another's educational and personal issues deriving from their professional effort.

Another presenter, an expert in "collaborative learning" had worked with the principals throughout the two years; I knew that they had engaged in various activities related to her specialty, but not much more. I was able to extrapolate assumptions about them from my general knowledge of school principals and from my practical experience as a principal and supervisor of principals in various venues.

The three sessions I was to teach at the conference were to be spread over two days, one for three hours, the other two, each for an hour and a half. These three sessions represented a single component in an enterprise to which I would be unlikely to contribute in the future. The challenge was to get the most out of the opportunity and time given me. Although I was involved in only one part of the program, my aim was to contribute to its overall goals.

My first task was to find out as much as I could about the backgrounds of the participants in the program, who were Solomon Schechter Day School principals. The program was a funded pilot program, indicating that there were some resources in the community for nurturing the qualities in which I was interested. In other words, the enhancement of the vitality and power of mentors and groups was recognized, a goal of this program. The principals all had good, some very good, Jewish backgrounds. Some were rabbis. Many had studied at the Jewish Theological Seminary of America or schools of education like Teachers College Columbia, receiving graduate degrees. Some had studied Philosophy of Education and Philosophy of Conservative Judaism and were interested in the implementation of both in their schools and communities. All worked hard at their personal relationships to Jewish tradition.

The principals had been paired in a two-year mentoring and peer-supervision program designed as a response to perceived lacks in the competencies of many principals. Aside from occasional in-service workshops and conferences similar to this one, most principals had tended to work in "splendid isolation." The cooperative aspects of this two-year pilot program differentiated it from the modal experience of most principals (Sarason, 1982). In the program, they had experienced peer-sharing along with relatively skilled supervision by their veteran mentors. They had found this relationship to be valuable and, in general, liked these collaboration formats.

The principals had, so far, experienced collegiality and competitiveness, and, over the two years, had learned to be open about their problems. They had a wealth of shared experience; yet, each pair and each individual had had, since the last conference, new experiences which might be of value to the others. They had not had many opportunities to engage teachers and parents in their own schools in Jewish learning, and especially in that of a collaborative nature.[8]

In sum, I was trying to connect to the overall goals of a group project

---

8   The same experience that the principals had had in this program might be a model for other programs that might be undertaken with the teachers in their schools. Further down the road, some analogous programs might be developed with and for parents and community leaders. In developing the "analogues" the question of *authority* will always be present, as will the types of relationships between principals and teachers or principals and parents that are different from those in the peer and group relationships the principals had experienced. These would be relevant distinctions for comparative analysis. For an important study of peer supervision among teachers, see A. Ofek, 1985.

already in process. My contribution was conceived as academic, but with a vague hope that it would be relevant.[9]

Choosing the text

I was told by the workshop organizers that they wanted me to teach a Jewish text, not "educational theory." I was also to relate to the "meaning of our work in Jewish education." I didn't have to be Sherlock Holmes to glean the following implications:

- The chosen text would have to have relevant links to the overall goals of the principals' program. I understood these to be focused on the topics discussed above.
- It would have to arouse active participation, in the group dialogue and in the interpretation of the text.
- It would have to differ in some significant respects from the conventional wisdom of modern educational thought, in this, exemplifying a Jewish slant or nuance.

Professor Joseph Schwab taught us, in his great essay, "Learning Community," that "shared recovery of meaning" in educational practice *is* the "experience" of community. He develops this idea forcefully in the essay, advocating the

"deliberate shaping of learning situations and classroom practices, whatever the subject matter and whatever the grade level, so that they will contain, as factors intrinsic to the learning process itself, certain basic components of community." (Schwab, 1987, p. 31).

The meaning of this is clear. Enquiry[10] not only discloses a content; the *way* something is studied always imparts other messages.[11] The experience of study in a group should communicate a visceral understanding of what

9   I am grateful to Dean Emeritus Sylvia Ettenberg of JTSA and Dr. Robert Abramson, Director of the Department of Education of the United Synagogue of America for inviting me to contribute to this program.
10 This spelling reflects Schwab's "trademark" distinction between enquiry (reading "out" in a rhetorical examination of a body of material) and inquiry of a more general sort. For almost everyone else, "inquiry" is used loosely for both.
11 Gregory Bateson called this "deutero-learning." See Bateson, 1972.

community means. How can the *medium* of study be constructed so that it conveys this deeper level to the brains and to the "bones" of the learners? This would be an important consideration in an attempt to relate to the dimension of mentors and colleagues in the principals' community.

The "medium is the message."[12] I strove to construct exercises that embodied the *message* of the text with regard to content and to the ways of learning it. My goal was to use the "medium," i.e., the *text and methods of learning*, as a resource for advancing the "message" of the overall program. If the medium is the message, how do you construct that medium so that it conveys the message of the text at a deep level?

At this stage, I sought to convey, through a classic source, a Jewish perspective on mentorship, colleagueship, continuity, pluralism, collaboration, teaching, collaborative learning, and community. Most important, the *way* the text would be studied would have to *enact* these values, beyond the cognitive understanding of the content. Participants would experience the text in its collaborative dimensions and would internalize it through partaking of the approaches used to unpack it.

An Important and Relevant Text

There might be no better classic source with which to engage these issues than the "Rabban Yohanan Ben Zakkai and students" section of Chapter two of *Pirke Avot* from 2:8 until the end of the chapter, including the teachings of Rabbi Tarfon.[13]

Jewish continuity, with its ambiguities (continuity *of* what? *for* what?) is a responsibility assigned to Jewish families, to the Jewish community and, especially, to Jewish education. The question is of relevance in the Diaspora, of course, but also in Israel, in light of its religious-secular conflicts and, as a response to the Shenhar Report[14] which portrays the

12 Marshall McLuhan's famous axiom from his *Understanding Media* is so widespread that it needs no footnote.
13 My treatment here is influenced by Jacob Neusner's commentary to *Pirke Avot*, *Torah From Our Sages*, Rossel Books, 1984. Source citations are from that edition. However, I take a different tack in many places, especially in my attempt to see the text from an educational perspective with a view to the curricular activity I was trying to create. I will focus mainly on the Mishnaic tractate *Avot* but the parallel text in *Avot D'Rabbi Natan* (*ARN*) is an expansion and enrichment of the latter, also potentially useful for our purposes.
14 *Am V'olam: Tarbut Yehudit B'olam Mishtaneh*, Jerusalem, Ministry of Education, August 1994.

decline of Jewish studies in Israel's *Mamlakhti* (national non-religious public school system) and in its secular universities. Many perceive in this a crisis of future Jewish identity in the making.

Jewish educators, by definition, take pains to create involving curricula that go beyond "knowing about" to the realms of commitment and the perpetuation of Jewish values. Curricula are optimally constructed to affect people, not merely to convey knowledge.[15]

The approach is not new. A kindred situation prevailed at the time of the destruction of the second *Bet Ha-Mikdash* by the Romans in 70 C.E. Rabban Yohanan ben Zakkai assured the continuity of the Jewish people and its tradition by creating a center for learning at Yavneh, and establishing the study of Torah as a replacement for the lost Temple. His method, subsumed tersely in *Avot* Chapter 2, needs articulation by students of the text.[16] My emphasis here will be on the structural elements in the text which help us to focus on the issues of colleagueship, discipleship and mentoring to which I have alluded above.

I will, however, make selected substantive comments which prepare the ground for the curricular suggestions I shall present later. I am doing this in line with Schwab's distinction between the subject matter as a "source" and as a "resource," from his approach in "The Practical: Translation into Curriculum." (Schwab, 1973). When the subject matter specialist is "the" *source*, then everything else is controlled by him. When the specialist or the subject matter is a *resource*, then it is one among other valid considerations, the latter deriving from the remaining curricular "commonplaces." (Schwab, 1973, Tyler, 1950).

I am going to relate to this subject matter insofar as it functions as a *resource*. This means that I take into account the group that will encounter the material, as well as the purposes for which the Principals' Program was created. I analyze the text stressing those aspects of it relevant to its proposed use. I am thereby claiming that, though it is rich enough to be viewed from many perspectives, I am choosing these, and not others, for their fit to the educational purposes designated.

---

15 I am thinking here of what Lee Shulman called "*Pedagogies of Engagement*" in his keynote address at the International Conference on Jewish Education at Bar Ilan University, December 2000. Shulman tried, with this concept, to bridge Bloom's cognitive and affective domains. (Bloom, 1956, and Krathwol et al., 1964).

16 Seymour Fox has advocated an authentic Jewish educational terminology for many years, opposing the unreflective embrace of concepts and terms from the general field without considering whether they are compatible with overall Jewish philosophical principles. The use of the Ben-Zakkai material in this exercise attempts to get at this issue.

Moreover, I am making another educational choice: I am leaving the most important questions open-ended. I want the group to work on them from the perspective of their own realities. (See lesson plan below for further discussion, especially #6). My preparation will serve as an example of "theoretical sensitivity" Glaser and Strauss, 1967; Glaser, 1978) but is not intended to control the end result. I consider the traditional approach of the *Tiferet Yisrael* commentary to the *Mishnah* (not in its specifics, but with regard to its overall assumptions)[17] a useful resource for our purposes, though I am not negating the place of critical scholarship which has also been useful to me.

I will make clear to the group that we are working within the frame of traditional assumptions about the text, along with the critical approach of Jacob Neusner.

The Text of the Ben Zakkai and Students Section of אבות, Chapter 2
A brief *structural* summary of the text:[18]

1. The text describes Rabban Yohanan Ben Zakkai as the student of Hillel and Shammai, and gives the *opening statement* of R. Yohanan. The quote represents his philosophy of Torah study:

    > *Im lamadata torah harbeh, al tahzik tova le'atzmeha ki lekah notzarta.*
    > "If you have learned much Torah, do not puff yourself up on that account, for it was for that purpose that you were created." (*Avot* 2:8)[19]

2. Then, the text lists his five (apparently "outstanding") students and his *characterizations* of them. (*hu haya moneh she'behen*) "He praises a different quality in each."[20] (*Avot* 2:8)
3. The characterizations of each student are followed by *two conflicting versions* of R. Yohanan's choice of the most "weighty" of them. In the first, he considers *R. Eliezer ben Hyrcanos* the most outstanding; in the

---

17 *Tiferet Yisrael. Pirush lemishnah me'et harav Israel Lipschitz.*
18 The text is well known, and readily available, so I will not reprint it here in full.
19 Neusner's translation in Neusner, 1984, pp. 74ff. All text references are to this edition of Neusner. See also Neusner, 1991.
20 R. *Joshua*'s characterization is problematic in that it is not parallel in form to the others. (see *ARN* version where, instead of *Avot*'s *Ashrei yoldato*, we have it that R. Yohanan *Kara lo hoot hameshulash shelo bimhera yenatek.*

second, reported by *Abba Shaul*, he chooses *R. Elazar ben Arakh*. The reasons for the choice, in each of the versions, are not completely clear. Presumably, each version supports *Ben Zakkai*'s previous characterizations of *Eliezer* and *Elazar*. The second version, reported by *Abba Shaul*, is supported by what follows.

4. *R. Yohanan* then "quizzes" his five students with regard to the most and least desirable qualities which a person should cleave to or reject. Each of the five students answers both questions. *R. Yohanan* indicates his preference for the answers of *R. Elazar Ben Arakh,* which supports the version of *Abba Shaul* in the previous section.

5. *Each of the five* students then makes three statements, with *R. Eliezer*, the first, presenting additional material.

6. Some teachings of *Rabbi Tarfon* are added, concluding the chapter. The connection is open to interpretation.[21]

The Yohanan Ben Zakkai Texts From Avot: A Pedagogical "Warm-up"[22]

Of the numerous possible constructions of this text, as adumbrated above as productive for the enquiry, I have chosen to focus on *mentoring* and *colleagueship*. They provide the parameters for the curricular-pedagogical suggestion that I constructed. This is not the only possible way to construe this material, but I claim it here as the most valid for our purposes, for using the material "in the service of the student." (Schwab, 1973, p. 377).

Yohanan Ben Zakkai and his students are, to quote Neusner, a spiritual "family," as contrasted with the lineal heirs of the other "chain of tradition" cited up to this point in the Avot text. Family is created by people who learn Torah together. (Neusner, 1984, pp. 74ff).

The text deals explicitly and implicitly with issues like: how to learn Torah, how to be a teacher, how to be a student of Torah, how to be a colleague, a neighbor, how to be a member of a community. Of these, we are stressing here three over-arching roles: students, peer-colleagues, teachers, and the interactions among them.

Neusner in his *Pirke Avot* commentary considers the whole Yohanan

---

21 Neusner sees no connection. I will suggest a possibility below.
22 By "pedagogical warm-up" I mean those inquiries and reflections useful for relating to the text as a resource. *Schwab*, 1973.

Ben Zakkai and students text as a unit. However, though he does try his hand at it himself a couple of times, he doesn't see much use in finding structural connections among the various components of the whole text. (Neusner, 1984, p. 77). The separate sayings are, in his view, conventional, reflecting the basic thrust of *Pirke Avot* as a whole, with emphasis on *Torah, Tefillah,* and *Good Deeds.* Moreover, he does not see the *R. Tarfon* section as connected. (p. 84). This may be good historical scholarship, but to adopt Neusner's view would be, again, to use the text as a source rather than a "resource." In this respect, it seemed useful to use the traditional commentaries which lend themselves more to providing for a legitimate educational perspective on our chosen themes.

The *Mishnah* commentary of the *Tiferet Yisrael,* among others, interprets the text in a way that enables the compilation of overall profiles of each of the five students. This assumption of a consistent personal identity for each of the five students throughout the text supports a valid educational conjecture about the text which I exploit, though I do not necessarily follow the specific leads of *Tiferet Yisrael.*

In this light, I also venture another hypothesis, open for exploration, that the rest of the material — from the praises of *Ben Zakkai* for each of the students *hu haya moneh shebehen,* to the tests he gave them, to the separate teachings of each of the students – lends itself to nuanced interpretations of *R. Yohanan*'s original teaching. In further developing an educational perspective, I'm suggesting that it is possible, imaginatively, to induce such connections.

For the priming of inquiry, it seems to me legitimate to make both of these broad assumptions, supported by educational considerations and by what we know about this text, formative as it is for Jewish historical *consciousness*, objective historical considerations aside.

Yohanan Ben Zakkai's initial statement is the key to the whole textual interpretation that I am offering, the basic fundamental theological and educational orientation lesson that his five outstanding students received from him:

> *Im lamadata torah harbeh, al tahzik tova le'atzmeha ki lekah notzarta.*

According to Neusner, (1984, 74ff) for Yohanan Ben Zakkai, Torah is all of the meaning of Life. But what does this mean? It is the *purpose* for which humans were created. It can't mean just "study for the sake of study." It has to mean Torah in a broader sense, the study of which gives one the potential to do things in depth, from a perspective. It provides a foundation beneath which one cannot fall. It makes life possible at a higher level. The one who studies much Torah has resources to interpret situations and to accomplish that which others cannot![23]

But Ben Zakkai's five students can be interpreted as having different "takes" on this foundational teaching. Each of the five is different, in character, style, and in the content he emphasizes. Yet, despite these differences, according to our text, Ben Zakkai considers the five to be *his students*. I will postulate, for purposes of inquiry, that all the presentations by each of them reflect unique transformations and applications of this teaching.

A support for this premise derives from R. Yohanan's positive responses. R. Yohanan honors each of them with a different praise, for what they are. He also honors what they say in response to his questions: he accepts their statements, implying that he doesn't see them as contradicting his view. We don't know his response to their separate teachings which may have been promulgated after his death. However, I propose that it is a legitimate hypothesis, in line with the earlier parts of the unit, that the editor's juxtaposition of his statement and those of the students implies some form of implicit approval.[24] This point, accepted for purposes of enquiry, is open to acceptance or rejection as the deliberation progresses. At the very least, it is an open question. There is, in any case, no grounds for an *a priori* rejection of the possibility that connections may be found.

It is worth examining the possibility, therefore, that each, in one way or another, is a reflection of the master, their mentor, and that the statements of each can be related to the original saying of R. Yohanan in a valid way. This becomes the stimulus for the pedagogic approach that will emerge below.

To recap our assumptions thus far, there is a tension: each of the five students reflects R. Yohanan's teaching, or they would not be *his* students;

---

23 I remember Seymour Fox making this very point many years ago: A doctor sees many possibilities in a "sore throat" which would be totally unavailable to a layman.

24 As an alternative possibility, one might posit that *Ben Zakkai* may reject a particular aspect of what a student individually says, but accept the overall potential of the statement or viewpoint, as a kind of pedagogic "strategy." (cf. Schwab, 1953: 109–21). In other words, he might disagree in part but still consider a particular statement as being "in the ballpark." At the same time, it is not clear what the parameters are of *R. Yohanan*'s approval. What would put a statement "outside?" These ambiguities are what lend themselves to educational exploration; the answers are to be determined through inquiry, as I will attempt to illustrate below.

yet, each also adds his own nuances, which R. Yohanan legitimates. Furthermore, just as he accepts their views, he also ranks and rates them; he is not afraid to judge them and does so in three different ways: in the loving praises of each student, in the rating of "weightiness" (the Abba Shaul mishna 2:8), and in the two "quizzes" that undergird his expressed preference. He expresses his opinion of them, and of their views. He encourages their best qualities as he sees them. He judges their responses as to which is the most valid. He models this kind of wise and forthcoming, yet gentle, assessment. He tells his preference for the views of Elazar ben Arakhh. (2:9) Yet, since he sees the others' views "included" in Ben Arakh's preferred answer (*shebihlal devarav devarehem*), they, therefore, should not be considered as rejected, and we may infer that their views are acceptable to R. Yohanan, just not broad enough.[25]

That the separate teachings of each of the students can also be examined as reflections of their teacher's original teaching is, again, an "educational" assumption, and the task would be to tease out the extent to which each is a valid reflection of the master's teaching, and how each differs from the others. Each of Ben Zakkai's students in their own teachings which follow, can be predicated as nuancing Ben Zakkai's teaching as it applies to different contexts. They are continuing his teaching but they are expanding its scope creatively. This is an essential offshoot of the rabbinic value *shimush talmidei hakhamim.*

Do disciples also affect their mentors? Yohanan Ben Zakkai chooses from the answers *that he gets* to his questions, from what the students give him. This can be interpreted as a pedagogic choice; in other words, there are some limitations to his response. He waits. He does not look for the answer that he already has in hand; he chooses the best answer that he gets!

The R. Tarfon material may be avowed as having a purpose here, (*contra* Neusner). It may be seen as clarifying R. Yohanan's teaching, a kind of commentary on the whole unit. It addresses more implicitly the issue of "reward" (really "credit") for the study of Torah which is ambiguous in the original statement of R. Yohanan. R. Yohanan doesn't bluntly say there is *no* reward; just that a person shouldn't focus on it. One shouldn't expect a "return" for studying Torah. This appears problematic to the students, indicated by the stand taken by R. Elazar in the last of his "three statements:" *ve'ne'eman hu melahtekha she'yishalem leha sahar poaletekha* (2:14).

---

25 He knows how to criticize, contra the modern view not to make distinctions between students, fearing for their "self-esteem."

R. Elazar doesn't necessarily disagree with R. Yohanan on the basic point, but there is a need for assurance. The Tarfon section seems complementary on this point as a summary which includes both perspectives, fulfilling the need to spell it out. Tarfon's statement, (2:16 *veda matan seharan shel tzadikim le'atid lavo*) thus clarifies the last statement of Elazar ben Arakh, and this seems possibly to be its purpose here.

The main point for our purposes is that there is enough tension in this issue to justify the exploration of the Tarfon material in this light by any group studying these texts.

In this section I have not presented a set of answers to all the questions that might arise in the workshop inquiry that I am going to propose now. It is rather spadework, a development of resources intended to raise the level of discourse.

The Lesson Plan for the Principals' Conference

In discussing the actual program as it was presented, I will write in the past tense, switching to the present tense for current reflections.

1. Individuals, then pairs, studied the complete text, noting, in the margins of the large-paper Xerox copy, difficult words and concepts, questions, comments and associations, indicated by drawing lines between sections. Examples of these were then collected orally with no concern for "best" or "correct" answers.[26] The purpose was to create a level playing field, in that everyone has now prepared the ground-level of the text thoroughly, struggling with problems encountered. The purpose is to get everyone involved, but not yet in a systematic way.

2. Stage one satisfactorily achieved, the leader presented an open-ended "basic question". Criterion: a "basic question" is one that is truly open-ended, whose answer is not determined *by the leader* in advance.[27] This is a crucial point that is absolutely necessary for our

---

26 Much of the approach in this section is based on the Great Books Foundation's approach as described in its *An Introduction to Shared Inquiry* (Second Edition) 1991. See also Lukinsky, 1997. The Great Books approach is especially important in its stress on *true* open-ended questions. In this method, the early stages of discussion do not necessarily have to come to conclusions.

27 *An Introduction to Shared Inquiry*. See also Lukinsky and Schachter, 1996.

purposes. If the leader has determined the "answer" to the basic question, there tends to be unconscious manipulation to make it "come out" that way. This eliminates the possibility of real collaborative discussion. Students, due to prior conditioning, may not believe that the discussion is truly open-ended. The leader may need to prove this by demonstrating openness to diverse possibilities.

This does not mean that the leader does not challenge the views that are proposed. It should be noted here that my earlier deliberations about the text were geared to advance my preparedness, to provide a broad framework, not specific answers.

Examples of basic questions that I was prepared to ask, chosen on the basis of the feedback on activity #1 above, are:

- Why does R. Yohanan Ben Zakkai prefer the opinions of R. Elazar ben Arakkh to the others?
- What is the meaning of *ki lekah notzarta*?
- Why does Ben Zakkai see R. Elazar's opinion as "including" all of the others?
- What do "lev-tov" and "lev-ra" mean?
- What is the purpose of the R. Tarfon material? How does it relate to the rest? It seems to be just added on.

In the actual program, I decided to use the question of why Ben Zakkai preferred the view of R. Elazar Ben Arakh to the others. The chosen question does not have to be comprehensive. It only has to be generative in important ways, with the potential for a wider discussion; it is a microcosm for the discussion as a whole. The image of a "spider's web" is useful; a good pathway is one that leads to many others. While the *basic question* may be chosen in advance, the leader should be prepared to make a change in mid-course. More than one basic question can be taken up if there is time, but it is likely that one is enough if it has this quality of generativity.

3. The group worked in pairs on the basic question. Each individual first wrote answers to it, followed by each pair discussing the results of their thinking. Writing slows down the process, enabling the deliberation to begin in a less pressured mode, with each person having the opportunity to articulate and to interact with one other before the discussion in the large group begins. The work in pairs enables people to think for themselves before they hear the views of

the more aggressive members of the group. Having a chance to work out their own views, they are better able to argue and defend them in the ensuing large-group deliberation. At this point general discussion followed, now more focused. It is still important at this point to have all views expressed, to give people a chance to speak and argue their viewpoints.[28]

4. The next activity took place after a break in the schedule and for a longer period of time. Each participant was asked to choose one sage from the five students of Ben Zakkai, to follow him up through the various levels of the text and to develop a profile of him. A profile combines all the sources on each sage, his characterization by R. Yohanan, his answers on the two quizzes, and then his individual teachings.

For example: R. Shimon Ben Netanel is characterized by R. Yohanan as a *yera het*, one who "fears sin." In answer to Ben Zakkai's first test question, R. Shimon sees the trait that should be "cleaved to" as *haroeh et hanolad*, to have "foresight. In the second test — the trait to be most avoided — he chooses (to be) *haloveh ve'aino meshalem* — one who borrows and doesn't repay. In the three statements of his own, he stresses the need for care and spontaneity in prayer, and the constant hope for God's mercy, reflected in never allowing oneself to be a *rasha* in one's own eyes.

The profile of R. Shimon is consistent. It reflects his concern with anticipating proper behavior, making up for inadvertent neglect, and, in the last resort, repenting of one's sins, and never viewing oneself as beyond hope of forgiveness.

5. The last activity, the writing and presentation of profiles, generated the next stage of the enquiry, an example of synthesis in which the reflection of R. Yohanan's original statement is sought in the profiles of each of the students, derived from R. Yohanan's statements about

---

28 At my class in the Hebrew University, students discussed the "basic question" of why R. *Elazar's* opinion was seen by *Ben Zakkai* "as including" all of the others? One student related "*lev-tov*" to the portrayal of R. *Elazar* by his teacher as a "*Maayan Ha-mitgaber*." (Neusner — A surging spring). She saw a parallel. A surging spring comes from a "deep place." The image represents the depths of his consciousness. His understanding surges from the depths of his person, symbolized by the "heart." Another student looked at the order of the speakers. Elazar ben Arakh is *last*; he speaks after he has heard what each of them said. He absorbs all of their statements and includes them in his response. He says something new, something that comes from the *depths* of *himself* in response to what he has heard; i.e. he doesn't just dredge up something from what he already knows, out of the computer, so to speak.

each, their answers to his questions, and their own teaching statements.[29] R. Shimon's "profile" can be related to R. Yohanan's opening dictum. R. Shimon's profile represents a consistency of character in one who learns Torah without expecting credit or reward: to learn Torah is to be sensitive, aware of the traps into which one can fall in life. A profile of this sort (and this is only one of the possibilities for R. Shimon) can be drawn for each of the five students from these texts alone.

6. A culminating exercise on two levels:

First, in an attempt to move a notch higher on the list of affective objectives, participants were asked to choose a sage with whom they identify and to give reasons for their choice. Here it is not desirable to use the term "*most* identify." This type of question often results in blocking. It is possible, even desirable, to identify with more than one. Each person therefore describes one identification, without having to worry about it being the strongest one.

A culminating exercise, (part two) was: Relate three lessons deriving from this two year training experience as a legacy to your colleagues. Each of the principals who had participated in the program thus *enacted* the text that they had studied. As Ben Zakkai's students each leave three statements for posterity, so did each of the principal-students have that opportunity. In order to do so they had to think about what they had learned, not only in this exercise, but also during the whole two year project.[30]

Summary and Conclusions:

This study is about how mentors affect their students, their disciples. It suggests that true students or disciples do not merely repeat what their mentors say or do, but rework what they learned from them. It brings a Jewish perspective by extrapolating from a classic Jewish text that deals with these same issues tersely, with open-ended possibilities that lend

29 The various stages of the program have obvious affinities with the levels of Benjamin Bloom's famous taxonomies. See Bloom, 1956; and Krathwol, et al. 1964. Regarding the latter, see Footnote # 15, Lee Shulman's "Pedagogies of Engagement." Shulman in his Bar Ilan address was reformulating the Bloom stages with some important nuances. His address will appear in the Proceedings of the Bar Ilan conference in the future.

30 Another possible task would have been to use the results of the whole activity as an opportunity to have the principals extrapolate from their own experience of learning the text to teaching it to their own teachers and parent community.

themselves to discovery in an alert group. The text is a classic; it has latent potentials for different circumstances.

I have tried to demonstrate that the Yohanan ben Zakkai and students texts (Avot Chap.2) embody concepts of Jewish continuity in its "deep structure." I have tried to facilitate the *internalization* of this paradigmatic meaning for a workshop setting for Jewish educators. The *study* of the text has the potential to enact and dramatize the *experience* of the paradigm, to energize it. To study the text *and* the students' involvement in it, is itself to research the question of Jewish continuity. My focus is an educational one, on the *student-teacher relationship*. I have described a "practical" curricular activity, but there are some research possibilities here too. If I were to do this again, I would record the results and do a "grounded theory" inquiry (Glaser and Strauss, 1967) based upon the resulting account.

In brief:
A. The Yohanan ben Zakkai sources in Avot Ch.2 help us understand Jewish continuity. They describe the ideal of Torah in R. Yohanan's thinking and its differentiated transmission to five outstanding students.
B. The source, its separate parts and overall context, is rich in its content and structure.
C. Students of the text can be involved in its levels of meaning. The medium is the message.
D. What is learned is potentially applicable to other contexts.
   A goal is the formative evaluation of the teaching of the text, but the result in each case will be not wholly predictable, following the qualitative "principle" of grounded theory which favors exemplarity and generativity over generalizability. (Glaser and Strauss, 1967).

References

Am V'olam: Tarbut Yehudit B'olam Mishtaneh. (1994). [People and world: Jewish culture in a changing world]. Jerusalem: Ministry of Education, August.

Bateson, Gregory. (1972/1987). *Steps to an ecology of mind: Collected essays in Anthropology, Psychiatry, Evolution and Epistemology.* Northvale: New Jersey: Aronson. (Originally, Chandler Publishing Co.).

Bloom, Benjamin. (1956). *Taxonomy of educational objectives: Handbook 1: The cognitive domain*, New York: David McKay Co.

Boyer, Ernest L. (1996). Forward. In Craig Kridel, Robert Bullough Jr. and Paul Shaker. *Teachers and mentors: Profiles of distinguished twentieth century Professors of Education.* New York and London: Garland Publishing.

Fish, Stanley. (1980). *Is there a text in this class? The authority of interpretive communities.* Cambridge, MA: Harvard University Press.

Glaser, Barney, and Strauss, Anselm. (1967). *The discovery of Grounded Theory.* Chicago, IL: Aldine.

Glaser, Barney. (1978). *Theoretical sensitivity.* Mill Valley CA: Sociology Press.

Great Books Foundation. (1991). *An introduction to shared inquiry* (Second Edition) Chicago, IL.

Heschel, Abraham Joshua. (1966). Jewish Education. In Abraham Joshua Heschel. *The insecurity of freedom.* Philadelphia PA: Jewish Publication Society of America.

Kadushin, Max. (1938). *Organic thinking.* New York: Bloch Publishing.

Krathwol, David, Bloom, Benjamin, and Masia, Bertram B. (1964). *Handbook 2 The affective domain.* New York: David McKay.

Kridel, Craig, Bullough Jr., Robert and Shaker, Paul. (1996). *Teachers and mentors: Profiles of distinguished twentieth century Professors of Education.* New York and London: Garland Publishing.

Lipschitz, Rabbi Israel. *Tiferet Yisrael: Pirush lemishna.*

Lukinsky, Joseph. (2002).Teaching *Hazal* and the thought of Max Kadushin. *Studies in Jewish Education 8: Teaching Classical Rabbinic Texts.* Jerusalem: Magnes Press.

Lukinsky, Joseph. (1997). Remembering Professor Bettelheim. *Melton Gleanings, 2 (1).* Autumn.

Lukinsky, Joseph and Schachter, Lifsa. (1996). Are questions necessary? *Jewish Education News.* Winter.

Moreno, J. L. (1987). Spontaneity and catharsis. In Jonathan Fox, *The essential Moreno.* New York: Springer Publishing Company.

Neusner, Jacob. (1991). *The Oral Torah: The sacred books of Judaism.* Atlanta: Scholars Press.

Neusner, Jacob. (1984). *Pirke Avot, Torah from our Sages.* Chappaqua NY: Rossel Books.

Ochs Peter. (Ed.). (1990). *Understanding the rabbinic mind: Essays on the hermeneutic of Max Kadushin.* Atlanta: Scholars Press.

Ofek, Adina A., (1985). Peer supervision from theory to practice: An exploratory study in the field of Jewish education (unpublished doctoral dissertation, JTSA).

Palmer, Parker J. (1998). *The courage to teach; Exploring the inner landscape of a teacher's life.* San Francisco: Jossey-Bass.

Sarason, Seymour. (1982). *The culture of the school and the problem of change.* Boston MA: Allyn and Bacon.

Schwab, Joseph J. (1987). Learning Community. *The Center Report.* May.

Schwab, Joseph J. (1978). Eros and education. In Ian Westbury and Neil J. Wilkof. (Eds.). *Science, curriculum, and liberal education: Selected essays, Joseph J. Schwab.* The University of Chicago Press.

Schwab, Joseph J. (1973). The Practical: Translation into curriculum. *School Review 81,* pp. 501–22; reprinted in Ian Westbury and Neil Wilkof. (Eds.). (1978). *Science, curriculum, and liberal education: Selected essays, Joseph J. Schwab.* Chicago and London: The University of Chicago Press.

Schwab Joseph J. (1953). John Dewey: The creature as creative. *Journal of General Education 7.* pp.109–21.

Shulman, Lee. (2000). Keynote Address at the International Conference on Jewish Education at Bar Ilan University, December.

Shulman, Lee. (1992). Toward a pedagogy of cases. In Judith Shulman. (Ed.). *Case methods in teacher education.* New York: Teachers College Press.

Tyler, Ralph. (1950). *Basic principles of curriculum development.* Chicago and London: The University of Chicago Press.

Paradigmatic Change: Towards the Social and the Cultural in Jewish Education
ZVI BEKERMAN

Liberal Jews around the western world seem to hold ambivalent views towards Jewish educational efforts. On the one hand, they believe these efforts to be central in preventing assimilation and its greatest threat, intermarriage, and on the other they seem regularly unhappy with its products. By liberal Jews I point to a wide variety of mostly non-orthodox, religious and non-religious, groups, which hold to open perspectives regarding the possible integration of tradition and modernity. This paper reflects critically on the choice of schooling as the vehicle for Jewish cultural transmission, suggesting not a total rejection of it but rather the need to review its paradigmatic bases.

Educational efforts with Jewish children have come to be considered almost solely responsible for the development of a strong sense of Jewish identity and commitment to the Jewish people (Wertheimer, 1999). The release in the USA of the National Jewish Population Survey in 1990 showing Jewish youth losing identity ground and too many Jews marrying outside the faith, gave these efforts greater urgency. The developments in the USA have influenced Jews elsewhere who also seek to lower assimilation rates through educational programs.

The current interest in Jewish education is expressive of a modernist trend in Jewish perceptions of the secrets of Jewish transmission. While in earlier times folk knowledge would have it that Jewishness is inherited or naturally absorbed from the Jewish environment in which children grow up, past/present modernity and contemporary globalization seem to have convinced Jews that formal schooling holds the secret for Jewish continuity and commitment. Unfortunately this turn to the support of formal Jewish schooling took place without much deliberation as to the nature and goals both of such education and of the context within which this education would make sense. But for a few scholars (Ackerman, 1969; Fox, 1973) who demanded serious consideration of the purpose, diversity, and complexity as well as the paradigmatic bases of the Jewish educational enterprise, Jewish education has concentrated on the transmission of specific textual knowledge and religious skills needed, for the most part, to participate successfully in bar/bat mitzvah ceremonies.

Schools, knowledge, individuals and culture

It is worth reminding ourselves that the current educational structure is not natural to the world; neither has it made its appearance by chance. The development of mass education, through schooling, is closely related to the industrial revolution and the development of the nation state. Both were in need of recruiting masses to their service; masses with basic cognitive and behavioral skills which could serve the needs of the nation state and its economic structure. Thus schools are in no way disinterested arenas within which neutral knowledge or skills are transmitted from the minds of specialists to those of passive individuals. In the modern era, schools have served as the primary means by which sovereigns have unified the different local groups inhabiting the areas they were successful in subordinating to their power, under one flag, one language, and one narrative. With this in mind, it is already surprising that liberal Jews have chosen the school structure to secure their future and continuity.

Yet on the other hand, it could be argued that this should surprise no one. Indeed Jews have adopted an already existing structure and have turned it into one that serves the Jewish minority and not just the sovereign under which it resides. Historically the path is similar to that taken by other religious denominations (e.g. the Catholics).

However, the central lynchpin of formal schooling's success is its structure and its functionality, both based on and expressive of a particular paradigmatic perspective which I doubt can be beneficial for Jews or any other minority. Schools are the central conduit for the transmission of two interrelated beliefs of the modern western world; the first: the belief in the individual self; and the second: the outside existence of knowledge which this self can absorb if properly guided.

These above-mentioned elements have been in the making for centuries in the functioning of schools. Over five thousand years ago, when the first schools were created in order to produce a cast of scribes able to sustain the bureaucratic needs of growing, powerful, centralized, urban, economic human enterprises, they developed the three central characteristics which hold to this day (Cole, 1990; Goody, 1987):

1. The student was trained by strangers, separated from his kin and family;
2. The knowledge slated for transmission was differentiated and compartmentalized into fields of specialization; and
3. Learning took place outside of the contexts of its intended implementation, i.e. students rehearsed knowledge "out of context."

It is doubtful whether a system structured around these premises could in any way serve the goals of liberal Jewish education, if indeed this education is interested in finding ways to strengthen and enliven ethnic/ religious identity, community structures and the individuals' affiliation to them, as well as an understanding of Judaism as a living tradition able to offer a variety of answers to real present socio-cultural issues.

While these three characteristics are amongst those that reformers have periodically tried to change, and in spite of the multiple efforts invested in this enterprise, most schools today are still basically structured like those of antiquity. Let us again ponder the questions: Can a framework that is premised on distancing the individual from the family and community core serve to engender Jewish identity and communal incorporation? Can a structure that conceives of and imparts knowledge in differentiated and compartmentalized chunks (Bible, Talmud, Israel, etc.), serve in the cultivation of Jews able to conceive of Judaism and its potential role in the world as a comprehensive whole? And, last, is it feasible to expect that school children would find what they learn relevant if they are 'educated' in environments in which the acquisition of knowledge is segregated from the places in which this knowledge can be functional, (and in which the knowledge transmitted does not reflect the knowledge implemented by the community itself in the world outside)?

When confronted with these questions some liberal Jews today might want to agree and add that those are exactly the central issues which need to be addressed if liberal Jewish education is to succeed in the modern West. They would readily point to the efforts being invested today to extend education into the surrounding school community to include parents and adults in general, and to the efforts to involve schools in community work and activities so as to achieve a better fit between school and the "real" outside world (Woocher, 1995). I react to these statements positively but immediately want to point out my conviction that they might not be helpful in the long run.

This is so because these structures and their operation, not satisfied with what was described above as their tools for shaping the masses, hide at least two paradigmatic features which, if left untouched, will not allow for the system to be reformed, thereby to become beneficial to those minorities wishing to sustain a level of cultural independence so as to compete in the interpretative work which takes place when shaping the world they inhabit. These paradigmatic features to which I have already hinted above are what modernity has come to call "universal cultural values" and their appointed recipients, "autonomous individuals" and their assumed identities (Bekerman, 2001; Bekerman and Silverman, 2000).

This not being the place to expound on a full fledged critique of these paradigmatic western bases, it will suffice to say that both culture, as a reified identifiable cast of behaviors and beliefs, and the individual as autonomous and universal have been the focus of a long and wide theoretical controversy within high and post modernity which has successfully demonstrated the link between these features and many of the world's current maladies (Giddens, 1991; Sampson, 1993; Taylor, 1994).

It is worth mentioning that these theoretical developments have pointed *inter alia* at two central issues related to our present understanding of culture and individual identity which are relevant to education. The first is that culture must be understood as a verb and not a noun; as something which grows, evolves and intermittently becomes when executed, to be promptly dissolved again into the doings of human activity which might be able, or not, to reproduce it again in similar or different ways (Bauman, 1999). Second, individual identity must be conceived as a similar dialogic (verb-like) process of becoming and shaping mostly through the use of the most human of human tools: language (Harre and Gillett, 1995; Holland, Lachicotte, Skinner, and Cain, 1998). Thus both culture and individual identity have come to be conceptualized as evolving processes widely dependant on languaging (Wittgenstein, 1953).

It is doubtful whether not exposing these ruling paradigms of a reified individual identity and culture, together with the practices through which these paradigmatic perspectives are framed and constructed within school participants, can be helpful to the education of Jews. The individual, separate and in isolation, might be a good item for domination, but is not a good one for community survival. Culture reified and segregated might be a good means of offering cheap recognition by politically correct multiculturalist, but equally serves to justify and perpetuate the ongoing suffering of minorities, now recognized but with their structural subordination left fully intact (Bekerman, in press).

Thus far I have discussed what I believe to be the unchallenged principles that define and support present Jewish educational efforts, thereby explaining my conviction that liberal Jewish education, in spite of its growth, will not help Jews to achieve at least their declared goals of strengthening a vital and active Jewish identification so as to make Jewish civilization a life option.

What, then, can be done? We can start by re-conceptualizing Jewish education as a particular case of Cultural Education (CE). By CE I mean the educational efforts invested by minority groups who seek to sustain what they perceive to be their socio-historical heritage in the face of the homogenizing assimilatory power of a hegemonic global west. Such a move would be similar to that taken by anthropologists (Verenne and McDermott, 1998) in their examination of the central paradigmatic perspectives of general education. It starts by restoring, respectfully, the concept of culture to its historical sources. Thereafter, it develops the restored meaning of culture into a methodology — cultural analysis — which, in turn, allows for a re-visioning of the crucial analytic unit for educational analysis, no longer focusing on the individual or the socializing group but, rather, on the production of cultural contexts. Finally, it leads to a new articulation of major policy issues, related no longer to Jewish education and its components — individual students, teachers, parents, curricula — but to the analysis of particular Jews in the particular context of particular western societies.

(i) The (re)concept(ualization) of culture

In the last decades, culture has become the focus of a variety of social scientific theorizing. Psychologists, sociologists, and linguists (Cole, 1996; Gee, 1992; Holzman, 1997; Wexler, 2000) have joined anthropologists in identifying culture as pivotal to the varied phenomena under examination. But in comparison to the advances in cultural analysis in these arenas, the field of Jewish liberal education lags far behind.

In examining the reigning paradigms of Jewish liberal education, two conceptual threads become evident. First, it becomes apparent that here, "culture" remains imprisoned in early modern European frames. In the perspectives of early modern Europe, culture has been interpreted primarily as the high achievements in literature and the arts of the [European] human spirit. Accordingly, culture becomes the locus of the superior and the universally relevant. For example, the English educator Matthew saw in culture "the best that has been taught and known" (Williams, 1961; Williams, 1976). Echoes of this view are heard in Jewish educational circles in the rhetoric surrounding questions regarding the "educated Jew," the ideal which successful products of the Jewish educational system should emulate. The second thread has been to see culture as synonymous with a psychologized internalized self. In its internalized sense, culture has become that which "belongs" to a person, a powerful force which shapes the individual from the outside, in.

Reestablishing the concept of culture as a relevant force for our purpose would mean, first, realizing how, in its present philosophized and psychologized interpretation, the concept of culture stands in direct opposition to its etymological roots. Culture (from the Latin cultura-ae) means, in its most basic form, "work," as in the compound agri-culture. The field of biology has maintained this primal sense when identifying cultures as environments for growth and development. From the field of anthropology, as early as the 1940s, Boas (Boas, 1940) opposed the conception of culture as a monad (one cell organ) isolated all by itself. Culture, he maintained, was an activity conducted in environments with others; culture, as is customary to put it today, is a situated and distributed activity. There is no such a thing as a culture that can be "known" or "learned."

Other anthropologists who, like Margaret Mead (Mead, 1942), emphasized the importance of enculturation processes, were careful to point out that the young, in disregard of their biological heritage, can become members in any group despite any level of dissimilarity between their adopted group and their group of origin. Claude Lévi-Strauss (Lévi-Strauss, 1955) went even further when he posited that any personality type could come into being in any culture because every human can reject the commands of the culture into which she was born.

Though we might not have a choice as to which culture we are born into, in principle we can choose the one to which we want to belong. Belonging to a culture is not a matter of identity, but of identification (Carbaugh, 1996; Lave and Wenger, 1991; Varenne and McDermott,

1998). Our identification, cultural or other, is built through our activity in the contexts in which these activities take place over the course of our personal historical trajectories. The activity is molded and interpreted as a certain class of cultural work (Jewish or other), when the activity is enacted with others, friends and foes. The same activity played out in different socio-cultural contexts can develop into different group identifications. From this perspective, being Arab or Jew, and yes — even man or woman, is not fate but an achievement; an achievement accomplished in concert with all partners to the interaction in the given historical event. Perceptions, beliefs, and primarily scripts scripted in concert with parents, siblings, teachers, and multiple others, (some committed and others hostile), become partners in the construction of each of our potential identifications. These scripted identifications are all the product of intensive and active social work, shaped in interaction in given historical trajectories. None of these identifications are qualities of our minds, but all are products of hard interactional work from which these qualities come to be inferred. (Harre and Gillett, 1994).

(ii) Cultural analysis, Culture as methodology

Culture is thus not a given and not a cause. Culture is the cooperative activity of many. Culture is never predictable in advance and creates not final but intermittent, risky, products. Such an understanding of culture should help us focus not so much on what it was, but on what it is that we are making, given the tools we are using, our near and distant associates and the historical, political, economic, institutional contexts in which our work gets done. So framed, our field of inquiry shifts from the traditional locale of psychology and sociology to the more inclusive and complex domain of cultural analysis.

While psychological and sociological perspectives have looked for the wrongs of education in the minds of autonomous individuals (Holzman, 1997; Wenger, 1998) or in explanations of social contexts and how they influence individuals (while at the same time pointing out the influences of specific individual agents on that context (Archer, 1995), in cultural analysis, positing causality and tracing clear historical paths becomes difficult.

Cultural analysis pays attention to the work done in concert and the meaning attached to this work by the participants in the interaction, given the historical trajectory of these and their contexts, and well knowing that they will soon be going with their interpretative work somewhere else. When applied to Jewish education, cultural analysis is neither about failure or success nor about who is responsible for these. Rather, it is about how people/groups in a given context organize their worlds through their activities. Cultural analysis asks how we have accomplished our present situations in concert and in developing contexts, knowing in advance that neither a particular agent nor a particular cause can be identified for the purpose.

Given the present economy of Jewish education, its founders, foundations and their gate keepers, (so much imbued in their positivist paradigmatic perspectives, long considered misguided from any serious scientific empiric position), the task is indeed too complex to warrant consideration. All seem to prefer fast recipes, linear and causal; those that will allow for investments with prompt returns that are successful in the long run, or not. Reform, in their view, is indeed needed, but it is of no concern if the reform does not transform and, after the lapse of five to ten years at best, all has to be reformed again. A cultural analysis would ask about change, and then question the options, tools, and co-participants available to produce such change, not only from within the narrow Jewish liberal educational context but from within the wider joint institutional, historical, political, and economic ones, indeed rendering the situation complex and almost unbearably difficult for those currently involved in Jewish education. Experts of sorts often answer queries with the terms suggested by the present paradigm, as if this were a given. Thus in Jewish education they tell us about the need to review curricula, better train teachers, invest more in more and more isolated schools. Indeed all these answers are guided by the (mis)understanding of culture we identified in the previous section of this paper. Cultural analysis asks about how these arguments are shaped so as to serve and perpetuate the same present situation the experts seek (or so they say) to change.

By simply stating that a cultural analysis should propel Jewish education in different directions does not necessarily mean that such an analysis would automatically fare any better, because cultural analysis is also well embedded in the cultural conditions it wants to overcome. The first task of cultural analysis, therefore, would be to uncover the conditions which encourage the present situation, paying careful attention to its own position in the setting. Second, it would strive to uncover the ways in which present answers in fact serve the causes of the problems which they purport to solve. Finally, cultural analysis, by crossing borders and producing new experimental associations and dissociations, both material and conceptual, would conclude by producing more inclusive questions which shuffle our present understandings.

A cultural analysis could start by identifying some problems. Cultural analysis as a methodology should guide us in this case to pay careful attention to how things, all things, get done. When properly looking at these doings in their contexts, we might come to identify multiple problematic items in Jewish liberal education, both in its strategies and their sustaining paradigms. Since the work has still to be done, here we can only summarize some partial and preliminary arguments, beginning with educational strategies.

Based on an understanding of culture as practices situated and distributed, it could be asked whether the perceived malfunctioning of Jewish liberal education is not due to the quality of systems rather than to that of individuals; those systems jointly and cooperatively built and sustained by all, while trying to preserve the appearance of creating a "worthwhile reality." A cultural analysis would question how educators and leaders, usually smart (at times too smart), have come to believe that the supposedly failing Jewish school system is the best option available. It would suggest, perhaps, that the failing Jewish educational system was adaptive to local needs to avoid generating types of Jewish knowledge and activity that, if displayed in relevant surrounding social contexts, would be considered inappropriate or dangerous in one way or another for the liberal Jews implementing them.

As they are today, given their guiding principles, Jewish liberal educational institutions contribute little to that which is central to present world realities — they offer little if anything at all, that may serve Jewish kids in their encounters with the fiercely competitive and global world of today; that same world in which their parents want them so much to succeed. Paradoxically the contents of the texts taught usually carry messages which attack this competitive spirit thus rendering them even less pertinent. Alternatively when supporting competition implicitly (through, for an example, a Bible quiz) these (always mediated) texts are so inconsequential and contribute so little to the true competitive spirit that they too become irrelevant. From this perspective, not learning would indeed be adaptive for Jewish children whose families want them both to be part of and successful in the modern global world that has little place for local Jewish particularities, while at the same time not wanting to suffer from a self perception of Jewish denial and betrayal.

In toto, Jewish educational institutions teach Jews a Judaism assumed to be unproblematic and descriptive of a "true" identifiable world outside.

This follows from the institutions' a-historical and a-contextual approach to the contents taught: what it calls "Jewish culture." Teaching this way means sustaining a worldview that has by now long been unacceptable by moral and empirical standards.

Indeed if Judaism "is" and Jews "are" givens, static and reified, and as they are not attractive to students because of their contents or forms, then there is little chance for anyone to become engaged. Moreover if Judaism is a learning and a Jew is a quality of mind, rather than Judaism being a doing and a Jew a becoming-in-activity, even when youth learn at schools, their functioning in the world will not allow them to apply their learning successfully. The world "can only pay attention" to material or interpretative differences. Students well know (or will soon learn) that for them to become lawyers (or doctors, or teachers, or parents) they are dependent mostly on hard interactional work built around languages to be rehearsed, fashions to be worn, and a whole set of practices recognizable in context. If they will fail to enact this work, at the right time, with the right people, in the right interpretative moment, they will risk forfeiting their chosen identities. Even without venturing into the far future, students already realize that they are Americans or Israelis in their conversational and behavioral modes while they are Jews in their feelings — indeed a cheap exchange. Cheap for Jews as Jews but worthwhile for Jews who want to succeed in the West; a West that has not necessarily been kind to difference in general and Jewish difference in particular.

By failing to learn "Jewish," students are being fully adaptive to a system which has little room for cultural variance in those domains that the larger context deems successful. Those "successful domains" of western culture are usually, in one way or another, homogenic and thus very western.

If the above analysis is correct, the question for Jewish education is not 'Why do individuals fail to learn?' but, rather, 'How do the world and communities get organized so as to make it worthwhile for particularistic educational efforts to fail?' In short, cultural analysis would shift the focus of Jewish liberal education from the heads of individual students to world systems and their politics.

Hence Jewish education could do well to move from focusing on children "failing" (not achieving "enough" literacy) at school to the study of cultural settings in which that failing can make sense. By so doing Jewish education will find itself dealing in politics, that one issue which is still messy in western homogenic educational culture — that is to say much disliked by the powers that be. It would call for a search for ways to make the world contexts in which students live amenable so as to allow for the knowledge teachers teach to become relevant; or, alternatively, to think about how to adapt the knowledge Jews care for so that it may be relevant in present contexts.

Again the present western world is not helpful here. It seems not to allow for much of Jewish knowledge to become relevant, so it is "it" that Jews might need to fight and not so much students or teachers. Otherwise they might realize that there is nothing more difficult than to expect learning to be maintained as useless memories. Learning, to be maintained, is in need of the many to be involved. Learning is a cumulative process which requires the ongoing participation and organization of people in settings who, while participating, put to use the things learned over time and in multiple like and other settings (Lave and Wenger, 1991; Rogoff, 2003; Wenger, 1998).

This aspect, if true, seems to be endangered by the western emancipatory message which, to this day, forms the basis of liberal Jewish functioning in the world. Particular cultures in the West, if allowed at all, seem to be expected to be secluded to the privacy of the individual sphere, far from the public eye (I) or present in the public eye but constrained to ritual events. But liberal Jews do not now seem to want to become Lubavitchers (playing in the "agora") any more than in the past, in spite of present multiculturalist trends, and rightfully so. These multi-culturalist trends are easily ready to offer recognition, but not necessarily equality, and liberal Jews seem to prefer things to work in exactly the opposite direction.

The central question that should be asked, then, is why are dominant cultures unwilling to accept cultural differences? Instead of opting for this path, Jewish liberal schools seem to teach types of intolerance thus, somehow, reproducing within Jewish culture that same sense which the dominant culture produces, not realizing that since Jews are not dominant things might not work in their case for the better. Paradoxically while caring "in" their education about their own, they serve the outside world which denies them and others like them. Intermarriage in this case could become an adaptive response disguised as a threat; the dissatisfaction with Jewish education another adaptive step towards the conquest of present hierarchical positions without passing as defector; and the ghettoization of Jewish education a secure path towards a successful assimilation.

Let me conclude this section by summarizing in brief the main points I have raised that run contrary to the accepted theory and practice of Jewish liberal education.

1) The (at times) perceived failure—or dissatisfaction with the products—of Jewish education has little to do with the quality of individual teachers or students and much to do with the quality of the systems we (all) cooperatively construct.

2) Failing to understand the above means confusing failure with what are adaptive moves to local and global systemic circumstances.

3) Western positivist paradigmatic perspectives in the social sciences are responsible for the present educational perspectives which guide Jewish liberal educational theory and practice. Change will only be available after these paradigmatic perspectives are abandoned.

4) Changing the above means revising our basic appreciation of the individual, of culture, and of the learning process. It means realizing that they, all, are interactional, contextualized, and historicized processes rather than isolated inside (individual), static and well defined outside (culture), and specific-task oriented and measurable transmissions (education).

5) I have asserted that from any feasible communicational perspective for Jews to be relevant to themselves they have to be relevant in and to the world; an almost trivial point when considering that meaning is by definition not a representational given but the outcome of the management of difference in an historical trajectory.

6) Last I have suggested that, if the above is correct, Jews would do well to look for educational solutions in the organization of present western world politics rather than in the limited parameters of their school settings or the solitude of their teachers' or students' minds.

So, if to date Jewish educationalists have been thinking about individual learning, group membership, and school failure, we need to try and change their views. There is nothing individual about the learning, there is nothing literate about the membership and schools are not necessarily the settings in which to achieve productive, adaptive, relevant learning.

(iii) Culture-guided educational policy

As we have shown above, the terms culture and identity have become independent reified nouns in contrast to their procedural, developmental, historicized meanings. This process of fixative reification is part of the problem we are seeking to ameliorate. We suggest that the restoration of the developmental process embodied in these historically re-contextualized concepts (culture and identity) constitutes a partial solution to these same problems, as well as an educational model.

Traditionally the basic humanities curriculum puts great emphasis on classical philosophical inquiry, mostly from an idealistic perspective concerned with the nature of reality and problems of virtue in political educational contexts. It also envisions traditional textual literacy as the heart of cultural (in our case Jewish) production and maintenance. Finally, humanities curricula suggest a strong connection between traditional views of "universal" humanism and traditional particularistic cultural world-views. Textual learning in these settings has been presented in a dislocated and mostly de-historicized way, unsuccessfully engaging learners in interpretative practices which might make these texts relevant to their present contexts.

The classic humanities curriculum implicitly (and partially explicitly) assumes certain modernist understandings of concepts such as culture, identity, and education, which are associated with individual, cognitive, and autonomous activities.

As discussed above, in the post-modern era the focus has shifted from the individual to the social arena and from the intra-psychological to the inter-psychological. This theoretical relocation into the social interactional sphere where historically situated participants calibrate their positions according to complex socio-cultural relations, has the potential to promote a re-thinking of educational aims and strategies.

Cultural Education is geared to cultivate in members of culturally, economically, or politically oppressed groups, a critical consciousness of their situation as the foundation of their liberatory praxis while recognizing that their greatest enemy is the fatalistic belief in the inevitability and necessity of existing beliefs and structures.

This relocation does not necessarily rule out the possibility of continuing, partially, with what has been done so far, but does imply the need to promote new representations of possible models of teachers and students responsive to the new and diverse challenges encountered in today's transnational, global world. The moment identity, culture and education recover their contextual historical dimensions and regain their process-like and dialogical co-constitution, they can no longer be presented in their glorified historical remoteness. Neither can they be conceived in their present detached solitude as static traits or pure forms; as cognitive/mental properties, available for proper transmission given a becoming context. Rather forceful consideration must be given to the contextual socio-historical character of social processes and meaning construction, emphasizing the interdependence of all such developments and phenomena.

This calls for a deep curricular involvement with all those human/social sciences which, in the last decades, have begun a critical reappraisal of modernity. Critical approaches are historically part and parcel of modern thought; what needs to be added is a critique of the critical process and its ownership, as well as reflexive systematic reflection on what has traditionally been considered to be unconscious/natural presuppositions about knowledge and its categories. This activity would guide audiences through a reflective process towards a new and, hopefully, better understanding of their own condition and social situation, and of the powers and processes involved in their becoming. These would then no longer appear as natural events but rather would be seen to be the result of human social activity that might first have to be understood so as to be wrestled for change when this is considered necessary.

CE is geared towards the joint production of participants/agents who are active in and aware of historical processes, the interdependence of social phenomena, and the participation of a multiplicity of powers and interests in the shaping of present meanings. This awareness should allow participants in the process to devise the strategies necessary for change (if change is indeed their goal), and to consider the feasibility of their implementation in the multiple arenas in which interested powers struggle for domination (i.e. educational institutions, media channels, political arenas, etc.). These are not uniquely Jewish educational challenges. They are salient for a multitude of other minority groups which have suffered from western social, cultural, political, and/or economic colonizing tendencies in the modern era.

A tentative analysis using these tools would unmask "modernity" as a homogenizing (middle-class, heterosexual, white, etc.) process which tends to control the particular narratives of "others" thereby subduing them to industrial commodifying forces at once national and global.

Teachers, parents and students should be trained to be sensitive to and uncover these processes as well as to consider possible alternative paths of action. Adopting this view would mean that teachers and students would thus, in one way or another, become engaged with the challenges posed by massifying homogenizing educational/socializing systems and cognizant of the risks they present to a variety of subgroups with diverse legitimate interests (be they ethnic, religious, cultural, political, etc.)

These massifying homogenizing forces have been unleashed by the processes of modernization which have taken place in much of the world by virtue of the expansion of the sphere of influence of western socio-political structures (i.e. nation-state, corporations, etc.) together with their related values (anonymity, literacy, homogeneity) and accompanying phenomena (migratory forces, diasporas, economic crises, ecological crises, detraditionalization, etc.)

If we can agree on the above, then what I propose is that we see Jewish education's task as the production (collaborative of course) of cultural participants/agents, socialized and/or enculturalized to particular (western peripheralized) socio-historical traditions with the aim of allowing for their future creative development and productive dialogic/cross-fertilization, while realizing that without an emphasis on Cultural Education, cognitive and social development become arduous and that when political systems create de-legitimizing educational settings, they cease to reflect human- istic/democratic — some would say Jewish values.

We should always remember that culture has little to do with the habits we train people to adopt and everything to do with the environments we build for people to inhabit (Varenne and McDermott, 1998). Indeed culture as activity in context is not so much something into which one is put, but an order of behavior of which one is part. In short our interaction in context is the one that continuously produces culture.

We should recall too that perhaps the greatest of all pedagogical fallacies is the notion that a person learns only the particular thing he is studying or being taught at the time. Collateral learning by way of the formation of enduring attitudes, of likes and dislikes, may be, and often is, much more important than the textual or managerial lessons that are taught. Finally we should consider that the most important attitude that can be fomented is that of a desire to go on learning. Good education is a social enterprise to which all individuals have an opportunity to contribute and to which all feel a responsibility. By way of illustration, we could say that what we are after are educational processes which invite us to uncover the conditions, as they are organized, for a group to be recognized, stereotyped, and/or become functional and adaptive.

Some change might be achieved by developing educational programs which bring to a level of awareness Judaism's own cultural processes in their manifold forms — assumptions, goals, norms, values, beliefs, and communicative modes — in their historical evolutionary context as they are expressed in institutional, political, and social, life; so as to permit us to see them as a potential bias in social interaction and in the acquisition or transmission of skills and knowledge.

For teachers, parents and students, this awareness is necessary so as to allow them to realize that their failures and successes are not so much theirs but, rather, are products of complex webs of relations taking place within and between cultural realizations, patterns, modes, etc. which, in their turn, are products of complex historical events. It is also relevant to make all aware of their own cultural assumptions and the effects these have on their educational planning and behavior. And last, but not least, it is necessary to raise consciousness about the unequal power relationships which are endemic to educational and state institutions (hegemony at large).

Jews are not only 'in' their (our) in-memorial texts but also "become" at the end point of numerous chains of production. These chains of production are contained in a financial structure of regional, national, and global circuits; in an aesthetic experience expressed in architecture and packaging, which brings about an ideological experience, an image of a community, a perspective on the use of time and the meaning of pleasure; and in a social-status-creating machine, a machine which organizes body, space and time and the relations between them, a fantasy machine, a place for the regulation of power.

Educational instructors/mediators need, first and foremost, to be able to read the world — theirs (ours) as well as any other. To do this they are in need of theory and descriptive power in abundance in order to uncover and cope with the complexity of the sites or the social phenomena. They need familiarity with a variety of disciplines and discourses:

- Economic discourse for discussing commodities, supplies, and management;
- Aesthetic discourse, to discuss architecture, advertising, display;
- Political discourse, to discuss bodies, policies, planning, discipline;
- Ethnographic discourse to find the beauty of the particular responses to all of the above;
- Historical discourse to talk about change in organization, consumption, community;
- Interpretative discourses, which will allow for the articulation of understandings of each of the texts which, in concert, create culture, Jewish or other, and their necessary intertextuality in practice.

All of the above is needed to read both the world and the activities that allow for its becoming, not only in the world outside but also inside the classrooms. This might not be all that is needed but it is a start, a critical one without which the rest will not follow.

All in all this discussion points first and foremost to the need to open the doors of Jewish liberal communities to the world that surrounds them (us) and to become active in it, as well as to enrich the communities' (our) "customers"– teachers and students alike – with descriptive powers, analytical points of view, critical perspectives, and competing languages. The central solution we offer rests in the artifact "language-in-action" as the originating tool for individual and social experience. Indeed we write assuming that it is expression which organizes experience and not the other way round. "Self" from this perspective is a becoming in dialogue, and social groups develop their own relatively stable coherent styles, though stylistic coherence never becomes a finished product.

Knowledge of the uses of language (gesture and verb), and the learning of "languaging" (Maturana and Valera, 1987) enables the recognition that we are not unrestricted agents authoring the world but that, if we author the world at all, we do so by drawing upon words authored by others (Becker, 1995). Choice in expression (identity, role, you have it) is the result of the development throughout history of "heteroglossia" (Bakhtin, 1981), the multiplicity of languages filled with their own semantic and axiological content, which rule social life.

The understanding of the contextual and historical situatedness of language supports the partial solution I have suggested regarding the possibility of overcoming the present Jewish liberal (our) educational stand. If indeed in their (our) present position they (we) "language western" and lack the potential to successfully "language Jewish" (because of western absolutism which has instituted its unitary universal language and semantic abstracted domains) then the learning of language might not be enough. In these circumstances they (we) might have to consider the option of counteracting it through the most powerful of linguistic devices — that of parody and carnavalesque.

Indeed since time immemorial the carnavalesque spirit has epitomized the popular counter-culture which rejects the "high culture" of officialdom, itself ultimately expressed in western hegemonic domination. Parody and the carnavalesque stand for the embodied, the ambivalent, and the generative, as opposed to the abstract, the fixed and the represented. The carnavalesque shocks our present epistemological comfort. By being grotesque, it distorts present understandings, transcends "natural" boundaries, invites fusion and communion, and thus becomes a threat to officialdom (Bakhtin, 1968).

True modernity has recognized the power of the carnavalesque and has retained it as a safety valve through which to secure its tyranny. Still the teaching and practice of heteroglossia, parody and historicized language might serve to counteract our present situation by supporting a new free and critical historical consciousness (Bakhtin, 1968).

The current Jewish liberal (our) understanding, like any ideology, is not a given; neither is it eternal. It does not inhabit an abstraction but rather is the product of socio-cultural practices expressed in utterances, scented by an ordained common language. Training in the way we suggest affords the possibility of de-centering the present authorial/hegemonic voice. If adopted these might be modest steps in the right direction.

Note

In this paper, I am deeply indebted to an unpublished manuscript by R. McDermott and Herve Verenne, who in no way share responsibility for the statements made and conclusions drawn. I am also grateful to Vivienne Burstein for her assistance in honing the arguments presented.

References

Ackerman, W. I. (1969). Jewish education — For what? *American Jewish Year Book, 70,* 1–35.

Archer, Margaret S. (1995). *Realist social theory: The morphogenetic approach.* Cambridge: Cambridge University Press.

Bakhtin, M. (1968). *Rabelais and his world.* H. Isowolsky. (Trans.) Cambridge: MIT Press.

Bakhtin, M. M. (1981). *The dialogic imagination: Four essays by M. M. Bakhtin.* (C. Emerson and M. Holquist, Trans.) Austin: University of Texas Press.

Bauman, Z. (1999). *Culture as praxis.* London: Sage.

Becker, A. L. (1995). *Beyond translation; Essays toward a modern philology.* Ann Arbor: The University of Michigan Press.

Bekerman, Z. (in press). Hidden dangers in multicultural discourse. *MCT-Multicultural Teaching.*

Bekerman, Z. (2001). Constructivist perspectives on language, identity and culture: Implications for Jewish identity and the education of Jews. *Religious Education, 96 (4),* pp. 462–473.

Bekerman, Z., and Silverman, M. (2000). The liberal Jewish discourse on culture and Jewish continuity. *Cultural Education in a multicultural society, 9.* Jerusalem: The Hebrew University, pp. 183–192. (In Hebrew).

Boas, F. (1940). *Race, language, and culture.* New York: Free Press.

Carbaugh, D. (1996). *Situating selves: The communication of social identities in American scenes.* Albany: SUNY Press.

Cole, M. (1990). Cognitive development and formal schooling: The evidence from cross-cultural research. In L. C. Moll (Ed.), *Vygotsky and Education*. Cambridge: Cambridge University Press.

Cole, M. (1996). *Cultural Psychology: A once and future discipline*. Cambridge: Belknap Press of Harvard University Press.

Fox, S. (1973). Towards a General Theory of Jewish Education. In D. Sidorsky (Ed.). *The future of the Jewish community in America*. New York: Basic Books. pp. 260–270.

Gee, J. P. (1992). *The Social Mind: Language, ideology and social practice*. New York: Bergin and Garvey.

Giddens, A. (1991). *Modernity and self identity*. Stanford CA: Stanford University Press.

Goody, J. (1987). *The interface between the written and the oral*. Cambridge: Cambridge University Press.

Harre, R., and Gillett, G. (1995). *The discursive mind*. London: Sage.

Holland, D., Lachicotte, W., Skinner, D., and Cain, C. (1998). *Identity and agency in cultural worlds*. Cambridge: Harvard University Press.

Holzman, L. (1997). *Schools for growth: Radical alternatives to current educational models*. Mahwah, New Jersey: Lawrence Erlbaum Associates, Publishers.

Lave, J., and Wenger, E. (1991). *Situated learning: Legitimate peripheral participation*. New York: Cambridge University Press.

Lévi-Strauss, C. (1955). *Tristes tropiques* (J. Russell, Trans.). New York: Atheneum.

Maturana, U., and Valera, F. (1987). *The Tree of Knowledge: The biological roots of human understanding*. Boston: New Science Library.

Mead, M. (1942). *And keep your powder dry: An anthropologist looks at America*. New York: W. Morrow.

Rogoff, B. (2003). *The cultural nature of human development*. Oxford: Oxford University Press.

Sampson, E. E. (1993). *Celebrating the other: A dialogic account of human nature*. Hertfordshire: Harvester Wheatsheaf.

Taylor, C. (1994). The politics of recognition. In D. T. Goldberg (Ed.), *Multiculturalism: A critical reader*. Oxford: Blackwell, pp. 75–106.

Varenne, H., and McDermott, R. (1998). *Successful failure: The schools America builds*. Colorado: Westview Press.

Wenger, E. (1998). *Communities of Practice: Learning, Meaning, and Identity*. Cambridge: Cambridge University Press.

Wertheimer, J. (1999). Jewish Education in the United States: Recent Trends and Issues. In D. Singer (Ed.), *American Jewish Year Book, 1999*. New York: The American Jewish Committee. pp. 3–125.

Wexler, P. (2000). *Mystical Society*. Oxford: Westview Press.

Williams, R. (1961). *Culture and society, 1780–1950*. Harmondsworth: Penguin Books.

Williams, R. (1976). *Keywords: A vocabulary of culture and society*. New York: Oxford University Press.

Wittgenstein, L. (1953). *Philosophical investigations*. (G. E. M. Anscombe, Trans.) Oxford: Blackwell.

Woocher, J. (1995). Towards a 'Unified Field Theory' of Jewish Education. In I. Aron, S. Lee and S. Rossel (Eds.) *A Congregation of Learners*. New York: UAHC Press. 33–51.

"It is My Brothers I am Seeking"[1]: Educational Responses to the Isolationist Trend of Contemporary American Jewish Spirituality

DANIEL GORDIS

With the outbreak of urban hostilities between Israelis and Palestinians in October 2000, many conceptions that had long prevailed among thoughtful Jews were deeply shaken. In Israel, much has been written about the demise of the political left in the aftermath of the loss of its "partner," the "assault" upon the right in the form of dramatic territorial compromises that were put on the table by the Barak government, and the changing nature of Israel-American governmental relationships, particularly in the aftermath of the horrific events of September 11, 2001.

But that is not all that has changed. Some observers of the relationship between American and Israeli Jews sense that something else is afoot; they feel that the dramatic number of cancellations of trips and visits by American Jews spells the beginning of a radically altered relationship between the two communities. To cite only one of the most commonly discussed dimensions of this "new" relationship, the rates of American youth visiting Israel on what had previously been one of the mainstays of American Jewish education — the high school trip to Israel — have decreased dramatically. Across the U.S., numbers of participants in all such programs decreased from 7,100 in 2000 to a mere 1,857 in 2001.[2] At the time of the now infamous decision of the UAHC to cancel its Summer Program 2000,

---

1 Genesis 37:16.
2 These figures provided by Dr. Elan Ezrachi of the Jewish Agency.

the number of participants in Reform movement-sponsored programs had dropped from an all-time high of 1,400 in the summer of 2000 to 300 on the eve of summer 2001. Even Birthright, a program much better protected against such a decline, experienced a drop of 37 percent enrollment.[3]

Faced with the perception of perceived increased danger in Israel (and in Jerusalem in particular) after the beginning of this urban war, some leaders of North American Judaism (the UAHC's Rabbi Eric Yoffie, for example) have sought to justify these decreases, arguing that they do not represent a lessening of the American Jewish community's commitment to the State of Israel. Beyond concern for the situation in Israel and the impact on those particular participants who did not visit Israel, they assert, the phenomenon is not a cause for alarm.[4] This paper suggests otherwise. In the pages that follow, I will suggest that while the events of October 2000 and beyond may be the proximate cause for the sharp decline in visits to Israel, what these events in Israel have really done is to focus a spotlight on a long-developing change in American attitudes to Israel, which in turn, is the result of a profound shift in American Jewish identity, a shift we might call the "spirituality revolution."

This "spirituality revolution," this advocacy of return to a "Judaism based on personal meaning," has been more problematic that we have suspected, I will argue, and needs to be countered by the American Jewish educational establishment. For while it is true that the turn to spirituality has enabled many American Jews to find a religious home in Jewish life in ways that they previously did not believe possible, it has also inculcated in American Jews a premium on individuality at the expense of community, and in so doing, has weakened the notion that Jewish belonging necessarily includes a notion of peoplehood and devotion to collective causes. The paper, offered more as a preliminary reflection on possible new

3   Without going into detail at this juncture, there are several reasons why Birthright should have been impacted less: (a) the participants are college students, who unlike the high school students of other programs, theoretically do not require their parents' approval to make the trip, (b) the trip is free, unlike many of the high school programs, and (c) Birthright had a long waiting list. The fact that even with the waiting list, a significant drop in participants was noted, illustrates that the actual drop off may well have been much higher than the 37 percent figure suggests.

4   Consider Rabbi Yoffie's comments upon the cancellation of the UAHC youth trips to Israel for the summer of 2001. "Our religious and Zionist commitments run deep and are known to all, but this movement never uses other people's children to make a political or ideological point" (June 3, 2001). Similarly, Rabbi Allan Smith, director of the UAHC's Youth Division, said "the decision to suspend the summer trips for teenagers was not an indication of a lessening of the Reform Movement's commitment to Israel." (*http://www.uahc.org/pr/2001/010603.shtml*)

agendas for Jewish education in North America than as a conclusive study or analysis, concludes by suggesting that a restoration of a sense of communal agenda, or to put it in other terms, an attempt to heighten the "social capital" of the Jewish community, must become a key agenda of Jewish education in the United States, and it urges renewed attention to educational ventures and objectives that might increase "social capital" in the North American Jewish community.

The subject of this brief reflection in a volume dedicated to Professor Seymour Fox is no accident. For years now, as I have been privileged to study with Professor Fox and work with him, it has become clear that he harbors serious doubts about the "spiritual revolution" in American Jewish life. Indeed, when I first met Professor Fox at a Goals Seminar sponsored by the Mandel Institute in July 1996, I was serving as dean of a rabbinical school in Los Angeles in which "spirituality" was a core component of our self-definition. Professor Fox questioned many of the assumptions of our work in a direct and extraordinarily productive fashion, making it clear that he had serious doubts about how serious a phenomenon the "spirituality movement" was. Since then, as either I or someone else has mentioned this "alleged" phenomenon, Professor Fox has often asked, "what are we talking about here? Five hundred people, or five hundred thousand? Or five million?" That, in his inimitable way, has been his way of saying that whatever this "movement" is, it requires and deserves more study.

Though Professor Fox and I have not always agreed on the significance of this movement in American Jewish life and its implications, this paper is a first and still inadequate response to his ongoing, and surely correct, assertion that the movement ought to be studied. What follows is not an attempt to measure the size or impact of the movement, but rather, to offer some preliminary reflections on its implications and the educational responses for which it calls. In calling for a specifically educational reaction to the possible liabilities of contemporary American Jewish spirituality, the inquiry at the heart of this paper has been enriched by Professor Fox's fundamental orientation to the Jewish world, an orientation shared by the many of us who are fortunate enough to call ourselves his students.

Section I: A New Found Focus on "Spirituality"

In the past 15 or 20 years, "spirituality" has become one of the key "buzzwords" of American Jewish life. In virtually all discussions of Jewish identity, Jewish continuity and even Jewish education, a "lack of spirituality" had been decried as one of the key causes of what many leaders see as a crisis in American Jewish life, and a "return to serious spiritual engagement" has been touted as one of the keys to repairing the breach.

Though the approach to and definitions of "spirituality" have been many and varied, the basic thrust of most of the arguments has been rather similar. Essentially, the arguments claim that one of the reasons for the crisis in American Jewish identity, assuming that there actually is such a crisis, is that American Jews as both individuals and as a group no longer find interest in a tradition which does not speak to their innermost struggles, their vulnerabilities and their emerging senses of self. Like all other human beings, American Jews struggle with sense of purpose, with questions about self. Having achieved social and economic success, they worry about finding and creating ultimate meaning for their lives (though in the days to come, we may see many more struggling to find meaning in the aftermath of the loss of that very success). They wonder about their place in the cosmos, the "big picture" and the creation of what much of the spirituality literature calls the "creation of a relationship with God."

However, as voices as disparate in their orientation as Paul Cowan, Rodger Kaminetz, Wade Clark Roof and I have argued,[5] when generations of younger Jews searched for a religious tradition that could address these intimate religious needs, the Jewish world in which they were raised and the Jewish tradition to which they were exposed did not seem to provide a likely setting in which seek the engagement with these questions. The Jewish world in which these now "forty-something" year olds were raised seemed to them perfunctory, focused on hollow ritual and virtually guaranteed predictability. Worship was passive and conducted in a language they did not understand; decorum counted for more than feeling. Synagogues seemed to be places where stability and a balanced budget seemed the preoccupying focus, where rabbis too often seemed intent on avoiding conflict and the discussion of any subject that might arouse the ire of their congregants; thus, to the minds of many members of this "generation of seekers,"[6] synagogues were part of the establishment, part of the problem, and

---

5   The literature on "spiritual searches" is vast. Consider Cowan, 1996 and Kamemetz, 1995 and 1998. Wade Clark Roof has made what is perhaps the most articulate set of claims about the search for meaning in American religious settings in Roof, 1993 and 1999. I have made a claim similar to Roof's in the opening chapters of Gordis, 1995.

6   The phrase is not mine, but rather, is the title of Wade Clark Roof's much discussed book on the subject. See note 5, Roof, 1993.

certainly not places where one sought intellectual ferment, spiritual grappling and a celebration of the inner turmoil that is often adult life.[7]

As a result, these writers began to claim that a spiritual re-awakening would of necessity be one of the keys to a renaissance of the American Jewish experience. Unless Judaism could find a language through which to speak to the human and to the vulnerable in all of us, they claimed, most American Jews would look elsewhere for the "spiritual" engagement and even satisfaction that they crave, and the crisis would only deepen.[8] Thus (in admittedly over-simplified terms) was born the "spirituality movement."

Over the past decades, hardly any dimension of the American Jewish experience went untouched by the focus on spirituality. Federations, long (and in some respects unfairly) considered by many young people the bastion of a non-religious or even anti-religious Judaism with a focus on institutional self-preservation at the expense of all else, have begun hiring rabbis to serve as full time scholars in residence to inject a sense of Jewish religiosity and substance into the daily work of their organizations.

Publishing, too, has been affected by this phenomenon. The market for books on Judaism and spirituality has become so large, that volumes of this sort emerge not only from the classic Jewish presses such as the Jewish Publication Society and Jewish Lights, but from the larger New York houses as well. It is worth recalling that when Michael and Sharon Strassfeld were writing the *Jewish Catalogue* Series (1973, 1976 and 1980), (the Jewish Publication Society's largest sellers after the *Tanakh*), the notion of publishing even a potentially major seller such as this in a mainstream New York house would have been a wild-eyed fantasy. But that, too, has changed. In recent years, however, Random House, Holt, Simon and

---

7   Popular culture in the United States made much the same point. That is a subject for a separate analysis, but in this context, it is perhaps worth noting that such films as Woody Allen's *Crimes and Misdemeanors* (1989) level a similar critique at the American Jewish establishment. In this film, the "hero" is an ophthalmologist, "Judah," who arranges for the murder of the flight attendant with whom he'd been conducting an affair. His rabbi, who effectively knows what has happened, refuses to confront him, and suffers with a disease that gradually renders him blind. Thus, it is the criminal who ironically gives the gift of sight (though unsuccessfully to this rabbi) and who goes unpunished, but it is the rabbi, whose fear of confrontation and genuine moral stance is his key characteristic, who goes blind and, Allen seems to suggest, bears the punishment for the failure to carry out dutifully the tasks of his office.

8   In fairness, given the implicit critique of the movement presented in this paper, I should note that I, too, shared this enthusiasm for "spirituality" as an important attraction for disaffected Jews. Particularly in Gordis 1995, I made a case for a spiritual re-engagement with Jewish life, which though also focused on the need for community, did not explicitly acknowledge any of the dangers of the individualist approach of the spirituality movement alluded to in this paper.

Schuster and many others have recognized the huge market for books on Jewish spirituality, so that today, when one walks into Barnes and Noble on the Upper West Side of New York or Borders on the West Side of Los Angeles, one of the major tables set out with volumes by subject is the Judaica table, filled with books on spirituality and the Jewish quest, most published by mainstream American houses, not the less known Jewish publishers. Rabbis of all the movements, including Irving (Yitz) Greenberg, Jeffrey Salkin, David Wolpe and even Adin Steinsaltz (among many, many others) have published books with these main stream publishers that just decades ago would have been "relegated" to the catalogues of the Jewish publishing world. Twenty-five years ago, who would have dreamed that Random House would publish an edition of the Talmud?[9]

Publishing aside, the focus on spirituality has also touched the mainstream institutions of American Jewish life. A focus on spirituality has touched synagogues, the world of Jewish music and even rabbinic education.

Not surprisingly, synagogues, too, have been impacted by this movement. Spirituality lies at the very core of what is called the "synagogue renewal" movement. This movement, which is probably best exemplified by Synagogue 2000, co-sponsored by the University of Judaism in Los Angeles and the Hebrew Union College, and the work of the STAR project on synagogue revitalization,[10] is quite explicit about its desire to bring a sense of spirituality to the world of contemporary American Jewish worship.[11]

Not all change in synagogue worship has been so carefully planned;

---

9   Cf., for example, *The Talmud: The Steinsaltz Edition, Volume I, Tractate Bava Metzia, Part I* (New York: Random House, 1989).

10 The STAR project is funded primarily by the Schusterman Foundation with the participation of the Steinhardt and Bronfman families.

11 Cf. *http://www.starsynagogue.org/*, the organization's web site. There, the site asserts that "the mission of STAR is to promote Jewish renewal by helping the North American synagogue find and implement innovative, collaborative, effective and transdenominational ways to meet the *spiritual*, educational and social needs of every member of the Jewish community [emphasis added]. Similarly, Synagogue 2000 makes a similar claim on its site (*http://www.syn2000.org/Information.html*). The site argues that "Since 1990, all evidence has pointed to a shifting of the Jewish agenda from the "emergency" requirement of saving Jews abroad to the domestic demand that we salvage Jewish identity at home. As recently as this very Fall (1998), a study by Professors Arnold Eisen and Steven Cohen underscored the rapid fall-off of Jewish ethnic identity and the rise in religious, or spiritual, interest. That finding is consonant with sociological literature in general that uncovers a search for religious meaning by unaffiliated Americans of all religions and ages. Only the synagogue is in a position to create local communities of meaning, where a religious vision is paramount."

much has been grass-roots, and has come not from mainstream foundations, but from sources seemingly at the opposite end of the spectrum of influence. Though it would take an entire paper to reflect meaningfully on the dramatic changes in liturgy in both the Conservative and Reform movements in recent years, one particular dimension of this trend may well be appropriate to our discussion. Debbie Friedman, the well known American Jewish folk singer, has written hundreds of melodies, many of which are very well know and sung in camps, youth groups and even in adult circles. But one of her compositions, *Mi She-beirakh* (Prayer for Healing), has now become common fare in synagogues in which this prayer was until recently virtually unknown to the vast majority of congregants. What has made this *Mi She-beirakh* so compelling to contemporary congregations is a series of several factors: a lilting, beautiful melody; a "gender-balanced" rendition in which first the forefathers, but then the "foremothers" are mentioned, and perhaps most important, Friedman's own custom of first singing the song to her audience, then asking them to sing it to each other. Even when she performs in a concert, this *Mi She-Beirakh* is not a "song," but a prayer; a prayer which has quite clearly spoken to the yearning, fears and needs of hundreds of thousands of Jews across the United States. This yearning, which can be explained in a variety of ways, is almost always referred to by the rabbis who introduced the melody to their congregations, as a response to the spiritual hunger of their congregations.

Even rabbinic training, often though of as a bastion of the "ancien regime," has been affected. Though a review of the ways in which rabbinic training has changed over the past years would require an entire excursus, several indications of the centrality of spirituality even in the sphere of rabbinic education can easily be provided.

First, the issue of spirituality as a component of rabbinic education is now the object of serious study and research, both in the Jewish world but outside it as well. Thus, the Cummings Foundation has funded conferences in which deans and key faculty members of rabbinical schools were invited to discuss and explore the teaching of spirituality in rabbinic education.[12] And outside the Jewish world, the Carnegie Foundation for the Advancement of Teaching, which is currently doing a study of training for the professions in the United States, recently began to focus on the clergy. At

12 "The Conference on Rabbinic Education," in April 1999. The Conference has been repeated each year since then. That year, the sponsors were The Mandel Foundation, The Nathan Cummings Foundation, The Shusterman Foundation and the Revson Foundation.

the initial two day meeting held to inaugurate this study,[13] a large proportion of the time was spent discussing spirituality, particularly the perceived tension between "critical methodologies" and the desire to provide a "spiritually positive and intensive" learning environment. This focus was a concern for Protestants and Catholics as well, of course, but it was keenly felt by the Jewish educators who were present, and much of the deliberation in that conference focused on this issue among both Jews and Christians.

Perhaps even more telling than the study of spirituality as a component of rabbinic education has been the creation of new rabbinical schools designed specifically to address the perceived need for a rabbinic education in which the "spiritual" is given much greater attention than had been the case in order institutions, where a focus on the methodologies of the "Wissenschaft" and historical schools had become the prevailing approach to Jewish study. Consider, for example, the creation of the Ziegler School of Rabbinic Studies, the newest "mainstream" rabbinical school in the United States. Though there were many factors that led to the creation of this rabbinical school, including longstanding tensions between the University of Judaism and the Jewish Theological Seminary over recruitment, control of curriculum and a host of other governance issues, the public face put on the decision to create the school was often one which stressed its focus on spirituality. That "read" of the creation of the new school was at the heart of the *Forward*'s main article on the subject:

> "If there is one thing [that the Dean[14]] hopes [the new school] will bring to the Conservative Movement, it is a more intense focus on spirituality…. Critics of the University of Judaism's recent move toward independence agree that the curriculum at JTS in the past has focused too narrowly on academia and scholarship at the expense of spiritual and leadership training. However, they see a return to spirituality already afoot at the seminary." (*Forward*, October 20, 1995, pp. 1–2).

What is interesting about the *Forward*'s description of the creation of the school is not simply its claim that a focus on spirituality lay at the core of the new school. More interesting, indeed, was the *Forward*'s suggestion that even the Seminary, from which the UJ was liberating itself, thought

---

13 The conference took place at the headquarters of the Carnegie Foundation for the Advancement of Education in Stanford, CA, in February 2001.

14 In the interests of "full disclosure," it should simply be noted that I was the Dean of the Ziegler School referred to in this *Forward* article.

that a "return" to spirituality was critical. The core disagreement, therefore, was not whether spirituality was critical and had previously been ignored, but the degree to which the Seminary had already modified its training, thus obviating the need for the new school that the University of Judaism was then creating.[15]

The Ziegler School's self-description also focused on the spirituality awareness of its curriculum, program and faculty. In its first academic bulletin, it alluded to this shift in a subtle way, by describing itself as a merger of the best of the university and yeshiva worlds.[16] Similarly, the ZSRS's language on its current web site continues to reflect the same focus and concern:

"The Ziegler School of Rabbinic Studies made history when it opened the first independent rabbinical school on the West Coast. While we take pride in being history-makers and serving as pioneers in the Conservative Jewish community, we are much more than innovators and pacesetters. First and foremost, we are a full-fledged five-year rabbinical school that values rigorous scholarship, embraces the splendors of spirituality, and provides our students with vast opportunities to grow intellectually and spiritually.

On the idyllic campus of the University of Judaism, in Los Angeles, and in an atmosphere that places great emphasis on personalized teaching, our students open their minds and hearts to the texts and traditions of our religion, feel the presence of God in their lives, and assume the ever-expanding roles and responsibilities offered to those entering the Conservative rabbinate of the 21st century."[17]

15 It is interesting to note that in the fall of 2001, the Ziegler School had more students in its entering class than did JTS. Whether this will remain a long term trend remains to be seen. But it is clear that the rapid growth of the school suggests that something about its nature is speaking to large number of students, many of whom would probably have gone to JTS had they not had a choice.

16 The Academic Bulletin of 1998–2000 (page 7), for example, introduces the school as follows: "The Ziegler School strives to combine the very best of the graduate school and academic training with an emphasis on supportive relationships in a nurturing and caring community. We believe that those emphases, along with our commitment to taking the best that the yeshiva model has to offer today's rabbinic students, yield a program that will shape your vision and passion for Jewish life for many years to come."

17 Web site of the University of Judaism, November 21, 2001. URL for this passage is *www.uj.edu*. The specific location of the passage quoted above is on that web site at *http://38.246.89.20/Content/ContentUnit.asp?CID=187&u=982&t=0*.

To anyone familiar with the vocabulary and sort of discourse that had been common at the Jewish Theological Seminary until recently, the change is clear. This is the Ziegler School's delicate way of saying that it intends to be different than the Seminary, and that it is moving beyond the historicist approach to Jewish learning (commonly called non-spiritual) that had long characterized the New York campus.

Thus, there is scarcely a corner of Jewish life in America that has not been touched by the renewed focus on spirituality. Particularly since the 1990 National Jewish Population Survey created a feeling of crisis around the issue of "continuity," synagogue worship, the publication of Jewish books, rabbinical schools and even federation staffs have all been deeply impacted by a call for a more intimate and "religious" approach to Jewish tradition. In many respects, it would be difficult to argue that this new phenomenon is anything but positive. Many Jews who might otherwise have left the confines of the Jewish community in their search for a religious tradition that addresses their most personal and primal needs might have turned elsewhere — to Christianity, as have some, or more likely, to the traditions of the Far East, with their more flexible theologies (though the word "theology" might not be technically appropriate to those schools of religious thought and reflection) and their focus on inwardness rather than on outward expressions of piety or communal conformity.[18]

Anecdotally, it appears that many Jews (though it is not clear exactly how many) now ground their religious lives in Judaism, and make the Jewish community a focus of their social, communal and even intellectual lives in ways that might well not have been possible without the injection of this new vocabulary into Jewish communal and institutional life.[19] This "movement", if it can be called that, clearly created a home for many Jews in Jewish tradition that they might not have otherwise discovered. It has revitalized synagogue worship for many, and it has even made the rabbinate a more attractive professional option for others.

However, now that this once renegade movement has become almost mainstream, the time has come to ask whether there have been unanticipated costs to this new way of speaking about what it is that lies

18 One of the most interesting descriptions of the attraction of Jewish to Buddhism, for example, is Kamanetz, 1995. Equally interesting, in part because it is written by a practicing Conservative rabbi in the congregational rabbinate, is Lew, 2001.

19 As of this writing, the results of the 2000 National Jewish Population Study have not yet been made public. When the statistics are more widely available, we will have a greater understanding of precisely how broadly this phenomenon extends in the American Jewish community.

at the heart of Jewish tradition. Has the focus on spirituality in American Jewish life altered the sense of what Jewishness at its core is, and if it has, has that change been exclusively positive? Those are the questions to which this brief analysis now turns.

Section II: The Darker Side of the Spirituality Movement: A Turn Toward America's Hyper-Individuality

As positive as the "spirituality" movement in America has been in many respects, some evidence is beginning to suggest that there may be cause for some concern, that the time may have arrived for a consideration of the possible dangers of the predominant focus on Judaism as a way of satisfying the emotional, spiritual and personal religious needs of individual Jews. This is not because there is anything wrong with "spirituality" as a Jewish focus, per se, but rather, because spirituality is of necessary a largely private, individualistic and thus in some respects, distinctly non-communal experience. Thus, an approach to Jewish life which focuses predominantly on the spiritual dimension of Jewish life has, at the end of the day, the capacity to lead to the privatization of the religious experience. This privatization, in turn, might well affect not only the expression of religious behavior, but the very understanding of what it means to be a Jew as well.

As we will soon note, observers like Arnold Eisen, Steven Cohen and John Ruskay[20] have argued that we are beginning to see a religious form of expression that stresses the individual over the collective, the inner search in place of social consciousness, and the comfort of safe religious involvement instead of a sense of peoplehood that can involve risk.[21] The

---

20 Eisen and Cohen are discussed extensively below. For Ruskay's sense that the job of the federation is to focus on community (and implicitly, therefore, to step away from the preoccupation with the individual that we have been describing, see, inter alia, Ruskay, 1995, and Ruskay, 2000.

21 Two points deserve mention at this juncture. First, this last notion, that dealing with the element of risk, has been written about less than the others. However, I believe that the notion of risk-avoidance is distinctly related to the other issues listed here, and deserves serious study and consideration.

   Second, it goes without saying, of course, that the individualist strain of an American sense of self is hardly new. Of the many classic works that are already aware of this, consider as only one example John Stuart Mill, 1956, and the chapter entitled "Of Individuality, As One of the Elements of Well-Being" (pp. 67–90). Note that Mill makes reference to the work of de Tocqueville (cf. p. 88), whose celebration of much of America, including its individualistic streak, is now canonical.

implications of this trend for Jewish community, certain forms of Jewish continuity and for American-Israel relations may well be very troubling. However, before turning our attention to the specifically Jewish dimension of this phenomenon, it is important to point to evidence that this inward turn, no matter how "Jewish" certain of its elements may be, reflects a much wider phenomenon, one that a variety of scholars have suggested has come to characterize much of American culture and society.

The popularity of Robert Putnam's relatively recent book, *Bowling Alone*, (2000) has given the impression for many that our awareness of this trend is rather new. That assumption, however, is not entirely correct. Although it is true that Putman documents the trend in a unique way, and creates the link to notion of "social capital" in a form that has captured attention more effectively than many others, others had pointed to this trend long before him. As far back as in Robert Bellah et al.'s now classic study, *Habits of the Heart*, this language of individualism, which Bellah called the "first language" of Americans, was the subject of study (Bellah et al., 1985, p. 22ff). Nor was Bellah the first. Nonetheless, since it was Putnam who brought the dilution of social capital to the attention of many more than had previously been the case, our brief discussion will take him as our starting point.

Putnam demonstrates quite clearly that this phenomenon of heightened individualism (and the resultant diminution of "social capital") is part of the larger milieu of American life, having nothing to do uniquely with the Jews. Though he does not address the issue of American Jews' recent silence, apathy and relative inaction on the subject of Israel since the outbreak of what some call "The Second Intifada," were he asked, Putnam might well say that this response is neither surprising nor atypical, and that, in fact, it is part of a much wider trend:

> "Like the decline in voting turnout, to which it is linked, the slow slump in interest in politics and current events is due to the replacement of an older generation that was relatively interested in public affairs by a younger generation that is relatively uninterested. Among both young and old, of course, curiosity about public affairs continues to fluctuate in response to daily headlines, but the base level of interest is gradually fading, as an older generation of news and politics junkies passes slowly from the scene. The fact that the decline is generation-specific, rather than nationwide, argues again the view that public affairs have simply become boring in some objective sense. (Putnam, 2000, p. 36).

For Putnam, then, what Israeli Jews (and some Americans, as well, of course) see as a "new" problem that has surfaced in light of the recent return to violence in the mid-East conflict, should be seen not as a new development, but rather, as a new illustration of a long-developing trend of individual isolationism in the American public. And for Putnam, some of the immediate causes of this isolationism are clear:

> "How did patterns of civic and political participation change over this period? The answer is simple: The frequency of virtually every form of community involvement measured in the Roper polls decline signifi-cantly, from the most common — petition signing — to the least common — running for office. Americans are playing virtually every aspect of the civic game less frequently today than we did two decades ago." (Ibid. p. 41, emphasis in original).

Though Putnam quite appropriately strives to be descriptive and not judgmental, there is no gainsaying the subtle message in his work that some of this phenomenon reflects a kind of selfishness, a notion of communal and civic involvement that involves giving over much less of the "self" than had been in vogue only decades early in the United States.

Today, Putnam asserts, the kind of memberships that people prefer involve "moving a pen, not making a meeting."

> "Probably the most dramatic example [of mass-membership organiza-tions growing in size and political significance] is the AARP[22], which grew from four hundred thousand card carrying members in 1960 to thirty-three million in the mid-1990's. But membership in good standing in the AARP requires only a few seconds annually — as long as it takes to sign a check. The AARP is politically significant, but it demands little of its members' energies and contributes little to social capital." (Ibid., p. 51).

This change, to Putnam's mind, results in a very different sort of connection between members of society, quite clearly, a kind of tenuous connection that is radically different from the sort of connection that was often seen as the desired "thicker" connection in Jewish communities. Says Putnam,

---

22 American Association of Retired Persons.

"The bond between any two members of the National Wildlife Federation or the National Rifle Association is less like the bond between two members of a gardening club or prayer group and more like the bond between two Yankee fans on opposite coasts (or perhaps like two devoted L. L. Bean catalog users): they share some of the same interests, but they are unaware of each other's existence. Their ties are to common symbols, common leaders, and perhaps common ideals, but *not* to each other." (Ibid, p. 52, emphasis in original).

Could that be part of the cause of the lack of American Jewish political activity on behalf of Israel in a critically trying hour? Perhaps. But whether or not we reach that conclusion, it is clear that the demise of social capital as a mainstay of American social intercourse has not at all been limited to the sphere of politics and civics.

The individualist turn in American culture has impacted religion no less directly than it has politics and other spheres, and though Putnam addresses the religious sphere as part of his book, other commentators on the religious scene of America have made even more pointed comments about this change. Consider the comments of Wade Clark Roof and William McKinney:

"Large numbers of young, well-educated, middle-class youth ... defected from the churches in the late sixties and seventies.... Some joined new religious movements, others sought personal enlightenment through various spiritual therapies and disciplines, but most simply "dropped out" of organized religion altogether.... [The consequence was a] tendency toward highly individualized religious psychology without the benefits of strong supportive attachments to believing communities. A major impetus in this direction in the post-1960s was the thrust toward greater personal fulfillment and quest for the ideal self... In this climate of expressive individualism, religion tends to become "privatized," or more anchored in the personal realms." (Roof and McKinney, 1987, pp. 18–19, 7–8, 32–33).

The search for religious communities of meaning has characterized the Christian world no less than it has the Jewish world. One need only point to work such as that of Wade Clark Roof, mentioned above, to track the trend. Just as the Jewish world has witnessed a renewed interest in Orthodoxy, perhaps because of the sense of authenticity it purveys, the Christian world has seen a rise in allegiance to the evangelical church. And that Church, as has been much documented, is much less civically concerned than had been the liberal Protestant Churches from which many of the newly loyal evangelicals came. Putnam himself notes that "[r]eviewing the sweep of American history, Robert Wuthnow, one of the country's most acute and sympathetic observers of religion, concludes that 'whereas the mainline churches participated in progressive social betterment programs during the first half of the twentieth century, evangelical churches focused more on individual piety.'" (Putnam, 2000, p. 77).[23]

One of the many reasons that this research should be of interest to Jews and to strategists for the Jewish community is that many observers of the American religious world claim that it is not clear that such a privatized religion can thrive or even survive. "Unless religious impulses find a home in more than the individual heart or soul," writes Martin Marty, the well-known observer of religion in America, "they will have few long-lasting public consequences."[24] Putnam agrees, writing that "both individually and congregationally, evangelicals are more likely to be involved in activities within their own religious community but are less likely to be involved in the broader community." (p. 77).[25] But if involvement in the broader community (both abroad, in Israel, and at home, in domestic social and political issues) is part and parcel of what a full Jewish identification should entail (and we will argue below that it is), these trends could well bring with them serious challenges to American Jewish life.

Before proceeding to an examination of this individualist trend in Jewish life, we should remind ourselves that the fact that this phenomenon is also a well documented facet of American life in general is not irrelevant to our strategic response, should there be one. Should American Jewish educators, communal leaders and philanthropists decide that it is necessary to try to counter this trend, we will need to do so in the full knowledge that this sort of change of direction will require us to cut against the grain of contemporary currents of American culture. This is not exclusively a Jewish issue or a Jewish problem; it is America, plain and simple. And more than anything, American Jews have wanted to be Americans (and

---

23 Citing Wuthnow, "Mobilizing Civic Engagement."
24 Professor Martin Marty, of the University of Chicago, as quoted in "Spiritual America," *U.S. News and World Report*, April 4, 1994. Cited in Putnam, 2000, p. 69.
25 Depending on what percentage of the newly-involved and highly committed Jews turn to Orthodoxy as their address, parallels to the Christian experience could bode poorly for the ongoing support of Jewish social concerns.

more recently, universalists), plain and simple.[26] Charles Taylor points to these seekers and claims that that "[t]here is always something tentative in their adhesion, and they may see themselves, as, in a sense, seeking. They are on a "quest." .... Not only do they embrace these traditions tentatively, but they also often develop their own version of them, or idiosyncratic borrowings from or semi-inventions within them."[27] All these observations basically suggest that if we are to urge these individualists, seekers, "spirituality driven Jews" to consider an alternate path, we will need to do so in full cognizance of the enormity of the request we are making.

Section III: Diminished Social Capital in North American Judaism

It should come as no surprise that the trends to which Putnam, Roof, Bellah and Taylor point in their work are clearly shown to be at play in the Jewish community as well. While a variety of sorts of evidence could be adduced for this, our brief review of this phenomenon will focus on two primary works, both relatively recent. They are Steven Cohen and Arnold Eisen's *The Jew Within* (2000) and Ari Goldman's *Being Jewish: The Spiritual and Cultural Practice of Judaism Today* (2000).

We begin with Cohen and Eisen, who ask their readers to consider Brad, a respondent, who said the following about participation in Jewish organizations:

"I am sort of thinking about why we haven't been involved with the Jewish community. I think that it's because I don't see that the need

26 Consider, for example, Amy Tobin, and her remarks to the General Assembly Convention in November 2001. Speaking of members of her generation, commonly called "Generation X," Tobin told the assemblage that the urgency that the organized community ascribes to the "continuity crisis" does not speak to her peers. "The messages we hear are that Jewish continuity is in danger, and it feels as if almost all organized Jewish efforts bend in that direction [sic].... This does not resonate for us, because we feel as connected to human survival as Jewish survival." Warning starkly that her Jewishness was only one part of her, she warned the assembled leadership, "Appeal to us in our totality, as multidimensional people and as Jews." And then, reported one writer, she warned that if that did not happen, "organized American Jewry can kiss her — *dramatic pause* — generation goodbye." (As reported in *The Forward*, November 23, 2001, p. 2, in Julia Goodman's "Hear Me, Says a Gen-Xer, or Kiss My Cohort Goodbye.")

27 Charles Taylor, *Sources of the self: The making of modern identity*, (Cambridge, MA: Harvard University Press, 1989), pp. 16–17. Cited in Cohen & Eisen, (2000) p. 195.

exists there. I think that there are other organizations that need us more. The people that the Jewish organizations benefit aren't in as much need as the people that we are helping." (p. 135).[28]

What people like Brad express is a new phenomenon, and a disturbing one to many in the field of Jewish education. It is a rather utilitarian calculus (to use Bentham's terminology) that precedes the decision to associate with or to contribute to a Jewish cause or organization. Whereas a generation ago it was a relative given that American Jews would associate with Jewish causes and institutions (indeed, Jonathan Woocher [1986] argued that such affiliation often became the very substance of their Jewish self-expression), a new generation of Jews carefully evaluates the work of these Jewish organizations, compares them to other general causes, and then decides on that basis of need where to focus their time, energy and financial resources. Simply being Jewish longer represents an effective *a priori* argument for selecting one organization over another. What matters now is not the specific sub-collective of which these people are part (viz., the Jewish community), but rather, the degree to which such communal and institutional involvement makes the individual feel that he is doing good work, that she is making a difference. Eisen and Cohen put the matter as follows:

"Personalism and privatization ... and the diminished salience of ethic identification examined in the previous chapter, have exerted a major impact upon Jews' engagement with the public sphere in recent years. That engagement ... has noticeably and sharply declined.... Personal Jewish meaning, as mediated through family, stands forth clearly as the paramount concern. Activity in the Jewish public sphere is approved or undertaken only to the degree that it serves that concern — a change that clearly bears consequences of major importance for the Jewish community." (p. 137).

This shift in Jewish priorities and sensibilities has had an impact even on those areas of Jewish identification which were once considered virtually automatic roads to the hearts and pocketbooks of American Jews, namely the Shoah and the State of Israel. Almost in unison, federation executives and campaign directors now point to a profound shift in these arenas,

---

28 Note, of course, the focus on the universal in this quotation, similar to that of Amy Tobin, cited above.

sounding the alarming cry that whereas only a decade or two ago, mere mention of the Shoah or the State of Israel was virtually guaranteed to elicit profound response, today, no response or contribution is assured.

Cohen and Eisen find the same thing. The Shoah, or the Holocaust as they refer to it, plays a much diminished role in the worldviews of most of their respondents, and many did not see any real need for organizations to preserve its memory:

> "Instead, the Holocaust was consistently presented to us as a *human* tragedy, albeit one that is personally very painful because it touched one's own extended family. Most interviewees readily drew critical universal lessons that aim at preventing similar tragedies from befalling other minority groups, who were often seen as more vulnerable today than Jews. The heart of our respondents' Jewish concern clearly lies elsewhere — and, they are convinced, rightfully so," (p. 142, emphasis in the original).

And the same was true with the status of the State of Israel for this new, independent, seeking, autonomous Jew that Cohen and Eisen call the "sovereign self." "Once again, the priority for American Jews is *individual* Jewish meaning,[29] and the question is whether Israel enhances or detracts from that meaning. All too often, we found, Israel has been judged on this score by our respondents — and found wanting."(p. 143). Though this is not the place to review the many statistics that Eisen and Cohen adduce for their claims, it is worth noting (in light of the concerns we have mentioned about public support for Israel since the outbreak of hostilities beginning in October, 2000) that in 1998, they found that when it came to being a "good Jew," just 20 percent felt that it was essential for a good Jew to support Israel. (p. 144).

Even at some length, it is worth summarizing the findings of Cohen and Eisen, for if they are right (and it is extremely unlikely, no matter what reservations one may have about certain elements of the project, that they are not basically on the mark), the implications for Jewish education in America (which they do not address in any depth) are profound:

> "The main thesis of this work, suggested in its title, can be succinctly stated: More and more, the meaning of Judaism in America transpires

---

29 The close parallel between the "individual Jewish meaning" to which Eisen and Cohen refer, and the "spirituality" to which we referred earlier, should be obvious.

within the self. American Jews have drawn the activity and significance of their group identity into the subjectivity of the individual, the activities of the family, and the few institutions (primarily the synagogue) which are seen as extensions of this intimate sphere. At the same time, relative to their parents' generation, today's American Jews … are finding less meaning in mass organizations, political activity, philanthropic endeavor, and attachment to the State of Israel. In broad strokes, that which is personally meaningful has gained at the expense of that which is peoplehood-oriented. American Jews today are relatively more individualist and less collectivist. Taken as a group, their patterns of belief and practice are more idiosyncratic and diverse, less uniform and consensual. No less important, they regard the ever-changing selection of Jewish activities and meanings from the broad repertoire available as part of their birthright as Jews. They celebrate the autonomy of this choosing and do not worry about its authenticity. Indeed, they welcome each change in the pattern of their Judaism as a new stage in their lifelong personal journeys," (pp. 184–85).

"The self — albeit in negotiation with others, particularly other family members — is the ultimate arbiter of Jewish expression…. Jewish selves now expect to be encouraged by Jewish professionals and institutions to change and develop in their own way, free of outside interference, and with the support of those near and dear to them" (p. 185).

Jonathan Woocher, whose book *Sacred Survival* (published in 1986) was considered a classic on the American Jewish community, has recently suggested that the phenomenon to which he pointed in that book, that of American Jews seeing the creation of national and international organizations to protect Jewish interests as their "sacred" Jewish work, has largely ended. "The limitations of civil Judaism," he writes, "have become obvious," (Woocher, 1999, p. 21). Because civil Judaism was rooted in an awareness of historical events, it weakens as those events become more distant, or as the causes which they subsequently engendered appeared less pressing (rescue of Jews) or legitimate (Israel in the face of the Palestinian efforts for independence, for example). Thus, Woocher admits, "we are clearly not the community we were in the 1980's, when I wrote about civil religion. Although it has not vanished, the Jewish civil religion is certainly no longer the dynamic force it was a decade and a half after the Six-Day War."(Woocher, ibid, p. 21). Rather, says Woocher, American Judaism now has, instead of this communal civil religion, a much more personal expression of Jewishness, which he sees as dangerous in certain ways. "What I fear unites today's indifferent Jews with many who are seeking (or claim to have found) a renewed Jewish spiritual commitment is precisely the assumption that religion is a 'personal thing,' highly individualized and valuable only to the extent that it contributes to one's sense of personal growth and fulfillment." (Ibid., p. 22).

More anecdotal, yet very interesting, is Ari Goldman's book *Being Jewish*, (2000) which points in more illustrative form to many of the same phenomena. What is interesting about Goldman's book is that while not a sociological treatise, it gives expression to many of the trends we saw in Cohen and Eisen. Goldman's book is designed for the lay reader, and is one of the many introductions to Jewish life on the American market that cover the life cycle, the holiday cycle and other common Jewish rituals. But what makes Goldman's book unique is that is expressly endorses the "quirky" and wide variety of practice in contemporary America that is a product of the individualism with which we are concerned. Goldman, himself an Orthodox Jew, claims not to be worried about this individualism. He endorses it, and in the process, offers us both a classic example of the worldview espoused by the individualists to whom he (and his mainstream publisher) are reaching out, as well as some memorable examples of how this individualism plays out in the lives of contemporary American Jews.

Reaching out to a wide and modern audience, Goldman uses language precisely designed to speak to those described by Cohen and Eisen. "Judaism can help ease the modern sense of isolation and loneliness," he writes, assuring his readers that though there are other sorts of introductions to Jewish life, "Judaism is much more fun than the Artscroll Series would have you believe." (Goldman, 2000, pp. 16–17, 18).[30] And Goldman reassures his readers that there is no way that they will "do it wrong." Again, his goal is to be reassuring: "Jews are not consistent. Jews pick and choose from among the wide panoply of religious practices. In the words of the late Jacob Rader Marcus, the preeminent historian of American Jewry … 'There are six million Jews in America, and six million Judaisms.'" (Ibid., p. 27).

Our purpose here is not to review Goldman's book, or to challenge his approach and his endorsement of this far-reaching individualism. The

---

30 The Artscroll references is to a widely used (but also pilloried) series of prayer books, bibles and others reference works produced by the traditional end of American Orthodoxy. The series is known for its footnotes and marginalia which focus on the "correct" way to perform the numerous rituals that constitute daily Jewish life.

purpose of this brief examination of Goldman's book is to suggest that even the literature designed for the very people that Eisen and Cohen describe, coincides perfectly with the descriptions they offer in *The Jew Within*. Eisen and Cohen focus on the Jew as the "sovereign self"; Goldman writes of the Jew in New Jersey who wears *tzitzit* all day, but eats non-kosher food (because he feels "naked" without the *tzitzit*), the couple who do not eat shellfish on Shabbat (even though they do eat shellfish the rest of the week, and not eating shellfish has nothing to do with any traditional semblance of Shabbat observance), or the family in Detroit who have three sets of dishes: one for dairy, one for meat, and one for non-kosher Chinese takeout (Ibid., pp. 28–29).

Goldman corroborates Cohen and Eisen's sense that something dramatic has changed in American Jewish life. Jews are seeking the spiritual, the personal, the personalized, satisfaction of the self. And as a result of these new priorities, a tremendous amount has changed in the subtle and implicit assumptions of American Jews. The primacy given to Jewish organizations has diminished. A sense that being Jewish is about being part of a larger entity has given way to the notion that Judaism is meant to satisfy an inner yearning, a personal search, a spiritual quest.

Despite all that there is to celebrate about the intensive Jewish search of many of these people, the distinct disadvantages of such an orientation for the Jewish body politic are obvious. Israel will not benefit from the level and sort of support that it had once been able to count on. Jewish communal institutions, both of the defense sort (ADL, American Jewish Committee, AIPAC, etc.) and of the social service sort (Federations, Homes for the Aging, Mazon[31] and many others) will suffer. But perhaps most importantly, some will argue, what is troubling here is that the image of what being Jewish actually is, is mistaken, mis-apprehended, skewed. The argument that many will make is that being Jewish has always meant something radically different than the way in which the "spirituality movement" and Generation-X wish to read it, some more communal, more inter-dependent, built more around a common core. Significantly, it is in this final claim that part of the response to this phenomenon may well be found.

---

31 "Mazon: A Jewish Response to Hunger" describes itself as "a national, nonprofit agency which allocates donations from the Jewish community to nonprofit organizations providing food, help and hope to hungry people of all faiths and backgrounds." Cf. *www.mazon.org*.

Section IV: An Educational Response to Radical Individualism?

If we accept the premise that something in American Jewish life is awry, and that part of the problem is the highly individualistic trend in contemporary Jewish discourse, what, if anything can be done? Given how deeply rooted the problem is in American life in general, might it not be foolish to assume that there is anything we can do to alter this trend?

Strategists unencumbered by a profound optimism might argue that no intervention has the capacity to succeed. In making their case, they could point not only to the profoundly American roots of this "problem," but to the fact that in asking American Jews to think differently, we would be asking them to do so not on the basis of what is good for them, but because of our sense of what is good for the community. And if Amy Tobin, cited above, is any indication, such arguments will not fall on receptive ears.

And it is precisely that sense of resignation on this issue that seems to have taken hold of much of our community's leadership, either unwittingly or out of a conscious sense of resignation. The problem is dissected, discussed and analyzed, but few interventions are suggested. And perhaps most interestingly, given the focus of this volume, educational interventions are hardly, if ever, suggested.

Consider, for example, the collected papers from a relatively recent conference hosted by the Ethics and Public Policy Center in Washington, D.C. in 1999. Edited by Elliot Abrams and David Dalin, the conference papers, entitled "Secularism, Spirituality, and the Future of American Jewry," do not even have a category for education as they seek to examine the nature of the problem and potential responses to it. The four elements that the conference proceedings discuss are (1) Post-War American Jewry: From Ethnic to Privatized Judaism, (2) Spirituality and the Civil Religion, (3) Sustaining Jewish Belief in a Secular or Christian America, and (4) The Rabbi, The Synagogue, and the Community. It is particularly astounding to note that in the last category, the "school" or the "educator" are nowhere to be found, and that of the four excellent writers invited to contribute to the latter category,[32] none are people who made their primary mark in the field of education in general or Jewish education in particular.

Why would such a conference not address the educational agenda?

---

32 They are Jack Wertheimer, Barry Shrage, Peter S. Knobel and Adam Mintz. Admittedly, Jonathan Woocher of JESNA did write a piece for the conference, but he dealt more with the thesis of his earlier book, *Sacred Survival*, than he did with matters of education. Education, for all intents and purposes, was not seen as a critical dimension of the discussion.

Could it be that the task seems overwhelming, that "mere" education cannot counter such a deeply rooted trend? Perhaps that is the reason, perhaps not. And it is true — a major reshaping of American Jewish education to increase Jewish social capital, to focus more on the collective, to advocate a spiritual search in a context of mutual engagement and involvement, would be enormously difficult. But that should not excuse us from the obligation to try if we conclude that that is the direction that needs to be pursued. It would be too facile to assume that no claims can be made to engage American Jews in a serious re-evaluation of their highly individualistic commitments. Instead, I would argue, it simply means that the appeal to their sensibilities has to be made not on the basis of what is good for them or for the establishment, but on what is an authentic reading of the Jewish tradition.

Not all of the people to whom we might wish to speak will care what "counts" as authentic, of course. Goldman's book, discussed above, makes amply clear that some Jews are creating their own brands and varieties of Jewish life without regard for any outwardly validated notion of authenticity. But we should not be quick to abandon authenticity as an argument. Much of the return to Orthodoxy (as well as the renewed search for tradition even in the Conservative and Reform movements) is clearly animated by a search for authenticity, a desire to allow Jewish texts and tradition to "speak for themselves." If we do that, I suggest, Jews will quickly have to engage a tradition that sees the very essence of Jewish life as being part of something far beyond their own selves. They will encounter a tradition that validates the spiritual search, but not at the expense of the collective. The educational aim here ought not be to force anything upon them, but rather, to allow them to discover for themselves the deep-seated commitment of Jewish traditions that run counter to the highly individualistic and personal lexicon that modern America has developed for such searches. The goal might well be to ask them to think anew about whether significant Jewish engagement is to be found in the popular culture, context and assumptions of American religious life at large, or in a more particular and communally engaged Jewish ethic, even if that ethic runs counter to the prevailing assumptions of the American culture in which these people were born, educated, nurtured and shaped.

The response to the radically diminished expressions of support for Israel since October 2000, then, ought to be the asking of a series of strategic and content questions. The strategic question has to do with whether the community can be convinced that something is awry, and that education may well be one of the critical ways of addressing that problem.

The content question has to do with what might be taught in order to begin to portray Jewish life as something other than a purely private search, an individual journey designed to satisfy personal "spiritual" needs. This paper has implicitly addressed that strategic question already; thus, by way of moving towards conclusions, it might useful to consider the kind of approach that might be taken to the content side of the response.

Let us consider one example of the sort of text that makes the sort of point we are advocating, namely, that Judaism at its best and in its very essence is much more communal and interdependent than the version of Jewish self-definition that is currently emerging in the United States. The text in question is the famous *baraita* about a prospective convert who comes to the court seeking permission to convert:

> "Our Rabbis taught: If at the present time a man desires,, to become a proselyte, he is to be addressed as follows: 'What reason have you for desiring to become a proselyte; do you not know that Israel at the present time is persecuted and oppressed, despised, harassed and overcome by afflictions'?

> If he replies, 'I know and yet I am unworthy,' he is accepted immediately and is given instruction in some of the minor and some of the major commandments. He is informed of the sin [of the neglect of the commandments of] Gleanings,,, the Forgotten Sheaf, the Corner and the Poor Man's Tithe. He is also told of the punishment for the transgression of the commandments. Furthermore, he is addressed thus: 'Be it known to you that before you came to this condition, if you had eaten forbidden fat you would not have been punishable with *karet*, if you had profaned the Sabbath you would not have been punishable with stoning; but now were you to eat suet you would be punished with *karet*; were you to profane the Sabbath you would be punished with stoning.'"

> And as he is informed of the punishment for the transgression of the commandments, so is he informed of the reward granted for their fulfillment. He is told, 'Be it known to you that the world to come was made only for the righteous, and that Israel at the present time are unable to bear either too much prosperity or too much suffering.' He is not, however, to be persuaded or dissuaded too much. If he accepted, he is circumcised forthwith. Should any shreds which render the circumcision invalid remain, he is to be circumcised a second time. As soon as he is healed arrangements are made for his immediate immersion, when two

learned men must stand by his side and acquaint him with some of the minor commandments and with some of the major ones. When he comes up after his immersion he is deemed to be an Israelite in all respects." (B.T. Yevamot 47a-b).

Even without analyzing this text fully, the anti-individualist elements of the *baraita* are obvious. The prospective convert is (ineffectively) dissuaded from joining the Jewish people because of the risk entailed in joining this *collective*; he is asked by the rabbis, "what reason have you for desiring to become a proselyte," and then, effectively warned, "do you not know that Israel at the present time is persecuted and oppressed, despised, harassed and overcome by afflictions?" To become a Jew is not to be on a solitary search for meaning or "spirituality." To be a Jew is to throw one's personal lot in with the lot of a larger community. To become a Jew means to be willing to be "persecuted and oppressed, despised, harassed and overcome by afflictions," not because there is anything particularly ennobling about such a fate, but rather, simply because to become a Jew is to become part of a collective.

Note also the specific *halakhot* that are enumerated in this text. Of all the possible laws to which the new convert might have been introduced, who would have imagined that the tradition would have chosen to teach him about "the sin [of the neglect of the commandments of] Gleanings,,, the Forgotten Sheaf, the Corner and the Poor Man's Tithe"? Could the reason possibly be that even here, in this phase of the conversion process, the point is being made that despite the fact that the Jews are the outsiders, the weak, the peripheral in larger society, what it means to be a Jew (himself or herself an outsider) is to continue to worry about the outsider, the weak, the peripheral? The Jew as outsider committed to those even less fortunate? There is nothing solitary or self-focused about this. Quite the contrary; to be a Jew, according to this *baraita*, is to be focused on the collective, the other, virtually anything but the self.

Such a text is only one of an enormous array of texts that could be adduced — in what is admittedly a conscious attempt to make a communitarian point — to further this agenda.[33] Nor is the world of text

---

33 It should be noted, of course, that it is hardly the case that only texts from the Jewish canon ought to be adduced here. Others, such as Taylor's *The Ethics of Authenticity* (Cambridge: Harvard University Press, 1992) and his particularly useful notion of "inescapable horizons" can serve equally critical purposes in engendering the sought-after conversation.

the only way in which this argument could or should be presented. Virtually every sphere of Jewish learning could be examined in such a way that the communal, interdependent nature of classic Jewish identity comes for the fore with great ease than it has thus far. There are the historical traditions of *kiddush ha-shem* (religious martyrdom) which clearly suggest that self-preservation is not the ultimate Jewish priority. As we focus on them, we might well recall Warner's claim that "the religious groups that seem to work best in cosmopolitan America are those that recognize the mobility of their members and bring them into contact with great cultural traditions by incessantly and elaborately recounting the founding narrative."(Cited in Cohen and Eisen, 2000, pp. 198–99).[34] What are these founding Jewish narratives? What to the narratives of Purim (and Esther's willingness to risk her life as she approaches the king, after Mordecai asks her "who knows if it was precisely for a moment such as this that you came to the throne?"), or Hanukkah (and the risks of the Hasmoneans as they prepared to risk everything for one last attempt at Jewish independence in Judea) tell us about collective responsibility and the place of risk for a larger good in Jewish life?

Nor ought this effort be limited to classic texts and history. The plastic arts, music, liturgy and certainly ritual could and should be included in this endeavor. Indeed, as the creation and re-creation of Jewish social capital becomes a central focus of North American Jewish education, the role of ritual not only in education, but in the lives of liberal Jewish communities more generally is likely to become an important issue.[35]

Ultimately, for those of us convinced that the erosion of Jewish social capital is a distinct problem for the future of the sort of Judaism we would like to see survive in America, the task is to reach out to those currently convinced that the highly individualist, "new-age spiritual" version of

34 Citing Warner, (1993) "Work in Progress toward a New Paradigm for the Sociological Study of Religion in the United States," *American Journal of Sociology 98*, no. 5 (March), pp. 1059–60, 1078.

35 With regard to ritual, educational strategists would do well to ask why preliminary indications are that this drop off in support for communal Jewish issues seems to be less of an issue among the more traditional elements of the Jewish community. Is this a function of the fact that the more committed tend to be more traditional, or (and these are not mutually exclusive options), is there something about the world of Jewish ritual that instills a sense of commitment to the larger body politic? If one were to determine that the latter is the case, then interestingly, even more liberal communities, who would certainly not wish to commit themselves to a halakhically rigorous way of life, might still wish to investigate the ways in which such rituals and their communal ethic might be injected into the life of liberal Jewish communities.

Jewish life is satisfactory, and to make the claim that a "fuller" reading of Jewish tradition advocates and offers something different, something richer, something much more communally and socially based that actuallybodes much better for the creation and sustenance of an interdependent Jewish community.[36]

Robert Bellah, as noted above, said that Americans have a "first language" — a language of individualism, personal choice and self-realization. The responsibility of Jewish educators in America is to mediate between that and what Jonathan Woocher calls a possible second language — a language of community, memory and responsibility.[37] It is the second that needs to be defended in contemporary America, and *that* needs to be the task of Jewish education. In light of that, the focus on spirituality, "my Judaism" (a phrase that is very problematic), personal meaning and creativity, is perhaps not the direction that education ought to take.

What is at question is not whether such a "read" of the tradition is a legitimate one (at least that does not seem in question to *IU*), or whether there is more than ample material to sustain a concerted effort to make this dimension of identity formation a key element of American Jewish education. What is really in question is whether the educational establishment and other elements of the strategists of American Jewish life can get sufficiently large portions of the community sufficiently concerned about what is happening in American Jewish life — both vis-à-vis Israel and vis-à-vis communal institutions in the United States — that they will be willing to engage in a relatively far-reaching re-assessment of the educational goals they have set for their community in the past decade of so. What it at stake, bottom line, is a debate about the vision of what American Judaism ought to be.

---

36 A fuller examination of this issue will also need to consider arguments such as those of Durkheim (1961). Given what he wrote therein, Durkheim might well have claimed that over and above the need to offer compelling reasons for American Jews to believe that an authentic Judaism is not focused on the self (in the way that we have been suggesting the spirituality movement is), it would also be necessary to organize the social experience of the young in educational settings in such a way that they develop sensibilities that fit them for and establish a decided preference for living towards collectivity. What precisely those means would be in the first decade of the 21st century is by no means obvious, and is a subject that merits the serious reflection of educators in all walks of Jewish education. I am grateful to Dr. Daniel Pekarsky for a series of illuminating conversations in which he suggested this line of inquiry.

37 See Bellah et al's point in *Habits of the heart*, particularly in the chapter on "Community, Commitment and Individuality." Woocher's use of the term "second language" (a play on Bellah, can be found in Abrams and Dallin, 1999), p. 24.

Conclusion

In brief form, in a fashion that raises many more questions than it answers, this paper offers some preliminary musings about the impact of the "spirituality movement" on American Judaism. What this brief paper calls for might be perceived as a Herculean task, for in a sense, it advocates a willingness to resist some of the critical dimensions of the American myth as it has been internalized by much of the American Jewish community. Yet we ought to be careful to distinguish between tasks that are Herculean and Sisyphean. That a task is enormous does not mean that it cannot be accomplished; that a goal is far-reaching does not mean that it ought not be undertaken.

The relative (and much discussed) success of American Orthodoxy in recent years (a success fraught with problematic elements, to be sure) suggests that American Jews are not entirely impervious to appeals to spirituality by way of commitment to a larger collective. The challenge for the leadership of the American Jewish community will be to create that same sense of devotion to the collective *outside* the halakhic context, in a community of people interested in spiritual intensity and possibly collective responsibility, but not in the context of the heteronomy implied by halakhic standards. If the portion of the American Jewish community that is not interested in halakhic commitment (the overwhelming majority, probably over 90%) cannot be reached with an educational program that stresses the communal over the individual, there is reason to fear that those dimensions of Jewish life that have always depended on a commitment of Jews to an enterprise beyond their own satisfactions might be in danger. That challenge to educators is to take this challenge seriously.

A number of years ago, the United Jewish Appeal (now the United Jewish Communities) decided to give up on its slogan, "We Are One" in favor of other, less memorable slogans, because the notion of Jewish "one-ness" simply didn't have the appeal that it used to, or perhaps, it no longer seemed plausible to many. Either way, it was a loss that should not simply be ignored. Now, years later, when Israel faces some of the most serious threats to her continued security, it has become clear that in many respects "We Are Not One." It is tempting to write off the statistics about decreasing travel to Israel and a distancing of American Jews from the Jewish States as reactions to physical danger, the tragedies of September 11, 2001, and other passing phenomena. This paper has sought to suggest that though these factors are undoubtedly at play, they may well not be the entire story, and other factors ought to be considered.

If we take this challenge seriously, and undertake the self-examination that these new trends call for, we may find in retrospect that as difficult as these days are, they afforded us an opportunity to rethink our goals, to sharpen our vision, and to redouble our efforts for the rich Jewish engagement that American Jews continue to seek.

References

Abrams, Elliot and Dalin, David G., *Secularism, Spirituality, and the Future of American Judaism*. Washington, DC: Ethics and Public Policy Center, 1999.

Bellah, Robert N. et al. (1985). *Habits of the heart: individualism and commitment in American life*. New York: Harper and Row.

Cohen, Steven M. and Eisen, Arnold M. (2000). *The Jew within: Family, self and community in America*. Bloomington, IN: Indiana University Press.

Cowan, Paul. (1996). *An orphan in history: Retrieving a Jewish legacy*. New York: William Morrow.

Durkheim, Émile. (1961). *Moral education: A study in the theory and application of the Sociology of Education*. New York: The Free Press.

Goldman, Ari L. (2000). *Being Jewish: The spiritual and cultural practice of Judaism today*. New York: Simon and Schuster.

Goodman, Julia. (2001). Hear Me, Says a Gen-Xer, or Kiss My Cohort Goodbye. *The Forward*. November 23, p. 2.

Gordis, Daniel. (1995). *God was not in the fire: The search for a spiritual Judaism*. New York: Simon and Schuster.

Kamemetz, Rodger. (1995). *The Jew in the lotus: A poet's rediscovery of Jewish identity in Buddhist India*. San Francisco: HarperCollins.

Kamemetz, Rodger. (1998). *Stalking Elijah: Adventures with today's Jewish mystical masters*. San Francisco: Harper SanFrancisco.

Lew, Alan. (2001). *One God clapping: The spiritual path of a Zen Rabbi*. Vermont: Jewish Lights Publications.

Mill, John Stuart. (1956). *On Liberty*. Indianapolis: Bobbs-Merrill Company.

Putnam, Robert D. (2000). *Bowling alone : The collapse and revival of American community*. New York : Simon and Schuster.

Roof, Wade Clark. (1993). *A generation of seekers: The spiritual journey of the baby boom generation*. San Francisco: Harper SanFrancisco.

Roof, Wade Clark. (1999). *Spiritual marketplace: Baby boomers and the remarking of American religion*. Princeton: Princeton University Press.

Roof, Wade Clark and McKinney, William. *American Mainline Religion*. Piscataway, NJ: Rutgers University Press, 1987.

Ruskay, John. (1995). From challenge to opportunity: To build inspired communities. In *Journal of Jewish Communal Service 72 (1/2)*, pp. 22–33.

Ruskay, John. (2000). Looking Forward: Our Three-Pronged Challenge and Opportunity. In *Journal of Jewish Communal Service 77 (2)*, pp. 69–75.

Strassfeld, Michael and Sharon. (1973). *The Jewish catalogue*. Philadelphia: The Jewish Publication Society.

Strassfeld, Michael and Sharon. (1976). *The second Jewish catalogue*. Philadelphia: The Jewish Publication Society.

Strassfeld, Michael and Sharon. (1980). *The third Jewish catalogue*. Philadelphia: The Jewish Publication Society.

Taylor, Charles. (1989). *Sources of the self: The making of modern identity*. Cambridge, MA: Harvard University Press.

Taylor, Charles. (1992). *The ethics of authenticity*. Cambridge: Harvard University Press.

The Forward. (1995). October 20.

The Talmud: The Steinsaltz edition, Volume I, Tractate Bava Metzia, Part I. (1989) New York: Random House.

Woocher, Jonathan. (1986). *Sacred survival: The civil religion of American Jews*. Bloomington and Indianapolis: Indiana University Press.

Contemporary Sensibilities and their Implications for Jewish Education

JENNIFER GLASER

Schwab's vivid metaphor of the educational milieu as Chinese boxes nestled one into another speaks to the way in which educational contexts are manifold and layered. (Schwab, 1980, p. 3). Such Chinese boxes ought not to be considered as discrete layers (like an onion, from the innermost milieu of the classroom to the outward milieu of society), but as the multiple dimensions of thick context. Bringing our attention to bear on the localized milieu of a particular school and classroom calls us at the same time to turn our gaze outward to broader aspects of the social and cultural climate. This turn outward is unavoidable not only because theories of knowledge; cultural traditions; conceptions of identity and of community are played out within the dynamics of classroom interactions, but because this "play" itself contributes to the development of the culture. (Rogoff, 2003, pp. 44–51).

This essay seeks to explore that broadest of Chinese boxes, our general worldview. It seems fair to say that in a large part of the western world this box is undergoing transformation, shifting both the way we make sense of our identity and the contexts in which Jewish education takes place. Our journals reflect this change — in their pages we marvel at the return to adult Jewish learning and text study; we struggle with questions of trans-denominationalism and Jewish pluralism; point to the successes of Limmud and Bnei Jeshurun; draw new insights about Jewish identity and identification from the latest Jewish population surveys; and turn our attention to ways of re-imagining models of meaningful Jewish community.[1]

While the sensibilities of which I speak are generally associated with the contemporary western milieu, I am suggesting that they are particularly important for us as Jewish educators because it is this milieu that richly suffuses the urban environments in which the vast majority of Jewish education takes place. There is also an implicit presumption here (one I will not be arguing for) that the way we come to make sense of our world shift over time; 'movements of thought" emerge as we come to reassess our understanding of the human condition in light of our experience on this planet. The effects of this reassessment impact on the way we view the world at a fundamental level, finding expression across disciplines, interests and diverse fields of inquiry.[2] In this paper I will not have the opportunity to do more than point generally to some of the ways in which elements of our shifting worldview are already surfacing in contemporary Jewish educational theory and practice, yet I hope that some of the positive challenges and difficulties I see associated with this shift become apparent.

The elements of the shifting worldview I take up in this paper may be characterized under four emerging themes in contemporary theory:

(i)   A recognition of "being within"
(ii) The turn to the narrated self
(iii) The empirical fact of plurality
(iv) The weight of contingency

In exploring each of these themes, I shall pay particular attention to the impact of the contemporary worldview on our conceptions of knowledge and identity, for the pursuit of knowledge and the development of personhood are central to the Jewish educational enterprise.

---

1   Limmud is a Jewish educational event in Britain, Bnei Jeshurun an innovative and successful synagogue community in New York, For studies on Jewish identity see the work of Cohen and Eisen, 2000, and Horowitz, 2000/2003. For re-envisaging Jewish Community see Eisen, 1996, and Aron et al., 1995.
2   For example the invention of the microscope and telescope in the 17th century altered our perceptions of reality and the human place within the universe in ways that permeated all aspects of human inquiry and endeavor.

(i) "Being Within"

Recognition of "being within" is a recognition that we dwell within a language, a perspective, a body, a culture and a community. To accept this is to acknowledge that the search for objectivity can only go so far. This has led us to become suspicious of Archimedean thinking and to turn our attention away from universals toward situated knowledge. To accept that we are bound by our language and interpretative structures leads us to a humbler position concerning knowledge; one born of our recognition that our understanding of reality and our knowledge claims are constructed using the resources of language and say as much about the construction of that symbol system (and our use of it) as they do about the way we think things are "out there." Taking such a stance does not require that we deny metaphysical realism (deny that there is something "out there" beyond language); only that we accept that language gives us access to the only truth we (humans) can have.

The recognition that we "dwell within" challenges the enlightenment emphasis on objective knowledge. Until the latter half of the 20th century, the perceived ontological gap between the sciences and humanities meant science was regarded as epistemologically superior.[3] In education too, mathematics and the natural sciences occupied a privileged position. Other disciplines and areas of knowledge either shaped themselves to this paradigm or reconciled themselves to a place that was largely secondary, optional and epistemologically inferior. Yet with the later 20th century's recognition of the ineradicability of language and context, this gap has been narrowed. Science too has taken a "linguistic turn" and metaphors of language and literature have come to replace scientific method as the dominant metaphor of human understanding. The famous 'two slit' experiment in quantum mechanics exemplifies this shift and illuminates its significance for education. In one version of the experiment, a series of individual photons or electrons are fired toward a screen with two small slits and their point of impact measured on a photographic plate set up on the other side. While the photons hit the plate at a single point, the pattern of imprints that builds up on the plate seems to imply that *each* photon passes through *both* slits. Each photon seems to act as a wave as it passes through the slits yet as a particle at the point of impact with the plate. This creates a paradox that Hilary Putnam likens to the Charles Addams cartoon

---

3   Where natural sciences and human sciences were seen to operate according to different systems of explanation and understanding.

of a skier skiing down a hill: "... [The skier's] tracks pass on opposite sides of a large tree. We do not see the skier pass through the tree — we never have seen such a thing, nor will we ever — but the tracks seem to force the inference that the skier passed through the tree before we looked." (Putnam, 1983, p. 48). This might seem strange enough, but the story gets even more bizarre when we *do* look. If further apparatus is set up to observe the electrons at the point at which they pass through the slits, we find that each electron is recorded as going through only one of the holes (not both). Furthermore, the resulting pattern now produced on the photographic plate changes to become consistent with half the photons (or electrons) going through each slit.

> "This is very strange. Whenever we try to detect an electron, it responds as a particle. But when we are not looking at it, it behaves like a wave. When we look to see which hole it goes through, it goes through only one hole and ignores the existence of the other one. But when we don't monitor its passage, it is somehow "aware" of both holes at once and acts as if it has passed through them both." (Gribbin, 1987, p. 230).

The first paradox challenges us to rethink the relationship between language and world. Terms such as "photon" or "electron" are no longer seen to be descriptions of a reality independent of us, but are now seen to be part of the system of signs we humans use to construct reality; that is, we become acutely aware of them as hypothetical models rather than as descriptions of independent "factual" entities. This ties our understanding of the world intimately to our linguistic practices (including the traditions concretized in our language), for it is in the context of culturally determined linguistic *practices* that theories are developed and attract support. Seyla Benhabib puts this well: "[theoretical] reason is the contingent achievement of linguistically socialized, finite and embodied creatures..." (Benhabib, 1992, p. 6).

Recognition that all knowledge is *situated* knowledge has affected the status of Jewish education in two ways. Firstly, whereas Jewish education has always been premised on the view that we "dwell within" a tradition, culture, language and community, the contemporary recognition that *all* dwelling is in-dwelling means that this commitment to particularity no longer labels us as parochial. The awareness that we are all born into a linguistic tradition and become who we are through negotiating its categories has shifted Jewish education from the educational periphery to the (multicultural) center. Indeed, in the current climate, any claim that schooling — including government schooling — is objective or culturally neutral leaves one to the charge of cultural hegemony and/or colonial blindness. Secondly; within a tradition that is heavily textual and interpretative, the general reclamation of the status of the humanities validates the status of text study in Jewish education as an activity that is capable of making an important *epistemological* contribution.

The linguistic turn in Western culture is reflected in a similar turn in Jewish exegesis; the turn to Midrash. As Moshe Idel notes, the affinity between midrashic hermeneutics and contemporary modes of literary criticism, together with a contemporary unease with metaphysics and an awareness that the generative capacity of texts extends beyond the intentions of the author, have led to a resurgence of interest in the midrashic mode. (Idel, 1993, p. 45). In keeping with contemporary sensibilities that locate the thinker within a living tradition, Gerald Bruns notes that *midrash* has come to symbolize a mode of engaged practice wherein interpretive activity is situated (located within a particular social context) and dialogical (with commentary evolving in a communal framework as part of an ongoing multi-vocal conversation) — an engagement in which the authority and force of a particular text is not antecedently given, but lies in its use and in the power of its interpretative possibilities (within the tradition and amongst interpreters):

> "Each rabbi's interpretation is, strictly speaking, ungrounded: it derives its meaning and authority not from its separate correspondence — at a distance — to a piece of original textual evidence but from its participation *in* the original, that is, from its place in the dialogue inaugurated on Sinai when God addressed the Torah to Moses....
>
> One understands by getting into the game, not by applying techniques. Do not think of yourself as an analytic spectator situated outside the text; think of yourself as belonging to the text. Only now you must picture the text not as a formal object (so many fixed letters) but as an open canon whose boundaries are shaped and reshaped by the give-and-take of midrashic argument." (Bruns, 1992, pp. 114 and 116).

The force of one's interpretation is in part a product of its being taken up and used by other interpreters — i.e., its generative capacity within the ongoing conversation. As with the linguistic turn, within the midrashic paradigm, "the text is treated as something moving rather than fixed, something that is always a step ahead of the interpreter, always opening

onto new ground... always calling for interpretation to be begun anew....
Midrashic interpretations stop but do not end." (Ibid. p. 111). Interestingly,
the expansion of the term "midrash" to denote a particular *educational*
paradigm (one reflecting commitments sympathetic with the linguistic
turn) not only makes it possible for the field of Jewish education to
appropriate the language of western interpretative theory, but also allows
for general postmodern interpretative theory to appropriate the concept of
midrash. Thus we find Neil Douglas-Klotz utilizing the concept of midrash
to explore a new paradigm in social science, one characterized by: "1) a
community process, 2) an open rather than closed field of research, 3) the
development of 'inter-penetrating' attention and 4) a spiral rather than a
closed circle of hermeneutic inquiry." (Douglas-Klotz, 1999, p. 181).

Within Jewish education, midrash as an *educational paradigm* has come
to characterize an approach to learning in which the student's engagement
in text-study is open, situated, responsive to multi-vocality, non-dogmatic,
evolving and in cognizant of the indeterminacy of textual meaning. Rather
than viewing midrashic interpretation as the engagement of an outside
"researcher" with a body of Jewish literature, midrash is seen as a *mode of
being* — a particular way of engaging with the world that is rooted in
Jewish tradition. Describing the style of Jewish engagement that
characterizes learning at the Pardes Institute in Jerusalem, Daniel Landes
speaks of the "Paradigm/Midrash that is Pardes" — a mode of engagement
which combines *DoReSH* ("What does God *demand* from you") with a
form of hermeneutic engagement in which students participate in Jewish
life through their encounter with classic Jewish texts. (Landes, 2000). Here
the term "text" is interpreted widely and the "midrashic mode" extends
beyond text study to one's mode of participation in *tiyulim*, Shabbat
hospitality and *tikkun olam* activities. Other examples of Jewish
organizations with an educational agenda which characterize themselves
according to a midrashic paradigm include the Jewish Renewal movement
and the Postmodern Jewish Philosophy Network.[4]

The second paradox identified with the linguistic turn challenges us in
another way — it forces us to recognize the way in which our participation
in the world affects how we see it. Observation can no longer be regarded
as neutral, merely recording an independent reality, but is now seen to give
us the world only *as it presents to us in the very activity of observing it*, with

4   For the Postmodern Jewish Philosophy network see Kepnes et al., 1996; for Jewish
    Renewal's claim that "Jewish renewal is rooted in a Midrashic response" go to: http://
    www.shalomctr.org/index.cfm/action/read/section/renew/article/comm36.html

the observer becoming an integral part of (contributing to the shaping of) the "event" of observation.

The impact of this dimension of the linguistic turn on education has been to emphasize the epistemological virtue of pedagogical strategies that embody constructivist principles. Drawing on D.C Phillips, David Perkins characterizes three understandings that lie behind varying forms of constructivism in education:

- The active learner: knowledge and understanding as actively acquired.
- The social learner: knowledge and understanding as socially constructed.
- The creative learner: knowledge and understanding as created or recreated (Perkins, 1999, p. 6).

Constructivism approaches language as the symbolic tool for fixing meaning and truth. If we see language as a social activity expressive of, and embedded in, a language tradition, then constructing meaning and establishing truth will be seen as an essentially *relational* activity. Engaging in social experiences that *challenge and stretch* our existing language use will thus become critical to our capacity to grow as individuals. While not all experiences may be linguistic to begin with (they may involve gesture, music, performance, ceremonies, feelings, etc.), such experiences need to be translated and analyzed using appropriate linguistic tools (vocabulary, theoretic constructs, texts) if they are to enable us to rethink, clarify and develop our understanding of the world and of ourselves. This emphasis on the primacy of relation in constructivism acts to soften the modernist emphasis on autonomy and independence.

The notions that: (i) the "fit" between language and world is mediated by tradition, (ii) meaning is constructed through experiences interpreted in a social (language) context, and (iii) knowledge is actively created; all connect strongly with traditional contents and pedagogies of Jewish education. From the social linguistic context of *hevruta* study (in which deliberation is mediated through text and linguistic tradition) to the experiential multi-generational "re-creation" of the exodus at the Pesach Seder, it becomes possible for Jewish educators to frame their practices within a language representing the cutting edge of mainstream education.

In their article on the Yeshiva, Moshe and Tova Halbertal illustrate well this comfortable fit between Jewish educational practices and a vocabulary embodying contemporary sensibilities and commitments:

"Yeshiva life is a life of ongoing conversation…. The students become attached to the tradition through their active participation in the ongoing argument. The text is the initial conversation which expands and develops by dialogue with it. Re-enactment is not a repetition: the student introduces a new interpretation, a novella or a *chidush* (a new way of approaching a problem)… In this respect, a talmudic page proceeds counter to Popper's 'Scientific method of reasoning'…" (Halbertal and Hartman-Halbertal, 1998, pp. 424, 462, 464).

Yet it needs to be stressed that this "fit" is not without its adaptations. To adopt traditional pedagogies in the 21st century is not to return to a pre-modern ethos, but to adapt these pedagogies to the current worldview.[5] As Steven Kepnes points out:

"The model of the Yeshiva is the model of a moral world built in and through the language game of Jewish texts. The postmodern "retrieved" Yeshiva is not the closed in and ghettoized Yeshiva of old but a Yeshiva modified by critique to include both men and women and to welcome visits by non-Jews. It is a Yeshiva not only open to internal critique but capable of mounting sustained ethical critique of the injustices in the larger Jewish and non-Jewish worlds outside of it." (Kepnes, 1996, pp. 7–8).

Such moral critique is matched by an epistemological critique that shapes the contemporary Beit Midrash around a moderate hermeneutic and an attentiveness to difference.[6] In the arena of the day school we find a similar phenomenon — schools are adopting the language of hevruta study and the dialogical context of the Beit Midrash, yet adapting the form in response to their needs. Hevruta study is no longer the domain of males learning Talmud in pairs; today's hevruta grouping may be of mixed gender, differing sized groupings, and students may be engaged with contemporary as well as traditional texts. Whereas the epistemological assumption underlying text-study in the traditional Beit Midrash places us in a

5   In Jerusalem, for instance, we see a spectrum of Jewish learning institutions — the Conservative Yeshiva, the Reform Beit Midrash, Pardes, Matan, and Elul — adopting the language and pedagogy of Yeshiva study, yet doing so in ways that respond to a contemporary critique of pre-modern commitments.
6   A striking example of which is Elul in Jerusalem, which explicitly seeks to construct mixed hevruta pairs between secular and religious students.

backward chain of tradition where we all stand in the same place vis-à-vis truth because we are all equi-distant from the past, in the contemporary Beit Midrash we all stand in the same place vis-à-vis truth because we are all interpreters and constructors of knowledge. This does not mean that "all interpretations are as valid as one another," but that our epistemological judgment of interpretations stands independent from hierarchies of authority.[7]

The tension created by adapting traditional pedagogies to the 21st century is well illustrated in Landes' description of the Pardes Institute's Beit Midrash. On the one hand, the Beit Midrash is described as providing an 'authentic' environment in which students experience the "timeless quality of a true and real Jewish experience of study;" while on the other hand, it is characterized as a Jewish learning environment, "egalitarian in spirit and practice" and responsive to the individual's search for meaning. Pardes' method of learning is described as responsive to the challenges of modern scholarship and providing an interface with Western culture and philosophy. Exactly how these adaptations of the traditional male Beit Midrash modify the notions of "authenticity" and "timelessness" would be intriguing to explore.

Perhaps one of the greatest tensions that needs addressing when looking at the fit between constructivism and Jewish education is how the notion of Sacred Text modifies the constructivist stance. As mentioned earlier, recognizing that we 'dwell within' does not require us to give up metaphysics; however, it does imply that truth and meaning are seen as to be shaped by *human* linguistic practices — practices located within the earthly domain and not beyond it. If we see linguistic tradition as a distinctly human tradition, then the power of speech and the capacity to speak lies with us. This places truth and meaning within a naturalized universe. Yet for those Jews who see Torah as God-given, the power of speech originates with God.[8] Speech may be human (it is our linguistic system, our system of meanings), but it is not *only* human because our language is predicated on the word of God. Biblical text thus bridges between human and transcendental realms, between the earthly and the mystical. It is at once a conversation amongst ourselves and a conversation

---

7   This too, I think, lies behind the way Midrash (and midrashic methodology) is being given more and more attention by contemporary Jewish thinkers.

8   Recognizing that there are many interpretations of what 'Torah as the Word of God' might mean.

initiated beyond ourselves. We see this expressed in Buber's *I-Thou*[9] and in Abraham Joshua Heschel's conception of the Holy and of sanctification.

This religious dimension of in-dwelling offers a different understanding of the emergence of language and boundaries of linguistic tradition than that of contemporary secular culture. While the linguistic turn places tradition (speech, text and interpretation) at the center, it raises a further hermeneutic problem: "One cannot put text/Torah at the center without facing the issue of its supposed sacredness. How do we understand the text/Torah as sacred text, as word of God? With text/Torah at center, questions of theology come before questions of anthropology." (Ochs, 1996, p. 25). Models of adult Jewish education that seek to combine insights from the Jewish mystical and Hassidic traditions with a Gadamerian or hermeneutical stance can be seen as one response to how we might maintain a sacred centre while drawing from a western hermeneutic tradition that understands linguistic tradition in human terms.[10] In Jewish day school education the awareness of this difference is implicitly expressed in the often voiced angst of teachers who, on the one hand, are committed to the constructivist view that students' linguistic play is of generative *epistemological* value (and thus want to empower their students to construct their own meanings through their encounter with biblical text), yet on the other hand, feel that, in doing so, they are denying the authority of the text *as* Sacred Text.[11] This raises an important challenge in the training of teachers for Jewish studies; suggesting that prospective teachers would benefit from being introduced to a range of contemporary Jewish hermeneutic responses that might help them negotiate this tension.

Finally, constructivism's emphasis on the social, active and creative learner provides a contemporary pedagogical language through which to interpret informal and formal Jewish practices that take place *outside* the

9 Here we need to recognize Buber's distinctly *theological* ontology. For Buber, the *I-Thou* encounter is an experience of direct engagement in which I and You lose our subjectivity in an encompassing oneness. This relation is one of genuine dialogue in which we receive something that is said and feel approached for an answer. Here the capacity for speech is not a linguistic capacity, but an *expressive* one; it is the capacity of 'that which is created' to express something. (see Buber, 1975, p. 62; and 1979, p. 36).

10 For instance, in the hermeneutic style adopted within the Pardes Institute's new spiritual education program that draws on Hassidic and mystical hermeneutic traditions; in the Hassidic orientation of the Matan Institute, and the mystical orientation of the Jewish Renewal movement.

11 I have seen this particularly amongst students who themselves view Bible as a revealed text, and at the same time see themselves teaching in community day schools where they are aware that students may not view the Bible in the same way.

classroom and school. Purim, youth movements, Holocaust Remembrance Day, B'nei Mitzvah and Jewish summer camps provide but a few examples of the spectrum of institutionalized experiential environments in which the *play* of Jewish life takes place. Such activity not only provides members of the community with opportunities to participate in (re-create) the practices, historic memory, commitments and debates internal to our tradition, but is productive of the tradition itself. What constructivist theory does here is to sharpen our focus on the distinctly epistemological value of such play.[12]

(ii) The Narrated Self

The contemporary awareness of "in-dwelling" outlined so far has not only had a strong impact on the way we approach texts, but has also had a strong influence on the way that we have come to understand and theorize about personhood and Jewish identity. Until the 1970s modernist (analytic) theories of identity were constructed on a division between mind and body, thought and action, and focused on questions of definition rather than meaning. The theoretical focus was on articulating necessary and sufficient conditions for ascribing and maintaining identity (What defines a person? What defines the same person over time/change?) and on logical problems concerning causation between, and the integration of, a non-physical mind and a physical body. This (positivist) theoretical focus gave rise to a particular — and often peculiar — set of problems concerning the definition of persons and personal identity.[13]

As philosophers and psychologists turned toward questions of meaning (an outcome of the general turn toward language and interpretation) they needed a new vocabulary that allowed *interpretation* to play a larger role in their theorizing about identity. Gaining impetus in the 1960s, it was the expanding language of persons as "selves" that filled this role.[14] Discourse on the self can be traced back to William James. At the turn of the 20th century James wrote about "The Consciousness of Self" in which he

12 See Chazan, (2003) p.78. In Israel, South Africa and Australia, we find schools that have institutionally incorporated both a Beit Midrash within the school and have employed full-time teaching staff as informal educators within the school community.

13 In philosophy, this can be seen in the variety of imagined scenarios used to investigate identity issues in the 1970s — scenarios of body-splitting, brain-swapping, placing of brains in vats, acute cases of amnesia, mind replication, etc.

14 This expansion of 'self' talk includes the rise of such identity terms as: the narrative self; the dialogical self; the ontological self. The term 'self' has become a noun "the Self" and this has spawned a verb "selfing" (the process of becoming a self).

linked personal identity with our awareness of ourselves as "I" and "Me."[15] For James, "I" designated the self as experiencing subject (the self as knower), while "Me" designated the self as object (the self as known). Both terms, however, located identity in the first-person *experience* of who "I" am. That is, the term "self" characterized *a person's phenomenological experience of him or herself as an "I."*

During the past 50 years the phenomenological experience of self has increasingly been understood in cognitive terms — that is 'who I am' has become increasingly characterized in terms of our reflective *consciousness* of ourselves as an "I".[16] Talk of *selves* — our constructed sense of who we are — has provided a vocabulary for talking about personal identity which focuses on meaning rather than definition.[17] For constructivists, selves emerge out of language (interpretative) activity; we are not *born* a self but *become* one. The question of language now becomes somehow strategic for the question of human nature. Here too the "researcher" has become implicated in the "observation" — for it is our *reflexive awareness* of who we are that is now seen as an integral part of what constitutes our identity. Identity is no longer a fact (or noun) but a hermeneutic *process*; we are constantly remaking ourselves as we reinterpret our past and (projected) future in light of present experiences, values, and meanings.[18] It is this interpretative process that has made narrative structure central to contemporary conceptions of identity — for identity will emerge out of the way we link past to prospective future and weave our life experiences into units of meaning. This narrative quality is well described by Richard Shusterman:

> "Once we abandon a foundationalist essentialism about the self, we can only constitute the self in terms of a narrative about it. Even if we try to constitute the self in terms of its actions, we find that the meaning (or even proper description) of any action is not atomistically given in

15 In 1890 William James published *The Principles of Psychology*, in which chapter ten was called "The Consciousness of Self." This is identified as one of the earliest publications (if not the earliest) explicitly on the self. Perhaps the most influential work in social psychology has been George Herbert Mead's *Mind, Self and Society* published in 1934.

16 We can see this in Charles Taylor and Paul Ricoeur. We also see it reflected in the way Abraham Heschel and Joseph Soloveitchik address questions of identity through an exploration of our consciousness of ourselves as "I".

17 For an exploration of the tensions between identity established through definition and meaning, see Tamir, 1996.

18 See: McAdams, 1997.

itself but is a function of the narrative context in which it appears...
The meaning of my actions and the definition of myself as agent
changes significantly according to the story told." (Schusterman, 1993,
p. 295).

Indeed *story* has become a favored metaphor for speaking about identity.
Replacing the enlightenment view of man as the "rational animal" we have
come to see ourselves as *language* animals — a view captured in
MacIntyre's oft-quoted thesis that: "Man is in his actions and practice, as
well as in his fictions, essentially a story-telling animal." (MacIntyre, 1987,
p. 216).

Importantly, since language gets its meaning from its relationship to
other language (rather than by correspondence to some reality 'out there')
— the notion of story suggests that we are able to *remake ourselves by
remaking our speech.* Here the metaphor of *journey* captures the sense in
which the construction of a life contains movement over time. In her study
of American Jewish Identity, "Connections and Journeys" Bethamie
Horowitz notes:

"The concept of journey appears to be both apt and necessary for
accurately portraying the nature of contemporary American Jewish
identity. The term 'journey' encompasses how Jewishness unfolds and
gets shaped by the different experiences and encounters in a person's
life. Each new context or life stage brings with it new possibilities. A
person's Jewishness can wax and wax, wane and change in emphasis. It
is responsive to social relationships, historical experiences and personal
events. It is worth noting how this concept of journey differs from the
more typical Jewish self-image of 'wandering Jew' in which the Jewish
people are forced to wander from place to place, holding fast to their
own fixed identities through a changing environment. In contrast, the
journeys described in this report are about the voluntary movements of a
consciously evolving self interacting with a changing environment."
(Horowitz, 2000/2003, p. viii).

Horowitz suggests that as a result of this move toward narrative identity,
contemporary studies of Jewish identity need to go beyond the traditional
sociological markers of affiliation and participation in community events
and look to examine the ways Jews reflexively speak about their identity
(their subjective relationship to being Jewish) — a narrative that will be
contingent and provisional, changing in response to life circumstances and

experience.[19] Given that "selfing" (becoming a self) is a life-long project, even strong identities may at the same time be extremely fluid, open to revision, adaptation, and transformation.[20] While Jewish practices may serve to stabilize "who" we are — for consistency of action is an important part of coming to stand *for* something — actions will be open to revision as our self-understandings and our sense of our own possibilities for a future change.

Once narrative interpretation is seen as crucial for the process of self-construction our capacity to engage with the narratives embedded in our cultural tradition and which function to orient it become centrally important to developing a sense of place as individuals. Here the distinction between "my narrative" and "our" narrative blurs, for it is *as a member of the community whose identity is constituted by the telling and retelling of the story* that I engage with it.[21] For children as well as adults, we might think of this sort of hermeneutic engagement not only as building content-knowledge and text skills, but as a means of character (identity) development. Grappling with the text, participants reclaim their narrative traditions (aggadic, legal, historic, etc.), and through this expanded language come to grapple with their identity in richer, more nuanced, ways.[22]

This increasing attention to cultural literacy amongst moderately affiliated Jews is reflected in the expanding number of Jewish day schools and in the increasing number of adults engaging in Jewish learning.[23] Within adult Jewish education, text study has come to be seen as both an important locus for developing *self*-knowledge (for example, coming to understand better where I stand on moral or social issues) and a forum for exploring the subjective experience of being Jewish. This is often what makes text-study so educationally powerful. This experience is not unique

---

19 Horowitz reports that: "60 percent of the people in her study experienced changes in their relationship to being Jewish over time, suggesting that Jewish identity is not a fixed factor in one's life but rather a matter that parallels personal growth and development.", ibid, p. vii.

20 Don MacAdams turns the noun "self" into the verb form "selfing" in MacAdams, 1997, p.56.

21 Paul Ricoeur elaborates on the relationship between individual and communal narrative through text in "Toward a Narrative Theology," Ricoeur, 1995, pp. 236–248.

22 For further reflections on the activity of adult text study see: Aron and Schuster, 1998. Note: "More than any other form of adult Jewish learning, text study offers the learner both direct contact with tradition and opportunities for learning about him or herself," p. 45.

23 For instance, the phenomenal growth of the Florence Melton Adult Mini Schools over the past eight years.

to America. Reflecting on the Orthodox British community, Jonathan Sacks describes what he sees as a new generation of British Jews:

> "They are searching for personal meaning, moral guidance, and stability and structure in their lives. They have been touched by the outreach movements, and they are beginning to reconnect with Jewish observance and *Talmud Torah*, the study of Jewish texts. Almost every adult education program we run in Britain is today oversubscribed, and there is a huge demand for new Jewish day schools." (Sacks, 1997).

In Britain, *Limmud* — a voluntary-led Jewish educational organization best known for its annual conference — suggests in its literature: "Come to Limmud and together we will strengthen our identities, inspire our faith and invigorate our community. Wherever you find yourself, Limmud will take you one step further along your own Jewish journey." (Quoted in Nicholls, 2003, p. 196). In December 2003 its annual conference drew 350 presenters, 900 sessions and over 2000 participants. The emphasis here is on individual journey and self-discovery, but such discovery takes place through participation in a learning community. The search for meaning may be personal, but it is carried out in a context with others; the "autonomous" self once portrayed as atomistic individual, has become thought of primarily as a *social* creature.

Finally, it is important to recognize that while a narrative view of identity places our sense of who we are firmly in the cognitive domain, this cognitive emphasis is balanced by a background reflexive awareness of our own embodiment and physical extension. Our reflexive sense of who we are incorporates a sensory-motor awareness of "being within" which is characterized as *kinesthetic* experience. Kinesthetic knowledge may be directed inwardly toward ourselves or outwardly to others. Inwardly, our kinesthetic sense:

> "...allows us to notice what we are feeling in our own interior, letting us know when we are stiff or fatigued or upside down, whether our fingers are stretched apart or close together. The kinesthetic sense both tells us about ourselves and connects us with others as embodied selves." (Stinson, 1995, p. 44).[24]

---

24 Stinson notes: "Most educators appear to want to suppress student physicality, not enhance it; even in the early grades.... Most often physicality is recognized as something that must be managed in order to obtain the best academic performance.... This body-mind duality in schools has been recognized by a number of theorists." p. 45.

As well as connecting us with our own interiority, kinesthetic experience connects us by inference to the sensory-motor experience of others — it enables us to connect to "the weighty sadness of a friend, [or] the tense anxiety of an unprepared student before an exam," (ibid). This awareness of our own interiority contributes to our awareness of acting in the world, and of being acted upon. Habits and repeated performances of ritual may lead us to experience a sense of comfort with doing things *this* way (rather than *that*), or may result in a feeling of belonging as we experience again patterns and structures of bodily sensual experience that already form part of our relationship to the world (e.g., the sense of belonging we feel when we find ourselves once again seated at the Pesach seder, or the sense of Jewishness that a seemingly otherwise assimilated Jew feels when she/he fasts on Yom Kippur). Yet while such habits and patterns of experience provide the non-cognitive background for identity, they will not form part of our self-concept or contribute to our self-understanding until we become cognitively aware of them.

The current attention being given to the role of habits and to the kinesthetic sense in self-formation speaks to the traditional relationship between action, identity formation, and meaning that is found within Judaism. It suggests that the role of habit and "doing" in Jewish education is not only one of acculturation toward normative practice, but establishes an internal spatial/physical orientation and competency which contributes to our sense of who we are. While this is closer to the traditional Jewish attitude toward the place of habits, what is illuminated by practice is different. Whereas traditionally, habits (or the practice of mitzvot) come before interpretation because the experience of doing contributes to our understanding of the *object* (the action, mitzvah); in relation to the development of self, action and habit come before interpretation because the experience of doing contributes to our sense of ourselves as subject (the actor). Practices kinesthetically reshape our internalized landscape and orientation. This aspect of self-formation has strong implications for educational theory and practice. (See O'Loughlin, 1998). While this dimension of Jewish education has largely not been the focus of researchers' work, two areas where focus as been placed on the contribution of the kinesthetic sense are the Jewish camping experience and the Israel experience. Barbara Kirschenblatt-Gimblett puts it thus:

"Tourism as a technique of the body is central to the pedagogy of the Israel Experience. That pedagogy... appeals to the truth of the senses, to body knowledge, and to forms of memory that are not only inscribed but incorporated… Incorporating practices consist of repeated actions that become habitual. They are remembered by the body. These tours stress embodied experience over language." (Kirschenblatt-Gimblett, 2000, p. 313).

In particular, bodily knowledge points to the need for educators to be aware of (i) the kinesthetic dimension of Jewish educational experiences and how such inner experience fits with cognitive contents (for instance, the kinesthetic dimension of one's feeling of connection to others in the context of hevruta study or in sitting at a school assembly on Yom HaAtzmaut); and (ii) the way in which kinesthetic experience contributes to the development of our imaginative landscape of possibilities (for instance, how the physical experience of being called to the Torah for the first time transforms a cognitive possibility into one in which we are aware of ourselves as participant, and through this awareness come to see ourselves differently).

(iii) The Empirical Fact of Plurality

Whether we face it reluctantly or with enthusiasm, globalization and technological advances in the 20th century have confronted us with the fact of plurality. Awareness of this plurality emerges through our experience of simultaneity and difference (our encounter with the multiplicity of values, cultures, and ways of life played out on this planet). This contemporary experience of plurality is reinforced by our awareness that each of us dwells within a particular framework, one that brings with it its own limitedness and biases. There is a growing awareness that living with plurality requires that we develop an ability to negotiate these differences. For many, this plurality is seen as a value rather than a problem — for without multiplicity we would have no choice and no autonomy.

If plurality is a necessary condition for *choice*, in today's world choices face us as never before — we can choose the nation we live in, the religion we identify with (or not), the kind of family we build, the profession or trade we learn, the countries we visit, etc. The currencies that help transform choice from theoretical domain to a practical one are education and capital — third world subsistence farmers with little or no formal schooling simply do not have as wide a range of plural possibilities as first world middle class tertiary educated individuals. In the contemporary world, taking advantage of plurality requires flexibility, mobility (both professional and geographical) and the ability to integrate change. Higher and higher levels of literacy are needed in order to handle responsibly the ranges of possibilities placed before us. In terms of Jewish identity, we might say that Jews who are not Jewishly literate will have a smaller range of Jewish options (ways of actualizing their Jewishness) than those with a higher level of Jewish literacy.[25]

Importantly, rather than placing emphasis on ways to resolve plurality (via convergence or consensus), the emphasis is now placed on educating toward skills that enable people to negotiate and bridge between these differences. (See Stone, 1993/4, p. 51). Minimally this requires education for tolerance; maximally it strives for an education that embraces such differences and sees itself as enriched by the dialogue between them. We see this in the growth of Community Jewish Day Schools and in the developing language of trans-denominationalism and non-denomination-alism. This awareness of plurality is also reflected in the increasing opportunities that invite Jews to mix diverse cultures in their search for meaning thus generating new possibilities for Jewish spiritual expression (for example, mixing Raiki with Jewish spiritualism, Buddhism with Judaism, Jewish mystic traditions with text study, etc.)

Plurality, however, may also confront us with differences that are incommensurate or that are so substantive that they become impossible to bridge. Understanding and intelligibility can fail. Not only will there be stances which we cannot condone, but there will be stances that leave us facing one another in silence with nothing left to say — or possible to say — to one another. Given plurality, different individuals and different communities may live parallel, rather than entwined, lives. More than ever before, the debate around the meaning of Am Yisrael — the meaning and limits of the very notion of Jewish peoplehood — is on the agenda.[26] Importantly, this does not stop us from talking generally about Jewish identity (after all, we do know the sort of thing we are talking about when we use the term), but the term is now seen to be radically over-determined — that is, there are many determinants that contribute to "Jewish" and different ones act as criteria for the identity of different Jewish individuals.

---

25 The opposite does not hold true — it does not follow that those with higher levels of literacy will necessarily have (or see themselves as having) more options.

26 However here we need to remember that people live in many overlapping communities, and people who are unintelligible to us (living parallel lives) on one level, may be members of our community on another. As Ann Diller notes: "...our contemporary world is so inter-dependent that we can rarely have coexistence without some encroachment from demands for cooperation.". See Diller, 1992, p.205.

While the term "Jewish identity" is spoken in the singular, when we speak about it we are really talking about Jewish *identities* — and some of these identities may share little in common with one another. Just as there is little we can say about games that is true of all games other than they require some concept of rules and some notion of playing (participatory action), there might be little we can say about the identity of Jews that is true for all cases other than that Jewishness too requires some concept of limits and some notion of participatory action (though there will be no particular limit and no way of playing that will fit all cases).

Recognizing the fact of plurality leads to a certain sense of decentering. We no longer view the community in terms of concentric circles whereby the core of the community is identified as "same" and the extending circles mark out levels of difference (in which case to be marginal is to deviate from the core). Rather, we see the community as the overlapping space of individuals each of whom have allegiance to many communities. In today's world, individually constructed eclectic Jewish identity is not *necessarily* seen as any weaker than a normatively defined one. Our place in the community is now shaped by the network of relationships that link us to each other. Belonging to communal institutional structures may still play an important pragmatic role (for it is most often through them that we have a practical community through which we can develop and express our Jewishness), but our membership alone will no longer define the kind of Jewish identity we characterize for ourselves (for *who I am* will never directly correlate with the institution's ideology.)

Plurality also has an internal dimension — the contemporary milieu is one in which we are increasingly aware that we are born into multiple traditions and are members of different communities that each impact upon our choices. In any given situation, there may be more than one way for us to "get it right" (fulfill our goals, our values, our commitments). What I then choose to do will not only depend on principled judgment but also on the way I construct my personal narrative and on practical expediency. What stops such plurality from dissolving into schizophrenia is that at the same time as we are aware of one possibility, we are aware of the other. I do not oscillate between different selves (each oblivious to the other), but in the very act of realizing one value, am aware that I could equally have realized another. Here the meaning of my Jewish identity is given through the personal construction of a unifying narrative that makes sense of these choices. Rather than seeing the fact that I eat Kosher at home but not in restaurants as a problem of inconsistency that needs to be resolved (either you keep Kosher or you don't), I acknowledge the inconsistency and seek to unify the conflicting actions under a single narrative ("one is about normative practice, the other about my autonomy as an individual.") In such cases I am aware of myself as someone who realizes contrary values and this awareness is with me in both contexts (home and restaurant), modifying my understanding of who I am in each situation. In such a situation, what this acceptance of plurality does is to enable us to let go of the *anxiety* that comes with a multiply-committed life.

Inner plurality may give us choice, but it also generates tension. Aware of multiple competing commitments, we may find ourselves simultaneously living radically divergent self-defining narratives. Inner plurality brings an awareness that we can never fully express all that we could be — for action will often require that we settle on one way of expressing who we are to the exclusion of the other. Negotiating such plurality makes identity complex and at times painful. Raimond Gaita describes this well:

> "Suppose someone whose nature is divided in something like this way: he is the child of two cultures and in him the two are sometimes in creative, sometimes in debilitating conflict, such that the results are interwoven in all that is significant in his character and personality; it is idle to wonder how he would be if he could resolve this conflict. The conflict is the root of his strengths and weaknesses; at times it seems to provide him with roots, his speech and action flow as from a firm, fertile center, whereas at other times, it is the opposite: he is as once rootless, unlocated, vacillating and wasted... His friends sorrow over his pain but cannot wish it otherwise, for it is so constitutive of him, that to wish it otherwise would be to wish him to be someone else." (Gaita, 1981, pp. 143–4).

It is a situation that is common to many of our students. In as much as Jewish educational contexts (such as school and synagogue) ignore the multiple contexts of their students, they may relieve themselves of the tension that comes with the fact of plurality ("everyone knows what this school stands for.") However ignoring students' plurality will come at a price, for it neither relieves their internal anxiety, nor takes responsibility for providing them with the tools for bridging the multiple worlds they inhabit and thereby constructing a positive sense of themselves as a whole. Elisheva, an American Conservative Jewish high school student, reflects on her experience of just this kind of plurality thus:

> "I remember one day I spent an entire morning in the office of my

rebbe... crying. I was so confused and did not know how to deal with my frustration. I felt I was living inconsistently. For nearly nine hours every day, I would go to school to learn and act like an Orthodox Jew. However when I would return home at the end of the day, I had to switch gears once again and resume my usual lifestyle....

Everyone wants to have an identity. Feeling lost can be a very scary thing.... Without anyone telling me how to observe Judaism, I am not sure which path I will choose to follow. Yet throughout all of my grappling, I have learned one thing. That is, for right now, I do not need to have a label. As long as I continue to search for my identity as a Jew in society, I am well on the way."[27]

Elisheva's response is to reject having to choose between American and Jewish identity (as if being one excludes the other) and to look instead for ways of relating to the world from her multiple commitments. The challenge plurality poses to Jewish education is substantive, and one of the key issues concerns the ways in which we might teach for commitment in the face of such diversity. If there are many good lives to live, what is needed for me to become committed to living this life rather than another? Choice in relation to our Jewish identity means (for the vast majority of us) *re*committing ourselves to something given through birth and/or upbringing.[28] For our students this suggests two things: first, if we want them to choose Jewish practice, we need to provide them with opportunities to develop and appropriate personal meanings that give significance to what they do; second, we can expect students both to be actively engaged in determining their own allegiances and practices (testing out possibilities to see where they may lead) and to see these determinations as less fixed; open to the possibility of revision as their life develops.[29]

In a world where Jewish identity is fundamentally interpretative, integrative and tied to meanings, reflexive deliberation that connects personal experience to Jewish content becomes critical for Jewish education. Here we need to distinguish between two ways in which teachers may draw upon the personal realm in classroom discussion: (i) we

27 From a public address, printed in Heilman, 1998, pp. 82–3.
28 Putting aside the role society (family, peers, culture) may play in training us for this role. For an excellent discussion of different ways in which we negotiate our identity see: Tamir, 1996.
29 Bethamie Horowitz's study "Connections and Journeys" (2000–2003) explores the changing ways people may give expression to their Jewishness at different points in their life, pp.154–158.

may bring personal narrative into the classroom by focusing on the student as the object of attention. This brings to mind the classic image of the teacher moving around a circle of children who each offer their own example in relation to the topic under discussion (for instance "Shabbat.") Students are asked to share their experience ("What my family does on Shabbat") in order for the class to learn something about one another's lives and see the link between the subject matter under discussion and their own lives. Our interest in offering such self-disclosure is to be affirmed or understood. Alternatively, (ii) we may bring personal narrative into the classroom for what it may contribute to the subject under discussion. In this case our interest in offering personal narrative is to further illuminate the topic of our inquiry. Here the teacher needs to go beyond eliciting personal experiences or meanings to reflective critical engagement with them ("What meanings might we ascribe to Shabbat through these narratives?" or "what do these different accounts tell us about the criteria people use for determining their own Shabbat practice?") Modeling this sort of engagement with the personal in the process of inquiry is critical for Jewish education if we are to help students internalize a model of reflexive deliberation in which they bring their own lives into an evolving dialogue with tradition over time.

Focusing on plurality and constructed identity does not mean that everything becomes a matter of choice simultaneously (indeed too much choice at any one time becomes radically disabling); rather, it means that there is no predetermined boundary between those aspects of our life we accept as given and those we choose for ourselves. This makes even the most incidental features of our identity a matter of purposeful action and choice. Those aspects of self which unreflectively provide the background against which we make choices today may themselves become a matter of choice (affirmed, rejected or transformed) tomorrow. Aspects of self that I choose not to see as central in defining my identity today may change in time as different parts of me come to play a more significant (or less significant) role in the way I construct my narrative. Maintaining identity now involves us in ongoing hermeneutic activity — an interpretative activity in which I re-appraise what I previously chose for myself in light of who I now take myself to be. In light of such re-appraisal, the smallest details of our lives take on symbolic (political/ritualistic) importance.

While the impact of choice on Jewish life is usually discussed in relation to its impact on the identity of Jews who do not accept halakhah as binding, its impact on contemporary Orthodoxy should not be under-estimated. Haym Soloveitchik describes this change well in his article

"Rupture and Reconstruction" in which he points to the loss of the "naturalness and inevitability" of Jewish life.

> "Alternatives now exist, and adherence is voluntary.... religious conduct is less the product of social custom than of conscious, reflective behaviour. If the *tallit katan* is worn not as a matter of course but as a matter of belief, it has then become a ritual object.... its essence lies in its accuracy.... A way of life has become a *regula*, and behavior, once governed by habit, is now governed by rule." (Soloveitchik , 1994, p. 71).

For Haym Soloveitchik, the central impact of this change can be seen in "the new and controlling role that texts now play in contemporary religious life" — a role that has a strong impact on education and the construction of identity amongst a segment of today's Orthodox Jewry. (Ibid., p. 65).[30]

(iv) The Weight of Contingency

Our contemporary awareness of contingency is an outcome of our recognition of plurality and choice. Contingency is experienced in two ways. Firstly, given that we choose between plural possibilities, we are aware that we may have chosen otherwise and that things might have been other than they are. Secondly, given that all projects, commitments, choices, values, etc. are open to future revision, contingency brings with it a rejection of certainty — all truth, all commitments, values and projects reflect the way we make sense of things "for now." This modifies modernity's teleological belief in progress. Progress will now be local, particular and contextualized — judged in relation to interpretations of the past and modestly (or tentatively) held in light of a projected future. Claims will always be relative to circumstances and frameworks. Indeed those who declare their own certainty boldly are likely to be viewed with suspicion (and this marks out the present postmodern moment from that of 20 years ago, for now the rhetoric of early postmodern movements is seen to reflect the same claims to certainty as the modernist positions they rejected).

---

30 While I do not want to claim that the change in the way text is viewed in Orthodoxy is generalizable outside the context Soloveitchik was addressing, it seems to me that there is something here to think about further regarding the changing relationship to text within other Jewish movements over the last 50 years (for instance, in Reform Judaism).

I refer here to the *weight* of contingency because contingency is a relatively heavy burden — it means living with (even making a virtue out of living with) a great deal of uncertainty, ambiguity, open-endedness, self-doubt and humility. This makes us a lot less certain of ourselves now than we were in the height of modernity. To be faced with multiple alternatives may threaten our inner sense of security. Following others into their culture and life experiences we may come to confront and question ourselves and our own culture — and in so doing we may put the security of our own identity at risk. Discomfort may emerge when we confront the need to revise our images of who we are — for instance, it may lead us to recognize an aspect of ourselves to which we had previously been blind, or discomfort may emerge from our realization that we are really more like "one of them" than "one of us." As theorists ask: "why expose ourselves to such discomfort?" "Why endanger one's established sense of self?" (Kimball and Garrison, 1996, p. 57; and Diller, 1992, p.209). Faced with too many choices, with too many conflicting values, desires and envisaged futures, the task of judging between alternatives becomes paralyzing. In widening the range of possibilities too far, our sense of self is diminished rather than enriched. We experience paralysis when we are overwhelmed by plural possibilities and a lack of criteria by which to choose between them. If I can be anyone, how do I choose who to be? If I can do anything, how do I choose what to do?[31] In her autobiography, Eva Hoffman describes this challenge to identity — a challenge faced when her family moved from post-war Poland to Canada:

"I'm a quantum particle trying to locate myself within a swirl of atoms. How much time and energy I'll have to spend just claiming an ordinary place for myself! ... 'There are no such places anymore,' my fellow student informs me. 'This is a society in which you are who you think you are. Nobody gives you your identity here, you have to reinvent yourself every day.' He is right, I suspect, but I can't figure out how it is done. You just say what you are and everyone believes you? That seems like a confidence trick to me, and not one I think I can pull off. Still, somehow, invent myself I must. But how do I choose from identity options available all around me? I feel, once again, as I did when facing those ten brands of toothpaste — faint from excess, paralyzed by choice." (Hoffman, 1990, p. 160).

---

31 Charles Taylor talks about this in terms of a crisis of identity in Taylor, 1992.

The anxiety here is not caused by choice alone, but by the contingency of our choosing. How do we decide what to stand for? Is there one brand of toothpaste that is the correct one for *me* to buy? Recognizing the contingency of our life choices suddenly puts the sheer given-ness of our place in the world under question. This is paradigmatic of the immigrant's experience — the person who is caught between the given-ness of a past and the uncertainty of a new future. They see themselves from the outside doing work that is often alien to their training and self-image, and they see themselves as they are perceived by others, "the stranger."

> "All immigrants and exiles know the peculiar restlessness of an imagination that can never again have faith in its own absoluteness. 'Only exiles are truly irreligious,' a contemporary philosopher has said. Because I have learned the relativity of cultural meanings on my skin, I can never take any one set of meanings as final. I doubt that I'll ever become an ideologue of any stripe… I know to what extent I'm a script. In my public, group life, I'll probably always find myself in the chinks between cultures and subcultures, between the scenarios of political beliefs and aesthetic credos. It is not the worst place to live; it gives you an Archimedean leverage from which to see the world." (Ibid, p. 275).

While the immigrant may stare contingency directly in the face, minority experience has the potential to develop in the individual a similar consciousness; a sense of living between two worlds that rejects a portrayal of any one culture as "absolute". This is the situation which describes much of Diaspora Jewish life today.[32] We live, mostly successfully, between a national culture and a Jewish culture — at home in, but differently oriented by, each one.[33]

In thinking about what it means to deal with contingency and plurality there has been a resurgent interest in the role of *imagination* and *imagining* in judgment. Imagining an alternate future for myself challenges the immutability of who I am now. Judging between multiple possibilities requires of us the capacity to project consequences, construct futures, engage in hypothetical reasoning ("what iffing.") Such exploration does not merely involve carrying out a cost/value analysis of likely outcomes,

---

32 The term Diaspora has entered into general discourse to characterize just this sort of hybrid cultural identity. The African diaspora, New European identities as "diasporian identities," etc.

33 And indeed we may experience this between Jewish cultures also — as in the case of Elisheva whom I quoted earlier.

but takes us into the world created by our choices in all their imagined complexity in order to understand what they would mean — for only then can we judge them as a whole and choose with responsibility between the possibilities that lie before us (for instance, only then can we ask ourselves whether this possibility constitutes a version of the good life, or whether this is a possibility *I* want to realize).[34]

Here the connection between commitment and action is important. Commitment is the stance taken by an agent — by someone who acts in the world. We would not normally consider someone to be committed to something — let's say justice or mitzvot– unless that value found some form of expression in the way they chose to live their life. As educators, the challenge we face is to make sense of the meaning of commitment in light of our awareness of plurality and contingency. If "who I am" is constantly revisited and left open to revision, if I see myself in terms of conflicting narratives and multiple possibilities, what does it mean for me to stand *for* something; to live my life (act in the world) in a committed way?

Educating for commitment in the face of such contingency requires that we avoid the polarization between descriptive and normative education. Recognizing plurality, we need to describe multiple possibilities for our students in a non-coercive way, but educating for commitment means that we present these possibilities in order to engage students with the further question "what ought *I* do?" For Isaiah Berlin, as for Joseph Schumpeter whom he quotes in this regard, developing commitment in the face of such contingency is: "to realize the relative validity of one's convictions and yet stand for them unflinchingly." (Berlin, 1969, p. 134). This means that developing commitment in the face of contingency requires us to develop an ironic sensibility; a sensibility that emerges out of juxtaposing that which *we actively choose for ourselves* with the *awareness of possibilities not pursued*.

Such a stance does not only have a reflexive dimension, but also a social, or communal, one; what *I* ought to do will not necessarily have direct correspondence to what *we* ought to be doing. If we accept the inter-relationality of human flourishing, then educating for commitment as a member of a community will mean educating students to respond to the question "what ought I do?" from the social point of view; that is, from a consideration of what I, *as a member of this community*, ought to do. Preserving the idea of individual autonomy, membership will not dictate

34 This has been described as embracing a responsibilist epistemology and ethic.

what I choose, but my autonomous choice will be made in light of my consideration of the community as a whole (consideration of its demands on me, of its needs and my place within it, etc.) Structurally, this means my response will emerge out of the juxtaposition of my own interests as interests situated amidst the community's interests. This involves an ability to imaginatively see our choices and our commitments within a larger frame of possibilities and interests. This kind of stance is what Richard Rorty describes as the stance of the liberal ironist who determines action according to an assessment of common purposes, but does so "against a background of an increasing sense of the radical diversity of private purposes, of the radically poetic character of individual lives." (Rorty, 1989, p. 67).

In summary we might say that the capacity to choose an orientation for ourselves in the face of plurality and contingency is strengthened or deepened as we come to (i) construct a narrative that enables us to make sense of who we are over time — to interpret the past and the prospective future in light of the present, and (ii) appreciate what is implied by the range of our commitments and possibilities at a time (e.g., where they are in tension with one another and where they reinforce one another). This kind of engagement places the capacity to engage in reasoned judgment high on the educational agenda. Such judgment requires that we are able to think from the social, or communal point of view and arrive at judgments that both (i) take into account others in all their particularity and difference from ourselves, and (ii) take into account multiple contingencies. The hermeneutics of such imaginative engagement has been described as 'visiting.'[35] In contrast to touring (where we take an observer's interest in others — other people, cultures, classrooms) and engrossment (where we seek to lose ourselves and experience another's experience as if we were them), visiting requires that we enter into an imaginary landscape, yet judge what we encounter there as ourselves. The paradigm of this kind of imagining is reading or storytelling — and it is no surprise that experiencing other's narratives (whether orally or through literature) and engaging in the imaginative playing out of possibilities (a rich playing out that sees consequences in all their complexity) are seen as excellent ways to nurture and develop the imaginative capacity needed for such judgment.

---

35 Hannah Arendt (1971) uses the term "visiting" (judgment requires letting your imagination go visiting — Book three of *The Life of the Mind*; Martha Nussbaum (1995) speaks of it as *Judicial Spectatorship* in *Poetic Justice*.) David Wong speaks of the process of imagining others "centrally" as a feature of children's development in Wong, 1998 (and here he refers to the work of child psychologist Melanie Klein).

Conclusion

Perhaps one of the biggest challenges posed by contemporary sensibilities are the challenge they pose regarding the way we re-imagine Jewish community The development of meaningful Jewish identity and the possibility for rich engagement in Jewish life emerge out of the relationships we play out within the context of the communities of which we are part. Speaking of the challenge this poses for the transformation of Reform Synagogues into learning communities, Jonathan Woocher puts it thus:

> "The key question from the standpoint of Jewish continuity is whether nontraditional Jews can be brought to see that their personal stories are connected to traditional and historical Jewish narratives ('master stories') and to a living community that tells and enacts these stories and then made to view these narratives as norm-giving.... The Jewish community must struggle with how to enact its master stories — how to realize and call attention to the behavioural implications implicit in them." (Woocher, 1995, pp. 27–28).

While much of this article has focused on participation in hermeneutic activity (self-construction, narrative, engagement with text), I also suggested that this cognitive engagement is intimately bound up with the world of action — a world we share with others. This connection between deliberation and action is captured in our understanding of participatory citizenship. In general education the democratic school movement and civic education are developing models of education for participatory citizenship which are driven by a concern for the flourishing of the *polis* as well as the flourishing of individuals. The implication for Jewish education is a strong one here — for it suggests the need for establishing Jewish educational environments that are not only inter-relational, and participatory, but ones that are integrated into (and build meaningful bridges between) the larger Jewish and civic communities of which are part. Indeed I would suggest that the area of citizenship education offers Jewish educators a rich literature to explore questions of engagement and commitment within the context of a contemporary social/communal imagination.[36]

36 Larry Cuban goes some way toward this in re-envisaging in Cuban, 1995. See in particular his description of a "mini-community" on p.133.

In the opening of this article I suggested that turning outward to explore the wider milieu might illuminate some of the contemporary sensibilities that are shaping the context in which much of Jewish education is taking place. While not entering Jewish education from Jewish thought, these sensibilities nevertheless give shape to the language and conceptual frame through which we interpret and understand Jewish educational theory and practice. Here I pointed to four such sensibilities: our awareness of indwelling; our reflexive sense of identity; our turn to narrative; and our awareness of plurality and contingency. In the case of in-dwelling, the trajectory for exploring the "fit" between contemporary sensibilities and Jewish education was mainly conceptual, following the turn in western culture away from enlightenment commitments toward a recognition of situatedness, and with it a recognition of the centrality of language, narrative, and text. In the case of the narrative self, the trajectory was by way of our phenomenological sense of who we are, and can be seen as part of the general turn toward self and narrative in contemporary culture. In the case of plurality and contingency, the trajectory was by way of presenting problems — challenges being taken up and explored within both western and Jewish contemporary theory concerning the internalisation of plurality, the contingency of identity, the challenge of preparing our students to negotiate this plurality, and the challenge of educating for commitment in the face of contingency.

In the introduction to this paper I also mentioned that while I can only touch lightly on these topics here and on their importance for Jewish education, I hoped that some of the positive challenges and difficulties I see this shift in sensibilities offering for the field of Jewish education would become apparent. In this I hope I have been successful.

References

Arendt, Hannah. (1971, 1978 edition). *The Life of the mind.* In Mary McCarthy. (Ed.). one-volume edition. New York, Harcourt Brace Jovanovich.

Aron, Isa and Schuster, Diane, (1998). Extending the Chain of Tradition: Reflections on the goal of adult text study. *Journal of Jewish Education 64 (1&2).* Winter/Spring.

Aron, Isa, Lee, Sara and Rossel, Seymour. (Eds.). (1995). *A congregation of learners: Transforming the synagogue into a learning community.* New York, UAHC Press.

Benhabib, Seyla. (1992). *Situating the self.* Cambridge U.K., Polity Press.

Berlin, Isaiah. (1969). *Four essays on liberty.* Oxford, Oxford University Press.

Boyd, Jonathan. (Ed.) (2003). *The sovereign and situated self.* London, UJIA.

Bruns, Gerald. (1992). *Hermeneutics ancient and modern.* Michigan, Yale University Press.

Buber, Martin. 1947, 1979 edition: *Between man and man,* Glasgow, Collins.

Buber, Martin. (1937, 1975 edition). *I and Thou,* Edinburgh, T. and T. Clark.

Chazan, Barry. (2003). Educating our children: Imagining the Jewish Day School of the future. In Jonathan Boyd. (Ed.). *The sovereign and situated self.* London, UJIA.

Cohen, Steven and Eisen, Arnold. (2000). *The Jew within; Self, family and community in America.* Bloomington and Indianapolis, Indiana University Press.

Cuban, Larry. (1995). Changing Public Schools and changing Congregational Schools. In Isa Aron, Sara Lee and Seymour Rossel. (Eds.). *A congregation of learners: Transforming the synagogue into a learning community.* New York, UAHC Press.

Diller, Ann. (1992). What happens when an ethics of care faces pluralism? In Clark Power and Daniel Lapsley. (Eds.). *The challenge of pluralism: Education, politics and values.* Indiana, University of Notre Dame Press.

Douglas-Klotz, Neil. (1999). Midrash and postmodern inquiry: Suggestions toward a hermeneutics of indeterminacy. *Currents in Research: Biblical Studies, 7.* Sheffield, Sheffield Academic Press.

Eisen, Arnold. (1996). *Taking hold of Torah.* Bloomington, Indiana University Press.

Gaita, Raimond. (1981). Integrity. *Proceedings of the Aristotelian Society.* Bristol, Element Books.

Gribbin, John. (1987). *In search of the big bang,* London, Corgi Books.

Halbertal, Moshe and Hartman Halbertal, Tova. (1998). The Yeshiva. In Amelia Rorty. (Ed.), *Philosophers on Education.* London, Routledge.

Heilman, Samuel. (1998). Building Jewish identity for tomorrow. In Ernest Krausz and Gitta Tulea. (Eds.). *Jewish survival: The identity problem at the close of the twentieth century.* New Jersey, Transaction Publishers.

Hoffman, Eva. (1989, 1990 edition) *Lost in translation.* New York, Penguin.

Horowitz, Bethamie. (2000/2003 revised edition). Connections and journeys: Assessing critical opportunities for enhancing Jewish identity. New York, UJIA-Federation of Jewish Philanthropies.

Idel, Moshe. (1993). Midrashic versus other forms of Jewish hermeneutics: Some comparative reflections. In Michael Fishbane. (Ed.). *The midrashic imagination.* Albany, SUNY Press.

Kepnes, Steven. (Ed.). (1996). *Interpreting Judaism in the postmodern age.* New York, NYU Press.

Kimball, Stephanie and Garrison, Jim. (1996). Hermeneutic listening: An approach to multicultural conversations. In *Studies in Philosophy and Education 15 (1–2).*

Kirschenblatt-Gimblett, Barbara. (2000). Learning from ethnography: Reflections on the nature and efficacy of youth tours to Israel. In Barry Chazan. (Ed.). *The Israel Experience: Studies in Jewish identity and youth culture,* Keren Karev publication.

Landes, Daniel. (Jan. 2000). *Pardes: Postmodern Paradigm/Midrash.* Jerusalem, Pardes Institute.

MacIntyre, Alasdair. (1987) *After virtue.* London, Duckworth.

McAdams, Dan. (1997). The case for unity in the (Post) Modern self. In Richard

Ashmore and Lee Jussim. (Eds.) *Self and identity*. New York, Oxford University Press.

Nicholls, Jacqueline. (2003). Case study 2: Limmud. In Jonathan Boyd. (Ed.), *The sovereign and the situated self*. London, UJIA publication.

Nussbaum, Martha. (1995). *Poetic Justice*. Boston, Beacon Press.

Ochs, Peter. (1988). Monological definitions. In Steven Kepnes, Peter Ochs and Robert Gibbs. (Eds.). *Reasoning after Revelation: Dialogues in postmodern Jewish philosophy*. Colorado, Westview Press.

O'Loughlin, Marjorie. (1998). Paying attention to bodies in education: Theoretical resources and practical suggestions. *Educational Philosophy and Theory 30 (3)*.

Perkins, David. (1999). The many faces of constructivism. *Educational Leadership 57 (3)*.

Putnam, Hilary. (1983). *Realism and reason*. Cambridge, Cambridge University Press.

Ricoeur, Paul. (1995). *Figuring the Sacred*. Minneapolis, Fortress Press.

Rogoff, Barbara. (2003). *The cultural nature of human development*. New York, Oxford University Press.

Rorty, Richard. (1989). *Contingency, irony and solidarity*. New York, Cambridge University Press.

Sacks, Jonathan. (1997). Love, hate, and Jewish identity. *First Things: Journal of Religion and Public Life 77*. (Nov.) web edition http://www.firstthings.com/ftissues/ft9711/articles/sacks.html

Schwab, Joseph. (1980). Translating scholarship into curriculum. In S. Fox. (Ed.). *From the scholar to the classroom*. New York, JTS Press.

Shusterman, Richard. (1993). Next year in Jerusalem: Postmodern Jewish identity and the myth of return. In David Goldberg and Michael Krausz. (Eds.) *Jewish identity*. Philadelphia, Temple University Press.

Soloveitchik, Haym. (1994). Rupture and redemption: The transformation of contemporary Orthodoxy. *Tradition*. (Summer).

Stinson, Susan. (1995). Body of knowledge. *Educational Theory 45 (1)*. (Winter).

Stone, Lynda. (1993/4). Modern to Postmodern: Social construction, dissonance and education. *Studies in Philosophy and Education 13 (1)*.

Tamir, Yael. (1996). The quest for identity. *Studies in Philosophy and Education 15*.

Taylor, Charles. (1992). *Sources of the self: The making of modern identity*. Cambridge Mass., Harvard University Press.

Wong, David. (1988). On flourishing and finding one's identity in community. *Midwest Studies in Philosophy 13*.

Woocher, Jonathan. (1995). Toward a "Unified Field Theory" of Jewish continuity. In Isa Aron, Sara Lee, and Seymour Rossel. (Eds.): *A congregation of learners: Transforming the synagogue into a learning community*. New York, UAHC Press.

On the Corruption of Jewish Education by Philosophy

Eli Gottlieb

It is a great honor to contribute to this volume celebrating Professor Fox and the Mandel School. Both have contributed immeasurably to my development as a student and practitioner of Jewish education. Indeed, this paper has its origins in one of my first conversations with Professor Fox. After listening to me talk about my interests in developmental psychology, philosophy, and Jewish education, Professor Fox suggested I read an article by his mentor, the late Joseph Schwab. Given the article's title — "On the corruption of education by psychology" — I took the suggestion as a not-too-subtle hint that some of my assumptions about the relations between education and psychology needed re-examining. If indeed such a hint was intended, he was right: They did.

In this chapter, I examine the relations between psychologies and philosophies of education in general, and between psychologies and philosophies of Jewish education in particular. I argue that just as education may be corrupted by psychology, so too may it be corrupted by philosophy. I show, citing examples from scholarship in the philosophy of Jewish education, that in deriving educational conclusions from philosophical analyses and reflections, philosophers of education import numerous questionable or distorted psychological assumptions. I argue that, in turn, these imported distortions lead to inadequate or one-sided characterizations of educational goals. I conclude by suggesting ways in which such distortions might be minimized. In short, here is my reply to Professors Schwab and Fox.

The philosophical presuppositions of psychologies of education

As Schwab taught us, there are no philosophically neutral educational psychologies (Schwab, 1958). Every psychological theory contains, either explicitly or implicitly, some conception of what it is to be a healthy, mature, well-adapted human being. This normative dimension is most blatant in the field of "pure" developmental psychology, where contrasts between the well-developed human being and the incompletely or inadequately developed one are generally explicit. In educational psychology (i.e., developmental psychology applied to educational problems and practices), however, it is sometimes less obvious. Not only educational practitioners, but also educational psychologists, tend to view theories of educational psychology as being concerned with the means of education, but not with its ends. Thus, having identified some educational goal (point B), they turn to educational psychology to provide them first with a reliable description of where their students are prior to instruction (point A) and then to suggest appropriate methods for bringing them to this desired endpoint (how to get from point A to point B). In doing so, they do not consider that the psychological theories themselves may contain, by design or by default, an implicit characterization of what point B ought to be.

Schwab's important contribution is to show in detail how various psychological theories, when applied to education, import premises about the ends of education that are unexamined, unsupported by empirical data, and often in conflict with the stated goals of the educators who employ them. In Schwab's examples, they do this by focusing one-sidedly on a particular aspect of human development and subordinating or ignoring all others. The net effect of such subordination is to produce psychological theories that are, at best, half-truths, and which lead in turn to the tacit legitimation of educational goals and practices that are similarly lopsided.

The examples Schwab cites are Freudianism, group dynamism, non-directivism and autonomism. Though Schwab's characterization of each of these educational psychologies is somewhat impressionistic, the broad theoretical trends he describes are not only recognizable, but still very much with us. These trends correspond more or less to contemporary psychodynamic, socio-cultural, and "child-centered" psychologies of education. Schwab shows that, by subordinating intellectual aspects of human psychology to emotional, social or motivational aspects, each of these theories is used to legitimate educational goals wherein intellectual achievement, scientific investigation, artistic creativity, and the pursuit of truth are either relegated to secondary priorities or absent altogether.

Schwab is careful to distinguish between psychological theories as formulated and defended in the field of psychological scholarship and the "same" theories as transformed into doctrines of instruction. Indeed, he seems keen to emphasize that the focus of his critique is less the psychological theories themselves than their translation into guiding principles for education. Nonetheless, the major thrust of Schwab's critique would appear to apply to psychological theories as such, and not just to the particular psychologies of education he mentions by name. There is no reason to expect that a "unified field theory" of human psychology will prove any less elusive than a unified field theory in physics. Accordingly, no psychological theory is ever likely to satisfy Schwab's desire for accounts of human development that are more than half-truths. Indeed, as Schwab notes elsewhere (for example, Schwab, 1971), psychological theories, compared with theories in other areas of the behavioral and natural sciences, are especially prone to partiality and distortion, on account of the unrivalled complexity and diversity of their subject matter. Moreover, as Schwab's student, Professor Fox demonstrated with respect to Freud, even psychological doctrines that are not explicitly educational in intent can turn out on closer inspection to entail complex networks of assumptions and proposals regarding both the ends and the means of education (Fox, 1975). This suggests that no psychological theory, however well supported and argued, would be able to withstand Schwab's accusation that it entails unjustified presuppositions about the desired endpoints of education.

It is interesting, therefore, that a mere decade and a half after Schwab's critique was published, an article appeared in the *Harvard Educational Review* which argued not only that such a psychological theory existed, but that it provided the only defensible rationale for preferring one set of educational objectives over any other. Even more interestingly, the authors based this claim on a Deweyian line of argument strikingly similar to Schwab's (see Dewey, 1902; Dewey, 1956). The article in question was Kohlberg and Mayer's (1972), "Development as the aim of education."

The psychological presuppositions of philosophies of education

Kohlberg and Mayer's essay makes no reference to Schwab's earlier article. Indeed, on the surface, the two papers address parallel but quite distinct problems. Whereas Schwab set out to demonstrate that there are no philosophically neutral educational psychologies, Kohlberg and Mayer set out to demonstrate that there are no psychologically neutral educational philosophies. However, as we shall see, the two papers paint remarkably similar pictures of the relations between philosophies and psychologies of education.

Kohlberg and Mayer's essay seeks to address what the authors describe as the most important issue confronting educators and educational theorists, namely, the rational selection of ends for the educational process. They begin by pointing out that a rational strategy for defining educational objectives must be not only philosophically coherent, but also consistent with empirical findings regarding the nature of learning. They identify three prevalent strategies for defining educational objectives — the "bag of virtues" strategy, the "industrial psychology" strategy, and the "developmental-philosophic" strategy — and argue that only the last of these strategies provides a rationale for defining objectives that is both philosophically sound and empirically valid.

In support of this conclusion, Kohlberg and Mayer present analyses of the psychological and philosophical assumptions of each strategy. The "bag of virtues" strategy defines the ends of education in terms of a set of traits considered to characterize the mature, healthy personality. This conception of the healthy personality is shown to rest on a romantic view of man as having a natural, inner self and on the maturationist assumption that this self can develop only at its own pace and along its own course. These philosophical and psychological assumptions are shown to be associated in turn with an existentialist epistemology in which knowledge is identified with self-insight and with a moral outlook in which the ultimate values are self-actualization and spontaneity.

In contrast with this subjectivist perspective, the "industrial psychology" strategy identifies the ends of education with the internalization of the objective standards of knowledge and behavior required for effective functioning within a given system. Kohlberg and Mayer show this strategy to rest on an equation of education with the transmission of cultural givens and on an associationist psychology in which development is viewed as the exclusive product of environmental conditioning. These philosophical and psychological assumptions are shown to be associated in turn with a positivistic epistemology in which knowledge is identified with that which can be experienced by the senses and objectively measured and tested, and on a relativistic moral outlook in which what is good or bad varies arbitrarily from society to society.

Finally, the "developmental-philosophic" strategy defines the ends of education as the attainment of higher levels of development. This strategy is shown to rest on the equation of education with the promotion of growth in a person's ability to solve the problems that arise in his or her interactions with the environment. Underlying this pragmatic philosophy of education is an interactionist psychology that views development as being driven neither by the unfolding of an innate sequence of predetermined patterns (as in maturationism) nor by the internalization of patterns observed in the outside world (as in associationism), but by transformations in the individual's own initial patterns for structuring their experience as they apply them to novel problems or situations. These philosophical and psychological assumptions are shown to be associated in turn with a functionalist epistemology that equates knowledge neither with inner experience nor with outer reality but with a coordinated relationship between an inquiring human actor and a problematic situation. Finally, whereas both the "bag of virtues" and "industrial psychology" strategies are shown to rest ultimately on forms of moral relativism, the "developmental-philosophic" strategy is shown to rest on a moral outlook in which goodness and badness are defined in terms of universal moral principles.

Kohlberg and Mayer go on to argue at length against the philosophical coherence and empirical validity of the assumptions underlying the "bag of virtues" and "industrial psychology" strategies and in support of those underlying the "developmental-philosophic" strategy. Their approach is to show that only a neo-Piagetian interactionist account of cognitive development provides a clear factual basis for characterizing objectively what is meant by mature thinking, deciding and acting, and thus that any philosophy of education that rests on psychological assumptions other than those of neo-Piagetian interactionism is ultimately baseless. However, the specific details of Kohlberg and Mayer's arguments need not detain us here. For, whatever we may think of their attempts here and elsewhere to crown cognitive-developmental psychology as queen of the educational sciences (see also Kohlberg, 1971), we cannot ignore the importance of their analysis for how we understand the relations between philosophies and psychologies of education in general. What Kohlberg and Mayer demonstrate most convincingly in their essay is how "merely" strategic choices and "purely" philosophical arguments regarding the selection of educational goals can turn out to entail or rest upon wide-ranging (and often unjustified) assumptions about matters of psychological fact.

The interdependence of psychologies and philosophies of education

Thus, ironically, both Schwab's critique and Kohlberg and Mayer's glorification of educational psychology appear to derive ultimately from very similar views about the relations between psychologies and philosophies of education. They are all in agreement that philosophies and psychologies of education are inextricably intertwined and implicated one in the other. Where they diverge is in their assessments of what such interdependence entails for educational deliberation.

For Schwab, this interdependence is primarily an obstacle to sound educational decision-making. Writing in the late 1950s, when the cognitive revolution in American psychology had yet to take root (see Bruner, 1983; Gardner, 1985), and when behaviorist, social-psychological and psycho-dynamic theories seemed to have carved up the human mind (and the university departments that studied it) into discrete behavioral, social and emotional chunks, Schwab saw all psychological theories as irredeemably one-sided and incomplete. In particular, he decried their failure to account for the development of higher mental functions such as scientific reasoning and artistic creativity. It is this incompleteness and partiality, according to Schwab, that is ultimately responsible for the distortions that psychologies of education import into educational reflection and practice. By applying psychological theories that brush over or ignore the cognitive dimension of human development, educational practitioners and decision-makers commit themselves tacitly to educational goals that undervalue intellectual achievement. Moreover, they do this under the spell of the supposed empirical soundness of the psychological theories in question, when, in fact, the subordination of cognition to other aspects of human psychology in these theories is based not on empirical investigation, but on philosophical presuppositions about the nature of mind.

Kohlberg and Mayer were more optimistic. By the early 1970s many psychologists believed that overwhelming evidence had been accumulated showing that people's thinking — be it in the areas of science, mathematics, morality or religion — develops through an invariant sequence of hierarchically ordered structural stages (see, for example, Elkind, 1971; Kohlberg, 1968; Piaget and Inhelder, 1969). Kohlberg and Mayer thus saw developmental psychology, and neo-Piagetian stage theory in particular, as having provided, at last, an empirically sound foundation on which to base decisions about educational goals. For Kohlberg and Mayer, therefore, the interdependence of psychologies and philosophies of education was not so much a problem as a solution. For, the reliance of philosophies of education on psychological assumptions is only a problem if those psychological assumptions are unjustified. If they are not only correct but demonstrably so — as is the case, according to Kohlberg and Mayer, with those of neo-Piagetian cognitive-developmental theory — they provide sound empirical grounds on which to prefer one educational philosophy over another. In other words, far from distorting educational goals, psychology provides the tools for their rational selection.

From the vantage point of the early 21st century, Kohlberg and Mayer's optimistic claims for developmental psychology smack of premature triumphalism. The last 25 years of research have brought wave after wave of empirical and conceptual challenges to neo-Piagetian stage theories. First came attacks by philosophers on their coherence, conceptual soundness, and susceptibility to empirical investigation (for example, Phillips and Kelly, 1975). Next came methodological critiques, backed up by devastating counterevidence, of many of their key claims about age differences (for example, Gelman and Baillargeon, 1983). Then came cross-cultural studies demonstrating their inherent ethnocentrism (for example, Shweder, Mahapatra, and Miller, 1990). In this "post-Piagetian era" (Gopnik, 1996), the field of developmental psychology looks much more like the breaker's yard of competing half-truths described by Schwab than the orderly showroom of universal facts described by Kohlberg and Mayer.

However, this does not mean that Schwab was right and Kohlberg and Mayer wrong. Although the empirical basis for Kohlberg and Mayer's "developmental-philosophic" justification of Deweyian progressivism has turned out to be much weaker than it may have seemed 30 years ago, their general point about the reliance of philosophies of education on assumptions about matters of psychological fact has lost none of its pertinence. Indeed, one need only open the latest issues of the major education journals to find both Schawb's suspicions about educational psychology and Kohlberg and Mayer's suspicions about the philosophy of education amply confirmed.

The corruption of Jewish education by philosophy

In this essay I have chosen to focus on the corruption of Jewish education by philosophy rather than on its corruption by psychology. However, this is not because I consider corruption of the latter kind to be any less problematic. Indeed, as I have argued elsewhere (Gottlieb, 2002), the philosophical presuppositions of developmental psychologists in studies of religious and cultural education have been a major source of distortion, both at the level of "pure science" and at the level of educational application. Rather, it is because, in my personal experience as a participant-observer in educational deliberations amongst scholars and practitioners of Jewish education, the empirical assumptions of philosophers have been less often challenged than have the conceptual assumptions of psychologists. In other words, it seems to me that the philosophers have been getting away with more for longer.

The sources of this imbalance are an interesting topic in their own right. One likely source is the sheer numeric advantage of philosophers of Jewish education over psychologists of Jewish education. (Indeed, this quantitative imbalance is, in itself, a phenomenon worthy of further investigation.) However, an equally important and perhaps related source is a deeply embedded institutional bias within key venues of Jewish educational scholarship towards abstract discussion of first principles, subject-matter, and general educational goals, as opposed to discussion of more concrete issues of child and adult learning. Indeed, it sometimes seems as if, in heeding Professor Fox's eloquent calls to place vision at the heart of Jewish education (for example, Fox, 1997), we have overcompensated, replacing myopia with hyperopia. It is in order to help redress this imbalance that I offer the following view of philosophy of Jewish education as seen through the convex eyeglasses of an educational psychologist.

Schwab as a philosopher of Jewish education

Schwab's major research interests were science and liberal education (see Westbury and Wilkof, 1978). However, at Professor Fox's urging, he became an active participant on the advisory committees and academic boards of a number of important programs of Jewish education, including the Melton Research Center at the Jewish Theological Seminary and Camp Ramah. In the course of his advisory work, Schwab was asked, together with a group of other experts, to respond to a question put to them by a group of educators and lay leaders about Jewish day schools in Philadelphia. The question was, "How shall we educate our children so that they will be committed to Jewish tradition and practices and yet encourage their intellectual curiosity and desire to question?" Schwab's written response to the question was published in the journal, *Conservative*

Judaism in 1964 as, "The religiously oriented school in the United States: a memorandum on policy."

As Professor Fox remarks in his preface to the article (Schwab, 1964, p. 1), the memorandum contains more than a suggestion for the specific day school problem: it provides an analysis of the problem of how to educate for commitment and openness in modern societies more generally. Thus, although the paper is "only" a memorandum, and although Schwab never saw himself as a philosopher of Jewish education, it seems appropriate to examine the underlying philosophical and psychological assumptions in terms of which Schwab's response is framed. For, as Schwab himself taught us, it is precisely in his relatively unguarded *practical* deliberations that a scholar's implicit theoretical assumptions are most apt to be revealed (see, for example, Schwab, 1971).

As Schwab notes at the outset, his analysis and policy recommendations rest on the assumption that the successful realization of religiously oriented life in modern, western society requires the union of two distinct styles of life and ways of meeting problems. Schwab first describes each of these styles and outlines in broad brushstrokes the kinds of education that will prepare for them. He then goes on to suggest ways in which these two components might be combined in an effective day school curriculum.

The first style or way of approaching problems is that of tradition. In traditional societies population size, social structures, loyalties, commitments and values are relatively stable from generation to generation. In such societies the difficulties facing each generation are similar to those that faced preceding ones. Accordingly, tradition-sanctioned knowledge and skills provide adequate ways of addressing the major concerns and problems of everyday life. According to Schwab (1964, p. 5), "education in such a society must mainly ingrain, habituate or internalize a definite body of material, moral, and emotional content. Originality and the questioning of tradition are vices except in the rarest of circumstances."

The second style or way of approaching problems is that of rational enquiry. In modern societies, demographic distributions, social structures, loyalties, commitments and values are subject to continuous change and bombardment from alien influences. In such societies, successive generations face radically different problems to those faced by their forebears. Accordingly, not only are tradition-sanctioned knowledge and skills inadequate to address these problems, but the character of knowledge itself is transformed, becoming less absolute and more susceptible to revision. In order to function effectively in such a society, children need to be taught to how to cope with change and to be at ease amongst the uncertainties of knowledge. This requires that they learn how to conduct independent and self-directed study, that they develop respect for and practice in the judicious use and evaluation of evidence, argument and interpretation, and that they be provided with opportunities to practice making and evaluating choices when no ready made answers are available.

Schwab argues that, whilst children in modern, western societies are undoubtedly in need of education in the latter style, a complete rejection of tradition brings in its wake serious social ills. Specifically, children raised without the benefit of some kind of tradition-oriented education are apt to be "rootless" in that they have no sense of historical continuity with preceding generations, no sense of membership in a group of peers with whom they share inherited values and customs, and no sense of having a part to play in the lives of the adult representatives of their community. In order to provide children with "roots and anchors for a modern society" (ibid., p. 7), a curriculum would need, therefore, to include, among other things, the teaching of lineal language and literature, the imparting of a sense of community through group history, daily actions in which children and adults have reciprocal goals, and collaborations with peers.

Schwab divides his practical recommendations for an integrated "roots" and rational enquiry curriculum into two sections, one covering elementary school, and the other secondary school. He prefaces his recommendations in each section with a brief sketch of the psychological needs, abilities and motivations of pupils at each type of school. According to these characterizations, children in the first ten to 12 years of life need routine and structure in their daily lives, secure relationships with one or more significant adults, as well as opportunities for success, mastery of the environment, and the expression of aggression. In addition, they can be encouraged under favorable conditions to engage in "exploratory, questioning behavior" (ibid., p. 10). Around the ages of 11 to 13, children experiment with selfhood, the outcome of such experiments determining the extent to which they will eventually become fully adult. They question what they have learned, reject control by significant adults, try and exert control on people and things by their own actions, and "put on" different personalities by imitating the mannerisms and behaviors of adults they have seen or read about.

Based on these characterizations and on his earlier discussion of the goals of a curriculum integrating roots and rational enquiry, Schwab sets out practical recommendations for both elementary and secondary schools. For elementary schools he recommends that there should be one home-room teacher per class, rather than many, and that learning activities should follow a regular rhythm, but avoid rigid timetabling and include frequent free periods. The timetabling of mastery in each subject area should also be flexible, so that it remains coordinated with the developmental tempo of each individual pupil. The curriculum itself should comprise of two components: tradition-centered activities, such as the learning of ritual, Jewish-cultural literature and participation in prayer, and secular activities, such as reading, arithmetic and geography (ibid., p. 11). However, these two components are to be treated quite differently. The tradition-centered activities are to be "*participated in* by the child as a privileged sharing in the adult world, not queried or 'whyed'" (ibid., Schwab's emphasis). The secular activities, however, "should not share in the not-queried, un-"whyed" treatment of tradition-centered activities. On the contrary, every effort should be made to develop materials and methods of instruction which favor acts of discovery, experimentation, self-teaching, and other active contributions of the child to the materials being learned" (ibid., p. 12).

Schwab's recommendations for the secondary school differ from those for the elementary school in two major respects. First, he recommends that, in general, the secondary school years should be years of adventure in learning, with an increased focus on rational enquiry and self-directed study. Second, he recommends that, in contrast to the elementary school years, this focus on rational enquiry should extend also to the tradition-centered component of the curriculum. Specifically, whilst tradition-centered activities should continue as shared practices, they should now become, in addition, subjects of questioning, exploration, and independent study. In addition to these two key shifts in focus in the move from the elementary to the secondary school, Schwab recommends that secondary pupils be exposed to multiple positive role models in order to help them put on different personalities and identities, and that they be given as many opportunities as possible for independent study so that they can gain experience in defining their own goals and methods of inquiry and in making independent judgments. He notes also that special care must be taken in the transitional years of seventh and eighth grade to allow for individual handling of pupils, since some may reach the stage of "testing" earlier than others.

Schwab's psychological assumptions

One can take issue with Schwab's psychological assumptions, and with his derivation therefrom of educational recommendations, on several levels. First, they are one-sided, focusing almost entirely on emotional and psychosocial development, while ignoring relevant findings and theory in the field of cognitive development (for example, Bruner, 1960; Bruner, Goodnow, and Austin, 1956; Piaget, 1929; Piaget, 1930; Piaget, 1952; Piaget, 1954; Vygotsky, 1962). Such one-sidedness is particularly ironic, given Schwab's earlier critique of one-sided psychologies of education (see Schwab, 1958). Second, even more so today than when Schwab wrote the memorandum, they are of highly questionable empirical validity. Though Schwab does not cite him explicitly, most of the psychological assumptions in the memorandum appear to derive from Erik Erikson's theories of psychosocial development (for example, Erikson, 1963). Erikson's theories, though highly suggestive, have scant basis in empirical research. The area of Erikson's work best supported by empirical data is his account of identity development in adolescence (Erikson, 1963; Erikson, 1968). However, most of this empirical research was not conducted until several years after Schwab wrote the memorandum (Marcia, 1966; Marcia, 1980). Moreover, this empirical research has since been subjected to significant criticism, with recent studies challenging the entire notion of a unitary direction of healthy identity development (for example, Gergen, 1991; Schachter, 2000). Regardless of whether or not we ultimately accept these critiques, their very existence demonstrates that assumptions Schwab accepted as given are actually the objects of significant controversy and debate. Third, many of Schwab's psychological statements are so broadly formulated as to verge on the banal, resulting in recommendations that are almost entirely devoid of content. For example, on the basis of the assumed psychological need of young children for routine and structure on one hand, and opportunities to gain mastery of the environment and express aggression on the other, Schwab recommends that the daily schedule of the elementary school follow a regular rhythm of learning activities interspersed with free periods for relaxation. This tells us nothing at all about the kind, length, number, content, structure or order of the learning activities, nor about whether or how they might differ from grade to grade. Of course, Schwab cannot be expected to tell us all this in the space of a short memorandum. Indeed, Schwab may well have considered such details inappropriate in a deliberation of the "quasi-practical" kind with which he is concerned in this article (see Schwab, 1969). But one cannot help wondering what exactly he has told us that we would not have been able to work out without the benefit of his prefatory analysis.

All of the above gripes relate to Schwab's uses of psychology. However, such criticisms are ultimately peripheral to the central concern of this essay. My aim is not to criticize philosophers of education for being clumsy or undiscerning educational psychologists. Rather, it is to show how their philosophical analyses *themselves* import into educational deliberations implicit and unjustified psychological assumptions. And in this respect Schwab is an exemplary case.

Schwab's recommendations for a two-component curriculum are based on a conceptual analysis of modern religiosity, which views it as an integration of two distinct styles of life. His approach is to describe two idealized forms of society, and to abstract from each its underlying epistemological and educational foundations. He then goes on to argue that if various social ills are to be avoided, these two styles must be combined. His curriculum recommendations are then presented as an example of how the two styles can be combined in the context of American Judaism. At no point in this analysis does Schwab provide any evidence that these two styles are represented in people's minds as distinct functional domains, each with their own unique modes and methods of inquiry and judgment. Indeed, he does not address at all the questions of what the relations are between these styles within individual lives, or of how children and adolescents actually think about religious and other matters. Yet, in moving from conceptual analysis to curricular recommendations, Schwab translates the tradition-enquiry dichotomy from a hypothetical abstraction into a psychological given.

Unfortunately for Schwab, such translation is not only logically unwarranted, but also empirically unjustified. As my own studies have shown, contemporary children and adolescents view the religious domain, like other domains of "enquiry," as one in which beliefs must to be coordinated with evidence, arguments and interpretations critically evaluated, and choices made when no ready made answers are available (Gottlieb, 2002). In other words, Schwab's dichotomy is, from a psychological perspective, a false one.

Psychology and indoctrination

Similar fallacies of translation infect many other philosophical discussions of Jewish education. However, rather than belabor the point, I will restrict myself to just one more example before moving on to consider what we can do to minimize such corruption. The example I have chosen is the indoctrination debate.

My argument in this essay is that there is a general tendency amongst philosophers of Jewish education to import unjustified psychological assumptions into their deliberations. It is essential, therefore, that my critique not be misconstrued as an *ad hominem* attack on Schwab. After all, some might argue, Schwab never considered himself a philosopher of Jewish education and is far from representative of scholarship in this field. If I am to defend myself against this easy rebuttal, I must provide examples of similar fallacies of translation in more mainstream instances of Jewish educational philosophizing. The indoctrination debate is an especially rich source of such examples. For, in addition to being a topic hotly disputed beyond the four cubits of Jewish educational scholarship (see, for example, Callan, 1988; Gardner, 1991; McLaughlin, 1984), it is one about which prominent philosophers of Jewish education have expressed conflicting points of view. It thus provides a unique window onto the kinds of assumptions philosophers of Jewish education share, even when they disagree amongst themselves.

My discussion will focus on three articles, one from each of the last three decades. The first is Barry Chazan's (1978) "Indoctrination and religious education," — one of the first systematic attempts to examine the relationship between Jewish education and indoctrination. The second is Michael Rosenak's (1983) "Jewish religious education and indoc-trination," which includes both a critique of Chazan's approach and a presentation of Rosenak's own perspective. The third is Hanan Alexander's (1992) "Recent trends in the philosophy of Jewish education: Chazan, Rosenak, and beyond," which critiques both Chazan's and Rosenak's analyses. I shall argue that each of these articles contains implicit psychological assumptions, and moreover, that these assumptions are contradicted by the findings of recent empirical research.

Chazan: Rationality versus religious conviction

Chazan's (1978) essay is an exercise in analytic philosophy. It sets out first to define indoctrination, then to examine to what extent religious education fits this definition, and finally to describe what a non-indoctrinary Jewish education might look like. Chazan reviews three criteria frequently employed to distinguish between indoctrination and education, and finds each wanting. Employing an approach reminiscent of Socratic elenchus, he considers in turn the criteria of method, content and intention, and rejects each as inadequate on the basis of counterexamples which meet the criterion but which are not considered indoctrinary. He then goes on to argue that, although none of these criteria is sufficient, indoctrination can ultimately be defined in terms of particular *combinations* of methods, contents and intentions. Specifically, he defines indoctrination as "the attempt to authoritatively impose on others beliefs and beliefs systems whose acceptance really should be dependent on the agent's own free and rational acceptance" (ibid., p. 70).

Chazan considers religious beliefs to be beliefs of this kind, and therefore to be candidate contents for indoctrination. However, religious education only becomes indoctrination, "at the moment when the educator's intention is to transmit a certain religious content and rationale in such a way that the student accepts it unquestioningly and without being able to re-examine it autonomously" (ibid., pp. 71–72). In this view, non-indoctrinary Jewish education is possible so long as its intention is "to prepare the child to freely choose" (ibid., p. 73) whether to accept or reject the beliefs, values and practices in which he is being instructed.

Chazan emphasizes that the educative goal of preparing the child to freely choose is a long-term one and need not define each step in the child's instruction. As Chazan puts it:

> "This goal does not imply that the child of two, four, six, nine, fifteen, or nineteen is able, or should be forced to do all his own choosing; rather, it claims that students should be prepared for that time when they are adequately equipped to choose, and they should choose only when they are adequately equipped. The principle of reasoned autonomy must stand before the educator every day as an ideal, although it is not equivalent to his proximate objective at all stages of the educative process." (ibid., p. 75).

Chazan recognizes that this approach depends on our being able to answer the crucial empirical question of when children become able to choose. Nonetheless, he brushes this question lightly aside, consigning it to the sphere of the social sciences (ibid., p. 76). It is fairly clear, however, what Chazan's intuitions are regarding the developmental constraints on rational autonomy. His admission that the "religious educator and indoctrinator sometimes may look alike when teaching early grades," suggests that it is only in later grades that students become capable of reasoned choice.

This is not the only empirical assumption implicit in Chazan's analysis. Chazan concludes his essay by noting that his analysis rests on a belief in religion "as a world view and a way of confronting life, rather than as divinely dictated truth" (ibid.) For, according to Chazan, religious belief of the latter kind legitimizes indoctrination. As he puts it:

> "If one assumes that there is a God, who has dictated the truth, and religion represents that truth, then the authoritative transmission and inculcation of beliefs systems is legitimized because of the unquestioned value of their contents." (ibid., pp. 75–76).

Clearly, Chazan's argument here is not a conceptual one, since he has already argued that authoritative transmission of religious content is an illegitimate form of instruction. Rather, it appears to be an empirical prediction that people who believe that they are in possession of divinely revealed truths will have no qualms about employing indoctrinary means to inculcate these truths in others. This prediction rests in turn on the empirical assumption that belief in divinely revealed truths is incompatible with a respect for rational choice and reflective judgment. In other words, Chazan seems to be subscribing here to a dichotomy much like Schwab's, only sharper. Where Schwab's implicit psychology posits "religion-oriented" and "rational" modes of thought that are distinct yet compatible, Chazan's implicit psychology views these two modes of thought as mutually exclusive.

As was the case with Schwab, such assumptions are neither logically warranted nor empirically justified. Not only does Chazan provide no evidence in support of his empirical assumptions, but the assumptions themselves are contradicted by existing data. In my recent investigations of religious thinking amongst students at religious and secular schools in Israel, I found a tendency amongst the former to believe in religion as divinely dictated truth and amongst the latter to believe in religion as a worldview or lifestyle preference. However, the majority of students at both types of school sought to back up their beliefs with rational justifications, were receptive to evidence and lines of reasoning opposed to their own, and were opposed to indoctrinary forms of persuasion. Chazan's pessimism about the capacities of preadolescents to engage in rational evaluation of competing religious claims seems also to be unwarranted. Although fifth-graders in my study tended less than twelfth-graders spontaneously to take opposed points of view and lines of reasoning into account in justifying their religious beliefs, they did so with remarkable ease and epistemological sophistication when asked explicitly to do so. This suggests that reflective judgment about matters of religious belief is within the grasp of schoolchildren, even as early as fifth grade. (Gottlieb, 2002).

Rosenak: Good religion and mental health

Rosenak rejects Chazan's equation of instruction in divinely revealed truths with indoctrination. He agrees with Chazan that none of the criteria of method, content or intention is sufficient to distinguish between education and indoctrination. However, he discounts Chazan's definition of indoctrination as the combination of authoritative methods, unverifiable contents and autonomy-curtailing intentions, on the grounds that "every educational system has unverifiable principles, standards of loyalty and cultural continuity, and models of ideal personality" (Rosenak, 1983, p. 126). Instead, he argues that education succumbs to indoctrination when it becomes corrupted philosophically, culturally, or existentially.

Philosophical corruption occurs, according to Rosenak, "when principles become avenues for escape from reality rather than making sense of it, and when the ideals that flow from the principles are made synonymous with them" (ibid., p. 135). Rosenak considers such corruption to be exemplified in attempts by particular theological perspectives or interpretative traditions to monopolize Jewish faith and practice. Cultural corruption occurs when the interpretations and customs of the past are elevated to dogmas, thereby stifling cultural creativity, as for example when aggadic interpretations are transformed into "thought Halachot" (ibid.). Existential corruption occurs when conceptions of the ideal person are narrowed to exclude people with specific temperaments, to require changes in basic dispositions, to deny some aspect of human personality or to stunt psychological growth, as for example when tender-mindedness, intellectual achievement, or self-denial are prized above all other aspects of human personality and development.

This is not the place to evaluate the philosophical soundness of Rosenak's approach. Rather, as with Schwab and Chazan, I shall focus on Rosenak's psychological assumptions. The first and most obvious point to note in this regard is that each one of Rosenak's criteria for distinguishing education from indoctrination rests on an implicit (if vague) characterization of healthy human functioning. The idea that philosophical corruption occurs, "when principles become avenues for escape from reality rather than making sense of it" implies a view of the healthy, mature human being as an intellectually honest sense-maker, who embraces responsibility for her beliefs and practices rather than seeking escape in blind conformism. Rosenak's description of cultural corruption introduces a further desirable trait into this implicit psychological portrait, namely, the capacity to adapt creatively to new situations rather than rely exclusively on the received wisdom of the past. Finally, Rosenak's description of existential corruption extends his portrait to include not only particular desirable traits, but also a particular conception of how these and other traits are to be held in healthy mutual balance. Thus, for example, "[d]iscipline harnessed to what Allport has called intention-orientation" is healthy, but some other kinds of self-discipline constitute instances of "crippled self-denial" (ibid., p. 136).

Normative psychological assumptions such as these are not restricted to Rosenak's criteria for distinguishing between education and indoctrination. They can be found in more explicit form at numerous other points in the paper. Thus, he cites as desirable ends of education such psychological traits as emotional maturity, integrated personality, and self-realization (ibid., pp. 130–131). And he concludes his paper by citing with approval Guttmann's (1976, pp. 120–121) statement that:

> "Religion formulates an answer to life's questions and is linked to every sphere of existence … To the religious man, not only is religious truth the most exalted, it is also the most authoritative and absolute." (Rosenak, 1983, p. 137).

This statement too contains implicit psychological claims, suggesting that people who subscribe to religious beliefs do so in a particular way. Specifically, it implies that religious believers seek to integrate their religious beliefs into every aspect of their lives and that they subscribe to them with absolute conviction.

Given all these psychological assumptions, it is interesting that Rosenak himself appears to view his argument as purely conceptual, rather than empirical. As he states at the outset (ibid., p. 127):

> "It is not the subject of our paper to explore how men and societies become attached to given principles, develop convictions with regard to them, initiate inquiries on their basis, and are prepared to die for them, though they are not objectively verifiable."

Nonetheless, as I have shown, his analysis is laden with implicit assumptions about matters of psychological fact. Moreover, as with Schwab and Chazan, these assumptions are neither logically warranted nor empirically justified. Not only does Rosenak fail to provide us with any reasons for preferring his particular conception of psychological health to rival conceptions, but the Guttmannian psychology of religion he advocates fares badly in empirical studies of religious thinking. Religious believers vary greatly both in the subjective intensity with which they subscribe to their religious beliefs (see, for example, Leslau and Bar-Lev, 1993; Levy, Levinsohn, and Katz, 1993) and in their epistemic evaluations of the objective certainty with which these beliefs can be held (Gottlieb, 2001). Furthermore, even believers who believe with similar intensity and who share similar epistemic conceptions of religious truth may vary greatly with respect to the extent to which they wish their religious beliefs to permeate and define all areas of their lives. (See Cohen and Eisen, 2000; Gottlieb, 2002; Horowitz, 2000; Schachter, 2000).

Alexander: The new challenges of postmodernity

Alexander takes issue with both Chazan's and Rosenak's approaches to philosophy of Jewish education, and with their approaches to the indoctrination problem in particular. His objection to Chazan's analytic approach is that it fails to provide any rationale for Chazan's own stated educational goals. As Alexander puts it:

"Having made the claim that Jewish education should be a form of non-indoctrinary education which has religious, moral, and political commitants, he is obliged to tell us why it should be so. Yet, the most that Chazan's analysis will yield is that, if we agree that indoctrination is bad, Jewish educators shouldn't do it. He does not offer an adequate argument as to why Jewish educators should not indoctrinate, why what he calls confrontation does not involve indoctrination, or why there must be religious, moral, and political aspects to Jewish education." (Alexander, 1992, p. 139).

In a similar vein, Alexander criticizes Rosenak's approach for failing to justify why Rosenak's own particular set of preferred "unverifiable principles, standards of loyalty and cultural continuity, and models of ideal personality" (Rosenak, 1983, p. 126) are any better than anyone else's. More specifically, Alexander complains that:

> "[Rosenak] offers no reasons as to why these criteria are preferable to Chazan's method, content, and intention arguments. Indeed, according to Rosenak's own critique of those arguments, even his theory of indoctrination is based on certain assumptions. Why are Rosenak's assumptions better than any others? If it is true that every educational system has assumptions that are immune from criticism according to the assumptions of other educational systems, then what is true for the secularists is right for them, and what is true for the religionists is right for them. In short, Rosenak's position is faced with a paradox. If his critique of the secularist claim that religious education is indoctrination is right, then it is wrong, because the secularists must also be right." (Alexander, 1992, p. 146).

In order to avoid the "superficiality" of Chazan's analytic approach and the "quagmire of relativism" into which Rosenak's normative approach leads, Alexander advocates what he calls a postmodernist approach to educational philosophy, wherein questions of educational goals are no longer framed in absolutist terms but rather by reference to specific cases, as questions of "how is one thing possible, given (or supposing) certain other things" (ibid., p. 150). Thus, argues Alexander, philosophy of Jewish education should proceed from the explicit normative assumption that Jewish education is valuable and ask, "not whether being educated as a Jew is meaningful, but rather how it can be given the tendency toward absolutism on the one hand and relativism on the other" (ibid., p. 151).

Alexander seems to be advocating a philosophy of Jewish education that takes something from Chazan and something from Rosenak; that starts, a la Rosenak, from particular norms, and proceeds, a la Chazan, with rigorous conceptual analysis. But what are the grounds for Alexander's preference? Why is this way of doing philosophy of Jewish education better than the ways in which Chazan and Rosenak do it themselves? More specifically, how does this way of doing philosophy of Jewish education avoid Alexander's own criticisms of Chazan's and Rosenak's shortcomings?

Alexander presents two arguments in support of his preferred mode of Jewish-educational philosophizing. Intriguingly, both are empirical rather than conceptual. His first argument is that, "the normative-analytic debate in educational philosophy has run its course," and that consequently Chazan's and Rosenak's reflections take insufficient account of, "recent developments in the field of philosophy" (ibid., p. 148). His second argument is that, "in this radically pluralistic society," in which, "modernity itself is now in a period of crisis," the question for many young Jews, "is no longer how to be Jewish. It is rather, why be Jewish, indeed, why be anything at all?" (ibid., p. 149). Chazan and Rosenak, however, remain "enmeshed in the problems of modern educational thought" as "defined by the Enlightenment and Emancipation" (ibid., p. 148), Alexander's implication being that they both address concerns that are no longer educationally relevant.

Philosophically speaking, these arguments are rather dubious. They do not show that Chazan's and Rosenak's preferred modes of philosophizing are any less adequate than Alexander's, only that they are less fashionable. More specifically, such arguments leave Alexander open to precisely the kind of objection that he raised against Rosenak: If Rosenak's reliance on unverifiable normative assumptions is unjustified then so is Alexander's, irrespective of how comfortably it sits with the prevailing philosophical *zeitgeist*.

However, our concern here is not with the philosophical soundness of Alexander's approach, but with its psychological accuracy. Alexander claims that the principal question with which young Jews are concerned today is not, "How to be Jewish?" but rather, "Why be Jewish?" But how does he know this? What is the evidence for his claim? Alexander cites no psychological, sociological, or anthropological studies. Instead, he cites comments by the philosophers Richard Bernstein and Richard Rorty to the effect that we are currently witnessing the death throes of the "modernist" intellectual agenda. In other words, his argument is based on data and arguments from the history of ideas rather than from psychological studies of what actually goes on the minds of individual Jews. And, as with the psychological assumptions of the other philosophers I have discussed, there are good empirical grounds for disagreeing with Alexander. Although recent studies have provided plentiful evidence that contemporary Jews are selective in their commitments to Jewish beliefs and practices, there is little evidence that they give much serious thought to the global question of whether or not to be Jewish. These same studies show, on the contrary, that most Jews view being Jewish as a given (for example, Cohen and Eisen, 2000; Horowitz, 2000; Levy et al., 1993; Schachter, 2000). Indeed, there is considerable evidence that such notions of "given-ness" extend beyond the global category of "Jew" to include also more specific adjectival categories of self-definition such as "modern Orthodox woman" "traditional Moroccan son" or "secular teacher of Jewish history"

(Gottlieb, 2002; Rapoport and Garb, 1998; Rapoport, Garb, and Penso, 1995; Schachter, 2000). In other words, it is precisely questions of how to be Jewish, and not questions of why to be Jewish, that contemporary Jews are most likely to ask.

Philosophical corruptions and what to do about them

In the preceding pages I have shown how philosophers of Jewish education incorporate implicit psychological assumptions in their educational deliberations. Furthermore, I have shown how such assumptions can lead to one-sided or downright false conclusions about what and how people actually think. Despite the many differences between Schwab, Chazan, Rosenak and Alexander, the path by which these distortions are introduced into their analyses is the same. It begins with a claim couched in the language of philosophical analysis and ends with the translation of this claim into a statement of empirical fact.

How can such distortions be minimized? Schwab himself provides us with a number of sound practical suggestions. Indeed, precisely those mechanisms and forms of educational deliberation that Schwab advocates as defenses against the excesses of psychologists may be invoked against the excesses of philosophers. First, we should recognize the limitations of philosophy, and take more care to scrutinize the assumptions and premises of philosophers, be they conceptual or empirical (Schwab, 1958; Schwab, 1971). Second, we should treat both philosophy and psychology (among other scholarly and practical disciplines) as resources for educational deliberation rather than as models for it (Schwab, 1973). In other words, we must not allow educational philosophers to intimidate us with their erudition and acuity, nor educational psychologists to blind us with science. Rather, we should demand of them that they speak to us in languages we can understand and that they respond with patience and intellectual honesty to our requests for clarifications of their theories and applications of their generalizations to specific educational questions and situations.

In Schwab's view, the most effective way to promote educational deliberations of this kind is to bring together scholars, practitioners, and other stakeholders who share a common commitment to addressing some particular set of educational problems but who differ in their areas of scholarly and practical expertise (Schwab, 1973). At the same time, however, Schwab is aware of the delicate balancing act that is necessary if such an approach is to succeed. Not only must no one expert or stakeholder be allowed to dominate the others. Even the chairperson, or "curriculum expert," must be monitored so as to ensure that his or her own ways of framing and summarizing the group's deliberations are not overly biased in favor of one particular methodological or normative preferences.

The Mandel School versus corruption

It is precisely this delicate balancing act that the Mandel School, under Professor Fox's guidance, has taken on as its primary challenge. Bringing together subject-matter experts, practitioners, policy-makers, social scientists and other agents of culture, it seeks to foster deliberations about the problems and prospects of Jewish and Israeli education that are at once intellectually profound, empirically grounded, and politically savvy. Needless to say, such ambitions are not easily realized. Any process of group deliberation about things that matter will include its fair share of conflicts, misunderstandings, reversals and wrong turns. Yet it is only through such engagement that genuine progress in educational thought and practice is possible.

That the Mandel School is committed to performing this balancing act does not mean that it has yet or ever will achieve some optimal equilibrium between competing educational disciplines and perspectives. On the contrary, its deliberations may turn out to oscillate continually from one kind of corruption to another as its faculty and students, and their problems and goals, change and interact over time. However, if the school succeeds in resisting the hegemony of any one kind of knowledge or model of scholarly expertise, such corruptions are likely to be seen eventually for what they are.

Moreover, at a time when communication across disciplinary boundaries is rare, and in a place where civilized debate about matters of social import is rarer still, the Mandel School's commitment to such deliberation takes on significance beyond the prevention of disciplinary corruptions of education. It provides the scholarly community and Israeli society at large with a working model of respectful, informed, and committed conversation about questions and problems that concern us all.

References

Alexander, H. A. (1992). Recent trends in the philosophy of Jewish education: Chazan, Rosenak, and beyond. In A. Shkedi (Ed.), *Studies in Jewish education, 6,* pp. 121–152.

Bruner, J. S. (1960). *The process of education.* Cambridge, MA: Harvard University Press.

Bruner, J. S. (1983). *In search of mind.* New York: Harper and Row.

Bruner, J. S., Goodnow, J. J., and Austin, G. A. (1956). *A study of thinking.* New York: Wiley.

Callan, E. (1988). Faith, worship and reason in religious upbringing. *Journal of Philosophy of Education, 22 (2)*, pp. 183–193.

Chazan, B. (1978). Indoctrination and religious education, *The language of Jewish education.* Bridgeport, CT: Hartmore House, pp. 57–76.

Cohen, S. M., and Eisen, A. (2000). *The Jew within: self, family and community in America.* Bloomington: Indiana University Press.

Dewey, J. (1902). The child and the curriculum. In R. D. Archambault (Ed.), *John Dewey on education.* New York: Modern Library, pp. 339–358.

Dewey, J. (1956). *Experience and education.* New York: Macmillan.

Elkind, D. (1971). The development of religious understanding in children and adolescents. In M. P. Strommen (Ed.). *Research on religious development: a comprehensive handbook* (pp. 655–685). New York: Hawthorn Books.

Erikson, E. H. (1963). *Childhood and society.* Second edition. New York: Norton.

Erikson, E. H. (1968). *Identity: youth and crisis.* New York: W. W. Norton.

Fox, S. (1975). *Freud and education.* Springfield, IL: Charles C. Thomas.

Fox, S. (1997). *Vision at the heart.* Jerusalem: Mandel Institute.

Gardner, H. (1985). *The mind's new science: a history of the cognitive revolution.* New York: Basic Books.

Gardner, P. (1991). Should we teach children to be open-minded? Or, is the pope open-minded about the existence of God? *Journal of Philosophy of Education, 27 (1)*, pp. 39–43.

Gelman, R., and Baillargeon, R. (1983). A review of some Piagetian concepts. In J. H. Flavell and E. M. Markman (Eds.), *Handbook of Child Psychology* (Vol. 3: *Cognitive Development*). New York: Wiley, pp. 167–230.

Gergen, K. J. (1991). *The saturated self.* New York: Basic Books.

Gopnik, A. (1996). The post-Piaget era. *Psychological Science, 7 (4)*, pp. 221–225.

Gottlieb, E. (2001, April). *Epistemic diversity in children and adolescents: a comparative study of religious and non-religious thinking.* Paper presented at the Annual Meeting of the American Educational Research Association, Seattle, WA.

Gottlieb, E. (2002). *Religious thinking in childhood and adolescence: argumentative reasoning and the justification of religious belief.* Unpublished doctoral dissertation, The Hebrew University of Jerusalem.

Guttman, J. (1976). *On the philosophy of religion.* D. V. Herman. (Trans.). Jerusalem: Magnes Press.

Horowitz, B. (2000). *Connections and journeys: Assessing critical opportunities for enhancing Jewish identity.* New York: Jewish Continuity Commission, UJA-Federation of New York

Kohlberg, L. (1968). The child as a moral philosopher. *Psychology Today, 2 (4)*, pp. 25–30.

Kohlberg, L. (1971). From is to ought: How to commit the naturalistic fallacy and get away with it in the study of moral development. In T. Mischel (Ed.). *Cognitive development and epistemology.* New York: Academic Press, pp. 151–235.

Kohlberg, L., and Mayer, R. (1972). Development as the aim of education. *Harvard Educational Review, 42 (4)*, pp. 449–496.

Addin-Enbu Leslau, A., and Bar-Lev, M. (1993). *Olamam hadati shel bogrei hahinukh hamamlakhti dati* [The religious world of graduates of state-religious education] *(Hebrew).* Ramat Gan: The Sociological Institute for Community Research, Bar Ilan University.

Levy, S., Levinsohn, H., and Katz, E. (1993). *Beliefs, observances and social interaction among Israeli Jews.* Jerusalem: The Louis Guttman Israel Institute of Applied Social Research.

Marcia, J. E. (1966). Development and validation of ego-identity status. *Journal of Personality and Social Psychology, 3*, pp. 551–558.

Marcia, J. E. (1980). Identity in adolescence. In J. Adelson (Ed.), *Handbook of adolescent psychology.* New York: John Wiley, pp. 159–187.

McLaughlin, T. H. (1984). Parental rights and the religious upbringing of children. *Journal of Philosophy of Education, 18 (1)*, pp. 75–83.

Phillips, D. C., and Kelly, M. E. (1975). Hierarchical theories of development in education and psychology. *Harvard Educational Review, 45*, pp. 351–375.

Piaget, J. (1929). *The child's conception of the world.* London: Routledge and Kegan Paul.

Piaget, J. (1930). *The child's conception of physical causality.* London: Routledge and Kegan Paul.

Piaget, J. (1952). *The child's conception of number.* New York: Basic Books.

Piaget, J. (1954). *The construction of reality in the child.* New York: Basic Books.

Rapoport, T., and Garb, Y. (1998). The experience of religious fortification: the coming of age of religious Zionist young women. *Gender and Education, 10 (1)*, pp. 5–20.

Rapoport, T., Garb, Y., and Penso, A. (1995). Religious socialization and female subjectivity: Religious Zionist adolescent girls in Israel. *Sociology of Education, 68*, pp. 48–61.

Rosenak, M. (1983). Jewish religious education and indoctrination. In B. Chazan (Ed.), *Studies in Jewish education, 1*, pp. 117–138.

Schachter, E. (2000). *Hitpat'hut zehut koherentit bematsav qonfliktuali: hitpat'hut datit uminit beqerev tse'irim ortodoksim moderni'im* [The development of a coherent identity in a conflictual situation: the case of religious and sexual development among young adult Modern Orthodox Jews] *(Hebrew).* Unpublished doctoral dissertation, The Hebrew University of Jerusalem.

Schwab, J. J. (1958). On the corruption of education by psychology. *School Review, 66*, 169–184.

Schwab, J. J. (1964). The religiously oriented school in the United States: a memorandum on policy. *Conservative Judaism, 18,* pp. 1–14.

Schwab, J. J. (1969). The practical: a language for curriculum. *School Review, 78,* pp. 1–23.

Schwab, J. J. (1971). The practical: arts of eclectic. *School Review, 79*, pp. 493–542.

Schwab, J. J. (1973). The practical: translation into curriculum. *School Review, 81,* pp. 501–522.

Shweder, R. A., Mahapatra, M., and Miller, J. G. (1990). Culture and moral development. In J. W. Stigler (Ed.), *Cultural psychology: essays on comparative human development*. New York: Cambridge University Press, pp. 130–204.

Vygotsky, L. S. (1962). *Thought and language*. Cambridge, MA: MIT Press.

Westbury, I., and Wilkof, N. J. (1978). Introduction. In I. Westbury and N. J. Wilkof (Eds.), *Science, curriculum, and liberal education: selected essays of Joseph J. Schwab*. Chicago: The University of Chicago Press, pp. 1–40.

A Jewish People Leadership Academy[1]

YEHEZKEL DROR

Assuring a Thriving Future for the Jewish People and Judaism

The history of the Jewish People and Judaism has been ruptured by the Enlightenment, the *Shoah*, the establishment and development of the State of Israel, and the emergence of a new type of Diaspora as epitomized by the Jewish communities in the USA. In consequence, the future of the Jewish People and Judaism in a humanity undergoing radical shifts is in doubt. Optimistically considered, the Jewish People and Judaism, with Israel as their core state,[2] will thrive in all respects, while also fulfilling a major role in the making of a new global civilization. Pessimistically considered, the Jewish People and Judaism will decline and dissipate, with Israel becoming "normal" and loosing its nature as the Jewish State of the Jewish People; or, to take a very low probability catastrophic view, Israel will be destroyed in a Middle East apocalypse, the Jewish People as such will practically disappear, and Jews will become no more than dispersed adherents to a "religion" with a glorious past but no significance whatsoever for the future.

Developments in any such direction as well as a mixture of them are within the evolutionary potential of present and foreseeable dynamics, with much depending on the policies and actions of the Jewish People and of Israel. What is clear is that present trends do not assure deterministically the realization of a more optimistic future, with many of them moving rather in a very undesirable direction. Taking into account such trends and global change as a whole, reliance on an automatic self-renewal and

---

1 In the classical sense of Plato's Academy — a place for learning and the advancement of knowledge through guided discourse and lectures. In the Hebrew version of this paper I use the term "Beit Midrash."
2 I am using this concept following Huntington, 1996.

existence-guaranteeing process, in line with Nachman Krochmal's theory of Jewish history,[3] is not only baseless but positively dangerous in that it de-motivates determined interventions with history as needed for reducing the probability of bad futures, increasing the probability of desirable ones and gearing for the unknown and inconceivable.[4]

It follows that the Jewish People must act, and this along three main lines: One, strengthen Jewish action resources and capabilities. Two, develop a "Jewish People Policy" designed to assure, as far as humanly possible, a thriving future. And, three, collectively, locally and personally realize this well-considered and suitably approved Jewish People Policy, as changing with time and adjusted to specific circumstances.

Put differently, the Jewish People must build up the capacity to govern itself and weave its future, so as to assure its long-term meaningful existence and thriving in the face of both promising opportunities and serious threats.[5] A crucial requirement for doing so is high quality Jewish People leadership[6] — to the development of which, with the help of a Jewish People Leadership Academy, this contribution of mine to the book in honor of Professor Seymour Fox is dedicated.

Political-Public and Spiritual Leadership

A distinction must be made between two main "pure types" of leadership, namely spiritual and political-public, (without ignoring additional categories such as social and communal, organizational, professional and other types of leadership). All types of "leaders" share some core characteristics that in part overlap, but many actual and desired features differ from one category to another, as well as from one period in history, its traditions, environments and circumstances, to another.

In this paper I focus on political-public leadership for the Jewish People and its parts. Since the situation of the Jewish People requires leaders who

3   Also discussed in Harris, 1991: Ch. 3.
4   In terms of Jewish religious commands too, reliance on miracles instead of human measures is anathema.
5   I am applying here to the Jewish People the *leitmotif* of my book (Dror, 2001), which is global in scope.
6   The "Jewish People Policy Planning Institute", established in February 2002 by the Jewish Agency, with some partners to join soon, as an independent think tank, meets another requirement of facilitating the future of the Jewish People. As will be explained, developing Jewish People policy and upgrading Jewish People leadership are interdependent measures reinforcing one another.

convince and educate rather than command, they must partake in part of the profiles of spiritual leaders. Therefore, and because of their crucial importance for the future of the Jewish People and Judaism, some comments will be included on spiritual leaders and the possible contributions of the proposed Jewish People Leadership Academy (in short "the Academy") to their emergence and development. Similarly, I will not discuss the special leadership needs of political leadership in Israel,[7] with all the complexities deriving from the country's double nature as a democratic state and as the core state of the Jewish People and of Judaism, again with the exception of some brief observations on possible contributions of the Academy.

Importance of Leadership

There is no need to dwell on the importance of leadership, which is obvious. However, it should be noted that the importance of political leadership, and especially of "rulers", is mounting in all countries as a result of a mutually reinforcing series of factors. These include, among others: the growing political and social importance of mass media; the increasingly personal and image-based nature of electoral competition; the increasing role of summit meetings and personal diplomacy; the traumatization of populations and consequent mass-psychological seeking of "father" images (and, when more women leaders emerge, also "mother" images); and the inter-departmental nature of main policy spheres which enhances the integrative functions of top decision makers.

These factors operate in part also in the Jewish People. In addition, a number of additional factors unique to the Jewish People both augment and also weaken the significance of leaders. The Jewish People is not a polity. Therefore, political-public leaders lack formal powers and enforcement instruments, weakening their standing. Furthermore, the dispersal of the Jewish People among different states and political cultures makes the emergence of a leadership accepted by all or most of the People difficult. At the same time, somewhat paradoxically, the very absence of a common authoritative political frame enhances the importance of leaders in providing coherence and enabling collective "voluntary" action– fusing

7   I speak about "political-public" leadership of the Jewish People and "political" leadership of Israel, making this conceptual differentiation because of the absence of a clearly "political" sphere in the Jewish People as contrasted with the situation in a state, including the State of Israel.

in many ways "political leadership" with "social leadership", as expressed — as noted — in the term "political-public leadership" which I shall use.

These special characteristics have important implications for the necessary and desirable profiles of Jewish political-public leaders, at the facilitation and development of which the proposed Academy aims.

Main Mission: Weaving the Future for the Better While Serving the Present

Before going into specifics, let me conceptualize the main mission of leadership, as applying with special force to the Jewish People, on which the proposed Academy is predicated, as follows: Weaving the future for the better while serving the present.

Firstly, leadership is a "mission" and a "calling", not a "job". This is true always, but is particularly so in regard to the Jewish People with its moral conceptions of leadership on one hand, and the difficulties and conditions of its leadership on the other.

Secondly, a main task, and perhaps *the* main one, is "weaving the future,"[8] in the sense of combining present elements and processes in ways that lead to a better future, paying due attention to plural views on what is "better" and their changes with time. This involves, to reiterate an important conception, reducing the probability of bad futures, increasing the probability of good ones and gearing for the uncertain and the inconceivable.

When an entity is doing well and the main pathways into its future are positive, and there are no serious dangers or radical challenges on the horizon, then weaving the future involves mainly incremental improvements which do not require much effort, and attention can be focused more on serving the present. At the other extreme, when trends are very bad and a society is in a historic trap, very difficult and even risky "leaps" onto a different curve and into a new space are essential, up to "throwing surprises at history", and taking care of the present becomes secondary to the main effort. This also applies, though differently so, when opportunities open for moving into a radically better future by bringing about mutations in present trends.

Historically, Zionism and the establishment of the Jewish state were a heroic and most successful attempt to "leap" into a radically different

---

8   I borrow this metaphor from Plato's *Statesman*.

future for the Jewish People. However, despite this historic metamorphosis for the better, the Jewish People as a whole and Israel as a Jewish state continue to face dismal possibilities on one hand and very promising opportunities on the other. Therefore, weaving the future, including from time to time radical interventions with history, is a main task of a Jewish People policy and leadership.

Thirdly, taking care of the present so as to improve the situation of the people in the here and now is always a task of leadership, both normatively and imposed on them democratically. The more there are pressing needs and the less other social actors, such as free markets processes, take care of them, the more leaders have to do so. This need is especially acute when parts of the Jewish People face dismal situations, because of anti-Jewishness (a term coined by Professor Irwin Cotler[9] which is much preferable to "anti-Semitism"), economic crises and more — when "rescue" operations become an urgent must.

A difficult moral and political dilemma is posed by the need to balance taking care of the present with weaving the future, both with what are always scarce resources. To mention a concrete illustration, the allocation of reparations between helping the survivors of the Holocaust and their descendants and using the money for taking care of the future of the Jewish People, such as through education, constitutes a difficult moral issue which leadership must decide with the help of their own moral stature and their moral reasoning capacities.

Dimensions of High-Quality Jewish People Leaders

Discourse on the "good leader" has fascinated the human mind since antiquity and continues to be a subject to which much attention is given.[10] To process what is relevant in available thinking and knowledge, with

---

9   See Irwin Cotler, 2002.
10 Thucydides' *The Peloponnesian War* and Plato's *Statesman*, mentioned above, are obligatory introductory reading for all who are seriously interested in leadership. I have not found any comprehensive study of leadership in Jewish thought and history, but some important observations and examples can be found in Halkin and Hartman, 1985; Kreisel, 1999; and Walzer et al., 2000. Reflecting recent better literature on leadership are: Bennis, 2000; Bennis et al., 2001; Cleveland, 2002; Hesselbein, Goldsmith and Beckhard, 1997; Goleman et al., 2002; and Terry, 2001. Especially relevant is Badaracco, Jr., 2002, with its emphasis on the importance of a large number of "quiet leaders."

some additions of my own,[11] the main dimensions of the qualities needed by political-public Jewish People leaders to fulfill their mission can be subsumed under 18 headings:[12] (1) morality; (2) charisma; (3) willpower combined with self-skepticism; (4) realistic visions and strategic long-term and systemic perspectives; (5) educational, with elements of spiritual leadership; (6) the ability to realistically estimate dynamics; (7) the ability to "think in deep history"; (8) possession of examined and up-to-date cognitive maps and reference theories; (9) moral reasoning; (10) policy pondering frames; (11) policy analysis and planning methods; (12) crisis management abilities; (13) fuzzy gambling sophistication; (14) decisiveness; (15) readiness to change one's mind; (16) multiple literacy and skills; (17) familiarity with main policy domains; and (18) the ability to use well advisors and knowledge resources.

Other classifications and different lists are possible, but these make little substantive difference for our limited purposes. More important, the dimensions suggested and others need semi-quantitative specifications, but for considering the idea of setting up a Jewish People Leadership Academy, it suffices to specify that leaders need "a lot" of each one of them and that it is the task of the Academy to upgrade these dimensions as far as possible, given the characteristics of participants and length of study activities.

Let me move on to exploring the dimensions, one after another.

1. Morality: Morality is especially crucial for Jewish People leaders, both because of the importance of morals in Judaism and because of these leaders' lack of formal authority. At the Academy this point can be explained and a code of ethics for Jewish People leadership should be elaborated and discussed.[13] But no real impact on the morality of the participants can realistically be expected, nor can improvement of moral reasoning, as discussed below, have much impact on personal morality.

It is important to explain this statement with its serious pessimistic implications. I differ from one of the basic assumptions of the classical Platonic Academy, as reflected in some, though not all, of the Platonic Dialogues: namely, that knowledge leads to virtue. The proposed Academy can provide knowledge and improve cognitive processes, including moral

---

11 See Dror, 1993.

12 These and other features of good political-public leadership for the 21st century in a global context will be elaborated in Dror, in a work in progress.

13 For an example of such a code for senior politicians in general, see Dror, 2001, pp. 102–3.

reasoning, and this is a lot. But the moral personality of participants is beyond the Academy's influence. The endeavor to upgrade the character and virtues of Jewish People leaders requires other approaches – such as discernment in the selection and advancement of leaders — which, regretfully, are very difficult and of doubtful effect, as illustrated by the moral failings of many political leaders around the world. (Hence the pessimistic implications of the impossibility of relatively easily improving the morality of leaders by conveying knowledge, as noted above). [14]

2. Charisma: Charisma is very important for Jewish People leaders because of the absence of common authoritative structures. But the Academy should not be expected to contribute to this personality characteristic, all the more so as the nature of charisma is not really understood.

This and the earlier point together with some additional ones, should make one wary of expecting too much from the Academy. As will be clarified in respect to other dimensions of high quality Jewish People leadership, the Academy can make important and also essential contributions, including some that cannot be achieved in any other way, while being very cost-effective. But expecting too much cannot but lead to waste of effort and resources and to frustrations, impairing what can and should be achieved.

3. Willpower combined with self-skepticism: Both are important for Jewish People leadership as for all political-public leaders, but — again – willpower is not a characteristic that can be augmented with the help of the Academy. However self-skepticism can be facilitated, not by exhorting on its importance but indirectly, by studies, exercises and projects which demonstrate to participants that what they accepted as "obvious" and "beyond doubt" is often very doubtful indeed, and by illustrating the necessity for alternative working assumptions on what seems to be "clear-cut." Indeed, "assumption-skeptical" thinking is potentially one of the more important qualities to be imparted to participants.

4. Realistic visions and strategic long-term and systemic perspectives: In this dimension the Academy can make a major contribution by presenting and exercising frames and modalities of preparing realistic

---

14 Even more pessimistic, up to fatalism, is Ludwig (2002). I think his biological-evolutionary deterministic reductionism is far from correct, but still his empiric findings are very disturbing.

visions and engaging in strategic thinking, and by demonstrating their practical utility.

Inter alia, presenting the principles of systems thinking, studying cases of systems analysis in action, and applying systems mapping and improvement approaches to cases, projects and main policy issues can habituate participants to using systems perspectives as part of their cognitive processes.

All this illustrates a main impact of the Academy applying to many of the dimensions, namely bringing about the "internalization" into the cognitive processes of participants — on deliberate and conscious as well as tacit and quasi-automatic levels — of concepts, approaches, frames, schemata and thinking modalities which upgrade reality understanding and efforts to influence the future.

5. Educational, with elements of spiritual leadership: One of the widespread weaknesses of contemporary political leaders is their inability or lack of effort to serve as educators of their society, with much more attention being given by them to "political marketing" than to the enlightenment and "maturing" of their populations. Such a weakness becomes a major failure for Jewish People leaders for whom the education of their publics is a critical function. This is so not only because of the lack of an inclusive Jewish polity, but because of the very nature of the Jewish People and Judaism as a civilization defined by values, norms and styles of behavior. This core characteristic of the Jewish People and Judaism makes educating the people fateful for survival and essential for thriving.

Here the Academy can do a lot, by alerting participants to their educational functions, providing them with at least some knowledge in the didactics of mass education and by supplementing whatever knowledge they have in Jewish traditions with adjustment to their educational functions.

In this crucial matter there is a significant overlap between political-public leadership for the Jewish People and spiritual leadership. Mutual exposure between leaders of these two types should be a regular feature of the life of the Academy so as to upgrade the functioning of both.

6. The ability to realistically estimate dynamics: The dispersal of the Jewish People imposes quite a load on capacities to estimate dynamics (not "estimate of situations" which is too static a concept, though widely accepted in intelligence communities), including identifying emerging threats and opportunities alike. This is an essential basis for deciding on action and therefore central to the tasks of Jewish People leadership.

The Academy can do a lot to help leaders with estimating dynamics, by studying estimation approaches and examining cases of estimation failures and successes. Concomitantly, readings, presentations and study-exercises should provide participants with realistic and penetrating estimations of the past, present and foreseeable dynamics of the Jewish People and its parts.

7. The ability to "think in deep history": Clinging to a "surface" view of events without penetrating into their deeper features and causes is a main weakness of ongoing efforts to influence present and future realities. This unavoidably leads to simplistic and often counter-productive action. Needed, instead, is the basing of "intervening with history" (which is a main task of leadership, central to weaving the future) on understanding and having a "sense" for "deep history" which is only in part reflected, and often misleadingly so, in "what meets the eye."[15]

Jewish People leadership should have a good understanding of the variables shaping the future and be able to identify the sub-set of those which can be "manipulated" — to serve as policy instruments to be applied in mutually reinforcing sets. This requires "thinking in deep history." Such understanding is especially essential for assuring the future of the Jewish People and Judaism because of the dangers inherent in present trends.

This requirement goes far beyond knowing the "behavior" history of the Jewish People and Judaism (however also essential), which is not difficult to convey to participants who lack it. What is needed, to put it differently, is thinking in terms of "theories of history of the Jewish People" with insight and understanding and a "sense" for the basic processes shaping the history of the Jewish People and Judaism, processes which are sure to be important also in shaping their future for the next one or two generations — even though unprecedented variables exert increasing influence making "what was" less reliable a basis for exploring what will be and what can be.

Helping leaders to acquire such an ability to "think in deep history" is not an easy task, and is made all the more difficult as suitable texts are scarce. Thus it will be necessary for the Academy to stimulate salient research and writing, as discussed later. Still, through innovative teaching methods, including for instance also simulation games of the type of

---

15 Very relevant is the approach of Fernand Braudel, which applies with special salience to the Jewish People. For a convenient collection of some of his essays, see Braudel, 1980.

"Civilization", but more sophisticated and applied to the Jewish People, much can be achieved.

8. Examined cognitive maps and reference theories: This dimension supplements the two last discussed and overlaps them. Cognitive maps are subjective images of the world, while reference theories are the subjective images of causal effects by which events are explained and predicted. An example is the widespread belief of Jewish leaders that more education to make pupils familiar with Jewish traditions assures greater adherence to Judaism.

Making cognitive maps and reference theories explicit, subjecting them to critical evaluation and correcting them as far as relevant knowledge is available, is a main conduit to improving the ability of leaders to weave the future. Thus, to return to the example, consideration of the possibility that more of the same in Jewish education may well cause "allergy" rather than adherence and the consequent awareness of the need to change the contents and didactics of Jewish education while expanding it, can well improve the effect of leaders on Jewish education, while alerting them to the pitfalls of trusting one's given images and understanding of realities.

9. Moral reasoning: As stated, I do not think that the Academy can change significantly the character, vices and virtues and moral stature of leaders. However, much can be done to improve the quality of moral reasoning, that is, the weighing of different values and goals essential for making a choice — as illustrated above when the need was posed to make a moral choice between allocating resources to improving the present or investing in bringing about a better future.

Moral reasoning can be improved by becoming acquainted with relevant approaches in moral philosophy and practicing them by application to concrete policy choices. Some of the processes of argumentation of the Talmud are also highly relevant. Taking care to upgrade moral reasoning is neglected and often ignored in nearly all leadership and executive development and training programs. This focus can therefore well be an important distinctive feature of the Academy.

10. Policy pondering frames: As emphasized by modern cognitive sciences and the philosophy of judgment, perspectives and "frames" condition thinking. Improving policy consideration frames is, therefore, a primary means of improving the choice capacities of leaders. This is true for all leadership, but carries special weight for Jewish People leaders because of the partly unique complexities of Jewish People policy spaces on the one hand, and the lesser availability of organizational supports which supply position papers based on advanced policy pondering frames on the other.

To illustrate, Jewish People leadership should consider options and make decisions on the basis of thought in terms of the rise and decline of civilizations, the evolutionary potentials of the Jewish People and Judaism, competition with other loyalties, the preservation of continuity while adjusting to radically changing environments, critical choice as "fuzzy gambling with history for high stakes," and more.

Much can be done at the Academy to upgrade the frames of thinking of Jewish People leaders, both by presenting and exploring alternative frames and perspectives and by exercising their application to concrete policy issues. Such practices lie at the core of improving the cognitive capacities of participants.

11. Policy analysis and planning methods: Leaders need some familiarity with the primary policy analysis and planning methods, such as systems approach, thinking in terms of benefit-cost-risk, prediction methods, coping with uncertainty and the inconceivable, uses and misuses of simulation, etc. In governments, as noted, the knowledge of such methods required by political leaders is limited because they have profession staffs at their disposal. In respect to Jewish People leaders, who are less equipped with professional staffs, required standards of familiarity with policy analysis and planning methods and the ability to use them at least qualitatively are higher, though detailed methodologies and technical skills are not required.

The Academy can quite easily provide the necessary knowledge by a combination of guided readings, lectures and demonstrations with hands-on exercises and projects.

12. Crisis management abilities: A paradox faced by all leadership, especially in an epoch, such as ours, of non-linear changes and shifts, is the need and desire for long-term and systemic weaving of the future based on thinking in deep history, on the one hand, and the certainty of many future crises that will require improvisation, on the other. This applies fully to the Jewish People. Therefore, upgrading crisis management is an important task for the Academy.

This too is a dimension where a lot can be achieved by much work on policy domains, which provides an essential cognitive basis for better improvisation, as well as by upgrading crisis coping abilities by learning and practicing "time compressed" choice and, especially, a series of diverse crises exercises.

13. Fuzzy gambling sophistication: As mentioned above, interventions with history are "fuzzy gambling for high stakes." The perception and understanding of the essence of choice as "fuzzy gambling" with uncertainties that often cannot be expressed quantitatively and with a high degree of inconceivability, is central for leadership. They need, therefore, fuzzy gambling sophistication, including both the emotional ability[16] to tolerate ambiguity and the cognitive ability to reason in terms of uncertainty and inconceivability, so as to manage risk and gear up for the unforeseeable and also the unthinkable.

The Academy can introduce participants to this view of choice and upgrade their understanding of uncertainty and inconceivability and ways to map and cope with them. The Academy can also point out the main pitfalls in trying to confront uncertainty, such as perceptional distortions, the use of misleading quantitative methods, and the search for "mystic" reassurances. Furthermore, in all cases, exercises and projects involving choice, its fuzzy gambling nature should be emphasized and ways to improve the gamble should be exercises, together with ways to benefit from expert advice and support in so doing.

14. Decisiveness: Much of the upgrading of leadership, including many of the dimensions already discussed, is directed at improving choice, also viewed as making up one's mind by pondering options and integrating a variety of considerations which are transformed, by a well-grounded act of "will" into a decision.

The main way to help participants to develop higher quality "decision-making" judgment, capacities and habits is by integrative exercises and projects which internalize a range of frames, perspectives, methods and approaches at both the conscious and the tacit levels. The Academy can do so with the help of cases, exercises and projects dealing with Jewish People issues and policy spaces.

15. Readiness to change one's mind: "Making up one's mind" must be supplemented and balanced by a willingness and ability to "change one's

---

16 In this article I do not enter into the questions of "emotional intelligence", which are in the main beyond the scope of Academy activities. But see Goleman, 1995; and Goleman at al., 2002.

mind"; that is to re-examine critically and also skeptically, with an "open mind,"[17] one's pre-dispositions, assumptions, policy orthodoxies etc. and to be able emotionally to revise one's made-up mind accordingly.

Again, explaining and illustrating the need is a preliminary recommended approach. But only exercises and projects in which changing one's mind is practiced, often with not easy confrontations between participants and mentors, can lead to increasing abilities and propensities to re-examine one's predispositions and be more ready and willing to change one's mind when evidence and analysis requires one to do so.

16. Multiple literacy and skills: Political-public leadership requires literacy in diverse domains of knowledge, such as social sciences including economics, science and technology, law, and a number of languages including numeracy. Also required are many skills, including skills in management, social relations and communication, and negotiations.

Some of this literacy and skills are of special importance for Jewish leadership, such as knowledge of Hebrew, and there are many courses and programs providing most of them.[18] Remote learning too can meet some of the needs.

Therefore, the Academy should limit itself to pre-entry requirements of salient literacy and skills, emphasizing the need for suitable literacy and skills, and help, when necessary, with referring participants to good programs providing them. "Outsourcing" by encouraging other bodies to provide suitable offerings may also be useful.

As mentioned, for some Academy programs, such as for young leadership trainees, demonstrating adequate literacy and pre-entry participation in relevant skill-training programs, together with other graduate studies requirements, (such as at a public policy school) should be a prerequisite for being accepted. However the Academy itself should not provide what others can do well, including language and skill-training. The exception are some skill requirements specific to Jewish People leadership and best dealt with by the Academy, such as dealing with mass media from a Jewish perspective.

Another type of skills that should not be taken up at the Academy, despite its attractiveness for leaders, is knowledge and advice on "how to gain power and keep it." The Academy should concentrate on enabling

17 In the sense used by Rokeach, 1960. Interesting to apply are parts of Kegan, 1994.
18 A glaring omission is the lack of opportunities for political and public leaders to gain science and technology literacy, despite its importance in the determination of the future.

leaders to use power for the better, not on how to win in the competition for power. A few guest lectures on political marketing and so on should be included in the activities so as to strengthen "realism" and meet the interests of participants, but not more.

A different approach is appropriate with leadership aspirants who have no experience in public life and politics. These must be provided with some sense for the realities of power, by appropriate studies and exercises, but again not on "gaining power" but on operating within force fields.

17. Familiarity with main policy domains: All leaders require familiarity with the main policy domains of their entity and penetrating knowledge and understanding of those of which they are in charge. In respect to Jewish People leaders, who operate less within elaborate state machineries, this familiarity has to be sharpened. They all require good and detailed knowledge of the main policy domains of the Jewish People as a whole and of its main parts in particular, with meticulous knowledge of the domains of which they are in charge.

The Academy can meet this need well by readings, lectures and study tours.

18. Using advisors and knowledge resources: All leaders have to work with advisors and know how to access information and manage knowledge. Jewish People leaders who, as already mentioned, have usually less staff and large-scale organizational support, have to be all the more able to access information and locate relevant knowledge. While they are working and should work more with advisors, they are less accustomed to doing so than government leaders who often have much experience in public organizations. Let me add that working with advisors on political-public issues is significantly different from working with advisors and consultants in the business world, from which not a few Jewish People leaders come.

Therefore, ways of working with advisors and utilizing sources of knowledge should be explored at the Academy, largely with the help of case studies.

Comments on Jewish Spiritual Leadership

As noted, spiritual leadership is crucial for the future of the Jewish People and Judaism. Whatever is done, the appearance of outstanding spiritual leadership, of the stature of Rabbis Kook and Soloveitchik, is beyond deliberate social action. While facilitation of good spiritual leadership is possible and constitutes a most urgent task, it is, however, in the main beyond the capacities of the proposed Academy. Emphasis on the educational tasks of political-public leaders, as proposed, may help. The crucial importance of spiritual leadership should be one of the insights conveyed at the Academy, so that political-public leaders better support spiritual leaders and work in close affinity with them. Other useful lines of action include shared retreats of political-public and spiritual leaders, as well as the participation of the latter in Academy activities as a whole.

The Academy can make a significant indirect contribution by encouraging the inclusion of political-public leadership knowledge and understandings in the teaching and training directed at developing spiritual leadership, for example at institutions like the Rabbi Isaac Elchanan Theological Seminary of Yeshiva University and the rabbinical training programs of the Jewish Theological Seminary.[19]

Comments on Israeli Political-Public Leadership

The quality of Israeli Jewish-Zionist political-public leadership is crucial for the future of the Jewish People and Judaism and raises difficult issues. Main difficulties stem from the failings of the Israeli political system. Others result from overloads with very difficult and divisive issues. But most vexing of all are the role conflicts stemming from the double nature of Israeli's leadership as both heading a democratic state and heading the Jewish core state of the Jewish People. Little wonder that the Israeli political leadership has in the main been negligent in fulfilling main leadership roles in the Jewish People as a whole and in taking special care to deepen the Jewish-Zionist nature of Israel, with due consideration for the democratic rights of minorities. This neglect carries with it very serious dangers for the future of Israel as a Jewish-Zionist state and for the future of the Jewish People and Judaism as a whole.

---

19 Very urgent are changes in the preparation of rabbis in Israel, so as to provide them with both high quality Jewish religious and traditional rabbinic knowledge and a comprehensive understanding of the problematics of the Jewish People within a changing world — which they too must understand well. Unless this is done, the future of Jewish spiritual leadership in Israel, which is crucial for its Jewish-Zionist nature and for the future of the Jewish People and Judaism as a whole, is left to chance and the present negative trend is likely to continue and become aggravated.

Coping with this, and other grave failings of the political leadership of Israel requires multiple measures including, first of all, reform of Israel's political and governmental system. But the Academy can help a lot, by involving Israeli Jewish leadership in all its activities and by running special activities for Israeli leaders on leading the Jewish People, on deepening the Jewish-Zionist nature of Israel, and on strengthening its functions and standing as the core state of the Jewish People and Judaism. Also, with time, the Academy can help with the establishment of a twin (but not identical) Israeli Policy College, outside the domain of the Academy, for upgrading the leadership of Israel as a whole, paying due attention to the security, social and economic problems of Israel as a state.

Participants and Offerings

The Academy should seek as participants persons fulfilling leadership roles in the Jewish People and candidates and aspirants for such positions. Offerings should range from intensive two to three days retreats and one to two weeks workshops, to study periods of one to three months. The shorter activities would be aimed mainly at experienced leaders and would focus on particular dimensions and policy domains, while the longer ones would be for younger leaders and leadership aspirants and cover the whole spectrum of dimensions.

Learning Methods and Materials

Time at the Academy should be used intensely, from morning till evening and often till late at night. Preparatory readings and studies should permit optimal utilization of the time spent at the Academy. Subjects that can be easily learned on one's own, by long-distance learning or by main stream executive training programs, should generally, as already suggested, be excluded from the Academy's curricula.

Learning should be directed in part at "professionalism" in the sense of cultivating capacities to build bridges between abstract and general knowledge and understanding, on the one hand, and concrete policy domains and specific issues, on the other.[20] Accordingly, learning methods

20 In line with Schon, 1984.

would mainly be active, lectures and presentations being limited to a maximum of about one-third of the time, with most of the time at the Academy going to projects, exercises, simulations, group deliberations, etc. Field trips and, especially for leadership aspirants, periods of internship provide additional learning avenues.

With time, the Academy may offer distance learning in select subjects not covered by other training and development institutes, such as the situation and dynamics of the Jewish People and Judaism.

All this requires suitable teaching materials fully adjusted to the needs of the Academy, including texts, cases, projects, simulation models and so on. Having sufficient high quality teaching material ready is a prerequisite for starting the study activities.

Follow-up and Network Effects

The Academy should engage in systematic follow-up activities to evaluate its short-range and long-range impacts in order to construct a network of "graduates" to whom various second-phase activities will be offered.

Such follow-up activities could be very helpful in improving cooperation and promoting joint activities.

Cooperation with various training programs for Jewish People leadership, such as at the recently established Public Policy School of the Hebrew University, various programs of the Wexner Foundation and more, should be encouraged. But no existing institution approximates the unique and urgently needed activities of the proposed Academy — leaving a wide scope for unique contributions.

Staffing and Structure

The single most important factor in determining the success or failure of the Academy is the quality of its staff. Visiting lecturers and mentors, selective outsourcing and cooperation with institutions engaging in overlapping activities — such as public policy schools and Jewish policy R&D organizations ("think tanks") — can help to keep the Academy staff streamlined. Nevertheless, a minimum critical size for commencing activity would, in my estimate, be at least five to seven full time professional core staff members with multiple disciplinary backgrounds and experience, and adequate administrative personnel headed by an outstanding director of recognized professional and public standing.

The structure would include a Board of Trustees, an Executive Committee and one or two advisory councils. Details are not important, but one requirement is crucial: namely professional independence subject to policy directives by the Board.

Budget

The Academy would need an adequate budget, to be supplemented by fees paid in part by the participants and the organizations sending them. The budget would have to be assured in advance for three years so as to enable the establishment of the Academy and its operation before achievements can be evaluated.

My estimate is that setting up the Academy would require about three million dollars per year for the staff and the preparation of learning material, to which the costs of adequate physical facilities and a project budget for each activity must be added.

This is a most cost-effective investment. Even quite limited achievements in improving Jewish People leaders are "worth" orders of magnitude far greater than these costs, and the significant achievements aimed at are worth even more. Therefore, in terms of cost-benefit-risk, it is hard to imagine an investment that has more potential to serve as a catalyst for ensuring and improving the future of the Jewish People and Judaism than the setting up the proposed Academy (together with the establishment of the Jewish People Policy Planning Institute).

Setting up the Academy

Finding the core staff could well take a year, accomplished in parallel with setting up the Academy structure, starting the collection and preparation of teaching materials, and finding at least provisional physical facilities. After the core staff is recruited, another year would be needed for preparing the initial program and learning materials, and for organizing the first set of activities. Accordingly, two years after a decision to set up the Academy is taken and the first three-year budget is assured, the Academy could start its activities, building them up into a full program within another year or two.

Three years after the Academy starts its learning activities, that is about five to six years after a decision has been taken on establishing and financing it, results should be evaluated by an independent committee. These would serve as a basis for the decision on whether or not the Academy would continue its activities and for instituting changes based on the running-in experience.

Relations with Jewish People Policy Development

The history of comparable executive training and leadership development endeavors indicates that learning and the production of policy recommendations do not go well together, with activities directed at one disturbing activities directed at the other. However, cooperation between a training institute and a policy R&D institute can be very fruitful, with the latter providing cases, projects, methods, mentors and internship opportunities and the former serving as a critical forum for discussing policy papers and proposals and as a channel for introducing policy study findings and recommendations into actual policy making.

Such a synergetic relationship is of special importance for the Jewish People where professional strategic analysis, policy planning and political-public leadership are underdeveloped. Therefore, the establishment of the Jewish People Policy Planning Institute in 2002 can significantly improve the success probabilities of the proposed Academy, while the establishment of the latter will help in both the substantive work of the Policy Institute and in translating its recommendations into actual decisions by the leaders participating in Academy activities.

The scope for cooperation between the proposed Academy and the Jewish People Policy Planning Institute goes much further. Both need to be grounded in a deep understanding of the dynamics of the Jewish People and of the potentials for weaving its future, and both require policy pondering and planning frames, methods, etc. Reaching such deep understanding requires fundamental research and creative theory building, while the development of policy methodologies requires grounding in prescriptive disciplines. Both are in the main beyond the tasks and capacities of the Academy as well as the Jewish People Policy Planning Institute, belonging rather to the domains of individual thinkers, universities, research and advanced study institutes, and so on. But relevant work needs encouragement and facilitation, and sometimes must be invited and contracted for. These initiatives would be up to the Academy and the Institute, which should identify shared needs for fundamental research, new theories, adjusted policy frames, and so on, and act together to stimulate relevant studies.

Mutually fruitful interfaces and overlaps between the Academy and the Jewish People Policy Planning Institute go further, for instance with the Institute providing briefings to leaders which can often be conveniently held at the Academy and integrated into the latter's program. And some "constructive competition" within complementary missions, can also be beneficial.

Therefore, moving ahead with the establishment of the Academy for Jewish People Leadership, and building from the beginning a cooperative and also synergetic relationship between it and the Jewish People Policy Planning Institute, including possibly locating them in adjunct facilities, is recommended.

Cooperation with the Mandel Institute

It is not for me to express views on the priorities of the Mandel Foundation and Institute. But, to my mind, there can be no doubt that the pioneering and well established education leadership activities of the Mandel Institute — as pioneered and led by Seymour Fox, with the Mandel family on one hand and with devoted colleagues on the other — can serve as an excellent basis for the proposed Academy. Therefore, with due respect and recognizing my ignorance of salient considerations, my tendency is to recommend to the Mandel Foundation to initiate and undertake, with suitable partners, the establishment of a Jewish People Leadership Academy, whether on the lines proposed in this paper or on others, with Seymour Fox to spearhead and lead this "peak" endeavor.

References

Badaracco, Jr., Joseph L. (2002). *Leading quietly: An unorthodox guide to doing the right thing*. Boston: Harvard Business School Press.

Bennis, Warren G. (2000). *Managing the dream: Reflections on leadership and change*. New York: Perseus.

Bennis, Warren G. et al. (Eds.). (2001). *The future of leadership: Today's top leadership thinkers speak to tomorrow's leaders*. New York: Wiley.

Braudel, Fernand. (1980). *On history*. Chicago: The University of Chicago Press.

Cleveland, Harlan. (2002). *Nobody in charge: Essays on the future of leadership*. San Francisco: Jossey-Bass.

Cotler, Irwin. (2002). *New anti-Jewishness. Alert Paper No. 1*, Jerusalem: Jewish People Policy Planning Institute.

Dror, Yehezkel. (1993). School for Rulers. In Keyon B. De Greene, (Ed.) *A systems-based approach to policymaking*. New York: Kluwen, pp. 139–174.

Dror, Yehezkel. (2001). *The capacity to govern: A report to the Club of Rome*. London and Portland, OR: Frank Cass.

Dror, Yehezkel. (in progress). *The superior ruler*.

Goleman, Daniel. (1995). *Emotional intelligence*. New York: Bantam Books.

Goleman, Daniel, Boyatzis, Richard and McKee, Annie. (2002). *Primal leadership: Realizing the power of emotional intelligence*. Boston: Harvard Business School Press.

Halkin, Abraham, and Hartman, David. translators and discussants. (1985). *Crisis and leadership: Epistles of Maimonides*. Philadelphia: The Jewish Publication Society of America.

Harris, Jay M. (1991). *Nachman Krochmal: Guiding the perplexed of the Modern Age*. New York: New York University Press.

Hesselbein, Frances, Goldsmith, Marshall, and Beckhard, Richard F. (Eds.). (1997). *The leader of the future: New visions, strategies, and practices for the next era*. The Drucker Foundation Future Series, San Francisco: Jossey Bass.

Huntington, Samuel P. (1996). *The clash of civilizations and the remaking of world order*. New York: Simon and Schuster.

Kegan, Robert. (1994). *In over our heads: The mental demands of modern life*. Cambridge, MA: Harvard University Press.

Kreisel, Howard T. (1999). *Maimonides' political thought: Studies in ethics, law, and the human ideal*. Albany: NY: State University of New York Press.

Ludwig, Arnold M. (2002). *King of the mountain: The nature of political leadership*. Lexington, Kentucky: The University Press of Kentucky.

Rokeach, Milton. (1960). *Open and closed mind*. New York: Basic Books.

Schon, Donald A. (1984). *The reflective practitioner : How professionals think in action*. New York: Basic Books.

Terry, Robert. (2001). *Seven zones for leadership*. Palo Alto, CA: Davies-Black.

Walzer, Michael et al., (Eds.). (2000). *Jewish political tradition, Vol. I*. New Haven: Yale University Press.

Visions of Educational Leadership: Sustaining the Legacy of Seymour Fox

LEE S. SHULMAN

A Personal Prologue

This paper has been prepared as both an act of scholarship and an act of friendship. Seymour Fox and I have known each other for 50 years. Our relationship has progressed through four stages. When we first met, in 1952, he was *the teacher of my teachers* at Camp Ramah in Wisconsin, a Jewish summer camp of the Conservative movement. I later became *the student of his teachers* at the University of Chicago between 1957 and 1963, primarily Joseph Schwab and Bruno Bettelheim. Still later, we both were simultaneously *teaching the same students* in 1969 and 1970 at the Hebrew University, in a program designed to educate curriculum specialists for the Israeli Ministry of Education. For the past generation, we have worked together as colleagues-at-a-distance — Seymour Fox as the leader of programs in Jewish Education and in the education of educational leaders at the Mandel Foundation and School, and I serving as a frequent advisor in those efforts.

   In this essay, I shall discuss the areas of education to which Seymour Fox has made singular contributions, with special reference to the connections between the earliest and most recent arenas for his efforts — the University of Chicago and the Mandel programs for educational leadership. The essay will combine equal parts reminiscence and reflection, nostalgia and analysis. It will give particular attention to a concept to which Fox has grown increasingly committed, the idea of "vision." Hence,

451

the title of the essay, "Visions of Educational Leadership" refers both to Fox's concern with vision as a theoretical construct, and with the central role of vision within a particular theoretical model of leadership that I will offer in this paper. In the essay, I will consciously engage in both quite personal observations about the contributions of Professor Fox, and more abstract principles which both exemplify and draw from his distinguished body of work.

I shall begin by looking back at the foundations of Fox's intellectual development, his experiences at the University of Chicago. These observations are not only intended to account for the conceptual and strategic trajectories of one man's thought; they also serve to connect a set of seminal ideas about leadership to their foundations in philosophy and the social sciences. Indeed, this is one of the central premises upon which the work of Professor Fox rests: *There is nothing as practical as good theory, nor is there anything that more powerfully contributes to enlightened vision than good philosophy.*

The University of Chicago: A Setting for Development

It is impossible to understand Seymour Fox's development, and the approaches to educating leadership with which he has become identified, without appreciating the profound effect of the ideas, methods and culture of the University of Chicago during the 1950s and 1960s. Fox's Chicago was an intriguing blend of the wonderful worlds of Robert Maynard Hutchins and John Dewey, brilliantly channeled through the extraordinary mind of Joseph Schwab and further elaborated by the psychoanalytic insights of Fox's dissertation director, Bruno Bettelheim.

From Hutchins came a perspective on the centrality of great books and great ideas and their importance in envisioning the good life and the roles of reason in the world. This is an idea that was exemplified in Fox's lifelong commitment to the study of the "great books" of both the Western and Jewish traditions in every program he ever designed. For Fox, as for the University of Chicago, there was no problem, topic or issue that could not be illuminated significantly by engaging the core ideas of Western philosophy. For Fox, these works were complemented by the wisdom inherent in the Jewish "sources," the equally important ancient and more modern works of Jewish thought. Thus, in every program that Seymour Fox has led, works in philosophy and original Jewish sources have played a central role.

From John Dewey came the emphasis on the centrality of connecting theory to practice, ideas to interests, and principles to problems. Dewey would, without question, become the central philosophical force in Fox's thinking. Although he never stopped teaching Plato and Aristotle, it was Dewey who regularly inspired his respect for the complex and subtle interplay of profound theory and engaged practice. For Hutchins, education began by stepping back. For Dewey, education begins by wading in, and yet thinking about it. And for Fox's teacher Joseph Schwab, education is a continuing dialectic between stepping back and wading in, between the philosophical analysis of great ideas and visions of the ideal, and the practical challenges of solving real problems with all their uncertainties and complexities. As we shall see, Seymour Fox's life-long conception of education for leadership rests on the intentional, artful and intensive engagement of the students of leadership both with the most important philosophical and theoretical sources and with pressing challenges of policy and practice.[1]

In addition to the lawyer-philosopher Hutchins and the biologist-philosopher Schwab, the psychoanalyst Bruno Bettelheim also played a powerful role in Fox's Chicago. Bettelheim offered three particularly important insights for understanding the work of Fox in the preparation of educational leaders. The first was the principle that nothing is more important and central to the quality of an education than the establishment of a potent context or setting. For Bettelheim, the Orthogenic School replaced the analyst's couch as the proper setting for educational change. From Camp Ramah to the Mandel School, Fox has constantly understood the importance of settings whose total impact scaffolds and nurtures the goals of the educational program.

A second principle was the inevitable and necessary importance of the interaction between emotion and learning. Bettelheim, like Schwab, was a fearsome teacher. He engaged his students by challenging their views, demanding that they personalize their observations of human nature, and creating a sense of profound anxiety in anyone who offered an opinion in his class. Nevertheless, his classes were always oversubscribed and his students were constantly engaged and attentive. In spite of the fear of vigorous questioning and possible humiliation, students spoke up, offering

---

1   I have elsewhere made the argument that the perspectives of Hutchins and Dewey are not as incompatible as they are often described, in my essay "Professing the Liberal Arts." (Shulman, 2004b).

themselves and their ideas as potential sacrifices on Bettelheim's pedagogical altar. When I once asked Bettelheim why he taught that way (years later when we had become friends and colleagues in California), he answered simply that without anxiety there is no real learning. Cognition without emotion, he would assert, yielded only shallow insight, not deep and abiding vision. While many of his students felt that, in his classes, the emotions associated with terror dominated those that more gently promoted studious vigilance, his impact on the thinking of his students was unquestionable.

A third of Bettelheim's most important insights was expressed in his classic work *The Informed Heart* (Bettelheim, 1960) as he attempted to characterize the value (and limitations) of psychoanalysis, the theory and movement with which he was most closely associated. He argued that *psychoanalysis*, most often characterized as either a specific technique of psychotherapy or as a personality theory, was best understood as *three* related but otherwise distinctive enterprises: a method of psychotherapy, a theory of personality, and a *way of seeing*. Psychoanalysis is least valuable and generalizable, he observed, in its most popular form, as a particular form of psychotherapy. As a psychotherapeutic technique, it applied best to a quite limited range of clients, those who are highly verbal, economically and dispositionally capable of sustaining prolonged periods of therapy, and suffering from a limited range of emotional disorders. It is, in contrast, somewhat more generally useful as theory of personality, although its limitations derive heavily from the narrow range of persons whose lives provided the basis for the theory and its overemphasis on individuals rather than settings. It has nevertheless proven heuristically useful as a personality theory for thinkers as different from one another as social scientists and novelists.

Psychoanalysis excels, Bettelheim asserted, as *a way of seeing*, as *a source for vision*, as a *set of lenses* for making sense of the world. And after all, Bettelheim would claim, ways of seeing are far more important than protocols of practice or theories of personality, in framing the day-to-day functioning of both laypersons and intellectuals. Ways of seeing are templates for the development of vision. They inspire the habits of mind and heart associated with psychoanalytic ways of knowing. These are approaches toward raising questions about the complex and often unconscious sources of human behavior, with an interpretive stance toward human motivation and action, and with the frequently symbolic character of human social and cultural initiatives. Taken together, they are powerful tools in our attempts to find meaning in the world.

Bettelheim's observations about psychoanalysis apply quite well to the models of leadership I present in this essay. One can distinguish among protocols or maxims of practice (analogous to the methods or techniques of psychotherapy), theories of leading, teaching or knowing (comparable to a theory of personality), and visions of leadership (comparable to ways of seeing). The most robust and enduring influences on leadership are the visions themselves, the ways of seeing that frame and orient the values, thoughts and actions of leaders. For Bettelheim, as for Fox, the ultimate goal of professional preparation is the inculcation of powerful visions of the possible, the desirable and the valued.

Taken together, I would propose that the impact of the University of Chicago's keen educational thinkers on Fox (and, of course, on many more of its students including myself) can be understood as a confluence of the thought of Hutchins, Dewey, Schwab and Bettelheim. Each exercised a distinctive influence, whose fingerprints can be discerned in the work of Seymour Fox and the programs of his educational creations.

I have quite purposely limited myself in this chapter to discussing the ways in which secular perspectives on education and philosophy have influenced and inspired Seymour Fox's work. It would be naïve and inaccurate to ignore the profound and continuing impact of the Jewish tradition on his life and work. Moreover, at the heart of Fox's conception of educational vision are those perspectives on learning, living and development that are rooted in Jewish thinkers. His recent book with Israel Scheffler and Daniel Marom, *Visions of Jewish Education* (Fox, Scheffler and Marom, 2003), brilliantly reflects the value of Jewish sources for his conceptions and images of education. I believe that this set of influences is richly represented in many other essays in the present volume.

Pedagogies of Leadership and Leadership as Pedagogy

The argument of this essay is that all forms of leadership are pedagogical in at least two senses. A leader (at least in a democratic institution) is inherently someone who must teach in order to lead; leading without educating is a form of tyranny. Moreover, no one ever knows fully how to be a leader; all leaders are in a continuing, unending process of learning from their own experiences, from the experiences of others, and from the thoughts and exemplars of others whom they encounter. Leaders for whom leadership ceases to be pedagogical (in both senses) will rapidly lose their capacity to lead effectively. Therefore, those who would teach others to lead must prepare them to teach others, as well as preparing them to learn, i.e., to teach themselves. In that sense, a pedagogy *of* leadership must entail the central function of teaching future leaders to become powerful pedagogues in their own right.

Readers will readily recognize that when I use the term "leader" I may be as likely to refer to teachers-as-leaders as I do to administrators or policy makers as leaders. For purposes of our discussion, I shall use "school" as a proxy for any institution of education or human development, knowing that not all educational institutions look like schools (they could, for example, be ministries, bureaus of education or entire communities, for example). But my central thesis will be to argue that effective leadership is itself a form of pedagogy, a genre of teaching.

In what more elaborated sense is leading a form of teaching? Teachers must engage students' attention, motivation and interest, must connect to their prior understandings in order to build new knowledge and skill, must challenge their students' prior beliefs and stereotypes to make way for new insights, must act prudentially in the face of uncertainty as they make judgments rather than act formulaically, must create and sustain classroom communities and school organizations that transcend individual action, and must themselves continue to grow by learning from their own experiences and those of their peers. Similarly, leaders face parallel challenges as they learn to work with both their colleagues and their clients. Indeed, I shall argue that a useful model of educational leadership can be derived from models of effective teaching, and that learning to lead and learning to teach are strikingly parallel processes.

The successful reform of schools and schooling requires a careful understanding of the conditions that are required for successful reform to occur (see McLaughlin and Talbert, 2001; Cohen and Hill, 2001; Elmore, 2000). At the heart of those necessary changes is the requirement that educational leaders develop the capacity to be the central agents of improvement and of change. In principle, no reform effort "gets it right" the first time. Therefore, the conception of reform must rest on both a vision of schooling and a conception of leadership with *learning* at its center, both institutional learning on the part of the schools and professional learning on the part of its leaders and teachers.

These two visions cannot be independent and disjunctive, however. In this essay, I shall begin with a discussion of the characteristics of *institutions* that can sustain successful educational reforms and continue to learn *qua* institutions. I shall then discuss the ways in which our models of school learning and leaders' learning are also connected to one another, and indeed depend heavily on one another. Finally, I will conclude with a brief discussion of the ways in which the more general policy community and the surrounding society need to invest important "capital" if both kinds of learning have a chance to succeed. In an epilogue, I will return to the work of Professor Seymour Fox, and briefly discuss how his own practices in the education of leaders over the past 50 years both exemplify and illustrate the principles and models I offer in this chapter.

Sources of this Work

Theory begins in wonder. Wonder is often motivated by the anguish of failure. The theoretical work on which the present chapter is based grew out of a teaching reform effort in which Judy Shulman and I collaborated during the 1990s (Shulman, 2004a). At the end of five years' work, we concluded that our efforts had generally failed to achieve their aims. We had not succeeded in preparing teachers who could teach in communities of learners. While we felt that some teachers had developed far more than others in our program, overall we concluded that while the general model appeared valid, we had been unable to create a practice that would effectively apply the theory.

We felt the need to develop a theoretical language to describe the differences between teachers and schools that had learned effectively (alas, a minority of those with which we worked) and the larger numbers that had not. Why had some learned and others failed to learn, or resisted applying what they knew? We wanted such a theory to be couched in the language of teacher learning, since our research objectives were to examine how teachers learned to teach in such settings. A theoretical formulation was needed to identify the components of teachers' capabilities for teaching, and to suggest how these functions related to one another, as well as the conditions under which they might change and develop. We have reported more fully on that effort (Shulman and Shulman, 2004), especially as related to differences associated with the subject matters being taught and learned — e.g., mathematics, science, social studies, English language and literature — in a special issue of the *Journal of Curriculum Studies* (Sherin and Shulman, 2004). In this chapter, I wish to focus on the adaptation of the conceptual model to an understanding of education for leadership.

A Note on Conceptual Models

Why draw pictures or diagrams to represent complex notions of theoretical relationships? I suppose one way of answering is to say that diagrams are helpful to the sorts of people who find pictures useful. I strongly believe that the most useful conceptual frameworks are either structural or narrative. That is, they either portray the dynamic interactions and connections among a set of key factors, or they represent the causal connections by weaving them into a story with a beginning, middle and end, as well as with multiple plots that can take different directions.

My goal in this section of the chapter is to present a set of conceptual models of educational leadership. These models will address these questions: What are the distinctive elements of a well-functioning organization whose participants — leaders and followers — are capable of engaging in intentional, purposeful, inspired and adaptive efforts at reform? What are the characteristics of a leader capable of leading such an organization? How does a leader learn to adapt and change in the context of her own and her organization's experience? What are the conditions needed for training someone to assume the roles of leadership?

Educational Leadership: The Level of the Teaching Community and Institution

I begin with the claim that any successful educational institution must embody a combination of at least six factors: a shared *vision* and ideology, a body of *knowledge* and understanding, a *community of practice*, adequate *incentives* and support, legitimate opportunities for *structured reflective critical deliberation*, and a supportive *professional learning community*. The role of any leader is to create and "manage" these factors, through understanding and discerning them, through making practical decisions to enhance and focus their functions, and to monitor and redesign their efforts in the direction of the educational missions of the institutions themselves. I will now elaborate each of these elements:

1) A vision or ideology of the educational goals shared by all or most members of the institution and consistently modeled by its leaders and those people and texts whose values embody the mission of the institution.
2) A knowledge base in the form of common "tools for thought" and a

shared lexicon — involving both the content or subject matter of learning and the theoretical foundations of education — appropriate to the vision and to the clients whom it intends to serve.

3) A shared set of practices and performances, in which participants — as members of a community of practice — are engaged in efforts of designing, teaching, school and classroom organization, as well as shared norms of evaluation.

4) An adequate set of incentives, rewards, recognitions and other sources of motivation and support sufficient to stimulate passion, zeal, and spirit needed to sustain the work and support commitment through difficult periods.

5) A capacity for honest, critical, evaluative judgment and deliberation — a structured, organized and supported set of institutional norms, practices and rituals for the documentation, critical review, reflective analysis, and systematic re-design of teaching and learning.

6) A supportive community of administrators, teachers, students and community members who can sustain the norms, practices and incentives needed. And what holds this community together is *commitment* to the shared norms and values articulated in their visions, not merely to responding adaptively to the immediate consequences of their efforts. Indeed, *commitment* and *community*

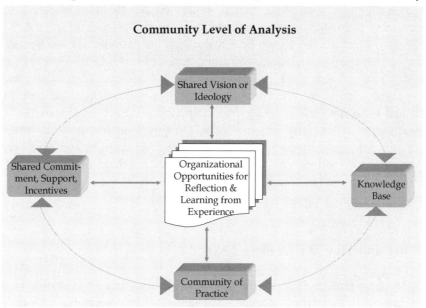

Figure 1

share an etymology. They share the concept of common, shared, exchanged, reciprocal relationships, interactions and trust. Community and commitment entail the development of identity that is both *intrapersonal* and *interpersonal*, that is, an identity based on a coherent integration of one's experiences and values as an individual, and a set of connections and relationships with the norms and values of a community within which one holds membership.

Thus, an educational institution capable of successful growth and reform is an effort characterized by a shared, vivid and committed vision of the desirable and possible character of education and human life, supported by a sufficient base of knowledge and understanding to support movement toward that vision. But understanding is not enough. There must be a set of practices that are consistently used by the professional community (hence, a community of practice) and which become the tools and vehicles for accomplishing the desired reforms. Yet, shared vision, distributed understanding and consistently effective practices are not sufficient. Since this kind of educational work is always difficult to sustain, the reform needs a set of incentives and motivators — both internal and external — to support the work of the educators and the students, even when difficulties are inevitably encountered. Figure 1 displays these interactions.

Nevertheless, even work that is supported by all these factors will inevitably produce surprises; uncertainties are the essence of all serious reform. Therefore, there must be a central and institutionalized mechanism for critical reflection, documentation and learning from experience. Institutions whose work is characterized by reform, innovation and experiment, must construct formal mechanisms and cultures that support critical reflection and learning from experience. Otherwise, yesterday's experiment will rapidly become today's dogma and tomorrow's superstition. All these features require a strong community of teachers, administrators and citizens to support and sustain them or these fragile efforts can crumble. A leader is someone capable of creating, sustaining, supporting and changing such an institution over time.

What and How do Leaders Learn?

If the above features describe the necessary elements of a successful school reform effort, they clearly depend on leaders who are compatible with such a view. Thus, in our model of educational leadership, we make the claim that the effective leader in a reform environment is characterized by a set of attributes that parallel those of the actively reforming institution: vision, understanding, performance, motivation, reflection and community membership. These six domains will then become the categories for the education of leaders and their continuing professional development. The elements and their interactions become the building blocks for designing a leadership curriculum.

Once again, for individuals, we examine a set of categories parallel to those I proposed for the analysis of a well-led institution. An accomplished leader is characterized by vision, understanding, a capacity for practice, motivation or passion for his work, both the disposition and skill to reflect critically on his practice, and membership in (as well as a capacity to create) a supportive, appropriately critical learning community whose attributes contribute to and scaffold his leadership efforts. As we can see in Figure 2, which represents the level of the individual, these attributes interact with one another in explaining the behavior and learning of an educational leader.

We can ask of any leadership education program how well it offers its students opportunities to develop, criticize and sustain their ideologies or visions for education. That is, how does it create learning experiences for

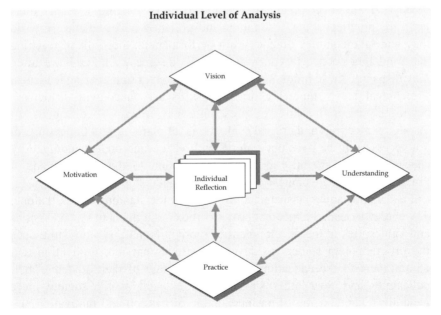

Figure 2

the development, enrichment and sharp critique of visions of educational excellence and humanity? Some future leaders bring well-developed visions with them into their training experiences, and those visions must be challenged and confronted with critical arguments. Others may enter programs with purely technical conceptions of leadership and educational ends. They will need to be engaged with texts, models and experiences that can nurture visions of the good and the worthy. A leader without vision will not be capable of leading well.

Vision is necessary but is not a sufficient element of leadership. Just as teachers must know their subjects deeply, both in substance and in syntax, and must also understand the processes of learning and development associated with the teaching of those subjects (Shulman, 1986; 1987), so leaders must develop deep and flexible understandings of the contents and processes central to the institutions they lead. We therefore must ask of training programs: How well do they ensure deep understanding of the subjects to be taught and learned, of the students to be educated, and of the theories of teaching and learning they must master? Naturally, as educational leaders they must be deeply engaged with understanding teaching and learning outside formal classrooms as well as within them. Much of the pedagogy of leadership occurs in non-formal settings; indeed these are often the most important contexts for learning.

Beyond the development of vision and understanding, a leader must learn the practical skills, techniques and practices of leadership. How do they learn the complex practices and performances, the skills of teaching and modeling needed to educate diverse colleagues? Although we often may disparage those programs that limit themselves to preparing leaders at a technical level alone, the practical skills associated with leadership cannot be ignored. Skills of presenting new ideas to colleagues, of managing meetings and critical evaluations, of planning and budgeting, all are necessary to be developed along with vision and understanding. Any successful program must give proper attention to the development of practical skills, the technical component of leadership.

Leadership cannot be sustained by vision, understanding and skill alone. The energy to lead, the fuel that provides the commitment to sustain visions and values, lies in the development of motivation and passion. How does the program help leaders to develop an inner passion, motivation and commitment to the education and to the welfare of their students, their colleagues and their other stakeholders, as well as the society more generally? The creation of an inner flame of passion and motivation is a responsibility of programs for preparing educational leaders.

There remains one more central component in this model, indeed it is *the* central element: the capacity, disposition and habits of mind and heart associated with critical reflection, analysis and evaluation of one's work and the work of one's institution. How do leaders learn to reflect, that is, develop the non-trivial skills, understandings and dispositions needed to critically analyze one's own actions and those of colleagues? Engagement in reflection is a double-edged sword, challenging the leader to confront the lessons of experience seriously yet without becoming a slave to those lessons. As I shall discuss in a later section of this essay, there must exist a dynamic tension between vision and experience, wherein one's goals are subjected to the empirical tests of practical experience as a crucible, yet not so easily sacrificed on the altar of expediency and practicality. The challenge of reflection is to strike a balance between learning to change one's views in light of experience and electing to sustain one's views in spite of experience.

Finally, it is clear that leadership is not an individual exercise or a solo performance. Leaders function as part of communities, both as creators and members, as subjects and objects. We need to ask of any program, therefore, how do leaders learn to function as members of professional communities whose commitments are tied to visions as well as to their passions, to their understandings as well as their practices? These are the questions which our models raise for us.

A model is a heuristic. One of the virtues of creating a visual model of a theory or conception is that one can play with the elements and relationships within a model to stimulate thinking and to raise questions. I am particularly interested in the interactions suggested by these representations. For example, by placing *Vision* at the intersection of *Understanding* and *Passion* I am proposing that we can understand the development of vision as a particular confluence of the intellectual and the emotional aspects of learning. Similarly, by placing *Practice* at the intersection of *Passion* and *Understanding* at the bottom of the figure, I am suggesting that direct practical experience results from a combination of conception and motivation. I shall develop this concept of the model as heuristic in the next section, especially with regard to the interactions of the various elements with the concept of *Vision*.

Vision as impassioned understanding. I remember once asking Joseph Schwab how Dewey would agree or disagree with Aristotle's definition "Man is a rational animal." Schwab responded that while Dewey would agree with the statement, he would understand it in a significantly different sense. For Aristotle, argued Schwab, "animal" and "rational" are two distinct analytic categories, which when joined together additively produce the special character of a human being. For Dewey, however, the two characteristics are in continuing dynamic interaction and interdependence. Man's rationality is permeated throughout with his animality; similarly, his animal nature is dynamically in interaction with his rationality. Thus the two are constantly influencing and modifying one another. I believe that this conception is also quite consistent with Israel Scheffler's (1991) lovely concept of the "cognitive emotions" and the psychologist Robert Abelson's (1963) notion of "hot cognitions."

This is the image I wish to communicate with these models of leadership. Each element of the model is in continuing dynamic interaction with its neighbors, especially those immediately adjacent. I am particularly interested in the concept of Vision, which sits imperially atop the model, both framing the other elements and being supported by them. Fox and his colleagues have been particularly interested in the role of vision as a primary determinant of thought and action among educators. In our model, we view vision as the development of images of the possible, the desirable and the attainable which serve to frame the directions that leaders take. Vision is at the intersection of understanding and passion, of knowledge and motivation, of cognition and will. In Freud's terms, it is akin to the ego-ideal which draws its inspiration from both the raw emotional energy of the libido and the more measured, deliberative intelligence of the ego. One also sees that practice or the consequences of action do not directly influence vision. Indeed, the role of reflection is to mediate the impact of experience on the other elements of leadership, most especially on vision. Thus, as Dewey observed repeatedly, we do not learn by doing, but by thinking about (i.e., reflecting upon or deliberating on) what we have done.

We can now see the elements of the model as they connect to a conception of curriculum for the preparation of educational leaders. There is a powerful interaction between several kinds of learning experience. Learners develop normative visions of the desirable and the valued in many ways. One method is through directly engaging with exemplary human beings who can serve as role models. Learners also develop norms and visions through reading inspiring accounts of the lives of women and men whom they never encounter directly. Accompanying that work is engagement with both compelling theories as well as vivid narratives of practice, which serve to join visions of the desirable with accounts of the possible and the accomplished. Practice can be both personal and vicarious, both directly experienced and encountered via cases. Accounts of courageous failures may be as inspiring as tales of success. Motivation, passion, persistence and commitment are essential features of the preparation of leaders.

James March (1999) has observed that passion also mediates the otherwise rational impact of experience on vision. That is, the fully "rational animal" would, upon experiencing repeated failures of action as motivated by visions of the possible, dilute those visions, moderate them or change them entirely in the face of countervailing experiences. But the truly committed leader will often permit deeply impassioned visions to trump the lessons of practice. Just because you fail repeatedly is no evidence that your visions of the desirable and possible are unwarranted. But if those visions rest only on the pillars of understanding, they may not withstand the assaults of unrequited quests.

For this reason, March has long treated the character of Cervantes' *Don Quixote* as a model of leadership. Quixote's quests are constantly failures. Yet, he manages to avoid processing experience objectively, instead permitting his illusions to reinforce his visions and values in spite of the calamities that befall him. Thus even direct experience must be mediated by vision and passion lest these images of the desirable be rendered far too fragile. The more ambitious and complex a vision of the possible, the higher the probability that it will fail in its execution or attain its objectives only partially. Visions of the *im*probable may be the most important of all to sustain. Thus, from Schwab's (1959) account of "The Impossible Role of the Teacher in Progressive Education" to many of the visions of Jewish education explicated in the volume by Fox, Scheffler and Marom (2003), we encounter visions that are sustained in spite of their failure to succeed wholly (or even substantially) in practice. The wisdom of leadership may lie in those judgments that dictate, as they say in poker, when to bet and when to fold, that is, when to persist in spite of experience and when to modify and adapt one's visions in response to experience. For such judgments there are no simple rules; there is only the imperative that one engages, both individually and communally in processes of deliberation.

The centrality of deliberation. Schwab also placed enormous weight on the value of practical deliberation, a form of collective reasoning in which carefully selected competing and complementary perspectives on a complex question of practical judgment were gathered together and supported in their dialogues (Schwab, 1969). It is no accident that a process of deliberation, reflection, critique and judgment occupies the central position in each of these models. Like Seymour Fox, I too am a student and disciple of Joseph Schwab. Moreover, as a cognitive psychologist, I have concluded that these "metacognitive" activities lie at the heart of both successes and failures of teaching and learning. At the individual level, learning depends directly on the capacity of learners to reflect critically on their own performances, to judge prudentially the meaning of their experiences and to apply those lessons to their understandings, their future practices and their emergent visions. "Yesterday's achievement is today's ability and tomorrow's aptitude" is an observation made about a set of definitions of intelligence and achievement, but applies equally well to this conception of learning. However, yesterday's achievements will fail to evolve into ability and aptitude in the absence of the kind of reflective effort described here.

At the institutional level, whether we are talking about a hospital, a law firm, a research laboratory or an educational institution, learning only occurs when the leadership has created organized, structured arrangements for reflective critique by the community of practice. These are called "clinical pathological conferences" in teaching hospitals and "case conferences" in good teaching institutions.

The Joint Models

It should be clear that both the communal and the individual levels of these models interact intensely and reciprocally. As the late Robert Merton observed, "We create our institutions and they, in turn, create us." An effective school reform initiative is a setting that is educative for its leaders and teachers as well as its students. An effective leader is someone who continues learning and contributes to the jointly produced community of practice of which he is a part. Thus, in order to grasp the full challenge of educating education leaders, we must represent in our models, not only the individual and institutional levels separately, but also their interactions. (See Figure 3).

This representation can be analyzed along several dimensions. From the outside-in and the inside-out, we see the interdependencies between the levels. Thus, individual passion and motivation must be sustained by incentives, support and commitments at the institutional level or it can dry up rapidly. Individual understanding grows when it draws upon and in turn contributes to the knowledge base of the community. Individual vision is both a product of the shared ideals and values of the larger community and

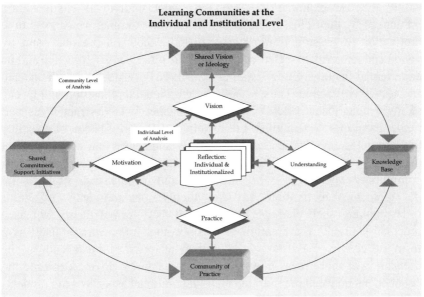

Figure 3

a resource for them. Individual practices are enriched by a larger community of practice that both scaffolds the efforts of the individual and creates an environment in which coherent and internally consistent patterns of teaching can be expected and built upon by all participants. And at the heart of the effort are both the individual and collective performances of critical review and reflection needed to learn from both experience and deliberation about ends and means. Experimentation without deliberation can be dangerous.

The notion of "shared" vision, ideals or practices can also be misleading. It is far more likely to be the case that each level of the model holds more variation, inconsistency and incoherence than the levels within. Moreover, it is unlikely that any individual is a member of only one institution, community or network. Therefore, the values, practices, understandings and incentives that influence an individual (and are, in turn, influenced by him) are likely to be inconsistent and even competitive with one another. Thus, just as an organization will engage in practical deliberation to resolve the competing perspectives of both its members and its missions, so an individual will need to engage in personal reflection and critical analysis to work seriously with the competing imperatives that influence her own judgments and choices.

Again, reminding ourselves that such visual models have heuristic value, we can examine the ways in which individual elements are influenced by their closest neighbors. Thus, for example, we can see how motivation or passion is most directly influenced, on the one hand by vision and its normative elements, and on the other hand by practice and its experiential features. Understanding is inspired by vision and both enacted and tested by practice. Thus, at both the individual and institutional levels, strongly held ideals often give emotional energy to abstract ideas and render them more operational. For example, a powerful vision of a society that promotes democratic ideals of equality and access can give important meaning to the study of theories of democratic leadership. Similarly, communal experiences with practices and rituals can support the development of motivations that strengthen visions and ideals.

By making such elements explicit, not as a formal theory but as a practical heuristic, the creation of a conceptual framework — itself as a form of vision — assists in the critical analysis of ideas and in the translation of those ideas into pedagogical practices. Having explored the connections between the individual and institutional aspects of the model, I will now turn to the final dimension, that of the society and polity.

Models of Leadership and Connections to the Larger Society and Polity

One of the distinctive characteristics of Seymour Fox as educator and education leader over the years has been his continued recognition that the challenges of education can never be adequately met by working solely within the educational community per se. The quality of education in any sector depends heavily on the resources, values, policies and practices of the broader community, society, polity and culture in which it is immersed. Thus, Fox has always worked closely with lay community leaders, political leaders and cultural leaders to enlist their support and investment in the work of education. Figure 4 attempts to represent the kind of interaction between and among the levels of individual leaders, their institutions and the broader social and policy communities that should guide serious and systemic efforts at reform. Visions do not only guide and inspire those who teach and those who lead educational systems. They are at the heart of the norms that guide a society to invest its resources in some initiatives and not others. An important lesson of Seymour Fox's work for all educators who take visions of educational leadership seriously, is that visions limited to the world of education *writ small* will suffer from myopia, tunnel vision, and

Levels of Analysis: Individual, Community, and Resources

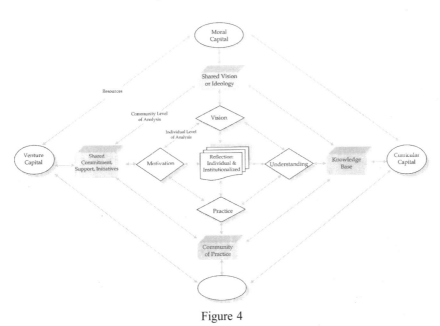

Figure 4

other maladies of limited imagination. (It is no accident that the root words for both "vision" and "imagination" refer to the experiences of "seeing.")

One of the most interesting conceptual developments in the last 50 years has been the elaboration of the metaphor of "capital" as a way of representing how a variety of social developments and commitments can be understood as forms of *investment* in the condition of the society. Thus, Schultz (1971) won the Nobel Prize in economics for his invention of the concept of "human capital" wherein he analyzed a society's investments in education as creating a new kind of resource (parallel to natural resources such as fossil fuels or agricultural productivity) from which society can subsequently draw. Similarly, Putnam (2000) wrote of the social capital created (or used up) in a society's norms and communal commitments. I have chosen to use a parallel language in describing the outer circle of the model of leadership.

Individual and institutional visions are either sustained or challenged by the norms, values and ideals that dominate the larger society and culture (or the potent sub-cultures within which the institutions function). I refer to these resources as the *moral capital* of the policy community, which can either enhance or weaken visions, but which is also influenced by the strongly held and communicated visions of significant groups. The motivations and incentives so important for leadership are strongly affected by the willingness of members of the society to invest the economic wealth of the society in support of those initiatives. I refer to this element as *venture capital.*

Educational reforms cannot flourish without significant investments in the basic curricular and instructional materials that teachers and students use in their everyday lives. This, too, entails significant investments in books and software, in computers and resource materials, and in the growing variety of educational resources needed to sustain educational improvement. The number of institutions that fail because of the absence of the most basic tools of learning — texts, tests, paper and pencils, laptops and networks — is shocking. I refer to these investments, which again depend on the policy choices of the larger community, as the role of *curricular capital.* Finally, administrators, teachers and students themselves need to be developed as the essential elements of the educational process. A society must make policy decisions to invest in professional and student development without which new and more ambitious visions of education will be impossible. I call this dimension *technical capital.* While the terms I have chosen may not be suitable to everyone, I trust that the larger point can be made: there is significant interaction among the levels of individual leadership, institutional effectiveness and policy-determined investments by the larger society that must be understood in any comprehensive conception of leadership.

Epilogue: The Fox Legacy

From the University of Chicago to the Mandel School, Seymour Fox has developed and enacted a conception of leadership that is layered, multidimensional and dialectical. It has combined attention to the individual, the institution, and society. It has respected the power of both singular leaders and of the larger culture and organized community. It has respected both the affective and the intellectual (both *Eros* and *education*, in Schwab's memorable phrase) dimensions of practice. Most important, from the days of Camp Ramah to the reinvention of the Hebrew University School of Education, and from the earliest stages of the Jerusalem Fellows programs to the continued inventions of the Mandel Foundation programs, Fox has recognized the power of vision, both as an educational construct and as a societal engine. For Fox, "visions of the possible" have driven his efforts. Like James March's version of Don Quixote, he is a man of vision who chose to "dream the impossible dream" but unlike the Man of La Mancha, Fox's efforts have succeeded far more widely than more prudent and cautious individuals could have possibly imagined.

Fox's own body of work also illustrates the rich complexity of the concept of educational vision. It would be misguided to assert that educational visions derive in some straightforward linear fashion from the religious or cultural traditions in which individuals are raised or socialized. One cannot deduce vision from an antecedent philosophy. Philosophies are constructed to be coherent and internally consistent. But visions are human accomplishments that reflect the full countenance of complexity and contradiction that characterizes the human condition. In Seymour Fox's thought, teaching and actions, we can observe a continuing effort to meld the powerful influence of the Chicago traditions of Hutchins, Dewey, Schwab and Bettelheim with the Jewish sources that lie at the heart of his identity. Fox's vision is a dynamic, evolving set of ideas and values that reflect the interplay among those enduring influences that, in their very collisions and contradictions, as well as their resonances and synergies, provide a stage for the development of educational ideas and programs. In this conception, one does not *have* a vision; one composes, revises, adapts and performs one's vision — and learns to endure the inevitable uncertainties and struggles associated with that quest.

If there is a living exemplar of the model of leadership that demonstrates the power of a dynamic interaction of vision, understanding, practical skill, deep passion and critical reflection in the interests of communities and societies, it is the continuing accomplishments of Professor Seymour Fox. He personifies a powerful vision of educational leadership; his ongoing leadership efforts can serve as a "vision of the possible" to those who follow in his footsteps. Indeed, Fox's own achievements provide an *existence proof* for the power of vision in the creation and sustenance of educational institutions.

References

Abelson, R. P. (1963). Computer simulation of "hot cognitions." In S. Tomkins and S. Messick. (Eds.). *Computer simulation and personality: Frontier of psychological theory.* New York: Wiley.

Bettelheim, Bruno. (1960). *The informed heart: Autonomy in a mass age.* New York: Avon.

Cohen, David K., and Hill, Heather C. (2001). *Learning policy: When state education reform works*. New Haven, CT: Yale University Press.

Elmore, Richard F. (2000). Building a New Structure for School Leadership. Washington, DC: Albert Shanker Institute. Accessed January 7, 2004 at http://www.shankerinstitute.org/Downloads/building.pdf.

Fox, Seymour, Scheffler, Israel, and Marom, Daniel. (2003). *Visions of Jewish education*. New York: Cambridge University Press.

March, James G. (1999). *The pursuit of organizational intelligence*. Malden, MA: Blackwell Publishers.

McLaughlin, Milbrey W. and Talbert, Joan. (2001). *Professional communities and the work of high school teaching*. Chicago: University of Chicago Press.

Putnam, Robert D. (2000). *Bowling alone: The collapse and revival of American community*. New York: Simon and Schuster.

Scheffler, Israel. (1991). *In praise of the cognitive emotions, and other essays in the Philosophy of Education*. New York: Routledge.

Schultz, Theodore W. (1971). *Investment in human capital: The role of education and of research*. New York: Free Press.

Schwab, Joseph Jackson, Westbury, Ian, and Wilkof, Neil J. (Eds.) (1982). *Science, curriculum and liberal education: Selected essays*. Chicago: University of Chicago Press.

Schwab, Joseph Jackson. (1969). The practical: A language for curriculum. *School Review, 78 (5)*, pp. 1–23.

Schwab, Joseph Jackson. (1959). The impossible role of the teacher in progressive education. *School Review, 67*, pp. 139–159.

Sherin, Miriam Gamoran, and Shulman, Lee S. (Eds.) (2004). *Journal of Curriculum Studies, 36 (2)*.

Shulman, Lee S. (1986). Those who understand: Knowledge growth in teaching. *Educational Researcher*, 15 (2), pp. 4–14.

Shulman, Lee S. (1987). Knowledge and teaching: Foundations of the New Reform. *Harvard Educational Review, 57 (1)*, pp. 1–22.

Shulman, Lee S. (2004a). Communities of learners and communities of teachers. P. Hutchings. (Ed.). In *Teaching as community property: Essays on Higher Education*. San Francisco: Jossey-Bass.

Shulman, Lee S. (2004b). Professing the Liberal Arts. In S. Wilson (Ed.). *The wisdom of practice: Essays on teaching, learning, and learning to teach*. San Francisco: Jossey-Bass.

Shulman, Lee S., and Shulman, Judith H. (2004). How and what teachers learn: A shifting perspective. *Journal of Curriculum Studies, 36 (2)*, pp. 257–271.

Seymour Fox

List of Publications

Fox, S. (1963) **The Melton Research Center: A Program for Jewish Education** (New York: The Research Center at the Jewish Theological Seminary of America)

Fox, S. (1967) "*Is Education a Discipline*" (delivered at the School of Education at the Hebrew University of Jerusalem)

Fox, S. (1969) "*A Prolegomenon to a Philosophy of Jewish Education,*" **Many Directions, One Purpose**, School of Education, Hebrew University, Jerusalem, pp.145-155, (Hebrew)

Fox, S. (1973) "*Towards a General Theory of Jewish Education*" in **The Future of the Jewish Community in America**, ed. D. Sidorsky (New York: Basic Books), pp. 260-270

Fox, S. (1973) "*A Practical Image of The Practical*" in **Curriculum Theory Network**, 10 (winter), pp. 45-57

Fox, S. (1975) **Freud and Education** (Sprigfield, Illinois: Charles C. Thomas Publisher)

Fox, S. and Rosenfield, G., eds. (1977, second edition 1980) **From The Scholar to the Classroom: Translating Jewish Tradition into Curriculum** (New

York: Melton Research Center for Jewish Education at the Jewish Theological Seminary of America)

Fox, S. (1977) *"The Scholar, the Educator and the Curriculum of the Jewish School"* in S. Fox, and G. Rosenfield, eds. (1977, second edition 1980) **From The Scholar to the Classroom: Translating Jewish Tradition into Curriculum** (New York: Melton Research Center for Jewish Education at the Jewish Theological Seminary of America), pp. 104-115

Adar, L. and Fox, S. (1978) *"Analysis of the Content and Use of a History Curriculum,"* School of Education, Hebrew University, Jerusalem (Hebrew)

Fox, S. (1981) *"Jewish Education: Can it lead to Revival?"* Institute for Contemporary Jewry at the Hebrew University, Shazar Library, (Hebrew)

Fox, S. (1983) *"The Role of the Principal in Curriculum Development,"* **Between Education and Psychology: Dedicated to the Memory of Prof. Avraham Minkowitz**, Eds. M. Nisan and U. Last, Magnes Press, Jerusalem, pp.179-189 (Hebrew)

Fox, S., ed. (1983) **Philosophy for Education** (Jerusalem, The Van Leer Jerusalem Foundation)

Fox, S. (1983) *"Theory into Practice (in Education)"* in S. Fox **Philosophy for Education** (Jerusalem, Van Leer), pp. 91-97

Fox, S. (1983) *"Ramah – A Setting for Jewish Education,"* in S. Ettenberg and G. Rosenfield, eds., **The Ramah Experience, Community and Commitment**, New York, The Jewish Theological Seminary of America, pp. 19-37

Fox, S. (1984) *"The Role of Israel in Jewish Education in the Diaspora,"* Jerusalem, The Samuel Mendel Melton Centre for Jewish Education in the Diaspora at the Hebrew University of Jerusalem

Fox, S. (1985) *"The Vitality of Theory in Schwab's Conception of the Practical,"* in **Curriculum Inquiry** 15, 1, pp. 63-89

Fox, S. (et al.), eds. (1990) **A Time to Act, The Report of the Commission on Jewish Education in North America**, Lanham, University Press of America

Fox, S. and Hochstein, A. (1991) *"Planning Perspectives on the Improvement of Jewish Education, Response to Reactions,"* in "Symposium, Reactions on 'A Time to Act'" in **Jewish Education**, vol. 59, no. 2, pp. 35-40

Fox, S. (1993) *"Zvi Adar's z"l Approach to Bible — as Part of his Humanistic World View,"* **In Memory of Prof. Zvi Adar z"l,** The School of Education, Hebrew University, Jerusalem

Fox, S. and Scheffler, I. (1996, second edition 2000), **Jewish Education & Jewish Continuity, Prospects & Limitations,** Jerusalem, Mandel Foundation

Fox, S. with Novak, W. (1997, second edition 2000), **Vision at the Heart, Lessons from Camp Ramah on the Power of Ideas in Shaping Educational Institutions,** New York and Jerusalem, Council for Initiatives in Jewish Education and the Mandel Foundation

Fox, S. and W. Novak, (2000) *"Vision at the Heart: Lessons From Camp Ramah on the Power of Ideas in Shaping Educational Institutions,"* Mandel Foundation Monograph series (Hebrew)

Fox, S. and Scheffler I. (2000) *"Jewish Education and Jewish Continuity: Prospects and Limitations,"* Mandel Foundation Monograph series (Hebrew)

Fox, S., Scheffler, I. and Marom, D., eds. (2003) **Visions of Jewish Education** (New York: Cambridge University Press)

Fox, S. *"The Art of Translation"* in Fox, S., Scheffler, I. and Marom, D., eds. (2003) **Visions of Jewish Education** (New York: Cambridge University Press), pp. 253-295

Fox, S. (2004) *"Prof. Moshe Greenberg: The Scholar and his Contribution to Education,"* in **Understanding the Bible in Our Times, Implications for Education,** edited by Marla L. Frankel and Howard Deitcher, volume 9, pp. 5-9, The Hebrew University Magnes Press, Jerusalem (Hebrew)

Fox, S. (2005) *Medabrim Hazon: Hazmana Lediyun Betachlit Hachinuch Hayehudi,* Jerusalem, Keter, edited by Seymour Fox, Israel Scheffler, Daniel Marom (Hebrew translation of **Visions of Jewish Education**)

Fox, S.
– Director and author of all curriculum programs of The Jewish Theological Seminary of America, 1960–1966
– Supervised writing of curriculum programs of the Melton Center, Hebrew University, Jerusalem 1969–1990

Contributors

Walter I. Ackerman *z"l* was best known for his work at both the University of Judaism in Los Angeles, and Ben-Gurion University of the Negev in Beersheba where he served for over 20 years as Dean of the Faculty of Humanities and Social Sciences, Shane Family Professor of Education and founding director of the School of Continuing Education. He was an advocate for making public education more accessible to culturally disadvantaged students in Israel, and was widely published in the United States and Israel.

Zvi Bekerman teaches Anthropology of Education at the School of Education and the Melton Center for Jewish Education of the Hebrew University of Jerusalem. His main interests are in the study of cultural, ethnic and national identity, including identity processes and negotiation during intercultural encounters and in informal learning contexts, as well as identity construction and development in educational computer-mediated environments.

Robert Chazan currently holds the Scheuer Chair in Jewish History at New York University. He completed his graduate training in medieval Jewish history at the Jewish Theological Seminary of America and Columbia University. His most recent books are *God, Humanity, and History: The Hebrew First Crusade Narratives* (2000) and *Fashioning Jewish Identity in Medieval Western Christendom* (2004).

Burton I. Cohen is Associate Professor of Jewish Education at the Jewish Theological Seminary of America. He served for over 30 years in senior administrative positions with the Conservative Movement's Ramah Camps and

Israel Programs. Among his publications are *Case Studies in Jewish School Management* and *Studies in Jewish Education and Judaica in Honor of Joseph S. Lukinsky* (co-editor).

David K. Cohen is John Dewey Professor of Education and Walter A. Annenberg Professor of Public Policy, at the University of Michigan. He has been a consultant to the Mandel Foundation, and has taught at the Mandel School. His recent research and writing concern the relations between policy and practice, and the effects of efforts to improve school systems. His most recent book is *Learning Policy: When State Education Reform Works.*

Jonathan Cohen is Senior Lecturer in Philosophy of Education at the School of Education and the Melton Center for Jewish Education of the Hebrew University of Jerusalem. He is also the academic coordinator of Jewish and Humanistic Studies for the Jerusalem Fellows Program of the Mandel School, and has published numerous articles in the areas of philosophy of education, curriculum theory and the philosophy of Jewish education.

Yehezkel Dror is Professor Emeritus in Political Science at the Hebrew University of Jerusalem, a member of the Club of Rome, and Founding President of the Jewish People Policy Planning Institute, established by the Jewish Agency for Israel. His most recent book is *The Capacity to Govern: A Report to the Club of Rome*, and his main areas of research include statecraft, global security, rulership, the Jewish people and Israeli policy issues and policy planning.

David Finn is Chairman of Ruder Finn Group. He has published more than 80 books, primarily on sculpture ranging from ancient Egypt and Greece to Michelangelo, Bernini, and artists of the 20th century. He is a graduate of City College (CUNY, 1943), and was an adjunct professor at New York University. He worked with Seymour Fox on the book, *A Time to Act*, which dealt with plans for the Mandel Foundation.

Jennifer Glaser is a faculty member of the Mandel Leadership Institute and the Melton Center for Jewish Education of the Hebrew University of Jerusalem. Her main areas of research include philosophy of Jewish education, pluralism, conceptions of self and community, and children's philosophical thinking.

Daniel Gordis is Vice President of the Mandel Foundation Israel, and Director of the Mandel Leadership Institute. Prior to making aliyah, he was Founding Dean of the Ziegler Rabbinical School at the University of Judaism. He has written a number of articles and several books, among them *If a Place Can Make You Cry: Dispatches from an Anxious State*, a description of Israeli society in the post-Oslo Intifada period.

Eli Gottlieb, Director of the Mandel Jerusalem Fellows program of the Mandel Leadership Institute. Prior to assuming this position, he was visiting professor in Cognitive Studies in Education at the University of Washington. His research examines the relations between cognition, culture, and identity, and how the development of each is mediated by formal and informal educational practices. In particular, it focuses on how children's and adolescents' religious thinking develops in different cultural and educational contexts.

Moshe Greenberg is Yitzhak Becker Professor of Jewish Studies Emeritus at the Hebrew University. He was Ellis Professor of ancient Semitic languages and literatures at the University of Pennsylvania until 1970 when he joined the Faculty of Humanities of the Hebrew University. He served as advisor on Bible instruction for the Israeli secular school system. In 1994 he was awarded the Israel Prize for Bible, and in 1996, the Samuel Rothberg Prize for his educational work in the Diaspora. His research and approach to the teaching of the Bible appear in his books *On the Bible and Judaism* (in Hebrew) and *Studies in the Bible and Jewish Thought*.

Pam Grossman is a Professor of English Education in the School of Education at Stanford University. Her research interests include the pedagogy of teacher education, the connection between professional knowledge and professional preparation in teaching and other professions, the teaching of English in secondary schools, and pathways into teaching in New York City schools. Her publications have appeared in a number of scholarly journals.

David Weiss Halivni is the Lucius N. Littauer Professor of Classical Jewish Civilization at Columbia University, and the author of 12 books and close to a hundred articles in Hebrew and English. The seventh volume of *Sources and Traditions*, a critical commentary on the Talmud will appear in the near future. His specialty is the composition of the Talmud and its theological implications.

Samuel C. Heilman is the Harold Proshansky Professor of Jewish Studies and Sociology at CUNY. He is the author of numerous articles and reviews as well as eight books, including *Synagogue Life*, *The People of the Book*, *The Gate Behind the Wall*, *A Walker in Jerusalem*, *Cosmopolitans and Parochials* (co-authored with Steven M. Cohen), *Defenders of the Faith*, *Portrait of American Jews*, and *When a Jew Dies*.

Barry W. Holtz is the Theodore and Florence Baumritter Professor of Jewish Education at the Jewish Theological Seminary of America and a long-time consultant to the Mandel Foundation. As author and editor, Professor Holtz's books include: *Back to the Sources: Reading the Classic Jewish Texts*, and, most recently, *Textual Knowledge: Teaching the Bible in Theory and in Practice*.

Benjamin M. Jacobs is a doctoral candidate and instructor in the Program in Social Studies at Teachers College, Columbia University. He also serves as coordinator of the doctoral program in Education and Jewish Studies at New York University. His research focuses on social studies curriculum history and theory, and the history of Jewish education in the United States.

Joseph S. Lukinsky is the Theodore and Florence Baumritter Professor Emeritus at the Jewish Theological Seminary of America. He has published articles in general and Jewish journals including the *Yearbook of the National Society for the Study of Education*, (84:1, 1985) and the *Yale Law Journal*, (July 1987) along with sponsoring over 35 doctorates in the field. In 2002 he was awarded the Samuel Rothberg prize for Jewish Education by the Hebrew University.

Daniel Marom is director of the Visions of Jewish Education Project at the Mandel Foundation in Israel. He is a faculty member of the education department of the Mandel School, where he has developed a tutoring program for educational leaders. Marom co-edited *Visions of Jewish Education* and has published articles on Zionist history, literature and education.

Daniel Pekarsky is a philosopher of education at the University of Wisconsin-Madison, and has served for many years as a consultant to the Mandel Foundation. His research focuses on questions at the intersection of ethics and education, as well as on Jewish education. Representative articles include "Socratic Teaching: A Critical Assessment," "Dewey's Conception of Growth Reconsidered," and "Burglars, Robber-Barons, and the Good Life."

Michael Rosenak is the Mandel Professor for Jewish Education Emeritus at the Hebrew University, and serves on the Faculty of the Mandel School. His teaching and writing focus on the philosophy of Jewish education, and his most recent book is *On Second Thought; Tradition and Modernity in Jewish Contemporary Education* (in Hebrew).

Jonathan D. Sarna is the Joseph H. and Belle R. Braun Professor of American Jewish History at Brandeis University. He also chairs the editorial and advisory board of the Jacob Rader Marcus Center of the American Jewish Archives in Cincinnati and is chief historian of the National Museum of American Jewish History in Philadelphia. His most recent book is *American Judaism: A History*.

Chava Shane-Sagiv is a senior research assistant at the Mandel Foundation. She is doing her graduate research in the Department of History and Education at the Hebrew University, Jerusalem, on the subject of the teaching of history in Israeli secondary schools in the 1950s. Her other research interests include conceptions of teaching and learning about the past, in both general and Jewish history. She teaches history and coordinates the history faculty in a Jerusalem high school.

Israel Scheffler is Victor S. Thomas Professor of Education and Philosophy Emeritus at Harvard University, and Scholar in Residence at the Mandel Center for Studies in Jewish Education at Brandeis University. He is the author of several books, among which are *The Anatomy of Inquiry, Science and Subjectivity,* and *Symbolic Worlds*. With Seymour Fox and Daniel Marom, he is co-editor of *Visions Of Jewish Education.*

Lee S. Shulman is President of The Carnegie Foundation for the Advancement of Teaching, and Charles E. Ducommun Professor of Education Emeritus at Stanford University. A two-volume collection of his essays, entitled *The Wisdom of Practice* and *Teaching as Community Property* was published in March 2004. He is a Fellow of the American Academy of Arts and Sciences, and his current work is on the scholarship of teaching and learning.

Philip Wexler is Professor of the Sociology of Education at the Hebrew University of Jerusalem. He teaches education and society across the programs of the Mandel Leadership Institute. His teaching and writing is in the areas of sociology of education, the relationship between education, society and religion, social theory and sociology of Jewish education. He is the author of a number of papers and books in these areas, most recently, *Mystical Society: An Emerging Social Vision.*

Sam Wineburg is Professor of Education at Stanford University. His book *Historical Thinking and Other Unnatural Acts: Charting the Future of Teaching the Past* was the 2002 Frederic W. Ness Award winner from the Association of American Colleges and Universities, and his work on teacher community (with Pam Grossman) won the 2002 "Exemplary Research on Teaching and Teacher Education Award" from the American Educational Research Association.